Contents

Credits and acknowledgments

The authors and publisher would like to thank the following for their permission to reproduce their photographs: (Key: b-bottom; c-centre; l-left; r-right; t-top)

Action Plus Sports Images: Glyn Kirk 88; **Alamy Images:** Adrian Sherratt 197, U11 26, Yoav Levy / Phototake U26 12, Kelly Redinger /Design Pics Inc Prep for HE 4, Richard Wareham Fotografie 386; **Corbis:** Ariel Skelley / Blend Images U14 1, / CHRISTOPHE KARABA / epa 423, / Duomo 310, Inspirestock 351, Steve Lipofsky 75, or Black 100 229, / Sam Bagnall / AMA 381, / SRDJAN SUKI / epa 314; **Coventry University:** 216; **Dartfish:** 393, 433; **Getty Images:** / AFP 416, AFP 459, / Chris Cole 409, / DEA / P.Martini 295, Gallo Images / Stringer 377, Goh Chain Hin U20 4, Hamish Blair / Staff 357, / Hill Creek Pictures 483, / Hulton Archive 326, Ian Walton / Staff 403, / Jamie MacDonald U14 18, Michael Kappeler 148, Matthew Lewis / Stringer 347, Peter Parks / AFP 60, Paul Gilham / Staff / 393br, Pascal Pavani / AFP 31, 34, Shaun Botterill / Staff 416tr, / Sports Illustrated 339, Stockbyte 129, U26 1, / Wire Image 305; **Imagestate Media:** John Foxx Collection 477; **iStockphoto:** / Andresr 471, / skynesher 169; **Paul Lonsdale:** 232; **University of Hull:** Mike Park, 201; **Pearson Education Ltd:** Gareth Boden 117, 141, 259, 278, 278tl, 279, 284, 291, 411, Jules Selmes 171, 325, 491, U11 3, U14 3, Lord and Leverett 231, Rob Judges 407, Studio 8. Clark Wiseman 87,195, 261; Mind Studio 59, 445, 469, 3 U20, 3 U26, Photodisc / Jeff Maloney 26 U20, Photodisc / Karl Weatherley 139, Photodisc / Photolink 52, Photodisc / Photolink / Rim Light 1 U20, Photodisk / Photolink 67, Robert Harding / Bananastock Prep for HE 1; **Photos. com:** © 2010 353, © 2010 U11 27; **Press Association Images:** / AP / Gerry Broome 338, Arne Dedert / DPA 457, John Giles / PA Archive 124, Rui Vieira / PA Archive 48; **Prozone:** 432; **Science Photo Library Ltd:** DAVID SCHARF 359; **Shutterstock:** 83, / Andresr 227, / Andrey Shadrin 379, 473, / Andrey Shadrin 379, 473, / Belova Larissa 293, Adam Borkowski Prep for HE 8, Neale Cousland 142, / Danny Warren 192, / Dusan Zidar 17 U14, / Eoghan McNally U11 1, / Frank Herzog U14 11, / Hannamariah 289, Hasa 1, JHershPhoto 199, / Karin Lau 349, Andrea Leone 464, Louis Louro 119, R McKown 33, Lorelyn Medina 121, / Monkey Business Images 181, 412, U14 20, 254, 167, Prep for HE 9, Nicholas Moore 57, / Morgan Lane Photography 292, Jim Parkin 443, / Patrizia Tilly 375, PJCross 3, Norman Pogson 29, / Poleze 187, / Roca 85, / Sportlibrary 5 U11, / Sportsphotographer.eu U11 10, / Steve Broer 323, StockLite 137, / thefinalmiracle 441, / Tonobalaguerf U14 5, / Tyler Olson 476, Csaba Vanyl 56, / Wolfgang Amri 345, Xsandra Prep for HE 2, Yamix U26 25, / Yuri Arcurs 257, 287, 321, U14 31, U20 31, / Zsolt Nyulaszi 220; **All other images** © Pearson Education

Picture Research by: Harriet Merry

The authors and publishers would like to thank the following individuals and organisations for permission to reproduce material:

p.202 Example of an informed consent form for strength tests. Reprinted with permission from The Cooper Institute, Dallas, Texas from a book called "Physical Fitness Assessments and Norms for Adults and Law Enforcement". Available online at www.cooperinstitute.org

p.205 Forestry non-adjusted aerobic fitness values for males table (ml/kg/min) for males. Adapted, with permission, from B. J. Sharkey, 1984, Physiology of fitness, 2nd ed. (Champaign, IL: Human Kinetics), 258

p.206 Forestry non-adjusted aerobic fitness values for females table (ml/kg/min) for males. Adapted, with permission, from B. J. Sharkey, 1984, Physiology of fitness, 2nd ed. (Champaign, IL: Human Kinetics), 259

p.206 Forestry age-adjusted aerobic fitness values table. Adapted, with permission, from B. J. Sharkey, 1984, Physiology of fitness, 2nd ed. (Champaign, IL: Human Kinetics), 260-61

p.207 Forestry aerobic fitness values table. Adapted, with permission, from B. J. Sharkey, 1984, Physiology of fitness, 2nd ed. (Champaign, IL: Human Kinetics), 262

p.207 Elite maximum oxygen uptake values. Brian Mackenzie/www.brianmac.co.uk (Sports Coach)

p.210 Lewis nomogram. © McGraw-Hill

p.384 Code of conduct: Coaches, Team Managers and Club Officials. The Football Association

Unit 26, p.13 Nomogram reproduced with permission from Wilmore, J.H. (1986) Sensible Fitness, Human Kinetics, Campaign'.

Unit 26, p.17 Heath-Carter Somatotype Rating Form reproduced with permission from J.E.L. Carter, Ph.D., www. somatotype.org.

Unit 26, p.19 Heath-Carter Somatochart reproduced with permission from J.E.L. Carter, Ph.D., www.somatotype.org.

Unit 26, p.20 Mean somatotypes of various female and male sports performers and non athletes, adapted from deGaray A., Levine L., Carter J (eds) (1974) Genetic and anthropological studies of Olympic athletes, Academic Press, New York.

Every effort has been made to contact copyright holders of material reproduced in this book. Any omissions will be rectified in subsequent printings if notice is given to the publishers.

BTEC
Level 3

edexcel
advancing learning, changing lives

SPORT
AND EXERCISE SCIENCES | LEVEL 3

BTEC National

Mark Adams | Ray Barker | Wendy Davies | Adam Gledhill
Julie Hancock | Chris Lydon | Pam Phillippo | Louise Sutton
Richard Taylor | Nick Wilmot

A PEARSON COMPANY

Published by Pearson Education Limited, a company incorporated in England and Wales, having its registered office at Edinburgh Gate, Harlow, Essex, CM20 2JE. Registered company number: 872828

www.pearsonschoolsandfecolleges.co.uk

Edexcel is a registered trademark of Edexcel Limited

Text © Pearson Education Limited 2010

First published 2010

13
10 9 8 7 6 5 4 3

British Library Cataloguing in Publication Data
A catalogue record for this book is available from the British Library.

ISBN 978 1 846908 97 2

Edited by Liz Cartmell
Designed by Wooden Ark
Typeset by Tek-Art
Original illustrations © Pearson Education Limited and Vicky Woodgate 2010
Cover design by Visual Philosophy, created by eMC Design
Cover photos: Front © Erik Isakson/Getty; Back © Shutterstock/Neale Cousland, Shutterstock/Jim Parkin, Shutterstock/PJCross
Printed in Malaysia (CTP-PPSB)

Websites
The websites used in this book were correct and up to date at the time of publication. It is essential for tutors to preview each website before using it in class so as to ensure that the URL is still accurate, relevant and appropriate. We suggest that tutors bookmark useful websites and consider enabling students to access them through the school/college intranet.

Disclaimer
This material has been published on behalf of Edexcel and offers high-quality support for the delivery of Edexcel qualifications.
This does not mean that the material is essential to achieve any Edexcel qualification, nor does it mean that it is the only suitable material available to support any Edexcel qualification. Edexcel material will not be used verbatim in setting any Edexcel examination or assessment. Any resource lists produced by Edexcel shall include this and other appropriate resources.

Copies of official specifications for all Edexcel qualifications may be found on the Edexcel website: www.edexcel.com

About the authors

Mark Adams is a Senior Verifier for Sport Levels 1 to 3. He has taught for ten years at schools and colleges across all qualifications. Mark is a consultant with the Premier League education and learning team. He is the series editor for our BTEC Level 3 National Sport and BTEC Level 3 National Sport and Exercise Science resources and has written for our BTEC Level 2 First Sport books.

Ray Barker has worked as sports manager and lecturer in a number of contexts for 30 years for companies and colleges in Scotland, Wales, the USA and France. He has written extensively on Sport topics and has assisted in the development of awards for various exam boards. He currently lectures at the University of Hull and is external examiner at Loughborough College and Cardiff School of Sport.

Wendy Davies has been a lecturer for the past 14 years after a varied career in the sport and leisure industry. She initially trained as a PE teacher and has worked in leisure management, sports development, coaching and lecturing. She is now on the management team in a busy department of a large Further Education college teaching a range of units and levels.

Adam Gledhill has nine years experience teaching throughout Further and Higher Education, has been involved with qualification development for five years and external verification for three years and was a co-author of the previous editions of this book for Heinemann. Alongside teaching, Adam is currently working towards a PhD in Sport Psychology around the area of talent development in football at Loughborough University and provides sport science support to youth athletes in a range of sports.

Julie Hancock is a Senior Verifier for Sport and Sport and Exercise Sciences. She has taught for 20 years and helped develop a range of educational resources and publications as well as training for tutor programmes. Originally a PE teacher, then a lecturer in Further Education and Higher Education, she now delivers training to teachers and lecturers to support the development of BTEC programmes.

Chris Lydon is a department manager and senior sports lecturer currently teaching BTEC courses at a Further Education college. In this role he is involved in the professional development of new staff and introduces them to BTEC assessment and verification. He has wide-ranging experience of teaching Further and Higher Education programmes and has contributed to a number of BTEC Sport textbooks published by Heinemann.

Pam Phillippo has played a key role in the redevelopment of the BTEC Sport qualifications and is an expert in psychophysiology. Formerly a lecturer in Further and Higher Education, and having worked with GB athletes, her specialist fields include fitness testing and training, exercise prescription, and experimental methods.

Louise Sutton is a principal lecturer in sport and exercise nutrition at Leeds Metropolitan University and currently manages the Carnegie Centre for Sports Performance and Wellbeing. She is a member of the Health and Fitness Technical Expert Group of SkillsActive, the Sector Skills Council for Active Leisure and Learning in the UK. In 2005 Louise was awarded the Re-Energise Fitness Professional of the Year award for her commitment and contribution to raising standards in nutrition training and education in the health and fitness industry.

Richard Taylor is a former rower and personal trainer with several years experience of teaching Further and Higher Education sports programmes. Currently Head of PE at an independent school, Richard has written several Higher Education sports programmes and also contributed to previous editions of this book. Alongside teaching, Richard also works as a freelance sports writer and is currently undertaking a PhD.

Nick Wilmot has worked in education for 9 years and has experience of teaching a range of Further and Higher Education courses. Nick has experience of writing high level curriculum and has also contributed to BTEC National Sport Student Book 1 and Student Book 2. Nick has an MSc Applied Sport and Exercise Science and specialises in the physiological assessment of athletes and sports psychology.

About your BTEC Level 3 National in Sport and Exercise Sciences

Every year the Sport and active leisure sector outperforms the rest of the UK economy and with the approach of the London 2012 Olympic and Paralympics Games the opportunities available within this sector are more varied than ever before. Sport and exercise scientists continue to be a growing presence in the world of sport and have increasing influence. Sport and exercise sciences' core elements of anatomy, physiology, psychology and biomechanics are seen in almost every aspect of and activity within the sport and active leisure sector. BTEC Level 3 National Sport and Exercise Sciences will help you succeed in your future career within the sport and active leisure sector. It's designed to give you plenty of flexibility in selecting optional units so you can meet your interests and career aspirations.

Your BTEC Level 3 National in Sport and Exercise Sciences is a **vocational** or **work-related** qualification. This doesn't mean that it will give you all the skills you need to do a job, but it does mean that you'll have the opportunity to gain specific knowledge, understanding and skills that are relevant to your chosen subject or area of work.

What will you be doing?

The qualification is structured into **mandatory units** (ones that you must do) (M) and your choice of **optional units** (O). How many units you do and which ones you cover depends on the type of qualification you are working towards.

- BTEC Level 3 National Certificate in Sport and Exercise Sciences: three mandatory units to provide a total of 30 credits

- BTEC Level 3 National Subsidary Diploma in Sport and Exercise Sciences: three mandatory units plus optional units to provide a total of 60 credits

- BTEC Level 3 National Diploma in Sport and Exercise Sciences: five mandatory units plus optional units to provide a total of 120 credits

- BTEC Level 3 National Extended Diploma in Sport and Exercise Sciences: six mandatory units plus optional units to provide a total of 180 credits.

The table below shows how the units in this book cover the different types of BTEC qualifications.

Unit number	Credit value	Unit name	Cert	Sub Dip	Dip	Ext Dip
1	10	Anatomy for sport and exercise	M	M	M	M
2	10	Sport and exercise physiology	M	M	M	M
3	10	Sport and exercise psychology	M	M	M	M
4	10	Research methods for sport and exercise sciences		O	M	M
5	10	Research project in sport and exercise sciences		O	M	M
6	10	Sports biomechanics in action		O	O	O
7	10	Exercise, health and lifestyle		O	O	O
8	10	Fitness testing for sport and exercise		O	O	M
9	10	Fitness training and programming		O	O	O
10	10	Sport and exercise massage		O	O	O
11	10	Analysis of sports performance			O	O
12	10	Sports nutrition		O	O	O
13	10	Current issues in sport		O	O	O
14	10	Instructing physical activity and exercise		O	O	O
15	10	Sports injuries		O	O	O
16	10	Sports coaching		O	O	O
17&18	10	Practical Individual sports & Practical team sports		O	O	O
20	10	Applied sport and exercise psychology				O
21	10	Applied sport and exercise physiology				O
23	10	Work experience in sport		O	O	O
26	10	Laboratory and experimental methods in sport and exercise sciences			O	O

How to use this book

This book is designed to help you through your BTEC Level 3 National Sport and Exercise Sciences course.

It contains many features that will help you develop and apply your skills and knowledge in work-related situations and assist you in getting the most from your course.

Introduction

These introductions give you a snapshot of what to expect from each unit – and what you should be aiming for by the time you finish it!

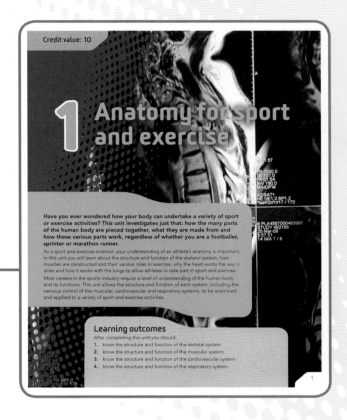

Assessment and grading criteria

This table explains what you must do in order to achieve each of the assessment criteria for each unit. For each assessment criterion, shown by the grade button **P**, **M**, **D** there is an assessment activity.

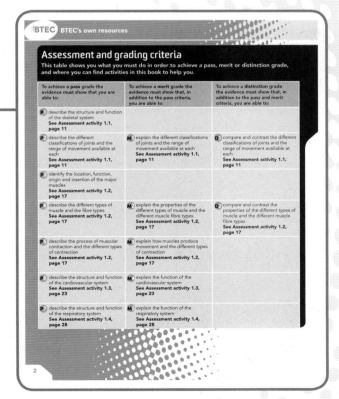

Assessment

Your tutor will set **assignments** throughout your course for you to complete. These may take a number of forms. The important thing is that you evidence your skills and knowledge to date.

Stuck for ideas? Daunted by your first assignment? These students have all been through it before…

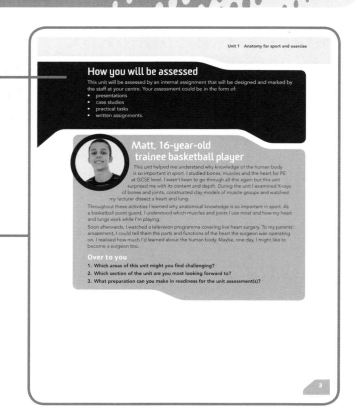

Unit 1 Anatomy for sport and exercise

How you will be assessed

This unit will be assessed by an internal assignment that will be designed and marked by the staff at your centre. Your assessment could be in the form of:
- presentations
- case studies
- practical tasks
- written assignments.

Matt, 16-year-old trainee basketball player

This unit helped me understand why knowledge of the human body is so important in sport. I studied bones, muscles and the heart for PE at GCSE level. I wasn't keen to go through all this again but this unit surprised me with its content and depth. During the unit I examined X-rays of bones and joints, constructed clay models of muscle groups and watched my lecturer dissect a heart and lung.

Throughout these activities I learned why anatomical knowledge is so important in sport. As a basketball point guard, I understood which muscles and joints I use most and how my heart and lungs work while I'm playing.

Soon afterwards, I watched a television programme covering live heart surgery. To my parents' amazement, I could tell them the parts and functions of the heart the surgeon was operating on. I realised how much I'd learned about the human body. Maybe, one day, I might like to become a surgeon too.

Over to you

1. Which areas of this unit might you find challenging?
2. Which section of the unit are you most looking forward to?
3. What preparation can you make in readiness for the unit assessment(s)?

3

Activities

There are different types of activities for you to do: **Assessment activities** are suggestions for tasks that you might do as part of your assignment and will help you develop your knowledge, skills and understanding. **Grading tips** clearly explain what you need to do in order to achieve a pass, merit or distinction grade.

Assessment activity 1.3

P5 M3 BTEC

Now you have to produce a presentation for gym users that explains the role of the cardiovascular system.

1. Give an oral presentation or use presentation software such as PowerPoint® to describe the structure and function of the cardiovascular system. You should complement your presentation by drawing the structure of the heart and blood vessels on a whiteboard and relating its function to exercise where appropriate. P5

2. During your presentation, explain the function of the cardiovascular system in a sports context – what it does and how each part of the system is designed to meet its function. M3

Grading tips

- To attain P5 you should be able to describe the structure and function of the cardiovascular system. If you can, provide real working examples that will help you show this.

- To attain M3 ensure you include plenty of detail in your response. 'Explaining' means showing the function of the cardiovascular system.

There are also suggestions for activities that will give you a broader grasp of the Sport and Exercise Sciences sector, stretch your understanding and deepen your skills.

Activity: Cardiovascular system

In small groups, gather in a sports hall. On the floor (using chalk, tape or ready-made cut-outs), mark the various chambers of the heart and the main arteries and veins that make up the cardiovascular system.

A volunteer should take on the role of 'blood'. Slowly walk around the marked-out areas of the cardiovascular system so that everyone understands blood flow within the human body.

The remainder of the group should take turns providing a running commentary of blood's progress as he or she makes their way around the cardiovascular system.

Personal, learning and thinking skills

Throughout your BTEC Level 3 National Sport and Exercise Sciences course, there are lots of opportunities to develop your personal, learning and thinking skills. Look out for these as you progress.

PLTS

If you identify questions to answer and problems to resolve in your poster and table, you can develop your skills as an **independent enquirer**.

Functional skills

It's important that you have good English, Mathematics and ICT skills – you never know when you'll need them, and employers will be looking for evidence that you've got these skills too.

Functional skills

Discussing the structure and function of the cardiovascular system could help you develop your **English** speaking and listening skills.

Key terms

Technical words and phrases are easy to spot. You can also use the glossary at the back of the book.

Key terms

Aerobic – requires oxygen.
Anaerobic – does not require oxygen.

WorkSpace

Case studies provide snapshots of real workplace issues, and show how the skills and knowledge you develop during your course can help you in your career.

There are also mini-case studies throughout the book to help you focus on your own projects.

WorkSpace

Katie Miller
Gym instructor

Katie works with a team of gym instructors and personal trainers in a large health and fitness centre. She is responsible for:
- contributing to the daily running and operation of the centre
- undertaking client health fitness assessments, including analysis of cardiovascular and respiratory function
- instructing clients in the gym
- planning and leading additional training sessions, such as spin or circuit training.

'A typical day for me involves arriving at the fitness centre in the morning and checking the gym equipment and swimming pool. I spend approximately two hours a day in the gym, helping clients with their routines. The rest of the time I carry out fitness assessments on clients, which involves checking their heart rate, blood pressure, respiratory function, muscular strength and body fat. I advise clients on the best training methods in light of their fitness test results and on any additional exercise classes they would find beneficial. I also instruct either a spin or a circuit-training class each day.

'I really enjoy meeting and helping people. Given my sports science background, I particularly enjoy the fitness testing. The procedures are quite complex and clients are often unsure what terms such as 'systolic' or 'vital capacity' mean when they're being tested and how to interpret their results.

'Whenever I perform a test, I always make clear to the client what I'm testing for and why it is important. Explaining complex anatomical terms is quite a challenge but so long as the client goes away happy with a basic understanding of, say, their lung function results and what they mean, that's my job done.

'Without the grounding in anatomy I received from my National Diploma course, I doubt if I'd be as confident or knowledgeable in this field. Studying anatomy for sport and exercise has definitely given me a head start in this career.'

Think about it!

- What areas have you covered in this unit that provide you with the knowledge and skills used by a fitness instructor?
- What other skills might you develop? Think about how you would explain to a client the implications of high cholesterol on the cardiovascular system and what exercise can do to help.

29

Just checking

When you see this sort of activity, take stock! These quick activities and questions are there to check your knowledge. You can use them to see how much progress you've made.

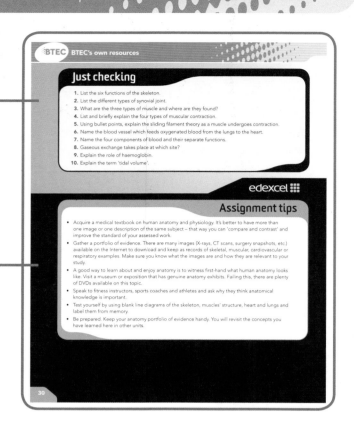

Edexcel's assignment tips

At the end of each unit, you'll find hints and tips to help you get the best mark you can, such as the best websites to go to, checklists to help you remember processes and useful reminders to avoid common mistakes.

Don't miss out on these resources to help you!

Have you read your **BTEC Level 3 National Study Skills Guide**? It's full of advice on study skills, putting your assignments together and making the most of being a BTEC Sport and Exercise Sciences student.

Ask your tutor about extra materials to help you through the course. The **Teaching Resource Pack** which accompanies this book contains interesting videos featuring Tottenham Hotspur, activities, presentations, a Podcast and information about the Sport and Exercise Sciences sector.

Visit www.pearsonfe.co.uk/videopodcast to view or download a free video podcast that you can use at home or on the go via your mobile phone, MP3 player or laptop. Wherever you see the podcast icon in the book you'll know that the podcast will help you get to grips with the content. You can also access this podcast for free on the internet by visiting www.edexcel.com/BTEC or via the iTunes store.

Your book is just part of the exciting resources from Edexcel to help you succeed in your BTEC course.
Visit www.edexcel.com/BTEC or www.pearsonfe.co.uk/BTEC2010 for more details.

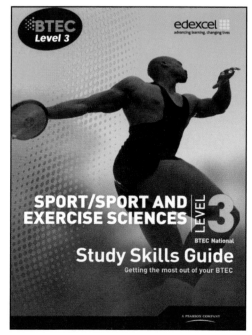

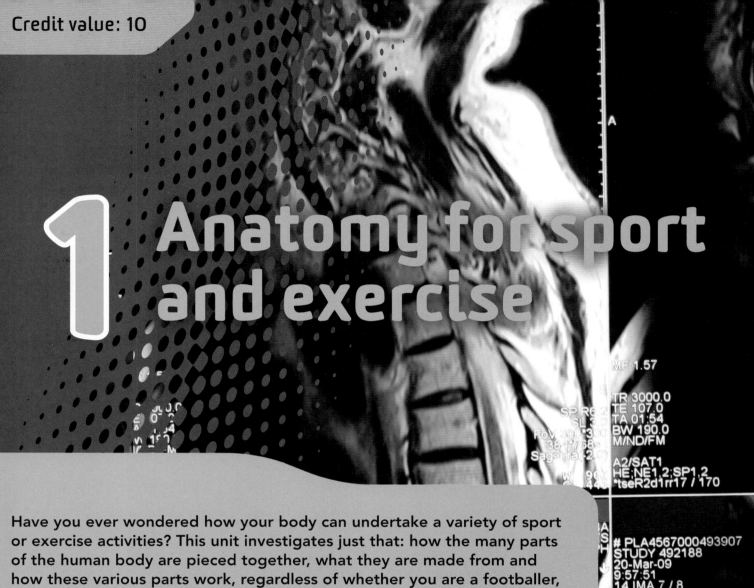

1 Anatomy for sport and exercise

Have you ever wondered how your body can undertake a variety of sport or exercise activities? This unit investigates just that: how the many parts of the human body are pieced together, what they are made from and how these various parts work, regardless of whether you are a footballer, sprinter or marathon runner.

As a sport and exercise scientist, your understanding of an athlete's anatomy is important. In this unit you will learn about the structure and function of the skeletal system, how muscles are constructed and their various roles in exercise, why the heart works the way it does and how it works with the lungs to allow athletes to take part in sport and exercise.

Most careers in the sports industry require a level of understanding of the human body and its functions. This unit allows the structure and function of each system, including the nervous control of the muscular, cardiovascular and respiratory systems, to be examined and applied to a variety of sport and exercise activities.

Learning outcomes

After completing this unit you should:

1. know the structure and function of the skeletal system
2. know the structure and function of the muscular system
3. know the structure and function of the cardiovascular system
4. know the structure and function of the respiratory system.

Assessment and grading criteria

This table shows you what you must do in order to achieve a pass, merit or distinction grade, and where you can find activities in this book to help you.

To achieve a **pass** grade the evidence must show that you are able to:	To achieve a **merit** grade the evidence must show that, in addition to the pass criteria, you are able to:	To achieve a **distinction** grade the evidence must show that, in addition to the pass and merit criteria, you are able to:
P1 describe the structure and function of the skeletal system **See Assessment activity 1.1, page 11**		
P2 describe the different classifications of joints and the range of movement available at each **See Assessment activity 1.1, page 11**	**M1** explain the different classifications of joints and the range of movement available at each **See Assessment activity 1.1, page 11**	**D1** compare and contrast the different classifications of joints and the range of movement available at each **See Assessment activity 1.1, page 11**
P3 identify the location, function, origin and insertion of the major muscles **See Assessment activity 1.2, page 17**		
P4 describe the different types of muscle and the fibre types **See Assessment activity 1.2, page 17**	**M2** explain the properties of the different types of muscle and the different muscle fibre types **See Assessment activity 1.2, page 17**	**D2** compare and contrast the properties of the different types of muscle and the different muscle fibre types **See Assessment activity 1.2, page 17**
P5 describe the process of muscular contraction and the different types of contraction **See Assessment activity 1.2, page 17**	**M3** explain how muscles produce movement and the different types of contraction **See Assessment activity 1.2, page 17**	
P6 describe the structure and function of the cardiovascular system **See Assessment activity 1.3, page 23**	**M4** explain the function of the cardiovascular system **See Assessment activity 1.3, page 23**	
P7 describe the structure and function of the respiratory system **See Assessment activity 1.4, page 28**	**M5** explain the function of the respiratory system **See Assessment activity 1.4, page 28**	

How you will be assessed

This unit will be assessed by an internal assignment that will be designed and marked by the staff at your centre. Your assessment could be in the form of:

- presentations
- case studies
- practical tasks
- written assignments.

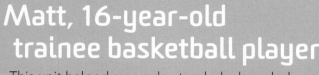

Matt, 16-year-old trainee basketball player

This unit helped me understand why knowledge of the human body is so important in sport. I studied bones, muscles and the heart for PE at GCSE level. I wasn't keen to go through all this again but this unit surprised me with its content and depth. During the unit I examined X-rays of bones and joints, constructed clay models of muscle groups and watched my lecturer dissect a heart and lung.

Throughout these activities I learned why anatomical knowledge is so important in sport. As a basketball point guard, I understood which muscles and joints I use most and how my heart and lungs work while I'm playing.

Soon afterwards, I watched a television programme covering live heart surgery. To my parents' amazement, I could tell them the parts and functions of the heart the surgeon was operating on. I realised how much I'd learned about the human body. Maybe, one day, I might like to become a surgeon too.

Over to you

1. **Which areas of this unit might you find challenging?**
2. **Which section of the unit are you most looking forward to?**
3. **What preparation can you make in readiness for the unit assessment(s)?**

1. Know the structure and function of the skeletal system

Warm-up

What happens during an 800 metre freestyle swimming race?

An 800 metre freestyle swimmer completes her event in approximately 9 minutes. At the finish she is tired, hot and out of breath and her muscles ache. She has covered 800 metres, taking only gulps of air at regular intervals throughout the race. How many times do you think her heart has beaten during the race and how many litres of air have passed in and out of her lungs?

Your skeletal system consists of bones and joints. Without bones you would be a shapeless heap of muscles and organs. Your joints allow movement. You need to know how the structure and the function of the skeletal system contribute to the range of motion required in sport and exercise.

1.1 Structure of skeletal system

The human skeleton consists of 206 bones held together by connective tissue known as ligaments, while joints at the junction between two or more bones provide mobility. Your skeleton forms a frame under which your internal organs sit and over which your muscles and skin are situated.

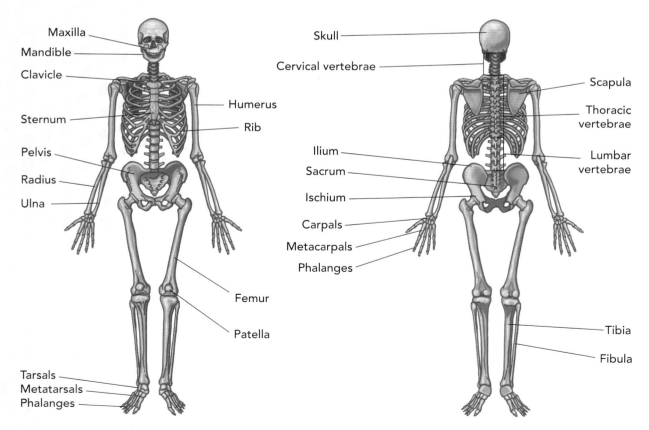

Figure 1.1: The bones of the human skeleton.

Axial and appendicular skeleton

The bones of the human skeleton are divided into two groups: axial and appendicular. This distinction helps you understand the functions of the skeleton.

- The axial skeleton forms the long axis of the body and includes the bones of the skull, ribcage and spine. These bones protect, support or carry other body parts. For example, the skull is part of the axial skeleton and it protects the brain.
- The appendicular skeleton consists of the bones of the upper and lower limbs, shoulders and pelvis. These bones direct and affect movement.

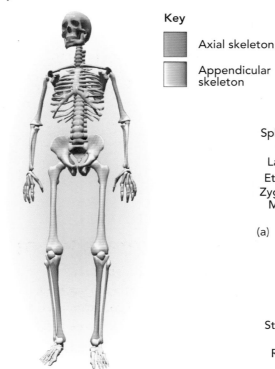

Key

Axial skeleton

Appendicular skeleton

Figure 1.2: The axial and appendicular skeleton.

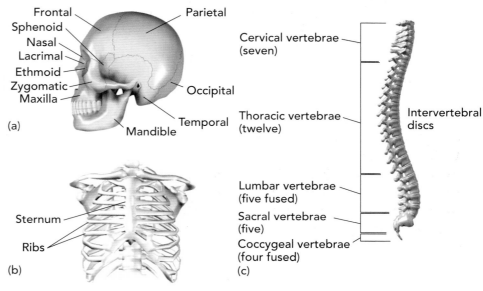

Frontal
Sphenoid
Nasal
Lacrimal
Ethmoid
Zygomatic
Maxilla

Parietal

Occipital

Temporal
Mandible

(a)

Sternum

Ribs

(b)

Cervical vertebrae (seven)

Thoracic vertebrae (twelve)

Intervertebral discs

Lumbar vertebrae (five fused)

Sacral vertebrae (five)

Coccygeal vertebrae (four fused)

(c)

Figure 1.3: The axial skeleton.

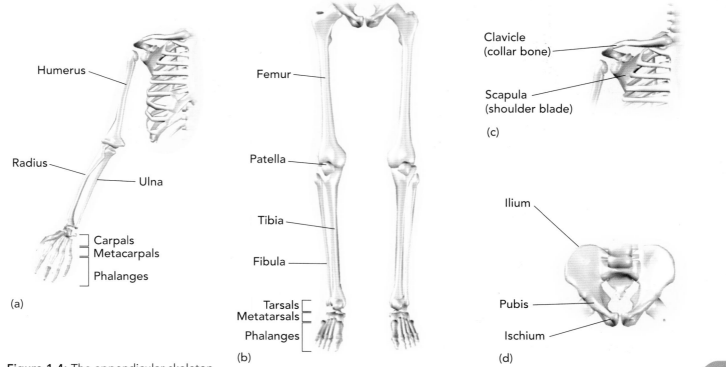

Humerus

Radius

Ulna

Carpals
Metacarpals

Phalanges

(a)

Femur

Patella

Tibia

Fibula

Tarsals
Metatarsals

Phalanges

(b)

Clavicle (collar bone)

Scapula (shoulder blade)

(c)

Ilium

Pubis

Ischium

(d)

Figure 1.4: The appendicular skeleton.

Activity: Axial and appendicular skeletons

Work in pairs or small groups. Using diagrams of the human skeleton, make a list of at least six major bones in both the axial and appendicular skeletons that play an important role in sport. For example, the phalanges of the hand are part of the appendicular skeleton and are used in tennis to help grip a tennis racket or hold a tennis ball. List the bones and roles in a table, like the one below.

Phalanges (appendicular)	Help grip a tennis racket or hold a tennis ball

Discuss which bones you think are most used in a variety of sports.

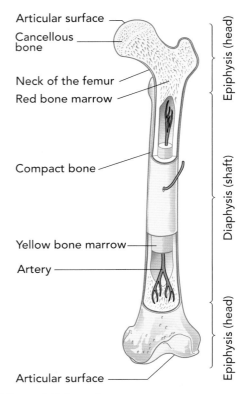

Figure 1.5: Long bone.

Types of bone

Bones come in a variety of shapes and sizes according to their functions and are classified by their shape.

- **Long bones** are longer than they are wide. A long bone has a shaft and two ends. All limb bones – with the exception of the patella (kneecap), wrist and ankle bones – are long bones. Examples are the fibula and tibia (bones in the lower leg).

- **Short bones** are small, cube-shaped bones consisting of **cancellous bone** surrounded by a thin layer of **compact bone**. They are like a sweet with a hard shell and a soft centre. Examples are the metacarpals, which are small bones in the hand.

Key terms

Cancellous bone – lightweight, honeycomb bone with a spongy appearance found at the ends of long bones and also in the centre of other bones.

Compact bone – forms the dense outer shell of bones. It has a smooth appearance.

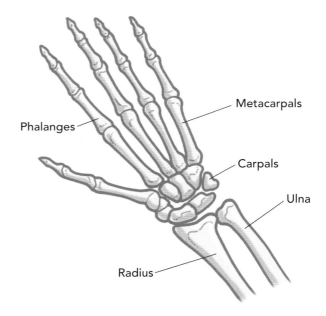

Figure 1.6: Short bone.

- **Flat bones** are thin, flattened and slightly curved. They have two outer layers of compact bone with cancellous tissue between them. The sternum (breastbone) and scapula are flat bones.

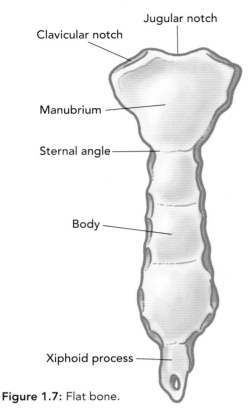

Figure 1.7: Flat bone.

- **Irregular bones** have complex shapes that fit none of the other categories of bone. The facial bone and vertebrae are good examples.

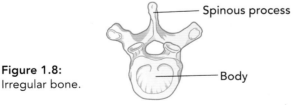

Figure 1.8: Irregular bone.

- **Sesamoid bones** have a specialised function: they ease joint movement and resist friction. They are covered with a layer of cartilage as they are found where bones articulate. Although small in appearance, sesamoid bones vary in size. The largest is the patella (kneecap).

Figure 1.9: Sesamoid bone.

Structure of a sesamoid bone

Location of major bones

From top to bottom, the human skeleton consists of the following groups that contain one or more of the major bones.

- Skull – bony framework of the head consisting of facial and cranial bones which form the cranium.
- Shoulder girdle – consists of four bones, two clavicles and two scapulae. The clavicle (collar bone) connects the humerus to the torso. One end of the clavicle is connected to the sternum and the other end to the scapula (shoulder blade).
- Chest (thorax) – consists of the ribs and sternum (breastbone) and protects the heart and lungs. The sternum is a flat bone situated in the middle of the chest. Ribs are thin and flat, and there are 24 in total (in 12 pairs). The first seven pairs from the top are connected to the spine and the sternum by cartilage. The next three pairs are attached to the spine at the rear and the rib above at the front. The last two pairs are known as floating ribs.
- Arm – made up of the humerus, radius and ulna. The humerus is the upper arm bone and fits into the scapula of the shoulder. The radius is located on the side away from the body (on same side as the thumb).
- Pelvic girdle – consists of three bones: the ilium, ischium and pubis. The pelvic girdle supports the weight of the body from the vertebral column and protects the digestive and reproductive organs.
- Hand – consists of 27 bones in three parts: the wrist, the palm and the fingers. The wrist contains eight small bones known as carpals. The palm contains five metacarpals, one aligned with each of the fingers which consist of 14 bones called phalanges.
- Leg – the thigh contains a bone called the femur, the longest, largest and strongest bone in the body. The lower leg contains the fibula and tibia (shin bone). The tibia is larger than the fibula because it bears most of the weight. The patella (kneecap) is a large, triangular bone located within a tendon between the femur and tibia.
- Foot – made up of 26 bones in three separate parts: the ankle, the instep and toes. The ankle contains seven tarsals. The metatarsals and phalanges of the foot are similar in number and position to the metacarpals and phalanges of the hand.

- Vertebral column – known as the spine, backbone or spinal column, it supports body parts, allows movement and protects the spinal cord. It consists of 33 vertebrae divided into five categories:
  - o cervical – seven cervical vertebrae support the neck and head and let you bend, tilt and turn your head
  - o thoracic – twelve thoracic vertebrae are connected to the ribs. They do not move much so the heart and lungs don't get squashed
  - o lumbar – five lumbar vertebrae allow twisting and turning. Powerful back muscles are attached to these vertebrae
  - o sacrum – five vertebrae fused to the pelvic girdle making a solid base for the trunk and legs
  - o coccyx – four fused vertebrae and the evolutionary remains of a tail.

Remember

You are born with over 300 bones. By the time you reach adulthood you have only 206 as many will have fused to form larger, stronger bones.

1.2 Function of skeletal system

Bones give your body shape, protect and support your organs, provide levers for your muscles to pull on, store calcium and other minerals, and are where your blood cells are produced.

Support

Bones provide a framework that supports the body and gives it shape. For example, the lower limbs support the torso. The 206 bones of the skeleton provide a framework and points of attachment for tissues.

Protection

Bones protect internal organs such as the brain, heart and lungs from damage. Our internal organs are delicate compared with our muscles and bones. Therefore, the bones of the skull protect the brain, whereas the vertebrae surround and protect the spinal cord.

Attachment for skeletal muscle and leverage

Skeletal muscles, attached to bones by tendons, use long bones as levers to produce movement. Therefore, we can walk, run, jump, etc. The type of joint determines the types of movement.

Source of blood cell production

Bones make blood. Bones such as the femur and ribs contain red **bone marrow**, which produces red blood cells, some white blood cells and platelets. The main bones responsible for red blood cell production are the sternum, the vertebrae and the pelvis.

Store of minerals

Bone is a reservoir for minerals such as calcium and phosphate. The stored minerals are released into the bloodstream when needed. These mineral bone stores are important for adolescents as they allow bones to grow and the body to take on a proportional appearance.

Bone growth

Bones are living tissue that grows and hardens. Bone growth is carried out at cellular level and involves three factors:

- Osteoblasts are bone-forming cells that create new bone tissue.
- Osteoclasts are specialised cells that remodel bone by destroying bone cells and reabsorbing calcium.
- Epiphyseal plate (or growth plate) is the only region of a long bone which can generate new cells.

1.3 Joints

A joint is a site where two or more bones meet. Joints are classified according to the movement between the **articulating surfaces** of a bone. There are three types of joint: fixed, slightly moveable and synovial.

Fixed

Fixed joints do not move. They interlock or overlap and are held together by bands of fibrous tissue. An example of this type of joint is between plates in the cranium.

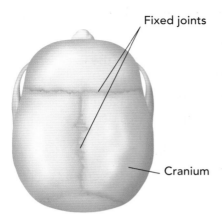

Figure 1.10: Fixed joint.

Slightly moveable

Slightly moveable (or cartilaginous) joints allow slight movement. The ends of the bone are covered in **articular (or hyaline) cartilage** separated by pads of white **fibrocartilage**. Slight movement at the surface is possible because the pads of cartilage compress. An example of this type of joint is between most vertebrae.

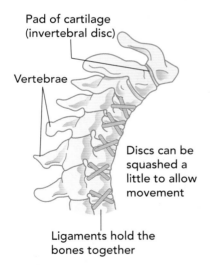

Figure 1.11: Slightly moveable.

Key terms

Bone marrow – fat or blood-forming tissue found within bone.

Articulating surface – acts as a cushion between joints.

Articular (or hyaline) cartilage – smooth, slippery covering over bones that reduces friction.

Fibrocartilage – tough cartilage capable of absorbing heavy loads.

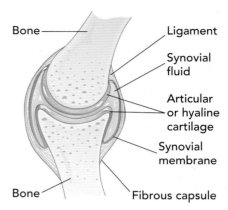

Figure 1.12: Synovial/freely moveable.

Synovial/freely moveable

A synovial joint is a freely moving joint in which the bones are separated by a joint cavity containing fluid. The bones are connected by ligaments while the ends of the bones are covered with articular cartilage.

All synovial joints contain the following parts:

- an outer sleeve or joint capsule – helps to hold the bones in place and protect the joint
- a synovial membrane – capsule lining that oozes a viscous liquid called synovial fluid that acts as a lubricant
- a joint cavity – gap between articulating bones where synovial fluid pools to lubricate the joint allowing bones to move more easily
- articular cartilage on the end of the bones – provides a smooth and slippery covering to stop the bones knocking or grinding together
- ligaments – hold the bones together and keep them in place.

Remember

Cartilage protects bone by:

- forming a gristly cushion between bones in a slightly moveable joint
- forming a slippery coating at the end of bones in a synovial joint.

Ligaments:

- are a strong binding material that fasten bones together
- hold joints in place
- are slightly elastic to allow bones to move correctly.

Synovial joints are divided into the following categories:

- **Gliding** – flat surfaces glide over each other providing a little movement in all directions. Examples include the joints between carpals in the hand.
- **Hinge** – the joint can swing open until it is straight, like a field gate. Examples include the elbow and knee joints.
- **Pivot** – a ring on one bone fits over the peg of another, allowing controlled rotational movement. Examples include the head of the radius rotating within a ring-like ligament secured to the ulna.
- **Condyloid** – a bump on one bone sits in the hollow formed by another. Movement is backwards and forwards or side to side. Ligaments often prevent rotation. An example is the wrist joint.
- **Saddle** – the ends are shaped like saddles and fit neatly together. Movement is backwards and forwards or side to side. An example is the joint at the base of the thumb.
- **Ball-and-socket** – the round end of one bone fits into a hollow in the other bone and can move in numerous directions. Examples include the hip and shoulder joints.

Movement available

- Flexion – to bend the limb, reducing the angle at the joint. This occurs at the knee when you prepare to kick a football or rugby ball.
- Extension – to straighten a limb, increasing the angle at the joint. This occurs at the elbow when you shoot in netball.
- Adduction – movement towards the body. This occurs at the shoulder when you pull on an oar while rowing.
- Abduction – movement away from the body. This occurs at the hip during a side step in gymnastics.
- Rotation – angular motion about an axis. This occurs at the shoulder during the 'dig' forearm pass in volleyball.
- Circumduction – a circular movement that combines flexion, extension, adduction and abduction. This occurs at the shoulder joint during cricket bowling action.
- Pronation – an inward rotation of the forearm so that the palm of the hand is facing backwards and downwards. This occurs at the wrist joint during a table tennis forehand topspin shot.

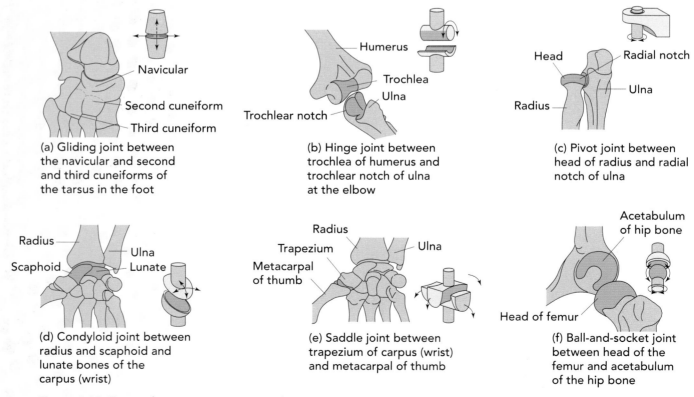

(a) Gliding joint between the navicular and second and third cuneiforms of the tarsus in the foot

Navicular
Second cuneiform
Third cuneiform

(b) Hinge joint between trochlea of humerus and trochlear notch of ulna at the elbow

Humerus
Trochlea
Ulna
Trochlear notch

(c) Pivot joint between head of radius and radial notch of ulna

Head
Radial notch
Ulna
Radius

(d) Condyloid joint between radius and scaphoid and lunate bones of the carpus (wrist)

Radius
Ulna
Scaphoid
Lunate

(e) Saddle joint between trapezium of carpus (wrist) and metacarpal of thumb

Radius
Trapezium
Metacarpal of thumb
Ulna

(f) Ball-and-socket joint between head of the femur and acetabulum of the hip bone

Acetabulum of hip bone
Head of femur

Figure 1.13: Types of movement at a synovial joint.

- Supination – an outward rotation of the forearm so that the palm of the hand is facing forwards and upwards. This occurs at the wrist joint during a table tennis backhand topspin shot.
- Plantar flexion – a movement that points the toes downwards by straightening the ankle. This occurs at the ankle when jumping to shoot in basketball.
- Dorsiflexion – a movement that brings the top of the foot towards the lower leg. This occurs when you perform a toe raise exercise.
- Hyperextension – involves movement beyond the normal anatomical position in a direction opposite to flexion. This occurs at the spine when a cricketer arches his or her back when approaching the crease to bowl.

- Inversion – involves inward rotation of the foot, turning it inwards and sideways. This occurs when you dribble a football.
- Eversion – the opposite of inversion, involves the outward rotation of the foot, turning it outwards and sideways. This action occurs in speed skating.

Take it further

Researching knee injuries

Carry out some research into three athletes from three different sports who have suffered knee injuries. In each case, record which part of the knee was affected and how long it took to heal.

Assessment activity 1.1

You are a fitness instructor at a gym and have been asked to produce some information for gym users on the skeletal system.

1. Create a poster of the human skeleton to describe its structure and function, and illustrate the major bones. **P1**
2. Draw a table that describes the different types of joint and the range of movement available to them. **P2**
3. Your table should explain in detail the different types of joint and the range of movement available to them. **M1**
4. Your table should compare and contrast joints, highlighting the differences in their construction and range of movement. **D1**

Grading tips

- To attain **P1** your poster should describe the axial and appendicular skeleton, and the different types of bone in the skeleton and visibly locate all major bones. You also need to list the five functions of the skeleton.
- To attain **P2** you should be able to describe the three different classifications of joints and the range of movement available at each. If you can provide real working examples, these will help show this.
- To attain **M1** you should be able to explain in detail the different classifications of joints and the range of movement available at each. If you can provide real working examples, these will help show this. Ensure you choose different sports to illustrate your explanations.
- To attain **D1** you should compare and contrast each of the different classifications of joints and the range of movement available at each and their relevance to sporting activities. Provide examples from different sports that illustrate your comparisons. Explain how the range of movement differs.

PLTS

If you identify questions to answer and problems to resolve in your poster and table, you can develop your skills as an **independent enquirer**.

Functional skills

Researching the structure and function of the skeletal system could help develop your **English** skills in reading.

2. Know the structure and function of the muscular system

The muscles that move your bones when you exercise are skeletal muscles. There are over 640 named muscles in the human body.

2.1 Muscular system

Muscle	Function	Location	Origin	Insertion	Exercise
biceps	flexes lower arm	inside upper arm	scapula	radius	arm curls, chin-ups
triceps	extends lower arm	outside upper arm	humerus and scapula	**olecranon process**	press-ups, dips, overhead pressing
deltoids	abducts, flexes and extends upper arm	forms cap of shoulder	clavicle, scapula and **acromion**	humerus	forward, lateral and back-arm raises, overhead lifting
pectoralis major	flexes and adducts upper arm	large chest muscle	sternum, clavicle and rib cartilage	humerus	all pressing movements
rectus abdominis	flexion and rotation of lumbar region of vertebral column	'six-pack' muscle running down abdomen	**pubic crest** and symphysis	**xiphoid process**	sit-ups
quadriceps – rectus femoris – vastus lateralis – vastus medialis – vastus intermedius	extends lower leg and flexes thigh	front of thigh	ilium and femur	tibia and fibula	knee bends, squats
hamstrings – semimembranosus – semitendinosus – biceps femoris	flexes lower leg and extends thigh	back of thigh	ischium and femur	tibia and fibula	extending leg and flexing knee (running)
gastrocnemius	plantar flexion flexes knee	large calf muscle	femur	calcaneius	running, jumping and tiptoeing
soleus	plantar flexion	deep to gastrocnemius	fibula and tibia	calcaneius	running and jumping
tibialis anterior	dorsiflexion of foot	front of tibia on lower leg	lateral condyle	by tendon to surface of medial cuneiform	all running and jumping exercises
erector spinae	extension of spine	long muscle running either side of spine	cervical, thoracic and lumbar vertebrae	cervical, thoracic and lumbar vertebrae	prime mover of back extension
teres major	rotates and abducts humerus	between scapula and humerus	posterior surface of scapula	intertubercular sulcus of humerus	all rowing and pulling movements
trapezius	elevates and depresses scapula	large triangular muscle at top of back	continuous insertion along acromion	occipital bone and all thoracic vertebrae	shrugging and overhead lifting
latissimus dorsi	extends and adducts lower arm	large muscle covering back of lower ribs	vertebrae and iliac crest	humerus	rowing movements
obliques	lateral flexion of trunk	waist	pubic crest and iliac crest	fleshy strips to lower eight ribs	oblique curls
gluteus maximus	extends thigh	large muscle on buttocks	ilium, sacrum and coccyx	femur	knee-bending movements

Table 1.1: The major muscles.

Major muscles

Remembering the names, locations and actions of the major muscles is a huge task. The main ones to remember are outlined in Table 1.1 with their function, location, **origin** and **insertion**.

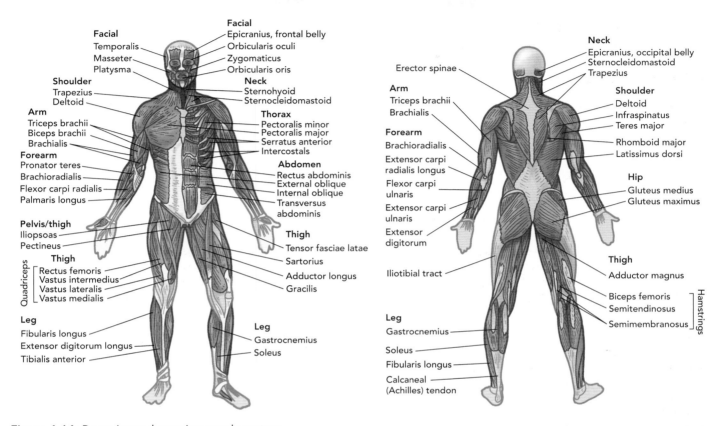

Figure 1.14: Posterior and anterior muscle system.

Key terms

Origin – a muscle's origin is attached to the immobile (or less moveable) bone.

Insertion – a muscle's insertion is attached to the moveable bone.

Olecranon process – forms part of the elbow; located at the end of the ulna.

Acromion – roughened triangular projection atop of the scapula.

Pubic crest – portion of the pelvis next to the pubic arc.

Xiphoid process – forms the end of the sternum.

Cardiac muscle – specialised muscle of the heart.

Skeletal muscle – voluntary muscle with obvious striations that attaches to the body's skeleton.

Smooth muscle – muscle with no visible striations found mainly on the walls of hollow organs, veins and arteries.

 # 2.2 Types of muscle

All movement occurring in the body depends on the actions of muscles. They work by shortening, lengthening and remaining static or still. There are three main types of muscle tissue: **cardiac**, **skeletal** and **smooth**.

Cardiac muscle

Found only in the wall of the heart, the cardiac muscle's contractions help force blood through the blood vessels to the whole body.

Activity: Muscles and muscle groups

Work in pairs or small groups. Find an anatomical model of a skeleton (preferably half-size), and a large piece of modelling clay. Use the clay to construct the following muscles and fix them over the skeleton in their correct positions:

- deltoids
- biceps
- triceps
- pectoralis major
- gastrocnemius.

Label their origin and insertion points, and prepare to comment on their function. Once completed, your tutor will ask you questions and check you have completed the task successfully.

Note that if you work in groups to identify the location, function, origin and insertion of the major muscles, you can develop your skills as a team worker.

Skeletal or voluntary muscle

This accounts for much of the muscle tissue in the body. Skeletal muscle is voluntary, which means you control the contraction. It is attached to bones and when stimulated, skeletal muscle moves a part of the skeleton such as the arm or leg.

Smooth muscle

This is an involuntary muscle that lines the walls of organs. It produces long, slow contractions that are not under voluntary control. Smooth muscle is found in the body where movement occurs without conscious thought, such as the passage of food. These long, slow contractions would be of little use to skeletal muscles, as they require fast or deliberate movement. Except for the heart, the muscles in the walls of all the body's hollow organs – such as the stomach – are almost entirely smooth muscle.

Muscle	Location	Speed of contractions	Respiration
Cardiac	Heart	Slow	**Aerobic**
Skeletal	Attached to bones	Slow to fast	Aerobic and **anaerobic**
Smooth	Hollow organs and arteries	Slow	Mainly aerobic

Table 1.2: The different characteristics of each muscle type.

Key terms

Aerobic – requires oxygen.

Anaerobic – does not require oxygen.

2.3 Fibre types

Two main types of striated skeletal muscle can be distinguished on the basis of the speed of contraction of their fibre types. These fibres include Type I, Type IIa and Type IIb, and all have different characteristics.

Type I

Type 1 fibres are also known as slow twitch muscle fibres. They are efficient at using oxygen to generate fuel (ATP) for continuous, extended muscle contractions over a long time. They fire more slowly than fast twitch fibres and can work for a long time before they fatigue. Slow twitch fibres are great at helping athletes run marathons and bicycle for hours.

Type IIa

Fast twitch muscle fibres (also known as intermediate fast twitch fibres) can use both aerobic and anaerobic metabolism almost equally to create energy. In this way, they are a combination of Type I and Type II muscle fibres.

Type IIb

Fast twitch fibres use anaerobic metabolism to create energy and are the 'classic' fast twitch muscle fibres that excel at producing quick, powerful bursts of speed. This muscle fibre has the highest rate of contraction of all the muscle fibre types, but it also has a much faster rate of fatigue.

Types of sports each are associated with

All types of muscle fibre are used in all exercise. Although Type I fibres are adapted to low intensity aerobic endurance work, they are generally employed at the beginning of exercise (regardless of the intensity of exercise). Type II fibres adapt to high intensity anaerobic exercise involving explosive or powerful movements, but they are also employed during low intensity endurance workouts as performer fatigue increases.

Type I	Type IIa	Type IIb
Red	Red	White
Contract slowly	Contract rapidly (but not as fast as Type IIb)	Contract rapidly
Aerobic	Aerobic	Anaerobic
Endurance-based such as cycling and long-distance running	Middle-distance such as ice skating	Speed- and strength-based such as sprinting and rugby
Can contract repeatedly	Fairly resistant to fatigue	Easily exhausted
Exert minimal force	Exert medium force	Exert great force

Table 1.3: The different characteristics of each muscle type.

Take it further

Long distance runners

Long distance runners, especially those running on the track, are generally able to end their race with a sprint finish if needed. If they have a dominant number of Type I fibres, how is this possible?

Force production

The forces involved in muscular contractions in Type II (fast twitch) fibres are far greater than in Type I (slow twitch) fibres. The greater force is related to the size of the individual fibres and the number of fibres making up the muscle unit. Both the size and number of fibres are greater in Type I muscles.

2.4 Muscle contraction

To understand the different types of muscle movement, you must know about the structure of muscle tissue. Skeletal muscle contains bundles of cells called muscle fibres, together with nerves that carry messages to and from the brain. A muscle contracts when messages from the brain race along the nerves to the fibres, telling them to shorten, lengthen or tense.

Each fibre is made up of contractile protein myofibrils. A myofibril is a rod-like bundle of myofilaments running the length of a muscle fibre. Each myofibril is made of overlapping protein threads or filaments known as myofilaments. Each myofibril is divided along its length into a series of units or sarcomeres.

Each skeletal muscle fibre is a long cylindrical cell surrounded by a sarcolemma, the cell membrane surrounding a muscle fibre. It consists of a multinucleate fibre and is designed specifically for contraction. The sarcolemma is thin to enable diffusion of oxygen and glucose into the cell, and carbon dioxide out.

Muscles work across joints. One end is usually attached to a fixed bone and the other end to a moveable bone. When the muscle contracts, it pulls on the moveable bone.

Remember

The origin is where the muscle joins the fixed bone. The insertion is where it joins the moving bones. On contraction, the insertion moves towards the origin.

Sliding filament theory

Sliding filament theory explains how muscles contract. During contraction, myosin filaments attach to actin filaments by forming chemical bonds called crossbridges. Muscle cells are composed of actin and myosin molecules in series. This basic unit of a muscle cell is known as a sarcomere. Sarcomeres give skeletal muscle tissue its striated appearance.

The mechanisms involved for muscular contraction are simple. The myosin molecules act like a ratchet, while the actin molecules form passive filaments that transmit the force generated by the myosin to the ends of the muscle tissue. The mechanism of the sliding filament theory involves the myosin progressing along an actin filament, constantly binding, ratcheting, and then letting go. This process of binding and ratcheting allows muscles to contract (i.e. shorten). When the muscle does not need to contract, thin strands of a further protein (called tropomyosin) are wrapped around the actin filaments to stop the myosin from binding. As a muscle undergoes contraction:

- molecules called troponin attach to tropomyosin
- calcium ions are introduced into the muscle cell and bind with troponin

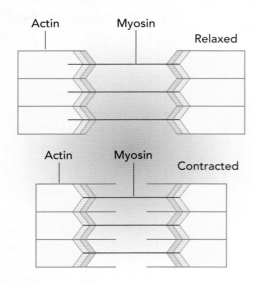

Figure 1.15: Sliding filament theory.

- calcium binding changes the shape of troponin, causing tropomyosin to move, exposing actin
- myosin is now free to bind with actin and the muscle contracts (according to the sliding filament theory).

Troponin and tropomyosin are proteins that form part of the thin or actin filament. Tropomyosin is a rod-shaped protein that spirals about the actin core to stiffen it. Troponin binds to the tropomyosin and helps it bind to the actin.

Calcium plays a vital role in cells. The skeleton is the major mineral storage site for calcium and releases calcium ions into the bloodstream under controlled conditions. Circulating calcium is either ionised or bound to blood proteins such as troponin. The ions are stored in the sarcoplasmic reticulum of muscle cells.

ATPase is an enzyme that catalyses (speeds up) the following reversible reaction enabling a quick supply of energy for muscle contraction:

$$APT + H_2O \longleftrightarrow ADP + Phosphate$$

Antagonistic pairs

Skeletal muscles are normally arranged in pairs, so that one muscle is contracting while its opposite is relaxing. The muscle shortening to move a joint is called the agonist (or prime mover). The muscle opposite that relaxes is called the antagonist. A muscle that acts as an agonist for one movement can act as an antagonist for the opposite movement. For example, the bicep contracts (agonist) while the tricep (antagonist) relaxes during the up-phase of an arm curl. During the down-phase, the reverse occurs. The tricep contracts (agonist) while the bicep (antagonist) relaxes.

Fixator

Fixators stabilise the origin so the agonist can achieve its maximum contraction.

Synergist

Synergists assist the agonist by effecting the same movement preventing undesirable movements by stabilising the joints in use.

2.5 Types of contraction

There are four types of muscle contraction: isometric, isokinetic, concentric and eccentric.

Isometric contraction

The muscle length does not change (compared to concentric or eccentric contractions) and the joint angle does not alter. As there is no movement, isometric exercises are done in static positions.

Isokinetic contraction

The muscle produces movement at a constant speed or angular velocity over a joint's range of motion. This contraction does not normally occur during sports actions, so it is used to test and improve muscular strength, especially after injury.

Concentric contraction

This is the main type of muscle contraction. The muscle shortens as the two ends of the muscle move closer together. This type of contraction is seen in the biceps muscle when performing a bicep curl.

Eccentric muscle contraction

The muscle increases in length while still producing tension. The two ends of the muscle move further apart. For example, in the lowering phase of a bicep curl, the biceps are working eccentrically to control the lowering of the weight.

Assessment activity 1.2

BTEC

Produce a guide or leaflet for gym users that aids understanding of major muscles, muscle types and muscle movement. Include the following in your leaflet or guide.

1. A muscle diagram or guide that indicates all the major muscles. Next to this, construct a table that indicates the origins and insertions of each major muscle. **P3**

2. Near your muscle diagram, describe each of the three classifications of muscle types and fibre types. **P4**

3. Explain why the three different classifications of muscle types have different properties related to their functions and how the various fibre types differ. **M2**

4. Compare and contrast why the three different classifications of muscle types have different properties related to their functions and how the various fibre types differ. **D2**

5. On the other side of your leaflet choose a number of exercises (for example, press-up, sit-up, plank, etc.) and describe how the muscles involved produce movement (agonist, antagonist, fixator and synergist) and the different types of contraction that occur. **P5**

6. Explain how the muscles of the body produce movement for your chosen exercises and the different types of contraction that occur, and further explain the sliding filament theory. **M3**

Grading tips

- To attain **P3**, with the aid of a suitable muscular diagram, you should identify the location of each of the major muscles. Consider constructing a table that lists the major muscles, their function and their corresponding points of origin and insertion.

- To attain **P4** you should describe the different types of muscle and the different muscle fibre types. If you can provide real working examples, these will help you show this.

- To attain **M2**, the merit criteria demand you do a bit more both in terms of the quality and what you produce as evidence and in terms of complexity, so pay attention to detail in your responses.

- To attain **D2** you should compare and contrast the properties of the different types of muscle and fibre types, giving suitable examples in each case.

- To attain **P5** you should be able to describe how muscles produce movement and the different types of contraction. Provide real working examples to help show this.

- To attain **M3**, 'explaining' means showing how the muscles produce movement and the different types of contraction.

PLTS

If you identify questions to answer and problems to resolve about muscle fibre types and muscular contraction in your leaflet, you can develop your skills as an **independent enquirer**.

Functional skills

Researching the structure and function of the muscular system could help develop your **English** reading skills.

3. Know the structure and function of the cardiovascular system

3.1 Structure

Heart

The heart is a muscular organ in the circulatory system that constantly pumps blood through the body. The size of your clenched fist, the heart is composed of strong cardiac muscle tissue which contracts and relaxes rhythmically and constantly.

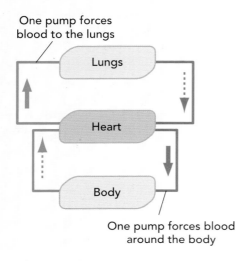

Figure 1.16: Double circulatory system.

The heart is two pumps in one. The right side receives oxygen-poor blood from the body and delivers it to the lungs. The left side of the heart receives the oxygen-rich blood from the lungs and delivers it to the rest of the body.

The heart wall is made up of three layers:

- Endocardium lines the inner heart chambers and allows blood to flow freely.

- Myocardium is the middle contracting layer composed mainly of cardiac muscle and forms the bulk of the heart.

- Epicardium is a superficial layer of the serous pericardium, a double-layered envelope surrounding the heart that prevents overextension during heart beats.

Other parts of the heart are described below.

- **Atria and ventricles** – the heart has four separate chambers: two atria and two ventricles. The upper chambers are called the left atrium and right atrium.

Key
← = oxygenated blood
← = deoxygenated blood

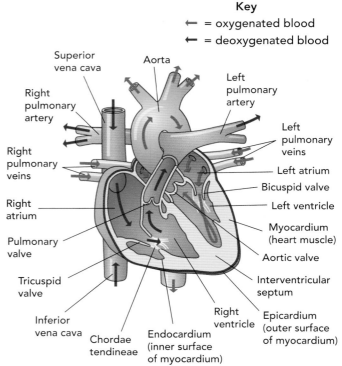

Figure 1.17: The heart.

The lower chambers are called the left ventricle and right ventricle.

The atria receive and collect the blood coming to the heart. They deliver blood to the lower left and right ventricles, which pump blood away from the heart through powerful, rhythmic contractions. The atria receive blood returning to the heart from the body. They need to contract only minimally to push blood into the ventricles, so are relatively small, thin-walled chambers.

The left and right ventricles make up most of the heart's volume. When ventricles contract, blood is pumped out of the heart into the circulation and around the body. The right ventricle pumps blood into the pulmonary artery, which routes blood to the lungs where gaseous exchange occurs. The heavily muscled left ventricle pumps blood into the aorta, the largest artery, which takes oxygenated blood away from the heart and around the body.

- **Bicuspid valve and tricuspid valve** – the bicuspid valve is situated between the left atrium and the left ventricle. It permits blood to flow from the left atrium into the left ventricle. The tricuspid valve is situated between the right atrium and the right ventricle. It allows blood to flow from the right atrium into the right ventricle. The job of the bicuspid and tricuspid valves is to prevent backflow into the atria when the ventricles are contracting and forcing blood into the circulatory system.

- **Chordae tendineae** – chord-like tendons that connect to the bicuspid and tricuspid valves. They prevent the valves from turning inside out.

- **Aortic valve and pulmonary valve** – guard the bases of the larger arteries attached to the ventricles and prevent backflow into the ventricles. The aortic and pulmonary valves are known as semilunar valves. They open and close in response to differences in pressure. When the ventricles are contracting, the valves are forced open as the blood rushes past them. When the ventricles relax, blood flows backwards toward the heart and the valves close.

- **Aorta** – the largest artery in the human body, originating from the left ventricle of the heart and transporting oxygenated blood to all parts of the body.

- **Superior vena cava** – a large short vein that carries deoxygenated blood from the upper half of the body to the right atrium.

- **Inferior vena cava** – the large vein that carries deoxygenated blood from the lower half of the body into the heart. It enters the right atrium at the lower right, posterior side of the heart.

- **Pulmonary vein** – carries oxygen-rich blood from the lungs to the left atrium of the heart.

- **Pulmonary artery** – carries deoxygenated blood from the heart to the lungs. It is the only artery in the body that carries deoxygenated blood.

Remember

- The heart acts as a double pump.
- The right side pumps blood to the lungs to collect oxygen.
- The left side pumps oxygenated blood to the rest of the body.
- Arteries carry blood away from the heart.
- The aorta is the largest artery.
- Veins carry blood back to the heart.
- The vena cava is the largest vein.
- The pulmonary artery is the only artery that carries deoxygenated blood.

Blood vessels

Blood vessels are similar to a system of plumbing for the body. They are vibrant structures that constrict and relax. They form a closed delivery system that starts and finishes with the heart. The walls of blood vessels have three layers. These layers surround the lumen, which is the blood-containing vessel.

The inner tunica initima lines the lumen and creates a slick surface minimising friction as blood passes

The middle tunica media layer is composed of smooth muscle cells and elastic tissue. Depending on the body's needs, either vasodilation or vasoconstriction results.

The outer tunica externa layer is composed of collagen fibres that protect and reinforce the vessel, and keep it in place in the body's structure.

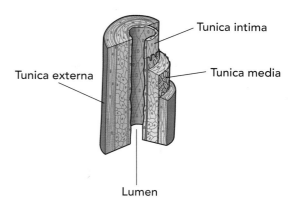

Figure 1.18: An artery wall.

There are five major types of blood vessels: arteries, arterioles, capillaries, veins and venules.

- **Arteries** take blood away from the heart for delivery around the body. The blood moves under pressure into smaller arteries, finally reaching the smallest branches known as arterioles, which feed into the **capillary beds** of body organs, skeletal muscles and other tissues.

  Thick-walled arteries near the heart are the largest in diameter and the most elastic. Elastic arteries transport blood under high pressure to the muscular arteries and contain more elastin in their tunica than any other vessel.

- **Arterioles** – smaller versions of arteries connecting arteries to capillaries. Major arterioles are thick-walled with small diameters. The tunica media consists of elastic tissue and a large amount of smooth muscle. This combination controls blood flow into the capillary bed. The smooth muscle controls the shape of the lumen by contracting and reducing the width of the vessel (vasoconstriction) and relaxing to allow the expansion of the vessel (vasodilation). Arterioles are responsible for the redistribution of blood flow and blood pressure.

- **Capillaries** – arterioles subdivide into capillaries, the smallest blood vessels in the body. They are microscopic – just one cell thick – to allow for **capillary exchange**. Capillary beds contain millions of capillaries for each muscle structure or body organ. As blood passes through the muscle or organ capillary system, it gives up oxygen and nutrients and takes up carbon dioxide and other waste products. Each capillary has a venous end, which connects to a vein, and an arterial end, which connects to an artery. On leaving the venous end of the capillary bed with waste products, the blood enters the venules, which transport the blood to the larger veins.

- **Veins** – these are supported by a thick tunica externa and contain less smooth muscle and elastic tissue than arteries. Veins also differ in that they are supported by valves. Valves prevent blood backflow. Veins act as low pressure reservoirs and move stored blood into general circulation during exercise.

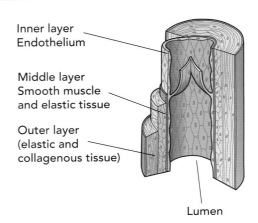

Figure 1.19: Structure of a vein.

- **Venules** – are small veins which, unlike capillaries, have some connective tissue in their walls. Venules collect the outflow of blood from the capillary bed at low pressure.

Key terms

Capillary bed – an interwoven network of capillaries.

Capillary exchange – where oxygen, carbon dioxide, nutrients and metabolic waste pass between blood and interstitial fluid by diffusion.

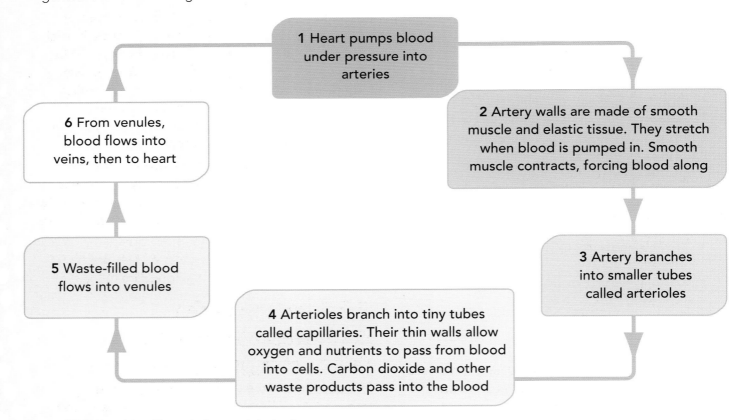

Figure 1.20: How blood is carried around the body.

Blood flow

Blood flow (or the amount of blood reaching parts of your body) within blood vessels, is regulated in part by two mechanisms: vasodilation and vasoconstriction.

- **Vasodilation** involves an increase in the diameter of the blood vessels resulting in an increase in blood flow to the muscle area that needs it most during exercise. For example, performing a bicep curl requires vasodilation of the blood vessels in the bicep muscle group.

- **Vasoconstriction** involves a decrease in the diameter of the blood vessels resulting in a reduction in blood flow to the muscle area. Vasoconstriction can occur when there is a fall in temperature, when you feel pain or when a muscle is less active.

Blood composition

Blood is a thick, tacky fluid that accounts for approximately 8 per cent of body weight. Average volume in a healthy adult male is 5–6 litres and 4–5 litres for a female. Blood is complex: it has cellular and liquid components that are visible under a microscope. Blood contains plasma, erythrocytes, leucocytes and thrombocytes.

- **Plasma** is a sticky, straw-coloured fluid composed mostly of water. It contains glucose and other nutrients for cells, hormones, gases, enzymes, antibodies and waste products.

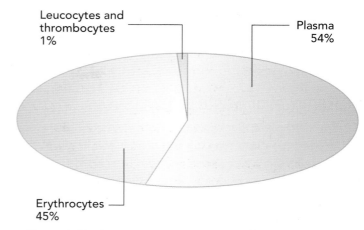

Figure 1.21: Approximate composition of blood.

- **Erythrocytes** (red blood cells) are a major factor of blood viscosity. They take on oxygen in the capillary beds of the lungs, and release this oxygen to tissue cells across capillaries throughout the body. They also remove carbon dioxide from the tissues, for excretion by the lungs.

- **Haemoglobin**, the protein that gives red blood cells their colour, binds with oxygen. A single red blood cell contains about 250 million haemoglobin molecules, so each red blood cell can transport a high level of oxygen.

- **Leucocytes** (white blood cells) account for less than 1 per cent of blood volume. They are crucial to defence against disease. They form a 'mobile army' that helps to protect the body from damage by bacteria, viruses and parasites. When white blood cells are mobilised, the body speeds up their production, and twice the number may appear in the blood within hours to fight infection.

- **Thrombocytes** (platelets) are essential for the clotting process. This is a complex process that starts when a blood vessel is ruptured or the lining damaged. Thrombocytes stick to the damaged area and to each other forming a temporary plug to seal the break. Red blood cells get trapped within the seal and form a blood clot. This turns into a scab.

3.2 Function of the cardiovascular system
Delivery of oxygen and nutrients

The main role of the cardiovascular system is transportation. Exercise increases the demand from cells for nutrients and oxygen. Blood is the tissue that carries these demands and the cardiovascular system is the method of delivery. The cardiovascular system also acts as a distribution network for hormones and heat around the body.

Removal of waste products

The cardiovascular system transports nutrients and oxygen to where they are required in the body, and removes the waste products from the organs and tissues to the lungs and kidneys, where they are excreted.

Thermoregulation

When the body experiences a temperature variation of more than 1°C the body's thermoregulation system activates. When too warm, blood vessels in the skin widen to allow greater blood flow. This allows increased heat loss to the surrounding environment with the help of the sweating process. When too cold, the blood vessels of the body's extremities (skin, limbs, etc.) narrow to allow greater warm blood flow to the body's internal organs.

Function of blood

Blood's functions include distribution, regulation and protection. Blood helps maintain body temperature by absorbing and distributing heat throughout the body, and to the skin, to encourage heat loss.

- **Oxygen transport** – using the circulatory system, blood delivers oxygen, nutrients and hormones to the parts of the body that require them for energy production.
- **Clotting** – a process during which blood forms solid clots. A damaged blood vessel wall is covered by a fibrin clot to assist repair. Platelets form a plug at the site of the damage and coagulation factors respond to form fibrin strands, which strengthen the platelet plug. This is possibly due to the constant supply of blood to the damaged site.
- **Fighting infection** – blood helps prevent infection. It contains antibodies and white blood cells, which defend against viruses and bacteria. They do this by attacking and destroying them once they enter the body or blood stream.

Cardiac cycle

The vessels that carry blood to and from the lungs form the pulmonary circuit which takes deoxygenated blood to the lungs and returns oxygenated blood to

the heart. The vessels that carry the blood supply to and from all other body tissues are collectively known as the systemic circuit. The right side of the heart is the pulmonary circuit pump. Blood returning from the body is oxygen-deficient and carbon dioxide-rich. Blood enters the right atrium and passes into the right ventricle, which pumps it to the lungs via the pulmonary artery. While in the lungs, the blood offloads carbon dioxide and takes on oxygen. The freshly oxygenated blood is then carried along the pulmonary vein back to the left side of the heart.

The left side of the heart is the systemic circuit pump. Freshly-oxygenated blood enters the left atrium and passes into the left ventricle, which pumps it around the body via the aorta. While it passes around the body, the blood gives out the oxygen and nutrients via a system of arteries and capillaries to organs and tissues. The blood is now oxygen-deficient and carbon dioxide-rich. It returns to the right side of the heart via the superior and inferior vena cava into the right atrium. This cycle repeats itself continuously.

The contraction of the cardiac muscle tissue in the ventricles is called **systole**. When the ventricles contract, they force blood into the arteries leaving the heart. The left ventricle empties into the aorta and the right ventricle into the pulmonary artery. The increased pressure due to the contraction of the ventricles is called systolic pressure.

The relaxation of the cardiac muscle in the ventricles is called **diastole**. When the ventricles relax, they allow the heart to accept the blood from the atria. The decreased pressure due to the relaxation of the ventricles is called diastolic pressure.

Key terms

Systole – cardiac-cycle period when either the ventricles or atria are contracting.

Diastole – cardiac-cycle period when either the ventricles or the atria are relaxing.

The heart is composed mainly of muscle tissue. A network of nerve fibres coordinates the contraction and relaxation of the cardiac muscle tissue to obtain an efficient, wave-like pumping action of the heart.

- **Sino atrial node** (SAN) – this is the natural pacemaker for the heart. Nestled in the upper area of the right atrium, it sends electrical impulses that trigger each

Activity: Cardiovascular system

In small groups, gather in a sports hall. On the floor (using chalk, tape or ready-made cut-outs), mark the various chambers of the heart and the main arteries and veins that make up the cardiovascular system.

A volunteer should take on the role of 'blood'. Slowly walk around the marked-out areas of the cardiovascular system so that everyone understands blood flow within the human body.

The remainder of the group should take turns providing a running commentary of blood's progress as he or she makes their way around the cardiovascular system.

heartbeat. The impulse spreads through the atria, prompting the cardiac muscle tissue to contract in a coordinated, wave-like manner.

- **Atrio ventricular node** (AVN) – the impulse that originates from the sino atrial node strikes the atrio ventricular node (AVN), situated in the lower section of the right atrium. The atrio ventricular node in turn sends an impulse through the nerve network to the ventricles, initiating the same wave-like contraction

of the ventricles. The electrical network serving the ventricles leaves the atrio ventricular node through the right and left bundle branches. These nerve fibres send impulses that cause the cardiac muscle tissue to contract.

- **Atrio ventricular bundle – Bundle of His** – this is a bundle of specialised fibres in the heart that transmit the cardiac impulses from the atria to the ventricles.
- **Purkinje fibres** – these are found in the inner ventricular walls of the heart, beneath the endocardium. These fibres are specialised myocardial fibres that conduct an electrical stimulus, enabling the heart to contract in a rhythmical routine.

Effect of the nervous system

The continual regulation of the heart rate is controlled by the sympathetic and parasympathetic nervous systems.

- **Sympathetic** – the sympathetic nervous system is activated by emotional or physical stressors (such as anxiety or exercise). Sympathetic fibres release a chemical called norepinephrine that makes the heart beat faster.
- **Parasympathetic** – this system opposes sympathetic effects and reduces heart rate when a stressful situation has passed. Parasympathetic responses are managed by a chemical called acetylcholine.

Assessment activity 1.3

Now you have to produce a presentation for gym users that explains the role of the cardiovascular system.

1. Give an oral presentation or use presentation software such as PowerPoint® to describe the structure and function of the cardiovascular system. You should complement your presentation by drawing the structure of the heart and blood vessels on a whiteboard and relating its function to exercise where appropriate. **P6**

2. During your presentation, explain the function of the cardiovascular system in a sports context – what it does and how each part of the system is designed to meet its function. **M4**

Grading tips

- To attain **P6** you should be able to describe the structure and function of the cardiovascular system. If you can, provide real working examples that will help you show this.

- To attain **M4** ensure you include plenty of detail in your response. 'Explaining' means showing the function of the cardiovascular system.

Functional skills

Discussing the structure and function of the cardiovascular system could help you develop your **English** speaking and listening skills.

4. Know the structure and function of the respiratory system

4.1 Structure

The respiratory system includes the nasal cavity, pharynx, larynx, trachea, bronchi and the lungs. Its job is to take in oxygen for the body cells and get rid of carbon dioxide. With each inhalation, air is pulled through the windpipe (trachea) and the branching passageways of the lungs (bronchi), filling thousands of tiny air sacs (alveoli) at the ends of the bronchi. These sacs (which resemble bunches of grapes) are surrounded by small blood vessels (capillaries). The respiratory tract is divided into two parts: the upper respiratory tract, consisting of the nose, nasal cavity, pharynx and larynx; and the lower respiratory tract, consisting of the trachea, bronchi and lungs.

Nasal cavity

The nose is the only external part of the respiratory system. The nose structure is divided into the external nose and internal nasal cavity. When you breathe, air enters the cavity by passing through the nostrils. The hairs of the nasal cavity filter particles of dust or pollen. The rest of the nasal cavity is lined with two types of mucous membrane that secrete a watery fluid containing antibacterial enzymes. The mucus traps inspired dust, bacteria and other debris, while the antibacterial enzymes attack and destroy bacteria chemically.

Epiglottis

This is a flap of cartilage at the entrance of the larynx which covers the opening of the airway during swallowing and helps prevent foodstuffs from entering the trachea.

Pharynx

The funnel-shaped pharynx connects the nasal cavity and mouth to the larynx (air) and oesophagus (food). Commonly called the throat, the pharynx is a small length of tubing that measures approximately 10–13 cm from the base of the skull to the level of the sixth cervical vertebra. The muscular pharynx wall is composed of skeletal muscle throughout its length.

Larynx

The larynx (or voice box) extends for about 5 cm from the level of the third to the sixth vertebra. Made of cartilage, it has a protruding section known as the Adam's apple. It is located between the pharynx and the trachea and has three functions:

- to provide an open airway
- to act as a switching mechanism to guide air and food into the correct channels
- to produce voice (it houses the vocal cords).

Trachea

The trachea (or windpipe) descends from the larynx through the neck and ends by splitting into two main bronchi prior to entering the lungs. The trachea is about 12 cm long and 2 cm in diameter and is very flexible and mobile.

Bronchi

The right and left bronchi are formed by the division of the trachea. The bronchi carry air into the lungs. The right bronchus is wider, shorter and more vertical than the left.

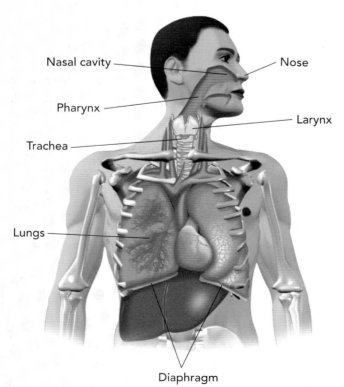

Nasal cavity — Nose
Pharynx —
— Larynx
Trachea —
Lungs —
Diaphragm

Figure 1.22: The respiratory system.

By the time inhaled air reaches the bronchi, it is warm, clear of most impurities and saturated with water vapour.

Bronchioles

Once inside the lungs, each bronchus subdivides into lobar bronchi: three on the right and two on the left. The lobar bronchi branch into segmental bronchi, which divide again into smaller and smaller bronchi. Overall, there are approximately 23 orders of branching bronchial airways in the lungs. Passages smaller than 1 mm in diameter are called bronchioles.

Lungs

The lungs occupy most of the thoracic cavity and extend down to the diaphragm. The heart is situated slightly to the left, so the lungs differ slightly in shape and size. The left lung is smaller than the right.

- **Lobes** – the lungs are divided into lobes. The left lung contains two lobes, the right lung has three. Each lobe is served by its own artery and vein, and receives air from an individual bronchus.
- **Pleural membrane** – each lung is enclosed in a pleural membrane that helps keep the two lungs away from each other and airtight. If one lung is punctured and collapses, the other pleural cavity will still be airtight and its lung will work normally.

- **Pleural cavity** – in between the parietal pleura and the visceral pleura is a thin space known as the pleural cavity or pleural space. It is filled with pleural fluid.
- **Parietal pleura** – outermost of the two pleural membranes, it covers the thoracic wall and the top of the diaphragm. It continues around the heart and between the lungs, forming the lateral walls of the mediastinal enclosure.
- **Thoracic cavity (chest cavity)** – is protected by the thoracic wall. It is separated from the abdominal cavity by the diaphragm.
- **Visceral pleura** – innermost of the two pleural membranes, it covers the surface of the lung and dips into the spaces between its lobes.
- **Pleural fluid** – pleural membranes produce pleural fluid, which fills the pleural cavity between them. This lubricating secretion allows the lungs to glide easily over the thorax wall during respiration. Although the membranes slide easily across each other, their separation is resisted by the surface tension of the pleural fluid. During breathing, the pleural cavity experiences a negative pressure (compared to the atmosphere) which helps adhere the lungs to the chest wall. This means that movements of the chest wall during breathing are coupled closely to movements of the lungs.
- **Alveoli** – bronchioles end in air sacs called alveoli. The 300 million gas-filled alveoli in each lung account for most of the lung volume and provide an enormous area for gaseous exchange. The external surfaces of the alveoli are covered with a host of pulmonary capillaries. Together, the alveolar and capillary walls form the respiratory membrane that has gas on one side and blood flowing past on the other side. Gas exchanges occur readily by simple diffusion across the respiratory membrane. Oxygen passes from each alveolus into the blood and carbon dioxide leaves the blood to enter the gas-filled alveoli.

Key

······· Lobe

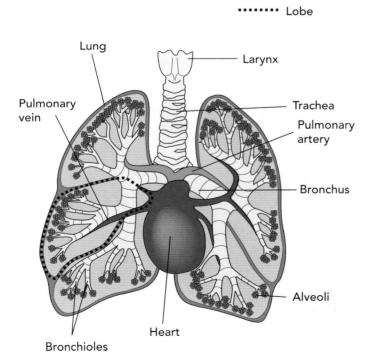

Figure 1.23: The lungs.

Remember

- Alveoli are where gaseous exchange takes place.
- Bunches of alveoli are surrounded by capillaries.
- Capillaries have thin walls to let the gases through.
- Each alveolus is smaller than a grain of sand.

Diaphragm

Contraction of the diaphragm increases the volume of the chest cavity, drawing air into the lungs during inspiration, while relaxation involves recoil of the diaphragm and decreases the volume of the chest cavity, pumping out air.

Intercostal muscles

These lie between the ribs. To help with inhalation and exhalation, the muscles extend and contract.

- Internal intercostals draw the ribs downward and inwards, decreasing the volume of the chest cavity and forcing air out of the lungs during expiration.
- External intercostals pull the ribs upwards and outwards, increasing the volume of the chest cavity and drawing air into the lungs during inspiration.

4.2 Function

Transport

Gaseous exchange occurs by **diffusion** between air in the alveoli and blood in the capillaries in the walls of the alveoli. **Partial pressure** applies to the diffusion of gases from a gas mixture to a gas in solution, and vice versa. Gases in contact with a liquid dissolve into solution by diffusion until equilibrium is achieved. At equilibrium, partial pressure of gases is the same in both gaseous and liquid states, and the gases are diffusing in and out of each state at the same rate. This same principle applies in the lungs: between the alveolar air (gaseous) and the blood circulating (liquid) in the capillaries of the alveoli walls. Blood entering capillaries from the pulmonary arteries has a lower oxygen content and higher carbon dioxide content than the air in the alveoli. To achieve equilibrium, oxygen diffuses into the blood via the surface of the alveoli, through the thin walls of the capillaries, through the red blood cell membrane and finally latches on to the haemoglobin. Carbon dioxide diffuses in the opposite direction to the oxygen.

Key terms

Diffusion – a substance moves by diffusion from a region of higher concentration to a region of lower concentration until equilibrium is reached.

Partial pressure – pressure exerted by a single gas in a mixture of gases (for example, the pressure of oxygen is different from the pressure of air).

- **Oxygen** absorbed into the blood combines with haemoglobin in the red blood cells to form oxyhaemoglobin. The concentration of red blood cells and their haemoglobin affects the amount of oxygen taken up by the blood. Red blood cells make up roughly 45 per cent of blood volume. These concentrations increase during exercise, as more fluid moves from the plasma to the tissues, and more water is lost from the plasma as sweat.
- **Carbon dioxide** is excreted as a waste product of aerobic metabolism. It is carried to the veins via the cardiovascular system and diffused into the lungs, where it is expired.
- **Haemoglobin** is a large protein that can combine reversibly with oxygen. Haemoglobin is the oxygen-transporting component of red blood cells.
- **Oxyhaemoglobin** – oxygen attaches to haemoglobin to form oxyhaemoglobin. Blood carries oxyhaemoglobin to tissue sites, where the oxygen is released during a process known as tissue respiration.

Mechanisms of breathing

Breathing in is referred to as inspiration and breathing out as expiration.

- **Inspiration** – when the air pressure inside the lungs decreases, more air flows in. Air pressure inside the lungs is decreased by increasing the size of the thoracic cavity. Due to surface tension between the two pleural membranes, the lungs follow the chest wall and expand.

  The muscles involved in expanding the thoracic cavity are the diaphragm and external intercostal muscles. As the diaphragm contracts, it flattens and so the dimension of the thoracic cavity increases. Contraction of the intercostal muscles lifts the ribcage and pulls the sternum upwards. Although this expands the thoracic cavity by only a few millimetres, it is enough to increase the thoracic volume by almost 500 ml – the usual volume of air that enters the lungs during normal inspiration.

  o *At rest* the external intercostal muscles contract and internal intercostal muscles relax. This action causes the ribs and sternum to move upwards and outwards, increasing the chest volume.

  o *During exercise* the thoracic volume increases further. Assistance from muscles such as the pectorals and trapezius help raise the ribcage, extending the thoracic volume beyond the normal 500 ml.

- **Expiration** – this is a passive process that depends more on lung elasticity than on muscle contraction. As the inspiration muscles relax, the ribcage descends and the lungs recoil.
  - *At rest*, the diaphragm and external intercostal muscles relax and return to their original positions. The ribs and diaphragm exert pressure on the pleural fluid. This reduces the lung volume and increases air pressure inside, so air is forced out via the respiratory passage.
  - *During exercise*, the combined contraction of the internal intercostal and abdominal muscles forces air out of the lungs.

Respiratory volumes

The average human lungs can hold about 6 litres of air, but only a small amount of this capacity is used during normal breathing. Lung volumes refer to physical differences in volume, while lung capacities represent different combinations of lung volumes, usually in relation to respiration and exhalation. These values vary depending on the age and height of the person.

- **Tidal volume** means that air goes into the lungs in the same way that it comes out and, under normal conditions, this equates to approximately 500 cm³ of air breathed (both inhaled or exhaled). Of this inhalation, approximately 350 cm³ reaches the alveoli in the lungs. The remainder fills the pharynx, larynx, trachea, brochi and bronchioles. This 150 cm³ is known as dead or stationary air. The 350 cm³ of air from the inhalation that makes it to the alveoli mixes with 150 cm³ of dead air in the pharynx, larynx, trachea, bronchi

and bronchioles (which was left from the previous exhalation), so that 500 cm³ reaches the alveoli in a single breath. Figure 1.24 illustrates the breathing rate of a healthy adult. The continuous oscillating line is an indication of a breathing pattern; a dip in the line denotes an exhalation, and a rise in the line denotes an inhalation. Much of the breathing is located within the tidal volume band. The exceptions on the diagram are as follows:
  - two sharp rises – forced deep inspirations (which are the inspiration reserve volume)
  - two sharp falls – forced deep exhalations (which are the expiratory reserve volume).

- **Inspiratory reserve volume** – by breathing in deeply, you can take in more than the usual 350 cm³ of air that reaches the alveoli. This is important during exercise. In addition to the tidal volume, you can also breathe in up to an additional 3000 cm³ of air, known as inspirational reserve volume.

- **Expiratory reserve volume** can be up to 1500 cm³ and is the amount of additional air that can be breathed out after normal expiration. At the end of a normal breath, the lungs contain the residual volume plus the expiratory reserve volume. If you then exhale as much as possible, only the residual volume remains.

- **Vital capacity** is the amount of air that can be forced out of the lungs after maximal respiration. The volume is around 4800 cm³.

- **Residual volume** is the amount of air left in the lungs after maximal respiration (when you breathe out as hard as you can). The volume is around 1200 cm³ for an average male.

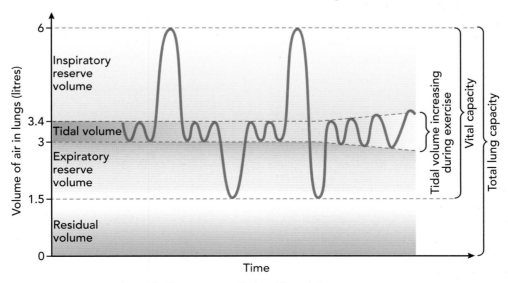

Figure 1.24: Lung volume and capacities of a healthy adult.

- **Total lung capacity** is the volume of air contained in the lungs after maximal inspiration. The volume is usually between 4000 cm³ and 8000 cm³, with 6000 cm³ for an average-sized male.

Activity: Total lung capacity

Working in small groups with guidance from your tutor, use a spirometer to determine your total lung capacity. Total lung capacity is the best and most accurate indicator of the size of your lungs available. Compare the results with your fellow learners and try to justify the largest reading and the smallest reading.

Control of breathing

Neural control – breathing control involves neurones (cells that conduct nerve impulses) in the reticular formation of the medulla and pons (both parts of the brain stem). The dorsal respiratory group (DRG) and the ventral respiratory group (VRG) are two areas of the medulla critical in respiration. The VRG is thought to be responsible for rhythm generation.

Chemical control – other factors that control breathing are the continually changing levels of oxygen and carbon dioxide. Sensors responding to such chemical fluctuations are called chemoreceptors. These are found in the medulla and in the aortic arch and carotid arteries.

Assessment activity 1.4   **P7** **M5**   BTEC

Your leaflet on muscles for gym users proved a success. You've now been tasked with producing a presentation using a program such as PowerPoint® to be discussed and later displayed on a continuous loop on monitors at the gym.

1. Your presentation is to describe the structure and function of the respiratory system for users of CV equipment. **P7**

2. You should explain the function of the respiratory system in a sports context, detailing why humans require such a system and how it works when using CV equipment. **M5**

Grading tips

- To attain **P7** you must be able to describe the structure and function of the respiratory system. If you can provide real working examples, these will help to show this.

- To attain **M5** ensure you include plenty of detail in your response. 'Explaining' means showing the function of the respiratory system.

Functional skills

Discussing the structure and function of the respiratory system could help you develop your **English** skills in speaking and listening.

Katie Miller

Gym instructor

Katie works with a team of gym instructors and personal trainers in a large health and fitness centre. She is responsible for:

- contributing to the daily running and operation of the centre
- undertaking client health fitness assessments, including analysis of cardiovascular and respiratory function
- instructing clients in the gym
- planning and leading additional training sessions, such as spin and circuit training.

'A typical day for me involves arriving at the fitness centre in the morning and checking the gym equipment and swimming pool. I spend approximately two hours a day in the gym, helping clients with their routines. The rest of the time I carry out fitness assessments on clients, which involves checking their heart rate, blood pressure, respiratory function, muscular strength and body fat. I advise clients on the best training methods in light of their fitness test results and on any additional exercise classes they would find beneficial. I also instruct either a spin or a circuit-training class each day.

'I really enjoy meeting and helping people. Given my sports science background, I particularly enjoy the fitness testing. The procedures are quite complex and clients are often unsure what terms such as 'systolic' or 'vital capacity' mean when they're being tested and how to interpret their results.

'Whenever I perform a test, I always make clear to the client what I'm testing for and why it is important. Explaining complex anatomical terms is quite a challenge but so long as the client goes away happy with a basic understanding of, say, their lung function results and what they mean, that's my job done.

'Without the grounding in anatomy I received from my National Diploma course, I doubt if I'd be as confident or knowledgeable in this field. Studying anatomy for sport and exercise has definitely given me a head start in this career.'

Think about it!

- What areas have you covered in this unit that provide you with the knowledge and skills used by a fitness instructor?
- What other skills might you develop? Think about how you would explain to a client the implications of high cholesterol on the cardiovascular system and what exercise can do to help.

Just checking

1. List the six functions of the skeleton.
2. List the different types of synovial joint.
3. What are the three types of muscle and where are they found?
4. List and briefly explain the four types of muscular contraction.
5. Using bullet points, explain the sliding filament theory as a muscle undergoes contraction.
6. Name the blood vessel which feeds oxygenated blood from the lungs to the heart.
7. Name the four components of blood and their separate functions.
8. Gaseous exchange takes place at which site?
9. Explain the role of haemoglobin.
10. Explain the term 'tidal volume'.

edexcel

Assignment tips

- Acquire a medical textbook on human anatomy and physiology. It's better to have more than one image or one description of the same subject – that way you can 'compare and contrast' and improve the standard of your assessed work.

- Gather a portfolio of evidence. There are many images (X-rays, CT scans, surgery snapshots, etc.) available on the Internet to download and keep as records of skeletal, muscular, cardiovascular or respiratory examples. Make sure you know what the images are and how they are relevant to your study.

- A good way to learn about and enjoy anatomy is to witness first-hand what human anatomy looks like. Visit a museum or exposition that has genuine anatomy exhibits. Failing this, there are plenty of DVDs available on this topic.

- Speak to fitness instructors, sports coaches and athletes and ask why they think anatomical knowledge is important.

- Test yourself by using blank line diagrams of the skeleton, muscles' structure, heart and lungs and label them from memory.

- Be prepared. Keep your anatomy portfolio of evidence handy. You will revisit the concepts you have learned here in other units.

2 Sport and exercise physiology

As you sit reading this book, your body is doing little physical exercise. Your oxygen and energy demands are low and are easily met by your shallow breathing and relatively low pulse rate. The blood circulating around your system delivers glucose and oxygen to your cells and takes waste products, such as carbon dioxide, away.

However, if you were to get up and run around a sports field, significant changes would take place. To fuel this activity and maintain its equilibrium, your body must adapt quickly and it does so in a variety of ways involving many processes. This unit is designed to examine these processes and the implications on sports performance.

Understanding these processes is essential in the sport and exercise industries. This is so that you can appreciate how the body copes with the stress of exercise, why you cannot continue to exercise indefinitely, and how you can train these systems to improve performance and fitness levels.

Learning outcomes

After completing this unit you should:

1. be able to investigate the initial responses of the body to exercise
2. be able to investigate how the body responds to steady-state exercise
3. know fatigue and how the body recovers from exercise
4. know how the body adapts to long-term exercise.

Assessment and grading criteria

This table shows you what you must do in order to achieve a pass, merit or distinction grade, and where you can find activities in this book to help you.

To achieve a **pass** grade the evidence must show that you are able to:	To achieve a **merit** grade the evidence must show that, in addition to the pass criteria, you are able to:	To achieve a **distinction** grade the evidence must show that, in addition to the pass and merit criteria, you are able to:
P1 investigate the initial responses of the cardiovascular and respiratory systems to exercise **See Assessment activity 2.1, page 41**	**M1** explain the initial responses of the cardiovascular, respiratory, neuromuscular and energy systems to exercise **See Assessment activity 2.1, page 41**	**D1** analyse the initial responses of the cardiovascular, respiratory, neuromuscular and energy systems to exercise **See Assessment activity 2.1, page 41**
P2 describe the initial responses of the neuromuscular and energy systems to exercise **See Assessment activity 2.1, page 41**		
P3 investigate how the cardiovascular and respiratory systems respond to steady-state exercise **See Assessment activity 2.2, page 46**	**M2** explain how the cardiovascular, respiratory, neuromuscular and energy systems respond to steady-state exercise. **See Assessment activity 2.2, page 46**	**D2** analyse the responses of the cardiovascular, respiratory, neuromuscular and energy systems to steady-state exercise **See Assessment activity 2.2, page 46**
P4 describe how the neuromuscular and energy systems respond to steady-state exercise **See Assessment activity 2.2, page 46**		
P5 describe fatigue, and how the body recovers from exercise **See Assessment activity 2.3, page 50**	**M3** explain fatigue, and how the body recovers from exercise **See Assessment activity 2.3, page 50**	
P6 describe how the cardiovascular and respiratory systems adapt to long-term exercise **See Assessment activity 2.4, page 54**	**M4** explain how the cardiovascular, respiratory, neuromuscular, energy and skeletal systems adapt to long-term exercise **See Assessment activity 2.4, page 54**	**D3** analyse how the cardiovascular, respiratory, neuromuscular, energy and skeletal systems adapt to long-term exercise **See Assessment activity 2.4, page 54**
P7 describe how the neuromuscular, energy and skeletal systems adapt to long-term exercise **See Assessment activity 2.4, page 54**		

How you will be assessed

This unit will be assessed by an internal assignment that will be designed and marked by the tutors at your centre. Your assessment could be in the form of:

- presentations
- case studies
- practical tasks
- written assignments.

Michael, 17-year-old mixed martial artist

This unit helped me understand how my body responds physiologically to the training I do and why, at the end of every training session, I feel tired and sometimes exhausted. Unit 1 taught me about the structure of the body, but I needed to know how my body responds and adapts to my training. The lectures and activities helped me understand the changes my body undergoes during long-term training.

I appreciate now that training is not all about lifting weights but a balance of fighting skills, strength and cardiovascular work to make sure my heart and lungs are in good shape, and that I recover properly. I was training hard on ground work recently and started to tire. I told the coach I was fatiguing and he asked me to explain what I meant by 'fatiguing'. I explained about the depletion of energy resources and the build up of lactate and carbon dioxide in my blood. Impressed with my knowledge, he asked me to explain fatigue to the other athletes. It was a proud moment having everyone listening and thinking about what I was saying.

Over to you

1. **What areas of this unit might you find challenging?**
2. **Which section of the unit is relevant to you and your training?**
3. **What preparation can you do in readiness for the unit assessment(s)?**

1. Be able to investigate the initial responses of the body to exercise

What happens during a marathon?

Paula Radcliffe holds the world women's marathon record. Over 26 miles, her muscles need a supply of fuel and oxygen while her lungs eliminate waste products such as carbon dioxide. Many physiological processes occur when Paula competes. These processes occur when you exercise. The difference is Paula can push them further. How much blood does Paula's heart pump around her body? How much air are her lungs processing in one minute? Which energy systems are fuelling her muscles? Why can't you run the same time as Paula?

For several years, Paula Radcliffe has been one of the world's elite female aerobic athletes due to her success in the marathon event. How does her body respond to the demands of this gruelling event? To fuel this activity and maintain her body's equilibrium, Paula must respond quickly and she does so using complex physiological processes. This unit examines these processes and the implications for sport and exercise performance.

1.1 Exercise

Aerobic

Aerobic means 'with oxygen' and involves the use of oxygen in energy production. During aerobic exercise, oxygen is used to burn fats and glucose to produce adenosine triphosphate (ATP), the basic energy carrier for all cells in the human body. During aerobic exercise, glycogen is broken down to produce glucose, but in its absence fat metabolism is used instead. This process can cause a decline in performance levels, as the switch to fats as the main fuel source causes what marathon runners call 'hitting the wall'.

In general, aerobic exercise is performed at a moderate level of intensity over a long period of time, such as long-distance running at a moderate pace. Playing badminton, with near-continuous motion, is aerobic activity, while rugby union or cricket bowling, with their more frequent breaks, may not be.

Anaerobic

Anaerobic means 'without oxygen'. It is a short, high-intensity activity where the demand for oxygen from the exercise exceeds the oxygen supply. Anaerobic exercise relies on energy sources stored in the muscles and, unlike aerobic exercise, is not dependent on oxygen. Anaerobic exercise includes heavy weightlifting, sprints (running, cycling) and isometrics (in which one part of the body is used to resist the movement of another part) or any rapid burst of hard exercise.

With 100 metres to go, many distance cyclists are sprinting at speeds approaching 40 mph using short bursts of intense anaerobic exercise. How do you think their bodies feel once they cross the finish line?

1.2 Cardiovascular responses

When exercising, changes occur within the cardiovascular system. You must understand these changes as they impact on an athlete's training and performance.

Heart rate

Heart rate changes according to the body's needs. It increases during exercise to deliver extra oxygen to tissues and remove carbon dioxide. At rest, a normal adult heart beats approximately 75 beats per minute, peaking at around 200 beats per minute for strenuous activity, depending on age. Heart rate is controlled by the sino atrial node (SAN). The rate goes up or down when the SAN receives information via nerves that link the SAN with the cardiovascular centre in the brain. When you exercise, information is communicated and the heart adapts accordingly. It does so in these ways:

- the **sympathetic nerve** speeds up the heart: the synapses at the end of this nerve secrete a hormone called noradrenalin
- the vagus nerve (**parasympathetic nerve**) slows down the heart: the synapses at the end of the nerve secrete a hormone called acetylcholine.

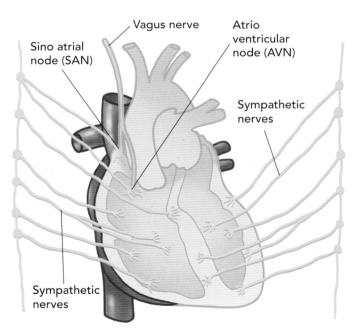

Figure 2.1: The heart is connected via the vagus nerve and sympathetic nerves to the brain. How does this work to make the heart beat continually?

When athletes are about to exercise an anticipatory increase in heart rate occurs following impulses originating in the brain. The anticipatory increase can depend on an athlete's emotional state, often belying his or her true resting state. For example, prior to the start of a race, an athlete's heart rate is likely to increase in anticipation of the event.

Stroke volume

Stroke volume is the amount of blood pumped by one of the ventricles in one contraction. About two-thirds of the blood in the ventricle is put out with each beat. During exercise, stroke volume increases progressively and gradually levels off at a higher level until the exercise has ended. Assuming normal stroke volume ranges between 70 and 80 ml per beat, a trained athlete's stroke volume can be 110 ml. During exercise blood flow increases sharply, allowing for a greater oxygen supply to the skeletal muscles.

Cardiac output

Cardiac output is the volume of blood pumped out of the heart in one minute. It is equal to the heart rate multiplied by the stroke volume. If a heart beats 70 times per minute, and 70 ml of blood is pumped each time, the cardiac output is 4900 ml per minute, typical for an average adult at rest. Cardiac output may reach up to 30 litres per minute during extreme exercise. An increase in heart rate, increased sympathetic nervous system activity and decreased parasympathetic nervous system activity can increase cardiac output.

Key terms

Sympathetic nerve – speeds up heart rate through the release of noradrenalin.

Parasympathetic nerve – slows heart rate through the release of acetylcholine.

Stroke volume – volume of blood pumped out of left ventricle per beat.

Cardiac output – volume of blood pumped out of left ventricle in one minute: cardiac output = stroke volume × beats per minute.

Blood pressure

Blood pressure is the pressure of the blood against the walls of the arteries and results from two forces. One is created by the heart as it pumps blood into arteries and through the circulatory system. The other is the force of the arteries as they resist the blood flow. During exercise, although both cardiac output and blood pressure increase, mechanisms act to restrict the blood pressure rising too high.

Calculating – blood pressure is the force exerted by the flow of blood against the walls of blood vessels. It is determined by two factors:

- resistance offered by vessel walls to blood flow (this can be dependent on several factors including blood vessel length and radius)
- cardiac output or blood volume pumped out of the left ventricle in one minute.

Therefore, blood pressure is defined as:

cardiac output × resistance

Blood pressure increases when either cardiac output or resistance increases.

Readings – medical staff sometimes measure blood pressure manually using the brachial artery. A blood pressure cuff is wrapped around the arm above the elbow and inflated until a brachial pulse cannot be felt or heard. The pressure is gradually released and the first sounds of forced blood through the brachial artery are listened for with a stethoscope. This gives the **systolic pressure**. As cuff pressure reduces the sounds of the forced blood disappear, giving the **diastolic pressure**. Alternatively, blood pressure can be easily measured at the touch of a button using digital instruments.

At rest, normal adult systolic pressure varies between 110 and 140 mm Hg, and diastolic pressure between 70 and 80 mm Hg. Blood pressure varies with age, sex, race and physical activity. Remember, what is normal for one person may not be normal for another.

Blood pressure around 120/80 mm Hg is optimal for adults. Systolic pressure readings of 120 to 139 mm Hg or diastolic pressure of 80 to 89 mm Hg is considered as **prehypertension** and needs to be watched carefully. A blood pressure reading of 140/90 mm Hg or higher is considered to be hypertensive. **Hypertension** is high blood pressure and increases the risk of cardiovascular diseases or kidney failure because it adds to the workload of the heart. During aerobic exercise, oxygen

consumption and heart rate increase in relation to the intensity of the activity. Systolic blood pressure rises progressively, while diastolic blood pressure stays the same or decreases slightly. Pulse rate rises and blood flow to the muscles increases.

Key terms

Systolic pressure – pressure exerted in the arteries when the heart contracts.

Diastolic pressure – pressure exerted in the arteries when the heart relaxes and fills with blood.

Prehypertension – means you don't have high blood pressure now but you are likely to develop it in future.

Hypertension – high blood pressure, which is when systolic blood pressure is above 140mm Hg and diastolic blood pressure is above 90mm Hg.

Activity: Blood pressure

Work in pairs or small groups. Under guidance from your tutor, use a digital blood pressure monitor to determine your own blood pressure and that of your friends

Note: interpreting exercise assessment data results when investigating the body's responses to steady-state exercise could develop your mathematics skills.

1.3 Respiratory responses

Your body is surprisingly insensitive to levels of oxygen required for exercise. However, it is sensitive to increases in carbon dioxide levels. The levels of oxygen in arterial blood vary little, even during exercise, but carbon dioxide levels vary according to the level of physical activity. The more intense the exercise, the greater the carbon dioxide concentration in the blood. To combat this, your body adapts by increasing its breathing rate to expel the carbon dioxide.

Increase in breathing rate

Physical exercise increases the oxygen consumption of skeletal muscles. For example, a trained athlete at rest might use 250 ml of oxygen per minute, but require 3600 ml per minute during maximal exercise. While oxygen consumption increases, the volume of carbon dioxide produced increases. Decreased blood oxygen and increased blood carbon dioxide concentration stimulates the respiratory centre to increase breathing rate. A minor increase in breathing rate before exercise is known as an anticipatory rise. However, when exercise begins, there is an immediate and greater increase in breathing rate due to receptors working in both the muscles and joints.

After several minutes of aerobic exercise, breathing continues to rise at a slower rate, levelling off (while exercise intensity remains constant) until exercise ends. If the exercise is maximal then breathing rate continues to rise until exhaustion. In both cases, after exercise is finished, breathing returns to normal – rapidly to begin with and then more slowly.

The increase in breathing rate during exercise demands an increase in blood flow to the skeletal muscles, placing demands on the respiratory and circulatory systems. Should either of these systems fail to keep up with demands, the athlete will feel out of breath. This is due to the inability of the heart and circulatory system to move enough blood between the lungs and the skeletal muscles, not necessarily an inability of the respiratory system to provide sufficient oxygen.

Intercostal muscles

During the breathing process, the external intercostal muscles contract, causing the ribs and the sternum to move upwards and outwards. The diaphragm muscles contract, causing the diaphragm to flatten. The combined movements of the ribs, sternum and diaphragm cause the thorax and lungs to increase in volume, while the air pressure within the lungs decreases below external air pressure. The result is that external air pressure forces air into the lungs.

During relaxed breathing, expiration is passive. The external intercostal muscles relax so the ribs and sternum move downwards and inwards. At the same time, the diaphragm relaxes and rises, regaining its dome shape. The combined movements of the ribs, sternum and diaphragm, aided by the recoil of the abdominal muscles, cause the thorax and the lungs to decrease in volume. Air pressure inside the lungs increases above external air pressure. The result is that internal air pressure forces air out of the lungs.

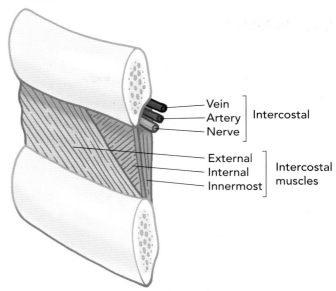

Figure 2.2 Eleven pairs of intercostals muscles occupy the spaces between 12 pairs of ribs. Their contraction and relaxation changes intrapulmonary pressure and contributes to the mechanics of breathing.

During exercise, forced breathing is used. This differs from normal breathing because, during expiration, the internal intercostal muscles contract, moving the ribs and sternum upwards and outwards forcibly. The abdominal muscles also contract, increasing the pressure of the abdominal cavity, helping the diaphragm to rise more forcibly. During exercise the muscles involved in the breathing process can utilise up to 10 per cent of total oxygen uptake. Cramp in these muscles is thought to be the cause of a 'stitch'.

Remember

Your ribs move approximately 5 million times a year, every time you breathe.

Increase in tidal volume

Tidal volume is air ventilated per breath. Exercise increases **minute ventilation** (the volume of gas ventilated in one minute). This rapid rise is due to nervous influences generated from receptors located in the working muscles and joints. Consequently, both tidal volume and breathing rate increase. After exercise, tidal volume and minute ventilation return to normal.

Key term

Minute ventilation – tidal volume × frequency of breaths per minute.

Valsalva manoeuvre

The Valsalva manoeuvre is forcibly exhaling with the mouth closed and the nose pinched, forcing air into the middle ear. This is used as a test of cardiac function and autonomic nervous control of the heart or to 'clear' the ears (equalise pressure) when external pressure increases. The normal physiological response consists of four phases:

- Initial pressure rise: pressure rises inside the chest and forces blood out. This causes a rise in blood pressure.

- Reduced venous return and compensation: return of blood to the heart is impeded by pressure inside the chest. Heart output is reduced and blood pressure falls. This fall causes blood vessels to constrict with some rise in pressure. During this time the pulse rate increases.

- Pressure release: the pressure on the chest is released, allowing the aorta to expand, causing a further initial slight fall in pressure. Venous blood can once more enter the chest and the heart. Cardiac output begins to increase.

- Return of cardiac output: blood returning to the heart is enhanced by the entry of blood which had been dammed back, causing a rapid increase in cardiac output and blood pressure. The pressure usually rises before returning to a normal level. With return of blood pressure, the pulse rate returns to normal.

Pulmonary ventilation

Pulmonary ventilation is the process of air flowing into the lungs during inspiration (inhalation) and out of the lungs during expiration (exhalation). Air flows because of pressure differences between the atmosphere and the gases inside the lungs. Air flows from a high pressure region to a lower pressure region. Muscular breathing movements create three changes in pressure that result in ventilation. These are:

- atmospheric pressure – air pressure outside the body

- intra-alveolar pressure – air pressure inside the alveoli of the lungs

- intrapleural pressure – air pressure within the pleural cavity.

The response of the body to exercise often results in an increased concentration of carbon dioxide in the blood following an increased utilisation of oxygen. It is this level of carbon dioxide that causes the respiratory centre to send impulses to the internal intercostal muscles to speed up the expiratory process.

Take it further

Catch your breath!

Paula Radcliffe completed a London Marathon in a time of 2 hours, 15 minutes and 25 seconds. Crossing the line, Paula was clearly tired, but did you notice her breathing? She took several rapid and deep breaths once she had stopped. Within a few minutes, her breathing rate had slowed enough for her to hold a brief television interview. Explain why it would be virtually impossible for Paula to give an interview immediately after she had crossed the finish line. Concentrate on the physiology of the pulmonary ventilation and why Paula needed those extra few minutes before holding a conversation.

1.4 Neuromuscular responses

The term 'neuromuscular' refers to both the nervous system and the muscular system. There are two kinds of nerves:

- sensory neurons (or nerves) which carry information from our extremities (the skin) to the central nervous system (the brain and spinal cord)

- motor neurons (or nerves) which carry information from our central nervous system to our muscles.

Nervous control of muscular contraction

Muscles contract when stimulated by nerves. Three basic types of contraction can occur during exercise, each with a variation of contraction pattern.

1. Isotonic contraction: the muscle shortens as it develops tension.

2. Isometric contraction: the muscle develops tension but does not change length.

3. Isokinetic contraction: the muscle contracts to its maximum at a constant speed over the full range of movement.

- **Neuromuscular junction** – a neuromuscular junction is the site at which a motor neuron communicates with a muscle fibre using nerve impulses.

- **Motor unit** – a motor unit is made up of a motor neuron and all the associated muscle fibres it affects. Motor units work together to coordinate contractions of a single skeletal muscle, although the number of fibres in each unit varies based on the muscle size and role.

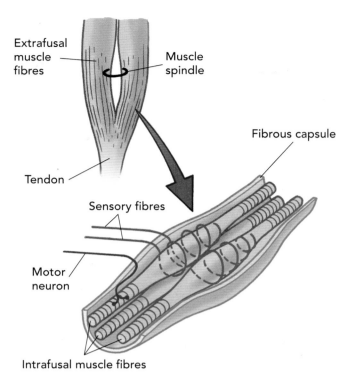

Figure 2.3 Muscle spindles provide information about any changes in length and tension of muscle fibres.

Muscle spindles

Muscle spindles are proprioceptors found in skeletal muscles. They detect muscle stretch and initiate a reflex that resists the stretch. When muscle is stretched, primary sensory sensors in the muscle spindle respond to the velocity and degree of stretch, then send this information to the spinal cord. Secondary sensory sensors detect and send information about the degree of stretch to the central nervous system. This information is transmitted to a motor neuron, which activates the muscle to contract, thus reducing stretch.

1.5 Energy system responses

The body takes in chemical energy in the form of food. This is stored in the body in the form of adenosine triphosphate (ATP). The movement of muscles requires ATP, so it follows that the ability of an athlete to move his or her muscles requires a continued supply of ATP.

ATP production

Energy is required for all kinds of bodily processes. Whether it is a 26-mile marathon run or one explosive movement like a tennis serve, skeletal muscle is powered by energy released by ATP. The body stores only a small quantity of this 'energy currency' in cells – enough to power only a few seconds of all-out exercise. Therefore, the body must replace or resynthesise ATP on a continual basis. Understanding how it does this is the key to understanding energy systems. ATP consists of a base (adenine) and three phosphate groups. It is formed by a reaction between an adenosine diphosphate (ADP) molecule and a phosphate. When a molecule of ATP is used, the last phosphate group splits off and energy is released.

Take it further

Aerobic and anaerobic metabolism

Consider the various movements and actions undertaken by Wayne Rooney during a football match (for example, heading, shooting, tackling, jogging, marking, etc.). Which of these rely primarily on aerobic metabolism and which rely primarily on anaerobic metabolism? Make a list and justify your decisions.

(a) ATP is formed when adenosine diphosphate (ADP) binds with a phosphate

(b) Energy is stored in the bond between the second and third phosphate groups

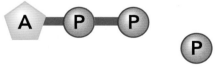

(c) When a cell needs energy, it breaks the bond between the phosphate groups to form ADP and a free phosphate molecule

Figure 2.4 ATP production (a) – (c)

Creatine phosphate system

ATP and creatine phosphate (phosphocreatine or PCr) make up the ATP-PCr system. PCr is broken down, releasing energy and a phosphate molecule (then used to rebuild ATP). The enzyme that controls the breakdown of PCr is called creatine kinase.

The ATP-PCr system can operate with or without oxygen, but because it does not rely on the presence of oxygen it is said to be anaerobic. During the first five seconds of exercise, regardless of intensity, the ATP-PCr system is relied on almost exclusively. The ATP-PCr system can sustain all-out exercise for three to 15 seconds. If activity continues beyond this period, the body must rely on an additional energy system to resynthesise ATP.

Lactic acid system

Glycolysis is the breakdown of glucose and consists of a series of enzymatic reactions. The carbohydrates we eat supply the glucose, which is stored as glycogen in the muscles and liver.

The end product of glycolysis is pyruvic acid and is used in a process called the **Krebs cycle** (see page 45) or converted into lactic acid. Traditionally, if the final product was lactic acid, the process was called anaerobic glycolysis; and if the final product was pyruvic acid, the process was called aerobic glycolysis. However, oxygen availability only determines the fate of the end product and is not required for the actual process of glycolysis itself. Alternative terms used are fast glycolysis if the final product is lactic acid, and slow glycolysis for the process that leads to pyruvic acid being funnelled through the Krebs cycle. The fast glycolysis system can produce energy at a greater rate than slow glycolysis. However, because the end product of fast glycolysis is lactic acid, it can quickly accumulate and is thought to lead to muscular fatigue.

Key term

Krebs cycle – a series of chemical reactions occurring in mitochondria in which carbon dioxide is produced and carbon dioxide atoms are oxidised.

Anaerobic glycolysis

Anaerobic glycolysis is the process by which the pathway of glycolysis produces lactic acid. It occurs at times when energy is required in the absence of oxygen. It is vital for tissues with high energy requirements or an insufficient oxygen supply.

Glycolysis forms pyruvic acid and hydrogen ions (H+). A build-up of hydrogen ions makes the muscle cells acidic and interferes with their operation, so carrier molecules called nicotinamide adenine dinucleotide (NAD+) remove the H+. The NAD+ is reduced to NADH, which deposit the H+ during the electron transport chain to be combined with oxygen to form water.

If there is insufficient oxygen, NADH cannot release the H+ and they build up in the cell. To prevent a rise in acidity, pyruvic acid accepts H+ forming lactic acid that then dissociates into lactate and H+. Some of the lactate diffuses into the blood stream. The normal pH of the muscle cell is 7.1, but if the build-up of H+ continues and pH is reduced to around 6.5, muscle contraction is impaired. Table 2.1 gives some examples of the three energy systems, their duration and their uses.

Remember

The energy systems do not operate in isolation; they interact to supply the energy required for muscular movement. Energy systems are like 'taps' that are never fully turned off – the energy flows continually (like water at differing pressures) according to the exercise being undertaken.

Energy system	Fuel	Duration	Intensity	By-products	Sporting Example
Creatine Phosphate	Creatine Phosphate (PC)	8–10 secs	High	Free creatine	100 metres/short sprints
Lactic acid/ anaerobic glycolysis	Carbohydrate	30–90 secs	Medium	Lactic acid and associated H+	400 metres/repeated runs in football or rugby
Aerobic*	Carbohydrate, fat, protein	Hours	Low	CO_2 and H_2O	10,000 metres/mountain hike

Table 2.1: The three energy systems, their duration and their uses.

* The aerobic energy system is a long-term energy system that is used in steady-state exercise and is discussed later in this unit.

Assessment activity 2.1

BTEC

As a newly qualified fitness instructor, you've been offered a great opportunity. The senior personal trainer is busy and has asked you to assist her with three important clients: a weightlifter, a 400 metre runner and a 1500 metre swimmer, all of whom compete at a high level.

The personal trainer is stepping up each of their preparations for competition and has asked you to prepare a handy A2 poster to illustrate each athlete's initial responses to exercise and the likely effects of their individual training programmes.

1. Your poster should illustrate the initial responses of the cardiovascular and respiratory systems for each client. **P1**

2. On the same poster, describe the initial response of the neuromuscular and energy systems to the clients' events. Illustrate your findings on a poster with two columns (neuromuscular and energy system responses) for each client and their event. **P2**

3. Further explain on your poster the initial responses of the cardiovascular, respiratory, neuromuscular and energy systems to the individual clients and their events. **M1**

4. Analyse the initial responses of the cardiovascular, respiratory, neuromuscular and energy systems to the individual clients and their events. **D1**

Grading tips

- To attain **P1** remember to include the following factors and describe what happens to them: heart rate, stroke volume, cardiac output, blood pressure, breathing rate, intercostal muscles, tidal volume and pulmonary ventilation. You may wish to complete this task using either a table or flow diagram. Don't forget to mention each of the clients and their specific events.

- To attain **P2** don't forget to mention each of the clients and their specific events as these responses may differ.

- To attain **M1**, 'explaining' means showing that you know why something happens and can give that explanation clearly.

- To attain **D1** you must analyse, which means showing you can break up the components of the question and respond to them with critical insight. In other words, you have the ability to see the important points to do with the initial responses to exercise of the cardiovascular, respiratory, neuromuscular and energy systems that might otherwise be overlooked.

PLTS

If you identify questions to answer and problems to resolve in your poster and table, you can develop your skills as an **independent enquirer**. Producing a poster to illustrate your findings will develop your **creative thinking** skills.

Functional skills

Discussing how to assess the body's initial responses to exercise will develop your **English** skills in speaking and listening.

2. Be able to investigate how the body responds to steady-state exercise

2.1 Steady-state exercise

Upon exercising, you increase your energy usage. This is reflected in the increased oxygen consumption. Under certain conditions where the work rate is constant, the pattern of this increased oxygen consumption shows an initial rise then levels off. Once this plateau is reached, oxygen consumption remains steady over the period of the exercise. For example, if you undertake 20 minutes of continuous same-speed jogging or 20 minutes of continuous same-speed swimming, a number of responses occur. Your heart and respiratory states increase to accommodate the demands placed on the body, more ATP is synthesised and neuromuscular changes occur. After three or four minutes your body adapts to the increase in exercise intensity and your physiological demands level out. For the remaining 15 minutes, you undergo what is known as steady-state exercise, and what this involves is discussed below.

2.2 Cardiovascular responses

Heart rate

Prior to exercise, the heart beats between 60 and 80 beats per minute in untrained men and women. The heart rate increases during exercise and it does so in relation to the intensity of the exercise performed, as shown in Figure 2.5.

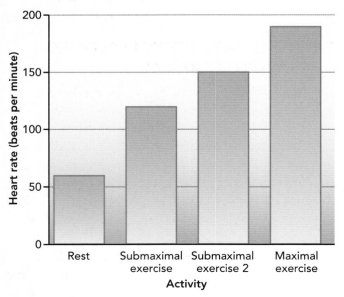

Figure 2.5: Heart rate during exercise. 'Submaximal exercise 2' is aerobic exercise of greater intensity than 'Submaximal exercise' given the increased heart rate.

Stroke volume

Stroke volume reaches a peak during submaximal exercise and does not increase further during **maximal exercise**. The greatest increase in stroke volume occurs in the transition from rest to moderate exercise. During maximal exercise, stroke volume does not increase as the left ventricle is, at this point, already full to capacity. The body tolerates maximal activity for as long as it can by increasing heart rate and maintaining stroke volume.

Key term

Maximal exercise – level of training intensity when an athlete approaches their maximal heart rate and performs exercise to an increasingly anaerobic level.

Cardiac output

Approximately 5 litres of blood are circulated each minute at rest for trained or untrained athletes, so approximately 1 litre of oxygen is available to the body. An increase in cardiac output has benefits for trained athletes as they can transport more blood to the working muscles and, therefore, more oxygen. Given the formula for cardiac output is stroke volume × heart rate, if the average stroke volume is 70 ml and the average resting heart rate is 70 beats per minute, the average cardiac output of a healthy adult is:

$$70 \times 70 = 4900 \text{ ml of blood per minute}$$

A key adaptation of steady-state exercise is that resting heart rate decreases while stroke volume increases. A trained athlete can have a stroke volume of 110 ml and a resting heart rate of 50 beats per minute. The average cardiac output of a trained athlete is:

$$110 \text{ ml} \times 50 \text{ bpm} = 5500 \text{ ml per minute}$$

Therefore, a greater cardiac output (oxygen to working muscles) maintained with fewer beats is an indication of increased fitness.

Blood flow

Increased energy expenditure due to exercise requires adjustment in blood flow that affects the entire cardiovascular system.

- **Vasodilation** – during exercise, the vascular portion of active muscles increases through dilation of arterioles, a process known as vasodilation that involves an increase in the diameter of the blood vessels resulting in an increased blood flow to the muscle area supplied by the vessel (or arteriole).
- **Vasoconstriction** – vessels can also shut down blood flow to tissues; this process is known as vasoconstriction and involves a decrease in diameter of a blood vessel by contraction of involuntary muscle fibres in the vessel walls. For example, at rest kidney function requires about 20 per cent of cardiac output. During maximal exercise blood flow to the kidneys decreases due to vasoconstriction to approximately 1 per cent of cardiac output as the kidneys effectively shut down during exercise.

Blood pressure

During steady-state exercise, dilation of the blood vessels in active muscles increases the vascular area for blood flow. The alternate rhythmical contraction and relaxation of the skeletal muscles forces blood through the vessels and returns it to the heart.

Thermoregulation

Increased plasma volume due to steady-state exercise supports sweat gland function during heat stress and maintains the correct plasma volume for the demands of exercise. A trained athlete stores less heat early during steady-state exercise, reaching a thermal steady-state sooner and at a lower core temperature than an untrained person.

Increased venous return

Veins solve the problem related to the low blood pressure of venous blood. Valves spaced at intervals within the vein permit one-way blood flow back to the heart. Veins compress because of low venous blood pressure or, in the case of steady-state exercise, muscular contractions aid the venous return.

Starling's law

Starling's law states that stroke volume increases in response to an increase in blood volume filling the heart. This stretches the ventricular wall, causing cardiac muscle to contract more forcefully. The stroke volume may also increase due to greater contractions in the cardiac muscles during exercise. Therefore,

the reduced heart rate of a trained athlete allows for greater filling during the longer diastole, so the stretch of the cardiac muscle is greater. This in turn increases the stroke volume.

Activity: Heart rate graph

Imagine you have undertaken a 20-minute steady jog at a steady 10 km/h. Draw a graph illustrating time along the horizontal and heart rate along the vertical. Sketch a line on your graph that indicates approximately how your heart rate has changed throughout the course of the 20-minute exercise. Assuming you didn't run to exhaustion, how do you think your graph will look at the beginning, throughout the majority of the run, and when you finally stop?

2.3 Respiratory responses

Tidal volume and breathing rate

Increases in breathing rate maintain alveolar ventilation during steady-state exercise. Trained athletes achieve the required alveolar ventilation by increasing tidal volume and only minimally increasing breathing rate. With deeper breathing, alveolar ventilation can increase from 70 per cent at rest to over 85 per cent of total ventilation in exercise. This increase occurs because deeper breathing causes a greater tidal volume to enter the alveoli.

Effects of pH and temperature on the oxygen dissociation curve

The **oxygen dissociation** curve is a graph that shows the relationship between the percentage of **oxygen saturation of blood** and the **partial pressure** of oxygen. During steady-state exercise, increased temperature and lower blood pH concentration affect the oxygen–**haemoglobin** dissociation curve in such a way that more oxygen can be unloaded to supply the active muscle. In prolonged high-intensity exercise, large amounts of **lactate** enter the blood from active muscle. At exhaustion, **blood pH** can approach 6.8. Only after exercise ceases does blood pH stabilise and return to 7.4.

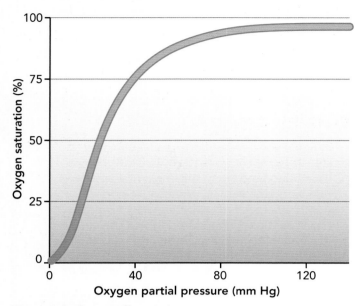

Figure 2.6: Oxygen dissociation curve.

Key terms

Oxygen dissociation – graph illustrating the relationship between oxygen saturation in blood and partial pressure of oxygen.

Oxygen saturation of blood – measure of oxygen dissolved or carried in blood.

Partial pressure – pressure applied by a single gas in a mixture of gases.

Haemoglobin – oxygen transporting component of red blood cells.

Lactate – product of lactic acid which occurs in blood.

Blood pH – measure of acidity or alkalinity of a solution.

Golgi tendon – a proprioceptor located within the muscle tendon.

2.4 Neuromuscular responses

Muscle spindles and **Golgi tendon** organs provide sensory information about the intensity of exercise, allowing smooth, coordinated movement patterns.

Increased pliability of muscles

Muscle spindles are located within muscle fibres known as intrafusal fibres. When the spindle is stretched, nerve impulses generate information about the degree of stretch and send this to the central nervous system (CNS). The CNS relays information concerning how many motor units should be contracted to implement smooth movement. The more your body is used to steady-state exercise, the more efficient the muscle spindles become at transmitting this information.

Increased transmission rate of nerve impulses

Golgi tendon organs are located within the tendons and are sensitive to stretch. Golgi tendon organs send information to the CNS concerning the strength of a muscle contraction and, together with muscle spindles, facilitate smooth movement patterns.

2.5 Energy system responses

Fuel is consumed with or without oxygen as muscles convert chemical energy to mechanical energy. This process is achieved using three energy systems. At any time, one of the three energy systems is the dominant contributor to the energy required for resynthesis of adenosine triphosphate (ATP). The contribution of each energy system depends on the intensity and duration of the exercise. The continual interaction of the three systems is known as the energy continuum.

Remember

During exercise, the body does not switch from one energy system to another – energy is derived from all systems at all times. However, the emphasis changes depending on the intensity and duration of the activity.

Adenosine triphosphate (ATP) production

Training to enhance intramuscular ATP energy transfer capacity requires repetitive, intense, short-duration exercise. The activities chosen should engage muscles in the movement for which the athlete desires improved anaerobic power. This achieves two goals:

- it enha es metabolic capacity of engaged muscle tissue or fibres
- it improves neuromuscular adaptations to the sport-specific pattern of movement.

When ATP is split, some of the energy is used to power muscle contractions but, as no system is 100 per cent efficient, some is always lost as heat. This is one reason why exercise produces heat.

Aerobic energy system

The aerobic energy system involves the oxygen transportation system and the use of mitochondria in working muscles for oxidation of glycogen and fatty acids. It is known as the aerobic energy system because of its reliance on oxygen.

This system involves prolonged work at low intensity and increases in importance the longer the sport duration. Lack of fuel, overheating or **dehydration** will end the exercise.

> ## Key term
>
> **Dehydration** – depletion of fluids that can impede thermoregulation and cause a rise in core body temperature.

Fuelling this system for combustion varies according to its duration and intensity. In prolonged aerobic exercise, the preferred fuel is free fatty acids because glycogen stores are limited compared to our plentiful fat stores.

Unlike glycogen, fatty acids can only be used in the aerobic energy system, whereas higher-intensity exercise involving aerobic and anaerobic energy systems prefer glycogen as fuel.

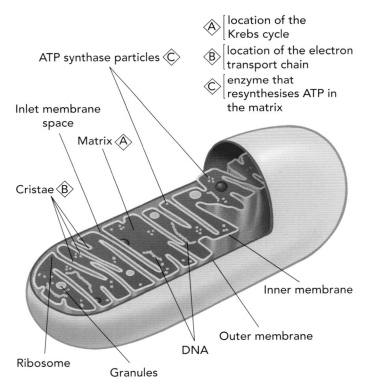

⟨A⟩ | location of the Krebs cycle
⟨B⟩ | location of the electron transport chain
⟨C⟩ | enzyme that resynthesises ATP in the matrix

Figure 2.7: A mitochondrion.

Anaerobic glycolysis

Anaerobic glycolysis involves the breakdown of glycogen (glycolysis) in the absence of oxygen, with the formation of ATP plus lactate. The accumulation of lactate ends the use of this energy system after 40 to 60 seconds of maximum effort, so this system is called upon by athletes (400 metre runners and rugby players) whose sports demand high-energy expenditure for up to 60 seconds.

Mitochondria

Mitochondria are the cellular site of aerobic respiration. Pyruvate oxidation and the Krebs cycle take place in the matrix (fluid) of the mitochondria, while the electron transport chain takes place in the inner membrane itself.

Krebs cycle

The Krebs cycle is a series of aerobic reactions that take place in the matrix in mitochondria. Carbon dioxide is produced and hydrogen is removed from carbon molecules and joins NAD to form $NADH_2$. The Krebs cycle provides a continuous supply of electrons to feed the electron transport chain. This cycle begins when the 2-carbon acetyl CoA joins with a 4-carbon compound to form a 6-carbon compound called citric acid. Citric acid (6C) is gradually converted back to the 4-carbon compound ready to start the cycle once more.

With each rotation, the Krebs cycle produces:

- 3 molecules of NADH
- 1 molecule of FADH2
- 1 molecule of ATP
- 2 molecules of CO2
- 1 molecule of oxaloacetate (allows the cycle to continue for another turn)

The Krebs cycle rotates twice for every glucose molecule used, producing six molecules of NADH. These molecules are important as they carry electrons into the next stage of glucose respiration, the electron transport chain (see figure 2.9, page 46).

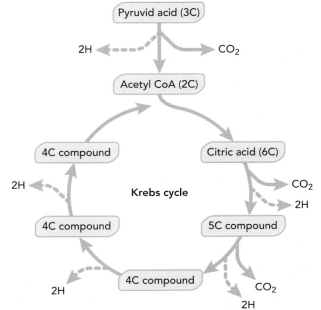

Figure 2.8: Krebs cycle.

Electron transport chain

The electron transport chain is a series of biomechanical reactions during which free energy contained within hydrogen (derived from the Krebs cycle) is released, so that it can be used to synthesise ATP during aerobic metabolism. The electron transport chain occurs in the many cristae in mitochondria. Each reaction involves a specific electron-carrier molecule which has a particular attraction for hydrogen. The final link in the electron transport chain is oxygen, which combines with the hydrogen and electrons to form water.

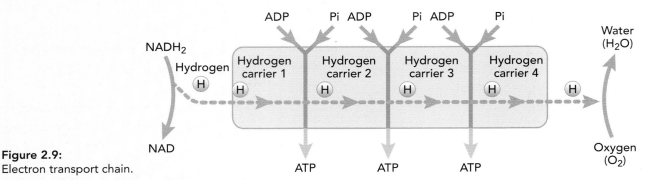

Figure 2.9:
Electron transport chain.

Assessment activity 2.2   P3 P4 M2 D2   BTEC

The 1500 metre swimmer has asked if you would assist his fitness and training programme. He is keen to learn more about physiology for sport and exercise and has asked you to explain his training programmes so that he understands the effects of his training.

You produce four large flashcards, one for each topic area. These flashcards are designed to keep in his kit bag and will describe the responses in bullet-point format for easy reference.

1. Describe on your flashcards how the cardiovascular, respiratory, neuromuscular and energy systems respond to the swimmer's steady-state exercise training (i.e. swimming front crawl at a constant rate for 20–40 minutes). **P3** **P4**

2. Further explain on your flashcards (use both sides if you need) how the cardiovascular, respiratory, neuromuscular and energy systems respond to the swimmer's steady-state exercise training. **M2**

3. Analyse the cardiovascular, respiratory, neuromuscular and energy systems' responses to steady-state exercise. Your flashcards might refer to fitness testing results taken by the senior personal trainer to illustrate your findings. **D2**

Grading tips

- To attain **P3** and **P4** use bullet points or flow diagrams to illustrate your findings.

- To attain **M2**, 'explaining' means showing that you know why something happens and can give that explanation clearly. Remember to keep your explanations in the context of the effects of the 1500 metre swimmer's training.

- To attain **D2** remember to keep your analyses in the context of the effects of the 1500 metre swimmer's training.

PLTS

If you identify questions to answer and problems to resolve how the cardiovascular, respiratory, neuromuscular and energy systems respond to steady-state exercise in your assignment, you can develop your skills as an **independent enquirer**. Undertaking practical assessments of the body's response to steady-state exercise will improve your **effective participator** skills.

Functional skills

Using ICT to research, retrieve, plan and evaluate exercise assessment data to investigate how the body's responses to steady-state exercise occur could develop your **ICT** skills. Interpreting exercise assessment data results when investigating the body's responses to steady-state exercise could develop your **Mathematics** skills. Discussing how to assess the body's response to steady-state exercise will develop your **English** skills in speaking and listening.

3. Know fatigue and how the body recovers from exercise

3.1 Fatigue

Fatigue involves the exhaustion of muscle from prolonged exertion or over-stimulation. We cannot exercise indefinitely because of neuromuscular fatigue, which occurs as a result of different methods and systems. The symptoms of fatigue include:

- depletion of energy sources, primarily creatine phosphate and glycogen
- increase in lactic acid
- dehydration
- **electrolyte** loss.

> **Key term**
>
> **Electrolyte** – a substance (usually salts) dissolved in water.

Exercise places demands on the body. Think about the changes that occur when you exercise:

- oxygen levels fall
- carbon dioxide and lactate levels increase
- body temperature increases
- blood glucose and glycogen levels fall
- fluid and electrolytes (salts) are lost as you sweat.

During short-term maximal exercise, insufficient oxygen and/or increased lactate levels can bring about fatigue. Reliance on anaerobic metabolism impairs energy transfer via glycolysis and inhibits the contractile mechanisms of muscle fibres.

> **Remember**
>
> A 2 per cent loss of body weight due to dehydration can lead to a 20 per cent drop in muscle performance.

Depletion of energy sources

The body needs energy to function effectively. When you exercise, your body needs a supply of energy so that heart rate increases, forcing more blood to the skeletal muscles so they can contract more frequently. The energy required comes from the food you eat.

- Carbohydrate (for example, pasta, rice and potatoes) is broken down into glucose in the body.
- Fats (for example, cheese, butter, oils) are broken down into fatty acids in the body.
- Proteins (for example, fish, meat, eggs) are broken down into amino acids that provide energy in extreme circumstances.

The breakdown of all three fuels in the body produces adenosine triphosphate (ATP). All forms of physiology – be it digestion, transmission of nerve impulses or muscular contractions – require energy in the form of ATP. Therefore, if an athlete fails to take in enough carbohydrate, fat or protein, it is likely they will deplete their energy sources quickly when exercise is undertaken.

- **Creatine phosphate** is synthesised in the liver and transported to skeletal muscles for storage. It is used to form ATP from ADP and is particularly important for intense efforts of physical exercise.
- **Muscle and liver glycogen** – a reduction in muscle and liver glycogen and blood glucose during submaximal exercise can occur despite the availability of sufficient oxygen and ATP. Once glycogen stores are depleted, muscles cease contracting – even during steady-state exercise – as the body is unable to use fat as the only fuel source. Marathon runners in particular must be careful not to deplete their glycogen stores early in a race by setting off too fast. To combat this, marathon runners run at a pace that metabolises fats so the rate at which glycogen depletes is lessened.

Effects of waste products

The main waste products of exercise are urea, carbon dioxide, water and lactic acid. Urea and water are filtered through the kidneys and expelled from the body. Carbon dioxide is carried in the blood to the lungs, where it passes into the alveoli and is then expelled from the body.

- **Blood lactate accumulation** – during exercise raised levels of carbon dioxide increase the level of blood acidity. One factor in this increased acidity is lactic acid, which dissociates into lactate and hydrogen ions in blood.

- **Carbon dioxide** – when carried in the blood, carbon dioxide combines with water producing carbonic acid.
- **Increased acidity** – carbonic acid is further broken down into bicarbonate and hydrogen ions. The hydrogen ions contribute to the blood's increased acidity.

> **Remember**
>
> - Muscle lactate is disposed of first by oxidation to pyruvate and then by dissimilation to carbon dioxide and water.
> - Some blood lactate is taken in by the liver, which reconstructs it to glycogen.
> - Remaining blood lactate diffuses back into the muscle to be oxidised then dismantled.

Neuromuscular fatigue

Depletion of acetylcholine – acetylcholine is a neurotransmitter released to stimulate skeletal muscles and the parasympathetic nervous system. Its effect is short-lived because it is destroyed by acetylcholinesterase – an enzyme released into the sarcolemma of muscle fibres to prevent continued muscle contraction in the absence of additional nervous stimulation.

Reduced calcium-ion release – as part of the sliding filament theory, calcium ions are known to be released allowing actin and myosin to couple and form actomyosin. If the store of calcium ions is reduced, the ability of the actin and myosin to couple is compromised, thus preventing continued muscle contraction.

> **Activity: Importance of calcium**
>
> Explain why the mineral calcium is important in the prevention of fatigue.

Fatigue is an unpleasant but often inevitable result of elite competition. Why do you think it is vital sport scientists understand the impact and consequences of fatigue and recovery?

3.2 Recovery

Four processes have to be satisfied before the exhausted muscle can perform to its optimum level. These are:

- restoration of muscle phosphagen stores
- removal of lactic acid
- replenishment of myoglobin stores with oxygen
- replacement of glycogen.

Excess post-exercise oxygen consumption (EPOC)

The need for additional oxygen to replace ATP and remove lactic acid is known as oxygen debt or excess post-exercise oxygen consumption (EPOC). The two major components of EPOC are:

- fast components (alactacid oxygen debt) – the amount of oxygen required to synthesise and restore muscle phosphagen stores (ATP and creatine phosphate)
- slow components (lactacid oxygen debt) – the amount of oxygen required to remove lactic acid from muscle cells and blood.

Bodily processes do not immediately return to normal after exercise. After light exercise such as golf or walking, recovery takes place quickly and often without realisation. With more intense steady-state exercise, however, it takes time for the body to return to normal.

Fast components

The restoration of muscle phosphagen stores – alactacid oxygen debt (without lactic acid) represents the oxygen used to synthesise and restore muscle phosphagen stores (ATP and creatine phosphate) that have been almost completely exhausted during high-intensity exercise. During the first three minutes of recovery, EPOC restores almost 99 per cent of ATP and creatine phosphate used during exercise (see Table 2.2).

Recovery time (seconds)	Muscle phosphagen restored (%)
10	10
30	50
60	75
90	87
120	93
150	97
180	99
210	101
240	102

Table 2.2: Restoration of muscle phosphagen.

The removal of lactic acid – lactic acid is catabolized and removed resulting in the feeling of pain or burning sensation in the muscles.

Slow components

The slow component of EPOC concerns the removal of lactic acid from the muscles and the blood. This can take several hours, depending on the intensity of the activity and whether the athlete was active or passive during the recovery phase. Around half of lactic acid is removed after 15 minutes, and most is removed after an hour. Once exercise is over, the liver synthesises lactic acid into glycogen while the remainder of the body can remove small amounts of lactic acid through respiration, perspiration and excretion.

- **Replenishment of myoglobin stores** – myoglobin is an oxygen-storage protein found in muscle. Like haemoglobin, it combines with oxygen while the supply is plentiful, and stores it until the demand for oxygen increases. During exercise, the oxygen from myoglobin is quickly used up and after exercise additional oxygen is required to pay back any oxygen that has been borrowed from myoglobin stores.

- **Replacement of glycogen** – the replenishment of muscle and liver glycogen stores depends on the type of exercise. Short-distance, high-intensity exercise may take two or three hours, whereas long endurance activities such as a marathon may take several days. Replenishment of glycogen is most rapid during the first few hours after training. Complete restoration of glycogen stores is accelerated with a high carbohydrate diet.

Take it further

Speeding up the recovery process

In groups, research the commercially available products designed to help athletes recover after exercise. What do these products contain that helps athletes with the recovery process? Discuss your answers.

Assessment activity 2.3 (P5) (M3)

Your swimmer has successfully completed his training programme and now understands the physiological responses to steady-state exercise. He is due to start an important competition soon and has asked about how the body recovers from exercise.

He has asked you to compile either a CD or MP3 that he can take with him and listen to while travelling or simply to remind him about exactly how his body recovers from exercise. He wonders if you would produce something he can take away to competition to remind him how to aid recovery while training and between swimming competition heats.

1. Your CD or MP3 should describe fatigue and how the body recovers from exercise such as long-distance swimming. (P5)

2. Your CD or MP3 should explain how fatigue and recovery apply to long-distance swimming training. (M3)

Grading tips

- To attain (P5) try to provide examples relating to long-distance swimming.

- To attain (M3) remember to keep your explanations on your CD in the context of the effects of the 1500 metre swimmer's training, fatigue and recovery.

PLTS

Producing presentation evidence to illustrate your findings on fatigue and recovery will develop your **creative thinking** skills.

4. Know how the body adapts to long-term exercise

There are differences between responses to exercise and how the body adapts to exercise. The immediate changes to the energy and neuromuscular systems during exercise are called responses. How the body adapts are permanent changes that take place as a result of long-term exercise. If you exercise regularly, your body adapts and you get fit. This means you are able to cope with exercise that previously you might have found difficult. Consequently, the human body is able to adapt and respond to exercise, allowing you to cope with your chosen sport.

4.1 Long-term exercise

A long-term exercise programme is one in which you exercise to a structured plan over a period of time. Examples might include an eight-week programme

of four 30-minute sessions per week or a six-week resistance programme. Responses to long-term exercise include changes to the heart, lungs and muscles, although the extent of the changes depends on the type and intensity of exercise undertaken.

4.2 Cardiovascular adaptations

Cardiac hypertrophy

An increase in heart size indicates the adjustment of a healthy heart to exercise training. Regular aerobic exercise (for example, four 30-minute jogging sessions per week for eight weeks) stimulates the increase in both the thickness of the muscle fibres and the number of contractile elements contained in the fibres.

Increase in stroke volume

Over time, aerobic training increases the size of the heart. This is due to an increase in the muscle mass of the heart chambers, especially the walls of the left ventricle. This increase in size increases ventricular contraction and the athlete's stroke volume.

Increase in cardiac output

An increase in stroke volume allows a greater cardiac output, so trained athletes are able to pump a greater volume of blood to the working muscles and organs.

Decrease in resting heart rate

As a result of increased stroke volume and cardiac hypertrophy, the athlete's resting heart rate decreases. When the heart can pump more blood per beat, it does not have to beat as often when the body is at rest. This is why getting fitter causes a decrease in resting pulse rate. Some of the world's top athletes have a resting pulse rate between 30 and 40 beats per minute.

Blood volume

Blood volume increases because of capillarisation during long-term exercise. Consequently, there is more space for blood to circulate which, in turn, allows for a greater supply of oxygen to skeletal muscles. In trained males, blood volume equates to approximately 75 ml per kg of bodyweight, and in females it is approximately 60 ml per kg of bodyweight.

Capillarisation

Long-term exercise can lead to the development of a capillary network to a part of the body. Aerobic training improves the capillarisation of cardiac and skeletal muscle by increasing the number of capillaries and the capillary density (the number of capillaries in a given area of muscle tissue).

4.3 Respiratory adaptations
Increase in minute ventilation

Minute ventilation depends on breathing rate and tidal volume. During exercise, adults can generally achieve 100 litres per minute or approximately 15 times the resting value. In trained athletes minute ventilation can increase by 50 per cent to 150 litres per minute.

Efficiency of respiratory muscles

An increase in strength allows the external intercostal muscles greater contraction, while the internal intercostal muscles relax during inspiration, forcing more air into the lungs. Likewise, during expiration the greater degree of contraction of the internal intercostals and relaxation of the external intercostals allows the athlete to breathe out a greater volume of air.

Increase in resting lung volumes

An increased surface area of the alveoli allows more deoxygenated blood access to the site of gaseous exchange. The carbon dioxide is offloaded and a greater amount of oxygen is diffused into the blood for its journey back to the heart. This increased ability of the blood to take on more oxygen due to the increased surface area of alveoli aids trained athletes tremendously.

Increase in oxygen diffusion rate

An increase in diffusion rates in tissues favours oxygen movement from the capillaries to the tissues, and carbon dioxide from the cells to the blood. Long-term exercise causes these rates to increase, allowing both oxygen and carbon dioxide to diffuse more rapidly.

4.4 Neuromuscular adaptations
Hypertrophy

Long-term exercise improves muscle tone and stamina. Training with a greater resistance brings about an increase in muscle size, a process known as hypertrophy. Muscular hypertrophy increases the cross-sectional size of existing muscle tissue due to the increase in the number of myofibrils and connective tissue (tendons and ligaments), which then become more pliable.

Increase in tendon strength

As the skeletal muscles of a trained athlete become larger, stronger or more efficient, the connective tendons have to adapt to meet these increased demands. Without such adaptations, serious injury may follow if the increased forces of contraction developed by the muscle cannot cause the lever or bone to move properly.

Increased myoglobin stores

With training, muscles increase their ability to store glycogen and myoglobin.

Increased numbers of mitochondria

With training, muscles increase their oxidative capacity. This is achieved by an increase in the number of mitochondria in the muscle cells, an increased supply of ATP and an increase in the quantity of the enzymes involved in respiration.

Increased storage of glycogen and triglycerides

With training (especially steady-state exercise), muscles increase the ability to use triglycerides as an energy store.

Neural pathways

Neural structures and pathways show changes as a result of long-term exercise training. These changes include **cellular adaptations**, modifications of **neurotransmitters**, alterations in reflex, and chemical and biochemical responses. For example, sprint training actually produces relatively small metabolic changes but has substantial effects on performance.

Key terms

Cellular adaptations – changes within the cell structure (for example, an increase in mitochondrial size).

Neurotransmitters – chemicals used to carry signals or information between neurons and cells.

4.5 Energy system adaptations
Increased anaerobic and aerobic enzymes

Long-term exercise brings about a number of cellular changes that enhance the ability of muscle tissue to generate ATP. Cellular adaptation such as the increase in size of mitochondria is usually accompanied by an increase in the level of aerobic system enzymes. A combination of these changes probably accounts for why an athlete can sustain prolonged periods of aerobic exercise as a result of longer-term training. The anaerobic system also undergoes a number of changes, including the increase in enzymes (especially in fast-twitch muscles) that control the anaerobic phase of glucose breakdown.

Increased use of fats as an energy source

The use of fats as an energy source occurs during low-intensity exercise. Fat combustion powers almost all exercise at approximately 25 per cent of aerobic power. Carbohydrate and fat contribute in equal measures during moderate exercise. Fat oxidation increases if exercise extends to over an hour as glycogen levels deplete. Beyond an hour of an exercise session, fats can account for approximately 75 per cent of the total energy required. Therefore, when considering the effects of long-term exercise, it is clear that trained athletes have far greater opportunity to burn fat as fuel than non-trained adults.

Explain how persistence with training and an understanding of the responses and adaptations to training can be a winning combination.

Higher tolerance of lactic acid

If your lactate threshold is reached at low-exercise intensity, your aerobic energy system in your muscles is not working well. As you get fitter, you begin to use oxygen to break down lactate to carbon dioxide and water, preventing lactate from pouring into the blood. If your lactate threshold is low, it is due to one or more of the following:

- not getting enough oxygen inside your muscle cells
- insufficient mitochondria in your muscle cells
- muscles, heart and other tissues are inefficient at extracting lactate from the blood.

A long-term adaptation to exercise is to saturate the muscles in lactic acid, which educates your body to deal with it more effectively. The accumulation of lactate in working skeletal muscles is associated with fatigue after 50–60 seconds of maximal effort. Therefore, training continuously at about 85–90 per cent of your maximum heart rate for 20–25 minutes improves the body's tolerance to lactic acid.

4.6 Skeletal adaptations

Increased calcium stores

Long-term exercise slows the rate of skeletal ageing. Athletes who maintain active lifestyles have greater bone mass compared with those who participate in less exercise. Exercise of moderate intensity provides a safe and potent stimulus to maintain and increase bone mass. Weight-bearing exercises such as running or walking are particularly beneficial, but this is also dependent on adequate calcium supply.

Increased tendon strength

Tendons attach muscles to bones or to muscles, whereas ligaments attach bone to bone and are usually found at joints. Both are able to withstand tensile stress when forces are applied. However, both types have poor blood supplies (vascularised). Both tissues are constructed of closely-packed bundles of collagen fibres. Crowded among the collagen fibres are rows of **fibroblasts**. The main function of the fibroblasts is to maintain the structural integrity by secreting compounds to help manufacture replacement fibres.

Key term

Fibroblast – connective tissue cell that makes and secretes collagen proteins.

Increased stretch of ligaments

An athlete requires stronger tendons and more pliable ligaments to handle heavy weights or an increased running distance. If an athlete lifts progressively heavier weights as part of a strength-training exercise programme, the athlete's muscles will gain strength. To accommodate this increase, tendons increase their load-bearing capacity relative to the increased strength of the muscle, while the ligaments need to adapt their pliability. This adaptation occurs when fibroblast secretions increase the production of collagen fibres relative to the training undertaken. Without this relationship, injury is likely to occur.

Remember

Strength training can have a positive effect on osteoporosis (brittle bone disease).

Take it further

On retirement?

Consider what happens to an athlete when he or she retires from competition: what do you think happens to the adaptations their body has developed over years of training?

Assessment activity 2.4

At his competition, your swimmer was successful and won his event. On return he commented that he owes part of his success to your hard work and advice. To remember exactly what he has achieved so far and how, he has asked for a series of reminders that he can take away with him.

1. First, he would like you to make him a poster that details how the cardiovascular and respiratory systems adapt to long-term exercise. He feels this will serve as a timely reminder every time he goes training. **P6**

2. Second, he would like a flipcard that summarises how the neuromuscular, energy and skeletal systems adapt to long-term exercise. He can keep this in his training bag and flick through it wherever he is. **P7**

3. Third, and in more detail, he would like a laminated A4 sheet of paper (which he can take on poolside) that explains how the cardiovascular, respiratory, neuromuscular, energy and skeletal systems adapt to long-term exercise. He says this will remind him of why he should train, especially when it gets really tough. **M4**

4. Finally, he has asked for a log of a six-month training period. This log should highlight times and instances that analyse how his cardiovascular, respiratory, neuromuscular, energy and skeletal systems adapt to long-term exercise. The log should provide evidence from his training regime (swimming, fitness testing, etc.) as to how these adaptations materialised. **D3**

Grading tips

- To attain **P6** and **P7** remember that both aerobic and anaerobic effects should be described, so perhaps have aerobic and anaerobic effects on the poster and flipcard.

- To attain **M4** show that you know why something happens or changes over a period of at least eight weeks, and give that explanation clearly.

- To attain **D3** you need to see important points that others miss, as well as identifying faults and making realistic suggestions as to how something could be improved for your 1500 metre swimmer's training.

PLTS

If you identify questions to answer and problems to resolve in your poster, you can develop your skills as an **independent enquirer**.

Functional skills

Interpreting exercise assessment data results when investigating the body's adaptations to long-term exercise could develop your **Mathematics** skills. Discussing how to assess the body's response to long-term exercise may help your **English** skills in speaking and listening. Accurately recording data and reproducing reports based on the findings of long-term exercise adaptations may help your **English** skills in writing.

Ian Fernandez

Trainee cardiac physiologist

Ian is in his first year as a trainee cardiac physiologist with a cardiac department at a large hospital. He is responsible for:

- taking blood pressure and electrocardiograph (ECG) readings
- making sure the patient examination areas are clean and tidy
- assisting senior cardiac physiologists
- taking telephone calls and enquiries from a range of sources
- maintaining a safe working environment.

'A typical day at the hospital involves me arriving at the department in the morning and making sure all the equipment, such as blood pressure monitors and electrocardio ECG equipment are working and clean. As this is my first year, the majority of my day in the department is spent assisting the senior cardiac physiologists. I welcome patients, take their details and make them feel comfortable. Under guidance, I sometimes take and record a patient's blood pressure or prepare the patient for an ECG. The latter is quite a complex procedure as there are lots of things to remember for the test to be carried out correctly.

'After completing my first year of study successfully, I will be able to perform these tests unsupervised – something I'm really looking forward to. I also make sure all the equipment is clean and ready to use and ensure all the patient filing is kept up to date.

'I enjoy meeting and helping people. I enjoyed the physiology unit on my sport and exercise science course, particularly the cardiac responses to exercise and how cardiac fitness develops. Given my sports background, I decided I wanted to specialise in cardiac physiology and help people with potential heart trouble through exercise.

'I'm required to undertake a three-year accelerated training programme that will provide all the necessary underpinning knowledge and practical skills required to become a registered cardiac physiologist with the Registration Council of Clinical Physiologists and gain my BSc in Clinical Physiology.'

Think about it!

- What areas have you covered in this unit that provide you with the knowledge and skills used by a cardiac or respiratory physiologist?
- What further skills might you need to develop? Think about how you might conduct lung function tests with a patient and whether you feel comfortable working in a medical environment.

Just checking

1. What is aerobic exercise?
2. What does 'systolic' refer to?
3. Explain what is meant by 'steady-state' exercise.
4. Explain what is meant by 'Starling's law'.
5. Give four symptoms of fatigue.
6. List the four processes of recovery after exercise.
7. Explain the concept of 'cardiac hypertrophy' as an adaptation to long-term exercise.
8. List three skeletal adaptations to long-term exercise.
9. Which node within the heart controls heart rate?
10. List three energy system adaptations to long-term exercise.

Assignment tips

- Physiology is a huge topic. It may be worth acquiring a medical textbook on human anatomy and physiology. It's better to have more than one view or description of the same subject, as that way you can 'compare and contrast' and improve the standard of your assessed work.

- Read sports magazines and their websites – magazines like *Health & Fitness* and *Ultrafit* often contain articles relating to performance physiology.

- Speak to physiologists or fitness instructors and ask why they think knowledge of physiology is important.

- Keep training diaries detailing your improvement in running times or lifting strength, and comment why you think these changes have occurred. Try to keep your explanations in terms of the adaptations you have studied.

- Make sure you are familiar with the pre-test procedures and testing methods before conducting cardiac, respiratory or strength tests.

- Be prepared. Keep a physiology portfolio of evidence handy. You will revisit the concepts learned in other units such as Unit 8 Fitness testing for sport and exercise, Unit 9 Fitness training and programming, Unit 10 Sport and exercise massage, and Unit 21 Applied sport and exercise physiology.

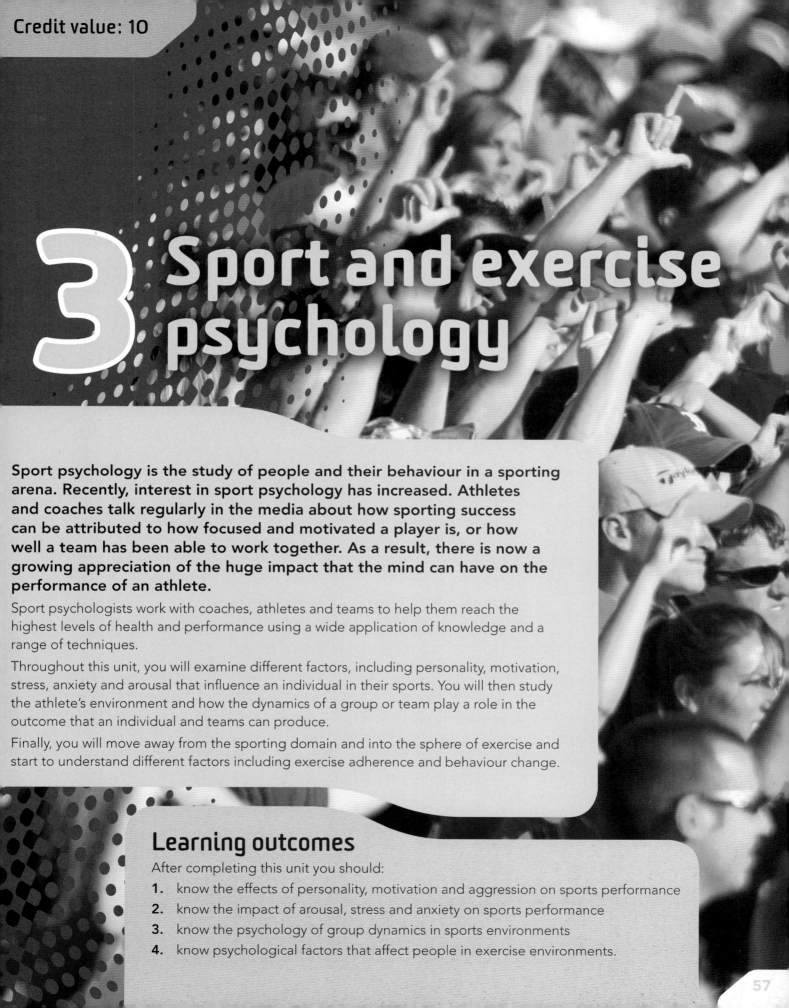

3 Sport and exercise psychology

Sport psychology is the study of people and their behaviour in a sporting arena. Recently, interest in sport psychology has increased. Athletes and coaches talk regularly in the media about how sporting success can be attributed to how focused and motivated a player is, or how well a team has been able to work together. As a result, there is now a growing appreciation of the huge impact that the mind can have on the performance of an athlete.

Sport psychologists work with coaches, athletes and teams to help them reach the highest levels of health and performance using a wide application of knowledge and a range of techniques.

Throughout this unit, you will examine different factors, including personality, motivation, stress, anxiety and arousal that influence an individual in their sports. You will then study the athlete's environment and how the dynamics of a group or team play a role in the outcome that an individual and teams can produce.

Finally, you will move away from the sporting domain and into the sphere of exercise and start to understand different factors including exercise adherence and behaviour change.

Learning outcomes

After completing this unit you should:

1. know the effects of personality, motivation and aggression on sports performance
2. know the impact of arousal, stress and anxiety on sports performance
3. know the psychology of group dynamics in sports environments
4. know psychological factors that affect people in exercise environments.

Assessment and grading criteria

This table shows you what you must do in order to achieve a pass, merit or distinction grade, and where you can find activities in this book to help you.

To achieve a **pass** grade the evidence must show that you are able to:	To achieve a **merit** grade the evidence must show that, in addition to the pass criteria, you are able to:	To achieve a **distinction** grade the evidence must show that, in addition to the pass and merit criteria, you are able to:
P1 describe personality and its effects on sports performance **See Assessment activity 3.1, page 63**	**M1** explain personality and its effects on sports performance **See Assessment activity 3.1, page 63**	**D1** analyse personality and its effects on sports performance **See Assessment activity 3.1, page 63**
P2 describe motivation and the factors which affect the motivation of athletes **See Assessment activity 3.2, page 66**		
P3 describe the types and causes of aggressive behaviour **See Assessment activity 3.3, page 68**	**M2** explain the types and causes of aggressive behaviour **See Assessment activity 3.3, page 68**	
P4 describe arousal and its effect on sports performance **See Assessment activity 3.4, page 74**	**M3** explain arousal and its effect on sports performance **See Assessment activity 3.4, page 74**	**D2** analyse arousal and its effect on sports performance **See Assessment activity 3.4, page 74**
P5 describe stress and anxiety and their symptoms and causes **See Assessment activity 3.4, page 74**		
P6 identify four different factors which contribute to the psychology of group dynamics **See Assessment activity 3.5, page 80**	**M4** explain four different factors which contribute to the psychology of group dynamics **See Assessment activity 3.5, page 80**	
P7 identify three psychological factors that affect people in exercise environments **See Assessment activity 3.6, page 82**	**M5** explain three psychological factors that affect people in exercise environments **See Assessment activity 3.6, page 82**	

How you will be assessed

This unit will be assessed by internal assignments that will be designed and marked by the tutors at your centre. Your assessments could be in the form of:

- written reports
- posters
- presentations
- booklets.

Jamie, 18-year-old sprint cyclist

This unit has helped me to understand that there is more to getting ready for games than just training all the time! I enjoyed looking at all the different aspects of sport psychology because they have helped me to understand myself more as an athlete.

There were lots of practical learning activities throughout this unit like playing different games that linked to group dynamics, and all of the different topics within the unit were brought to life using lots of famous examples that I had seen on the television and the news.

The exercise psychology part was also really good for me because it actually drew my attention to the different things that I do and say to try and get out of being active and it taught me that I can get round all of these different barriers with a little bit of planning!

Over to you

1. **Which areas of this unit are you looking forward to?**
2. **Which bits do you think you might find difficult?**
3. **What do you think you will need to do to get yourself ready for this unit?**

1. Know the effects of personality, motivation and aggression on sports performance

What is the role of psychology in sport?

Has there been a time when you have not played a sport as well as you could have done, even though you had trained really hard? Has there been a time when you have got something wrong in a game even though you know how to perform the skill well? Why do you think this could be?

1.1 Personality

Personality and the effect it has on sports participation and performance has interested sport psychologists since the late 1800s. However, evidence on whether personality affects sports performance is limited and inconclusive.

Key term

Personality – the sum of the characteristics that make a person unique.

What keeps athletes going when their bodies want them to stop?

Theories

There are different theories and approaches that try to explain personality and how it influences sports performance. The main theories you will examine are:

- Marten's schematic view
- psychodynamic theory
- trait theory
- situational approach
- interactional approach.

Marten's schematic view

In this view, personality is seen as having three different levels that are related to each other:

- psychological core
- typical responses
- role-related behaviour.

The psychological core is what people call 'the real you' and contains your beliefs, values, attitudes and interests; these are seen as being relatively constant or stable.

Typical responses are the usual ways that you respond to the world around you or different situations you find yourself in. For example, you may get angry and shout after being intentionally fouled in football because you feel that deliberate fouls are unsporting, but you may be quiet and shy when you meet people for the first time because you don't want to overawe them. These are your typical responses to these situations and are seen as good indicators of your psychological core.

Your role-related behaviour is often determined by your circumstances. This is the most changeable aspect of personality. Your personality changes as your perception

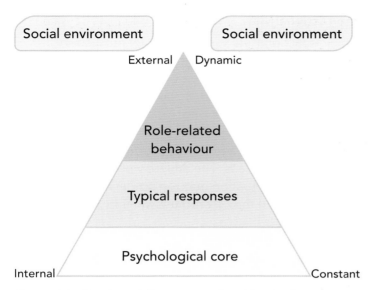

Figure 3.1: The three different interrelated levels of personality.

of your environment changes. For example, in the same day you might be captaining your college sports team where you show leadership behaviours, then working as an employee at your part-time job where you have to follow instructions.

Psychodynamic theory

The psychodynamic approach to personality says that personality is made up of conscious and unconscious parts. The first part is called the 'id' which stands for instinctive drive. It is the part of your personality that is unconscious and makes you do things without thinking. A sprinter on the start line in the Olympic final may feel so threatened by the expectations on them that they respond with high anxiety and their muscles automatically freeze. The second part of your personality, your ego, is the conscious part. The final part is your super ego, which is your moral conscience. The effect of the ego and super ego can be seen in sport when a football player refuses to take a penalty in a penalty shoot-out because they are worried about missing and letting their team down.

Rather than looking at different parts of personality, the psychodynamic approach tries to understand the individual as a whole. This approach is not often used in sport as it focuses on the reasons for behaviour that come from within the individual and tends to ignore the athlete's environment. However, this theory is useful when sport psychologists try to explain

behaviour as it helps you to understand that not all behaviour is under an athlete's conscious control.

Trait-centred views

Trait theories suggest that individuals have characteristics that partly determine how they behave.

> ## Key term
>
> **Trait** – a stable and enduring characteristic that is part of your personality.

Traits are stable aspects of personality and early trait theorists like Eysenck and Cattell argued that traits were inherited. There are two dimensions to personality:

- an introversion–extroversion dimension
- a stable–neurotic dimension.

Introverts are individuals who don't actively seek excitement and would rather be in calm environments. They prefer tasks that require concentration and dislike the unexpected. Extroverts become bored quickly, are poor at tasks that require lots of concentration and seek change and excitement. Extroverts are less responsive to pain than introverts. Extroverts are said to be more successful in sporting situations because they can cope with competitive and distracting situations better than introverts.

Stable individuals are more easy-going and even tempered. Neurotic (unstable) people are more restless, excitable, have a tendency to become anxious and are more highly aroused.

The conclusions are that trait views are simplistic and that personality alone cannot predict success in a sporting environment. It can, however, be used to help explain why individuals choose certain sports.

> ## Remember
>
> Although personality traits can be used with physiological and situational factors to try to predict who will do well in sport, there is no such thing as the right personality for all sports that will guarantee sporting success.

Situational-centred views

The situational approach says that behaviour is dependent on your situation or environment. It argues that this is more important than traits. There is some support for the situational approach in explaining sporting behaviour, as individuals may be introverted – displaying characteristics such as tolerance and shyness – but may participate in a sport that requires them to be extroverted.

> **Remember**
>
> A situation can influence a person's behaviour but it cannot predict sporting behaviour. To be able to do this, you need to consider the individual's personality traits as well.

Social learning theory suggests that personality is not a stable characteristic, but constantly changing and a result of experiences of different social situations. The theory states that individuals learn in sporting situations through two processes: modelling and reinforcement. Modelling occurs when individuals try to emulate the behaviour of athletes that they can relate to. Reinforcement is important because, if an individual's behaviour is reinforced or rewarded, it is likely that the behaviour will be repeated. Bandura, a leading psychologist, identified four main stages of observational learning that demonstrate how modelling influences personality and behaviour.

1. **Attention**: to learn through observation, you must have respect and admiration for the model you are observing. The amount of respect depends on the model's status. If the model is successful and dominant, they will hold your attention.

2. **Retention**: for modelling to be effective, you must retain the observed skill or behaviour in your memory, to be recalled when needed.

3. **Motor reproduction**: you must be able to physically perform the task you are observing. You need time to practise the skill and learn how it should be performed.

4. **Motivational response**: unless you are motivated, you will not go through the first three stages of modelling. Motivation is dependent on reinforcement (for example, praise, feedback, sense of pride or achievement), the perceived status of the model and task importance.

Interactional view

The interactional view is accepted by most sport psychologists when explaining behaviour as it says that you must consider how the situation and personality traits link and work together. It suggests that when situational factors are strong, for example, during competitive sporting situations like penalty shoot-outs in football, they are more likely to predict behaviour than personality traits. The athlete who is quiet and shy in an everyday situation may run screaming towards an ecstatic crowd if they scored the winning penalty.

Personality types

Another approach in sport psychology suggests that personality traits can be grouped under two headings: type A and type B.

- **Type A personalities** lack patience, have a strong urge for competition, a high desire to achieve goals, rush to complete activities, will happily multi-task when under time constraints, lack tolerance towards others and experience higher levels of anxiety.

- **Type B personalities** are more tolerant towards others, more relaxed and reflective than their type A counterparts, experience lower levels of anxiety and display higher levels of imagination and creativity.

> **Key terms**
>
> **Social learning theory** – states that individuals learn in sporting situations through two processes: modelling and reinforcement.
>
> **Type A personality** – typified by a strong competitive urge and a lack of patience. These people rush to finish activities, multi-task successfully under time constraints, lack tolerance towards others and experience higher anxiety levels.
>
> **Type B personality** – people with this personality type are relaxed and reflective. They have higher levels of imagination and creativity and experience lower anxiety levels.

Effects on sports performance

There is no direct link between personality type and successful sporting performance. Some research says that certain personality types may be more attracted to certain sports, but there is little to suggest that your personality will make you a better athlete.

Remember

Introverts tend to be drawn to individual sports like long-distance running while extroverts prefer team- and action-orientated sports like football.

- **Athletes versus non-athletes and individual versus team sports** – there is no such thing as a universal athletic personality. However, there are differences between athletes and non-athletes and between athletes in different sports. Compared with non-athletes, athletes who participate in team sports are more extroverted. Compared to non-athletes, athletes in individual sports are more introverted. This suggests that to study the differences between athletes and non-athletes, you should consider the sports the athletes play before reaching meaningful conclusions.

- **Elite versus non-elite athletes** – psychologists originally thought that successful athletes display lower levels of depression, fatigue, confusion and anger, but higher levels of vigour. However, evidence used to draw these conclusions was insufficient because it was based on small numbers of athletes. Recent research shows that personality accounts for less than 1 per cent of performance variations.

- **Type A versus type B** – type A personalities are more likely than type B personalities to continue participating in a sport when the situation becomes unfavourable or when they are not motivated.

Assessment activity 3.1

You are working with a youth sports team. The coach complains to you about some of his youth athletes, saying that they don't have the right personality to make it as athletes in his team.

Educate the coach about the role of personality in sport by preparing a short written report that looks at all of the different factors surrounding personality and environmental factors and their role in sports participation and performance.

1. Define personality and describe how it influences sport participation and performance. **P1**

2. Explain different theories that try to explain the link between personality and sports participation and performance. Explain how these theories try to explain that link. **M1**

3. Evaluate differing or contrasting arguments that relate to the personality and sport performance link. **D1**

Grading tips

- To attain **P1** make sure that you first tell the coach what personality is and then give them a brief overview of whether personality alone should determine whether or not people should be picked for sports teams.

- To attain **M1** use different theories and examples to explain how personality can influence sports performance.

- To attain **D1** make sure that you use a range of theories and supporting materials that give contrasting arguments so that you are giving the coach as full a picture as possible to allow them to make an informed decision about their players.

PLTS

By exploring each of the different theories and judging their value when making your arguments, you can develop your skills as an **independent enquirer**.

Functional skills

By writing your report on personality and its effects on sports performance, you could provide evidence of your **English** skills in writing.

1.2 Motivation

Most definitions of **motivation** refer to having a drive to take part and persist in an activity. A sport-specific definition is the tendency of an individual or team to begin and continue with the activities relating to their sport. There are two types of motivation: **intrinsic** and **extrinsic**.

Key terms

Motivation – the direction and the intensity of your effort; it is critical to sporting success.

Intrinsic – internal factors, such as enjoyment.

Extrinsic – external factors, such as rewards.

Intrinsic

Intrinsic motivation is when someone is participating in an activity without an external reward and/or without the primary motivation being the achievement of external reward. Intrinsic motivation in its purest form is when an athlete participates in a sport for enjoyment. When people are asked why they play sport, if they say 'for fun', or 'because it makes me feel good' they are intrinsically motivated. There are three parts of intrinsic motivation:

- **accomplishments** – when athletes wish to increase their level of skill to get a sense of accomplishment

- **stimulation** – seeking an 'adrenaline rush' or extreme excitement

- **knowledge** – being curious about performance, and wanting to know more about it and to develop new techniques or skills to benefit performance.

Extrinsic

Extrinsic motivation is when someone behaves the way they do because of an external mechanism. Common forms of extrinsic motivation are tangible and intangible rewards. Tangible rewards are physical rewards, like money and medals, intangible rewards are non-physical rewards such as praise or encouragement. For extrinsic motivation to be effective, rewards must be effective. If a reward is given too frequently, it will be of less value to the athlete, invalidating its impact on performance. A coach needs to have an in-depth knowledge of their athletes to maximise the effectiveness of extrinsic rewards.

Take it further

The effects of intrinsic and extrinsic factors on motivation

A group of children are playing football, to the annoyance of a man whose house they are playing outside. He asks them to stop playing but they carry on because they enjoy it. After a while, the man offers them £5 each to play for him. As the children like playing anyway, they accept his offer. The next day, they return and play outside his house again. He offers them money to play again but this time only pays them £4. The children agree to continue playing even though the amount is less. This pattern continues for a few days until one day the man says he can't afford to pay them. Disgruntled, the children refuse to play if he won't pay them.

1. **What motivates the children to play initially? Is this intrinsic or extrinsic motivation?**

2. **At the end of the case study, what is the motivating factor for the children? Is this intrinsic or extrinsic motivation?**

3. **What effect has extrinsic motivation had on intrinsic motivation?**

4. **Do you think that intrinsic or extrinsic factors are more important for long-term motivation?**

Extrinsic motivation can decrease intrinsic motivation. If the extrinsic motivator is used to control the athlete, intrinsic motivation will decrease. If the extrinsic motivator provides information or feedback to the athlete, this can benefit intrinsic motivation. The ways an athlete perceives and understands the original extrinsic motivator determines whether it will benefit or hinder intrinsic motivation.

Achievement motivation theory

Achievement motivation was proposed by Atkinson (1964), who argued that achievement motivation comes from your personality and is your drive to succeed. This drive makes athletes continue trying even when there are obstacles or they fail. Atkinson suggested two categories: the need to achieve (nach) and the need to avoid failure (naf). Everyone has aspects of nach and naf, but it is the difference between the two motives that makes up somebody's achievement motivation.

Attribution theory

The **attribution** theory examines how people explain success or failure. It helps you understand an athlete's actions and motivation.

Key term

Attribution – the reason you give to explain the outcome of an event.

Attributions fall into one of the categories below.
- Stability – is the reason permanent or unstable?
- Causality – does it come from an external or an internal factor?
- Control – is it under your control or not?

Table 3.1 details attribution theory with examples of explanations that are often given after winning and losing.

Factors contributing to a motivational climate

The motivational climate is the athlete's environment and how this affects their motivation positively and negatively. A motivational climate focused on mastery of tasks – where athletes receive positive reinforcement and there is greater emphasis on teamwork and cooperation – develops motivation by improving the athlete's attitudes, effort and learning techniques. When an athlete's environment focuses on the outcome (where they feel they will be punished if they make mistakes, competition is strongly encouraged and only those with the highest ability receive attention) this leads to less effort from athletes and failure is often attributed to lack of ability.

Factors affecting motivation

Intrinsic and extrinsic factors (see page 64), your personality and different situational factors (such as your coach) affect your motivation. The best way to understand your motivation is to consider how these factors interact.

Type of attribution	Winning example	Losing example
Stability	'I was more able than my opponent' (stable) 'I was lucky' (unstable)	'I was less able than my opponent' (stable) 'We didn't have that bit of luck we needed today' (unstable)
Causality	'I tried really hard' (internal) 'My opponent was easy to beat' (external)	'I didn't try hard enough' (internal) 'My opponent was impossible to beat' (external)
Control	'I trained really hard for this fight' (under your control) 'He wasn't as fit as I was' (not under your control)	'I didn't train hard enough for this fight' (under your control) 'He was fitter than I was' (not under your control)

Table 3.1: Attribution theory with typical examples.

Assessment activity 3.2

The coach of a local handball team has asked you to come to speak to Matt, a player he is struggling with. Matt is completely focused on winning trophies for their team and gets annoyed and frustrated when the team doesn't win. When the team loses, Matt says that it was the fault of the other players and bad luck. However, when the team wins he makes a point of telling everyone how well he has played.

Matt always seems to want to play when he is playing against teams that he knows he can beat, but he really doesn't like to play against teams when the players are just as good as him.

1. Describe motivation and different types of motivation.

2. Describe how the different types of motivation influence sports participation and performance.

3. Describe the different theories of motivation.

4. Describe how these different theories try to describe the relationship between motivation and sport participation and performance. **P2**

Grading tips

- To attain **P2** make sure that you define motivation and the different types of motivation. Look at how both intrinsic and extrinsic motivation influence sport performance. Describe each of the different theories of motivation and how people have tried to use them to understand motivation in sport.

- Use the attribution theory to explain how Matt explains success or failure and how this can affect future expectations of sport performance. Explain how having a high need to achieve (nach) or a high need to avoid failure (naf) can affect sports performance and motivation to perform against certain individuals. Explain some methods the coach could use to increase motivational climate.

- Evaluate how intrinsic motivation can be affected by extrinsic motivation. Highlight strengths and limitations of each of the different theories of motivation. Discuss how and why the different suggestions to improve motivational climate can influence Matt both positively and negatively.

PLTS

By asking lots of different questions to explore all of the possibilities within the activity, you could develop your skills as a **creative thinker**.

Functional skills

Using ICT to independently select and use a range of theories of motivation could provide evidence for your skills in **ICT**.

1.3 Aggression

Definition

Aggression is behaviour with a goal of harming or injuring another being who is motivated to avoid such treatment.

Gill's criteria for aggressive behaviour

Aggression has four main criteria, which were identified by Gill in the 1980s.

- It is a form of behaviour: aggression can be either physical or verbal behaviour.

- It involves causing harm or injury: aggression is designed to cause either physical or psychological harm.

- The injury or harm is directed towards another being.

- The aggression must be intentional: an accident cannot be classed as aggression.

Why do you think people become aggressive in sport?

Aggressive and assertive behaviour

There are two types of aggression: hostile and instrumental. They should not be confused with assertive behaviour, which is another key aspect of sport.

- **Hostile aggression** – this is inflicting harm (physical or psychological) on someone else (for example, an opponent). It is sometimes referred to as reactive aggression and can be accompanied by anger.

- **Instrumental aggression** – this is displaying aggressive behaviour in the pursuit of a non-aggressive goal. Sometimes referred to as channelled aggression, most aggression in sport falls into this category. Instrumental aggression often occurs in contact sports.

- **Assertive** behaviour differs from aggressive behaviour because the individual is playing with emotion and within the rules of the game. Assertive behaviour demonstrates four main criteria; it:
  o is goal-directed
  o is not intended to harm or injure
  o uses only legitimate force, even if this amount of force could be classed as aggression in a non-sporting or non-game setting
  o does not break any of the rules of the game.

Causes of aggression

There are different causes of aggression including instinct theory, social learning theory and frustration–aggression theory (and revised versions).

- **Instinct theory** suggests that we have an instinct to be aggressive that builds up until we can release that aggression in some way. This aggression can be released by being aggressive towards another being or can be released through socially

Activity: Aggression or assertion?

Decide which type of behaviour is being shown in the following scenarios. Choose from hostile aggression, instrumental aggression or assertion, and justify your answer.
- a boxer delivering a knockout blow in a boxing match
- a rugby player tackling an opponent hard to gain possession of the ball
- a boxer biting an opponent's ear during a clinch
- a basketball player blocking hard off of the boards
- a kick boxer delivering a low blow
- a footballer tackling a player hard, winning the ball fairly but injuring the player in the process.

acceptable means such as sport. This release is known as **catharsis**. However, while we often relate to this idea, there is little research-based evidence to support the instinct theory so few people use this theory to explain causes of aggression.

Key term

Catharsis – the release of aggression through socially acceptable means, such as sport.

- **Social learning theory** says that aggression is a behaviour that we learn by observing others and experiencing reinforcement for such behaviours. For example, if a child was watching a game on television with his parents and saw his favourite player foul an opponent off the ball and not get punished, and his parents cheer this action, he is likely to imitate that behaviour when playing.

Take it further

Learning by example?

Earlier in this unit (see page 62), we discussed the different stages associated with the social learning theory. Try to explain the situation described above using those different stages.

- **Frustration–aggression theory** says that aggression comes from you being frustrated by not achieving goals or having progress towards goals blocked. You will be able to think of times when you've been frustrated and become aggressive, so this theory made sense to sport psychologists until the point where the theory said that frustration will always result in aggression. This theory doesn't have a lot of support because you know that when you get frustrated, you can control that frustration. There is a revised version of this theory that is more widely accepted which is called the revised frustration–aggression theory.

- **The revised frustration–aggression theory** combines elements of the original frustration–aggression theory with elements of the social learning theory by stating that aggression occurs in situations where you become frustrated, as when you are frustrated you experience anger and arousal; and if you cannot control that arousal and anger you are more likely to become aggressive. This theory states that you are only more likely to become aggressive if the aggressive acts are supported.

Case study: Responses to aggression

A fullback in hockey is being beaten by the opposing winger all the time during a game which is frustrating the fullback greatly. After the winger's team scores a goal that the winger set up, the fullback hits the winger in the knee with his stick and injures the winger. This is not noticed by an official and the fullback's coach simply nods in their general direction after the incident.

1. **Which theory do you think can be used to explain the cause of aggression in this scenario?**

2. **What type of aggression has the fullback displayed?**

3. **How do you think the fullback is going to respond in future situations like this?**

4. **What do you think of the coach's actions in this scenario?**

Assessment activity 3.3

You are working as a sports journalist and you have been asked to write a magazine article based on the impact of aggression in sport.

Aim to give people a general description of the types and causes of aggression in sport. **P3**

Expand on this by providing explanations of each type of aggression and their causes using sporting examples. These sporting examples could be high profile examples (such as Zinedine Zidane's headbutt in the 2006 World Cup Final) or more general examples (such as a hard tackle in Rugby). **M2**

Grading tips

- To attain **P3** give a general introduction that tells people what aggression and assertion are, and provides the criteria for both. Define hostile and instrumental aggression.

- To attain **M2** discuss each of the different theories, looking at how they try to explain aggression and talk about any key strengths or limitations of the theories. Make sure that you provide examples of hostile aggression, instrumental aggression and assertion.

PLTS

By asking lots of different questions to explore all of the possibilities within the causes of aggression, you could develop your skills as a **creative thinker**.

Functional skills

Using ICT to independently select and use a range of theories of aggression could provide evidence towards your **ICT** skills.

2. Know the impact of arousal, stress and anxiety on sports performance

2.1 Arousal

Arousal is a state of alertness and anticipation that prepares the body for action. It involves both physiological activation (increased heart rate, sweating rate or respiratory rate) and psychological activity (increased attention). Arousal is typically viewed along a continuum, with deep sleep at one extreme and excitement at the other. Individuals who are optimally aroused are mentally and physically activated to perform.

Theories

The relationship between arousal and performance is demonstrated through the following theories:

- drive theory
- inverted U hypothesis
- catastrophe theory
- **Drive theory** – the drive theory view of the relationship between arousal and performance is linear. This means that as arousal increases, so does performance. The more 'learned' a skill is, the more likely it is that a high level of arousal will result in a better performance. However, there is little research support for this theory as there is evidence to suggest that athletic performance is benefitted by arousal only up to a point, after which the athlete becomes too aroused and their performance decreases. This argument is put forward through the inverted U hypothesis.
- **Inverted U hypothesis** states that at optimal arousal levels, performance levels will be at their highest, but when arousal is too low or too high, performance levels will be lower. It argues that at lower levels of arousal, performance will not be as high as it should be because the athlete is neither physiologically nor psychologically ready (for example, heart rate and concentration levels may be too low). As arousal levels increase, so does performance, but only up to an optimal point. At this optimal point of arousal (normally moderate

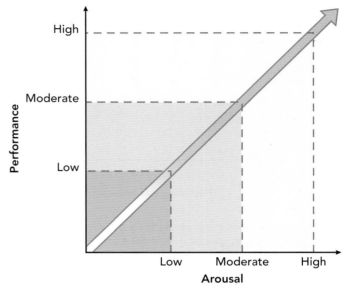

Figure 3.2: How does the drive theory explain the relationship between arousal and performance?

levels of arousal), the athlete's performance will be at its highest. After this optimal point performance levels start to decrease gradually.

Remember

The inverted U hypothesis states that arousal will only affect performance positively up to an optimal point; after this you will get a steady decrease in performance.

The inverted U hypothesis is more widely accepted than drive theory because most athletes and coaches can report personal experience of under-arousal (boredom), over-arousal (excitement to the point of lack of concentration) and optimum arousal (focus on nothing but sport performance). However, there are questions over the type of curve demonstrated: does it give an optimal point, or do some athletes experience optimal arousal for a longer period of time?

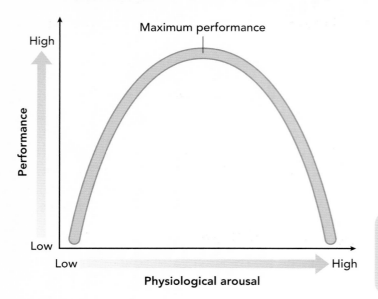

Figure 3.3: How does the inverted U theory explain the relationship between arousal and performance?

- **Catastrophe theory** says performance is affected by arousal in an inverted U fashion only when the individual has low levels of **cognitive anxiety** (see Figure 3.4a). If the athlete is experiencing higher levels of cognitive anxiety, and arousal levels increase up to the athlete's threshold, the player experiences a dramatic (or catastrophic) drop in performance levels (see Figure 3.4b). The key difference between catastrophe theory and the inverted U hypothesis is that the drop in

performance does not have to be a steady decline when arousal levels become too high. Catastrophe theory does not argue that cognitive anxiety is completely negative. The theory suggests you will perform at a higher level if you have a degree of cognitive anxiety because your attention and concentration levels increase; it is only when levels of cognitive anxiety are combined with hyper-elevated levels of arousal that performance levels decrease dramatically.

Key term

Cognitive anxiety – the thought component of anxiety that most people refer to as 'worrying about something'.

Activity: Arousal in sport

In pairs, produce a poster presentation explaining the three theories of arousal. Make sure you include:

- a diagram and explanation of each theory
- practical, sport-based examples of each theory to develop your points
- the key differences between each theory
- a note about which theory you think is the most likely to explain the relationship between arousal and performance and why.

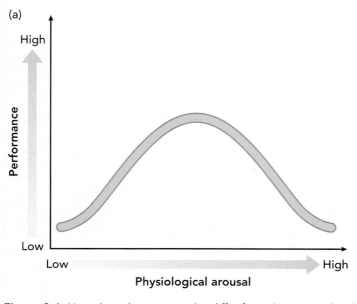

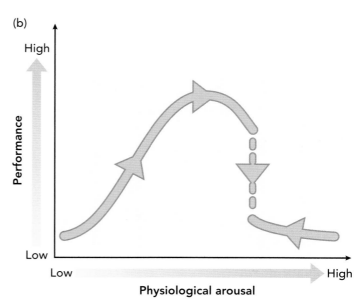

Figure 3.4: How does the catastrophe differ from the inverted U theory?

Effects of changes in arousal level

- **Improvements and decrements in performance level** – arousal doesn't necessarily have a negative effect on sports performance – it can be positive depending on the perception of the athlete. If the changes due to arousal are interpreted by the performer as positive, this can have a positive effect on performance or prepare the athlete for their event (psyching up the performer). But, if the changes are viewed as negative, this can negatively affect performance or preparation for performance (psyching out the performer).

- **Changes in attention focus** – during heightened states of arousal, the attentional field becomes narrowed, which focuses attention and concentration. This means that the more aroused you become, the lower the number of relevant cues you can concentrate on. For example, in a game of netball, when at optimal states of arousal, the centre player will focus on the opposing player in possession of the ball as well as her position on the court and the position of other players. During heightened states of arousal, the centre may be able to focus only on the opposition player who has the ball and may disregard other cues. Just as a heightened state of arousal can narrow the player's attention, it can broaden it to the point where performance is decreased. In this scenario, the netball player would be concentrating on irrelevant information, like crowd noise, as well as relevant game cues.

- **Aggression** – as discussed earlier through the revised frustration–aggression theory, aggression can be caused by increases in arousal levels that are accompanied by increases in anger and other emotions; but only in situations where the aggression response is likely to be supported.

2.2 Stress

Lazarus and Folkman (1984) defined stress as: 'a pattern of negative physiological states and psychological responses occurring in situations where people perceive threats to their well-being, which they may be unable to meet'. Two terms have been introduced in sport to explain stress: eustress and distress.

- **Eustress** is a good form of stress that gives you a feeling of fulfilment. Some athletes actively seek out stressful situations as they like the challenge of pushing themselves to the limit. This helps them increase their skill levels and focus their attention on aspects of their sport. The benefit is that increases in intrinsic motivation follow.

- **Distress** is a bad form of stress and is normally what you mean when you discuss stress. It is an extreme form of anxiety, nervousness, apprehension or worry as a result of a perceived inability to meet demands.

Symptoms of stress

When you are in a situation you find threatening, your stress response is activated. The way you respond depends on how seriously you view the threat. The response is controlled by two parts of your nervous system: the sympathetic nervous system and the parasympathetic nervous system.

The **sympathetic nervous system** is responsible for the fight or flight response. It gives you the energy you need to confront the threat or run away. To do this, the sympathetic nervous system produces these physiological responses:

- blood diverted to working muscles to provide more oxygen
- increased heart rate
- increased breathing rate
- increased heat production
- increased adrenaline production
- increased muscle tension
- hairs stand on end
- dilated pupils
- slowed digestion
- increased metabolism
- a dry mouth.

Key terms

Eustress – 'beneficial' stress that helps an athlete to perform.

Distress – extreme anxiety related to performance.

Sympathetic nervous system – part of the system responsible for the 'fight or flight' response.

Once stress has passed, the **parasympathetic nervous system** begins working. The parasympathetic system helps you relax by producing these responses:

- makes muscles relax
- slows metabolism
- increases digestion rate
- decreases body temperature
- decreases heart rate
- constricts the pupils
- increases saliva production
- decreases breathing rate.

Key term

Parasympathetic nervous system – part of the system that helps you to relax.

Remember

A lot of people see the symptoms of stress as negative aspects when they play their sport, but without some of these responses your body would not be able to meet the demands of your sport.

Causes of stress

It is common to have lots of athletes in similar situations yet with entirely different individual responses to those situations. Some of the main causes are discussed below.

- **Internal** causes of stress include:
  - illnesses/infections
  - psychological factors such as cognitive anxiety
  - not having enough sleep
  - being overly self-critical or being a perfectionist.
- **External** causes of stress include:
  - your environment, for example, too noisy, too quiet
  - negative social interactions, for example, somebody being rude to you
  - major life events, for example, a death in the family
  - day to day hassles, for example, travel to and from games, training schedules.

Remember

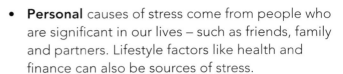

The key difference between internal and external sources of stress is that internal causes of stress are things that we think about whereas external sources come from the environment.

- **Personal** causes of stress come from people who are significant in our lives – such as friends, family and partners. Lifestyle factors like health and finance can also be sources of stress.
- **Occupational** causes of stress are related to your job, for example, lack of job satisfaction or unemployment. In a sporting situation, having a disagreement with a coach or a manager and being dropped from the team could cause you to suffer from stress.
- **Sports environments** – there are two key aspects of sport performance that cause stress: the importance of the event and the amount of uncertainty that surrounds it.

The effects of stress on performance

The effects of stress on performance are shown in Figure 3.5.

- At stage 1 of the stress process, some form of demand is placed on the athlete in a particular situation.
- At stage 2 the athlete perceives this demand positively or negatively. At this stage you start to understand how the negative perception of the demand causes a negative mental state, lack of self-confidence and lack of concentration. If the demand is perceived as too great, you will feel unable to meet the demand (negative mental state and loss of self-confidence) and find it difficult to concentrate on what you must do to meet the demand.
- It is this perception that increases the arousal levels of the performer (stage 3). During this stage you experience heightened arousal, higher levels of cognitive and somatic anxiety and changes in your attention and concentration levels.
- Ultimately this determines the outcome of performance (stage 4).

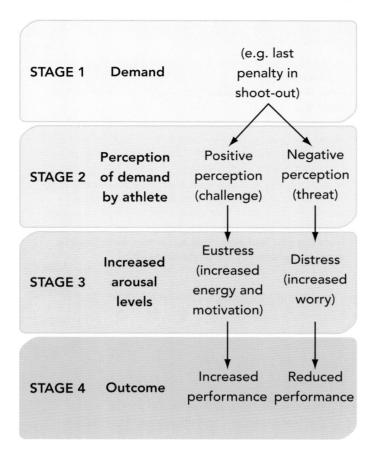

STAGE 1	Demand	(e.g. last penalty in shoot-out)	
STAGE 2	Perception of demand by athlete	Positive perception (challenge)	Negative perception (threat)
STAGE 3	Increased arousal levels	Eustress (increased energy and motivation)	Distress (increased worry)
STAGE 4	Outcome	Increased performance	Reduced performance

Figure 3.5: The stress process helps explain the relationship between stress, arousal, anxiety and performance.

2.3 Anxiety

Anxiety is a negative emotional state that is characterised by, or associated with, feelings of nervousness, apprehension or worry. There are two types of anxiety: **state anxiety** and **trait anxiety**.

Trait and state anxiety

Trait anxiety is an aspect of personality and part of an individual's pattern of behaviour. Someone with a high level of trait anxiety is likely to become worried in a variety of situations, even non-threatening situations.

State anxiety is a temporary, ever-changing mood state that is an emotional response to any situation considered threatening. For example, at the start of a showjumping event, the rider may have higher levels of state anxiety that drop once the event begins. State anxiety levels may increase again when coming up to high jumps and be at their highest level when coming towards the final jump which, if they were to clear quickly and cleanly, would result in a win.

The symptoms of anxiety

Cognitive anxiety refers to negative thoughts, nervousness or worry experienced in certain situations. Symptoms of cognitive anxiety include concentration problems, fear and bad decision-making.

Somatic anxiety relates to the awareness and perception of physiological changes (such as increases in heart rate, sweating and increased body heat) when you start to play sport. For example, an athlete could be concerned because they sense an increased heart rate if they have gone into a game less prepared than usual. This increase in heart rate is necessary for performance, but the athlete perceives it as negative. The symptoms of increased somatic anxiety range from increases in heart rate, respiratory rate and sweating to complete muscle tension that prevents the athlete from moving (known as 'freezing').

Causes of anxiety

Athletes experience all of the day-to-day causes of anxiety that everyone else does. Major life events and the hassles of daily routines are sources of anxiety, but athletes have other factors that are anxiety-provoking such as injuries, training schedules, contractual issues and concerns about levels of performance.

Effects of anxiety on sports performance

Constantly worrying about an event can make you think that you are not good enough to succeed (decreased self-confidence). This can make you feel like you are less likely to win (decreased expectations of success). Heightened cognitive anxiety means there is an increase in nervousness, apprehension or worry. One of the things athletes worry about is failing. Once you start to worry about it, you are focusing on it, which increases the likelihood of it happening. A heightened fear of failure could result in negative physiological responses like freezing or a lack of movement coordination, which negatively affect performance.

Take it further

The three main causes of anxiety

There are three main causes of anxiety: the importance of the event, uncertainty about the opposition and the competition itself.

1   **Importance of the event:** the more important the event, the greater the levels of stress and anxiety.

•   **Do you agree?**

2   **Uncertainty:** think back to when you have played against an opponent who was equally matched to you in terms of skill and ability levels. Now think about when you played against someone who was far less skilled than you and also against someone who you knew you had no chance of beating.

As a rule, greater levels of uncertainty lead to greater levels of anxiety.

•   **Who did you experience the greater levels of anxiety against?**

3   **Competition:** when a player is constantly anxious about competing, they are said to have high levels of competitive trait anxiety. Think back to when you have been in a competitive situation.

In athletes, this evaluative situation creates a threatening situation for the athlete, and as the athlete has high levels of competitive trait anxiety this can lead to higher levels of competitive state anxiety.

•   **How did you feel when you knew that people were watching you and your performance?**

Assessment activity 3.4

You are working as an assistant to a sport psychologist and you have been asked to produce an educational poster that will help sports performers and coaches understand the relationships between stress, arousal, anxiety and sports performance.

1.   Describe the different theories of arousal and the effect on sports performance. **P4**

2.   Explain the different theories of arousal and the effect on sports performance. **M3**

3.   Analyse the theories of arousal and say which you think best explains the relationship between arousal and performance, providing support for your answer. **D2**

4.   Describe stress and anxiety and then go on to describe the causes, symptoms and effects of stress and anxiety. **P5**

Grading tips

•   To attain **P4** describe three theories of arousal that you think provide the best explanations for the relationship between arousal and performance. Follow this up by describing the positive and negative effects of arousal on performance.

•   To attain **M3** use sport-based examples and advice for coaches and athletes to explain the different theories of arousal and the positive and negative effects of arousal on performance.

•   To attain **D2** look at each of the different theories of arousal in detail then provide a strong argument to support which you think best explains the relationship between arousal and performance.

•   To attain **P5** prepare some coach- and athlete-friendly notes that describe stress and anxiety, their causes, symptoms and effects on performance. Use sport-based examples wherever possible.

PLTS

Organising your time and resources, and prioritising the work that you need to do, will help you to develop skills as a **self-manager**.

Functional skills

Selecting, comparing, reading and understanding texts and using them to gather information, ideas, arguments and opinions could provide evidence of your **English** skills in reading.

3. Know the psychology of group dynamics in sports environments

3.1 Group processes

Groups or teams

There must be interaction between individuals in order for them to be classified as a group. This is characterised by communication over a period of time. The individuals need to get on (interpersonal attraction) and there should be a collective identity – the members of the group must perceive themselves to be a distinct unit that is different from other groups. The group must have shared goals, targets, norms and values, and be prepared to achieve these goals collectively. All these characteristics are common in teams, but there are some key differences between a group and a team.

The main difference relates to the pursuit of shared goals and objectives, both team and individual. For a group to be classed as a team, the members must depend on each other and offer support to each other to try to achieve team goals. The members will interact with each other to accomplish these goals and objectives.

Stages of group development

For a group of people to become a team, they must go through four developmental stages (Tuckman, 1965):

* forming
* storming
* norming
* performing.

All groups go through all stages, but the time they spend at each stage and the order in which they go through the stages may vary. Once a team has progressed through the four stages, it does not mean that they will not revert back to an earlier stage. If key members leave, the team may revert back to the storming stage as others begin to vie for position within the team.

* **Forming** – during the forming stage, group members familiarise themselves with each other, trying to decide if they belong in that group. Group members assess the strengths and weaknesses of other members, and test their relationships with others in

Michael Jordan once said 'Talent wins games; teamwork and intelligence wins championships'. What do you think his opinion is on the importance of team cohesion?

the group. Individuals get to know their roles within the group and make decisions about whether or not they feel they can fulfil (or want to fulfil) their role within the group. Formal leaders in the group tend to be directive during the forming stage.

* **Storming** – during the storming stage, conflict begins to develop between individuals in the group. Individuals or cliques start to question the position and authority of the leader, and start to resist the control of the group. Often, conflicts develop because demands are placed on the group members and some individuals try to acquire more important roles. During the storming stage, the formal leader in the group takes on more of a guidance role with decision-making and helps the team move towards what is expected in terms of professional behaviour.

- **Norming** – during the norming stage, conflict that occurred in the storming stage is replaced by cooperation. Members of the group start to work towards common goals rather than focusing on individual agendas, and group cohesion begins to develop. As group cohesion develops, group satisfaction increases (due to satisfaction from achieving tasks) and levels of respect for others in the group increase. In the norming stage, the formal leader expects group members to become more involved in the decision-making process, and the players to take more responsibility for their professional behaviour.

- **Performing** – the performing stage involves the team progressing and functioning effectively as a unit. The group works without conflict towards the achievement of shared goals and objectives and there is little need for external supervision as the group is more motivated. The group is now able to make its own decisions and take responsibility for them.

Steiner's model of group effectiveness

Steiner's model was put forward to explain group effectiveness. It is described as:

actual productivity = potential productivity – losses due to faulty group process

Actual productivity refers to how the team performs (the results they get and their level of performance). Potential productivity refers to the perfect performance the team could produce based on the individual skill and ability of each athlete in the team and the resources available. Losses due to faulty group processes relate to the issues that can get in the way of team performance, preventing the team from reaching its potential performance. Losses are normally due to two main areas: **motivational faults/losses** and **coordination faults/losses**.

Key terms

Motivational faults/losses – these occur when some members of the team do not give 100 per cent effort.

Coordination faults/losses – these occur when players do not connect with their play, the team interacts poorly or ineffective strategies are used. Generally, sports that require more interaction or cooperation between players are more susceptible to coordination faults or losses.

Activity: Motivational and coordination losses in volleyball

In a volleyball team, two players seem to be putting in little effort. When they are setting, they don't appear to be on the same wavelength as the other players on the team, and when they are blocking they don't seem to be putting a great deal of effort into their jumps. The other players on the team appear to be working harder to try to make up for this. However, despite their efforts, there is little interaction between spikers and setters.

1. **Where are the coordination losses in this scenario?**
2. **Where are the motivational losses in this scenario?**
3. **What do you think would be your role as the coach to improve these faults?**

Ringelmann effect

The Ringelmann effect is a phenomenon where, as the group size increases, the individual productivity of the people in the group decreases. The Ringelmann effect is caused more by motivation faults or losses than coordination losses and occurs when people are not accountable for their own performance (as the group gets larger athletes can hide behind other athletes and not get noticed).

Social loafing

Social loafing is when group members do not put in 100 per cent effort when they are in a group- or team-based situation. The losses in motivation that cause social loafing are evident when the individual contributions of group members are not identified or are dispensable. It occurs when some players appear to be working harder than others. Individuals who display social loafing lack confidence, are afraid of failure and tend to be highly anxious. Players who display social loafing don't feel they can make a useful contribution to overall team performance, which can be why they don't want to participate.

Interactive and coactive groups

Interactive teams require team members to work together to achieve a successful performance. Their successful performance is dependent on interaction and coordination between members.

Coactive teams require individuals to achieve success in their individual games, events or performances to achieve overall team success. There is no direct interaction between team members during the performance.

3.2 Cohesion

Cohesion is a dynamic process reflected in the tendency for a group to stick together and remain united in the pursuit of its goals and objectives:

- **Social cohesion** relates to how well the team members get on. In recreational sport, all the players may get on well and enjoy playing the game regardless of whether they win or lose.
- **Task cohesion** relates to how well group or team members work together to achieve common goals and objectives.

Remember

Although both types of cohesion influence performance to a certain degree, task cohesion is more closely related to successful sporting performance.

Factors affecting cohesion

Carron's conceptual model of cohesion (1982) explains factors affecting cohesion. It says four factors affect team cohesion: environmental, personal, leadership and team.

- **Environmental** – groups that are closer to each other (in terms of location), and which are smaller, are more cohesive because members have greater opportunities to interact and form relationships.
- **Personal** – the individual characteristics of group members are important in group cohesion. If players are motivated to achieve the group's aims and objectives, are from similar backgrounds, have similar attitudes and opinions and similar levels of

commitment, there will be more satisfaction among group members and the group is more likely to be cohesive.

- **Leadership** styles, behaviours, communication styles and compatibility of the coach's and athlete's personalities are key leadership factors that affect cohesion.
- **Team** – if the team stays together for a long time, experiences successes and failures together and can be involved in the decision-making process, the group is more likely to be productive and cohesive.

Relationship between cohesion and performance

It is easy to say that the greater the level of cohesion, the higher the level of performance. Interactive sports like football and volleyball require direct interaction and coordination between players so cohesion (especially task cohesion) is important. Coactive sports like golf and archery require little, if any, direct interaction or coordination. Cohesion has a greater influence on performance in interactive sports than it does on coactive sports.

3.3 Leadership

Qualities and behaviour

The best leaders can match their styles, behaviours and qualities to different situations. The following qualities contribute to making a good leader:

- **Patience** – a good leader gives athletes time to develop.
- **Self-discipline** – the leader should lead by example. If the leader expects players to always display professional standards, the players expect the same of the leader.
- **Intelligence** – a good leader is expected to come up with ideas and formulate plans to improve team performance.
- **Optimism** – the leader must remain positive and enthusiastic at all times to motivate team members
- **Confidence** – the leader must be self-confident and instil confidence in their colleagues. A good leader gives people they work with the responsibility and capabilities to make decisions and supports them in their decisions.

Prescribed versus emergent leaders

Leaders are either prescribed or emergent.

- **Prescribed leaders** are appointed by some form of higher authority. For example, Fabio Capello was appointed England manager by the FA.
- **Emergent leaders** achieve leadership status by gaining the respect and support of the group. These leaders achieve their status through showing specific leadership skills or being skilful at their sport. For example, Wayne Rooney emerged within the Manchester United team, became an informal leader of the team and has been touted as a future captain. He emerged because of his impressive performances, gaining the respect of others.

Styles of leadership

- **Autocratic** leaders have firm views about how and when things should be done. They are inflexible with their approach to the group. This type of leader dictates who does what tasks and when to do them, and often how the task should be done. They use phrases like 'do this', or 'do it the way I told you to'. The leader does not seek the views of people within the group, and rarely gets involved on a personal level with group members. When working with this type of leader, group members work less productively when the leader is not there and become aggressive when things go wrong.
- **Democratic/consultative/group** leaders make decisions only after consulting with group members. They encourage group involvement, adopt an informal and relaxed approach to leadership and listen to ideas relating to the prioritisation and completion of goals. They use questions like 'How do you think we can do this?'

  Democratic leaders maintain their status by making the final decision based on the information collected from group members and their own thoughts and ideas. When the leader is not present, group members tend to continue working towards agreed goals and do not become aggressive when things start to go wrong.

Theories of leadership

The four main theories of leadership are trait, behavioural, interactional and multi-dimensional. They are outlined below.

- **The trait approach** (often referred to as the great man theory) says there are certain personality characteristics that predispose an individual to being a good leader and that leaders are born, not made. This theory says that leadership is innate and a good leader would be good in any situation. This approach has not had much support and it is now accepted that there is no definitive set of traits that characterise a good leader.
- **Behavioural approach** – behavioural theories of leadership argue that a good leader is made, not born, and anyone can be taught to be a good leader. The behavioural approach is based on social learning theory and says people can learn to be good leaders by observing behaviours of other good leaders in a variety of situations, reproducing those behaviours in similar situations and having behaviours reinforced.
- **Interactional approach** – trait and behavioural approaches to leadership place emphasis on the personal qualities of a coach. The interactional approach considers interaction between the individual and their situation. Two main types of leader are identified through the interactional approach:
  - **Relationship-orientated leaders** are focused on developing relationships with individuals in the group. They work hard to maintain communication with members; always help to maintain levels of social interaction between members and themselves; and develop respect and trust with others. Relationship-orientated leaders are more effective with experienced, highly skilled athletes.
  - **Task-orientated leaders** are concerned with meeting goals and objectives. They create plans, decide on priorities, assign members to tasks, and ensure members stay on task, with the focus of increasing group productivity. Task-orientated leaders are effective with less experienced, less skilled performers who need constant instruction and feedback.

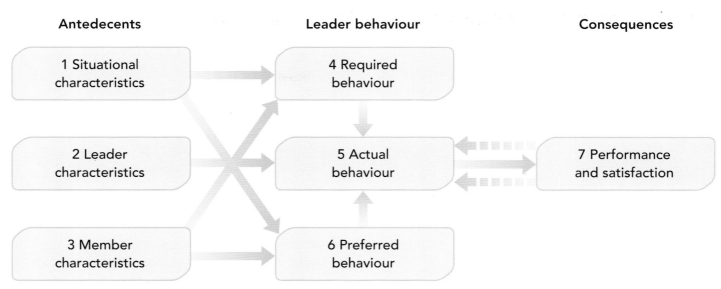

Figure 3.6: The multi-dimensional model of leadership (Chelladurai, 1990). How do the different leadership factors interact to influence performance?

Different athletes will have a preference for task-orientated or relationship-orientated leaders. In principle, a leader who gets the right balance between providing a supportive environment and focusing on getting the job done is the most effective leader. It is a leader's role to get to know their performers so they know where to concentrate their efforts.

- **The multi-dimensional model** says the team's performance and satisfaction with the leader will be highest if the leader's required behaviours, preferred behaviours and actual behaviours all agree. This is shown in Figure 3.6.

The behaviour required by the leader is generally determined by the situation the leader is in and should conform to the norms of the group.

The preferred behaviour is determined by the people within the group or team. Their preferences are related to factors including personality, experience and skill of the athletes; and non-sport related aspects like age and gender.

The actual behaviour is determined by the characteristics of the leader, the situational factors and the preferences of the group.

3.4 Social facilitation

Have you been in a sporting situation when you played better with an audience? If so, you have experienced social facilitation. How about playing worse when you play in front of an audience? If so, you have experienced impairment of performance, which is another aspect of social facilitation.

- **Audience effect** – social facilitation suggests that the effect of the audience increases arousal levels in athletes. In skills that are well learned or simple, increased arousal levels improve performance levels. However, in skills that are not well learned, or complex, performance levels can be reduced.

- **Co-action effect** – co-action is when other people are performing at the same time as you, but not in direct competition with you. The presence of these individuals can influence your thoughts and effort. Generally, you will perform a simple or well-learned skill better in the presence of co-actors whereas a more difficult skill or a skill you don't know well could be made worse in the presence of co-actors.

- **Home advantage** suggests that a team is more likely to be successful when playing at home than away. There is a body of research that supports this idea, claiming that home advantage is greater in indoor sports than outdoor sports. A number of reasons have been suggested to explain home advantage including physical (for example, related to the location of the event) and psychological (for example, players choking under the pressure of fans). As the importance of the game increases, home advantage can decrease in certain sports.

For example, as a basketball game becomes more important, the away team's performance remains constant but the home team's performance decreases in certain areas such as free-throw shooting, because of increased pressure.

Assessment activity 3.5

  P6 M4 **BTEC**

You are an assistant coach at a sports team. You have been watching one of your team's games trying to look at the different factors that can influence group dynamics and performance. You have been asked to prepare a presentation for the manager and coaches about your observations of the match, commenting specifically on the key factors you have identified that influence group dynamics and sports performance.

1. Identify four factors which influence group dynamics and performance in team sports. **P6**
2. Explain four factors which influence group dynamics and performance in team sports. **M4**

Grading tips

• To attain **P6** you need to identify four factors which influence group dynamics and performance in team sports. These could be aspects of group processes, cohesion and leadership.

• To attain **M4** you need to follow this by explaining each of the different factors that you have identified and provide examples to support how they can influence group dynamics.

PLTS

If you communicate the results of your observations effectively, you could develop your skills as a **reflective learner**.

Functional skills

By presenting the different factors that can affect group dynamics and team performance, you could develop your speaking and listening skills in **English**.

4. Know psychological factors that affect people in exercise environments

4.1 Psychological factors

Reasons why people exercise

There are different reasons why people take part in exercise, including health benefits, enjoyment, self-esteem and social reasons.

• **Health benefits** – these relate to weight management, cardiovascular risk and mental health issues.

• **Enjoyment** – this is a main reason for taking part in exercise. Women and young people are more likely to report enjoyment as an important factor.

• **Self-esteem** – regular exercise plays an important role in building self-esteem. Increased self-esteem results from achieving exercise goals (for example, managing to walk around the block, lifting a target weight).

• **Social reasons** – people often start exercise programmes as an opportunity to meet new people and socialise. Social opportunities are a big reason why exercisers attend group-based exercise sessions, such as aerobics.

Barriers to exercise

Barriers to exercise can be classified under five main headings: physical, emotional, motivational, time and availability. Most of these barriers can be overcome by planning or education.

- **Physical** – individuals report physical barriers to some degree as reasons not to exercise. The most common forms of physical barriers relate to injuries or disabilities, health, age (for example, 'I'm too old') and weight (for example, 'I'm too fat'). Generally, men give physical reasons more than women do for not taking part in exercise.

- **Emotional** – these relate to some form of fear relating to health (for example, 'I might get injured', 'It may damage my health'), being too shy to take part, being too embarrassed and considering themselves not the 'sporty type'.

- **Motivational** – not having the commitment to maintain an activity programme due to other factors is another barrier. The most common motivational barriers are needing time to relax, needing rest in spare time, not having any energy, not enjoying physical activity and not thinking the exercise programme would last.

- **Time** – is seen as the most important barrier to exercise, but lack of time is a perceived barrier rather than an actual barrier. The most common time factors relate to work or family commitments (for example, having to look after children). However, people have enough time to watch television or socialise with friends, so time can be down to an individual's priorities.

- **Availability** – this relates to finances, facilities, equipment and other individuals to exercise with.

Determinants of exercise

Determinants of exercise adherence are grouped as personal factors, environmental factors and activity-related factors.

- **Personal factors** include demographic variables (such as income and education), cognitive variables (such as motivation) and behaviours (such as a previous history of exercise participation).

- **Environmental factors** include social environmental factors (such as the support of friends and family) and physical environmental factors (such as the weather conditions outside).

- **Activity-related factors** include group versus individual activities and the frequency, intensity and duration of exercise.

> **Take it further**
>
> ### Exercise adherence
>
> Looking at each of the different determinants of exercise adherence, discuss with your friends how you think each of those could positively and negatively affect exercise adherence.

Behaviour change models

Models of behaviour change such as the transtheoretical model, the health belief model and the theory of planned behaviour are used to try to explain exercise behaviour.

The transtheoretical model (sometimes known as the stages of change model) suggests that to change behaviour, individuals go through a series of stages of:

- precontemplation
- contemplation
- preparation
- action
- maintenance
- termination.

This process is a dynamic (ever-changing) one. It is often the case that people move through the different stages several times while trying to change their behaviour. An additional stage is added to the model which is known as relapse. When people fall back from their current stage, relapse occurs. Relapse can happen at any stage and individuals begin the cycle again from the stage before.

> **Take it further**
>
> ### The transtheoretical model
>
> Using books and the Internet, research each of the different stages of the transtheoretical model and find out what they mean.
>
> After this, why not research some of the other models of behaviour change such as the health belief model and the theory of planned behaviour and try to find out how they can be used to help people alter their health behaviours?

Assessment activity 3.6

You are working as a personal trainer. June is a client that has been referred to you by her GP as he feels she would benefit from more exercise and would like you to work with June. The GP has provided you with the following case notes:

'June is 50 years old and lives on her own. Her children have left home and she has few friends. She has a poor lifestyle and she drinks frequently and smokes, is clinically obese and refers to herself as a bit of a 'slug' (she has very low self-esteem). June understands the benefits of regular exercise but she does not take part in any physical activity. She says she has no intention of doing so, as she does not feel she would be able to take part in it effectively and says that she has very little money.'

From the case notes, write a letter to the GP where you complete the following:

1. Identify three psychological factors that June gives for not wanting to exercise. **P7**

2. Explain how June feels that these factors can stop her from exercising. **M5**

Grading tips

- To attain **P7** identify what you see as the main factors for June not participating in exercise.

- To attain **M5** try to use the different theories of behaviour change to discuss why June doesn't exercise. Why not try suggesting some ways in which you could get June to be more active?

PLTS

If you communicate your thoughts regarding June's situation effectively, you could develop your skills as a **reflective learner**.

Functional skills

By writing to the GP, and making your letter fit for purpose, you could develop your writing skills in **English**.

Louise Smith
Personal trainer

Louise works as a self-employed personal trainer. She works with a wide range of clients from people training for marathons, to rugby players wanting strength and conditioning advice, to less active clients who just want to be active to improve their quality of life.

'Being a personal trainer is a great job. I get to work with lots of different people and you get a great sense of satisfaction knowing that you are helping people to meet their targets, either within their general health or related to their sport. In order to be able to meet the needs of all these different people, I need to have a really good understanding of exercise psychology so that I can make sure that everybody stays motivated to train or be active.

'One of the biggest problems that I face is when I get clients who start to lose their motivation. There are lots of different factors that can influence why a person will start to exercise and there are also a lot of factors that can make that same person want to stop – a big part of my job is to make sure that the factors that the client will use as reasons to stop don't become too powerful!'

Think about it!

- If you were Louise, what strategies could you use to make sure that your clients stayed motivated?
- What do you think could be some of the different factors that people would give for starting an exercise programme?
- What do you think are some of the reasons people would give for quitting an exercise programme?

Just checking

1. What is personality and how does it affect sports participation and performance?

2. What are the main theories that have tried to explain the relationship between personality and sports participation and performance? What are the main arguments of each of these different theories and which is the most widely supported?

3. What is aggression and what are the different types of aggression?

4. What is motivation and what are the different types of motivation?

5. What is the attribution theory and what are the different types of attributes we give?

6. What is stress and what are the different sources of stress?

7. What is arousal and what are the different theories that try to explain how arousal affects performance?

8. What is anxiety and what are the different types of anxiety?

9. What is cohesion? Explain the key factors that can affect team cohesion.

10. What are some of the different factors that can affect exercise adherence?

Assignment tips

- Try to use as much supporting information as you can for this unit. This will be helpful in achieving higher grades in some cases. The Internet is full of websites based on sport psychology so you might want to try these:

  o Athletic Insight (www.athleticinsight.com)

  o Mind tools (www.mindtools.com)

  o Zone of Excellence (www.zoneofexcellence.ca)

- Try to use plenty of examples to support your points throughout your work. The more you bring your work to life with examples, the more you will understand it.

- Where there is a range of theories to consider in different topics, always try to consider each of the theories and then look at how they try to explain a particular topic.

- If there is a particular topic that you are interested in, you may want to try to stretch your knowledge even further using subject-specific textbooks – speak to your tutor about which may be appropriate for you.

- Always try to look at how sport psychology can be used to benefit athletes. Don't be satisfied with just understanding the topic from a theoretical perspective. This will also help to prepare you for Unit 20 Applied sport and exercise psychology.

4 Research methods for sport and exercise sciences

Why do we play sport? How does a good player become an elite player? How useful is exercise in combating childhood obesity? Research is vital to understanding all aspects of sport, exercise and health and it is only through research that questions such as these can be answered.

Sport and exercise scientists are playing an ever more significant role within society, often leading the way with developments in sport performance and health sciences. However, to stay at the forefront of applied work and provide the highest quality of service to clients, you need to base your advice on a sound knowledge base. This can only be developed through high-quality research.

Throughout this unit, you will develop a knowledge and understanding of some of the key issues that are associated with research methods. This will range from examining some different quality indicators such as validity and reliability, to looking at how you can make sure that you are meeting the necessary professional standards associated with research in sport and exercise sciences. After this, you will do more applied work examining how you can structure and organise research, and look at the different ways that you can collect and analyse data using both qualitative and quantitative methods.

Learning outcomes

After completing this unit you should:

1. know key issues in research methods for the sport and exercise sciences
2. know data collection techniques for the sport and exercise sciences
3. know qualitative data analysis techniques for the sport and exercise sciences
4. know quantitative data analysis techniques for the sport and exercise sciences.

Assessment and grading criteria

This table shows you what you must do in order to achieve a pass, merit or distinction grade, and where you can find activities in this book to help you.

To achieve a **pass** grade the evidence must show that you are able to:	To achieve a **merit** grade the evidence must show that, in addition to the pass criteria, you are able to:	To achieve a **distinction** grade the evidence must show that, in addition to the pass and merit criteria, you are able to:
P1 describe qualitative and quantitative research **See Assessment activity 4.1, page 90**		
P2 identify key issues that affect research in sport and exercise sciences **See Assessment activity 4.1, page 90**	**M1** explain key issues that affect research in sport and exercise sciences **See Assessment activity 4.1, page 90**	**D1** analyse key issues that affect research in sport and exercise sciences **See Assessment activity 4.1, page 90**
P3 outline the types, techniques, and classifications of data that are common in research in the sport and exercise sciences **See Assessment activity 4.2, page 97**		
P4 describe two ethical and legal issues associated with research in sport and exercise sciences **See Assessment activity 4.3, page 100**	**M2** explain the implications of not working both ethically and legally when conducting research in the sport and exercise sciences **See Assessment activity 4.3, page 100**	**D2** analyse the implications of not working both ethically and legally when conducting research in the sport and exercise sciences **See Assessment activity 4.3, page 100**
P5 describe the three main stages of qualitative data analysis in the sport and exercise sciences **See Assessment activity 4.4, page 103**	**M3** justify, for a selected research-based example, the most appropriate research design and techniques for qualitative data collection and data analysis **See Assessment activity 4.4, page 103**	
P6 describe two contrasting quantitative data analysis techniques used in the sport and exercise sciences **See Assessment activity 4.5, page 116**	**M4** justify, for a selected research-based example, the most appropriate research design and techniques for quantitative data collection and data analysis **See Assessment activity 4.5, page 116**	

How you will be assessed

This unit will be assessed by internal assignments that will be designed and marked by the tutors at your centre. Your assessments could be in the form of:

- written reports
- oral presentations
- discussions
- posters.

Simon, 19-year-old trainee performance analyst

This unit has helped me to understand that there is more to research than just reading things. It's all about discovering things through your own investigations and there are lots of different ways of carrying out these investigations.

There were lots of practical learning opportunities throughout this unit where we could collect our own data and analyse it – so we got a feel for the overall process and it felt more like doing sport science rather than just being given lots of number crunching to do. I'd definitely recommend it to you!

I enjoyed looking at the different ways in which I can apply the work on statistics to a performance environment. When I was at school, I was always a bit scared of maths but the way I learned about doing statistics in this unit helped me to get over that fear and now I'm doing a job where using maths is a major part of what I do!

Over to you

1. **Which areas of this unit are you looking forward to?**
2. **Which bits do you think you might find difficult?**
3. **What do you think you will need to do to prepare for this unit?**

1. Know key issues in research methods for the sport and exercise sciences

Warm-up

What is the role of research in modern sport and exercise science?

What do you think about when you hear the term 'research'? For some people, it means people in white coats dropping things into petri dishes whereas for others it could mean big needles and complex machines. How do you think research is applicable to sport and exercise environments?

1.1 Research

Research is a systematic process of investigation and study carried out with the goal of advancing knowledge.

Before conducting research, you need to consider which type of research would be the most suitable to answer your research questions. There are two main types of research:

- quantitative
- qualitative.

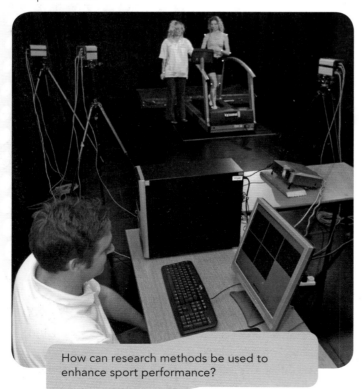

How can research methods be used to enhance sport performance?

Quantitative and qualitative research

Quantitative research is a formal, objective and systematic process in which numerical data is used to obtain information. It involves testing a hypothesis or trying to discover relationships. It is generally deductive research (this means that a scientist would start from a hypothesis and then begin observations to prove the hypothesis). It is designed to establish differences, relationships or causality (does one thing cause another?).

Qualitative research is generally subjective and involves words rather than numbers. It looks at feelings, opinions and emotions and is concerned with trying to explain *why* rather than *what* or *how many*. It tends to be inductive, which means a hypothesis can be developed through the research. It tries to explain differences, relationships or causality. Qualitative data can also produce quantitative data, for example, you may record how many people said that they like playing sport because they can spend time with their friends.

1.2 Key issues

Key issues influence the quality of your research. These are:

- **validity**
- **reliability**
- **accuracy**
- **precision**.

Key terms

Quantitative research – a formal, objective and systematic process in which numerical data is used to obtain information.

Qualitative research – a more subjective form of research that tries to explain differences, relationships or causality using non-numerical data such as words.

Validity – whether you are measuring what you are supposed to be measuring.

Reliability – the repeatability of a set of results.

Accuracy – how close a measurement is to the true value.

Precision – how fine or small a difference a measurement can detect.

Validity

Validity is essential in research because it relates to whether you are actually measuring what you planned to measure. There are different types of validity, but two key types are internal validity and external validity. Internal validity relates to whether the results of the study can be attributed to the different treatments in the study. This means that for your research to claim internal validity, you need to ensure that you have controlled everything that could affect the results of the study. External validity relates to whether or not the results of the study can be applied to the real world.

Reliability

Reliability relates to whether, if you carried out the research again, you would get the same or similar results. However, reliability can be claimed without results being correct. For example, if you always ask the wrong questions in research, you will always get the same wrong answers. This will mean the test is reliable because you have received the *same* wrong answers, even though they are not the ones you wanted.

In quantitative research, reliability can be one researcher conducting the same test on the same individual on a number of occasions, and getting the same or similar results. Alternatively, it can be different researchers conducting the same test on the same individual and getting the same or similar results.

In qualitative research, reliability relates to the same researcher placing results into the same categories on different occasions, or different researchers placing results into the same or similar categories.

There are certain factors you should take into account that can affect reliability. For example:

- Errors can happen when researchers don't know how to use the equipment correctly.
- The equipment may be poorly maintained.
- The wrong type of equipment may be selected.

There are two types of reliability: inter-researcher reliability and test-retest reliability.

Inter-researcher reliability examines whether different researchers in the same situation would get the same (or similar) results. An example of when inter-researcher reliability is a problem is body composition assessment. When people are learning to use the skinfold calliper technique of assessing body composition, it is difficult to take accurate measurements from the correct sites. Researchers come up with different values. When this happens, you cannot claim to have achieved inter-researcher reliability.

Test-retest reliability relates to doing the same test on different occasions and getting the same (or similar) results. An example of a test-retest reliability issue in sport or exercise research is the measurement of heart rate. Heart rate can be affected by different factors, such as temperature, time of day, diet, sleep patterns, physical activity levels and alcohol. If you measured the heart rate on the same person at the same time of day, but on different days, you could get different measurements.

Accuracy

Accuracy relates to how close your measurement is to the 'gold standard', or what you are intending to measure. Imagine you are looking at the weight of a boxer before a fight. If the boxer has an actual weight of 100 kg and your weighing device shows he weighs 100.1 kg, you could say this is accurate. However, if the measuring device shows he weighs 103 kg, you would say this isn't accurate as it isn't close to his body weight.

Precision

When working in a research setting, any measurement you take will have some unpredictability. The degree of unpredictability relates to the amount of precision the tool selected for measurement has. Precision is related to the refinement of the measuring process.

It is concerned with how small a difference the measuring device can detect. Precision is closely related to repeatability/reliability. An easy way to get to grips with accuracy and precision is to think about target sports, such as archery. If you were to hit the bullseye on the archery board with all of your arrows, you would say that you had been both accurate and precise. However, if you missed the board completely in different directions with your arrows, you would say that you had been neither accurate nor precise. This is shown in the diagram below.

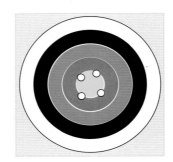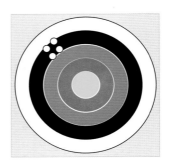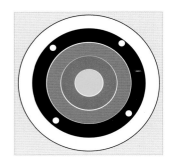

Figure 4.1: Can you explain the accuracy and precision shown on each archery target?

Assessment activity 4.1 P1 P2 M1 D1 BTEC

You are applying for a job as a performance analyst within a national cricket organisation. As part of the application process, the head of sport science support for the organisation has provided you with a sample data set and asked you to produce a presentation using a program such as PowerPoint® that interprets the data set. The data set is below with the accompanying presentation guidance.

Bowler	Speed gun results			Timing gate results		
1	75 mph	80 mph	77 mph	76.98 mph	77.02 mph	76.95 mph
2	81 mph	84 mph	83 mph	80.02 mph	80.05 mph	80.06 mph

1. Describe qualitative and quantitative research. Then say whether the table contains qualitative or quantitative data. **P1**

2. Name the different key issues that could have affected the quality of data in the data set. **P2**

3. Using the data set, explain the different key issues (for example, the bowling speeds of bowler X are more reliable because…). **M1**

4. Using the key issues, analyse which method of data collection has provided you with the best quality of data. **D1**

Grading tips

- To attain P1 include a description of qualitative and quantitative research in your PowerPoint.

- To attain **P2** and **M1** make sure that you look at all of the different key issues when analysing your data set.

- To attain **M1** and **D1** try to provide as much detail in your presentation as you can and make sure that you link your arguments to the data set.

PLTS

By asking questions to extend your thinking about how the key issues in research methods relate to the data set, you can develop your skills as a **critical thinker.**

Functional skills

If you produce a presentation that is fit for purpose, you could provide evidence of your **ICT** skills in communicating information.

2.   Know data collection techniques for the sport and exercise sciences

2.1 Types of data

Primary data

Primary data is data that you collect through questionnaires, interviews and observations which you use to investigate your research problem.

Secondary data

Secondary data is previously published data found in books, journals, government publications, websites and other forms of media. Secondary data is used to form rationales for your research and to support or counter-argue your research findings.

2.2 Classifications of data

Discrete data

Discrete data is a form of data where only separate, isolated or opposite values can be achieved (for example, male/female, win/lose, yes/no).

Nominal data

A nominal scale is where participants are put into categories and counted, for example, grouping basketball players under the team they play for. You will group the players in this way to count them, not necessarily to say that one group is better than another.

Ordinal data

Ordinal data is ranked data that gives no indication of the difference between levels. It allows you to say who is best and second best, but does not tell you the difference between the two. This type of data provides the researcher with a rank order, but does not give an exact value. For example, on a badminton ladder, the person at the top is assigned a rank of 1, the person

second down is awarded a rank of 2, the third person is awarded a rank of 3, and so on. There is nothing to say, however, that the person at the top of the ladder is three times as good as the person in third place on the ladder.

Continuous

Continuous data is data that can have any numerical value with any number of decimal places. For example, lap times in a MotoGP race can be classed as continuous data because of the values they are given (1 minute, 35.37 seconds).

Interval

Interval data is based on a scale that has equal intervals of measurement with equal intervals between each score. For example, in a figure skating scoring scale there is the same difference between scoring 5 and 5.5 as there is between scoring 5.5 and 6.

Ratio

Ratio data has proportional equal units of measurement. Ratio scales range from zero upwards and cannot have negative scores. For example, if a rugby team scores 40 points, it is worth twice as much as their opponents who have scored 20 points.

2.3 Qualitative data collection techniques

Three main types of data collection are involved with qualitative research:

- interviews
- focus groups
- observations.

Each type of data collection method has its advantages and disadvantages which we will discuss in this section.

Interviews

An interview is a conversation with a purpose. There are four types of interview: **structured**, **unstructured**, **semi-structured** and **focus groups** (focus groups will be covered separately as they are a group-based interview whereas the others are individual interviews).

Key terms

Structured interview – a set interview guide that you adhere to without change in light of participant responses.

Unstructured interview – this type of interview has a start question and then the conversation goes from there. You must be skilled at focusing your conversation to get a lot out of this type of interview.

Semi-structured interview – an interview that follows the guide but allows scope for probing further with your questions if a topic of interest is brought up. This is a good technique as it allows you to get deeper information from your participant through additional questioning as well as giving the participant the opportunity to discuss things further.

Focus group – a group-based interview where the group interaction is an essential aspect of data collection. This tends to be a semi-structured interview.

Advantages and disadvantages of interviews

No one type of interview is ideal – it should be matched to the situation or participant. Interviews are used in qualitative research because they are a useful way for researchers to understand the beliefs, opinions and emotions of participants. They are useful because the researcher gets a view of what the participant thinks in the participant's own words. This gives the researcher a greater understanding of the meanings that the participant attaches to their experiences.

Interview techniques

Interviews are used in qualitative research as they help you get lots of information about a topic quickly, but this only works if you have developed your interview skills. In interviews, you will only get answers to the questions you ask. If you ask the wrong questions, or the wrong types of question, you will never find out what you want. If you want to get the most from an interview, first establish some form of relationship with your participant. Do this by setting the tone of the interview; have a friendly chat before starting or break the ice with more general questions at the start of the interview which don't need much thought or effort to answer. If you can do this and then progress to more specific questions, you are likely to get more detailed responses. To get the most out of an interview, guide the conversation around your research problem. Gently probe the participant further, and get them to provide you with examples of things they have experienced, rather than hypothetical examples. When interviewing, a three-stage technique is often used in research.

- The researcher asks the main guiding question (for example, 'What motivates you to...?'). This 'gets the ball rolling'.

- This is followed up with probe questions (for example, 'Can you give me a specific example of...?'). This clarifies or deepens understanding or knowledge.

- The final aspect is a follow-up question (for example, 'So, am I correct in saying that...?'). This gives the researcher the opportunity to check they have understood what the participant has said and that it is taken in the correct context.

Advantages	Disadvantages
Participants can express their views in their own words.	They require more resources and are more time-consuming than using questionnaires.
Participants can provide information from their own perspective.	They tend to use small sample sizes as interviews are time-consuming.
Unexpected data may come out in the interview.	The participant can take the interview off in a number of directions.
Body language, tone and pitch of voice, and speed of speech, can be assessed.	Data analysis is more difficult and takes longer than using questionnaires.
The researcher can establish a rapport with the participant and investigate target groups.	The quality of the data is dependent on the quality of the questioning and quality of responses.

Table 4.1: Advantages and disadvantages of interviews and focus groups.

The listening part of an interview is as important as the speaking part. A good interviewer knows when to keep quiet and listen and when to speak. Don't interrupt the participant when they are speaking as this can prevent them from wanting to answer further questions.

Focus groups

Focus groups are similar to interviews, but involve more than one participant. There are usually between 6 and 12 participants and the researcher acts as a discussion facilitator rather than an interviewer. In this context, your role as the researcher is to ensure that the focus group stays on topic and doesn't wander. Focus groups are more effective if everyone has a say in the discussion. They can provide you with a better quality of data because the discussion gets deeper as the group develops ideas. They are a good way of finding out opinions and ideas.

Activity: Let's talk it through

Work with a partner to produce an interview guide on your favourite topic within sport and exercise science. When you have finished the interview guide, conduct the interview, taking it in turns to be the interviewer and interviewee. Record your interview on a dictaphone and keep the recording safe as you will need it later in the unit. When you have finished the interview, discuss the strengths and areas for improvement for your interview with your partner and make some notes about how you could improve the interview guide and the interview process.

Observations

Two main types of observation are used in qualitative research: participant and non-participant.

- **Participant observation** means that the researcher is actively involved in the topic they are researching. For example, if you were studying team cohesion in rugby, you could join a rugby team, to observe 'from the inside' and gain your own experiences of cohesion as a player. Data would then be recorded in the form of field notes, with you recording your own thoughts, feelings, opinions, emotions and experiences. This method is useful when trying to discover the more delicate aspects of group behaviour that are not easy to see from the outside.

- **Non-participant observation** involves the researcher observing 'from the outside'. There is no interaction with the individuals or the activity being observed. For example, if you wanted to look at injuries during a basketball match, you could watch how many injuries happened, what types of injuries they were and record the numbers on a data recording sheet.

Below there is a summary of the advantages and disadvantages of observational methods.

Recording observational data

Observation checklists and field notes are methods of recording data in observational research. Observation checklists are used more frequently in quantitative research, or in qualitative research for observing more simple forms of data. For example, if you were observing a young developing footballer while researching two-footedness in football, you could use an observation checklist similar to the one in Figure 4.2.

Advantages	Disadvantages
Observations can be 'here and now' rather than being dependent on recall.	There is potential for the researcher to misunderstand what they are seeing.
They can take place in natural settings rather than research settings.	It can be difficult to identify and record the correct type of data.
They allow for the identification of behaviours that may not be apparent to the person and may not have been discovered through interviews.	The Hawthorne effect: if the person knows they are the subject of research, they may act differently and could invalidate the whole project – the researcher must be very careful exactly how they approach the people in observational research.
They allow for the identification of behaviours that the person may not wish to disclose.	

Table 4.2: Advantages and disadvantages of observational methods.

Tick the box each time the behaviour occurs	Player number							
Controlled ball left foot								
Controlled ball right foot								
Passed ball left foot								
Passed ball right foot								
Shot left foot								
Shot right foot								
Shifted ball from left foot to right foot								
Shifted ball from right foot to left foot								

Figure 4.2: An example of an observation checklist.

Activity: What do you see?

Imagine you are a talent scout for your favourite sport. Using the observation checklist as a guide, produce a checklist of your own so that you can complete an observation of your favourite sport. Remember that you need to decide on exactly what it is you are looking for before you can produce your checklist.

When you have produced your checklist, conduct an observation of your sport and then answer the following questions:

- **Were you conducting participant or non-participant observation?**
- **How useful was your checklist?**
- **How could you adapt your checklist to make it more useful?**

Field notes are more commonly used in qualitative data collection than in quantitative data collection. They allow the researcher to record their observations. They are more flexible than observation checklists and allow you to collect more complex data. Field notes should include:

- descriptive notes that tell you about the setting of the research, the participants that are the subject of research and how they behave in a particular setting
- detailed notes to help you remember certain details over time

- reflective notes which should contain the researcher's thoughts, opinions, beliefs, evaluations and experiences and form an integral part of the data analysis.

2.4 Quantitative data collection techniques

Several data collection techniques can be used for quantitative data collection. You have covered how non-participant observation can be used in both qualitative and quantitative research – don't forget about this technique when considering quantitative research. Other techniques used in quantitative research include questionnaires. The settings in which data will be collected are either field-based data collection settings or laboratory-based data collection settings.

Questionnaires

Questionnaires are used when you are trying to collect a large amount of data from large groups and when the data you want to collect is not in-depth. If you need to obtain more in-depth information, questionnaires would not be suitable alone. However, they could be effective if used alongside other qualitative methods of data collection (such as interviews). As with other data collection methods, questionnaires have advantages and disadvantages.

Advantages	Disadvantages
They are people-friendly if the form is designed correctly.	Questions can be too complex if the form is designed incorrectly.
They are an opportunity to reduce participant bias.	There are control issues.
The participant can be anonymous.	There is no opportunity for probing questions.
The data is structured.	There is a potential for a low response rate.
They are usually accessible to most people.	

Table 4.3: Advantages and disadvantages of questionnaires.

Questionnaire design

If your questionnaire looks poorly organised and unprofessional, it may be thrown away, particularly if you decide to post your questionnaires to people. If it looks well organised and purposeful, you have a better chance of it being completed. The use of coloured paper, artistic designs, dotted lines and tick boxes all help, but ensure your design is geared towards the audience it is aimed at. For example, make it easy and simple to use for young children. When designing your questionnaire, remember that if it is more than one page long it is much less likely to be filled in – so keep it short.

Always consider why you are asking a question. This will stop you including unnecessary questions. The quality of your questionnaire will increase as its validity increases. Decide which format would be most appropriate for the question you want to ask. Should it be an open question or a closed question? When you start to design your questionnaire, you need to consider a number of factors including:

- What you want to find out.
- Your sample (this will affect how you write your questionnaire).
- The length and appearance of your questionnaire (when you design it, don't make it too long or difficult to answer).
- How and when you are going to distribute your questionnaire. If you are going to distribute it by hand, wait for it to be completed rather than going away and returning later. Another way you can distribute your questionnaire is by post or email, but this reduces the chances of it being returned. Include a return address and a covering letter to explain why your questionnaire is being sent out.
- How to analyse the results.

Remember that there are different types of questions: open and closed.

- **Open questions** are used more in qualitative research than in quantitative research. They allow people to express ideas, opinions and sentiments in words. They are used when asking questions that could lead to complex or in-depth answers, or if you are unsure of what the answers to the question could be. Open questions can take longer to answer than closed questions, so make sure that you plan your research to account for this. An example of an open-ended question could be 'What are your thoughts on the promotion of sport for people with disabilities within the UK?'

- **Closed questions** are used when a specific response is required and answers involve ranking, scales or categories. These questions are used more in quantitative data collection as they generate numbers for you to analyse using statistical methods. The participants respond to answers that the researcher has included on the questionnaire. The responses are in less depth than those from open questions. An example of a closed question could be 'Do you like playing rugby? Yes/No'.

Remember

When designing your questionnaire, the following are important:
- Make sure that the first questions are straightforward and ask for facts.
- Do not put questions at the start that require lengthy answers.
- Leave personal or potentially sensitive questions to the end.
- Group questions together when they follow a similar theme or topic.
- Don't ask leading questions.
- Don't include questions that ask for responses on two different topics.
- Keep your questions simple and clear.
- Use an appropriate structure to make it attractive to your audience.
- Use tick boxes to make it easy to fill in.
- Don't make the questionnaire too long.

Laboratory-based data collection

Laboratory-based data collection involves collecting data in an environment where all the conditions and variables are controlled, so that you are only measuring the variables in question. One advantage of laboratory-based data collection is that it has high levels of internal validity; you are controlling all your variables so you know that you are only measuring the aspect you mean to measure. One disadvantage of laboratory-based data collection is that it has low levels of ecological validity because the data is not collected in an environment that reflects the situation in which the activity is performed. Another disadvantage of laboratory-based data collection is that it normally requires the use of expensive or technical equipment to collect data, making it difficult to use this if you don't have a lot of resources.

Field-based data collection

Field-based data is collected in the environment that simulates the one in which the sport is played. One of the key strengths of field-based data collection is that it mimics the performance environment so you can claim ecological validity when you are collecting data in this setting. Field-based data collection can be cheaper than laboratory-based collection, making it more accessible to people without lots of resources. However, one limitation is that you don't control all the variables in this data collection setting, so it can be difficult to claim internal validity.

2.5 Research designs

A number of research designs are used within sport and exercise sciences. A research design is the overall structure of your research. Some of the common designs that you need to understand are experimental research, cross-sectional research, case study research, longitudinal research and comparative research.

Experimental

The aim of experimental research is to look at the effects of an independent variable on a dependent variable. To use this research design effectively, you need to understand the terms independent and dependent variable. The independent variable affects the dependent variable. For example, an athletics coach wants to find out if her lower back flexibility training is benefiting the athlete's high jump performance. She has asked you to research the topic for her. As the coach wants to find out if flexibility affects performance, flexibility is the independent variable and performance is the dependent variable.

Cross-sectional

Cross-sectional research involves using a range of participants with different backgrounds, ages and genders from the overall population.

For example, if you want to look at preferences for team sports or individual sports in people in the UK, cross-sectional research would be useful. This would allow you to obtain opinions from a range of people.

Case study: Taking it to the max!

Jamie is a sport scientist going through his supervised experience at the youth team of a professional football club. It is pre-season and he is trying to assess the VO_2 max of some of the players. As he has a number of methods available to him, Jamie has decided to use both field-based and laboratory-based data collection methods to try to find out which is most effective. To measure VO_2 max in a field-based way, Jamie has decided to use a multi-stage fitness test to get an indirect prediction of VO_2 max, and to measure it in a laboratory setting, Jamie has decided to use a gas analysis system.

1. **Which method do you think will be the most accurate and why?**

2. **Which method do you think will be most valid and why?**

3. **If you were Jamie, which do you think you would want to use and why?**

You would send your participants a survey-type questionnaire that allowed them to say which type of sport they preferred. Then you could produce some descriptive statistics for the results of the study (for example, 73 per cent of men prefer team sports, 20 per cent of men prefer individual sports and 7 per cent of men have no preference).

Case study

Case study research is where you investigate a particular phenomenon (e.g. an individual or team) over a long period of time. It takes into account the development of the area of investigation over time and the environment in which the research resides. For example, to investigate the psychological effects of injury at different stages of injury and recovery, a case study design would be suitable. It allows you to investigate one person over a period of time and at different times throughout the stages of injury. This means you can draw conclusions relating to that individual and suggest these conclusions as directions for future research on a larger scale.

Longitudinal

Longitudinal research involves measuring the same variables over a long period of time and requires greater resources than other types of research, so be careful when approaching this design. Longitudinal research is useful if you want to examine the developmental characteristics of a group; for example, to investigate factors associated with talent development in a particular sport, longitudinal research would be a good option. It allows you to focus completely on developmental issues over an extended period of time.

Comparative

In comparative research, the researcher compares two or more things with the aim of discovering something about one or all of them. For example, if you wanted to see if there were any similarities between boys' and girls' opinions on hooliganism in football, you could use a comparative design.

Assessment activity 4.2

You are working as a sport and exercise scientist and you have been asked to do some promotional work with less experienced sport and exercise scientists to try to increase their interest in research.

In order to do this, produce an information leaflet to introduce people to the different types and classifications of data and the different methods of data collection in sport and exercise sciences. **P3**

Grading tip

To attain **P3** try to make your leaflet as interesting and informative as possible by including lots of examples to demonstrate your points.

PLTS

If you explore the different types of data and data collection methods and make judgements about how they could be applied to different examples, you can develop your skills as an **independent enquirer**.

Functional skills

By writing your leaflet on types of data and data collection methods you could provide evidence of your **English** skills in writing.

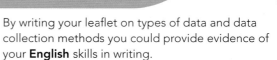

2.6 Ethical and legal issues

The British Association of Sport and Exercise Sciences (BASES)

BASES produced a code of conduct that governs how sport and exercise scientists work as practitioners and as researchers. The code of conduct outlines ethical and legal issues that are essential to safe research within the sport and exercise sciences.

- **Ethical clearance** – when conducting research, ensure that you are working ethically and legally. One of the first things you have to do before starting is to gain ethical clearance from an appropriate body. If you conduct any research as part of your course, ethical clearance will come from your tutor, college or school ethics committee. An ethics committee is an organisation that looks at your research proposal and says whether it is safe and ethical. It will confirm whether you can start work on your project.

- **Informed consent** – once you have gained ethical approval for your research project, you need to get informed consent from your participants. This is an ethical and legal requirement of research. It can be verbal but it is safer for both you and your participant if you obtain it in writing. An informed consent form consists of:
  - o a description of the investigation
  - o details of the procedure to be followed
  - o details of any risks to the participant
  - o details of the potential benefits of taking part in the research
  - o a section that offers to answer any questions and confirms that any questions asked have been answered fully
  - o an indication that the participant can withdraw at any time without being penalised
  - o a section that explains that any information collected about the participant will remain confidential.

- **Confidentiality/data protection** – where confidentiality is concerned, you may disclose only information that is important to the study you are conducting. Any data you collect is protected under the terms of the Data Protection Act (1998). No data that makes the participants personally identifiable should be included in your research project. Data collected should be stored in a locked filing cabinet or on a password-protected computer accessible only by you and your research supervisor.

- **Safety of the participants** – when conducting research, the key concern is the participants' safety. The researcher must maintain the highest professional standards so as not to endanger participants or themselves. The researcher should treat all participants equally and only work within their own area of competence.

- **Acting with due regard for equality and impartiality** – to preserve the reputation of sport and exercise science, you must remain totally unbiased in your actions and practices when working within sport and exercise science. This means that you cannot let factors such as race, age or gender affect the way you work with clients. You must not exploit personal relationships for personal gain. Any decisions you make must be completely objective (based on facts rather than on opinions).

Importance of ethical and legal issues

- **Ensure the welfare and safety of participants and the researcher** – the ethical and legal guidelines are in place to maintain the safety of the participants and the researcher.

- **Ensure that researchers only work within area of expertise** – if you think about the dangers that participants could be placed in through some areas of research, you will understand why the ethical and legal guidelines need to be in place so that researchers work only within their own areas of competence. For example, someone who has never used a syringe must not be allowed to take blood from participants.

- **Preserving and developing the reputation of the sport and exercise sciences** – the guidelines exist to promote excellence in sport and exercise sciences. This means that someone who works in a research capacity must maintain the reputation of sport and exercise sciences by following the procedures.

Implications of not working ethically and legally

The implications of not working within the ethical and legal procedures are severe. The most obvious is that you are risking your participants' welfare and safety. If you do this in a professional setting, restrictions can be placed on you.

Name		
Age	Date of birth	Gender Male/Female

Name of test	
Protocol to be followed	
Details of protocol	
Potential risks/benefits	

Participant to read and sign
- The details of the test have been explained to me fully. I have read and fully understand all of the procedures that are to be used in the test and have had the potential benefits and risks associated with the test explained to me fully.
- All questions that I have about the test and my involvement in the test have been answered.
- I am aware that I am free to cease participation in the test at any time.
- I am aware that my test results and any information that makes me personally identifiable will remain confidential and will be protected under the Data Protection Act (1998).

Signature of participant	Date	Signature of parent/guardian (if under 18)	Date

Investigator to read and sign
- I have explained the test procedure fully and have answered any questions the participant had regarding the test and their involvement in the project.

Signature of investigator	Date

Figure 4.3: An example of an informed consent form.

- **Tribunals** – if you do not work within ethical and legal guidelines, you could be subject to a tribunal leading to a fine, a written warning or not being allowed to conduct research again.
- **Legal or civil action** – if you work without due regard for ethical and legal issues within sport and exercise science, you are leaving yourself open to legal or civil action if something goes wrong. Ensure you follow the code of conduct when working in an applied setting, so you are not open to this type of action.
- **Measures to stop future research** – when working as a member of BASES, you are subject to the BASES disciplinary procedure if you do not work ethically and legally. You could be called before a tribunal where a group of BASES officers and the chair of BASES will review your particular case to discover if you have been working ethically and legally. From this tribunal, significant measures can be put in place to stop research temporarily or permanently, such as temporary suspension or permanent expulsion from BASES.

Assessment activity 4.3

You are working as a trainee sport scientist. You are preparing to do some research into the developmental experiences of female youth athletes. Your research will involve you interviewing and observing the female athletes over an extended period of time so your supervisor wants you to produce a presentation on the ethical and legal issues associated with the work you are doing. Prepare a 10-minute presentation that includes the following information:

1. A description of two ethical and legal issues associated with the research project you are going to be doing. **P4**

2. An explanation of the implications of not working ethically and legally in a research setting. **M2**

3. An analysis of the implications of not working ethically and legally in a research setting. **D2**

Grading tips

- To attain **P4**, before starting your presentation, download and read a copy of the BASES code of conduct and decide what you think are the two most important ethical and legal issues for this project. Describe these two issues as the basis of your presentation.

- To attain **M2**, provide examples of things that you would class as not working ethically and legally in this setting and then discuss what could happen to you if you were to do any of these things.

- To attain **D2**, for the same examples, think about, and then communicate, why you would be subject to different implications of not working ethically and legally. Support your arguments with specific sections of the BASES code of conduct.

PLTS

If you support your arguments relating to which ethical and legal issues are most strongly linked to the activity, you can develop your skills as an **independent enquirer**.

Functional skills

If you interpret the information in the BASES code of conduct for relevance against the activity, you could provide evidence of your **English** skills in reading.

3. Know qualitative data analysis techniques for the sport and exercise sciences

Before analysing your qualitative data, you must prepare it for analysis. In the case of individual interviews and focus groups, you should transcribe the recorded interviews verbatim (word for word).

3.1 Stages of data analysis

After transcribing your data, you will go through three stages of qualitative data analysis:

1. data reduction
2. displaying data
3. drawing conclusions and verifying data.

Data reduction

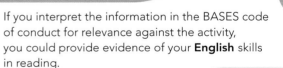

Data reduction involves reducing large amounts of data into manageable chunks. The most common form of data analysis in the data reduction stage is coding. If you choose to conduct a qualitative research project, you need to code your data as part of your data analysis. Coding is when you organise raw data (sentences, phrases or words from your questionnaires or interviews) into categories. The categories are given a valid heading and must have a rule for inclusion.

Having a rule for inclusion helps to guide which data you place in each category. For example, if you were researching 'factors affecting talent development in football', you could have a category called 'importance of parental tangible support'. Your rule for inclusion could be 'statement made refers to concrete support given to player from parent (for example, the purchase of playing kit or transport to matches) being either a positive or negative influence on the player's development'.

Coding

Coding techniques are simple when you get used to them. When coding data, all you are doing is breaking it down into smaller parts. You then put it back together in parts that relate to each other, before making sure that all your categories are valid. Coding involves the line-by-line analysis of data in minute detail and is used to generate categories.

Coding involves three stages: open coding, axial coding and selective coding.

- **Open coding** – in open coding, data is broken down and examined. Your aim is to identify all the key statements in the interviews that relate to the aims of your research and your research problem. After identifying the key statements, you can start to put the key points that relate to each other into categories, but you need to give each category a suitable heading to do this. When you start to organise your data under different categories, you have started the coding process.

- **Axial coding** – after the open coding stage, the next stage is to put the data back together. Part of this process means re-reading the data you have collected so you can make precise explanations about your area of interest. To do this, you need to refine the categories that you started to create during open coding. During this stage you may develop new categories. To allow you to refine your codes at this stage ask more questions about the categories (and the codes) you have created. Some questions you may consider are:
  - o Can I relate certain codes together under a more general code?
  - o Can I place codes into a particular order?
  - o Can I identify any relationships between different codes?

- **Selective coding** is the final stage of coding. It involves aiming to finalise your categories (and codes) so that you can group them together. When you group them together, you will produce different diagrams to show how your categories link together. The key part of this is to select a main category, which will form the focal point of your diagram. You also need to look for data that contradicts previous research, rather than data that supports it. This helps you to make better arguments and draw more conclusions based on your data.

Remember

Sometimes you may not go all the way through to selective coding. In smaller research projects, and projects where you are not necessarily trying to produce a theory or a model, you may find that open and axial coding provide sufficient data analysis.

Other techniques

As well as being able to manually analyse your data, there are electronic packages that you can use to analyse data (although in the early stages of your research career it is unlikely that you will use these and it is better to manually analyse your data so that you get used to handling the data). Some of the different packages available include ATLAS.ti and NVivo.

Take it further

Research electronic packages

Using the Internet, research the different electronic packages that are available for qualitative data analysis and find out what their advantages and disadvantages are.

Displaying data

There are different ways to display your data. The way that you display it will affect the argument or point you are trying to make. The different types of diagram used are network diagrams, Venn diagrams, radial diagrams and cycle diagrams.

Network diagrams

Network diagrams show hierarchical relationships between different ideas. The example below shows that there are a number of benefits to the use of imagery (the top of the hierarchy or the most important part of information to take away) and that these benefits include increased self-efficacy, skill acquisition and injury rehabilitation.

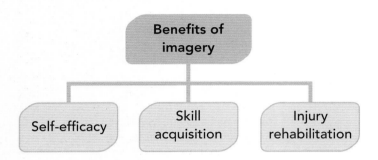

Figure 4.4: Why would you use a network diagram?

Venn diagrams

Venn diagrams consist of two or more overlapping circles. They show how different topics relate to each other. In the example below, you can see how the different disciplines within the sport and exercise sciences (SES) interact to make up the overall discipline.

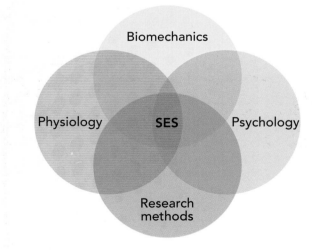

Figure 4.5: Why would you use a Venn diagram?

Radial diagrams

A radial diagram (also known as a spider diagram) illustrates a relationship where each item is linked to a central item. This diagram can be thought of as a simple organisation chart that starts from the centre rather than the top.

Figure 4.6: Why would you use a radial diagram (or spider diagram)?

Cycle diagrams

A cycle diagram shows the stages in a process as a continuous cycle. The process is shown as a circle, with a break at each stage, and an arrowhead to show the direction of the process. In the example below, the diagram shows that team cohesion affects team performance, which in turn affects team cohesion further, and so on.

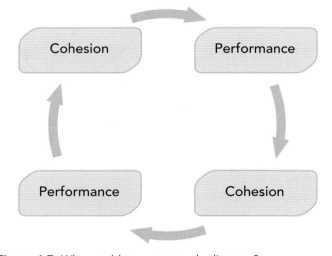

Figure 4.7: Why would you use a cycle diagram?

Drawing conclusions and verifying data

Your conclusions must be valid and reliable. Two common techniques used to do this are triangulation and member checking.

Triangulation refers to using different data collection methods in the same study. For example, you could use interviews and questionnaires or you could use the same interviews with different types of participants (such as athletes and coaches). Alternatively, you could ask different researchers to collect data and independently draw conclusions before checking their findings with each other.

Member checking – during member checking, you complete your data analysis and draw conclusions relating to the aims of the study. You then show the analysis to the participants who took part in the research so that they can check that you have understood and communicated everything correctly. If they decide that your analysis is correct, you can claim that the data is valid.

Remember

Triangulation is designed to improve the validity and reliability of your work, but sometimes it can make things worse so you need to be careful! Think about a study where you were interviewing both players and coaches of a rugby team – do you think that you would always get the honest answers from the players if they thought that the coaches would find out what they had said?

Activity: Analyse this

Using the interview that you completed earlier in the unit, transcribe and analyse the data that you collected so that you can produce a summary of the findings. Use the different stages of data analysis to analyse your data.

Assessment activity 4.4

P5 **M3** · BTEC

You are working as a sports therapist and you want to find out about how different athletes respond psychologically to chronic sports injuries that mean they cannot play or train for a long period of time. Ideally, you would like to study individual athletes, over an extended period of time, with a variety of age ranges and experiences.

Before you can do the research, you need to complete a discussion with your supervisor that includes the following information:

1. The best research design to use and a justification of your choice. **M3**

2. The best data collection technique (or techniques) to use and a justification of your choice. **M3**

3. A description of the different stages of data analysis. **P5**

4. The best way of analysing your data and a justification of your choice. **M3**

Grading tips

- To attain **P5** describe the stages of data reduction, displaying data, and drawing conclusions and verifying data.

- To attain **M3** try to relate the research methods that you select to specific aspects of the project that you want to complete as this will allow you to make a stronger justification. If you think it is more appropriate to use a combination of different research methods, make sure that you justify each method.

PLTS

By presenting a persuasive case for your choices of research methods, you could develop your skills as a **reflective learner**.

Functional skills

By discussing your ideas for the most appropriate research methods, you could provide evidence of your **English** skills in speaking and listening.

4. Know quantitative data analysis techniques for the sport and exercise sciences

4.1 Organising data

There are different methods of organising your data during quantitative data analysis, each of which provides a good starting point to the appropriate research project. The methods include range, rank order distribution, simple frequency distribution and grouped frequency distribution.

Range

Range is the distance in numerical value from the highest to the lowest value collected. You calculate the range by subtracting the lowest value from the highest value.

Rank order distribution

Rank order distribution means placing your data into an ordered list from the lowest to the highest in a single column, ensuring you include all the scores. Rank order distribution is used when the number of participants is less than or equal to 20 ($n \leq 20$).

Simple frequency distribution

Simple frequency distribution is used when the number of participants is greater than 20 ($n > 20$) and when the range is less than or equal to 20 ($r \leq 20$). You use simple frequency distribution with a table that has two columns, one for raw data scores (X) and one for frequency scores (f). The frequency column is the number of times that particular score was achieved.

Table 4.4 is an example of how to lay out your data. A basketball coach is looking at the number of free throws missed in each game over a season. He has 25 games to assess ($n > 20$) and the number of missed shots per game ranges from 1 to 7 ($r \leq 20$), so simple frequency distribution is suitable. The data is set out as shown below.

Number of missed shots (X)	Frequency (f)
7	3
6	5
5	14
3	2
1	1
	$n = 25$

Table 4.4: Why is simple frequency distribution used here?

Grouped frequency distribution

In quantitative research, you often work with ranges greater than 21 ($r > 21$) and with more than 20 participants ($n > 20$). This is when to use grouped frequency distribution. As with simple frequency distribution, the table has two columns: X and f – except this time the X column is for groups of scores and the f column is for frequency.

To keep your data on a single sheet of paper, you normally have between 10 and 20 groups of scores – the ideal number is 15. You need to decide on the interval size for each group, which is calculated using the formula $i = $ range $\div 15$.

Here is an example: an athletics coach is looking at the times recorded (in seconds) of athletes who want to represent the college at 5000 m. She has 30 times to look at ranging from 900 seconds to 1094 seconds. Grouped frequency distribution is a suitable method because both $r > 21$ and $n > 20$. The interval size for each group is 13 seconds ($r = 194$ seconds; $194 \div 15 = 12.93$ seconds, which is rounded up to 13). The data is shown in the table below.

Time (X)	Frequency (f)
1082–1094	1
1068–1081	1
1054–1067	1
1040–1053	1
1026–1039	5
1012–1025	8
998–1011	3
984–997	2
970–983	2
956–969	1
942–955	1
928–941	1
914–927	1
900–913	2
	$n = 30$

Table 4.5: Why is grouped frequency distribution used here?

Although using grouped frequency distribution is a useful way of organising large amounts of data, some information is lost through this process. Once scores have been placed into groups, it is impossible to know the individual values. For example, if you look at the 1012–1025 seconds row in the table above, it is only possible to identify that eight athletes fell within that range, but you won't know what the individual times were.

4.2 Displaying data

There are different ways of displaying your data including graphs, histograms, bar charts and cumulative frequency graphs. However, before conducting statistical analysis you must understand distribution curves. There are three types: normal distribution curves, positively skewed curves and negatively skewed curves.

A normal distribution of data means that most of the examples in a set of data are close to the 'average', while a few examples are at one extreme or the other. Normal distribution graphs have these characteristics:

- the curve has a single peak
- it is bell-shaped
- the mean (average) lies at the centre of the distribution and the distribution is symmetrical around the mean
- the two 'tails' of the distribution extend indefinitely and never touch the x axis
- the shape of the distribution is determined by the mean and standard deviation (see page 106).

Not all sets of data have graphs that look as perfect as the one in Figure 4.8. Some have relatively flat curves, others will be steeper. Sometimes the mean will lean a little bit to one side or the other. However, all normally distributed data will have something similar to this

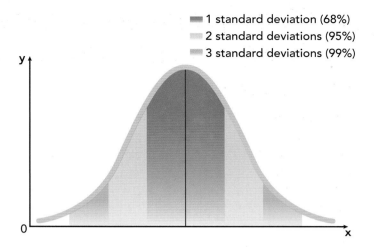

■ 1 standard deviation (68%)
■ 2 standard deviations (95%)
■ 3 standard deviations (99%)

Figure 4.8: What should you look for when trying to identify normal distribution?

bell-shaped curve. Generally, if you go right or left one standard deviation from the mean (the red area on the graph) you will include about 68 per cent of the scores in the distribution. Two standard deviations away from the mean (the red and yellow areas) account for about 95 per cent of the scores, whereas three standard deviations (the red, yellow and green areas) account for about 99 per cent of the scores.

Positively skewed curves and negatively skewed curves

If the shape of the curve is asymmetrical, your data is not distributed normally and is said to be positively or negatively skewed. Positively skewed means the longer tail of the curve points to the positive (higher) end of the scale and the scores are bunched to the left of the centre. Negatively skewed means the longer tail of the curve points to the negative (lower) end of the scale and the scores are bunched to the right of the centre.

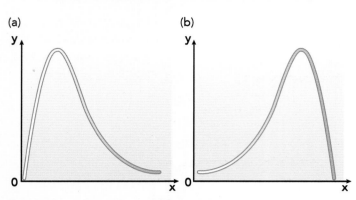

(a) (b)

Figure 4.9: How can you identify positively skewed and negatively skewed curves?

4.3 Measures of central tendency and variability

Measures of central tendency are numbers that describe what is average or typical of the distribution. These measures include the **mean**, **median** and **mode** (measures of central tendency) and standard deviation (measure of variability).

Key terms

Mean – the measure of central tendency that is calculated by adding up all of the values and dividing the answer by the number of values. You may also know this term as the 'average'.

Median – the middle value in a series of numbers.

Mode – the value that occurs most frequently.

Identification of outliers

Another important concept within central tendency and variability is that of outliers. Outliers are results that are radically different from what you would consider normal scores. Statistics that are drawn from data sets that contain outliers can be misleading.

Standard deviation

Standard deviation is a number that indicates how much each of the values in the distribution deviates from the mean (or centre) of the distribution. If the data points are all close to the mean, then the standard deviation is close to zero. If many data points are far from the mean, then the standard deviation is far from zero. If all the data values are equal, then the standard deviation is zero.

The formula for calculating standard deviation (sd) is as follows:

$$sd = \sqrt{\frac{\Sigma (X - M)^2}{n - 1}}$$

where:

sd = standard deviation
Σ = sum of
X = individual score
M = mean
n = number of participants

Here is how to calculate standard deviation:

- Calculate the mean.
- Subtract the mean from each subject's score $(X - M)$.
- Square the answer $(X - M)^2$.
- Sum the squared scores $\Sigma (X - M)^2$.
- Divide by the number of participants minus 1 $(n - 1)$.
- Take the square root of the answer.

4.4 Data analysis

Commonly, data analysis in quantitative research comes through the use of statistical tests. Statistics can seem frightening but they are more time-consuming than difficult, and you will have seen and used some of these methods before. There are two types of statistics: descriptive and inferential. Descriptive statistics are measures of central tendency and variability. Inferential statistics assess relationships or differences between data sets; they are further subdivided into two groups: **parametric tests** and **non-parametric tests** (see Figure 4.10).

Tests – selecting, types and explanations

Throughout this next section, you will look at a range of parametric and non-parametric tests, an explanation of each one and examples of different tests, and ways of selecting appropriate tests.

A good way to select your test is to use a decision tree like the one in Figure 4.11. If you follow the decision tree using the information available, you will find the test that you need to use. The process of using the decision tree is similar to planning a bus or a train journey – follow the line and find your stops to get to the destination!

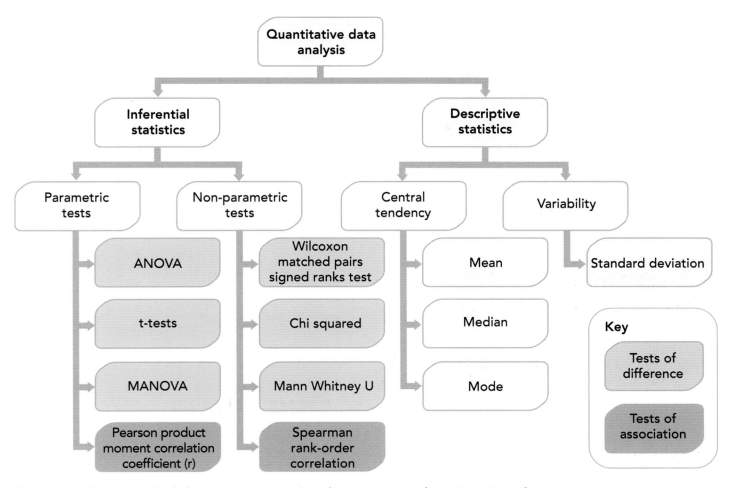

Figure 4.10: Why do you think there are so many statistical tests in sport and exercise sciences?

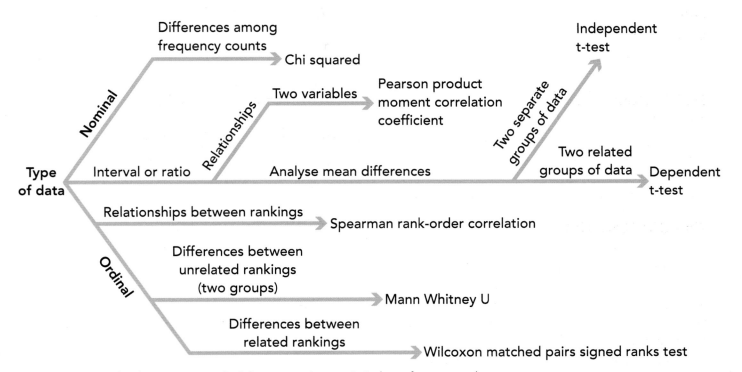

Figure 4.11: Use the decision tree to find the appropriate statistical test for your work.

Parametric tests – t-tests

The most common t-tests are the dependent t-test (also known as the paired samples t-test) and the independent t-test.

When you complete your t-test and want to see if your result is significant or not, you need to know whether you are completing a **one-tailed test** or a **two-tailed test**.

Dependent t-test

The dependent (paired samples) t-test examines significant differences between two sets of related scores, such as whether the mean high jump scores of one group are different when measured pre- and post-training (see the example below). The test is calculated using the formula below:

$$t = \frac{\Sigma D}{\sqrt{[n\Sigma D^2 - (\Sigma D)^2] \div (n-1)}}$$

where:

D = difference between before and after

n = number of paired scores

Σ = sum of

Instructions:

- Calculate your t value using the formula.
- Calculate your **degree of freedom** (df). For the dependent t-test, use the formula $df = n - 1$.
- Compare your t value to the table of critical values.
- After calculating your t value, compare your result to the critical value of t (use Table 4.7). Find your

df value (in this case 9), then go across and see if your result is greater than or equal to the number in the column below the 0.05 level. If the value achieved for your t-test is equal to or greater than the number shown, your results are significant to that level. Note that if $df > 120$, use the infinity row at the end of table 4.7 (∞).

As you can see from the example below the t value calculated (5.09) is greater than the critical value of t (2.262) meaning your result is significant to the 0.05 level. This means that you can say that there is a significant difference between high jump scores pre- and post-training.

Key terms

Parametric tests – statistical tests that use interval or ratio data. They assume that the data is drawn from a normal distribution and has the same variance.

Non-parametric tests – statistical tests that use ordinal or nominal data.

One-tailed test – a test that assumes one group will be better than the other, or at least no worse than the other. For example, girls will be better than boys.

Two-tailed test – a test that assumes there will be a difference between both groups, but doesn't say which will be better. For example, there will be a difference between girls and boys.

Degree of freedom – used as a correction factor for bias and to limit the effects of outliers, and based on the number of participants you have.

Example of a dependent t-test

Subject	Pre-training height (cm)	Post-training height (cm)	D (post-training minus pre-training)	D²
1	176	179	3	9
2	169	172	3	9
3	171	175	4	16
4	173	177	4	16
5	164	166	2	4
6	170	171	1	1
7	161	168	7	49
8	159	169	10	100
9	163	166	3	9
10	170	176	6	36
n = 10			D = 43	D² = 249

$$t = \frac{43}{\sqrt{[2490 - 1849] \div 9}}$$

$$t = \frac{43}{\sqrt{641 \div 9}}$$

$$t = \frac{43}{\sqrt{71.22}}$$

$$t = \frac{43}{8.44}$$

$$t = 5.09$$

Table 4.6: Investigating the effects of a 12-week plyometric training programme on high jump performance.

	Level of significance for one-tailed test					
	.10	.05	.025	.01	.005	.0005
	Level of significance for two-tailed test					
df	.20	.10	.05	.02	.01	.001
1	3.078	6.314	12.706	31.821	63.657	636.619
2	1.886	2.920	4.303	6.965	9.925	31.598
3	1.638	2.353	3.182	4.541	5.841	12.941
4	1.533	2.132	2.776	3.747	4.604	8.610
5	1.476	2.015	2.571	3.365	4.032	6.589
6	1.440	1.943	2.447	3.143	3.707	5.959
7	1.415	1.895	2.365	2.998	3.499	5.405
8	1.397	1.860	2.306	2.896	3.355	5.041
9	1.383	1.833	2.262	2.821	3.250	4.781
10	1.372	1.812	2.228	2.764	3.169	4.587
11	1.363	1.796	2.201	2.718	3.106	4.437
12	1.356	1.782	2.179	2.681	3.055	4.318
13	1.350	1.771	2.160	2.650	3.012	4.221
14	1.345	1.761	2.145	2.624	2.977	4.140
15	1.341	1.753	2.131	2.602	2.947	4.073
16	1.337	1.746	2.120	2.583	2.921	4.015
17	1.333	1.740	2.110	2.567	2.898	3.965
18	1.330	1.734	2.101	2.552	2.878	3.922
19	1.328	1.729	2.093	2.539	2.861	3.883
20	1.325	1.725	2.086	2.528	2.845	3.850
21	1.323	1.721	2.080	2.518	2.831	3.819
22	1.321	1.717	2.074	2.508	2.819	3.792
23	1.319	1.714	2.069	2.500	2.807	3.767
24	1.318	1.711	2.064	2.492	2.797	3.745
25	1.316	1.708	2.060	2.485	2.787	3.725
26	1.315	1.706	2.056	2.479	2.779	3.707
27	1.314	1.703	2.052	2.473	2.771	3.690
28	1.313	1.701	2.048	2.467	2.763	3.674
29	1.311	1.699	2.045	2.462	2.756	3.659
30	1.310	1.697	2.042	2.457	2.750	3.646
40	1.303	1.684	2.021	2.423	2.704	3.551
60	1.296	1.671	2.000	2.390	2.660	3.460
120	1.289	1.658	1.980	2.358	2.617	3.373
∞	1.282	1.645	1.960	2.326	2.576	3.291

Table 4.7: Critical values of t

Remember

When calculating statistics, a good tip is to change all the letters in the formula into the numbers you will be working with, and then rewrite the equation using the numbers – it will seem much friendlier then!

Independent t-test

The independent t-test is the most frequently used t-test. It is used when you have two groups and are trying to discover if the mean scores of two groups can be considered to be significantly different. The independent t-test is suitable when the data you have collected is interval or ratio data, when your groups are randomly assigned, and when the variance (or spread) in the two groups is equal. The independent t-test is calculated using the formula:

$$t = \frac{M_1 - M_2}{\sqrt{s_1^2/n_1 + s_2^2/n_2}}$$

where:

M_1 = mean value of group 1
M_2 = mean value of group 2
s_1 = standard deviation of group 1
s_2 = standard deviation of group 2
n_1 = number of participants in group 1
n_2 = number of participants in group 2

Parametric test – Pearson product moment correlation coefficient (r)

A correlation is the value of the relationship between two or more variables, which can be positive or negative. Whether it is positive or negative depends on the direction of the line when the results are plotted on a graph. The graphs in Figure 4.12 show examples of perfect positive and perfect negative correlations, but it is rare to record such correlations during data analysis.

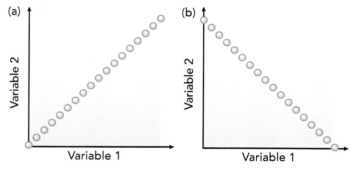

Figure 4.12: Graph (a) shows perfect positive correlation and graph (b) shows perfect negative correlation.

Example of an independent t-test

Using the Cooper 12-minute run data in Table 4.8, and the independent t-test formula, see if there is a significant difference between the two groups. Calculate the degrees of freedom (df) using the formula: $df = n_1 + n_2 - 2$ and then compare the t value calculated to the table of critical values in Table 4.7.

Where:

$s_1 = 238.3$ $M_1 = 3183.3$ $s_1^2 = 56786.89$ $n_1 = 10$
$s_2 = 94.6$ $M_2 = 2468.7$ $s_2^2 = 8949.16$ $n_2 = 10$

$$t = \frac{3183.3 - 2468.7}{\sqrt{(238.3)^2 \div 10 + (94.6)^2 \div 10}}$$

$$t = \frac{714.6}{\sqrt{(56786.89) \div 10 + (8949.16) \div 10}}$$

$$t = \frac{714.6}{\sqrt{5678.69 + 894.92}}$$

$$t = \frac{714.6}{\sqrt{6573.61}}$$

$$t = \frac{714.6}{81.07}$$

$$t = 8.81$$

Subject	Group 1 (12-minute run after 70% VO$_2$ max training)	Group 2 (12-minute run after 40% VO$_2$ max training)
1	3200 m	2513 m
2	3600 m	2601 m
3	2894 m	2444 m
4	3001 m	2361 m
5	3187 m	2541 m
6	3651 m	2486 m
7	3109 m	2611 m
8	2997 m	2419 m
9	3056 m	2400 m
10	3138 m	2311 m
Mean	3183.3 m	2468.7 m
Standard deviation	238.3	94.6

Table 4.8: Cooper 12-minute run data.

The Pearson product moment correlation coefficient is a parametric test that is suitable when you have interval or ratio data and you are trying to identify a relationship between two variables. It is a test of association, which means it looks at whether two or more variables are related. The test can be used in two ways. Either you can try to find out a relationship between two variables or you can try to predict one score from another. In a simple correlation which is trying to find out a relationship between two variables, it doesn't matter which variable is assigned X and which Y. If you are trying to predict one score from another, then X is the independent variable and Y is the dependent variable. There are three stages to using the Pearson product moment correlation:

1. Summing each set of scores.
2. Squaring and summing each set of scores.
3. Multiplying each pair of scores and obtaining the cumulative sum of these products.

The formula for this is outlined below:

$$r = \frac{n\Sigma XY - (\Sigma X)(\Sigma Y)}{[\sqrt{n\Sigma X^2 - (\Sigma X)^2}]\,[\sqrt{n\Sigma Y^2 - (\Sigma Y)^2}]}$$

where:

n = number of paired scores
Σ = sum of
X = scores for one variable
Y = scores for the other variable
$\Sigma(X)^2$ = sum of raw scores for X, squared
$\Sigma(Y)^2$ = sum of raw scores for Y, squared
ΣX^2 = sum of all of the X^2 scores
ΣY^2 = sum of all of the Y^2 scores

To interpret the significance of your r value, select your level of significance (remember that in sport and exercise science this is normally 0.05) and find your degree of freedom (df) for your test. For this test, use the formula df = n − 2 and compare your r value to the table of significance (see Table 4.7 on page 109) to find whether your results are significant. If your result is equal to or greater than the critical value in the table, your result is significant.

Non-parametric tests

If the data is non-parametric, t-tests cannot be used. In this case, the Wilcoxon matched pairs signed ranks test is used in place of the dependent t-test, and the Mann Whitney U test is used in place of the independent t-test.

Activity: Pearson product moment correlation coefficient (r)

Get together with a group of ten friends. Measure each other's vertical jump score and then measure each other's 30 metre sprint times. Use the Pearson product moment correlation coefficient to find out if there is a relationship between the two variables. Use the table of critical values in Table 4.9 to assess the strength of the relationship.

	Level of significance for one-tailed test				
	.05	.025	.01	.005	.001
	Level of significance for two-tailed test				
df	.10	.05	.02	.01	.001
1	.9877	.9969	.9995	.9999	1.000
2	.9000	.9500	.9800	.9900	.9990
3	.8054	.8783	.9343	.9587	.9912
4	.7293	.8114	.8822	.9172	.9741
5	.6694	.7545	.8329	.8745	.9507
6	.6215	.7067	.7887	.8343	.9249
7	.5822	.6664	.7498	.7977	.8982
8	.5494	.6319	.7155	.7646	.8721
9	.5214	.6021	.6851	.7348	.8471
10	.4973	.5760	.6581	.7079	.8233
11	.4762	.5529	.6339	.6835	.8010
12	.4575	.5324	.6120	.6614	.7800
13	.4409	.5139	.5923	.6411	.7603
14	.4259	.4973	.5742	.6226	.7420
15	.4124	.4821	.5577	.6055	.7246
16	.4000	.4683	.5425	.5897	.7084
17	.3887	.4555	.5285	.5751	.6932
18	.3783	.4438	.5155	.5614	.6787
19	.3687	.4329	.5034	.5487	.6652
20	.3598	.4227	.4921	.5368	.6524
25	.3233	.3809	.4451	.4869	.5974
30	.2960	.3494	.4093	.4487	.5541
35	.2746	.3246	.3810	.4182	.5189
40	.2573	.3044	.3578	.3932	.4896
45	.2428	.2875	.3384	.3721	.4648
50	.2306	.2732	.3218	.3541	.4433
60	.2108	.2500	.2948	.3248	.4078
70	.1954	.2319	.2737	.3017	.3799
80	.1829	.2172	.2565	.2830	.3568
90	.1726	.2050	.2422	.2673	.3375
100	.1638	.1946	.2301	.2540	.3211

Table 4.9: Critical values of correlation coefficient.

Non-parametric test – Wilcoxon matched pairs signed ranks test

The Wilcoxon matched pairs signed ranks test is used when you are trying to find out if there is a significant difference between two scores that are taken from the same participant (or from matched participants). It is used when the data is ordinal (ranked). To do the test, follow the instructions below.

1. Disregard any results for participants who scored the same in both conditions, then count up the number of paired scores left. This is your n score.
2. Calculate the difference between the two scores of each participant, assigning plus or minus signs (d).
3. Rank the differences, giving the smallest a rank of 1 (ignoring plus or minus signs, i.e. +2 is of the same value as –2). When two scores are tied, each is given the mean of the two ranks and the next rank is missed out (for example, if two participants are in level sixth place, they are both given the rank of 6.5 and the next place is given a rank of 8).
4. Add up the ranks of all the minus scores.
5. Add up the ranks of all the plus scores.
6. Take the smaller of the two figures calculated in points 4 and 5 to gain your w value.
7. Look up your value for w in a significance table (you can find one here: www.social-science.co.uk). If it is equal to or less than the figure in the 0.05 column, the result is significant at that level.

Non-parametric test – Chi square

The Chi square test assesses the significance of the discrepancy between results that were actually achieved and the results that were expected. The formula for calculating the Chi square is given below:

$$x^2 = \Sigma[(O - E)^2 \div E]$$

where:

Σ = sum of
O = observed frequency
E = expected frequency

The degree of freedom (df) is calculated using the formula $df = c - 1$, where c is the number of cells.

Activity: Wilcoxon matched pairs signed ranks

Imagine you are working with a sport psychologist and you want to find out if imagery training has an influence on sprint times in youth 100 metre sprinters. You could do this by using the Wilcoxon matched pairs signed ranks test. Look at the data in Table 4.10 and, using the steps above, find out whether the imagery training programme has been successful.

Subject pair	Condition A (run times pre-imagery training)	Condition B (run times post-imagery training)	d (A minus B)	Rank of d	Rank of plus differences	Rank of minus differences
1	11.09	11.00				
2	11.23	11.25				
3	11.55	11.32				
4	11.46	11.36				
5	11.22	11.73				
6	11.13	11.43				
7	11.01	10.86				
8	10.93	10.55				
9	10.99	10.90				
10	11.39	11.10				
					Total	Total
						$w =$

Table 4.10: 100 m sprint times pre- and post-imagery training.

Activity: Chi square

Imagine you are working with a superstitious squash coach. One of his main players plays on four courts on a regular basis and the coach believes that one of the courts is an unlucky court for the player. He believes the player loses more on that court than on any of the others. The coach aims to prove his point by comparing the number of losses on each of the four courts. The player has lost a total of 40 matches over the course of the season. From this, it could be expected that the player would lose an equal number of matches on each court (i.e. 10).

Using the Chi square test, find out whether there is a significant difference between observed and expected losses. In this example, $df = 4 - 1$, as there are four courts.

Use Table 4.11 to work out your answer.

	Court number				
	1	**2**	**3**	**4**	**Total**
Observed losses (O)	7	8	11	14	40
Expected losses (E)	10	10	10	10	40
$(O - E)^2$					
$(O - E)^2 \div E$					
$\Sigma[(O - E)^2 \div E]$					

df	.10	.05	.02	.01	.001
1	2.71	3.84	5.41	6.64	10.83
2	4.60	5.99	7.82	9.21	13.82
3	6.25	7.82	9.84	11.34	16.27
4	7.78	9.49	11.67	13.28	18.46
5	9.24	11.07	13.39	15.09	20.52
6	10.64	12.59	15.03	16.81	22.46
7	12.02	14.07	16.62	18.48	24.32
8	13.36	15.51	18.17	20.09	26.12
9	14.68	16.92	19.68	21.67	27.88
10	15.99	18.31	21.16	23.21	29.59
11	17.28	19.68	22.62	24.72	31.26
12	18.55	21.03	24.05	26.22	32.91
13	19.81	22.36	25.47	27.69	34.53
14	21.06	23.68	26.87	29.14	26.12
15	22.31	25.00	28.26	30.58	37.70
16	23.54	26.30	29.63	32.00	39.29
17	24.77	27.59	31.00	33.41	40.75
18	25.99	28.87	32.35	34.80	42.31
19	27.20	30.14	33.69	36.19	43.82
20	28.41	31.41	35.02	37.57	45.32
21	29.62	32.67	36.34	38.93	46.80
22	30.81	33.92	37.66	40.29	48.27
23	32.01	35.17	38.97	41.64	49.73
24	33.20	36.42	40.27	42.98	51.18
25	34.38	37.65	41.57	44.31	52.62
26	35.56	38.88	42.86	45.64	54.05
27	36.74	40.11	44.14	46.96	55.48
28	37.92	41.34	45.42	48.28	56.89
29	39.09	42.56	46.69	49.59	58.30
30	40.26	43.77	47.96	50.89	59.70

Table 4.11: Critical values of Chi square.

Non-parametric test – Spearman rank-order correlation

The Spearman rank-order correlation test is similar to the Pearson product moment correlation coefficient in its purpose. However, it is a non-parametric equivalent and is used when your data is ordinal (ranked). This test should be used when you want to find a relationship between two sets of ordinal data (for example, goals scored and final league position in football, serving accuracy and final ladder position in badminton, golf driving distance and final leader board position).

The first step is to rank your data (goals scored/serving accuracy/golf driving distance) from highest to lowest, with 1 being the highest. After this, determine the difference between your data and the place in the tournament. This must be squared and then summed.

Remember

When two or more scores are tied, each is given the mean of the ranks and then the next rank is missed out. For example, if two participants are in level fourth place, they are both given a rank of 4.5 and the next place is given a rank of 6.

The formula used for the test is shown below:

$$r_s = \frac{6(\Sigma D^2)}{n(n^2 - 1)}$$

where:

n = number of ranked pairs

D = difference between each pair

ΣD^2 = the sum of the squared differences between rank

To interpret the significance of your r_s value, select the level of significance (0.05) and calculate the degree of freedom (df) for your test. For the Spearman rank-order correlation test, this is calculated using the formula $n - 2$. Compare your value to the table of significance (see Table 4.12) to find whether your results are significant.

Take it further

More statistical tests

Using books and the Internet, research the following examples of statistical tests:

- Mann Whitney U
- ANOVA
- MANOVA

Use the descriptions and worked examples above to guide your reading. You should try to find the following information:

- a description of the test including the formula
- an explanation of the formula
- when you would use each test.

Remember

It is important to select the correct test when conducting statistical analysis. Your choice of statistical test will depend on whether the data you have collected is interval, ratio, ordinal or nominal, and on the number of groups that you have and/or the number of variables that you have.

ICT-based techniques

It is common to use ICT-based techniques to conduct your statistical analysis. However, at this early stage in your research career, it is recommended that you conduct your statistical analysis by hand so you become familiar with data handling. When you are comfortable with manual data handling, the two main ICT programmes you could use for your data analysis are the Statistical Package for Social Sciences (SPSS) and Microsoft Excel. ICT-based techniques are used as they are a powerful way of interpreting statistics and give you more precise results (they can calculate results to a higher level of significance than can sometimes be done by hand).

Activity: Spearman rank-order correlation

You are interested in the influence of home advantage in sport – a lot of people talk about it but you want to find out if it actually exists. For your favourite sport or a famous sport, find a league table from the end of the season and find out if there is a relationship between final league finishing position and the number of games won at home. Use the formula and the table below to calculate your answer; and use the accompanying table of critical values to interpret the significance of your result.

Subject	Rank of league position	Rank of games won at home	d	d²
				$\sum d^2 =$

df	.10	.05	.01
5	0.90		
6	0.83	0.89	
7	0.71	0.79	0.93
8	0.64	0.74	0.88
9	0.60	0.68	0.83
10	0.56	0.656	0.79
11	0.52	0.61	0.77
12	0.50	0.59	0.75
13	0.47	0.56	0.71
14	0.46	0.54	0.69
15	0.44	0.52	0.66
16	0.42	0.51	0.64
17	0.41	0.49	0.62
18	0.40	0.48	0.61
19	0.39	0.46	0.60
20	0.38	0.45	0.58
21	0.37	0.44	0.56
22	0.36	0.43	0.55
23	0.35	0.42	0.54
24	0.34	0.41	0.53
25	0.34	0.40	0.52
26	0.33	0.39	0.51
27	0.32	0.38	0.50
28	0.32	0.38	0.49
29	0.31	0.37	0.48
∞	0.31	0.36	0.47

Table 4.12: Critical values of rank order correlation coefficient.

Assessment activity 4.5

You are working as a performance analyst for a football team. You have been asked to find out if there is a relationship between goals scored and the final league finishing position because the manager cannot decide whether to spend his transfer budget on a new striker or a new goalkeeper as your team desperately needs both but can only afford one. To do this, rank teams in relation to their final league position, look at the goals scored and then rank them in relation to the number of goals scored – before investigating the nature of the relationship between the two. You are in the planning stages of the project at the moment and need to discuss the approach you will take for this research with your research team. In your discussion, you need to include the following:

1. The best research design to use and a justification of your choice. **M4**

2. The best data collection technique (or techniques) to use and a justification of your choice. **M4**

3. A description of two contrasting data analysis techniques. **P6**

4. The best way of analysing your data and a justification of your choice. **M4**

Grading tips

- To attain **M4** you should choose the best data analysis technique for the problem and say why it is the most suitable.

- To attain **P6** you should describe one parametric test and one non-parametric test.

- Try to relate the research methods that you select to specific aspects of the project that you want to complete as this will allow you to make a stronger justification.

- If you think it is more appropriate to use a combination of different research methods, make sure that you justify each method.

PLTS

By presenting a persuasive case for your choices of research methods, you could develop your skills as an **effective participator**.

Functional skills

By discussing your ideas for the most appropriate research methods, you could provide evidence of your **English** skills in speaking and listening.

Amy Jacobs
Performance analyst

Amy is a performance analyst for a professional football club. One of her key job roles is to analyse football matches to see how well the team and players are performing from a statistics perspective.

'Professional football is such big business now that football teams are looking for as much detail as they can get about the performance of the team as a whole, and of the individual players, so that they can start to see who is performing well, and who isn't. This has lots of influence over team selections as the statistics that I produce are often good indicators of whether or not a player is tired and needs a rest, or even if they look like they're not putting in enough effort.

'I can also give players detailed breakdowns of what they have done during the game. For example, how many passes they have completed, how far they have run, how many shots they've had on target (you know – like the ones you see on the television when a game is on). I can keep a record of this for them over the course of a season and we can use this to help develop the players.

'As well as being able to analyse players and our own team, I analyse lots of games of opposition teams if we have a big game coming up (for example, I might look at their star striker and be able to give the staff a breakdown of where they prefer to shoot from and how they score most of their goals) which the manager and the coaching staff find really useful – and sometimes they might even get me to compare the performance statistics of a couple of players that they're interested in buying.

'One of the key problems I face is that sometimes the playing and coaching staff don't understand some of the statistics that I present them with, so I do need to spend some time with them to explain what is going on.'

Think about it!

- What type of statistics do you think would be useful to use in this type of sporting environment?
- How do you think you could make the statistics easier to understand?
- How much do you think players would appreciate this type of feedback?

Just checking

1. What is research?
2. What is qualitative research?
3. What is quantitative research?
4. What are the key issues associated with research methods?
5. What are the different types and classifications of data?
6. What are the common designs used in research?
7. What is the BASES Code of Conduct and why is it important?
8. What are the different stages of qualitative data analysis?
9. What are the different ways of organising quantitative data?
10. What are the different ways of displaying quantitative data?
11. What are the different measures of central tendency and variability?
12. What are the different types of inferential statistics used in quantitative research?

edexcel

Assignment tips

- To justify something, remember that you need to say why it is appropriate for its intended purpose.
- It is a good idea to try to bring your work to life by using lots of examples as this will demonstrate a greater level of understanding.
- There are some useful websites that can help you with this unit such as www.socialresearchmethods.net, www.sportsci.org and openlearn.open.ac.uk/. However these are quite high level so you will need to take your time when reading the information you find.
- Try to read as many journal articles as you can when you are going through this unit. It will benefit your understanding if you can see the different research methods that are used in a range of projects.
- Developing research is all about generating ideas so discuss your ideas with your classmates and try to work with each other to extend each other's thinking around this topic.
- At this level, when conducting research, you should try to limit yourself to looking at a maximum of two groups or a maximum of two variables so that you are getting a good understanding and a challenging experience but you are not pushing yourself too far.

5 Research project in sport and exercise sciences

Why do people take part in sport? Why do some people not exercise? How does a talented athlete become an elite athlete? These are just some areas of research in sport and exercise sciences. There is still much to learn about the different disciplines within sport and exercise sciences. It is the role of research to advance knowledge, to guide the applied work of sport and exercise scientists; and it is part of the role of sport and exercise scientists to conduct this research.

The work of sport and exercise scientists, in a research-based setting, involves planning research projects, collecting and analysing data, communicating research findings with others and using reflective practice to evaluate the research undertaken.

This unit will help you to learn how to conduct all of these aspects of the research process so that you can effectively plan, conduct, produce and evaluate your research.

Learning outcomes

After completing this unit you should:

1. be able to plan a sport science- or exercise science-based research project
2. be able to conduct a sport science- or exercise science-based research project
3. be able to produce a sport science- or exercise science-based research project
4. be able to review a sport science- or exercise science-based research project.

Assessment and grading criteria

This table shows you what you must do in order to achieve a pass, merit or distinction grade, and where you can find activities in this book to help you.

To achieve a **pass** grade the evidence must show that you are able to:	To achieve a **merit** grade the evidence must show that, in addition to the pass criteria, you are able to:	To achieve a **distinction** grade the evidence must show that, in addition to the pass and merit criteria, you are able to:
P1 plan a sport science- or exercise science-based research project **See Assessment activity 5.1, page 127**	**M1** explain how the selected research design and research methods will ensure that data collection and analysis is valid and reliable **See Assessment activity 5.1, page 127**	
P2 carry out sport science- or exercise science-based research **See Assessment activity 5.2, page 136**		
P3 collect and record data from the research project conducted **See Assessment activity 5.2, page 136**	**M2** correctly analyse collected data, describing techniques used **See Assessment activity 5.2, page 136**	**D1** correctly analyse data, explaining techniques used **See Assessment activity 5.2, page 136**
P4 produce a full research report using a standard scientific structure **See Assessment activity 5.2, page 136**		
P5 carry out a review of the research project conducted, describing strengths, areas for improvement and future recommendations **See Assessment activity 5.2, page 136**	**M3** carry out a review of the research project, explaining strengths, areas for improvement and future recommendations **See Assessment activity 5.2, page 136**	**D2** carry out a review of the research project, justifying future recommendations for further research **See Assessment activity 5.2, page 136**

How you will be assessed

This unit will be assessed by internal assignments that will be designed and marked by the tutors at your centre. Your assessments could be in the form of:

- research proposals
- research projects
- discussions
- oral presentations.

Jamie, 19-year-old research assistant for sports manufacturer

I work as part of a research team on the development of sports footwear for a range of sports including football and athletics. Being a research assistant is great! I meet loads of interesting people and have a direct input in the production of many of the football boots and sprint spikes that you might wear when taking part in your sport. I really enjoy the testing part of my job – we get different athletes coming in to see how good the sports shoes are that have been designed. I get to see the full elements of the research process. I get feedback from the athletes and closely monitor their performance. I like talking to athletes about how they have found the shoes and whether the shoe improved their shooting accuracy or their foot comfort during their sprint start.

The job is difficult sometimes. I'm under pressure to make sure that the data collection procedures are spot on as the slightest mistake in data collection could mean that the whole session has been wasted. When you're working in such a competitive environment you can't afford to waste time or money or get the testing wrong.

Over to you

1. How would you ensure that everything went well during data collection?
2. What type of information could you give athletes from this research?

1. Be able to plan a sport science- or exercise science-based research project

What is research?

For some people, research means looking things up in books, whereas for others it makes them think about things like people in white coats and expensive kit. What images do you get in your mind when you think of research? Why do you think research is so important in sport and exercise sciences?

1.1 Plan

The first thing you need to do is to decide on a topic that you would like to study. If you think carefully about the topic, your project will be far easier to complete than if you just come up with an idea from the top of your head and run with it. Figure 5.1 shows the overall planning process, from deciding on your idea to completing the proposal.

Remember

When you start to think about what you want to research, you might think that if your idea isn't original, it isn't any good – but this isn't true! Any research that you will do at this level will be based on something that has been done before and will use current knowledge. There is nothing wrong with this at all.

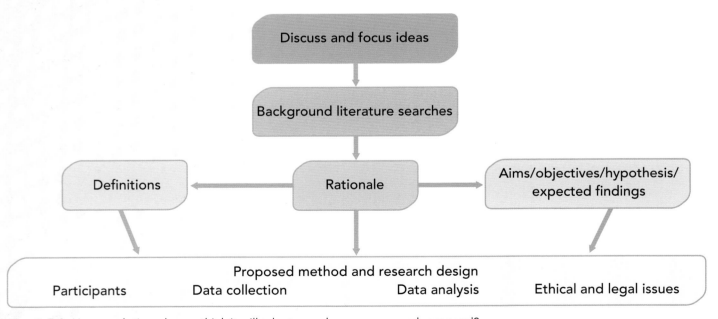

Figure 5.1: How much time do you think it will take to produce your research proposal?

Focus

You might not be able to identify a focused research project straight away, so try these guidelines.

* Think about what interests you and what you know about. If you choose a topic you are interested in

and know about, it will make your project easier to complete. You will also find it more interesting and you are likely to be more motivated to complete it.

- Use existing literature as this will provide you with a range of ideas that you may want to develop further. This will help you to form a **rationale** for your project. When you present your research proposal, you should include a mini-review of the literature that demonstrates your rationale.
- Think about current popular issues that might be worth researching, such as childhood obesity or how to improve performance in sport.
- Go over some ideas with friends. Talk about any ideas you have with others in your group and perhaps mind map some of these thoughts, to develop your ideas further.
- Speak to your tutor – they will be able to help you develop ideas.

Remember

When looking at whether your research project is worth pursuing, some people may ask 'So what?' Your rationale for the project is your way of answering this question – your reason for doing the project. It should be based on some form of problem that has been identified or a current 'hot' topic.

Activity: Deciding on your research ideas

Working in groups, produce an expanded mind map that covers the following areas.

1. **Name three areas that really interest you within sport and exercise science.**
2. **For each of these areas, write down what it is that interests you about them.**
3. **For each of the different individual interests, write down something that you would like to learn more about.**
4. **Using your previous knowledge from Unit 4 Research methods for sport and exercise sciences, write down some ideas about how you could find this information.**

Key terms

Rationale – the reason for completing the research project.
Aim – what you want to achieve through the research project.
Objective – how you will go about achieving the aims of the research project.

Title

After you have decided on the focus of your project, start to think about the title. Your title does not have to be a question, but it must clearly demonstrate the problem you are trying to solve and say what the project is about. It can be a 'working title' – you can alter it as you progress with your project. As well as deciding on the title, you should have some research questions in mind – some of the best titles can be let down if they are not supported by good research questions. These research questions will link in with the aims and objectives of your project.

Aims and objectives

The **aims** of your project are what you want to achieve through your research. They provide a clear statement of what you want to achieve and guide your research. The **objectives** are what you need to do in order to achieve your aims. They identify measurable tasks that need to be done to complete the project.

Hypothesis/null hypothesis/expected findings

A hypothesis is the predicted relationship between two variables. A null hypothesis is the prediction that there will not be a relationship between the two variables. When you are writing the hypothesis and null hypothesis, be careful to not write two separate hypotheses. This is easily done, so be careful about how you phrase your sentences. In some cases, it may not be appropriate to report a hypothesis and null hypothesis, so you should report expected findings instead.

Remember

Generally speaking, you will provide a hypothesis and null hypothesis when you are conducting quantitative research and you will provide an expected findings statement for qualitative research.

What role do you think research has played in Team GB's cycling success?

Scope

Your plan should indicate the **scope** of the project. This means who the research could be applicable to, whether the study is large or small scale, and the expectations of the research. For example, if you conduct a study of injury rates in ten international netball players, you would not be able to claim that your results were a good indicator of injuries in all athletic populations because your sample is too small and too focused.

Research design

In Unit 4 Research methods for sport and exercise sciences, you learned about different research designs that can be applied to research projects. As part of your proposal, you should report the research design that you will use and say why you will use it. In your research design section, it is good practice to say what your variables are (if applicable).

Sample

Your **sample** is the group(s) of participants in your study. There are different sampling techniques in research including:

- random sampling: a method where everybody has an equal chance of being selected
- stratified random sampling: choosing your participants for a specific reason then choosing people at random from within that group
- purposive/strategic sampling: choosing your sample because they meet criteria for your study or can provide information to help you answer your research questions.

In this section of your proposal, you need to say what sampling techniques you will use and why you have chosen this particular type of sampling and go on to discuss the details of your participants in the study. When you are writing about the proposed sample, you should discuss key details such as gender, age, sports or activities they play, level of training, level of performance, etc., but make sure you only report the details that are key to your study. For the research projects you will conduct, you will probably want to consider using your classmates, local sports teams or friends as participants.

Key terms

Scope – who and where your research is applicable to.

Sample – the participants in your study.

Remember

The people you choose as participants will depend on the type of project you want to conduct, but as a general pointer you need to get people who are easy to contact and who will help you to answer the research problem.

Data collection and analysis

How you will collect and analyse your data are two of the most important aspects of the proposal. This is because they show that you have given the project careful thought and have planned the kind of information you need to collect to achieve good-quality results. When planning this section, ask yourself questions like 'Which data collection and analysis methods are best for my project and why?', 'How many times do I need to collect data and why?' and 'What resources will I need to collect and analyse my data?' If you don't plan your data collection and analysis sections, you may find yourself with data that will not answer your research questions. When planning data collection and analysis, write about which techniques you have chosen to use, why you chose them and how you have planned to make sure your data is valid and reliable. The more detail you can supply the better your proposal will be.

> ## Remember
>
> You will need to use the knowledge and understanding that you gained from Unit 4 Research methods for sport and exercise sciences when writing your section on data collection and analysis.

As well as planning the data collection and analysis techniques that you will use, consider the resources that you will need to complete the collection and analysis. There are three main types of resource: physical, human and fiscal.

- **Physical resources** are the equipment or facilities that you need to complete your project.
- **Human resources** are the people you will need to help you complete your research project, such as a supervisor, participants and research assistants.
  - **Supervisor** – your tutor usually acts as your research supervisor. You have only one project to complete but your supervisor will have a number of students to work with, so you need to plan your time effectively to make the most of your supervisor.
  - **Participants** – you need to think of ways you can commit your participants to the study as you need to make sure they will complete the project so that your research is not worthless.
  - **Research assistants** – you may like to use research assistants. These are people who help you to collect your data, organise equipment, etc. Your friends can be really useful for this purpose, so why not ask some of them to help you set up your equipment? You can act as their research assistant in return, which makes the whole research process easier for everyone.

- **Fiscal resources** – are there any economic or financial resources you need to complete your project, such as money needed to buy supplements if you are carrying out a nutrition project? If you need to buy things to be able to conduct your project, how will you find the money to pay for them? Where will the money come from?

Validity and reliability considerations

Whenever you conduct research, you need to ensure your data is valid and reliable. There are a number of ways this can be achieved, including pilot studies, the use of repeated measures, triangulation and member checking.

- **Pilot studies** are smaller versions of your study that you use to test the research methods you have selected, before you start to conduct your research. They allow you to identify problems with the research methods and correct mistakes that could affect the internal validity and reliability of the data collected.
- **Repeated measures** are commonly used in quantitative research with experimental research designs. They are when data is collected from the same individual or groups over a period of time on more than one occasion to help you to assess the reliability of your data. If you collect data that is the same or similar on more than one occasion when all of the test conditions are the same, you can say that you have achieved reliability.
- **Triangulation** is the use of a range of research methods, sources of data or a number of researchers to try to increase the validity of the data you collect. For example, if you used semi-structured interviews, non-participant observations and two researchers, and you drew the same conclusions from each method and each researcher, you would be able to say you had ensured the validity of your research.

> ## Key terms
>
> **Pilot study** – a smaller scale version of your study used to check the data collection and analysis procedures.
>
> **Repeated measures** – using more than one data collection session to assess the reliability of your research.
>
> **Triangulation** – using more than one data analysis method to ensure the validity of results.

- **Member checking** happens at the final stage of qualitative data analysis (drawing conclusions and verifying data – see Unit 4: Research methods for sport and exercise sciences for a reminder). It involves giving the conclusions you have made back to the participants in the study to ensure you have interpreted what they have said correctly, thus increasing the validity of the research.

Ethical and legal considerations

The next aspect of your proposal should show that you have considered the ethical and legal issues as laid out by the British Association of Sport and Exercise Sciences (BASES) code of conduct. In Unit 4 Research methods for sport and exercise sciences, you learned about ethical and legal issues (for example, informed consent, confidentiality, data protection, ensuring the welfare and safety of the client throughout the research process, ethical clearance and working competently) that you should include in your proposal.

- **Informed consent and confidentiality** – within the area of ethical and legal issues, as part of your proposal, you need to produce a sample **informed consent** form. Informed consent is gained through asking participants to read and sign a document that sets out all the information relevant to the research project. When you produce your informed consent form, you could use the example on page 99 of Unit 4 Research methods for sport and exercise sciences to guide how you produce your form. You should include:

  o a description of the investigation, the aims and objectives

  o the procedures to be followed

  o an outline of any possible risks and benefits for the participants

  o an offer to answer any questions that the participants may have

  o an instruction that the participants are free to withdraw from the project at any time without penalty

  o a section that explains how you will maintain the confidentiality of participants and who will have access to the data

  o a section where the participant signs the form to say that they are happy to take part in the research, that you have answered any questions that they had and that they are happy with the answers that you gave.

Key terms

Member checking – allowing the participants of the study to check your interpretations and conclusions for validity purposes.

Informed consent – the knowing permission or agreement of your participants (or legal representative in the case of a child) to take part in the research as you have described it to them. The participant must be willing and should not be unfairly persuaded into taking part.

Activity: Informed consent forms

Produce an informed consent form for the research project you have planned. After you have produced your informed consent form, show it to your tutor for approval. Once your form has been approved by your tutor, give copies of it to your participants. Make sure you receive the signed copies back, to keep with your research records.

- **Health screening** – as part of your research project, you may need to conduct health screening with your participants (for example, if you are investigating any form of physiological testing). If you do need to carry out health screening, this must be done before you begin research and stored away securely with your signed informed consent forms. Within sport and exercise sciences research, health and medical screening is conducted to ensure the health and safety of the participants by identifying any contraindications to the research they will be taking part in. Refer to Unit 8 Fitness testing for sport and exercise for more information about health screening.

- **Ensuring the welfare and safety of participants** – you must ensure the welfare and safety of your participants throughout the research process. All participants have the right to expect the highest standards of professionalism, consideration and respect from you when you are conducting research. There are a number of ways that you can ensure the welfare and safety of your participants including child protection, Criminal Records Bureau (CRB) checking and having knowledge of all of the equipment in the project.

- **CRB checking** – if you are going to work with children or vulnerable adults, you may be asked to apply for a Criminal Records Bureau (CRB) check. This is a check that will help to show (in this context) if you are able to work with children or vulnerable adults, or if there is any reason why you should not. You can refuse to complete a CRB check if you wish, but this will limit certain types of research you can conduct. Your tutor will be able to tell you whether

or not you need to be CRB checked and will be able to help you organise going through the process.

- **Ethical clearance for your project** – before you start your project, somebody will have to look at it to make sure that it doesn't pose any unnecessary threats to anybody involved with the project and that it is a project that you will be able to complete. This process is called ethical clearance and in your school or college it will normally be your tutor that approves your research.

Remember

After you have completed your research proposal, you will need to show it to your tutor so that they can check it is ok. This is a process of ethical approval and is essential before you start your project.

Assessment activity 5.1   P1 M1   BTEC
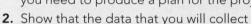

You have been approached by a company within the sport and active leisure industry to conduct a research project.

1. Before you can start your research project, you need to produce a plan for the project. **P1**
2. Show that the data that you will collect will be valid and reliable. **M1**

Grading tips
To attain P1 and M1, use the following format to write your proposal as this will help you to get all of your information across:
- Title
- Introduction
  - o Discuss the background information for your research project that will help provide the rationale for your study.
  - o Include any key definitions.
  - o Include your aims, objectives, hypothesis, null hypothesis or expected findings (where appropriate).
  - o Include your key research questions.
- Proposed method
  - o Research design
    - – Which will you use and why.

- o Participants
  - – Give as much detail as you can (for example, number, age, gender, performance level, sports played, etc.).
- o Data collection techniques
  - – Which you will use and why.
  - – Which resources you will need to collect data.
- o Data analysis techniques
  - – Which you will use and why.
- o Methods of ensuring validity and reliability
  - – Which you will use and why.
- Ethical and legal issues
  - o Which are important for your project and why?
  - o How will you make sure that you adhere to the ethical and legal guidelines?

PLTS
If you generate ideas and explore possibilities about how the research could be conducted, you could develop your skills as a **critical thinker**.

Functional skills

If your proposal is fit for purpose, you could provide evidence of your **English** skills in writing.

2. Be able to conduct a sport science- or exercise science-based project

When you conduct research, there are several things that you should take into account to be able to research effectively including resources required, any ethical and legal issues arising, data issues and the use of a research diary.

2.1 Resources

Resources needed

In the planning stage, you looked at how you decide which resources you need for data collection. In this section, you will look at what you need to do to make sure that the resources you need are available.

Considerations

You need to think about how you will access the resources that you need and how you will use them correctly. Think about the following areas:

- **Availability and booking** – there's nothing worse than wanting to start your project and not having the resources that you need, so remember that there will be lots of people wanting to use the same resources as you and book the resources that you need well in advance of starting your data collection.

- **Make arrangements with participants** – ensure that all your participants, supervisor and research assistants (if any) know where to be and when.

- **Familiarity with research techniques** – it is part of the BASES code of conduct that you only conduct a research project when you know what you are doing, so if you want to use a research technique (for example, focus groups) you should make sure that you know how to use that technique.

- **Familiarity with equipment and facilities** – as well as knowing how to use the different research techniques, you should also know how all your equipment works. Check with your tutor about equipment, read instruction manuals, use your class notes and practise using equipment to make sure that you know exactly what to do when it comes to your data collection session.

2.2 Ethical and legal issues

Simply planning the ethical and legal issues into your research project isn't good enough – you must make sure that you adhere to the ethical and legal issues while conducting your project. Look back at page 126 in this unit and to page 98 in Unit 4 Research methods for sport and exercise sciences to remind yourself of the implications of ethical and legal issues.

Activity: Working ethically and legally

Go back to your copy of the BASES code of conduct (available from www.bases.org.uk) and go through each of the sections, looking at what you need to do to be working ethically and legally. Look at the following areas: informed consent, health screening and confidentiality, data protection, ensuring the welfare of your clients and working within your own areas of competence.

2.3 Data

When completing your data collection think about three things: how you will collect data, how you will record your data and how you will store it.

Collecting data

By the time you are ready to complete your data collection, you will have already planned how you are going to do it but keep the following areas in mind (depending on which are appropriate to your project): accuracy, precision, correct use of field-based data collection, correct use of laboratory-based data collection, the use of spreadsheets or databases, interviews, questionnaires, surveys and observations. You looked at each of these techniques in Unit 4 Research methods for sport and exercise sciences, so if you need a reminder of how to use these techniques refer back to it.

Analysis

To produce a good project, make sure that you get your data analysis right and in as much detail as possible. One of the ways that you can do this is by using a research diary so that you can:

- record your thoughts and feelings about the research process
- have an ongoing evaluation of your project
- have the opportunity to conduct manual data analysis
- make initial conclusions about your analysed data.

All these will benefit your understanding of your project and will make it easier for you to evaluate your research project after you have completed it.

Recording thoughts and feelings regarding the research process

Record your thoughts and feelings about different aspects of the research project as you go along. This will help you to evaluate your project at later stages. Pay particular attention to any problems with data collection or data analysis. Throughout the research project, you will have meetings with your supervisor. It will be important that you use your research diary to record the guidance that they have given you through your meetings and your initial thoughts about how you could action their guidance.

- Ongoing evaluation of the project – write down any problems that you have had with the research project. Include some ideas for how you could overcome these difficulties or problems if you were to complete the project again.
- Opportunity to conduct manual data analysis – your data analysis should start as soon as possible. This is normally after the first round of data collection has been completed. When you start your data analysis you will be able to see how it is progressing and look at any themes that are emerging.
- Making initial conclusions regarding analysed data – just as you should start analysing your data as soon as you have finished your first round of data collection, you should start drawing your first conclusions as soon as you have finished your first round of data analysis so that you don't have to think back a long way when it comes to writing up your project.

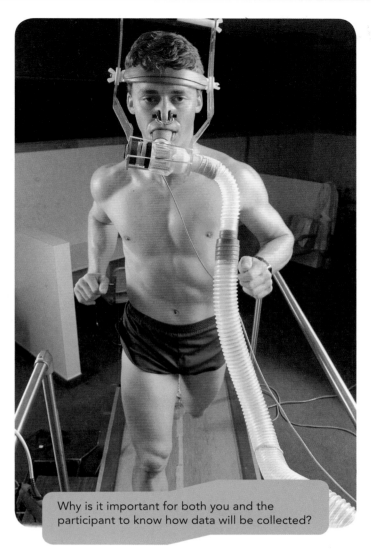

Why is it important for both you and the participant to know how data will be collected?

Recording data

In Unit 4 Research methods for sport and exercise sciences, you learned how to use techniques including the different types of distribution (rank order, frequency and cumulative frequency) and range in quantitative research; as well as looking at audio recording and video recording the data that you collect through qualitative research. You should use the appropriate technique to record your data in your research project.

Storing data

Your data should be stored confidentially, with access restricted to you and your supervisor only. To maintain confidentiality keep your data in a secure setting (such as a locked filing cabinet at your school or college) or in the case of electronic data, stored on a password-protected computer.

3. Be able to produce a sport science- or exercise science-based research project

Conducting your research can be time-consuming and you may need to invest a lot of time and effort in completing it. The last thing you want to do is let yourself down by producing a poor report. Follow the guidelines in this section and they will help you to produce a good report. Here are some points to get you started.

- Make sure that you demonstrate use of appropriate ICT when writing your research report and ensure that your report is coherent and well structured.

- It is likely that you will not be able to write your report 'off the bat' first time around. You will need to draft and redraft it several times. To make this easier, do not leave this task to the last minute. Make sure that you plan how you will write the report and leave time for this.

- Make sure you save your work regularly. This is probably the longest assessment you will complete as part of your course, so you do not want to have to start it all over again. Print out the work you have done on a regular basis so that you have a hard copy in your file. This will also help you with proofreading and editing your work.

- Proofread and edit your work yourself – do not rely on the computer's spell checking function. The spellchecker is useful if you have spelt something incorrectly, but it will not detect misuse of words such as 'too' instead of 'two' or 'one' instead of 'won'. Check for cases where the writing is in the first person; your project should be written in the third person and the past tense. For example, 'I noticed that' should be changed to 'It was noted that'.

- Use your research diary to help you write your report. You will get ideas as you go through the research process that you will want to include in your project write-up. Make notes as you go along in your research diary because you won't be able to remember them when you come to your write-up.

3.1 Scientific structure of the research report

When writing your project, try to make the report as readable as you can for your audience – one of the main things is to make it interesting. It is likely you will be conducting your research project on a topic that you are interested in. You need to demonstrate this level of interest through your writing because that will keep your readers interested. When students start to produce a research report, they sometimes fall into one of two traps.

- They make the report overly complicated, long-winded and full of complex technical terms because they think that this will impress the reader. However, this will not impress anyone.

- They make the report too 'chatty' and avoid using technical terms because they are worried that the audience will not understand it or because they do not understand it themselves. This style often lacks any form of academic rigour.

Remember

Try to find a happy medium between these writing styles. Try to demonstrate your enthusiasm for the topic in an academic manner, using appropriate terminology (such as key terms at relevant times), while at the same time showing your opinions, thoughts and arguments.

To produce a coherent and well-structured research report, you should use the format described below in this section. You should produce this report using appropriate ICT, for example, using an appropriate word-processing programme to type the report up and using appropriate database and spreadsheet programmes to produce necessary graphs and charts, etc.

Title page

Your title page should include the following information, usually in this order:

- project title
- your name
- your course (include qualification and level)
- the unit title
- the date when the project is due to be handed in.

Abstract

An abstract is a short summary of your research. It is normally about 150–200 words long at this level. This is an important section because it is the first thing people will look at and so it often determines whether they want to carry on reading or not. The abstract should include a brief description of your topic, aims, objectives, hypothesis, null hypothesis/expected findings, rationale, a brief description of your method, and a summary of the main results and conclusions.

Acknowledgements

In this section, you should acknowledge all the people without whom it would not have been possible to complete the research. This could include those who have given you information, such as your tutor, and the participants in the study.

General contents page

The contents page shows the layout of the report and what is in each section. Each aspect of the contents should be given a specific heading and the page number recorded next to it. Any major subdivisions of each section should also be shown in the general contents page in the same way.

Contents page for figures and tables

This should show the table or figure number, the title of each item and the page location within the report, so that it can be sourced easily should the reader need to refer to it.

Contents page for appendices

As for the general contents page, and for figures and tables, you need to have a section that shows the content of your appendices. This gives the appendix number and the content of the appendix.

Introduction

The introduction should describe your topic and give the rationale for conducting the project. It should identify and explain your research question, your aims and objectives and the hypothesis and null hypothesis. It should also define any key terms used in the project. You will have done this already in your proposal, so the key terms can often be transferred from your proposal (after changing from future tense to past tense). Alternatively, they may need to be altered slightly before being included in the introduction. If the area you are looking at has more than one definition from a number of people, you need to choose the definition that you are going to use for your project. This is known as the operational definition.

It is good practice to include a purpose statement in your introduction. There are different types of purpose statements for qualitative and quantitative research. Table 5.1 summarises the two types of purpose statement.

Quantitative purpose statements	Qualitative purpose statements
Words like 'test' or 'measure'	Words like 'understand'
Research design and variables	Research design
Who/what you are testing or measuring	Data collection methods

Table 5.1: The two types of purpose statement.

The purpose statements for both qualitative and quantitative research need to include the information in Table 5.1, but the details do not need to be in the same order.

Literature review

In the literature review you start to think about arguments that have been made in previous research. A common mistake with literature reviews is that students simply list a lot of research from other areas and leave it at that. However, this does not make up a literature review.

For your literature review, you should:

- give important details about the literature you have studied

- discuss strengths and areas for improvement from previous research
- highlight key arguments from previous research and say how they apply to your project.

Effectively, the literature should set the scene for your project. The literature you use should relate to the aims, objectives and research problem in your study, otherwise you will not be able to produce a coherent research project report.

Method

The purpose of the method section is for you to set out how you achieved your research objectives. As with the introduction and literature review, there will be aspects of the method section that you can adapt from your proposal (and you will simply need to change from future tense to past tense). This section will be the focal point of your project write-up because it tells the reader exactly what you did, how you did it and why you chose to do it that way.

For your method to be effective it must be in enough detail for somebody to be able to pick up your report, read your method and reproduce your study in exactly the same way as you. Your method should be written in the third person, past tense and continuous prose. For example, instead of writing 'I collected data from 20 participants and then I analysed it using Spearman's rank order correlation' you should say 'Data was collected from 20 participants and analysed using Spearman's rank order correlation'.

The method section should be split into three main parts: participants, data collection and data analysis.

- **Participants** – this section needs to provide all the important details about your sample. The style of writing needs to be in the past tense and you need to take into account any changes to your participants since the planning stage. Other than that, this section will be almost identical to the participants section of your proposal. The

main difference is that you will now know all of the participants' details, so you will be able to include all the mean and standard deviation data in the method section.

- **Data collection** – in this section of your method there are a number of details you need to include, such as research design, the methods you used (for example, interviews) and the data collection procedures (for example, how many interviews you did, how long the interviews took, how they were recorded, etc.).

- **Data analysis** – the data analysis section outlines all the methods you used that contributed to the overall analysis of your data, along with an explanation of why you used those methods. This section should include any aspects of the data analysis that you used. For example, 'Data was analysed using the independent test because the aim of the study was to find out if there was a significant difference between the mean scores of the two groups and the data collected was ratio in nature'.

Results

Your results are a descriptive account of what you found out. You do not interpret any of your results in this section – you simply say what you found. A common mistake is to report every single finding you have and let your reader find their way through it. You need to report the results that are important to the aims of your study in a concise, well-organised way. The overall aim of data analysis in your research project is to provide the reader with a coherent and logical development of answers to all the questions you raised throughout the introduction and literature review. You don't want to spoil this by reporting everything regardless of its relevance because you think it looks good.

There are some items that should always be reported in the results sections, including the descriptive statistics you calculated such as the mean and standard deviation data. These results are important because they give the reader an easy way to evaluate the results and, if possible, the data should be presented in one table. You must present the results in a way that is easy to understand and not daunting, but without using too many colours, fonts and special effects. The correct combination of tables and figures will make

Case study: Writing the method section

A typical write-up of the method used in a research project involving 100 elite ice hockey players might include the following:

Section 1
For this study, 45 males ranging in age from 21 to 25 were randomly selected from the overall available population ($N = 100$) of ice hockey players who have played at an elite level for at least three years ($m = 4.1 \pm 0.7$). After this, participants were randomly assigned to one of three groups ($n = 15$).

Section 2
Before research was started, a pilot study was conducted and necessary alterations made to the design of the questionnaire. Informed consent was obtained from the participants before any aspect research was conducted. Questionnaires were used as the primary data collection tool. The questionnaires consisted of a range of open and closed questions because… Interviews were then used as a follow-up data collection tool. Semi-structured interviews were selected because…

Section 3
A total of 100 questionnaires were given out by hand to the participants. These were completed in the presence of the researcher. From this, 10 follow-up semi-structured interviews were completed, ranging from 40 minutes to 60 minutes ($m = 47 \pm 4.6$) and then transcribed. Interviews were conducted in a setting familiar to the participants to ensure they were comfortable with the research process and to increase the quality of response from each participant. Ethical approval for the overall test procedure was obtained before research started and all data collected was kept confidential, with no details that made the participants personally identifiable included.

Section 4
The independent test was used because the aim of the study was to find out if there was a significant difference between the mean scores of the two groups and the data collected was ratio in nature.

1. **Which section relates to participants?**
2. **Which section relates to data collection?**
3. **Which section relates to data collection procedure?**
4. **Which section relates to data analysis?**

---

your data analysis easy to follow, and less detail is more beneficial to the reader. A simple graph or chart in black and white is preferable to a three-dimensional graph in a multitude of colours. Make sure you describe the key aspects of figures and tables in the results section – do not include them without saying what they show. Say what the tables show, but do not repeat the information in them as this is a waste of time. Another important part of the results section is to consider how you should report quantitative data analysis and qualitative data analysis. Although the principles are largely the same, the technical aspects are different.

- **Quantitative data** – as with the general principles of completing the results sections, when reporting your statistics a general guide is: the easier something is to understand, the better. Tutors don't want to be blinded with statistics – they want you to correctly analyse your data in the best way to suit your project. Make sure you report only the relevant data analysis, always include the level of significance and report your data using the appropriate number of decimal places. If you can place your results in an appropriate context, this will improve the quality of the results section.

- **Qualitative data** – just as with the use of statistics where you report only the relevant numbers, with qualitative data analysis you report only the relevant words, phrases or quotes. Select the correct type of organisational diagram or chart to make sure that you are not saying one thing with your quotes but another with your diagrams. For example, do not report results that show an interaction between different concepts and then use a radial diagram instead of a Venn diagram.

Discussion and conclusion

The discussion section is where you interpret your results, review and evaluate your research project, and provide future recommendations for research, generally in that order.

Your discussion should start by restating the aims of your project and saying whether they were achieved or not (including any evidence to support this). When you have done this, interpret your results in relation to previous research. This means that you compare your results to previous research, saying whether they are similar or different and try to explain why your results have happened. Next, explain what your results mean and who they can be applied to.

When writing the discussion, do not feel you have to use a thesaurus to write every word, in the hope that it will make the text sound more technical and detailed. The best discussion you can write is based on your observations and analysis of the results and written in such a way that you understand them. If you complete your discussion in this way, your arguments should be effective and convincing. Table 5.2 gives some examples of how a perfectly good argument can be changed into an overly complex sentence (or, in some cases, paragraph) that makes far less sense.

What they said	What they meant
There is a large body of experimental evidence which clearly indicates that smaller members of the genus Mus tend to engage in recreational activities while the feline is remote from the locale.	While the cat's away, the mice will play.
From time immemorial, it has been known that the ingestion of an 'apple' (i.e. the pome fruit of any tree of the genus Malus, said fruit being usually round in shape and red, yellow or greenish in colour) on a diurnal basis will with absolute certainty keep a primary member of the healthcare establishment from one's local environment.	An apple a day keeps the doctor away.
Even with the most sophisticated experimental protocol, it is highly unlikely that you can instil in a superannuated canine the capacity to perform novel feats of legerdemain.	You can't teach an old dog new tricks.

Table 5.2: Examples of complex and simple sentences

Use the checklist below to make sure you have written a good discussion section.

- Have you said what your results mean and who they are important for?
- Have you said whether the results are similar to, or different from, previous research or what you would have expected?
- Have you discussed the results that relate to the aim first and then any other important results afterwards?

The last section of your discussion is the conclusion and future recommendations section. This is where you summarise the main findings of the project (conclusion) and discuss the project's successes and areas for improvement, providing specific examples as evidence for future recommendations (see page 135 for more detail). The conclusion is an important part because it brings together and summarises the arguments made throughout the discussion.

Remember

The conclusion should be drawn from the discussion you have just finished writing and the future recommendations should be based on the overall research process.

References section

The reference section is where you list all of the authors whose work you have used in the text. It is a list of the sources you have used, written in alphabetical order of the lead author's surname (the author that is first on the front of the book) and is produced using a technique known as the Harvard reference system. When you write the reference list, there are slightly different techniques for referencing work from different sources. Try using the examples below to guide you when you write your reference section:

- To reference a book: author's surname, author's initials, year, *title of book*, place of publication, publisher.

  For example: Thomas, J. R., Nelson, J. K. and Silverman, S. J. (2005) *Research Methods in Physical Activity* (5th ed.), Champaign, IL, Human Kinetics.

- To reference a chapter in an edited book: author's surname, author's initials, year, title of chapter, editor(s) of book, *book title*, pages of chapter, place of publication, publisher.

  For example: Griffin, P. and Hemplin, T. J. (1989) An overview of qualitative research, in P. W. Darst, D. B. Zakrajsek and V. H. Mancini (eds.) *Analysing physical education and sport instruction* (2nd ed., pp.399–410), Champaign, IL, Human Kinetics.

- To reference a journal article: author's surname, author's initials, year, title of journal article, *title of journal*, **volume number**, pages.

  For example: Harwood, C. (2008). Developmental consulting in a professional football academy: The 5C's coaching efficacy program. *The sport psychologist*, **22**, 109–133.

- To reference an Internet source: author (if known) or title of article, full website address of Internet site, date accessed.

  For example: FA Structural Review Update, www.thefa.com/TheFA/NewsFromTheFA/Postings/2006/10/StructuralReview.htm (accessed 29/10/2006).

Remember

You should start your reference list as soon as you have included your first reference – this will save you a lot of work in the long run!

Appendices

The appendix section is where you insert any information that helps to provide support for anything you have said or done in your report. Pieces of information that are found in the appendices include: sample questionnaires or interview guides, sample informed consent forms and detailed protocols about the calibration of equipment. Any appendices that you include should be referenced in the text, for example, 'The gas analysis testing equipment was calibrated prior to each data collection session (for full details of the calibration protocol followed, see Appendix 1)'.

4.   Be able to review a sport science- or exercise science-based research project

4.1 Review

Refer back to page 133 where 'reviewing your project' is covered under the heading 'Discussion and conclusion'.

4.2 Future recommendations

Again, this section is referred to on page 134 under the heading 'Discussion and conclusion'.

Remember that your future recommendations should be based on what you see as the areas for improvement for your project. You should try to produce future recommendations that relate to the alternative research methods that could be used to develop the research project and how these methods would be of benefit. Below are some questions to ask yourself when you are writing this section.

- What could I have done differently to make this project better?
- What went well with the project that could be developed in the future?
- Why would these changes be beneficial for future research?

Take it further

Reviewing your research project

Throughout your discussion, you should review your research project. How do you think that you could expand on your review using the following questions?

- **How well did the project meet the original project aims?**
- **What are the strengths and areas for improvement?**
- **What evidence do you have to support this?**
- **Can you give specific examples?**

Case study: Future recommendations

An example of a future recommendations section could be:

The semi-structured interviews used in the research project allowed for the investigation of the participants' feelings about hooliganism in football which produced a number of key themes. Future research could seek to adopt focus groups as a data collection method as this would allow the participants to discuss their ideas with each other and could generate more opinions regarding the research topic. As all of the participants in this study were male *football fans, it would be interesting to use a range of participants to see if the views of people that are not football fans differ from those who are.*

For the case study above, answer the following questions:

1. **What could you have done differently to make this project better?**
2. **What went well with the project that could be developed in the future?**
3. **Why would these changes be beneficial for future research?**

Assessment activity 5.2

You are working as a sport and exercise scientist and somebody has seen the proposal that you have written as part of Assessment activity 5.1. They think it is a really good idea and would like you to:

1. carry out the research project **P2**
2. collect, record and analyse the data, describing and explaining the techniques you have used **P3 M2 D1**
3. write up the research for them. **P4**

When you have completed the project and are producing the research report, you will need to:

4. review the project, describing and explaining its strengths, areas for improvement and suggesting future research directions **P5 M3**
5. justify your future recommendations for further research. **D2**

Grading tips

- To attain **P2** complete the research project that you planned for Assessment activity 5.1.
- To attain **P3** collect your data for the research project, and record the data in an appropriate ICT programme such as Microsoft Access or Microsoft Excel.
- To attain **M2** describe how you analysed your data in the data analysis part of your method section.
- To attain **D1** provide a detailed explanation of the data analysis methods used in the data analysis part of your method section.
- To attain **P4** use the format for producing your research project so that you can produce a full research report using standard scientific structure, and produce the project using appropriate ICT.
- To attain **P5**, in the discussion section, describe the strengths and areas for improvement of your research project, and describe some future recommendations that could address these limitations of research.
- To attain **M3**, in the discussion section, explain in detail the strengths and areas for improvement of your research project, and explain some future recommendations that could address these limitations of research.
- To attain **D2** say how your suggested future directions would improve the limitations of your research project or how they would make the strengths even better.

PLTS

If you ask questions to extend your thinking about the conclusions of the research project, you could develop your skills as a **critical thinker**.

Functional skills

If your project is fit for purpose, you could provide evidence of your **English** skills in writing.

Jack Lowe
Sports nutritionist

Jack works for a sports nutrition company to help with product development and provide recommendations for athletes.

'Working as a sports nutritionist is a great job! I spend time working with athletes to help them develop the best eating habits, design dietary recommendations and give them advice on different training aids like sports drinks. As part of my job, I also work in the research and development unit for a major sports nutrition company.

'This involves me running research projects to test our sports drinks to make sure that they are the best on the market and so we can provide evidence to support marketing campaigns when we need it. I play an important role in finding evidence to support the testing of new ingredients that we might need to use to develop our range even further.

'The thing that I enjoy most about my job is knowing that the work I do is used to directly benefit athletes at all levels. It's not all easy going though. At times the work I do can be quite complex and it involves a lot of planning and effort to make sure that I am testing the products correctly. If I don't plan it all well and something goes wrong, it could mean that my company would end up selling a below standard product that wouldn't be much good to anybody!'

Think about it!

- Why do you think it is important for professionals like Jack working in the sports industry to be aware of research going on in their area?
- If you were Jack, how could you make sure that you plan sports drink research well?
- How could professionals like Jack use research to benefit their work with athletes?

Just checking

1. What is the purpose of research?
2. How should you structure your research proposal?
3. What are the key resource considerations when conducting research?
4. What are the key ethical and legal issues to consider when conducting research?
5. Why is informed consent important?
6. How can you ensure the welfare and safety of the participants you are working with?
7. How can you make sure that your data is valid and reliable?
8. What is the standard scientific structure of the research report?
9. What questions should you ask yourself when you are reviewing your research project?
10. What questions should you ask yourself when you are looking at future recommendations?

Assignment tips

- When planning your research project, look on websites, in magazines or newspapers, or read other journals to help you choose your research idea.
- When you have decided on your research idea, do as much background reading as you can so that you have a good depth of knowledge before starting your proposal.
- When completing your proposal, make sure that you refer to Unit 4 Research methods for sport and exercise sciences as this will remind you of the key research methods used.
- Complete your data collection early. Without any data, you don't have a research project and if you leave it too late you will panic and end up not doing a very good job!
- Check your data analysis with your tutor as you complete it. It is essential that your data analysis is correct.
- Write up your project as you go along. If you leave it all to the last minute, you will end up having to rush your work and it probably won't be as good.
- To make sure you have written a good conclusion section, when you have finished writing your first draft of the research project report, read the introduction and then read the conclusion without anything else in between. If you have written both of these sections correctly, they should make perfect sense without reading anything else.

6 Sports biomechanics in action

Have you ever watched sport and wondered how an athlete manages to perform at such a high level; for example, how Usain Bolt manages to set off so quickly or how Cristiano Ronaldo can make a football dip so quickly? These are questions that can be answered using biomechanics.

Sports biomechanics examines the causes and consequences of human movement and the interaction of the body with apparatus or equipment through the application of mechanical principles in sporting settings. It is one of the key areas to understand if you want to analyse the performance of individuals and teams.

You will start this unit by looking at how the performance of athletes and teams is analysed using notational analysis of performance criteria. You will then look in more detail at how you can analyse individual performance against 'model' performances. Throughout the unit, you will examine how you can effectively feed back to an athlete or team about their performance.

Learning outcomes

After completing this unit you should:

1. be able to perform notational analysis for sport
2. be able to compare a numerical model to sporting performance
3. be able to compare a technical model to sporting performance
4. be able to provide feedback on performance to an athlete or team.

Assessment and grading criteria

This table shows you what you must do in order to achieve a pass, merit or distinction grade, and where you can find activities in this book to help you.

To achieve a **pass** grade the evidence must show that you are able to:	To achieve a **merit** grade the evidence must show that, in addition to the pass criteria, you are able to:	To achieve a **distinction** grade the evidence must show that, in addition to the pass and merit criteria, you are able to:
P1 describe five relevant performance criteria for an individual or team-based sport **See Assessment activity 6.1, page 146**		
P2 perform two notational analyses on a chosen sport, with some support **See Assessment activity 6.1, page 146**	**M1** compare the two notational analyses, using statistics, data representation and literature to explain the strengths and areas for improvement **See Assessment activity 6.1, page 146**	
P3 produce a numerical model, using three numerical components, and compare it to a sporting performance, with some support **See Assessment activity 6.2, page 157**		
P4 produce a technical model, using four technical components, and compare it to a sports performance, with some support **See Assessment activity 6.3, page 163**	**M2** explain and justify the methodology for either the numerical or technical models **See Assessment activity 6.2 page 157, 6.3 page 163**	**D1** evaluate findings for either the notational analyses, numerical or technical models commenting on their influence on performance within the chosen sport **See Assessment activity 6.1 page 146, 6.2 page 157, 6.3 page 163**
P5 provide feedback on performance, to an athlete, or team, using information gathered from one of the analyses performed, prescribing future action, with support **See Assessment activity 6.4, page 166**	**M3** provide detailed feedback and prescribe future action for the athlete or team from either the notational analyses, numerical or technical models **See Assessment activity 6.4, page 166**	**D2** justify the prescribed future actions for either the notational analyses, numerical or technical models **See Assessment activity 6.4, page 166**

How you will be assessed

This unit will be assessed by internal assignments that will be designed and marked by the tutors at your centre. Your assessments could be in the form of:

- analyses of team and individual performances
- numerical and technical modelling of performance
- verbal or written feedback to athletes and teams.

Michaela, 20-year-old sports coach

This unit was really good for me as it helped me to understand that biomechanics isn't all scary maths and physics. I found it's more about how you can use these scientific principles to make athletes and teams perform better, and that's what really got me interested in it.

There were lots of practical learning activities in this unit that helped me to gain a better understanding of how the different techniques can be used in sport. We spent a lot of time going through different case studies, analysing our own performance and watching lots of recordings of sporting actions, all of which really helped my understanding and skill set.

I enjoyed learning about notational analysis the most because it was good for me to see how I can analyse both team and individual performances in matches and training, then use all of that information to feed back to (and help develop) different athletes.

Over to you

1. **Which bits of the unit do you think you will enjoy the most?**
2. **Which parts do you think you may find difficult?**
3. **What will you do to prepare for these difficulties?**

1. Be able to perform notational analysis for sport

How can we use biomechanics to improve performance?

Sports performers at all levels are always looking for an extra advantage over their opponents by improving their performance. Biomechanists use knowledge from a number of areas including coaching, performance analysis and traditional sciences to develop overall individual and team techniques and tactics. Can you think of any ways that this could be used in your sport?

Think about when you have watched sport on television. You will be able to think of examples where the commentators have talked about lots of different statistics that relate to aspects of sport performance. The statistics they discuss are produced using a technique called **notational analysis** and are based on aspects of sport performance known as **performance criteria**.

How do you think biomechanics can help to improve a tennis serve?

Key terms

Notational analysis – analyses of sport performance involving counting different observations of performance, for example, how many shots were successful versus unsuccessful.

Performance criteria – aspects of sport performance which, if performed well, should lead to successful sport performance.

1.1 Performance criteria

Performance criteria are factors (for example, shot accuracy, saves, headers, dribbling) that are important for successful sport performance. Some sports, if simple in nature (such as snooker), may have only a few performance criteria (such as safety success). In comparison, more technical sports (such as football) will have more, including factors such as tackle success. As well as different sports having different performance criteria, different positions within the same sport have different performance criteria, for example, a goal keeper has different performance criteria from a striker in football.

Unforced errors

An unforced error is an error that comes from your own actions (and not as a consequence of an opponent's actions). If an athlete (for example, a tennis player) can reduce the number of unforced errors they make in a match, then this should increase their chances of success. When analysing unforced errors, count the number made during a match. Then repeat this over a number of performances to see if there is a trend forming. You could then look further into the performance criteria by categorising the unforced errors such as from the serve, backhand shots, forehand shots, etc.

Forced errors

Forced errors are as a direct result of the actions of your opponent. In tennis, a player is likely to make forced errors because the other player is more powerful in their shots or is using uncontrollable spin on the ball. By getting your opponent to make many forced errors, you are more likely to win the match.

Shot success/failure/accuracy

Shot success is a determining factor in the match outcome in many sports. Shot success in its most basic form is how many attempts you score, whereas shot failure is how many attempts you miss and shot accuracy refers to how many shots were on or off target; you can look at these in more detail. For example, if you analysed Wayne Rooney's shot success, failure and accuracy, you could examine these factors:

- left-footed shots
- right-footed shots
- shots inside the box
- shots outside the box.

Crosses

A cross in team-based sports is another key performance criterion and relates to when the ball is played into an attacking area from a wide position and can be analysed either from a defensive or an attacking perspective. Decide which aspect of crossing you are interested in. If you want to analyse crosses, look at issues beyond the cross being cleared or an attempt at goal. This is because, for example, when defending, the cross may be cleared initially but this may lead to:

- another cross
- a shot on target
- a goal
- a penalty
- other negative outcomes for the defending teams.

When analysing crosses, look at the number of crosses cleared first, and then look at the overall outcome.

Heading

Heading is a key performance criterion in football. As with crosses, heading can be subdivided into defensive and attacking categories. Although there is some value in considering the number of headers won in defensive or attacking situations, you should analyse the outcome of the header, such as another header, keeping possession or losing possession.

Passing

In interactive sports such as football, rugby and basketball, passing is an essential performance criterion that influences the overall result of the game. When analysing passing look at success (i.e. received by a teammate) or failure (i.e. intercepted) and expand further into factors including pass direction, passes to particular teammates or long and short passes.

Dribbling

Dribbling involves a player trying to take the ball around an opposition player or players with the aim of gaining an advantage and is a key component in lots of team-based sports (for example, hockey, football and basketball). When dribbling the ball the end product must be a positive one. This means that it leads to:

- a shot at the target
- successfully passing the ball to a team member
- drawing a foul from the opposition
- gaining field advantage.

For example, you may record that a winger made 50 dribbles in the match, but only 30 led to an end product (a 60 per cent success rate).

Saves

For goalkeepers in sports, saves are an important performance criterion. This criterion can be analysed using success (i.e. saved the ball) or failure (i.e. attempted to save but was unsuccessful) and you could then look at more detail, such as any particular areas where the goalkeeper has differing success rates (for example, low–right, high–right, low–left, high–left) which could then be used to develop any necessary training programmes for the goalkeeper.

1.2 Notational analysis

Notational analysis is used by sport scientists to collect objective data on the performance of athletes. You can use notational analysis to observe tactics, technique, individual athlete movement and work rate, which can then help coaches and athletes to learn more about performance and gain an advantage over their opponents.

Movement

Think about when you have watched sport on television and they show lots of statistics and diagrams that show a player's distance covered in a game or the directions they have made most of their runs in. These are different examples of the term 'movement' that is used in sports. Other factors to look at when examining a player's movement include:

- work rate (for example, measuring heart rate using heart rate monitors)
- positional play and movement pattern (for example, how well a player fulfils the positional roles in a team or the movements a player performs during a game)
- distance covered (for example, how far a player has travelled during a game, sometimes broken down into walking, jogging and sprinting)
- movement patterns.

The image below shows an example of how the movement patterns and positional play of an athlete can be analysed.

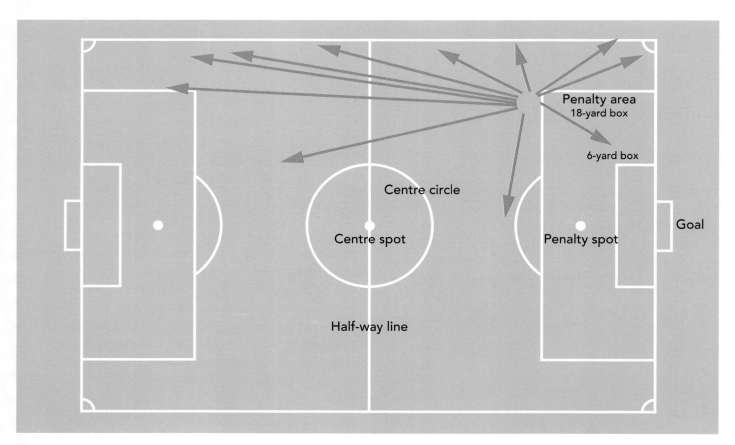

Figure 6.1: How can analysing the movement of players during a game assist managers and coaches?

Performance criteria

A central part of notational analysis is selecting the performance criteria (see page 142) to assess the sporting performance.

Statistics and data analysis

In Unit 4 Research methods for sport and exercise sciences, you learned how to analyse data using appropriate descriptive (for example, mean, median, mode, standard deviation) and inferential (for example, parametric and non-parametric tests) statistics. Use the skills you developed to complete the statistical analysis of the notational analyses. (For example, what was the mean number of shots on target by the team? Was there a significant difference in the performance criteria across the two games?)

Data representation

In Unit 4 Research methods for sport and exercise sciences, you learned how to correctly represent your data (for example, using spreadsheets, tables and databases). Use this information to correctly represent the data from your notational analyses. A useful way to record your data as you are completing the notational analyses is to use tally charts. They are a quick and easy method of recording the number of times you have observed a particular performance (such as a shot on target) which can be transferred into the appropriate table or spreadsheet.

Graphical representation

In Unit 4 Research methods for sport and exercise sciences, you learned about methods of representing data such as bar charts, pie charts and line graphs. Use the appropriate method of graphical representation when completing your notational analysis.

Activity: Analysing goals scored

The data in the table below was produced prior to the Bolton Wanderers versus Manchester United game in the Premier League 2009/10 season. The data shows when each team has scored the majority of their goals throughout the season up to, and including, 26 March 2010.

Scoring minutes	BWFC	MUFC
0–10	5.56% (2)	3.08% (2)
10–20	19.44% (7)	3.08% (2)
20–30	11.11% (4)	4.62% (3)
30–40	8.33% (3)	10.77% (7)
40–50	16.67% (6)	13.85% (9)
50–60	5.56% (2)	13.85% (9)
60–70	11.11% (4)	15.38% (10)
70–80	8.33% (3)	12.31% (8)
80–90	13.89% (5)	16.92% (11)

- Why is it appropriate to display this information in a table?
- What types of statistics are used in the table?
- What types of graphs or charts could be used to represent this data? When you have chosen which you think is best, produce your chart and see if it shows what you want it to.
- How could sports coaches use this information to benefit performance?

Assessment activity 6.1

You are starting a job as a performance analyst. After your first week in the post, the performance director asks you to analyse the upcoming games for your team.

1. Describe the five performance criteria that you have decided on as the start of a notational analysis process. **P1**

2. Conduct two notational analyses of your chosen sport using the performance criteria selected. **P2**

3. When you have collected the data through the notational analysis, compare the results of the two notational analyses using appropriate statistics, data representation and graphical representation; and then use literature to explain the strengths and areas for improvement for the team you have analysed. **M1**

4. Finally, evaluate the findings, looking at how they could be used to influence the performance of the team. **D1**

Grading tips

- To attain **P1** describe the five most important performance criteria for the sport you are examining.

- To attain **P2** it would be good to just analyse a section of each of the events you are analysing as full matches can be very difficult to analyse on your own.

- To attain **M1** you should appropriately analyse and display your result, then use literature (such as appropriate books, journals and websites) to explain the team's strengths and areas for improvement.

- To attain **D1** you should use the findings of the notational analysis to provide recommendations to improve team performance.

PLTS

If you ask questions to extend your thinking, you could develop your skills as a **critical thinker**.

Functional skills

If you use numerical information to feed back to your athlete or team, you could provide evidence of your **Mathematics** skills.

2. Be able to compare a numerical model to sporting performance

Numerical models (sometimes known as quantitative models) use numerical data to tell you the ideal performance level that you would like to achieve and give you something that you can compare your performance against. For example, a javelin coach may look at the velocity of release, height of release and the angle of release of their javelin throwers against a model performance to provide them with specific feedback (such as, 'Your javelin is "nose diving" because your angle of release is too big. Therefore, you need to reduce your angle of release by seven degrees to get a better flight path.').

Key term

Numerical model – a model of sport performance based on numerical factors.

Remember

To produce your numerical model, you will need to use the numerical factors that are appropriate to the sport performance you want to analyse.

2.1 Numerical model production

There are three ways of producing numerical (and technical – see page 158) models: literature-based, athlete-based or combined approaches.

Literature-based

Literature-based models are based on information found in journal articles, key textbooks, coaching publications and literature from websites. Once you know the key numerical factors that you would like to assess, you can research the ideal values for each of the numerical factors and place them in a numerical model of ideal performance.

> **Remember**
>
> If you are using literature to produce your numerical model, you need to make sure that the numerical values are from a valid and reliable source.

Athlete-based models

Athlete-based models can be based around elite athletes or other specific athletes. For example, if you wanted a numerical model of the ideal tennis serve, you could watch a video of Rafael Nadal and then analyse the different numerical factors in that serve. Alternatively, you could monitor your performance against a model based on your own performance. This can be particularly useful if you have been through a long injury period as you could compare current performance to pre-injury performance and identify where you need to improve to return to your pre-injury performance levels.

Combination approach

The combination approach involves using information from both literature and observations of athletes to produce your numerical model.

2.2 Numerical components

The numerical components that can influence sport performance fall into one of four categories:

* linear motion
* angular motion
* projectile motion
* measurements of movement.

Before you can understand these categories fully, you must understand two terms: **scalar quantities** and **vector quantities**. A scalar quantity has a magnitude (for example, how big, how fast something is) whereas vector quantities have a magnitude and a direction (for example, how fast you moved up or down).

Linear motion

Linear motion can occur in a straight line (**rectilinear motion**) or in a curved line (**curvilinear motion**). Some sports, such as the 200 metres in athletics, are part rectilinear and part curvilinear as the athlete needs to run in a straight line for one part and then a curved line for another part. When you look at linear motion, you will look at factors such as distance, displacement, speed, velocity and acceleration.

Linear motion factors	
Scalar quantities	**Vector quantities**
Distance	Displacement
Speed	Velocity
Acceleration	Acceleration in a direction

Table 6.1: Linear motion factors separated into scalar and vector quantities.

> **Key terms**
>
> **Scalar quantities** – a quantity that only has a magnitude (for example, speed).
>
> **Vector quantities** – a quantity that has a magnitude and a direction (for example, velocity).
>
> **Rectilinear motion** – movement in a straight line (for example, 100 metre sprint race in athletics).
>
> **Curvilinear motion** – movement in a curved line (for example, 200 metre sprint race in athletics).

* **Distance and displacement** – when describing linear motion, you can look at distance and displacement. The distance travelled is the sum of all movements regardless of direction whereas displacement is the straight line distance from point A to point B travelled in a particular direction. For example, if you look at a 200 metre sprint race, the sprinter in the inside lane will have sprinted a distance of 200 metres from start to finish, but will have only displaced 123.8 metre at an angle of 36°.

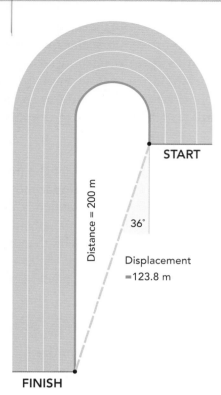

START

Distance = 200 m

36°

Displacement =123.8 m

FINISH

Figure 6.2: Is distance or displacement more important in a 200 metre sprint race?

- **Speed** is how quickly a body moves and is measured in metres per second (m.s⁻¹). You calculate speed by using the equation:

  speed = distance ÷ time

- **Velocity** is how quickly a body has moved and in what resultant direction and is also measured in m.s⁻¹. You calculate velocity by using the equation:

  velocity = displacement ÷ time

You can use this equation to find the average velocity (the velocity over the full race) or velocity during specific parts of a race (for example the velocity from 150 to 200 metres during a 200 metre race).

Remember

Sometimes you may have an average velocity of zero because the displacement is zero (for example, in a 400 metre race the distance travelled is 400 metres but the displacement is zero as you have started and finished in the same place). Therefore it is important to look at changes in velocity during a particular part of the race.

- **Acceleration** is the rate of change of velocity (or speed) and is measured in metres per second per second (m.s⁻²). You calculate acceleration by using the equation:

  change in velocity (or speed) ÷ time

To calculate the change in velocity (or speed), you use the equation:

  final velocity (or speed) – starting velocity (or speed)

Using Newton's laws, can you explain how Usain Bolt starts so quickly and then accelerates between 0 to 50 metres? Do you think it is more important to accelerate at a faster rate or decelerate at a slower rate when you want to win a sprint race?

Case study: Lightning Bolt!

At the IAAF World Championships in Berlin in 2009, Usain Bolt broke the 200 metre world record by running a time of 19.19 seconds. You know that the distance travelled was 200 metres and that the time was 19.19 seconds, so you can calculate the speed using that information.

Calculating speed:

distance (200m) ÷ time (19.19 seconds) = 10.42 m.s^{-1}

You can also calculate the velocity as you know from earlier that the displacement in a 200 metre race is 128.3m at an angle of 36°, so you can calculate velocity using that information.

Calculating average velocity:

displacement (128.3m) ÷ time (19.19 seconds) = 6.68 m.s^{-1} at an angle of 36°

Sometimes you will want to know the velocity or speed at different points during the race to help your performer improve their overall performance. You can calculate these values using the split times (the times for particular parts of the race). Each split time (below) is for a 50 metre interval.

Calculating speed at each interval:

0 – 50m = 5.60 seconds = 8.93 m.s^{-1}

50 – 100m = 4.32 seconds = 11.57 m.s^{-1}

100 – 150m = 4.52 seconds = 11.06 m.s^{-1}

150 – 200m = 4.75 seconds = 10.53 m.s^{-1}

As you know the speed for each of the different stages of the race, you can now calculate the acceleration through each of the different stages. Remember that at the start of a race, the starting velocity is always zero.

Calculating acceleration:

0 – 50m change in speed (8.92 m.s^{-1}) ÷ time (5.60 seconds) = 1.59 m.s^{-2}

50 – 100m change in speed (2.65 m.s^{-1}) ÷ time (4.32 seconds) = 0.61m.s^{-2}

100 – 150m change in speed (-0.51) ÷ time (4.52 seconds) = - 0.12m.s^{-2}

150 – 200m change in speed (-0.54 m.s^{-1}) ÷ time (4.75 seconds) = - 0.11m.s^{-2}

1. **Where do you get the greatest rate of acceleration and why?**

2. **Why is Usain Bolt's time from 100 to 200 metres faster than his time from 0 to 100 metres?**

3. **Where do you get the greatest speed or velocity during a race?**

4. **At what distance do you think fatigue starts to set in during the race?**

5. **How could you get a more precise measurement of speed, velocity and acceleration over 200 metres?**

Newton's laws

Sir Isaac Newton was a scientist who discovered important things such as gravity. He produced three laws that are essential if you are going to understand linear motion.

- **Newton's first law (the law of inertia)** says that every body will remain at rest or in uniform motion unless compelled to change by a force.

- **Newton's second law (the law of acceleration)** says that the acceleration of a body is proportional to the force causing the acceleration, and the acceleration takes place in the direction that the force acts.

- **Newton's third law (the law of action/reaction)** states that for every action, there is an equal and opposite reaction.

Angular motion

How can you stop a tennis player from returning your serve well? You can answer this question using the quantities of angular motion.

You can use the same quantities to explain angular motion as you did for linear motion. However, in this section they become angular displacement, angular velocity and angular acceleration.

To understand angular motion, you need to understand how angular motion is created. This is achieved through knowing about planes and axes of movement and understanding the terms torque and eccentric force, which are explained on page 152.

Case study: Planes and axes of movement

Human movements are based on planes and axes of movement. There are three planes known as the:

- **sagittal plane** – splits the body into imaginary left and right halves
- **frontal plane** – separates the body into imaginary front to back halves
- **transverse plane** – splits the body into imaginary top to bottom halves.

An **axis** is an imaginary straight line around which you rotate when you move. There are three axes of rotation (see Figure 6.3):

- **vertical axis** – is an imaginary line drawn from your head to your toe
- **sagittal axis** – is an imaginary line drawn from your back to your front

- **transverse axis** – is an imaginary line drawn from left to right.

So, using Figure 6.3 and the descriptions above, you can see that:

- Tom Daley performing a tuck front somersault as part of his dive would be moving about the sagittal plane around the frontal axis.
- Lionel Messi performing a Maradona turn would be moving about the transverse plane around the vertical axis.
- Beth Tweddle performing a cartwheel in her floor routine would move about the frontal plane around the sagittal axis.

1. **Can you describe any more sporting actions using the planes and axes of motion?**

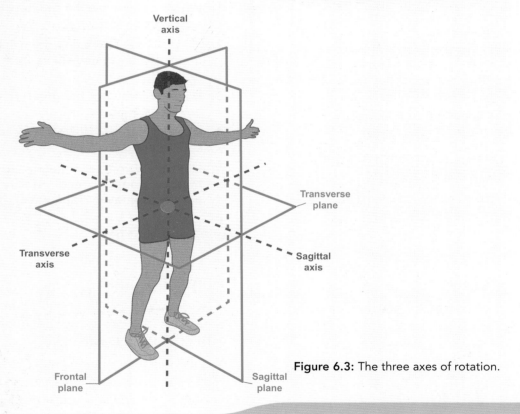

Figure 6.3: The three axes of rotation.

Take it further

Exploring combinations of plane and axis

Figures 6.4, 6.5 and 6.6 show the different movements that occur in the different planes and axes of motion. Using these diagrams, think of at least three different sporting actions for each combination of plane and axis.

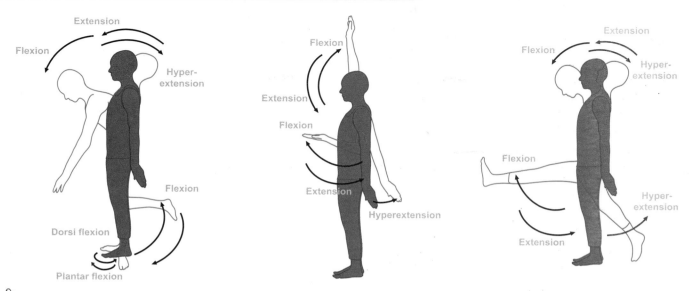

 Figure 6.4: Movements in the sagittal plane about the frontal axis.

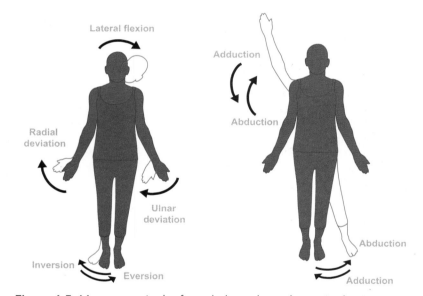

Figure 6.5: Movements in the frontal plane about the sagittal axis.

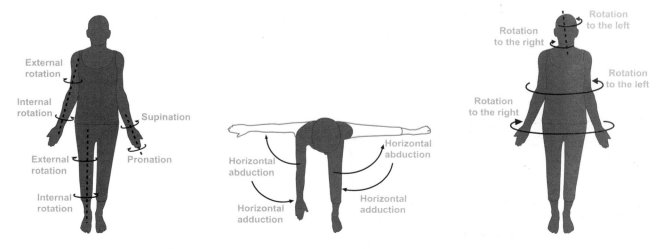

Figure 6.6: Movements in the transverse plane about the horizontal axis.

- **Torque** is the turning effect of an applied force. It is created when a force is applied at a distance from the axis of rotation of an object. As torque is the product of the size of the force and the distance from the axis, the further away you apply the force, the greater the torque will be.

- **Eccentric force** – to move on an angle, the force that is creating the movement has to be applied outside the centre of mass of an individual rather than through it. This 'off centre' force is known as the eccentric force.

- **Angular displacement** is the rotation of a body around an axis and is usually measured in degrees. If the direction of the rotation is stated, then the term angular displacement is used. Angular displacement is measured in radians (rad) and one radian is equivalent to 57.3°. For example, a 360° motion would equate to 6.28 rad.

- **Angular velocity** is the angle through which a body travels in one second and is measured in radians per second (rad.s^{-1}). Angular velocity is calculated using the equation:

    angular displacement (radians) ÷ time taken

- **Angular acceleration** is the rate of change of angular velocity and is measured in radians per second per second (rad.s^{-2}). You calculate angular acceleration by using the equation:

    change in angular velocity ÷ time

Activity: Tennis serving

Earlier, you were asked how you could stop a tennis player from returning your serve well. If you can aim your serve so that it lands close into their body so that your opponent cannot swing their racquet at the ball effectively, they are going to create less torque (as there is a shorter distance) which means that they won't be able to hit the ball back as fast or with as much spin, thus making it easier for you to maintain control of the rally or win the point!

- **Can you think of any other sports where this could be a key factor in performance?**

Analysing Tom Daley's back somersault

Using the concepts of angular motion, you can work out how quickly Tom Daley performs a back somersault as part of his dive 6 in the 2009 world championships. It took Tom approximately 0.4 seconds to go through one full back somersault (a 360° movement or 6.28 rad).

You can now work out how quickly he went through the somersault.

To calculate angular velocity:

angular displacement (6.28 rad) ÷ time taken (0.2 seconds) = 15.7 rad.s^{-1}

Tom had a starting angular velocity of 0 rad.s^{-1} and a final angular velocity of 15.7 rads.s^{-1}.

You can now calculate his angular acceleration through his first back somersault.

To calculate angular acceleration:

change in angular velocity (15.7 rad.s^{-1}) ÷ time taken (0.4 seconds) = 39.25 rad.s^{-2}

Take it further

Newton's laws of angular motion

Just as there are laws to explain linear motion, Newton's laws of motion can be adapted to explain angular motion.

- *Newton's first law of motion* says that a rotating body will continue to turn about its axis of rotation with constant momentum unless an external couple or eccentric force is exerted upon it. For example, a figure skater will continue to spin quickly in circles unless they redistribute their mass. This can be achieved by them extending their arms out.

- *Newton's second law of motion* says that the angular acceleration of a body is proportional to the torque causing it and takes place in the direction in which the torque acts. For example, a gymnast will try to create greater torque while preparing for a difficult dismount from the high bar.

- *Newton's third law of motion* says that for every torque that is exerted by one body on another, there is an equal and opposite torque exerted by the second body on the first. For example, in the long jump, the legs are brought forwards and upwards to land which makes the arms come forwards and downwards.

1. **Can you think of how these laws of motion could be applied to different types of sporting movements?**

Projectile motion

Projectile motion relates to the motion of an object (such as a javelin or a human being) that has been projected into the air. In most athletic events that involve projectile motion (such as the javelin and the long jump) the most important performance criterion is the distance the object travels before hitting the ground (or the maximum height achieved if thinking about high jump or pole vault). The distance travelled (or height achieved) by the object is dependent upon three major performance criteria:

- angle of release (also known as projection angle)
- velocity of release/velocity of take off
- height of release/height of take off.

- **The angle of release** is the angle between the projectile's velocity vector and the horizontal at the instant of release or take off. Different sports require different angles of release. Figure 6.7 shows that theoretically, if the height of release and velocity of release are the same, an angle of release of 45° is the angle that provides optimal performance. However, in sports that require maximum horizontal distance, such as the long jump, smaller angles are required. In comparison, in sports like the high jump where height is key, the optimal angle is larger.

- **The velocity of release** is recorded at the instance of release (for example, when the long jumper leaves the take off board).

- **The height of release** is the distance from the ground (in metres) at which the object leaves the thrower. If the angle and velocity of release are the same for two shot putters, the athlete who has a greater height of release will have a longer flight time and, therefore, record a greater range.

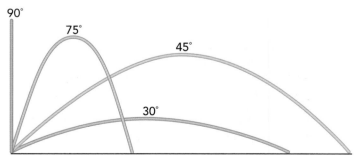

Figure 6.7: What do you think will happen to the projectile if the angle of release is too great or too small?

Measurement of movement

Different measurements of movement are important aspects of performance. You may want to include these in your numerical model.

- **Range of movement** – successful technique and performance is based on an athlete performing the correct movements at specific joints (for example, flexion and extension). As a sports biomechanist, you can analyse the range (in degrees) of the movement during the performance. For example, you may consider:
  - elbow extension during the shot put
  - knee extension during an instep kick in football
  - hip rotation during the golf swing.

- **The centre of gravity** is an imaginary point at which the weight of an object (for example, the athlete) can be considered to act. Objects with a low centre of gravity have better balance and are more difficult to tip over. If you stand in the anatomical position, your centre of gravity is around your belly button, but this point is constantly changing. For example, if you raise an arm above your head, your centre of gravity will move upwards; sometimes, the centre of gravity can actually be outside the body, such as in the 'Fosbury Flop' technique in high jump (see Figure 6.8).

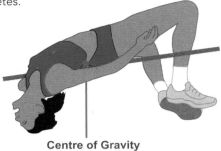

Centre of Gravity

Figure 6.8: How does the centre of gravity move outside a body and how can it benefit performance?

- **Limb angles and goniometry** – direct measurement of joint angles can be made using a goniometer. It is plastic or metal and comes in different sizes depending on which joint requires assessment. The range of motion at a joint is measured by placing the centre of the goniometer at the axis of rotation of the joint. The arms of the goniometer (similar to a basic ruler) are lined up with the long axis of the specified bones. After the athlete has made the movement, the change in position is recorded by measuring the angle in degrees on the goniometer. Another method to measure a joint angle is to record the image and then take the reading off the display. The angle, in basic terms, can be seen by using an acetate and marker pen to draw the lines of the two relevant bones. You should then be able to record the angle using a protractor.

2.3 Methodology

When you have decided which performance criteria you are interested in assessing, you may have to record the image(s). This allows you to take the data from the recording after the performance. This is important because sport is dynamic and fast moving, and as the tester, you won't always be able to record all the data at once.

Two-dimensional (2D) recording

You will probably record your athlete using two-dimensional filming in your school or college. In comparison to three-dimensional filming, two-dimensional filming:

- is quicker at recording the images
- is faster to extract the relevant data from the images
- requires less sophisticated software
- requires less technical and mathematical knowledge.

Two-dimensional filming allows you to film the athlete with consideration of the width and height of the image, but not the depth.

Measuring

- **Horizontal scaling** – before you start filming, you should scale the **field of view**. The field of view is the area that will be filmed that contains the sporting action. You will need to record a tester by placing a 1-metre rule in the field of view to scale the image. Once you have scaled your image, do not move the camera or use the manual focus as the scaling will be incorrect and will lead to invalid data. The scaling allows you to take measurements from the playback and convert them to real-life measurements. For example, if you are interested in the stride length of a long jumper, you may calculate that: 1 metre (real life) = 2 cm on screen. Therefore if you have recorded that the stride length on screen is 4 cm, using the scaling process means the real-life stride length was 2 metres.
- **Vertical reference** – the principle of vertical reference is the same as horizontal scaling. The vertical plane may be useful in activities based around vertical movement (for example, the high jump).

- **Perspective error** – when filming your athlete there is a chance that your recording may have perspective error because you are filming a dynamic action. This is easily explained using a 100 metre sprinter. You may be interested in recording the time at 10-metre intervals, with the camera positioned at the 50 metre point. Figure 6.8 shows that you would need to film the athlete going through all the points at 10-metre intervals. The perspective error can be seen at the 80 metre point as the camera is not in a direct line with the athlete so you cannot say exactly when the athlete reaches the 80 metre point. How do you think you could resolve this problem?

Key terms

Horizontal scaling – providing a scale of measurement that will allow you to convert on screen measurements to real-life measurements.

Field of view – the area you are recording that contains the sporting action.

Vertical reference – as for horizontal scaling, but on a vertical plane.

Perspective error – an error where objects seem to get bigger or smaller as they move towards and away from the camera and you can't effectively judge their position.

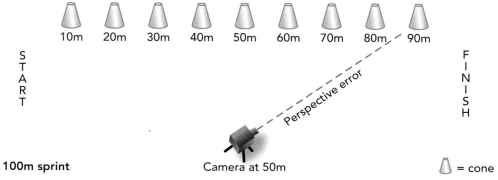

Figure 6.9: How can the wrong camera position produce invalid or unreliable data?

Activity: Numerical model of long jump

There is a variety of numerical factors important for the long jump. Three key factors are the velocity of run up, stride length and take off angle. They could be placed into a numerical model similar to the one here to allow you to analyse the performance of an athlete.

Performance criteria	Desired value	Observed value
Velocity of run up	9 m.s^{-1}	
Stride length	2 metres	
Take off angle	20° – 22°	

Using the numerical model above and the recording techniques outlined in the methodology section, record a friend doing the long jump and compare their performance to the numerical model.

- **How does their performance compare to the 'desired' performance?**

- **Can you suggest any training or coaching points that would allow them to improve their performance?**

Remember

To get the most accurate and valid images, it is important that you consider issues such as horizontal scaling, vertical referencing and perspective error when recording your image.

Case study: Analysing the shot putt

You can use the techniques of numerical modelling and video recording to analyse performances such as the shot put. In Figure 6.10, you can see how the performance criteria of height of release, angle of release and velocity of release could be analysed using a simple video recording and some clear plastic or thin paper. Figure 6.10a shows how you can highlight key points from two different frames of video and 6.10b shows how these can then be used to analyse performance.

The technique used to analyse this diagram is outlined below:

- Horizontally and vertically scale the filming.
- Record the shot put.
- Play the film back, pausing it at the point of release of the shot.
- Place a piece of thin plastic or clear paper over the screen and mark on the toe and hand – you can then measure the distance between the two to give you the height of release.
- Next, mark the position of the shot on your sheet.
- Move the film on one frame and mark on the position of the shot on your sheet again.

- Join the two dots using a ruler and pencil, then measure the distance of the line – you can then calculate the velocity of release.
- Draw a horizontal straight line on your paper from the shot in frame 1. You will then be able to use the two lines you have drawn (as can be seen in Figure 6.10b) to measure the angle of release using a protractor.

For this example, you can assume that the two frames of video are 0.04 seconds apart; that 2 cm on the screen is equal to 1 metre (horizontal) and that 1 cm is equivalent to 1 metre (vertical) in real life.

Calculating height of release: if the distance between the toe mark and the hand mark is 1.8 cm on screen, you can convert that to 1.8 metres in real distance which means that the height of release is 1.8 metres.

Calculating velocity of release: if the distance travelled by the shot between frame 1 and frame 2 on screen is 1.2 cm horizontally, you can then scale that to 0.62 metres in real distance. As you know that the time taken to travel that distance is 0.04 seconds, you can then calculate the release velocity: $0.62 \div 0.04 = 15.5 \text{m.s}^{-1}$.

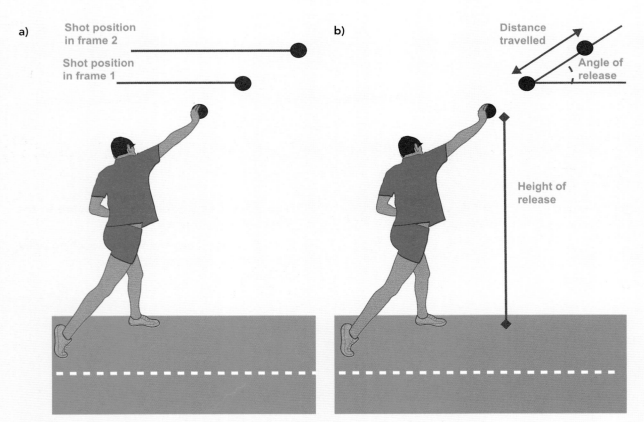

a) Shot position in frame 2
Shot position in frame 1

b) Distance travelled
Angle of release
Height of release

Figure 6.10: a) image without example analysis, b) image with example analysis.

Assessment activity 6.2

You have just started working as a biomechanist for a local sports club. They have asked you to produce a numerical model to compare performance against and want you to explain how and why you have produced the model in that way.

1. Choose a sport and produce a model that has three numerical components that allows you to compare observed performance criteria to a desired level of performance. **P3**

2. Then compare the model to a performance. **P3**

3. Explain and justify the methodology that you have followed to produce and compare the model. **M2**

4. After this, evaluate the findings of your observations, looking at the implications of your findings for future performance. **D1**

Grading tips

- To attain **P3** produce a model that includes three different numerical factors and compare it to an observed sport performance.

- To attain **M2** say how you collected your data, how you produced your model and why they were suitable methods.

- To attain **D1** look at how your findings could be used to benefit the athlete. For example, if you looked at the take off angle in long jump as one of your performance criteria, you could look at how changing the take off angle could improve performance.

PLTS

If you plan and carry out research to produce your numerical model, you could develop skills as an **independent enquirer**.

Functional skills

If you present a model that is fit for purpose, you could provide evidence of your **ICT** skills.

3   Be able to compare a technical model to sporting performance

3.1 Technical model production

Earlier you looked at how to produce a numerical model of performance (page 147). Producing a technical model is similar to numerical modelling but here you are looking at the technique used by the athlete and – in most cases – do not consider numerical aspects. Therefore, your model will be more **qualitative** in nature, will **describe** the athlete's performance more and will be more **subjective**.

Key terms

Qualitative model – a model that uses words, rather than numbers, to examine performance.

Descriptive – saying what you see in the sport performance.

Subjective – a performance analysis based on your own opinion.

While all of the technical models for sports are different, the way you produce the model (the way you draw the model out) will be the same. Use the model in Figure 6.11 as a guide for producing the overall model (you can see a sport-specific example later).

Remember

Technical modelling uses the same approach that a coach may use to comment on the performance of an athlete. A football coach may inform a player to keep their head down when shooting. Although there is no statistical data to support this, the coach has years of experience which provide valid information. As a sports biomechanist, the more you analyse performance the easier it will be to make subjective comments.

3.2 Technical component

The technical components that you will look at in your technical model are dependent on the sport or activity you have chosen. You may produce your technical model around 'coaching points' of the different sports or activities based on the key performance criteria for that sport. Throughout this section, you will see examples of different technical components linked to different sports.

Body position

One of the most important aspects from a technical perspective is the body position of the athlete. If you consider the golf swing, every stage must be coordinated and executed correctly.

Footwork

A tennis player's movement on the court is vital. Tennis performance depends on quick bursts of speed interspersed with variations of fast side-to-side movements. It also depends on the player's ability to make necessary adjustments as they get to the ball to maintain balance throughout the stroke. Statistics show that 70 per cent of missed or poorly hit shots are due to poor footwork. These components are important for footwork in tennis and can be analysed using descriptive terms:

- starting position when ball is struck
- acceleration to the ball
- agility
- balance
- stride length
- stride frequency.

Balance

Static and dynamic balance are basic skills needed in practically every sport and exercise activity. From football to cricket, changing your centre of gravity to match your moves is the key to skill execution.

Grip

In some sports, one important technical aspect that influences an athlete's performance is grip. The grip is important for a golfer or javelin thrower. The importance of placing the hands in the correct position

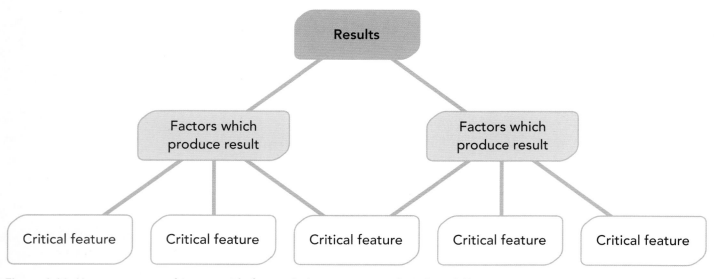

Figure 6.11: How can you use this as a guide for producing your own technical model?

on the golf club cannot be over-exaggerated. There is no such thing as the perfect grip, but there are factors when holding the club in an orthodox way that have proved to be successful for the majority of players. A 'V' must be formed on the right hand by the thumb and lower section of the forefinger, pointing between the chin and the right shoulder, and only two knuckles are visible on the left hand to the player.

Stance

In martial arts such as judo and combat sports such as boxing, the stance (the position of the body, particularly the feet) of the athlete is paramount. These types of sport require good balance and coordination, combined with the optimal stance. Failure to do this results in a loss of balance, which gives the opponent a big advantage. Within boxing, the most important factor when considering the stance is perfect balance, enabling the boxer to move quickly and smoothly, to shift the weight constantly from one leg to another and punch effectively. The stance recommended is flexible and allows a boxer to attack or defend, move in or out, lead or counterpunch. An example stance could be:

1. The left foot is flat on the floor and turned inwards slightly.
2. Both legs are bent slightly – the left is relatively straight, but the knee is not locked.
3. The right foot should be offset to the right of the midline of the body to afford a firm base.
4. The right heel is raised with the right knee bent and weight taken on the ball of the foot.
5. The left side of the body forms an approximate straight line with the left leg. The trunk should be kept as upright as possible to allow the hips and shoulders to pivot when punching.
6. The body weight is evenly distributed between both feet and acts through an imaginary line running through the centre of the trunk, which acts as the pivot.
7. The left hand is carried loosely clenched about shoulder height in front of the body (the distance from the body is entirely personal) and the elbow is tucked in comfortably.
8. The right hand is carried with the palm open towards the opponent at shoulder height, directly in front of the right shoulder.
9. Elbows should be tucked in comfortably to offer protection to the ribs.
10. The chin is dropped towards the chest; the opponent should be watched through the eyebrows.

Passing

Although passing is a general technical term, each sport uses a different action to complete a pass. For example, a pass in football is different from one in rugby.

Kicking

The following six key stages detail a kicking action, which is general in nature to football, rugby league and union, plus many others. Within each sport, a variety of kicking styles has evolved to suit different ball types, game rules and the part that kicking plays in the game. You can break the kick action into six stages:

- the approach
- planting of standing foot
- start of movement (kicking foot)
- hip flexion and knee extension (kicking foot)
- foot contact with ball
- follow-through.

Shooting

Shooting is another technical component required in lots of sports. Here are some technical points associated with shooting in netball.

- Keep your balance, find your aim and use your whole body to make the shot.
- Have a clear view of the ring.
- Stand with your feet a shoulder width apart and keep your body straight.
- Balance the ball on the fingertips of one hand and use your other hand to steady it.
- Bend your knees.
- Keep your back straight and your head up. As you prepare to release the ball, drop your hands back behind your head.
- Try to focus on a point at the back rather than the front of the ring, and let the ball go at the same time as you straighten your legs.

- Move your arms as little as possible when you release the ball.
- End your shot standing on tiptoes with your arms following through towards the ring.

Throwing

Throwing is a central component for many sports (such as cricket, American football, football). Due to the differences in the type of ball (in addition to the reason for throwing), there are different techniques for the different sports. Within cricket, throwing is a key aspect of fielding and leads to run outs, and can also save runs for the fielding side. The technical basics for throwing the ball in cricket are as follows.

- Once the ball is in your throwing hand, stand sideways to the wickets.
- Pull the throwing hand so it is behind your head.
- Aim your non-throwing hand at the wickets.
- Push the throwing arm through, keeping the elbow joint at a similar height as the shoulder joint.
- Turn the chest to the target and release the ball from a firm standing position.

Catching

One of the most difficult balls to catch in sport is the high kick in rugby. It is an important skill every rugby player should learn. As it is likely that the opposition will be surrounding you, you will need to catch the ball in the air. Before you leave the ground look at the surrounding area so that you are aware of what is happening. Bear in mind the following technical points.

- Call for the ball so that another player from your team does not jump for it.
- Get into a direct line with the ball's path (this will be difficult when the wind is blowing).
- Start to reach out your arms towards the direction of the ball.
- Bend your elbows slightly – to ready yourself for the impact of the ball.
- Make sure you are side on – to soften the blow from an oncoming tackle.
- Catch the ball at or above eye level, then bring it into your hands, then your body – so it is less likely to be knocked from your body (when back on the ground).

Fielding

In cricket, when fielding you should 'attack' the ball (move towards the ball if it is hit towards you, rather than standing still and waiting for it). If you can do this, it puts more doubt in the batsman's mind.

- As the bowler is running in to bowl, you as the fielder should start walking in from a few steps behind your original fielding position.
- When the bowler releases the ball, stop and 'spring' with your knees. This allows you to transfer your weight off either foot, enabling you to react to the left or the right.
- The main technique used to stop balls along the ground is called the 'long barrier'. This occurs when your body forms a 'barrier' behind the ball, giving you the best chance of stopping the ball. Keep your eye on the ball until it reaches you, as it could be costly.

Batting

In cricket, there are many shots that require a high level of technical ability. For example, in a forward defensive shot the aim is to put the bat in front of the wicket to stop the ball from hitting the wicket. This shot has no strength behind it, is usually played with a light or soft bottom-hand grip and merely stops the ball moving towards the wicket. The basic technical points are as follows.

- The head and front shoulder should lean into the line of the ball.
- The front leg should stride towards the pitch of the ball, bending to take the weight.
- The back leg remains straight.
- The bat should swing down and make contact with the ball beneath the eyes.
- The face of the bat should be angled towards the ground.

Striking

The term 'striking' relates to sports such as rounders or baseball. The player usually strikes the ball as far as possible or to a specific area of the field of play to gain an advantage.

Figure 6.12: What do you think would be the key performance elements of other shots in cricket?

Dribbling

In dribbling, there must be an end product, for example a shot at the goal or basket depending on the sport. From a technical perspective, the key elements for dribbling in basketball are outlined below.

- Spread your fingers evenly and cup your hand over the basketball (it is almost like you are trying to palm the basketball, although your palm does not touch the basketball).

- The only parts of your hand that touch the basketball are the bases and seams of the fingers.

- As you dribble the basketball, keep your upper body fairly steady while moving your forearm up and down as you push the basketball to the floor with a wrist snap.

- Dribble the basketball by pushing it down to the floor, then lower your hand to receive the basketball (suck it off the floor).

- When the basketball touches your hand, raise your forearm slightly to absorb the dribbling pressure. Release the basketball as you push it down again.

- Move forward on the balls of your feet and bend your knees to maintain your balance.

- Keeping your body over the ball will help to shield it from your opponents.

Sprinting

Sprinting is a key aspect of many team sports (for example, the football winger who sprints after the ball to make a cross). However, the technique for sprinting in athletics (100 metre, 200 metre, etc.) is completely different and requires special consideration. The sprinting technique can be split into seven separate phases.

1. Pre-race start (block position).
2. On your marks (fingers behind the line).
3. Set position (eyes focused on the track).
4. Go (driving of the arms).
5. Acceleration (face and neck muscles relaxed).
6. Drive (on the balls of your feet).
7. Finish (dip for the line at the appropriate point).

Stride length and frequency

Two key elements in the sprint technique are stride length and stride frequency. Stride length is defined as the distance the athlete covers with each stride (measured in metres). In comparison, stride frequency is the number of strides made in a specific time (one second).

Jumping

In track and field, there are a number of jumping events (such as the long jump, triple jump, high jump and pole vault) where there are five clear phases to the performance:

- run up
- take off and release
- flight phase
- landing phase
- recovery phase.

To make the performance successful, the athlete must execute all five phases correctly with a good level of transition between the stages. These events are described as being highly technical, since if the athlete has a poor technique in one phase, it can have a knock-on effect with the other stages.

You will only cover the long jump in relation to the five phases identified. However, the key elements described are also applicable to the other events (for example, body position at take off).

Figure 6.13: How could you use technical modelling to assess the long jump?

Run up

The key aim for the long jump is to obtain the greatest horizontal distance possible without making a foul jump. You will now cover the key technical aspects (highlighting numerical factors where possible). In the long jump you could say that the athlete with the greatest sprinting speed has a huge advantage in the run up. Yet, this is not always the case because the run up depends on other factors. As the sports biomechanist, you may consider the run up speed. From a technical perspective you should look for:

- stride consistency during the sprinting stage (excluding the last three to four strides)
- a trunk which is brought upright (or close to upright) during these last three to four strides
- a lowered centre of gravity in the final few strides
- increased stride length of the second to last stride
- a decreased stride on the last stride
- accuracy at take off (i.e. where they hit the take off board).

Take off

In take off, the athlete wants to gain vertical lift while retaining as much vertical speed as possible generated during the run up stage. When assessing performance, look for the following points at take off.

- The take off foot should be a heel strike (for most athletes).
- The take off leg should show some flexion at the hip, knee and ankle joints for cushioning the high impact.
- The centre of gravity should move from behind to over the take off point.
- The lead leg, coupled with the arms at take off, should drive in an explosive upward motion.
- Height of take off (numerical).
- Angle of take off (numerical).
- Speed at take off (numerical).

Release phase

During this key phase the athlete must maintain the optimum body position. Due to the take off or release phase (released from the take off board) the athlete, to some extent, will be fighting forward rotation. The forward rotation will bring the legs back underneath the athlete and therefore, when landing, will reduce the horizontal distance.

Flight phase

As with other track and field events, there are different techniques that the athlete may use to maximise performance during the flight phase. These are the sail, the hitch kick and the hang.

Landing

As in most sports, the difference between winning and losing is very small and, in this case, centimetres make the difference. A few centimetres can be gained or lost due to the landing phase. When considering the landing phase look for the following.

- In the last stages of the flight phase, the athlete should lean forward as this raises the legs.
- The knees should be flexed at the landing point for shock absorption.
- After landing, the athlete should push their head forward to aid forward rotation (so they do not fall backwards into the pit).

Recovery phase

The athlete knows the importance of the recovery process although it is a small phase in comparison to the other four. After landing the athlete should leave the pit without making a mark (before the landing mark). The rules state that if the athlete falls back into the pit towards the take off board, then the mark made would be recorded as the final distance.

Comparing your model to performance

After you have produced your technical model based on your technical components, compare your performance to the desired performance. This can be done easily using a table where you have the technical component, a description of the desired performance and a space for you to write the observed performance (see Assessment activity 6.3).

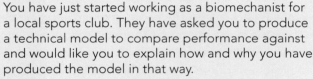

Assessment activity 6.3   P4 M2 D1   BTEC

You have just started working as a biomechanist for a local sports club. They have asked you to produce a technical model to compare performance against and would like you to explain how and why you have produced the model in that way.

1. Produce a technical model for a sport of your choice that has four technical components and then compare the model to a performance. **P4**

2. Explain and justify the methodology that you have followed to produce and compare the model. **M2**

3. After this, evaluate the findings of your observations, looking at the implications of your findings for future performance. **D1**

Grading tips

- To attain **P4** produce a model that includes four different technical components and compare it to an observed sport performance.

- To attain **M2** say how you collected your data, how you produced your model and say why they were suitable methods.

- To attain **D1** look at how your findings could be used to benefit the athlete. For example, if you looked at the point of contact with the ball as one of your technical components, you could look at how changing the point and type of contact could improve kicking performance.

PLTS

If you ask questions to extend your thinking, you could develop your skills as a **critical thinker**.

Functional skills

If you read a variety of documents when researching your technical model, you could provide evidence of your skills in **English**.

4. Be able to provide feedback on performance to an athlete or team

4.1 Feedback

You must be able to feed back to your athlete or team regarding their performance. There are a number of factors to consider when feeding back to your athlete including:

- confidentiality
- appropriate use of language – make it athlete-/coach-friendly
- strengths and areas for improvement
- positive and negative feedback
- clarity of information
- type of feedback (for example, written or verbal)
- having evidence to support the feedback you are providing
- acknowledgement of biomechanical limitations
- any other factors that have influenced performance.

Confidentiality

Make sure that all data you collect from your athletes remains confidential (see Unit 4 Research methods for sport and exercise sciences).

Appropriate use of language

When providing feedback to the athlete or coach you should make the information friendly and easy to understand. Therefore, consider the following points.

- Consider the use of language – avoid using over-technical points unless the athlete and coach are used to this level of technicality.
- Provide the feedback in stages and break it down – avoid too much information in one session.
- Avoid excessive amounts of text and numbers – use sparingly by using the key information only.
- Avoid an over reliance on tables, charts, etc. as too many can lead to confusion.
- Provide a report after verbal feedback to allow for reflection at a later date.

Strengths and areas for improvement

Always look for both strengths and areas for improvement when working with your client. When looking at strengths and areas for improvement consider:

- past performances (look for a pattern or profile)
- the influences on performance (such as motivation)
- separating the individual's strengths from the team's strengths
- the ability of the athlete and competition
- what the athlete needs to develop first (this will be the things that affect performance most significantly).

Positive and negative feedback

Positive feedback is what you give when the outcome of an event is what you wanted (for example, a player has improved their shot technique). Provide positive feedback quickly after the event, make it very specific and provide more detailed feedback if required. Avoid using too much positive feedback as this could lead to your athlete undervaluing the feedback and suffering motivation reductions. Negative feedback is often what the athlete receives when the outcome of the event was not desired (for example, a player sent off at a critical point of the game). Rather than taking this as an opportunity to criticise your athlete, you should help the athlete learn through it by producing specific action plans and providing specific feedback.

Clarity of information

Make sure that the information you give your athlete is simple and easy to follow and provides them with sufficient detail to help them develop. Too much scientific jargon could baffle them whereas very little detail is useless.

Remember

Summarise your information in graphs, charts or diagrams, rather than using huge amounts of text, to give your feedback greater clarity, making it easier to understand.

Type of feedback

Consider the type of feedback to use with your athlete. Generally, you will give less detailed verbal feedback soon after the event and then follow this up with more detailed written feedback. Make sure that you consider equality factors when working with athletes of different populations such as young children or disabled athletes.

Supporting evidence

There is a term used in sport and exercise science which is 'evidence-based practice'. This means that you should base your recommendations on appropriate sources of information (such as recent books or journals) and that your recommendations are linked directly to your athlete's performance.

Acknowledging biomechanical limitations

No technique you will ever use in sport and exercise science is perfect; everything has its limitations and biomechanics is no different. For example, you could find that your recording techniques have suffered from perspective error. You must consider these limitations when feeding back to your athlete and appreciate the role that these limitations could have played in the results you have obtained.

Any other factors that have influenced performance

Consider other factors such as motivation, injury, age, health, diet, previous training, confidence, ability level, temperature, time of day and group dynamics that could have affected the performance of the athlete. If you do not consider these factors and how they have influenced performance, you could end up providing misleading information or recommendations to your athlete.

4.2 Future actions

Goals and targets

Unit 3 Sport and exercise psychology and Unit 20 Applied sport and exercise psychology look at setting goals (long, medium and short term) and targets (SMARTs) for your athlete. You should use these techniques effectively when you are working with your athlete to develop future actions.

Recommendations

Part of the role of the sports biomechanist is to provide possible recommendations to the athlete and coach. There are a number of factors that you could consider that range from future coaching needs to different elements of fitness training.

- **Priority of future coaching and training** – as part of the feedback process, you need to prioritise future coaching and training sessions. You must be realistic. You can't coach or train all the areas for improvement at once, so base your decisions on:
  o   competition schedule
  o   access to coaches and training facilities
  o   current fitness status
  o   identification of key performance criteria
  o   individual and team-based performance criteria.

- **Team skills and drills** – within this unit you have looked at the key performance criteria for a variety of sports (such as catching, crossing and shooting). You may have identified how the influence of these basic sports skills has affected team skills and drills (for example, how to defend a corner in football). Future action for the team could concentrate on improving these team skills and drills.

- **Individual skills training** – many sports require a number of very precise movements, which require good coordination and application of force. An athlete's training programme must be specific and involve movements that are similar or identical to those performed in competition. The concept of matching training to performance is known as movement pattern specificity. For example, the tennis serve involves the whole body at some point in the movement. Precise training for the speed, power, flexibility, coordination and balance will train the player to make the serve effective. This type of movement pattern training also trains the muscle groups that will be used in competition.

- **Fitness training for specific components of fitness** – one factor which helps the athlete improve their biomechanical performance is to train a specific component of fitness. Fitness can be divided into two parts: health-related fitness and skill-related fitness. Use the information you acquire in Unit 9 Fitness training and programming to develop these recommendations.

• **Technique coaching specific to movement** – a coach who has specialist knowledge within a given sport should be able to improve the athlete's performance from a technical perspective. It is the role of the sports biomechanist to work with the coach in identifying strengths and areas for improvement. The sports biomechanist should continue to work with the coach on a regular basis providing specialist support to maximise the athlete's performance.

Assessment activity 6.4

1. Using any of the analyses that you completed for the previous three assessment activities, produce appropriate feedback for your athlete or team based on that analysis and provide future actions. **P5**

2. You should try to provide detailed feedback. **M3**

3. Justify the future actions for your athlete. **D2**

Grading tips

• To attain **P5** provide feedback that is appropriate for your athlete and include future actions in your feedback. Make sure that your feedback is clear and athlete friendly and considers some of the factors that could have affected performance.

• To attain **M3** include as much detail as you can about their performance when feeding back, highlighting as many specific areas of strength and improvement as possible. Include statistics and data representation, and have goals that are clearly linked to future performance and competition targets.

• To attain **D2** support your future actions by linking them to specific areas for improvement and using appropriate supporting evidence from books, journals or appropriate websites.

PLTS

If you present a persuasive course of action for performance development, you could develop your skills as an **effective participator**.

Functional skills

If you effectively communicate your information through your feedback, you could present evidence of your speaking and writing skills in **English**.

Shelley Kendal

Sports development centre coach

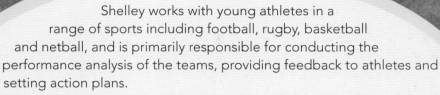

Shelley works with young athletes in a range of sports including football, rugby, basketball and netball, and is primarily responsible for conducting the performance analysis of the teams, providing feedback to athletes and setting action plans.

'Working with the sports development centre is great as I am interested in lots of different sports so I like to get involved in as many as I can. I first became interested in sports biomechanics because I was working with sports teams doing lots of fitness training every week and I thought, "Why are they doing all this fitness training when they're already really fit? Surely there's something else I can look at to help improve their performance?"

'From there, I started looking at analysing technique and tactics more and really saw the benefits of biomechanics that way. I now regularly have both team and individual performance reviews with players so that the coaches and myself can make sure their performance is as close to the model as possible, both in numerical and technical ways.

'Working in so many different sports is very challenging. As well as needing a detailed knowledge of a range of different sports and the requirements of different levels of athletes, I often have to use a range of techniques with different players and different teams – and feed back to players in different ways. Quite often, overly technical language can be confusing for athletes so I need to make sure that I feed back in language that they can understand. All of the athletes have different needs so it is important that I cater for those needs by using effective performance analysis, feedback and goal setting with action plans.'

Think about it!

- Why do you think that you would need to use different techniques with different athletes?
- What techniques would you like to use the most with athletes?
- How could you make sure that you meet the needs of both individuals and teams?

Just checking

1. What does the term 'performance criteria' mean?
2. What is notational analysis?
3. What is meant by the terms 'scalar' and 'vector' quantities?
4. What is the difference between a numerical model and a technical model?
5. What are the different sources of information for numerical and technical models?
6. What are the different numerical components that you could include in a numerical model?
7. What are Newton's Laws of motion?
8. What are the different scaling techniques used when video recording?
9. What are some of the different areas you can comment on when feeding back to athletes?
10. How do you structure your future actions with your client?

Assignment tips

- You may want to supplement your knowledge from this section with more subject specific books, journals and websites; so you could speak to your tutor about different resources that could be appropriate for your level.

- Have you heard the saying 'a picture paints a thousand words'? That phrase certainly applies here! Make your performance assessments and feedback as detailed as possible using different images, graphs and charts, but with as little text as possible.

- Always remember that any mathematical equations used in areas like biomechanics and research methods are basically just shorthand. When you are reading them, if you change the letters in the equation into numbers or words that you understand, the work will seem much easier.

- Try to read the work in such a way that you understand it. You may find it useful to put information into different pictures and flow diagrams to help you understand the different processes that you go through.

- Relate as much of the theory as you can to your favourite sport. This will help you to put the information into a context that you understand better and will stimulate your interest even more!

7 Exercise, health and lifestyle

This unit is particularly relevant to anyone aiming to work in health promotion or the fitness industry. It aims to develop your understanding of a range of different aspects which help maintain health and wellbeing. Good health helps you to achieve your maximum potential. Those who take part in regular physical activity, eat a healthy diet, do not smoke, drink alcohol in moderation and manage their level of stress, are likely to live longer and cope better with the demands of daily life.

You will gain the knowledge and skills to assess an individual's lifestyle, provide advice on lifestyle improvement and plan a health-related physical activity programme. You will explore the physical, social and psychological benefits of regular exercise, as well as barriers to participation, the importance of a balanced diet, not smoking and avoiding stress; and become informed about exercise and lifestyle programming for individuals. You will gain an understanding of behaviour change and models of change that can be adopted in the promotion of improved health behaviour.

Learning outcomes

After completing this unit you should:

1. know the importance of lifestyle factors in the maintenance of health and wellbeing
2. be able to assess the lifestyle of a selected individual
3. be able to provide advice on lifestyle improvement
4. be able to plan a health-related physical activity programme for a selected individual.

Assessment and grading criteria

This table shows you what you must do in order to achieve a pass, merit or distinction grade, and where you can find activities in this book to help you.

To achieve a **pass** grade the evidence must show that you are able to:	To achieve a **merit** grade the evidence must show that, in addition to the pass criteria, you are able to:	To achieve a **distinction** grade the evidence must show that, in addition to the pass and merit criteria, you are able to:
P1 describe lifestyle factors that have an effect on health **See Assessment activity 7.1, page 178**	**M1** explain the effects of identified lifestyle factors on health **See Assessment activity 7.1, page 178**	
P2 design and use a lifestyle questionnaire to describe the strengths and areas for improvement in the lifestyle of a selected individual **See Assessment activity 7.2, page 181**	**M2** explain the strengths and areas for improvement in the lifestyle of a selected individual **See Assessment activity 7.2, page 181**	**D1** evaluate the lifestyle of a selected individual and prioritise areas for change **See Assessment activity 7.2, page 181**
P3 provide lifestyle improvement strategies for a selected individual **See Assessment activity 7.3, page 188**	**M3** explain recommendations made regarding lifestyle improvement strategies **See Assessment activity 7.3, page 188**	**D2** analyse a range of lifestyle improvement strategies **See Assessment activity 7.3, page 188**
P4 plan a six-week health-related physical activity programme for a selected individual **See Assessment activity 7.4, page 194**		

How you will be assessed

This unit will be internally assessed by a range of assignments that will be designed and graded by your tutor. Your assignment tasks will allow you to demonstrate your understanding of the unit learning outcomes and relate to what you should be able to do after completing this unit. Your assignments could be in the form of:

- presentations
- practical tasks
- written assignments
- case studies.

Simon, 18-year-old gym user

I am a keen fitness enthusiast. I am a member of my local health and fitness club and attend three or four times a week. This unit gave me the knowledge and skills required to work as a health and fitness instructor. I particularly enjoyed learning about health and fitness screening and the consultation process. I have adopted the principles of training in my own exercise regimes and have begun to notice the benefits.

The practical tasks and activities made this unit more exciting for me. The bit I enjoyed most was interviewing my client for the assessment activities for the unit. I chose my uncle who has been sedentary and a smoker for much of his adult life. Helping him to explore ways of giving up smoking and embarking on a programme of physical activity has been extremely rewarding.

Over to you!

1. **What aspects of this unit might you find challenging?**
2. **What preparation could you do to overcome these potential challenges?**
3. **What aspect of the unit are you most looking forward to?**

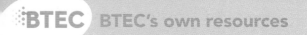

1. Know the importance of lifestyle factors in the maintenance of health and wellbeing

Warm-up

Factors influencing your health and fitness

Take five minutes to think about all the factors that might influence your health and fitness. Awareness of these factors and their effect on health and wellbeing will help you to formulate realistic and achievable lifestyle goals and programmes when meeting some of the assessment requirements of this unit.

1.1 Lifestyle factors

Evidence suggests that leading a healthy lifestyle by following a sensible diet, participating in regular physical activity, maintaining a healthy body weight and avoiding smoking, excessive alcohol consumption and stress, is important to **health** and longevity.

Key term

Health – as defined by the World Health Organization, is a state of complete physical, mental and social wellbeing and not merely the absence of disease and infirmity.

Lifestyle refers to the way a person lives and reflects an individual's attitudes, values and behaviours. There are five lifestyle factors that are significant in maintaining health and wellbeing:

- physical activity
- a healthy diet
- not smoking
- avoiding excessive alcohol intake
- avoiding excessive stress.

Physical activity recommendations and guidelines

To gain health benefits the Department of Health recommends you do at least 30 minutes of moderate exercise on at least five days of the week. This recommendation should be viewed as the minimum required to achieve health benefits. The good news is it does not have to be achieved in a single bout. Several short bursts of activity can count towards your total. This approach may make it easier for some individuals to meet their daily physical activity target. Greater benefits will be gained from increasing the amount to 40–60 minutes each day, especially for those at risk of weight gain and associated diseases. The same recommendations apply to older people dependent on ability, but children are encouraged to achieve at least one hour of moderate intensity activity every day.

What is moderate activity and what type of activity should you undertake? Moderate means you must get a little warmer and slightly out of breath – the more vigorous the activity the greater the gains in cardiovascular health. In terms of type, it can be anything that raises your energy expenditure above resting level, enough to expend about 200 calories, and includes brisk walking, swimming, cycling and jogging, dancing, heavy housework and gardening.

Benefits of physical activity

There is overwhelming scientific evidence to prove that individuals leading active lives are less likely to die early or suffer from chronic disease such as coronary heart disease and diabetes, and are better able to cope with stress.

Remember

Physical activity is any activity that increases energy expenditure above resting level. Exercise is physical activity that is structured and undertaken usually for fitness gains. Physical activity undertaken for health benefits would be targeted at avoiding disease and delaying death. Exercise undertaken for fitness benefits would be targeted at improving one or more components of health-related fitness.

Activity: The benefits of exercise

Before you read on, take a few minutes to consider all the benefits a regular programme of physical activity or exercise can bring.

Are you able to group the benefits you have identified into the following categories:

- physical
- social
- psychological
- economic and environmental?

Many studies have demonstrated the numerous health benefits of physical activity and exercise.

Social	Economic
• Encourages connectedness. • Improves social skills. • Reduces isolation. • Enhances self-esteem and confidence.	• Reduces health costs. • Creates employment. • Supports local business. • Reduces absenteeism. • Enhances productivity.

Table 7.1: The wider benefits of physical activity and exercise.

As you can see from Table 7.1, when considering the health and wellbeing of the nation, there are wider social and economic benefits to an active lifestyle. At an individual level you can examine the short- and long-term benefits of physical activity in maintaining health and wellbeing:

- It's an opportunity for fun and enjoyment.
- The body is relaxed and revitalised, reducing muscular and mental tension.
- Exercise boosts self-esteem and confidence.
- It clears the head and improves concentration.
- It lowers the risk of heart disease and stroke.

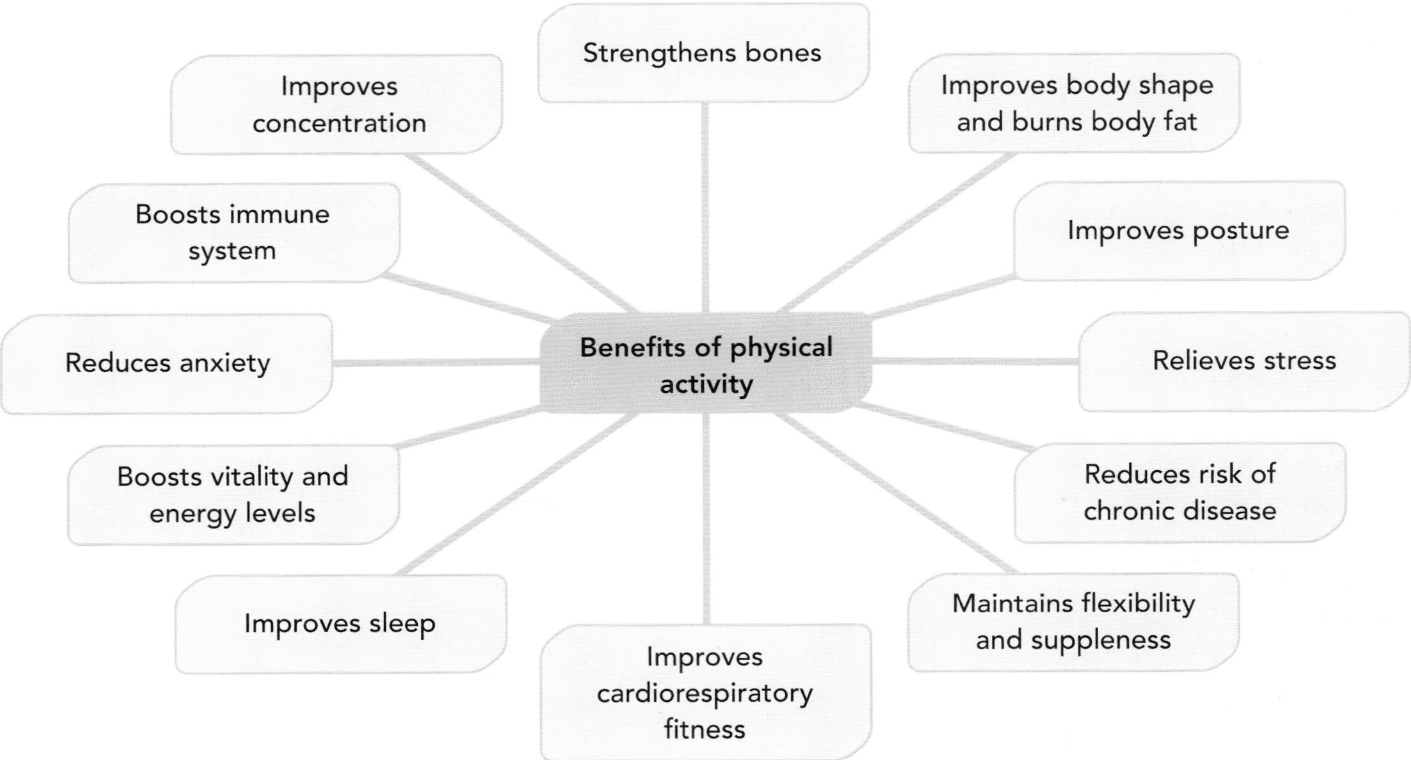

Figure 7.1: Consider the impact of these benefits of exercise and physical activity on your own health and wellbeing.

- It lowers body weight and body fat assisting in the maintenance of optimal body weight and composition.
- The risk of type 2 diabetes is lowered and the uptake of glucose in those who are sufferers is increased.
- It lowers the risk of certain types of cancer.
- It lowers the risk of osteoporosis.
- It alleviates the symptoms of arthritic pain.
- It combats ageing by maintaining the effectiveness of body systems, such as the respiratory, circulatory and musculoskeletal systems.
- Digestion is improved as exercise and activity support the proper functioning of the gut.

In addition, the **psychological** benefits of exercise should not be overlooked. Studies have shown that exercise brings about short- and long-term psychological benefits to health and wellbeing. Regular physical activity can improve mood, self-confidence and body image. Researchers have also found that regular physical activity reduces depression and anxiety and makes you better able to manage stress and tension.

Remember

Physical activity enhances mood, reduces anxiety and raises self-esteem and confidence. Surveys suggest that physically active individuals feel happier with life; even single bouts of activity can improve mood and energy. But for physical activity or exercise to have optimal benefits it is required to be current and continued.

Take it further

Research the benefits

While low levels of physical activity give some health benefits, moderate to high levels deliver major benefits to health and wellbeing. Undertake your own research of scientific journals and key authoritative sources on physical activity participation, such as the American College of Sport Medicine (ACSM) and British Association for Sport and Exercise Sciences (BASES), to investigate the scientific basis for this statement.

Alcohol

Alcohol is a drug that affects every organ in your body. It is a central nervous system depressant that is readily absorbed from your stomach and small intestine into your bloodstream. Binge drinking (excessive alcohol consumption) is a major public health concern.

Moderate alcohol consumption is thought to be beneficial in reducing the risks of heart disease. However, excessive intake causes health problems such as malnutrition, cirrhosis of the liver, certain forms of cancer and psychological health problems. Current safe limits recommended for alcohol consumption are up to three to four units per day for men, and for women up to two to three units per day. It is advised to spread alcohol intake throughout the week to avoid binges and include two or three alcohol free days each week. One unit is the equivalent to 8 grams of alcohol, typically a small glass of wine, or a half pint of beer, lager or cider and a single pub measure of spirits.

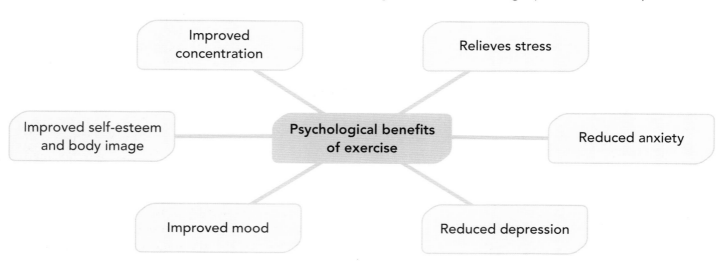

Figure 7.2: Consider the psychological benefits of regular physical activity on health and wellbeing.

Excessive consumption can have a detrimental impact on social and psychological health with the following associated risks.

- **Stroke** – this occurs when brain tissue dies as a result of a sudden and severe disruption of blood flow to the brain. Heavy alcohol use is associated with increased risk of stroke.
- **Cirrhosis** – chronic abuse of alcohol over a prolonged period can lead to cirrhosis of the liver, which may result in liver failure and death.
- **Hypertension** – the relationship between alcohol use and blood pressure is important as hypertension is a key factor in the risk of coronary heart disease and stroke. Hypertension is defined as a systolic blood pressure above 140 mm Hg and a diastolic pressure above 90 mm Hg.
- **Depression** – excessive alcohol consumption plays a part in causing depression. Alcohol dependence and depression may occur together. Depression is commonly reported in those being treated for alcohol dependence.

Smoking

Tobacco smoke contains nicotine and tar which are both damaging to health. Nicotine is a very powerful drug that causes addiction. It stimulates the central nervous system and increases heart rate and blood pressure. Tar is a complex mixture of chemicals, many of which cause cancer. It is largely deposited in the respiratory tract and gradually absorbed.

The risk of disease increases with the volume of smoking and number of years smoked, but also how deeply the smoke is inhaled. Some of the health risks associated with smoking include:

- **Coronary heart disease (CHD)** – a generic term to describe conditions caused by an interrupted or reduced flow of blood through the coronary arteries to the heart muscle. Smokers appear to have a higher risk of developing atherosclerosis (the build up of fatty deposits in the arteries) which is a primary contributor to CHD. Smoking presents an increased risk alone but when coupled with other risk factors such as high blood pressure, high cholesterol and physical inactivity it increases the likelihood of the blood to clot resulting in a heart attack.

- **Cancer** – worldwide, lung cancer is the most common form of cancer and the type most commonly associated with smoking. In terms of the risk of developing lung cancer the age at which smoking commences appears to be significant. Results of a study of ex-smokers showed that those who started smoking before the age of 15 had twice as many cell mutations (an instrumental factor in the development and initiation of cancer) than those who started after the age of 20. The impact of smoking on cancer risk is not limited to its effect on the lungs. Smoking is also implicated in cancers of the mouth, oesophagus, bladder, breast, cervix, colon, liver and kidneys.
- **Lung infections** – smokers are likely to suffer more respiratory tract infections than non-smokers. They are more prone to suffer from colds and flu, and take longer to recover. Pneumonia is a serious lung infection and is more common amongst smokers and more likely to be fatal. Bronchitis is a condition that inflames the lining of the bronchial tubes; it can be an acute or chronic condition. The most common symptom of bronchitis is a cough. Acute bronchitis is most often caused by a viral or bacterial infection, while chronic bronchitis is most often seen in smokers. Smoking causes damage to the cilia that line the airways; over time they become less efficient at clearing debris and irritants making the lungs more susceptible to infection.

Overall smokers have a higher risk of heart attack than non-smokers (a two- to three-fold increase in risk) while smokers under the age of 40 are five times more likely to suffer a heart attack than non-smokers. Exposure to other people's smoke (passive smoking) increases the risk of CHD in non-smokers. Passive smoking is becoming an increasing public health concern and has resulted in a ban on smoking in public places in the UK.

Stress

Stress can be defined as a physiological and mental response to triggers in our environment. Factors that produce stress are known as 'stressors' and they take different forms. Potential stressors include major life events, such as marriage, divorce and moving house, injury or trauma, and environmental situations such as a demanding work environment, but whatever the stressor the physical and mental responses usually include the feelings of anxiety and tension.

Chronic stress exposes your body to persistently elevated levels of stress hormones such as adrenaline and cortisol. The effects of chronic stress may manifest themselves in different ways, such as lowered resistance to disease, increase risk of heart disease, hormonal imbalances, back or joint pain and emotional and eating disorders. Other health risks associated with excess stress levels include:

- **Hypertension** – scientists remain unsure about the possible links between stress and hypertension. It is thought that long-term stress can contribute to hypertension through repeated blood pressure elevation. In the case of short lived stress we know that stress causes blood pressure to rise for a while, but once the stress is relieved blood pressure returns to normal.

- **Angina** – a pain or constricting feeling in the centre of the chest that can radiate down one or both arms, but most usually the left. This pain or tightness results from ischemia, or lack of oxygenated blood reaching the heart. It is an indicator of coronary heart disease caused by the build up of fatty deposits (atheroma) in the coronary arteries that supply blood to the heart muscle, which results in their narrowing. When stress causes an increase in blood flow to the heart, angina can occur.

- **Stroke** – stress can cause blood pressure to rise. Evidence suggests that those whose blood pressure rises with exposure to stress have a greater risk of stroke.

- **Heart attack** – stress is thought to increase the risk of coronary heart disease (CHD), although the direct links are unclear. It appears likely that stress may contribute to the development of other risk factors for CHD, such as smoking, inactivity, obesity and high blood pressure.

- **Ulcers** – the majority of ulcers (75 per cent) are caused by bacterial infection. There is support for the theory that stress is another cause. Stress may act by stimulating gastric acid production or by promoting behaviour that causes a risk to health.

Diet

The term 'diet' refers to your typical pattern of food consumption, while the term 'balanced diet' describes a diet that provides the correct amount of nutrients required by your body without excess or deficiency. A healthy diet should fulfil two primary objectives; it should:

- provide adequate energy and nutrients to maintain your normal physiological functioning, allowing for growth and replacement of your body tissues
- offer you protection against disease.

Scientific research provides evidence of direct links between good eating habits and disease prevention. The benefits of a healthy diet include increased energy and vitality, improved immune system function, maintenance of healthy body weight and reduced risk of chronic disease.

Deficiencies, excesses and imbalances in dietary intakes all produce potentially negative impacts on health which can lead to a range of dietary related disorders. Disorders of deficiency include scurvy (lack of vitamin C), osteoporosis (lack of calcium) and anaemia (lack of iron), while disorders of excess include obesity (excess calories) and coronary heart disease (excess fat). Imbalances of dietary intake may occur during periods of high nutritional demand such as growth or pregnancy, or when physical or psychological difficulties impact on meeting adequate nutritional intake such as during old age.

Targets for dietary intakes of the UK population were first established in the 1980s. These were reviewed in the 1990s in the COMA (Committee on Medical Aspects of Food Policy) report on Dietary Reference Values for UK Subjects. Healthy eating principles aim to assist the population in meeting these dietary targets. The current dietary targets for the UK population are listed in Table 7.2.

Table 7.2: How do you think your eating meets these dietary targets for the UK population? What activities could you undertake to assess if you meet them?

Nutrient	Recommendation
Total fat	Less than 35% of total energy
Saturated fat	No more than 11% of total energy
Protein	Less than 15% of total energy
Carbohydrate	50% of total energy
Fibre (non-starch polysaccharide)	18 g per day
Salt	6 g per day

A simple guide to healthy eating

- Eat the correct amount to maintain a healthy body weight.
- Reduce your fat intake, particularly from saturated sources.
- Eat plenty of foods with a high starch and fibre content.
- Don't eat sugary foods too often.
- Use salt sparingly and reduce your reliance on convenience foods.
- Ensure adequate intakes of vitamins and minerals by eating a wide variety of foods.
- If you drink alcohol keep within sensible limits.
- Enjoy your food and don't become obsessed with your diet or dieting.

The **Eatwell Plate** is the UK's national food guide. The model identifies the types and proportions of food groups you require to achieve a healthy, balanced diet. As you can see, the model shows a plate with divisions of varying sizes representing each of the five main food groups. Those that have a larger slice of the plate should feature in larger proportions in your diet, while those with the smallest slice should be consumed in smaller proportions or used only as occasional foods especially in the case of those with a high fat and/or sugar content.

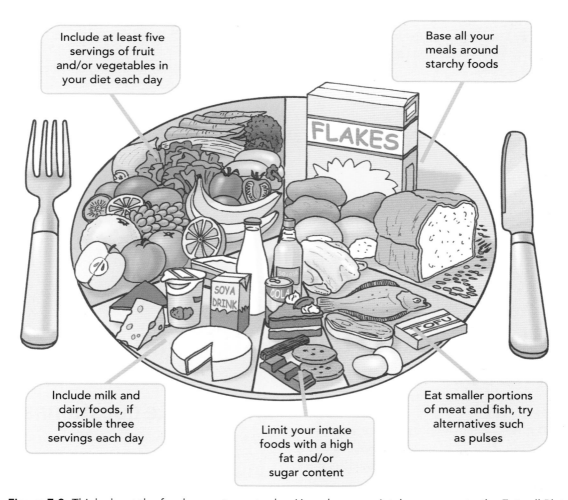

Figure 7.3: Think about the foods you ate yesterday. How does your intake compare to the Eatwell Plate?

Figure 7.4: Do you practise these simple guidelines of healthy eating and lifestyle on a daily basis?

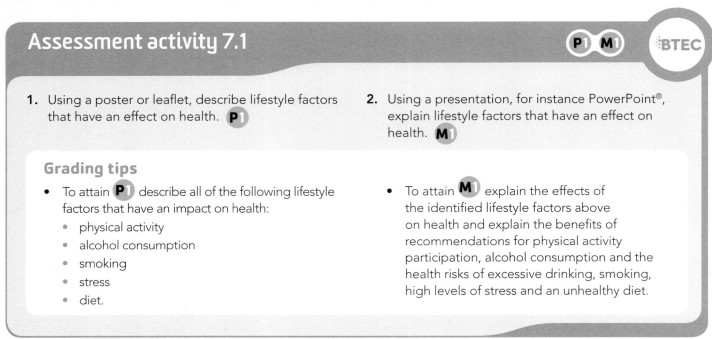

Assessment activity 7.1   **P1** **M1** BTEC

1. Using a poster or leaflet, describe lifestyle factors that have an effect on health. **P1**

2. Using a presentation, for instance PowerPoint®, explain lifestyle factors that have an effect on health. **M1**

Grading tips

*   To attain **P1** describe all of the following lifestyle factors that have an impact on health:
    *   physical activity
    *   alcohol consumption
    *   smoking
    *   stress
    *   diet.

*   To attain **M1** explain the effects of the identified lifestyle factors above on health and explain the benefits of recommendations for physical activity participation, alcohol consumption and the health risks of excessive drinking, smoking, high levels of stress and an unhealthy diet.

Functional skills

By using the Internet to research the lifestyle factors that have an effect on health, and by writing a poster or leaflet, or designing a presentation, you are providing evidence towards skills in **ICT** and **English**.

2. Be able to assess the lifestyle of a selected individual

To provide advice on lifestyle improvement and plan a health-related physical activity programme you must be able to assess the lifestyle of an individual. One way to achieve this is via a questionnaire that assesses the five lifestyle behaviours already identified as important in adopting a healthy lifestyle.

2.1 Lifestyle questionnaire

You should assess health status prior to planning a health-related physical activity programme. An objective evaluation of current exercise, health and lifestyle provides information on the individual's strengths and areas for improvement. This provides the basis for the establishment of realistic goals and the avoidance of injury. Testing initial fitness levels is a useful benchmark against which progress can be measured, with periodic testing providing motivating feedback as the physical activity or exercise programme progresses.

Levels of physical activity

Fitness assessment may form part of the overall screening process. It is essential that health and lifestyle screening takes place prior to this assessment and to exercise prescription, preferably by a medical or fitness practitioner. This is particularly important for anyone who is contemplating starting a physical activity or exercise programme, particularly if they are unaccustomed to exercise. Pre-exercise health screening can take different forms and can range from a self-administered physical activity readiness questionnaire to a complete medical examination carried out by a medical practitioner. The choice of method will depend on a number of factors such as age and health status, previous training history and resources. Comprehensive lifestyle and pre-exercise screening helps to identify medical conditions that may prevent the participant from exercising safely. It will highlight the participant's objectives and ensure that the exercise and lifestyle prescription fulfils their needs.

An example of a Physical Activity Readiness Questionnaire is available from the **Canadian Society for Exercise Physiology** at **www.csep.ca.** This questionnaire is designed for use by individuals between the ages of 15–69 and aims to identify the small number of individuals for whom physical activity might be inappropriate, or those who would require medical advice before embarking on a programme or supervision during physical activity or exercise participation.

The key features of a good lifestyle screening protocol are that it:

- takes account of the participant's past and current medical history
- takes account of family medical history

Remember

When in doubt about an individual's suitability or readiness to exercise ensure they consult their doctor. Any information obtained from health and lifestyle screening should be stored in a secure place to maintain confidentiality. This information should only be accessed by authorised personnel.

- measures body composition
- measures current fitness status and exercise history
- records diet and alcohol history
- records smoking history
- investigates stress and sleep patterns.

Alcohol consumption

Questionnaires aimed at assessing alcohol consumption should address volume (units) and frequency (days) of consumption.

Smoking

Questionnaires aimed at assessing smoking habits should consider the type of smoking (cigarettes, cigars, pipe), the duration of smoking (the number of years) and volume (amount per day).

Stress levels

Questionnaires aimed at assessing stress levels may consider major life events and recent changes in personal situation such as marriage, divorce, bereavement, loss of job, but also issues related to recent health status, eating habits and sleep patterns.

Diet

There are five basic methods for assessing dietary intake. Two of these methods use records of food consumption made at the time of actual eating, one with the actual weight recorded, the other using estimates of weights of food consumed using standard household measures. The other three methods attempt to assess diet and food consumption in the recent past by asking about food intake during the previous day (24 hour recall), over the past few weeks (diet history), or in the recent or distant past (food frequency questionnaire).

2.2 Consultation

One-to-one consultation

You are likely to gather information to assess the lifestyle of an individual through a one-to-one consultation. Key factors in a successful consultation include effective communication skills and client confidentiality.

The activity on the next page should help you highlight which aspects of your lifestyle require changes to improve your health. If you have many aspects to change, prioritise these and begin with the easy things.

Communication: questioning, listening skills and non-verbal communication

Effective communication is crucial in the consultation process. Communication is about giving and receiving information. Your questioning, listening and non-verbal communication skills are important in ensuring you set the correct tone for the consultation. Whether the subject feels at ease and whether your information is received in the way you intend it to be will depend on the effectiveness of your communication skills. Remember, non-verbal communication such as facial expressions, hand gestures and general body language sends out messages without you even speaking.

Key factors to ensure effective communication in the consultation process include:

- maintaining eye contact with your subject
- making them feel at ease by welcoming them, introducing yourself and explaining the consultation process
- maintaining a professional approach and avoiding being over familiar
- seeking permission if you intend to keep notes of your consultation
- maintaining an open and friendly posture at all times.

Client confidentiality

Information about a client belongs to the client. The principle of client confidentiality ensures that you should not release information about your clients to a third party without their consent.

Activity: Lifestyle assessment questionnaire

Complete the following lifestyle assessment questionnaire. The purpose of this questionnaire is to raise your awareness of the healthy and unhealthy lifestyle choices you make before you move on to working with a selected individual. Please answer **True** or **False** to the following questions:

Diet

1. I usually try to eat three balanced meals each day.	True/False
2. I usually eat at least five servings of fruit/vegetables each day.	True/False
3. I eat the right amount to be a healthy body weight.	True/False
4. I only consume alcohol within the recommended guidelines.	True/False

Physical activity and exercise

5. I undertake at least 30 minutes of moderate intensity physical activity at least 5 times per week.	True/False

Stress

6. I get plenty of rest.	True/False
7. I seldom feel tense or anxious.	True/False

Sleep

8. I usually get at least 8 hours of sleep each night.	True/False

Smoking

9. I never smoke.	True/False

Drugs

10. I never take drugs.	True/False

To calculate your score, give yourself one point for each question you answered True.

- 9–10 = very healthy lifestyle
- 7–8 = generally healthy lifestyle
- 5–6 = average lifestyle
- Below 5 = unhealthy lifestyle with many improvements needed

Why is the consultation process an important part of assessing the lifestyle of a particular individual?

Assessment activity 7.2

Your college has invested in a new health and fitness suite with the primary emphasis on improving the health and wellbeing of staff and students. Your class has been asked to design a lifestyle screening questionnaire for use in this facility.

1. Design a lifestyle questionnaire to describe the strengths and areas for improvement in the lifestyle of a selected individual. **P2**

2. To assess the usability of the questionnaire, use it on a client and explain the strengths and areas for improvement in their lifestyle. **M2**

3. Evaluate the lifestyle of a selected individual and prioritise areas for change. **D1**

4. Write up your findings in a report format.

Grading tips

- To attain **P2** you need to collect information on the lifestyle of an individual using a self-designed questionnaire and one-to-one consultation.

- To attain **M2** you must explain the strengths and areas for improvement of a selected individual's lifestyle and explain your recommended lifestyle improvement strategies.

- To attain **D1** you need to evaluate the lifestyle of a selected individual and prioritise areas for change. In doing this you may need to make some value judgements about the strengths and areas for improvement.

PLTS

Using your questionnaire, seeking feedback on it and refining it will help you develop your skills as an **independent enquirer**, **creative thinker** and **reflective learner**.

Functional skills

By researching and designing your lifestyle questionnaire you are providing evidence towards skills in **ICT** and **English**.

3. Be able to provide advice on lifestyle improvement

Poor health is a drain on national resources. It increases the amount spent on healthcare by the government. As individuals we may encounter difficulties in attaining **wellness**. Our age, ethnicity and socio-economic status may present challenges to achieving wellness.

3.1 Strategies to improve lifestyle

Take it further

The health of the nation

Use the Internet or your local health promotion office to investigate the range of local and national initiatives aimed at improving the nation's health. Awareness of these initiatives will assist you in meeting assessment requirements for the unit.

Ways to increase physical activity levels

Despite the strong case for keeping active, many find it difficult to take up exercise. The mere notion of physical activity or exercise conjures up unpleasant thoughts, images of boring exercise classes, or rough competitive sports where the risk of injury is a deterrent. Those who have never exercised before, or who are in poor shape, should not expect immediate results. Achieving physical fitness requires time and consistency. Ways of getting fit are explored below.

- **Walking** – scientific evidence supports the benefits of regular walking for health and wellbeing. It is an easy and economical way to become and stay active. All ages can participate and it is a social activity.

  To achieve the health benefits associated with walking, a target of 10 000 steps a day (about 5 miles) is required. The average sedentary individual achieves around 2000–3000 steps per day. A **pedometer** can be used as a motivational tool to measure progress towards achieving this target. A sensible approach to reaching the

10 000 a day target is to aim to increase average daily steps by 500 each week until the 10 000 target is reached.

Key terms

Wellness – can be viewed as our approach to personal health that emphasises individual responsibility for wellbeing through the practice of health promoting lifestyle behaviours.

Pedometer – a portable electronic device usually worn all day on the belt which counts each step taken.

- **Stair climbing** – encouraging the use of stairs in the workplace and other settings may have significant health benefits. Evidence suggests that moderate intensity lifestyle activities like taking the stairs (instead of the lift or escalator) may be more successfully promoted than vigorous exercise programmes. Stair climbing can be accumulated throughout the day and with an energy cost of approximately 8–10 kcals per minute, it can help with weight control. It also has benefits in terms of leg power and bone strength and cardiovascular fitness.

- **Cycling** – this can be an effective and enjoyable aerobic exercise. Daily cycling has been shown to be sufficient to lead to significant health benefits. People of most fitness levels can participate in cycling, although anyone with heart disease or other pre-existing conditions should consult their doctor before they start a cycling programme. Cycling offers a healthy leisure activity and with around 70 per cent of all car trips reported to be less than 5 miles, it is an alternative mode of transport.

Remember

The risks associated with participation in a regular programme of physical activity or exercise are commonly less than the risks associated with that of living a sedentary lifestyle. However, the potential benefits of exercise must outweigh the potential risks to the participant.

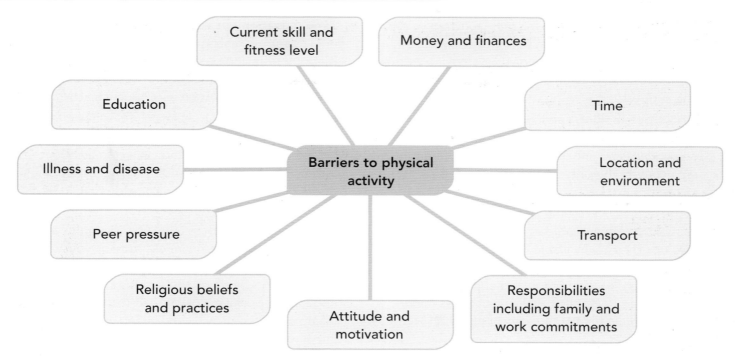

Figure 7.5: Consider the impact of these potential barriers to physical activity participation. How might they be overcome?

Alcohol

When alcohol consumption becomes so excessive and frequent that it has a severe and negative impact on health it is termed alcoholism. Alcoholics exhibit intense cravings for alcohol and become physically dependent on it.

Problem drinking and alcoholism is serious, but recovery is possible if the alcohol user is strongly motivated to stop drinking. Treatments might include counselling and therapy, self-help groups, either face-to-face or online, or alternative treatments and therapies.

Individual or group counselling is provided by specially trained therapists; often this might involve other family members. Exploring and developing awareness of triggers for alcohol consumption and the breaking of habitual behaviours are areas of focus for counselling and therapy. Relapse is often high for alcohol abusers and preventing relapse is a key feature of the counselling and therapy process.

Treatment for alcohol abuse often begins with detoxification and withdrawal from alcohol. This is necessary when alcohol consumption has continued for long periods of time. It can be an uncomfortable process with unpleasant withdrawal symptoms.

In extreme cases it can be fatal (which is why detoxification is usually undertaken under supervision within an alcohol treatment facility).

Successful treatment of alcoholism depends on recognition of the problem by the sufferer. Self-help groups such as Alcoholics Anonymous (AA) have helped many sufferers through a step-by-step programme of recovery. Some alcohol users may seek alternative treatments and therapies such as acupuncture and hypnosis which are thought to lessen the symptoms of withdrawal. However, there are mixed views about their value within the medical fraternity.

Smoking

Smoking increases the risk of lung and heart disease. As with most behaviour modification goals, in order to quit smoking the smoker must want to stop. Once this is realised there are a number of approaches than can be taken to help them.

- **Acupuncture** – a traditional Chinese therapy which may help someone to stop smoking by increasing the body's production of mood enhancing endorphins that reduce or alleviate withdrawal symptoms.

- **NHS smoking helpline** – this was launched in 2000 as part of a government initiative to encourage 1.5 million people in the UK to give up smoking by the year 2010. The helpline offers information, advice and support.

- **NHS stop-smoking services** – the range of services promoted include group and one-to-one counselling and information on nicotine replacement therapy.

- **Nicotine replacement therapy** – this refers to a range of products (gums, patches, lozenges and sprays) that are available to help the smoker to give up. They are available on prescription and are suitable for most smokers, although those that are pregnant or taking regular medication should consult their doctor first. Unlike cigarettes they do not contain the harmful cancer-causing toxic chemicals.

Stress management techniques

To control stress there are two general approaches that can be taken:

- Try to reduce the amount of overall stress.
- Develop coping or stress management techniques.

To reduce overall stress, the factors that promote stress, usually known as stressors, should be identified and, if possible, eliminated or reduced. Careful time management and prioritisation of workload and commitments may help an individual to manage their stress better.

It is not possible to eliminate all the stresses faced in daily life. Therefore, having techniques or participating in activities that reduce levels of stress will have a positive impact on health and wellbeing. Exercise can be viewed as a positive stress for the body. Other ways to manage stress are outlined below.

- **Assertiveness** – the ability to express your feelings and rights while respecting those of others. While assertiveness may come naturally to some, it is a skill that can be learned. Once mastered, it can help you deal with conflict situations that may be a cause of stress in daily life.

- **Goal setting** – properly set goals can be motivating and rewarding – achieving these goals can build self-confidence and reduce stress.

- **Time management** – this is a critical element of effective stress management. Time management is about achieving our tasks in good time by using techniques such as goal setting, task planning and minimising time spent on unproductive activities.

- **Physical activity** – this can have a positive effect on anxiety, depression, self-esteem and mood. It can be a stress reliever by producing an outlet for frustration, releasing endorphins, the 'feel good' hormones that lift mood, and providing a distraction from the stressor.

- **Positive self-talk** – this is the inner dialogue you have with yourself. It influences most of your emotional life and reflects how you respond to your thoughts, feelings and actions and it can be negative or positive. Positive self-talk involves taking an optimistic view of life and your situation. In daily life you face constant challenges, difficulties and deadlines – being able to take a positive view of these and have constructive ways of dealing with them helps to reduce and manage stress.

- **Relaxation and breathing exercises** – focusing on breathing exercises is a simple way of trying to control or reduce stress. It involves controlled inhalation and exhalation, best undertaken when you are quiet and comfortable.

Diet

To meet the learning outcomes of this unit it is necessary for you to be able to critically evaluate your own eating habits and what influences them.

The timing of meals is a key component of food habits. Food habits develop over time and are resistant to change. They are subconscious as they are acquired at a young age. In areas of the world where food is readily available 24 hours a day, intake can occur at any time. However, most of us do not eat continually but stick to reasonably defined mealtimes with snacks between. In western culture this has lead to a 'three meals per day' approach supplemented by snacking. As lifestyles become more busy and flexible, more snacking may occur, but overall nutritional density of the diet remains important.

Activity: You are what you eat

Keep a record of all food and fluid intake for at least a **3 day period** which should include **1 weekend day**. For a more detailed evaluation you can record your intake for a full week.

Write down **everything** you eat and drink. Be as accurate and honest as possible and don't modify your diet at this stage, otherwise you will not be evaluating your typical diet. Carry your record around with you at all times. This will allow you to record food and drink as it is consumed to avoid forgetting anything.

Record as much information as possible to include:

- the type of food and drink consumed and how much, either as an estimation of portion size using household measures such as slices of bread, pints of fluid, tablespoons of vegetables, etc. or as an actual weight, either weighed or recorded from the packaging

- the time that the food and drink was consumed and where you were when consumed (these points are often useful to consider when assessing external factors that affect your dietary intake)

- the cooking method and type of food preparation.

Once you have completed your record, compare it to the eatwell plate guidelines and write a short account of your evaluation on the strengths and areas for improvement in your diet.

The government has set targets or dietary intake goals aimed at improving the nation's health and reducing the risk of chronic disease. Your diet should be balanced across the five main food groups to ensure adequate energy and nutrients without excesses or deficiencies. As a population we are advised to eat more wholegrain starchy carbohydrate food and fruits and vegetables and to eat less fatty and sugary foods. This is expressed in the percentage contribution of food groups within the **Eatwell Plate** model.

Most foods require some form of preparation before consumption. Food preparation depends on cooking skills and facilities and the time available to prepare it. Awareness of these factors is important when suggesting strategies for improving dietary intake to ensure realistic and achievable goals are set. Food handling and safety are also important aspects of food preparation in ensuring health and wellbeing.

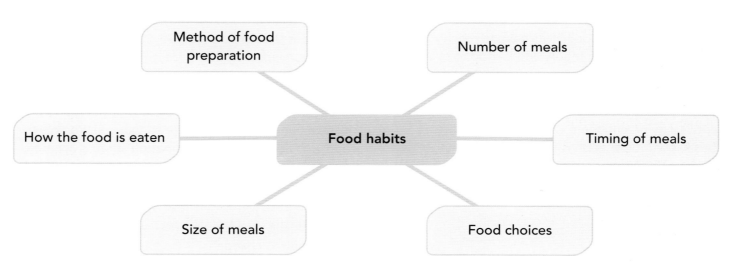

Figure 7.6: How do the main components of food habits impact on your diet?

Activity: What, when, where and why you eat

Your food record should allow you to further examine your normal eating patterns. As well as the types and amounts of food consumed, it should give you an idea about how your lifestyle dictates what, when, where and why you eat. Take another look at your record and consider the following questions:

- In relation to healthy eating principles, is your diet better than you first thought or is there room for improvement? What healthy eating goals might you not be achieving and why?

- Are your mealtimes structured and regular? Do you eat any differently at weekends? Does where and what time you eat dictate your food choice and selection?

- Do you rely heavily on convenience foods and takeaways? If yes, what influences this?

- What constraints do you foresee that may prevent you from making any changes you have identified as a result of your evaluation? Do you think you will be able to overcome them?

Suggest realistic strategies for improvement where necessary. Try to implement these changes over the coming weeks while studying this unit.

To monitor the effectiveness of your dietary changes, repeat this exercise in a month's time to see if you have successfully managed to implement the changes you identified to eat a healthier diet.

Take it further

Information and leaflets

Visit your GP surgery or local health promotion unit to collect information and leaflets on the treatment and management of lifestyle issues such as smoking, physical activity, diet, drug and alcohol use. You may find this exercise useful in assisting you with providing lifestyle improvement strategies for a selected individual.

Behaviour change

Behaviour modification has its basis in psychological principles of learning theory and is used to change or modify a person's behaviour. Behaviour modification techniques can be used to eliminate unhealthy lifestyle behaviours. One of the most common approaches applied by practitioners in promoting lifestyle behaviour modification is the Stages of Change Model (Prochaska, Diclemente and Norcross, 1992).

This model recognises that change occurs through a process of stages identified as:

- pre-contemplation
- contemplation
- preparation
- action
- maintenance
- termination.

In the **pre-contemplation** stage you are not considering changing behaviour in the near future. In fact, most people in this stage will fail to notice or have any concerns about a particular behaviour (for example, overeating or a lack of physical activity). When you become aware that a change may be desirable you are considered to be in the **contemplation** stage (for example, you've decided you can't fit into your clothes and need to lose weight by eating less and exercising). In the **preparation** stage, you will begin to set yourself targets and goals to improve behaviour. During the **action** stage you start to implement your plan of behaviour change – obstacles should be expected and strategies for overcoming them may need to be considered. In the **maintenance** stage you should be able to acknowledge that setbacks will come along from time to time, but you remind yourself of your goals and the positive benefits of the change so that you are able to cope with relapses. The **termination** stage is achieved when you are able to overcome all temptation towards your previous behaviour.

Simple steps to behaviour modification include:

1. Identify the problem (or problems) and understand the need to change.

2. Understand the influences on the problem.

3. Establish short-, medium- and long-term goals for tackling the problem and record them.

4. Develop a strategy to facilitate change and understand the resources or skills required for success.

5. Implement the strategy and record and monitor progress.

6. Evaluate progress and consider strategies to maintain change in behaviour if successfully achieved.

Different **barriers** may present themselves in tackling the five health behaviours identified in this unit. However, some common barriers may apply across all including:

- lack of knowledge about the benefits of the behaviour change
- lack of self-efficacy (or confidence) in making the behaviour change
- setting unrealistic goals for behaviour change
- lack of commitment or motivation to make the change
- lack of control over your environment to make the change
- lack of support from others to make the change
- falling at the first hurdle (relapse).

Cognitive and behavioural strategies are approaches to behaviour change based on concepts and principles derived from psychological models of human behaviour. They include a broad range of approaches along a continuum from structured individual psychotherapy at one end to self-help at the other. In cognitive behavioural therapy (CBT), a 'skills based' approach, the client and therapist work together to identify and attempt to understand the client's problem behaviour. A key element of this approach is to help the client to understand the relationship between thoughts, feelings and behaviour. The client and therapist then attempt to establish a shared understanding of the problem. This leads to some personalised goals and strategies for tackling the problem that are monitored and evaluated over time. During this process the client learns to develop psychological or practical skills for problem solving or management. The overall aim of cognitive and behavioural approaches is for the client to attribute improvements in their behaviour to their own efforts and not those of the therapist.

Case study: Beat the bulge

Carl is a 43-year-old male maintenance worker who was screened at his company's occupational health centre and found to have a high percentage of body fat. The occupational health nurse has told him he needs to lose some weight and begin a programme of physical activity. He smoked 40-a-day up until three years ago when he quit on his 40th birthday, but since giving up smoking he has gained weight.

He admits to a sedentary lifestyle away from work, preferring to watch sport, rather than participate in it, from the comfort of his armchair. He was a competitive athlete in his early youth, winning medals for distance running, but can't seem to get motivated to do any exercise at present. He has thought about joining his local health club but is sensitive about his current size and poor level of fitness.

1. **What benefits would a regular programme of physical activity or exercise bring for Carl and how long might it take before he would notice these benefits?**

2. **What do you think would be the most appropriate types of exercise to include in a regular programme of physical activity or exercise at this stage?**

3. **What strategies could you use to overcome Carl's current barriers to participation in a regular programme of physical activity or exercise and get him motivated to start?**

How would Carl benefit from lifestyle improvement strategies?

Possible approaches for helping people change unhealthy lifestyle behaviours include:

- individual advice and leaflets
- individual counselling and support
- group counselling and support
- campaigns and displays
- community-based activities.

Assessment activity 7.3

Select an individual who would benefit from lifestyle improvement. This could be a friend or relative who wishes to lose weight, follow a more healthy diet, give up smoking, reduce their alcohol intake or increase their physical activity.

1. Provide the individual with appropriate lifestyle improvement strategies. **P3**

2. Explain the recommendations you have made regarding lifestyle improvement strategies. **M3**

3. Analyse the range of lifestyle improvement strategies that are appropriate for your selected individual and how you can monitor and evaluate their effectiveness. **D2**

Grading tips

- To attain **P3** include advice where appropriate on stress management, smoking cessation, alcohol reduction and diet. You could achieve this though the production of a written report or a video recording of your consultation.

- To attain **M3** explain the lifestyle improvement strategies in terms of their suitability for the selected individual.

- To attain **D2** investigate the strengths and weaknesses of different strategies and how you can monitor and evaluate their effectiveness with your selected individual.

PLTS

By providing lifestyle improvement strategies for an individual, you are developing your skills as an **effective participator** and as a **creative thinker**.

Functional skills

By providing lifestyle improvement strategies for an individual you are demonstrating your skills in **English**.

4. Be able to plan a health-related physical activity programme for a selected individual

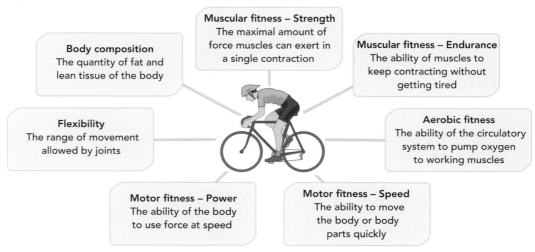

Body composition
The quantity of fat and lean tissue of the body

Muscular fitness – Strength
The maximal amount of force muscles can exert in a single contraction

Muscular fitness – Endurance
The ability of muscles to keep contracting without getting tired

Flexibility
The range of movement allowed by joints

Aerobic fitness
The ability of the circulatory system to pump oxygen to working muscles

Motor fitness – Power
The ability of the body to use force at speed

Motor fitness – Speed
The ability to move the body or body parts quickly

Figure 7.7: Evaluate each component of fitness in relation to your own health and fitness.

Health-related fitness has several components and you require a minimum level of fitness in each of these individual components to cope with everyday living with ease.

4.1 Collect information

Before you plan a health-related physical activity programme for a selected individual it is necessary to collect relevant information. This will help you to produce a plan which meets their personal goals and takes account of their relevant lifestyle, medical and physical activity history. There should also be some consideration of their attitude towards physical activity and exercise, and their motivation to adhere to your plan.

In order to maintain interest and motivation, you should carry out regular evaluations of the individual's fitness. Monitoring fitness goals and outcomes can provide useful information in the design and progression of physical activity and exercise programmes.

Personal goals

An individual's motivation to embark on a physical activity or exercise programme is influenced by a wide range of personal goals ranging from improving all or specific elements of health-related fitness, to weight loss and maintenance, to getting fit for a particular occasion or challenge. Knowing what these are will allow you to tailor your programme and provide a focus for boosting motivation if it dips.

Lifestyle

The key features of lifestyle screening have been covered on pages 178–180, but the most important elements in a lifestyle history should relate to:

- type of occupation and family commitments
- smoking and alcohol use
- perception of stress
- perceived challenges or barriers to success in achieving personal goals.

Medical history

The most important elements of a medical history should relate to:

- any current existing medical condition(s)
- any previous medical history
- any family history of chronic disease
- previous medical examination results if available
- medications or drug use.

Physical activity history

The most important elements of a physical activity history should relate to:

- exercise and activity history (frequency, intensity, time, type)
- exercise and activity preferences.

Attitude and motivation

It is vital that progress is monitored in order to sustain motivation and to develop a lifetime commitment to staying fit. Progress can be monitored by keeping training logs or diaries which record the distance walked or run, or the amount of weight lifted.

4.2 Goal setting

Goals (short-, medium- and long-term)

The first step in undertaking a physical activity or exercise programme is to commit to it. It is important to set short-, medium- and long-term goals to keep you on track. Setting goals, providing they are realistic, will give you a target and an incentive to continue, especially if the going gets tough or your motivation starts to wane – attaining your goals will improve self-esteem and motivation.

Short-term goals should be achievable within the first six to eight weeks of a programme, while long-term goals might look ahead to 12 months; medium-term goals aim at the first three, six and nine months. Long-term goals can be modified to meet changes in need or circumstances, or if progress is faster than expected and the goals are achieved.

Remember

Achieving short-term health-related fitness goals provides great motivation to continue with the programme.

SMART targets

By setting SMART targets or goals you are much more likely to be successful. Remember that 'SMART' stands for specific, measurable, achievable, realistic and timed (refer to Unit 9 Fitness training and programming, pages 249–250 for more details).

4.3 Principles of training

Being physically fit is about having enough energy, strength and skill to cope with the everyday demands of your environment. Individual fitness levels vary greatly from the low levels required to cope with daily activities to optimal levels required by some performers who are at the top of their sport.

The preparation and construction of an effective exercise or physical activity programme must be based on the way the body adapts to different training regimes. Programmes can be constructed to emphasise one or many aspects of fitness, for example, strength, aerobic endurance and flexibility, but the following factors should be given careful consideration:

- individuality
- specificity
- reversibility
- overload
- progression.

Overload

To achieve a higher level of fitness it is necessary to stress your body systems and place them in a state of overload. This is a point above and beyond that which is usually achieved. If this greater level is not achieved, adaptation will not occur. To avoid the problems associated with injury, illness and motivation, it is important that the training load is progressively increased. Rest and recuperation are also important too. Remember that when working with the general population to develop health-related fitness, the overload required may be very small and could take some time to achieve.

Consider the novice gym user who at the start of their training programme can only perform six repetitions of a press-up. After training two or three times a week for two to three weeks, they should be able to increase the number of repetitions achieved beyond this. They can then think about including sets of repetitions.

Specificity

Adaptations to training are specific to the type of activity undertaken and the intensity at which it is performed. Specificity relates to the muscle groups involved and the energy sources used. Training for one sort of activity does not lead to fitness for all activities. For example, a squash player can sprint around the court returning every shot, and keeps going long after their opponent looks exhausted and concedes defeat. Enter the same squash player in a long distance road race and they may manage to get round the course, but they are unlikely to win the event and may even get out of breath and have to stop along the way. Similarly there is little transfer of training from strength training to cardiovascular efficiency. For example, a marathon runner would not spend a great deal of time lifting heavy weights or doing short sprint intervals. The power lifter would not overemphasise distance running or low intensity resistance training, while prolonged long distance running is unlikely to improve endurance swimming time.

Progression

When exercise is performed over a period of weeks or months, your body adapts. The physiological changes that occur with repeated exposure to exercise improve your body's exercise capacity and efficiency. With aerobic training, such as running and cycling, the heart and lungs become more efficient and endurance capacity increases, while the muscles become stronger with resistance modes of training such as weight training. Adaptations derived from training are highly specific to the type of exercise or activity undertaken.

Individual differences

Genetics plays a large part in determining how quickly and to what degree you will adapt to a specific exercise regime. Two individuals are unlikely to show the same rate and magnitude of adaptation in response to the same training programme. As a result the principle of individual differences must be taken into account when designing health-related physical activity and exercise programmes.

Variation

Variation in a physical activity or exercise programme is important to progression of fitness goals, but also motivation to continue with the programme. Variation can be achieved by manipulation of the training variables:

- frequency (how often you undertake the activity)
- duration or time (for how long)
- intensity (how hard)
- the type of activity.

Reversibility

Training effects are reversible. This means that if the benefits of adaptation to an exercise programme are to be maintained and improved, then regular activity must be adhered to. It is possible to 'lose it by not using it'. All components of fitness can be affected by non-activity. However, once a level of fitness has been achieved, this level can be maintained with a

lower degree of effort than was initially required for its development.

FITT principles of exercise prescription

- **Frequency** of exercise refers to the number of times the exercise is undertaken, usually expressed in times per week.
- **Intensity** of exercise refers to how hard, or the amount of stress or overload that is to be applied.
- **Time** (duration) of exercise refers to how long the activity is to be carried out.
- **Type** of exercise refers to the mode of exercise performed.

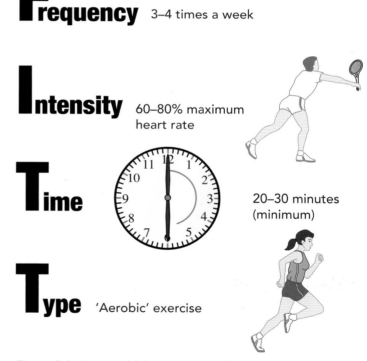

S	M	T	W	T	F	S
✔		✔	✔		✔	

Frequency   3–4 times a week

Intensity   60–80% maximum heart rate

Time   20–30 minutes (minimum)

Type   'Aerobic' exercise

Figure 7.8: How could the principles of exercise programming be applied to the case study of Carl on page 187?

Take it further

Exercise prescription

Undertake your own research to investigate the American College of Sports Medicine's guidance on exercise prescription.

4.4 Appropriate activities

Different types of exercise provide different health benefits. Once fitness goals have been set, the exercise prescribed must lead to the desired benefits, such as weight control, stress management, prevention of disease, muscle definition or the maintenance of flexibility. Important factors to be taken in to consideration are convenience, cost, motivation and enjoyment.

Walking

Do not underestimate walking as a form of exercise – it is possibly the perfect aid to weight loss and improving general fitness.

Cycling

A study carried out by the Department of Transport found that even a small amount of cycling can lead to significant gains in fitness. One study found that aerobic fitness was boosted by 11 per cent after just six weeks of cycling short distances four times per week.

Hiking

Hiking trails range from the easy to challenging. Beginners are advised to start on the flat while those with more experience and fitness may take on the challenge of a mountain trail. Hiking is generally free and usually involves covering longer distances over more varied and rugged terrain than walking, but this is not always the case. It also requires more specialised equipment to ensure personal safety, such as a good pair of boots, windproof and waterproof clothing, a backpack to carry food and fluid, and a map and compass.

Hiking conditions the cardiovascular system and also the major muscles of the legs, while carrying a backpack will increase energy expenditure and burn more calories to assist with weight loss.

Swimming

Swimming is a great aerobic activity to improve cardiovascular fitness. Nearly all major muscle groups are recruited when you swim, offering a total body workout to improve muscle tone and strength. However, as swimming is non-weight bearing it does not offer the same benefits as other forms of aerobic activities in terms of bone strength. It is appropriate for all fitness levels, particularly those who are unaccustomed to exercise, overweight, pregnant or who suffer from joint problems or injury.

Investigate the walking and hiking groups in your local area.

4.5 Exercise intensity

Exercise intensity is usually set at a percentage of maximal capacity, communicated as a percentage of maximal heart rate and provides a measure of how hard you are working (see page 191).

Rating of perceived exertion (RPE)

The best way to monitor intensity during exercise is to use a combination of heart rate measures and ratings of perceived exertion or RPE. Heart rates can be taken manually or by wearing a heart rate monitor. RPE is a ten point scale that focuses on tuning in the body to physical cues for recognising intensity of effort, such as a quickened breathing rate, breathlessness or flat out effort. The RPE scale provides a way of quantifying subjective exercise intensity, but has been shown to correlate well with heart rate and oxygen uptake.

Table 7.3: Modified rate of perceived exertion (RPE) chart.

Rating of perceived effort (RPE)	Intensity of effort
0	Nothing at all
1	Very weak
2	Weak
3	Moderate
4	Somewhat hard
5	Hard
6	Moderately hard
7	Very hard
8	Very, very hard
9	Near maximal
10	Extremely strong or maximal

The original scale was from 6 to 20, with 6 representing complete rest and 20 exhaustion. The reason for this numbering was reflected in the subjects that were used in the original exertion studies. They were all fit individuals who had heart rates that corresponded to around 60 beats per minute (bpm) at rest and a maximum heart rate of around 200 bpm.

Maximum heart rate

Heart rates are dependent on age (children have relatively higher rates than adults). When the body is in action, cardiac output can increase five to seven times in order to accelerate the delivery of blood to exercising muscles, and meet their demand for increased oxygen.

During participation in sport and exercise, cardiac output will be increased as a result of increases in either heart rate, stroke volume or both. Stroke volume does not increase significantly beyond the light work rates of low intensity exercise, therefore the increases in cardiac output required for moderate to high intensity work rates are achieved by increases in heart rate. Maximal attainable cardiac output decreases with increasing age, largely as a result of a decrease in maximum heart rate. Maximum heart rate can be calculated using this formula:

maximum heart rate = 220 – age (in years)

Exercise heart rates are used to assess the strenuousness of the exercise. This information is then used in the formulation of training intensities in the exercise programme.

Maximum heart rate reserve

Maximum heart rate reserve (or the Karvonen method as it is also known after the Finnish physiologist who introduced the concept) provides somewhat higher values for exercise intensity compared to heart rates calculated simply as a percentage of maximum heart rate. The Karvonen formula calculates training heart rate threshold as:

heart rate threshold = heart rate at rest + 0.60 (heart rate maximum – heart rate at rest)

For example, the heart rate training threshold for a sedentary adult female with a heart rate at rest of 85 beats per minute and a maximum heart rate of 185 beats per minute would be calculated as:

heart rate threshold = 85 + 0.60(185 – 85)
= 85 + 0.60(100)
= 85 + 60
= 145 beats per minute

Talk test

The best way to monitor intensity during exercise is to use a combination of heart rate measures and ratings of perceived exertion – but when neither is available the talk test method can be applied. It is a simple method that sets a marker to avoid overexertion; if you are able to comfortably talk during exercise you are likely to be exercising at an appropriate intensity.

Take it further

Your own plan

Now that you have been introduced to a variety of training methods for different components of fitness, plan a six week training programme suitable for yourself. Before you start you will need to give consideration to the fitness components that you wish to develop.

Assessment activity 7.4

Using the same individual you worked with in Assessment activity 7.3, devise a six week health-related physical activity programme taking into account current recommendations for physical activity. **P4**

Grading tips

- To attain **P4** ensure you give consideration to the principles of training when you design of your programme.

PLTS

By drawing up an activity programme, you are demonstrating your **creative thinker** skills.

Functional skills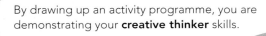

When you produce your activity programme, you have the opportunity to use your **ICT** skills.

Jay Stevens
Health and fitness instructor

I work in an independent health club as part of a team of ten fitness instructors and studio teachers who deliver health and fitness services to a wide range of clients. Everyone in our team is a qualified fitness instructor and a member of the Register of Exercise Professionals (REPs). My work responsibilities include:

- client health and fitness assessments
- exercise prescription and programming
- individual and group exercise instruction
- maintenance of health and safety
- mentoring junior colleagues.

A typical day for me involves making sure all health and safety checks of the equipment and gym environment have been undertaken. I also spend time in individual consultations carrying out lifestyle and fitness assessments. I may spend one or two hours each day on the development and review of health-related exercise programmes for clients, instructing them on new programmes or new equipment. If I have time I'll try to fit in a training session of my own.

The best thing about my job is that I enjoy meeting people and helping them set realistic and achievable goals for improving their health. Most people join the gym to lose weight but once they see all the other benefits of a regular programme of physical activity and exercise, they find it easier to maintain their programme, even if weight loss doesn't happen. It gives me a sense of satisfaction knowing that I have helped clients to achieve their personal fitness goals.

Think about it!

- What knowledge and skills have you covered in this unit that would provide you with an understanding of the role of the health and fitness instructor?

- How would you rate your current level of competency at using the knowledge and skills you have developed in this unit? What further knowledge and skills might you need to develop to pursue a career in the fitness industry?

- Investigate the requirements for joining the Register of Exercise Professionals (REPs). You can do this at www.exerciseregister.org.

Just checking

1. Identify five major benefits of regular physical activity and exercise participation.
2. Explain why it is important to undertake a thorough health, fitness and lifestyle assessment prior to formulating a health-related physical activity programme for an individual.
3. What key components would you include in the design of a lifestyle assessment questionnaire?
4. Define stress and consider why the control of stress is important to maintain health and wellbeing.
5. Describe the components of a healthy balanced diet.
6. Describe and evaluate three strategies to support the cessation of smoking.
7. What dietary modification techniques could be implemented to assist with weight loss?
8. Describe behaviour modification and the steps that might be involved in changing unhealthy behaviours.
9. In relation to physical activity and exercise prescription, what is overload and why is it important?
10. How would you determine maximum heart rate?

Assignment tips

- Take a look at the following websites for information on lifestyle factors that affect health and wellbeing:
  American College of Sports Medicine   www.acsm.org
  British Nutrition Foundation   www.nutrition.org.uk
  Department of Health   www.dh.gov.uk
  Food Standards Agency   www.eatwell.gov.uk
  The World Health Organisation   www.who.int

- Visit a range of health and fitness environments to gather information on lifestyle improvement. You may choose to use some of this information in meeting the assessment requirements of this unit.

- Remember, prior to being able to plan a health-related physical activity programme for a selected individual, it is necessary to collect relevant information. This will help you in the planning process that will meet the personal goals of the individual and take account of their relevant lifestyle, medical and physical activity history, as well as consider their attitude towards physical activity and exercise and their motivation to adhere to your plan.

- Before you embark on your assessment activities, role play activities with your fellow students and gain feedback from your tutor on your consultation skills. This will help you to effectively carry out a successful consultation with your client and design an appropriate six week health-related physical activity programme. You could also practise your technique on friends and relatives. This will help you to gain confidence in your interview technique.

8 Fitness testing for sport and exercise

Fitness is vital for success in sport, and fitness testing plays a valuable role in the development of fitness levels. Sports performers participate in fitness tests in order to determine their baseline measures and training needs. Fitness testing is built into the elite performer's training regime so that they can push their bodies to the maximum, recording progress and fitness gains.

Results from fitness tests are used to predict performance potential and provide feedback on the effectiveness of a training programme. Coaches can use results to identify the performer's strengths, areas for improvement and types of training needed to achieve optimum performance.

Fitness testing is also carried out in health clubs where instructors screen clients for contraindications to exercise, administer fitness tests, and use the results to design exercise programmes that meet the clients' personal goals. When conducting fitness assessments, instructors adhere to strict health and safety procedures, test protocol guidelines, and can identify those clients requiring medical referral.

In this unit you will gain experience of a range of laboratory- and field-based fitness tests. You will administer these tests, providing feedback to an individual on their fitness levels. You will conduct health screening techniques and health monitoring tests for two contrasting individuals, interpreting the results, and provide recommendations for lifestyle improvement.

Learning outcomes

After completing this unit you should:

1. know a range of laboratory-based and field-based fitness tests
2. be able to use health screening techniques
3. be able to administer appropriate fitness tests
4. be able to interpret the results of fitness tests and provide feedback.

Assessment and grading criteria

This table shows you what you must do in order to achieve a pass, merit or distinction grade, and where you can find activities in this book to help you.

To achieve a **pass** grade the evidence must show that the learner is able to:	To achieve a **merit** grade the evidence must show that, in addition to the pass criteria, the learner is able to:	To achieve a **distinction** grade the evidence must show that, in addition to the pass and merit criteria, the learner is able to:
P1 describe one test for each component of physical fitness, including advantages and disadvantages **Assessment activity 8.1, page 218**	**M1** explain the advantages and disadvantages of one fitness test for each component of physical fitness **Assessment activity 8.1, page 218**	
P2 prepare an appropriate health screening questionnaire **Assessment activity 8.2, page 222**		
P3 devise and use appropriate health screening procedures for two contrasting individuals **Assessment activity 8.2, page 222**		
P4 safely administer and interpret the results of four different health monitoring tests for two contrasting individuals **Assessment activity 8.2, page 222**	**M2** describe the strengths and areas for improvement for two contrasting individuals using information from health screening questionnaires and health monitoring tests · **Assessment activity 8.2, page 222**	**D1** evaluate the health screening questionnaires and health monitoring test results and provide recommendations for lifestyle improvement **Assessment activity 8.2, page 222**
P5 select and safely administer six different fitness tests for a selected individual recording the findings **Assessment activity 8.3, page 225**	**M3** justify the selection of fitness tests commenting on suitability, reliability, validity and practicality **Assessment activity 8.3, page 225**	
P6 give feedback to a selected individual, following fitness testing, describing the test results and interpreting their levels of fitness against normative data **Assessment activity 8.4, page 226**	**M4** compare the fitness test results to normative data and identify strengths and areas for improvement **Assessment activity 8.4, page 226**	**D2** analyse the fitness test results and provide recommendations for appropriate future activities or training **Assessment activity 8.4, page 226**

How you will be assessed

This unit will be assessed by an internal assignment that will be designed and marked by the staff at your centre. Your assessment could be in the form of:

- practically assessed activities
- laboratory reports
- presentations
- case studies
- written assignments.

Damian Silva, 17-year-old gymnast

This unit gave me an insight into conducting a client health fitness assessment and the knowledge, understanding and skills needed to perform well. Having studied the Edexcel BTEC Level 2 Diploma in Sport, I had some experience of fitness testing and had participated in fitness tests like the multi-stage fitness test and step test. In this unit we covered other fitness tests which I hadn't experienced before like the Wingate test of anaerobic power – which really pushes you to your max! We looked at the advantages and disadvantages of fitness tests and why different clients might need different types of test.

The thing I enjoyed most was working with clients in a real-world setting and administering health screening techniques, health monitoring tests and fitness tests. It was challenging giving detailed feedback to clients on what their results meant and how they could improve.

By studying this unit I've gained some great practical experience in assessing people's fitness and it has helped me to develop my confidence and skills when working with people.

Over to you

- What areas of this unit might you find challenging?
- Which section of the unit are you most looking forward to?
- What preparation can you do in readiness for the unit assessment(s)?

1. Know a range of laboratory-based and field-based fitness tests

1.1 Fitness tests

To safely and effectively administer laboratory-based and field-based fitness tests, you need good knowledge and understanding of tests for different components of fitness, and the procedures and protocols to follow. You'll need to be aware of the advantages and disadvantages of different fitness tests and the implications these have for test selection and administration. In this section you'll gain practical experience of different fitness tests, the standard methods to follow and how to interpret test results. You will look at the advantages and disadvantages of fitness tests and how these need to be taken into account when selecting appropriate tests to administer to a client. In particular, you will look at the following test methods for these different components of fitness:

Component of fitness	Fitness test
Flexibility	Sit and reach
Strength	Grip strength dynamometer 1 repetition maximum (1RM)
Aerobic endurance	Multi-stage fitness test Forestry step test 1.5 mile run test 1 mile walk test
Speed	35 metre sprint
Power	Vertical jump Wingate test
Muscular endurance	1 minute press-up 1 minute sit-up
Body composition	Skinfold testing (Durnin and Womersley, 1974) Bioelectrical impedance analysis

Table 8.1: The different components of fitness and types of fitness tests

Flexibility – the sit and reach test

This test is an indirect measure of static flexibility. Its aim is to measure trunk forward flexion, hamstring, hip and lower back range of motion. A standard sit and reach box is used.

1. Perform a short warm-up prior to this test. Don't use fast, jerky movements as this may increase risk of injury. Remove your shoes.

2. Sit with your heels placed against the edge of the sit and reach box. Keep your legs flat on the floor, i.e. keep your knees down.

3. Place one hand on top of the other and reach forward slowly. Your fingertips should be in contact with the measuring portion of the sit and reach box. As you reach forward, drop your head between your arms and breathe out as you push forward.

4. The best of three trials should be recorded.

Rating	Males (cm)	Females (cm)
Excellent	25+	20+
Very good	17	17
Good	15	16
Average	14	15
Poor	13	14
Very poor	9	10

Table 8.2: Interpreting the results of the sit and reach test

Alternative direct methods used to measure static flexibility include use of a goniometer or a Leighton flexometer. These devices can be used to measure joint range of movement (ROM) with norms available for interpretation of ROM achieved at the neck, trunk, shoulder, elbow, radioulnar, wrist, hip, knee and ankle joints.

Use of goniometry to assess joint ROM. Which flexibility test will you choose to administer?

Static strength – grip strength dynamometer test

This measures the static strength of the power grip-squeezing muscles, where the whole hand is used as a vice or clamp. A grip dynamometer is a spring device – as force is applied, the spring is compressed and this moves the dynamometer needle which indicates the result. Digital dynamometers are also available.

1. Adjust the handgrip size so that the dynamometer feels comfortable to hold/grip.
2. Stand with your arms by the side of your body.
3. Hold the dynamometer parallel to the side of your body with the dial/display facing away from you.
4. Squeeze as hard as possible for 5 seconds, without moving your arm.
5. Carry out three trials on each hand, with a 1 minute rest between trials.

Rating	Males aged 15–19 (kg)	Females aged 15–19 (kg)
Excellent	52+	32+
Good	47–51	28–31
Average	44–46	25–27
Below average	39–43	20–24
Poor	<39	<20

Table 8.3: Interpreting the results of the grip strength dynamometer test

Dynamic strength – bench press 1 repetition maximum (1RM)

The bench press 1 repetition maximum (1RM) is a test of the dynamic strength of the bench pressing pectoral muscles of the chest. It is a dynamic test used to assess upper body strength. The test can be safely carried out using a bench press resistance machine.

1. An informed consent form must be completed before undertaking this maximal test. An example of a consent form is shown on page 202.
2. Carry out a standard warm-up and stretching of the major muscle groups.
3. Determine a comfortable weight to start to press.
4. Breathe out on exertion, i.e. as the weight is lifted. Ensure you don't hold your breath as this will cause an increase in blood pressure.
5. Each bench press weight successfully lifted should be noted.
6. Allow a 2 minute rest between trials before increasing the weight by 5–10 lb.
7. Continue this protocol until a maximum weight is successfully lifted. This is recorded as your 1RM.
8. Perform a standard cool down.
9. Divide your 1RM result (lb) by your body weight in lb. Use the table below to interpret your results.

Rating	Males (1RM lb/lb body weight)	Females (1RM lb/lb body weight)
Excellent	>1.26	>0.78
Good	1.17–1.25	0.72–0.77
Average	0.97–1.16	0.59–0.71
Fair	0.88–0.96	0.53–0.58
Poor	<0.87	<0.52

Table 8.4: Interpreting the results of the bench press 1RM test

Remember

If you measure your body weight and weight lifted in kg, convert these figures to lb by multiplying by 2.2.

To use the interpretation table above divide the weight lifted in lb by your body weight in lb.

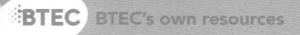

INFORMED CONSENT FOR STRENGTH TESTS

FITNESS TESTS TO BE UNDERTAKEN
• **1-RM for Chest** • **1-RM for Back** • **1-RM for Legs**
1. The purpose of these tests is to determine the maximal strength of the muscle groups used. 2. The participant will carry out standard warming-up and cool down procedures for the test. 3. The participant will be required to perform a one-repetition maximum (1-RM) for the tests cited above. 4. All participants will receive method details in full. 5. The tutor/assessor is available to answer any relevant queries which may arise concerning the test. 6. The participant is free to withdraw consent and discontinue participation in the test at any time. 7. Only the tutor/assessor and participant will have access to data recorded from the test which will be stored securely. Participant confidentiality is assured.

I FULLY UNDERSTAND THE SCOPE OF MY INVOLVEMENT IN THIS FITNESS TEST AND HAVE FREELY CONSENTED TO MY PARTICIPATION.

Participant signature: _____ **Date:** _____

Tutor/assesssor signature: _____ **Date:** _____

I (insert participant name), **UNDERSTAND THAT MY PARENTS/GUARDIAN HAVE GIVEN PERMISSION FOR ME TO TAKE PART IN THIS FITNESS TEST, WHICH WILL BE SUPERVISED BY** (insert tutor name). **I AM PARTICIPATING IN THIS FITNESS TEST BECAUSE I WANT TO, AND I HAVE BEEN INFORMED THAT I CAN STOP THE TEST AT ANY TIME WITHOUT ANY ISSUES ARISING.**

Participant signature: _____ **Date:** _____

Assesssor signature: _____ **Date:** _____

Parental/Guardian Signature: _____ **Date:** _____

Figure 8.1: Example of an informed consent form for strength tests

Aerobic endurance – multi-stage fitness test

This test is used to predict your maximum oxygen uptake (aerobic fitness) levels and is performed to a pre-recorded audio tape. It should be conducted indoors, usually in a sports hall using two lines (or cones) placed 20 metres apart.

1. Perform a short warm-up.
2. Line up on the start line and on hearing the triple bleep run to the other line 20 metres away. You must reach the other line before or on the single bleep that determines each shuttle run.
3. Don't get ahead of the bleep – you need to make sure you turn to run to the other line on the bleep.

4. You will find that the bleeps get closer and closer together, so you'll need to continually increase your pace.

5. Continue to run to each line. A spotter is used to check you have reached each line in time with the bleep. If not, you will receive two verbal warnings before being asked to pull out of the test.

6. Continue running until you are physically exhausted, i.e. you have reached maximum exhaustion, at which point your level and shuttle reached is recorded.

7. Use Table 8.5 to predict your maximum oxygen consumption (ml/kg/min).

8. Use Table 8.6 on page 204 to interpret the maximum oxygen uptake result.

Level	Shuttle	VO$_2$ max	Level	Shuttle	VO$_2$ max	Level	Shuttle	VO$_2$ max	Level	Shuttle	VO$_2$ max
4	2	26.8	10	2	47.4	15	2	64.6	19	2	78.3
4	4	27.6	10	4	48.0	15	4	65.1	19	4	78.8
4	6	28.3	10	6	48.7	15	6	65.6	19	6	79.2
4	9	29.5	10	8	49.3	15	8	66.2	19	8	79.7
5	2	30.2	10	11	50.2	15	10	66.7	19	10	80.2
5	4	31.0	11	2	50.8	15	13	67.5	19	12	80.6
5	6	31.8	11	4	51.4	16	2	68.0	19	15	81.3
5	9	32.9	11	6	51.9	16	4	68.5	20	2	81.8
6	2	33.6	11	8	52.5	16	6	69.0	20	4	82.2
6	4	34.3	11	10	53.1	16	8	69.5	20	6	82.6
6	6	35.0	11	12	53.7	16	10	69.9	20	8	83.0
6	8	35.7	12	2	54.3	16	12	70.5	20	10	83.5
6	10	36.4	12	4	54.8	16	14	70.9	20	12	83.9
7	2	37.1	12	6	55.4	17	2	71.4	20	14	84.3
7	4	37.8	12	8	56.0	17	4	71.9	20	16	84.8
7	6	38.5	12	10	56.5	17	6	72.4	21	2	85.2
7	8	39.2	12	12	57.1	17	8	72.9	21	4	85.6
7	10	39.9	13	2	57.6	17	10	73.4	21	6	86.1
8	2	40.5	13	4	58.2	17	12	73.9	21	8	86.5
8	4	41.1	13	6	58.7	17	14	74.4	21	10	86.9
8	6	41.8	13	8	59.3	18	2	74.8	21	12	87.4
8	8	42.4	13	10	59.8	18	4	75.3	21	14	87.8
8	11	43.3	13	13	60.6	18	6	75.8	21	16	88.2
9	2	43.9	14	2	61.1	18	8	76.2			
9	4	44.5	14	4	61.7	18	10	76.7			
9	6	45.2	14	6	62.2	18	12	77.2			
9	8	45.8	14	8	62.7	18	15	77.9			
9	11	46.8	14	10	63.2						
			14	13	64.0						

Table 8.5: Predicted maximum oxygen uptake values for the multistage fitness test (ml/kg/min)

Rating	Males (aged 15–19) (ml/kg/min)	Females (aged 15–19) (ml/kg/min)
Excellent	60+	54+
Good	48-59	43-53
Average	39–47	35–42
Below average	30–38	28–34
Poor	<30	<28

Table 8.6: Interpreting maximum oxygen uptake results (VO$_2$ max, ml/kg/min)

Aerobic endurance – forestry step test

Developed in 1977 by Brian Sharkey, this test is a modified version of the Harvard Step test. It is widely used in fitness selection procedures (for example, by the police) and predicts aerobic endurance levels.

A different bench height is used for males and females. For males, the height of the bench should be 40 cm (15.75 in.), for females, 33 cm (13 in.). The stepping rate of 22.5 steps per minute is the same for both males and females, which means the metronome should be set at a cadence of 90 beats per minute.

1. Stand directly facing the bench and start stepping in time with the beat of the metronome. As soon as you start stepping, the tester will start the stopwatch.

2. Keep to the beat of the metronome, which means you will put one foot onto the bench, then your other foot, then the first foot will be lowered to the floor, then your other foot, i.e. 'up', 'up', 'down', 'down'.

3. Straighten your legs when you fully step up onto the bench.

4. Keep stepping for 5 minutes, at which point the tester will stop the metronome and you will need to sit down immediately and locate your radial pulse.

5. At 5 minutes and 15 seconds (15 seconds after you have sat down) you will need to count your pulse for 15 seconds (stopping at 5 minutes and 30 seconds).

6. Record your 15 second pulse rate and perform a short cool down.

Use the tables to obtain your non-adjusted aerobic fitness level:

- Use either Table 8.7 or 8.8 (depending on your gender) on pages 205 and 206 to locate your 15 second pulse in the 'Pulse count' column and your body weight (to the closest kg). You will find your non-adjusted aerobic fitness level (in ml/kg/min) where these two values intersect.

- Next, adjust your fitness level to take into account your age, which will provide a more accurate prediction of your aerobic endurance. In Table 8.9 on page 206, locate your nearest age in years (left-hand column) and locate your non-adjusted aerobic fitness level (fitness score) along the top. You will find your age-adjusted fitness level (ml/kg/min) at the point where these two values intersect.

- Use Table 8.10 on page 207 to interpret your aerobic fitness level.

Pulse count	Maximal oxygen consumption (VO$_2$ max)												
45	33	33	33	33	33	32	32	32	32	32	32	32	32
44	34	34	34	34	33	33	33	33	33	33	33	33	33
43	35	35	35	34	34	34	34	34	34	34	34	34	34
42	36	35	35	35	35	35	35	35	35	35	35	34	34
41	36	36	36	36	36	36	36	36	36	36	36	35	35
40	37	37	37	37	37	37	37	37	35	35	35	35	35
39	38	38	38	38	38	38	38	38	38	38	38	37	37
38	39	39	39	39	39	39	39	39	39	39	39	38	38
37	41	40	40	40	40	40	40	40	40	40	40	39	39
36	42	42	41	41	41	41	41	41	41	41	41	40	40
35	43	43	42	42	42	42	42	42	42	42	42	42	41
34	44	44	43	43	43	43	43	43	43	43	43	43	43
33	46	45	45	45	45	45	44	44	44	44	44	44	44
32	47	47	46	46	46	46	46	46	46	46	46	46	46
31	48	48	48	47	47	47	47	47	47	47	47	47	47
30	50	49	49	49	48	48	48	48	48	48	48	48	48
29	52	51	51	51	50	50	50	50	50	50	50	50	50
28	53	53	53	53	52	52	52	52	51	51	51	51	51
27	55	55	55	54	54	54	54	54	54	53	53	53	52
26	57	57	56	56	56	56	56	56	56	55	55	54	54
25	59	59	58	58	58	58	58	58	58	56	56	55	55
24	60	60	60	60	60	60	60	59	59	58	58	57	
23	62	62	61	61	61	61	61	60	60	60	59		
22	64	64	63	63	63	63	62	62	61	61			
21	66	66	65	65	65	64	64	64	62				
20	68	68	67	67	67	67	66	66	65				
Weight (kg)	54.5	59.1	63.6	68.2	72.7	77.3	81.8	86.4	91	95.4	100	104.5	109

Table 8.7: Forestry non-adjusted aerobic fitness values (ml/kg/min) for **males**

Pulse count	Maximal oxygen consumption (VO$_2$ max)											
45										29	29	29
44								30	30	30	30	30
43							31	31	31	31	31	31
42			32	32	32	32	32	32	32	32	32	32
41			33	33	33	33	33	33	33	33	33	33
40			34	34	34	34	34	34	34	34	34	34
39			35	35	35	35	35	35	35	35	35	35
38			36	36	36	36	36	36	36	36	36	36
37			37	37	37	37	37	37	37	37	37	37
36		37	38	38	38	38	38	38	38	38	38	38
35	38	38	39	39	39	39	39	39	39	39	39	39
34	39	39	40	40	40	40	40	40	40	40	40	40
33	40	40	41	41	41	41	41	41	41	41	41	41
32	41	41	42	42	42	42	42	42	42	42	42	42
31	42	42	43	43	43	43	43	43	43	43	43	43
30	43	43	44	44	44	44	44	44	44	44	44	44
29	44	44	45	45	45	45	45	45	45	45	45	45
28	45	45	46	46	46	47	47	47	47	47	47	
27	46	46	47	48	48	49	49	49	49	49		
26	47	48	49	50	50	51	51	51	51			
25	49	50	51	52	52	53	53					
24	51	52	53	54	54	55						
23	53	54	55	56	56	57						
Weight (kg)	36.4	40.9	45.4	50.0	54.5	59.1	63.6	68.2	72.7	77.3	81.8	86.4

Table 8.8: Forestry non-adjusted aerobic fitness values (ml/kg/min) for **females**

Fitness score		30	31	32	33	34	35	36	37	38	39	40	41	42	43	44	45	46	47	48	49	50
Nearest age	15	32	33	34	35	36	37	38	39	40	41	42	43	44	45	46	47	48	49	50	51	53
	20	31	32	33	34	35	36	37	38	39	40	41	42	43	44	45	46	47	48	49	50	51

(cont.)

Fitness score		51	52	53	54	55	56	57	58	59	60	61	62	63	64	65	66	67	68	69	70	71	72
Nearest age	15	54	55	56	57	58	59	60	61	62	63	64	65	66	67	68	69	70	71	72	74	75	76
	20	52	53	54	55	56	57	58	59	60	61	62	63	64	65	66	67	68	69	70	71	72	73

Table 8.9: Age-adjusted fitness levels

Example 1: If your age is 16 years and you score 36 on the step test, your age-adjusted score is 38.

Example 2: If your age is 20 years and you score 65 on the step test, your age-adjusted score is 66.

Age and gender	Fitness category						
	Superior	Excellent	Very good	Good	Fair	Poor	Very poor
	Maximum oxygen consumption (ml/kg/min)						
15-year-old male	57+	56–52	51–47	46–42	41–37	36–32	<32
15-year-old female	54+	53–49	48–44	43–39	38–34	33–29	<29
20-year-old male	56+	55–51	50–46	45–41	40–36	35–31	<31
20-year-old female	53+	52–48	47–43	42–38	37–33	32–28	<28

Table 8.10: Aerobic fitness levels

Aerobic endurance – 1.5 mile run test

This test is best performed on an indoor athletics track, or use an outdoor track on a day when weather conditions will not adversely affect test results.

1. Perform a warm-up and stretching of major muscle groups.
2. On the starter's orders, run a distance of 1.5 miles as fast as you can.
3. Record the time taken.
4. Perform a standard cool down and stretching of major muscle groups.

To interpret the results:

- use Table 8.11 to provide an estimate of maximal oxygen consumption (VO_2 max ml/kg/min) according to the time taken to complete the run
- then use Table 8.6 on page 204 to obtain the fitness rating.

Time (mins) for 1.5 mile run	VO_2 max (ml/kg/min)	Time (mins) for 1.5 mile run	VO_2 max (ml/kg/min)
<7.31	75	12.31–13.00	39
7.31–8.00	72	13.01–13.30	37
8.01–8.30	67	13.31–14.00	36
8.31–9.00	62	14.01–14.30	34
9.01–9.30	58	14.31–15.00	33
9.31–10.00	55	15.01–15.30	31
10.01–10.30	52	15.31–16.00	30
10.31–11.00	49	16.01–16.30	28
11.01–11.30	46	16.31–17.00	27
11.31–12.00	44	17.01–17.30	26
12.01–12.30	41	17.31–18.00	25

Table 8.11: Results of the 1.5 mile run test

Take it further

Amazing VO_2 max!

Cross country skiers and cyclists have some of the highest maximum oxygen uptake values ever reported. Check out the levels they have reached in Table 8.12. Spain's Miguel Indurain, the road racing cyclist and Tour de France winner, also had a reported resting heart rate of 28 beats per minute. How does your VO_2 max and resting heart rate compare?

VO_2 max (ml/kg/min)	Athlete	Gender	Sport/event
96.0	Bjorn Daehlie	Male	Cross country skiing
92.5	Greg LeMond	Male	Cycling
88.0	Miguel Indurain	Male	Cycling
85.0	John Ngugi	Male	Cross country runner
73.5	Greta Waitz	Female	Marathon runner
71.2	Ingrid Kristiansen	Female	Marathon runner
67.2	Rosa Mota	Female	Marathon runner

Table 8.12: Elite maximum oxygen uptake values

Aerobic endurance – 1 mile walk test

This low intensity test is used to predict maximum oxygen uptake and, because of the non-stressful nature of the test, it can be particularly useful in assessing those who are unfit. The test is best performed on an indoor athletics track, or use an outdoor track on a day when weather conditions will not adversely affect test results.

1. Perform a warm-up.

2. On the starter's orders, walk a distance of 1 mile as fast as possible.

3. Record the time taken and convert to decimal minutes:

   where: decimal minutes (t) = [min + (s/60)]

4. On crossing the finishing line, take pulse rate for 15 seconds.

5. Convert the 15 second pulse into heart rate (beats/minute):

   where: 15 second pulse rate x 4 = beats per minute

6. Use the equation **below** to predict maximum oxygen uptake (VO$_2$ max l/min)

   VO$_2$ max (l/min) = 6.9652 + (0.0091 x wt) – (0.0257 x age) + (0.5955 x gender) – (0.2240 x t) – (0.0115 x HR)

   Where: wt = body weight (lb)

   age = years

   gender = 0 = female; 1 = male

   t = time in decimal minutes

   HR = heart rate (beats/minute)

Key terms

Absolute VO$_2$ max – maximum oxygen consumption expressed in litres per minute (l/min).

Relative VO$_2$ max – maximum oxygen consumption expressed relative to the individual's body weight in kg. The units of relative VO$_2$ max are ml of oxygen per kilogram of body weight per minute (ml/kg/min).

Case study: Conducting the 1 mile walk test

Paul is a 19-year-old male who completed the 1 mile walk test in a time of 13 minutes and 26 seconds. His body weight is 174 lb. On crossing the finishing line, Paul's 15 second pulse was 29.

Calculate Paul's maximum oxygen uptake (VO$_2$ max ml/kg/min).

Workings

- To convert 13.26 to decimal minutes (where decimal minutes (t) = [min + (s/60)])

  = [13 + (26/60)] = 13.43 decimal minutes.

- To convert the 15 second pulse into beats per minute

  = 29 x 4 = 116 beats/minute.

- Use the equation to predict maximum oxygen uptake (VO$_2$ max ml/kg/min):

  VO$_2$ max (l/min) = 6.9652 + (0.0091 x wt) – (0.0257 x age) + (0.5955 x gender) – (0.2240 x t) – (0.0115 x HR)

  Therefore:

  VO$_2$ max (l/min) = 6.9652 + (0.0091 x 174) – (0.0257 x 19) + (0.5955 x 1) – (0.2240 x 13.43) – (0.0115 x 116)

  VO$_2$ max (l/min) = 4.31

- Convert **absolute VO$_2$ max** (l/min) to **relative VO$_2$ max** (ml/kg/min):

  VO$_2$ max (ml/kg/min) = [(4.31 x 1000) ÷ Body weight (kg)]

  Therefore:

  VO$_2$ max (ml/kg/min) = [(4.31 x 1000) ÷ 79 kg] = 54.6 ml/kg/min

- Using Table 8.6 on page 204, Paul's fitness rating is good.

1. How does your predicted VO$_2$ max from the 1 mile walk test compare to normative data?

2. How do your results compare to data for elite performers?

3. How do your results compare to those of your peers?

4. Calculate your results and discuss in small groups.

Maximal treadmill tests

Maximal treadmill tests require participants to exercise until physical exhaustion is reached. Informed consent is required prior to undertaking the test. Tests are performed on a motor-driven treadmill which can be adjusted for both incline and speed, and specialist equipment is required to collect and measure respiratory gases.

Maximal treadmill test methods are usually continuous and progressive in nature, where at prescribed time intervals, the tester will increase the percentage of incline and/or the speed of the treadmill. Due to the physically stressful nature of maximal treadmill tests, they are not suitable for certain people, for example, the elderly.

Remember

During maximal treadmill testing, maximum oxygen uptake (VO_2 max) is reached when:

- the individual reports a Rating of Perceived Exertion (RPE) of 20 (Borg 6–20 RPE scale)
- there is less than 150 ml/min increase between exercise workloads
- blood lactate is greater than 8 mmol/l.

Speed – 35 metre sprint

The test is best performed on an indoor athletics track, or using an outdoor track on a day when weather conditions will not adversely affect test results.

1. Perform a warm-up.
2. Three people should keep time for the sprint, using stopwatches capable of measuring to one-tenth of a second.
3. Line up on the start line, in a standing start position.
4. As soon as you start sprinting, the timers will start their stopwatches.
5. Sprint as fast as you can, crossing the 35 metre line.
6. When you cross the 35 metre line, the timers will stop their stopwatches.
7. Your time for the sprint is recorded to the closest tenth of a second. An average result can be taken from the three timers.
8. A maximum of two to three trials are performed in one day. Allow at least 3 minutes recovery between trials. A third trial should only be performed if the difference in times between your first and second trial is greater than 0.20 seconds.

9. The best time from your two or three trials is recorded as your 35 metre sprint result.
10. To prevent muscle soreness, perform a cool down followed by static stretching.

Rating	Males (s)	Females (s)
Excellent	<4.80	<5.30
Good	4.80–5.09	5.30–5.59
Average	5.10–5.29	5.60–5.89
Fair	5.30–5.60	5.90–6.20
Poor	5.60+	6.20+

Table 8.13: Interpretation of results from the 35 metre sprint test

Anaerobic power – vertical jump test

This is a test of the anaerobic power of the quadriceps muscle group. A standard vertical jump board is used for the test, which may digitally record the jump height, or alternatively gymnast's chalk may be used.

1. Perform a short warm-up prior to the test.
2. Stand with your dominant side against the board, feet together, and reach up as high as you can to record your standing reach height.
3. Only one dip of the arms and knees is permitted; make the jump while simultaneously touching the vertical jump board at the peak of your jump.
4. Perform three trials. No rest is required between trials. The time taken to observe and record the height of the jump is all that is needed for recovery between consecutive trials.

To obtain the results of this fitness test, a nomogram can be used. Use the Lewis nomogram to predict the power of your quadriceps in kgm/s.

- Plot the difference (D) between your standing reach height and your best jump height (cm) on the nomogram line (D).
- Plot your weight in kilograms on the nomogram line (Wt).
- Using a sharpened pencil and ruler, join up the two plots, which will cross over the power line (P) to give a prediction of the anaerobic power of your quadriceps muscles (in kgm/s).

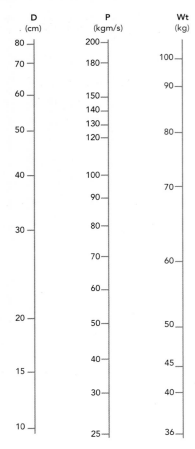

Figure 8.2: Lewis nomogram

Rating	Males (kgm/s)	Females (kgm/s)
Above average	105+	90+
Average	95	80
Below average	<85	<70

Table 8.14: Interpretation of anaerobic power results from the vertical jump test

Anaerobic power – Wingate cycle test

The Wingate cycle test predicts the anaerobic power of the quadriceps muscle groups using a 30 second all-out maximal sprint on a mechanically-braked cycle ergometer (for example, Monark 824E). The test was developed by scientists at the Wingate Institute in Israel.

1. Informed consent is required before participating in this arduous test.
2. You will need to wear a heart rate monitor for the warm-up. You need to cycle for between 2 and 4 minutes at an intensity sufficient to cause the heart to beat at 150–160 bpm. During the warm-up include two or three all-out bursts of cycling for 4–8 seconds each.
3. Following the warm-up you should rest for approximately 3 to 5 minutes during which you can carry out stretching of the major muscle groups.
4. Measure your body weight in kg. To calculate the weight to add to the cycle ergometer basket, use this formula:

weight to add to basket = body weight x 0.075 minus 1 kg for the basket weight

= weight to add to basket

- On command from the timer, pedal as fast as possible to overcome the inertia of the flywheel. The weight will then be lowered onto the basket.
- When the final load has been added to the basket, timing will commence. Continue to pedal as fast as possible for 30 seconds.
- An assistant will note the revolutions per minute (RPM) achieved for each 5 second period. This can be noted electronically from the cycle ergometer display.
- The subject will require motivation from peers to help them continue to sprint on the bike as fast as possible and keep the pedals turning for the full 30 seconds of the test.
- For cool down, and to minimise the risk of fainting, continue cycling with no load on the basket, for 2 to 3 minutes after the test. The subject will need to be given help from assistants to get off the bike and should then, as a precaution, assume the instructed recovery position.
- This is an extremely arduous test, requiring an all-out maximal effort. Tutors should be aware that such effort may cause participants to faint or be sick following the test and should ensure that procedures are in place should this happen.

Case study: Conducting the Wingate cycle test

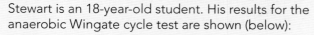

Stewart is an 18-year-old student. His results for the anaerobic Wingate cycle test are shown (below):

Calculation of weight to add to cycle ergometer basket:

Stewart's body weight	= 70 kg
Weight to add to basket	= Body weight x 0.075
	= 70 x 0.075
	= 5.25
Minus 1 kg for basket weight	= 4.25

Revolutions per minute for each 5 second period:

Time (s)	RPM
5	115
10	118
15	118
20	109
25	106
30	105

Calculation of anaerobic power:

anaerobic power (W) = total weight on basket (kg) x revolutions x 11.765

Time (s)	Anaerobic power (w)
5	5.25 x (115/60 x 5) x 11.765 = 592.0 W
10	5.25 x (118/60 x 5) x 11.765 = 607.4 W
15	5.25 x (118/60 x 5) x 11.765 = 607.4 W
20	5.25 x (109/60 x 5) x 11.765 = 561.0 W
25	5.25 x (106/60 x 5) x 11.765 = 545.6 W
30	5.25 x (105/60 x 5) x 11.765 = 540.5 W

Calculation of total revs in 30 seconds:

Time (s)		5s revs
5	115/60 x 5	9.58
10	118/60 x 5	9.83
15	118/60 x 5	9.83
20	109/60 x 5	9.08
25	106/60 x 5	8.83
30	105/60 x 5	8.75
Total revs		55.90 = 56 (closest rev)

Anaerobic capacity = total revs in 30s x 6m* (kgm-30s)   x force (kg)
= 56 x 6 x 5.25
= 1764 (kgm-30s)

*This is dependent on the cycle ergometer used. For a Monark cycle ergometer, one revolution of the flywheel is equal to a distance of 6 metres. For a Tunturi cycle ergometer, the flywheel travels through 3 metres for each pedal revolution. Insert the appropriate figure for the type of ergometer used.

Calculation of anaerobic capacity:

Calculation of anaerobic capacity (W)
= kgm-30s/3
= 1764/3
= 588 W (average mean power)

Calculation of power decline:

$$100 \times \frac{\text{(peak anaerobic power – low anaerobic power)}}{\text{peak anaerobic power}}$$
= % fatigue rate

$$= 100 \times \frac{(607.4 - 540.5)}{607.4} = 11.0\text{ % fatigue rate}$$

1. Undertake the maximal anaerobic Wingate cycle test.

   From your results, calculate:
   a) peak anaerobic power (W)
   b) anaerobic capacity (W) – your average mean power
   c) your power decline (percentage of fatigue rate).

2. Plot a graph to show your data results. On the Y-axis plot anaerobic power (W) achieved for each 5 second period (plot time in seconds on the X-axis).

3. Show your average mean power (w) by drawing a straight line across your graph intersecting the Y-axis at your power result.
   a) What is your average mean power result (w)?
   b) How do your anaerobic power results compare to those of your peers?

4. A high peak anaerobic power and low fatigue rate indicates an individual who has good anaerobic power. Discuss and compare your results in small groups.

Muscular endurance – press-up test

This test is used to assess the endurance of the muscles of your upper body.

1. Position yourself on a mat, with your hands shoulder width apart and arms fully extended.
2. Next, lower your body until the elbows are at 90 degrees.
3. Return to the starting position, with your arms fully extended.
4. Make sure your push-up action is continuous, with no rests in between.
5. The total number of press-ups is recorded for 1 minute.

Due to reduced upper body strength, females may choose to use a modified press-up technique. The positioning is similar to the standard method, but in the starting position a bent knee position is assumed.

Rating	Males	Females
Excellent	45+	34+
Good	35–44	17–33
Average	20–34	6–16
Poor	<19	<5

Table 8.15: Interpretation of results from the full body press-up test

Rating	Number of reps
Excellent	39+
Good	34–38
Average	17–33
Fair	6–16
Poor	<6

Table 8.16: Interpretation of results from the modified press-up test

Muscular endurance – sit-up test

This test assesses the endurance and development of your abdominal muscles.

1. Lie on a mat with your knees bent, and feet flat on the floor, with your arms folded across your body.
2. Raise yourself up to a 90 degree position and then return to the floor.
3. Your feet can be held by a partner if you wish.
4. The total number of sit-ups is recorded for 1 minute.

Rating	Males	Females
Excellent	49–59	42–54
Good	43–48	36–41
Above average	39–42	32–35
Average	35–38	28–31
Below average	31–34	24–27
Poor	25–30	18–23
Very poor	11–24	3–17

Table 8.17: Interpretation of results from the sit-up test

Body composition – skinfold testing

Skinfold testing can be used to predict percentage of body fat. A relationship exists between subcutaneous, internal fat and body density. Skinfold testing for the prediction of percentage of body fat is based on this relationship. In this section you will be using Durnin and Womersley's (1974) generalised prediction equations to predict your percentage of body fat.

For males and females, skinfolds are taken on the following four sites:

1. **Biceps** – a vertical fold on the anterior surface of the biceps muscle midway between the anterior axillary fold and the antecubital fossa.
2. **Triceps** – a vertical fold on the back midline of the upper arm, over the triceps muscle, halfway between the acromion process (bony process on the top of the shoulder) and olecranon process (bony process on the elbow). The arm should be held freely by the side of the body.
3. **Subscapular** – a diagonal fold taken at a 45 degree angle 1–2 cm below the inferior angle of the scapulae (point of the shoulder blade).
4. **Suprailiac** – a diagonal fold above the crest of the ilium, taken in the anterior axillary line above the iliac crest (just above the hip bone and 2–3 cm forward).

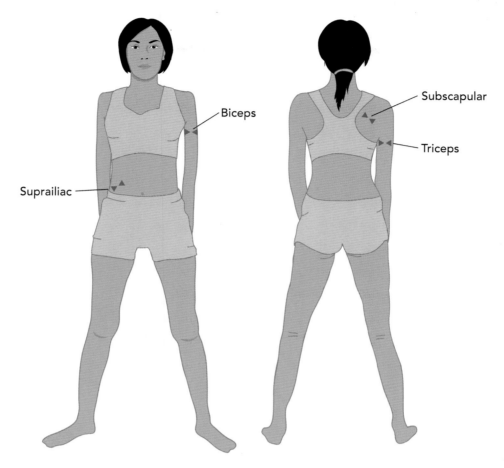

Figure 8.3: Skinfold testing: biceps, triceps, subscapular and suprailiac

Following a standard method will help ensure your results are valid. You will need skinfold calipers (such as Harpenden or Slimguide) to take the skinfolds as well as a tape measure and pen to mark each site. Work in pairs or small groups for skinfold testing.

1. Measurements should be taken on dry skin on the right side of the body. Exceptions to this would be if the participant has a tattoo or deformity on the site location, which means the left side of the body would need to be used.

2. The participant should keep their muscles relaxed during the test.

3. Mark each skinfold site with a pen and use a tape measure to find the midpoints.

4. Grasp the skinfold firmly between your thumb and index finger and gently pull away from the body. The skinfold should be grasped about 1 cm away from the site marked.

5. Place the skinfold calipers perpendicular to the fold, on the site marked, with the dial facing upwards.

6. Maintaining your grasp, place the calipers midway between the base and tip of the skinfold and allow the calipers to be fully released so that full tension is placed on the skinfold.

7. Read the dial of the skinfold calipers to the nearest 0.5 mm, 2 seconds after you have released the calipers. Make sure you continue to grasp the skinfold throughout testing.

8. Take a minimum of two measurements at each site. If repeated tests vary by more than 1 mm, repeat the measurement.

9. If consecutive measurements become smaller, this means that the fat is being compressed, and will result in inaccurate results. If this happens, go to another site and then come back to the site to be tested later.

10. Make sure you record each measurement as it is taken.
11. The final value is the average of the two readings (mm).

Remember

Body fat is affected by:
- age
- gender (females have essential fat)
- level of training and type of activity – population-specific equations exist for the prediction of percentage of body fat for elite gymnasts, footballers, swimmers and sprinters
- ethnicity (for example, Chinese people have lower body fat levels).

Calculation of percentage of body fat

1. Add up the results for the four skinfolds (mm).
2. Insert them into the body density calculation (see Table 8.18) according to gender:

males (16–19 years)
body density (d)
= 1.162 − [(0.063) ($\sum$ log of four × skinfolds)]

females (16–19 years)
body density (d)
= 1.1549 − [(0.0678) ($\sum$ log of four × skinfolds)]

3. Next, complete the following calculation for the prediction of percentage of body fat:

$$\left[\frac{(4.57)}{d} - 4.142\right] \times 100 = \text{\% body fat}$$

Rating	Males % body fat (16–29 years)	Females % body fat 16–29 years
Very low fat	<7	<13
Slim	7–12	13–20
Acceptable	13–17	21–25
Overweight	18–28	26–32
Obese	28+	32+

Table 8.18: Interpretation of percentage of body fat results

Case study: Calculation of percentage of body fat

Lilley is a 17-year-old student who completed the skinfold testing and the following results were recorded:
- biceps   = 9 mm
- triceps   = 15 mm
- subscapular   = 14 mm
- suprailiac   = 18 mm
- sum of skinfolds   = 56 mm
- log of skinfolds   = 1.748188

Using the calculation for females, Lilley's calculation of body density is:
= 1.1549 − [(0.0678) ($\sum$ log of four skinfolds)]
= 1.1549 − [(0.0678) (1.748188)]
= 1.1549 − (0.1185271)
body density (d) = 1.0363729

Lilley's calculation of percentage of body fat is:

$$\left[\left(\frac{(4.57)}{d}\right) - 4.142\right] \times 100 = \text{\% body fat}$$

$$\left[\left(\frac{4.57}{1.0363729}\right) - 4.142\right] \times 100 = \text{\% body fat}$$

[(4.4096097) − 4.142] × 100 = % body fat
[0.2676097] × 100   = % body fat
                           = 26.8% = overweight

1. What validity and reliability issues should you consider when undertaking skinfold testing?
2. How do your percentage of body fat results compare to normative data and to data for elite performers?
3. What other factors could affect body fat results?

Activity: Hydrodensitometry

Hydrodensitometry or underwater weighing is often thought of as the best method for the prediction of percentage of body fat. Many universities have underwater weighing tanks so that learners can undertake practical assessments to predict their percentage of body fat.

- Use the Internet or textbooks to research the rationale behind hydrodensitometry.
- Find out about the specialist equipment needed, what the test method involves and how it works.

Body composition – bioelectrical impedance analysis (BIA)

Bioelectrical impedance analysis (BIA) is a method used to predict the percentage of body fat of an individual. A BIA machine is required to conduct the test (for example, Bodystat 1500). The method is based on the fact that fat free mass in the body (muscle, bone, connective tissues) conducts electricity, whereas fat mass does not. Therefore, the higher the resistance to a weak electrical current (bioelectrical impedance), the higher the percentage of body fat of the individual.

1. Hydration levels can affect validity of test results. To ensure the test is valid, the subject should not:
   - exercise for 12 hours prior to the test
   - drink or eat within 4 hours of the test
   - drink caffeine prior to the test.
2. The subject should urinate 15 to 30 minutes before conducting the test.
3. The subject should lie down and remove their right sock and shoe.
4. Place the BIA electrodes on the right wrist, right hand, right ankle and right foot.
5. Attach the cable leads (crocodile clips) to the exposed tabs on the electrodes.
6. Enter data into the BIA machine (for example, the subject's age, gender, height, weight and activity level).

7. The test only takes a few seconds. The subject should lie still as the weak electrical current is passed through their body.
8. The percentage of body fat test result will be shown on the LCD display of the BIA machine.

1.2 Fitness tests: advantages and disadvantages

The best way to understand the advantages and disadvantages of different fitness tests is to gain first-hand experience by direct participation. By participating in fitness tests yourself you can gain knowledge and understanding of:

- why some tests might not be as valid and reliable as others
- how factors which affect test **reliability** and **validity** can be controlled or reduced
- other test advantages and disadvantages such as cost, time, equipment, practicality and the skill level required of the person administering the test
- the implications of the test advantages/disadvantages for test selection and administration.

Key terms

Reliability – the consistency and repeatability of the results obtained. That is, the ability to carry out the same test method and expect the same results.

Validity – the accuracy of the results. This means whether the results obtained are a true reflection of what you are actually trying to measure.

Maximal versus submaximal fitness tests

One of the main considerations is whether the fitness test you have conducted is maximal or submaximal.

The advantages and disadvantages of maximal fitness testing

A maximal fitness test requires the individual to make an 'all-out' effort with measurements taken at the all-out effort stage. Examples include maximal treadmill tests for the measurement of maximum oxygen consumption.

If the individual is able to reach their true maximum, then results obtained are more valid compared to submaximal testing, because physiological data is

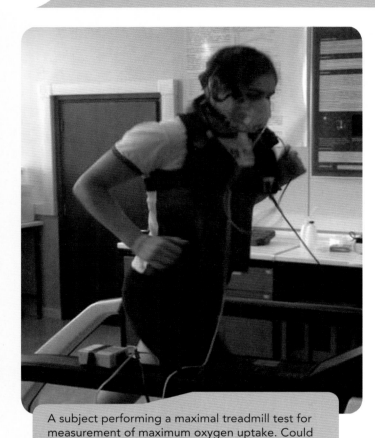

A subject performing a maximal treadmill test for measurement of maximum oxygen uptake. Could you reach your VO_2 max?

of data is made to an unknown maximum and small inaccuracies or uncontrolled variables can result in errors in prediction of the maximum because these are magnified by the process of extrapolation.

Now we'll go on to consider some of the advantages and disadvantages of fitness tests you will be familiar with.

Flexibility: sit and reach test – advantages and disadvantages

Advantages

- It is easy to complete – can use a bench and ruler if a sit and reach box is unavailable.
- The test is quick to administer.
- Published tables of norms are available.
- Modified tests exist which take into account the distance between the end of the fingers and the sit and reach box.

Disadvantages

- The test is assumed to be valid for all populations. However, research by Jackson and Baker (1986) reported that sit and reach results for 13–15-year-old girls were only moderately related to hamstring flexibility and poorly related with measures of total, upper and lower back flexibility. They concluded that the sit and reach test does not validly assess lower back flexibility in teenage girls.
- There is the potential for inconsistency of test methods. Has a warm-up been allowed or not?
- Performance may be influenced by length or width of the body segments (Wear, 1963).

Aerobic endurance: step test – advantages and disadvantages

Advantages

- There is minimal cost.
- It can test large numbers of subjects at once.
- There is no need for calibration of equipment.
- It provides good predictions of aerobic endurance as long as subjects keep good time with the metronome.

actually *measured* as opposed to 'predicted'. However, there can be difficulty in ensuring the individual is exerting maximal effort, and there are issues around motivating individuals to achieve their true maximum. There is the possibility of overexertion with some individuals and their more 'risky' nature means maximal tests are not appropriate for everybody. Maximal testing requires informed consent.

The advantages and disadvantages of submaximal fitness testing

A submaximal fitness test means that the individual performs the test at less than their maximal effort. Submaximal fitness tests require projection or extrapolation of data to estimate the individual's maximal capacity. Examples include the Astrand cycle ergometer test of aerobic fitness. Submaximal fitness tests are less 'risky' in nature and can be applied to a wider variety of populations. However, results only give a prediction, not a measurement. The extrapolation

Disadvantages

- Reliability and validity of the test depend on the correct stepping technique being used, which can be difficult for the subject to maintain.

- The stepping technique can be affected by length and proportion of the subject's legs.

- Any changes in technique can affect the work done by the subject. For example, not keeping up with the set stepping rate (dictated by a metronome), not maintaining the correct stepping rate throughout the test, not achieving correct leg extension as the subject steps up onto the bench.

- Efficiency of stepping may vary due to differences in hip angles and leg length when using a fixed bench height for all subjects.

- It is difficult to make ancillary measurements.

- It is difficult to accurately record your own radial pulse for fitness prediction.

- It is not suitable for certain populations, for example, the elderly.

- There is a risk of tripping if the step test is maximal (as exhaustion approaches).

- Well-motivated subjects are needed for maximal testing.

- The specificity of the step test favours sports performers who make endurance demands of the leg muscle groups (for example, cyclists and runners).

Accuracy of the step test: how can results be improved?

With any fitness test you need to be aware of **test variables** and how these can be controlled or reduced. Taking the step test as an example, test validity will improve if subjects have the opportunity to practise the stepping technique before the data is collected. This way, you will be able to make sure and check that the subject is aware of the correct timings and technique for stepping, i.e. full leg extension is achieved. The subject will also be able to practise locating and taking their radial pulse.

Key term

Test variable – this is any factor which could affect the validity and/or reliability of fitness test results.

Many of the published step tests that you will be familiar with use a standard bench height, which is sometimes different for males and females. However, the ideal would be for step test methods to alter the bench height to suit individual differences in the hip angles or leg length of subjects, thus ensuring efficiency of stepping movement.

Aerobic endurance: cycle ergometry tests – advantages and disadvantages

Advantages

- They can test a wider variety of populations.

- The subject is seated, which helps with taking ancillary measurements (for example, blood pressure).

- The digital display of the ergometer helps ensure correct revs/minute.

- There is a conversion of external work rate into approximate power demand.

- The seat height can be altered to suit individual differences in leg length to ensure efficiency of movement.

Disadvantages

- Subjects are tested individually, so it can be time-consuming.

- Loadings must be adjusted for differences of body mass.

- The equipment is expensive.

- There is overloading of the quadriceps at higher intensities of effort. Maximum effort can be prevented by local muscular fatigue rather than a general exhaustion of the cardiorespiratory system.

- There can be difficulty in dismounting from the ergometer in an emergency.

- The tests favour cyclists.

Cycle ergometry fitness tests are considered more accurate than stepping tests. This is because fewer variables need to be controlled than in step tests, for example, the pedalling rate is more accurately controlled than the stepping rate. The pedalling rate is shown on the digital display of the ergometer, and a metronome can also be used to help the subject with revs/minute timing. The cycle ergometer seat height can be altered according to the leg length of the subject, whereas for step tests a standard bench height is used. Therefore cycle ergometry tests enable subjects to perform more efficiently, leading to improved accuracy of test results.

The preferred method for maximal aerobic endurance testing is a graded treadmill test; higher values are obtained when a large muscle mass is involved in testing, resulting in improved accuracy of results. Individuals are not affected by local muscular fatigue; and provided they are well motivated, they can reach their maximal exhaustion of the cardiorespiratory system. During graded treadmill testing, VO_2 max is reached when:

- the individual reports a Rating of Perceived Exertion (RPE) of 20 (Borg 6-20 RPE scale)
- there is less than 150 ml/min increase between exercise workloads
- blood lactate is greater than 8 mmol/l.

Activity: Fitness test – advantages and disadvantages

Work in pairs or small groups. Choose a fitness test that you are familiar with, for example, the multi-stage fitness test.

- List the test advantages and disadvantages. Think about practicality, cost, ease of administration and potential issues like keeping in time/turning with the bleeps and motivation levels of subjects.
- Discuss the advantages and disadvantages you have listed and how test variables could be controlled or reduced.

Assessment activity 8.1

 **BTEC**

You are an athletics coach in charge of a squad of county athletes covering a variety of events. You have been asked to prepare a presentation to give to the athletes focusing on how fitness testing can be used to enhance their future performance and the types of tests available.

1. Describe one test for each component of physical fitness, including advantages and disadvantages. **P1**
2. Explain the advantages and disadvantages of one fitness test for each component of physical fitness. **M1**

Grading tips

P1 To attain P1 provide a clear description of each test that includes all the relevant features, together with their advantages and disadvantages. Think of your description as if you are 'painting a picture with words'.

M1 To attain M1 provide details and give reasons and/or evidence to clearly support the advantages and disadvantages you have put forward. Draw examples from personal experience of participation or observing others performing the tests. Use research evidence to support the points you are making. Don't forget to cite references in text as well as in an overall references section to support your work.

PLTS

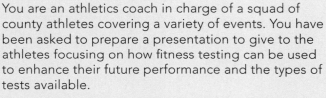

Describing and explaining the fitness tests for each component of physical fitness and preparing a presentation on the topic will develop your skills as an **independent enquirer**.

Functional skills

When you are discussing how to test each component of physical fitness, you can provide evidence of your **English** skills.

2.   Be able to use health screening techniques

2.1 Health screening procedures

Questionnaires

Health screening involves collecting information regarding an individual's current physical activity levels, dietary habits and lifestyle. Health screening questionnaires can be used to collect such information. Questionnaire results identify those who have risk factors of heart disease and highlight where lifestyle changes are required.

Health screening questionnaires are likely to contain specific questions relating to the following areas:

- physical activity history
- current physical activity levels
- injuries
- personal training goals
- alcohol consumption
- smoking
- stress levels
- dietary habits.

Client consultation

During the screening you'll need to ensure the individual feels at ease – develop a rapport, keep them fully informed and show discretion. Remember that it is just as important to listen to your client as it is to ask questions. Be aware of your body language and the non-verbal messages you are giving out. Finally, you must clearly communicate your findings and the implications of these.

Client confidentiality

During the health screening process, a client will provide you with information relating to their personal health and fitness. In addition to this, you will also collect data and information from the health monitoring tests and administration of fitness tests.

Such personal data and information must be treated with the utmost care. It is your responsibility to maintain client confidentiality by ensuring that:

- such records are used and viewed only by yourself as the fitness instructor, and your supervisor/ assessor (your clients should be made aware of this)
- your records are kept securely – they must not, at any time, be left in a public place and electronic records should be password protected
- the contents of the health screening and fitness assessment are not discussed in public with anyone else including your family or friends.

Remember

Medical and health records are confidential documents which contain sensitive data. It is your responsibility to ensure you maintain client confidentiality at all times when you have direct knowledge of, and/or access to, information which is confidential. Disclosing information about your client(s) to anyone who does not require it is a breach of their confidentiality.

Informed consent

Before administering any health or fitness tests, the individual to be tested should complete an informed consent form. This is documented evidence that shows that you have provided the individual with all the necessary information to undertake the tests. The individual to be tested will need to complete an informed consent form to confirm that they:

- are able to follow the test methods
- know exactly what is required of them during testing
- have fully consented to their participation in the fitness tests

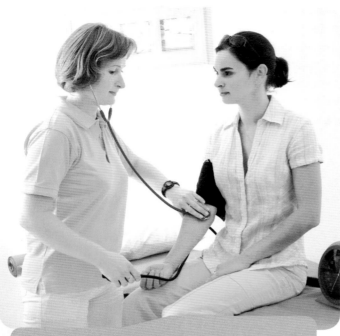

Conducting health screening: what checks will you carry out?

- know that they are able to ask you any questions relating to the tests
- understand that they can withdraw their consent at any time.

The consent form should be signed and dated by:

- the individual to be tested (the participant)
- their parents/guardians (if under 18)
- you (the tester)
- a witness (usually your tutor/assessor).

Coronary heart disease risk factors

The five major coronary risk factors are:

1. high blood pressure (hypertension), where on at least two separate occasions:
   - systolic blood pressure is higher than 160 mmHg
   - diastolic blood pressure is higher than 100 mmHg
2. cholesterol is higher than 6.20 mmol/l
3. cigarette smoking
4. diabetes mellitus
5. a family history of coronary heart disease in parents or siblings prior to age 55 years.

Medical referral

Questionnaire results and results from health monitoring tests can be used to identify risk factors and those individuals requiring referral to their GP. Factors for medical referral include: heart conditions, chest pain, breathlessness, high blood pressure (hypertension), diabetes mellitus, pregnancy and bone or joint problems.

2.2 Health monitoring tests

Health monitoring tests include heart rate, blood pressure, lung function, waist-to-hip ratio and body mass index (BMI).

Heart rate (HR)

This can be measured manually via the radial artery in the wrist or via a digital blood pressure monitor. Heart rate is measured in beats per minute (bpm).

The average resting heart rate for a male is 68 bpm and for a female is 72 bpm. Males generally have larger hearts than females, which can pump a greater volume of oxygenated blood around the body, thus the average resting heart rate for a male is lower compared to females. A high resting heart rate (tachycardia) is >100 bpm.

Blood pressure (BP)

Blood pressure can be measured using a digital blood pressure monitor, which provides a reading of blood pressure as: **systolic blood pressure/diastolic blood pressure** (mmHg).

Key terms

Blood pressure – can be measured using a digital blood pressure monitor, which provides a reading of blood pressure in mmHg (millimetres of mercury).

Systolic blood pressure – the highest pressure within the bloodstream, which occurs during each beat when the heart is in systole (contracting).

Diastolic blood pressure – the lowest pressure in the bloodstream, which occurs between beats when the heart is in diastole (relaxing, filling with blood).

Rating	Blood pressure reading (mmHg)
Average (desirable)	120/80 mmHg
Above average (borderline)	140/90 mmHg
High blood pressure (hypertension)	160/100 mmHg*

* An individual should seek advice from their GP if BP is >160/100 mmHg on at least two separate occasions.

Table 8.19: An interpretation of BP results

Lung function

Spirometry can be used to monitor health and to check if an individual is suffering from chest or lung problems. A spirometer is a hand-held device which can be used to measure the volume of air that you can blow out against time, which provides information about your lung function. To undertake spirometry:

- enter your age, gender and height into the spirometer
- wearing a noseclip, take a deep breath in and then tightly seal your lips around the mouthpiece of the spirometer
- blow out as hard and fast as you can until your lungs are completely empty
- repeat the spirometry test again to ensure reliability of results.

The spirometer will compare and interpret your results according to the values predicted for your age, gender and height. Spirometry can be used to obtain various readings including the following.

- **Forced Vital Capacity (FVC):** the total volume of air that you can expire following maximal inspiration
- **Forced Expiratory Volume in one second (FEV1):** the total volume of air that you can expire within one second
- **Ratio of FEV1 to FVC (FEV1/FVC or FEV%):** from the total volume of air that you can expire, this is the proportion that you are able to blow out in one second

- **Peak Expiratory Flow (PEF):** the maximal speed (flow) resulting from a maximally forced expiration following maximal inspiration.

Spirometry can help diagnose and monitor conditions such as chronic obstructive pulmonary disease (COPD), asthma and pulmonary fibrosis. A narrowing of the airways reduces the amount of air that you are able to blow out. In general, you are likely to be suffering from a disease which causes narrowing of the airways if:

- your FEV1 is less than 80 per cent of the predicted value according to your age, gender and height
- your FEV1/FVC ratio is 0.7 or less.

Waist-to-hip ratio

This ratio can determine levels of obesity and those at risk of heart disease. Use a tape measure placed firmly against the individual's skin to measure the waist circumference in centimetres at the narrowest level of the torso. Next, measure the individual's hips by placing the tape measure at the maximum circumference of the buttocks. Make sure the tape measure is level when taking measurements. Divide the waist measurement (cm) by the hip measurement (cm) to obtain the waist-to-hip ratio.

Body Mass Index (BMI)

BMI is a measure of body composition in kg/m^2 and is used to determine to what degree someone is overweight. It is only an estimate, as the test does not take into account the individual's frame size or muscle mass. Research shows a significant relationship between high BMI and incidence of cardiovascular disease, and high BMI and diabetes.

To obtain BMI, measure the individual's body weight (kg) and height in metres, and calculate the BMI as: kg/m^2.

For women, a desirable BMI is 21–23 kg/m^2. For men, a desirable BMI is 22–24 kg/m^2. The risk of cardiovascular disease increases sharply at a BMI of 27.8 kg/m^2 for men and 27.3 kg/m^2 for women.

Assessment activity 8.2

You have been asked to undertake health screening procedures and safely administer four different health monitoring tests for two contrasting individuals. They need to be quite different in terms of their fitness levels and lifestyles. For example, you could ask a peer (someone who trains and competes regularly) and you could ask an older individual (perhaps a relative who doesn't participate in regular physical activity).

1. Prepare an appropriate health screening questionnaire. **P2**

2. Devise and use appropriate health screening procedures for two contrasting individuals. **P3**

3. Safely administer, and interpret the results of, four different health monitoring tests for the two contrasting individuals. **P4**

4. Describe the strengths and areas for improvement for the two individuals using information from their health screening questionnaires and health monitoring tests. **M2**

5. Evaluate the health screening questionnaires and health monitoring test results and provide recommendations for lifestyle improvements. **D1**

Grading tips

P2 To attain P2 think about the range of topics you need to cover in your questionnaire. Consider different ways of presenting your questionnaire and the types of question you could use, for example, open/closed.

P3 To attain P3 the individuals selected need to be *contrasting*. For example, you could choose to test an elite/county level sports performer and an individual who doesn't train. Your two clients will need to complete your self-designed health screening questionnaire and informed consent forms. You will need to show evidence of conducting the client consultation, including an awareness of coronary heart disease risk factors and the need for medical referral.

P4 To attain P4 you need to safely administer four different health monitoring tests for your two contrasting individuals and interpret

their results against normative published data, defining what their results mean.

M2 To attain M2 use the results from the clients' health screening questionnaires and health monitoring tests in order to describe their strengths and areas for improvement. In doing this you should compare their responses from the screening questionnaires and results from the health monitoring tests against normative published data and accepted health ranges.

D1 To attain D1 you need to evaluate their responses to the screening questionnaires and results from the health monitoring tests conducted, reviewing the information and then bringing it together to form your conclusions for each client. You will need to provide valid recommendations of how each client can improve their lifestyle, giving evidence for your views or statements.

PLTS

During the health screening, if you identify questions to answer and problems to resolve you can develop your skills as an **independent enquirer**. If you generate ideas, explore possibilities and ask questions to extend your thinking you can develop skills as a **creative thinker**.

Functional skills

By researching and preparing a health screening questionnaire, and recording the results of health monitoring tests, you could provide evidence of your **ICT** skills. By interpreting the results of your health monitoring tests, you can develop your **Mathematics** and **English** skills.

3. Be able to administer appropriate fitness tests

In this section you'll need to select and safely administer six different fitness tests for a chosen individual, recording the findings.

3.1 Fitness tests and their administration

You need to develop and apply your skills in assessing fitness to be able to select and administer, in a safe and effective manner, six different fitness tests for a chosen individual. Refer back to the fitness tests covered on pages 200–215 of this unit.

You must be able to successfully prepare for six different tests. In your preparation you will need a clear understanding and justification of why you have selected these particular tests for your chosen individual, together with an understanding of the validity, reliability and practicality issues of the tests that you are to administer (refer back to Section 1.2 on pages 215–218). It is important that you have a sound understanding of the purpose of each test and be fully confident in how you will administer it.

Following fitness testing, when you give feedback to the individual, you will be able to apply your knowledge and experience to describe what their fitness results mean, interpreting their levels of fitness against normative published data (population norms). This will provide the individual with baseline fitness measures from which you can put forward recommendations and suggestions for future activities and/or training methods which will help them to improve their fitness levels.

Remember

Before you administer any fitness test, it is extremely important that pre-test procedures are followed.

Pre-test procedures

As previously stated, before administering any fitness tests, the individual to be tested should complete an informed consent form (refer back to page 202).

Prior to testing, equipment should be checked carefully. It is also essential that you calibrate any equipment you will be using. This means checking (and if necessary adjusting) the accuracy of fitness testing equipment before it is used by comparing it to a recognised standard. If equipment isn't correctly calibrated it could lead to inaccurate (invalid) results.

Activity: Informed consent

Use the Internet to find examples of informed consent forms. Following the guidelines outlined (see Section 2.1 on pages 219–220), design your own informed consent form that is appropriate for the fitness tests you have selected to administer for the individual.

Test sequences and protocols

To conduct a fitness assessment and administer fitness tests in a professional, safe and valid manner, you need to ensure that you are fully familiar with the test procedures and protocols. This means that you have had sufficient time to practise the administration of each fitness test method, and how to collect and interpret data results before you go on to administer the tests for an individual.

Remember

- For effective administration of fitness tests you need to be well practised and very familiar with the test methods. If you are well rehearsed in techniques, your results are more likely to be valid and reliable.
- Good planning will help you to feel more confident in administering fitness tests, particularly if you are administering tests to an individual you don't know.
- You will need to use published data tables to interpret results and give feedback to the individual.
- Practising test procedures and protocols will give you more experience in how to interpret results obtained. Results should be interpreted in a valid, effective and appropriate manner.

Recording test results

You'll need to be well planned and organised throughout the administration of the fitness tests. Use an appropriate data collection sheet to record the individual's results as you go along (see Figure 8.4). Ideally, for reliability of results, all fitness tests selected should be repeated. However, owing to availability of time this may not be possible, and you may need to take this factor into account when giving feedback to the individual.

Use the correct units of measurement for the fitness tests you have chosen to administer. For some fitness tests you may need to use tables to process raw data before you can interpret what the test results mean and provide feedback to the individual. For example, the multi-stage fitness test result is recorded as the level and shuttle achieved. Use a conversion table to look up the predicted aerobic fitness level (VO_2 max,

ml/kg/min) for the level and shuttle obtained (for example, see Table 8.5 on page 203). You can then provide feedback to the individual on their VO_2 max result, and by using a published data table you can let them know their fitness rating and what this means (for example, see Table 8.6 on page 204).

Reasons to terminate a fitness test

Individuals should be closely monitored while they are undertaking fitness tests. Reasons to terminate a test include your subject:

- requesting to stop the fitness test
- reporting chest pain
- experiencing severe breathlessness, wheezing
- showing signs of poor circulation, for example, pale, cold clammy skin
- showing signs of poor coordination, confusion and/ or dizziness.

Administering fitness tests – recording test results

Name:

Age (yrs/mths):

Height (m):

Weight (kg):

Body mass index (BMI kg/m²):

Informed consent form completed (*insert date*):

Fitness component	Fitness test [insert 6 different fitness tests]	T1	T2	Av. result	Units	Interpretation of test results (rating)
Flexibility	Sit and reach				cm	
Strength	Handgrip dynamometer				kg	
		Result				
Aerobic endurance	1.5 mile run test				ml/kg/min	
Speed	35 metre sprint				s	
Muscular endurance	1 minute sit-up				Number of reps	
Body composition	Bioelectrical impedance analysis (BIA)				% body fat	

Figure 8.4: A fitness testing data collection sheet

Assessment activity 8.3

You need to conduct a fitness assessment and administer fitness tests to an individual. You could use one of your subjects from Assessment activity 8.2.

1. Select and safely administer six different fitness tests for a selected individual recording the findings. **P5**

2. Justify the selection of fitness tests commenting on suitability, reliability, validity and practicality. **M3**

Grading tips

P5 To attain P5 ensure you have documented evidence of how you have administered the tests, for example, that you have followed pre-test procedures, have completed informed consent form(s), have used disclaimers where appropriate etc. You will also need to show evidence of documenting results, e.g. see Figure 8.4 on page 224.

M3 To attain M3, in your feedback to the individual, justify why you selected the fitness tests you did. Why were these the most appropriate for the individual? In your selection of the fitness tests, did you take into account their goals, needs and general level of fitness? Give reasons or evidence to support your views and how you arrived at these conclusions.

PLTS

If you identify questions to answer and problems to resolve in your selection and safe administration of six different fitness tests for a selected individual, you can develop your skills as an **independent enquirer**.

Functional skills

When conducting the fitness assessment, if you use the Internet to search for published data tables and follow safety and security practices for client confidentiality, you can develop your **ICT** skills. Through the selection and safe administration of six different fitness tests for a selected individual, you can develop your **English** skills. When recording data results, you can develop your skills in **Mathematics**.

4. Be able to interpret the results of fitness tests and provide feedback

4.1 Interpret results against normative data

Data interpretation tables presented earlier in this unit can be used to aid your interpretation of test results against normative data. You can also use published data interpretation tables to compare judgements against data for sports performers and elite athletes. Your choice in selection of data tables for interpretation of fitness test results will depend on your selected individual, their needs and personal goals. However, most individuals will be interested to know how they compare against normative data (population norms).

4.2 Feedback

Having administered six different fitness tests for an individual, you now need to provide feedback to the individual regarding their test results, discussing what they mean and giving your recommendations for future activities or training. Your feedback may be given verbally to the individual, supported by a written copy of their data results and interpretation of their levels of fitness against normative data. You may be asked to adopt the role of a fitness instructor and conduct the fitness assessment as would be expected in a real-life vocational context. Your centre of learning will provide you with advice and guidance on how they would like you to present your assessment evidence.

In your feedback, recap the tests carried out and why these particular tests were appropriate for the individual. Discuss in detail their data results and what these mean in terms of their fitness levels. Complete your feedback by discussing the strengths, areas for improvement and your recommendations for appropriate future activities or training. Give the individual the opportunity to ask questions about your statements or views, and be prepared to justify your reasoning.

Assessment activity 8.4

 **P6 M4 D2** BTEC

You now need to provide verbal face-to-face feedback to the individual tested.

1. Following fitness testing, give feedback to a selected individual, describing the test results and interpreting their levels of fitness against normative data. **P6**

2. Compare the fitness test results to normative data and identify strengths and areas for improvement. **M4**

3. Analyse the fitness test results and provide recommendations for appropriate future activities or training. **D2**

Grading tips

P6 To attain P6 interpret and describe the results from the six fitness tests the individual has completed in your verbal feedback to them.

M4 To attain M4 use published data tables to interpret their fitness levels against normative data according to the individual's age and gender. Use the individual's completed data collection form to aid your discussion.

Use data interpretation tables to help make comparisons and verbally highlight their strengths and areas for improvement.

D2 To attain D2, in your analysis, relate the individual's results back to the fitness components tested. Use test results and information collected about the individual to provide your recommendations for appropriate future activities or training and give your reasons for these recommendations.

PLTS

In your feedback to the individual, if you analyse and evaluate information, judging its relevance and value, supporting your conclusions using reasoned arguments and evidence, you can develop your skills as an **independent enquirer**. If you adapt your behaviour to suit different roles and situations, showing fairness and consideration to others, you can develop your skills as a **team worker**. If you assess yourself and others, identifying opportunities and achievements, you can develop your skills as a **reflective learner**.

Functional skills

When you interpret your client's fitness test results, you can show evidence of your **ICT**, **Mathematics** and **English** skills.

Frieda Peterson

Senior fitness and lifestyle coach

Frieda is 21 and works in a private health and fitness centre. She is responsible for: instructing clients in the gym; undertaking health screening and client fitness assessments and designing personal coaching programmes; monitoring and evaluating client progress towards meeting goals and objectives and contributing to the club's programme of promoting lifestyle and health awareness.

'Each day is different depending on my schedule and whether clients require health screening and monitoring tests and/or a fitness assessment.

Individual one-to-one client consultations begin with a comprehensive screening process where the client completes questionnaires covering their medical, physical activity and lifestyle history.

We also look closely at diet. I then carry out health monitoring tests like blood pressure and lung function and give the client feedback on their results and the implications for future health. Health screening is usually followed by an assessment of their fitness. The club has a purpose-built fitness centre where we can carry out several tests for the different components of fitness. I then meet with the client to give feedback on their fitness test results and health monitoring and to discuss and agree their training goals. I then design a personal programme for the client to work to and closely monitor their progress throughout. Every six weeks or so, a client will book in with me for a reassessment of their health and fitness.

My other duties involve organising our internal programme of lifestyle and health awareness. This involves coordinating visits, events and guest speakers covering a range of topics from healthy eating to how to reduce stress levels. Last month a local GP visited and carried out free cholesterol testing for our club members. A lot of people just aren't aware of the damage they can do to their body through poor diet and lack of exercise.

You need good communication skills for this job and to be able to motivate people, develop a rapport and lead by example. I find the job very rewarding. Providing good education helps people to recognise where they may need lifestyle improvement and my role is to help clients to implement positive lifestyle changes.'

Think about it!

- What areas have you covered in this unit that provide you with the knowledge and skills used by a fitness and lifestyle coach?
- What further skills might you need to develop?

Just checking

1. The sit and reach test is an indirect measure of static flexibility. Name two direct measures of static flexibility.

2. Give two advantages and two disadvantages of the 1 repetition maximum bench press test.

3. What is the difference between absolute and relative VO_2 max?

4. Stacey weighs 65 kg. She completes the vertical jump test and achieves a difference of 30 cm between her standing reach and jump height. What is Stacey's predicted anaerobic power (kgm/s)?

5. Skinfold testing for the prediction of percentage of body fat is based on the existence of what relationship?

6. State two factors which affect body fat.

7. Why is it important not to exercise or drink caffeine prior to the bioelectrical impedance analysis test?

8. Why is health screening important?

9. Tom weighs 77 kg and his height is 1.83 m. What is Tom's BMI (kg/m²) and how would you interpret the result?

10. Becky reaches level 8 shuttle 2 on the multi-stage fitness test. She is 17 years old. Interpret her test result.

edexcel

Assignment tips

- The Internet has a wealth of information on health screening procedures. Check out the different types of health screening questionnaires available to give you some ideas for the design of your own questionnaire.

- Speak to practitioners with experience of conducting health screening procedures. Examples include health fitness instructors, personal trainers and GPs. Check to see whether your local pharmacy conducts health screening and the methods they use.

- Search the Internet for published data interpretation tables for the fitness tests you intend to administer. Having more than one data source for interpretation of test results can help you provide comprehensive and detailed feedback to the individual.

- When administering the six different fitness tests for an individual, you should also consider any sports they participate in. Do they excel in a certain sport? If so, are there sport-specific fitness tests you can administer?

- By employing sport-specific fitness tests the results obtained will be a more accurate reflection of the individual's physiological sporting demands. For example, if the individual is a keen cyclist, you could use cycle ergometer tests to predict their aerobic endurance and anaerobic power. By doing this you will be testing the specific working muscles that the individual uses regularly in their sport, thus leading to greater accuracy of results.

9 Fitness training and programming

What does it takes for Wayne Rooney to be able to sprint for a football in the final minute of a football match? Consider the novice marathon runner and what they put their body through to complete the London Marathon and raise money for charity, or the injured youth basketball player entering the later stages of rehabilitation and training more purposefully – what must they do to get back to competition? Regardless of your ability in sport, you need certain levels of fitness to perform at your best. It is important for health, self-confidence, injury prevention and peak performance in sport that you have the required level of fitness. The role of people such as sports conditioning specialists, fitness instructors or personal trainers is to help different people improve or maintain their fitness level.

Throughout this unit, you will examine a range of topics within fitness training and programming. These range from understanding different components of fitness, and the training methods used to improve them, to being able to plan, take part in and review training sessions and programmes; these are useful for you if you wish to progress into fitness instructing, personal training, sports coaching or sports therapy.

Learning outcomes

After completing this unit you should:

1. know different methods of fitness training
2. be able to plan a fitness training session
3. be able to plan a fitness training programme
4. be able to review a fitness training programme.

Assessment and grading criteria

This table shows you what you must do in order to achieve a pass, merit or distinction grade, and where you can find activities in this book to help you.

To achieve a **pass** grade the evidence must show that the learner is able to:	To achieve a **merit** grade the evidence must show that, in addition to the pass criteria, the learner is able to:	To achieve a **distinction** grade the evidence must show that, in addition to the pass and merit criteria, the learner is able to:
P1 describe one method of fitness training for six different components of physical fitness **Assessment activity 9.1, page 241**	**M1** explain one method of fitness training for six different components of physical fitness **Assessment activity 9.1, page 241**	
P2 produce training session plans covering cardiovascular training, resistance training, flexibility training and speed training **Assessment activity 9.2, page 249**	**M2** produce detailed session plans covering cardiovascular training, resistance training, flexibility training and speed training **Assessment activity 9.2, page 249**	**D1** justify the training session plans covering cardiovascular training, resistance training, flexibility training and speed training **Assessment activity 9.2, page 249**
P3 produce a six-week fitness training programme for a selected individual that incorporates the principles of training and periodisation **Assessment activity 9.3, page 255**		
P4 monitor performance against goals during the six-week training programme **Assessment activity 9.4, page 256**		
P5 give feedback to an individual following completion of a six-week fitness training programme, describing strengths and areas for improvement **Assessment activity 9.4, page 256**	**M3** give feedback to an individual following completion of a six-week fitness training programme, explaining strengths and areas for improvement **Assessment activity 9.4, page 256**	**D2** give feedback to an individual following completion of a six-week fitness training programme, evaluating progress and providing recommendations for future activities **Assessment activity 9.4, page 256**

How you will be assessed

This unit will be assessed by internal assignments designed and marked by the tutors at your centre. Your assessments could be in the form of:

- written reports
- posters
- presentations
- session plans
- training diaries
- practical observations of performance.

Paul Cooke, 17-year-old gym enthusiast

This unit has been really beneficial because it has taught me all sorts of things about fitness and training that I didn't know before. I really like being physically active and exercising so I spend a lot of my time in the gym which means this unit was tailor-made for me!

The parts of the unit that I really enjoyed were the ones where I learned about the different methods of training, how to plan sessions correctly and how to plan training programmes effectively. I go to the gym a lot but up until starting this unit I didn't really know what I was doing in there – I just went in and lifted weights after doing some cardio work but I didn't really structure anything or have any specific goals. This unit has helped me to improve the quality of my own training and I'm starting to see the benefit of it now. I've also just started fitness instructing for my part-time job and I want to be a personal trainer so this unit has helped me out a lot with that too!

Over to you

- **How do you think this unit can help you?**
- **What are you looking forward to learning about?**
- **What might you find especially challenging?**

1. Know different methods of fitness training

The importance of fitness training

Consider how athletes meet the physical demands of their sport at an elite level. Now consider the rising levels of obesity in the world, particularly in the UK. These examples tell you about the importance of fitness training and programming. How can a knowledge of fitness training and programming help in these different scenarios?

When designing training programmes, there are two key questions:

- What am I trying to improve?
- How am I going to improve it?

You need detailed knowledge of the different components of fitness, and the different training methods used to improve them, to answer these two questions.

📱 1.1 Components of fitness

When you think about fitness, different things spring to mind, such as people who can run far, people with big muscles and people that are slim and toned. Fitness is the ability to meet the demands of your environment. It relates to an optimal quality of life and includes social, spiritual, psychological, emotional and physical well-being and can be classified under the following areas:

- Physical/health-related fitness: this focuses on your health-related aspects of fitness, with good scores in components in this area meaning you have only a small chance of developing health problems.
- Skill-related fitness: this is a level of fitness that allows the individual to perform an activity, task or sport (this is also sometimes known as motor fitness).

Fitness involves six main components:

- **aerobic endurance**
- **muscular endurance**
- **flexibility**
- **strength**
- **speed**
- **power**.

What do you think are the main reasons behind people starting training programmes?

Key terms

Aerobic endurance – the ability of the cardiovascular and respiratory systems to supply the exercising muscles with oxygen to maintain the aerobic exercise for a long period of time, for example over two hours during a marathon.

Muscular endurance – the ability of a specific muscle or muscle group to sustain repeated contractions over an extended period of time.

Flexibility – the ability of a specific joint, for example the knee, to move through a full range of movement. As with muscular endurance, an athlete can have different flexibility levels in different joints.

Strength – the ability of a specific muscle or muscle group to exert a force in a single maximal contraction to overcome some form of resistance.

Speed – the ability to move a distance in the shortest time.

Power – the ability to generate and use muscular strength quickly over a short period of time.

Aerobic endurance

A physical-related aspect of fitness, this is also known as stamina or cardiorespiratory endurance. It is the ability of the cardiovascular and respiratory systems to supply the exercising muscles with oxygen to maintain the exercise. It is important for daily tasks such as walking to work or doing the gardening and housework, but is also important for a range of sport, leisure and recreational activities. There are a number of events that rely almost exclusively on aerobic endurance, such as marathon running, long-distance swimming and cycling. Aerobic endurance forms the basis of fitness for most sports. If an athlete has a reduced aerobic endurance, possibly due to a long-term injury, this leads to a decrease in other fitness components such as muscular endurance. Poor aerobic endurance leads to poor sporting performance in some sports.

Muscular endurance

Another physical-related aspect of fitness, muscular endurance is needed where a specific muscle or muscle group makes repeated contractions over a significant period of time (possibly over a number of minutes). Examples include:

- a boxer making a repeated jab
- continuous press-ups or sit-ups
- 400-metre sprint in athletics.

Flexibility

Another physical-related aspect of fitness, flexibility is important for all sports and for health. There are two main types of flexibility: **static flexibility** and **dynamic flexibility**. Static flexibility is the range of movement that a muscle or joint can achieve and is limited by the structure of bones and joints, as well as factors such as muscle size and muscle tone. Dynamic flexibility is the range of movement that a muscle or joint can achieve while you are moving and is limited by your levels of static flexibility and coordination.

Key terms

Static flexibility – the range of movement that a muscle or joint can achieve.

Dynamic flexibility – the range of movement that a muscle or joint can achieve when in motion.

Poor flexibility may lead to:

- a decrease in the range of possible movement
- an increased chance of injury and stiffness
- a decrease in sporting performance.

Possible improvements in flexibility are limited by an individual's:

- body composition (for example, the percentage of body fat)
- genetics (characteristics inherited from parents)
- age (flexibility levels generally decrease with age)
- gender (females tend to be more flexible than males)
- muscle and tendon elasticity (the capacity to stretch before injury occurs).

While flexibility is important for all sports, any joint should not become too flexible because an excessive range of movement can lead to injury.

Strength

A physical-related aspect of fitness, strength is the ability of a specific muscle or muscle group to exert a force in a single maximal contraction. When you think about strength, you may think about athletes such as weightlifters or boxers, but strength is required in most sports, just in varying degrees.

Speed

A skill-related component of fitness, speed is required by an athlete to maximise performance. It is the ability to move over distance in the quickest possible time. Athletic sports such as the 100-metre sprint and long jump require high levels of speed. Speed endurance is a secondary element to speed and combines with anaerobic endurance. It is the ability of an athlete to make repeated sprints over a period of time and is important in different team sports. For example, a midfield player in football often has to make 10–30 metre sprints continuously throughout the game.

Power

Power is also a skill-related component of fitness. It is the ability to generate and use muscular strength quickly. Athletes who are stronger tend to produce a greater amount of power during an action. Generally, an athlete interested in health-related fitness does not train for power as it is needed more by athletes in specific sports and can only be developed by using advanced training methods. Power is important for sprinters when pushing away from the blocks, footballers striking a long range drive and boxers delivering a punch, as well as other sports.

Other components of physical fitness

In addition to the components above relating to skills and physical fitness, there are others:

- **Body composition** – the amount of body fat and lean body tissue the athlete has. It is important from a health and a sports performance perspective.
- **Agility** – the ability of an athlete to change direction many times quickly and accurately during sporting performance while maintaining control of the movement.
- **Balance** – being able to maintain stability or equilibrium while performing. There are two forms of balance: static balance, where the athlete is stationary, for example, in a handstand in gymnastics; dynamic balance, where the athlete is moving, for example, a footballer sprinting with the ball.

- **Coordination** – most sporting movements require athletes to use different joints and muscles in a specific order or sequence.
- **Reaction time** – the time between a stimulus to move and the start of a movement, such as a starting pistol (the stimulus) and the sprint start (the movement) in sprint events.

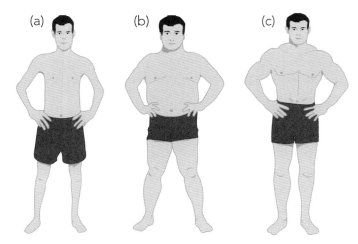

Figure 9.1: The three types of body frame: (a) ectomorph, (b) endomorph and (c) mesomorph. Which appears to be the most athletic and why?

Activity: Components of fitness in sport

- Complete the table that examines the importance of the different components of fitness in different sports. Give each component of fitness a rating from 1 to 10, with 1 being not important and 10 being very important.

- On a separate sheet of paper, choose your favourite sport out of the three and justify why the components of fitness are important: for example 'reaction time is important in goalkeeping because the quicker the goalkeeper reacts, the more chance they have of saving the ball and then distributing it to their teammates'.

Components of fitness	Boxing	Goalkeeper in football	100-metre sprinter
Aerobic endurance			
Muscular endurance			
Flexibility			
Speed			
Strength			
Power			
Body composition			
Agility			
Balance			
Coordination			
Reaction time			

1.2 Methods of training

Consider all the components of fitness and the different sports that you have covered so far. To develop each of these components of fitness to meet the needs of different sports, athletes, coaches and personal trainers can't just use one type of training – they need to use a range of appropriate training methods.

Aerobic endurance

The three most common methods used to improve aerobic endurance (also known as **VO$_2$ max**) are:

- continuous training
- fartlek training
- interval training.

There is not enough evidence to determine which method is best, but all will lead to improvements in aerobic endurance. Aerobic endurance training is often used by people who want to lose or manage their weight by reducing their body fat content, which is why aerobic training is often used during the pre-season by football teams and rugby teams. Body fat is reduced by aerobic endurance training because training results in increased levels of hormones, **epinephrine** and **norepinephrine**, which then activate enzymes which break down **triglycerides** into **free fatty acids**. These are used as an energy source. This reduces your body fat levels. As well as the health-related benefits of aerobic endurance training methods, they have different benefits for sport performance. They can help to improve blood volume, mitochondrial size and density, develop neuromuscular patterns and improve muscle tone; all of which benefits performance levels in a range of sports.

Key terms

VO$_2$ max – the maximum amount of oxygen that can be taken in by and be utilised by the body. Also, a measure of the endurance capacity of the cardiovascular and respiratory systems and exercising skeletal muscles.

Epinephrine – a chemical in the body used for communication between cells in the nervous system and other cells in the body. It works with norepinephrine to prepare the body for the 'fight or flight response'.

Norepinephrine – a chemical in the body used for communication between cells in the nervous system and other cells in the body. It works with epinephrine to prepare the body for the 'fight or flight response'.

Triglycerides – the most concentrated energy source in the body. Most fats are stored as these.

Free fatty acids – the parts of fat that are used by the body for metabolism.

- **Continuous training** is also known as steady-state or long, slow, distance training. It involves the athlete training at a steady pace over a long distance. The intensity of continuous training should be moderate intensity (approximately ≤70% VO$_2$ max) over a long distance and time.

This method of training is suited to long distance runners or swimmers. Due to the lower level of intensity, an athlete can train for longer. It can also be useful for:

  o beginners who are starting structured exercise

  o athletes recovering from injury

  o 'specific population' individuals such as children or elderly people.

Some of the disadvantages of this type of training include a higher risk of injury when running long distances on harder surfaces, it can be boring and it is not always sport specific; the sport specific benefits are small.

- **Fartlek training** is designed to improve an athlete's aerobic endurance. It is based on running outdoors, and varies the intensity of work according to the athlete's requirements. The intensity of training is changed by varying terrain, such as sand, hills, soft grassland or woodland. Some of the benefits of this training method include improving aerobic endurance, improving muscular endurance and improving balance and proprioception in the ankle, knee and hip; all of which have a variety of benefits ranging from improved sport performance during a game to helping with injury rehabilitation. Fartlek training can be more useful than continuous training for some people because it can be individual and sport specific. In addition, this training method uses both aerobic and anaerobic energy systems to improve aerobic endurance and can involve changes in direction, so it is useful for team sports players as it can closely mimic the requirements of the sport. In fartlek training there is no rest period, but the athlete has more control and is able to decrease intensity at any time to rest. The benefits of fartlek training are:

  o it is less technical than other methods (such as interval training) making it easier to use

  o athletes control their own pacing

  o the boredom of conventional training is reduced.

Some common examples of fartlek sessions include Astrand, Gerschler, Saltin and Watson methods.

- **Interval training** improves anaerobic endurance components and aerobic endurance by varying the intensity and length of the work periods. In interval training, athletes perform a work period, followed by a rest or recovery period, before completing another work period. When designing an interval training programme, you should consider:
  - o the number of intervals (rest and work periods)
  - o the intensity of the work interval
  - o the duration of the work interval
  - o the duration of the rest interval
  - o the intensity of the rest interval.

An example of an interval training prescription for aerobic endurance could be 1 set of 3 repetitions of 5 minute runs interspersed with 2 minutes and 30 seconds of rest. This would be written in a training diary as 1 x 3 x 5:00 Work:Rest 2:30. This method of training allows clear progression and overload to be built into the programme by increasing the intensity of work periods, increasing the number of intervals, decreasing the duration of the rest period or increasing the intensity of the rest period (for example, using a slow jog rather than a walk).

Activity: Benefits of training methods

You are applying for the position of strength and conditioning coach at a multi-sport organisation. The head of athlete support would like you (as part of the interview process) to produce a presentation that describes different aerobic training methods and the physiological benefits of each of the different methods. You should use the Internet, books and journals to produce your presentation. Your presentation should include:

- the names of the different training methods
- a description of each of the training methods (including strengths and limitations)
- an example of different training routines that could be used
- a general description of the physiological benefits of aerobic training
- the specific physiological changes that can occur as a result of each type of training so that you can justify the use of the different training methods with your specific sport.

Muscular strength and muscular endurance training

Think about when you have been in your gym or your fitness suite at school or college. You will have seen people lifting different weights at different speeds. Have you ever looked around and not known what to do or why? This is because a number of the training methods used to improve muscular strength can also be used to improve muscular endurance simply by doing the training differently, for example by altering the weight, the number of repetitions and the number of sets. Common training methods used to improve muscular strength and muscular endurance include:

- resistance machines
- free weights
- medicine ball training
- circuit training
- core stability training.

- **Resistance machines** – your local fitness centre will have a number of fixed resistance machines, which allow individuals to change the load based on their training programme schedule. The variable resistance ranges from 0–100 kg on most machines, allowing the programme to include overload and progression. These machines are expensive, making them impractical for use at home. Due to their design they are limited to specialist exercises such as a bench or leg press. On the positive side, they have an increased safety element compared to free weights, they can be useful for novice trainers who are still learning different movement patterns and an individual can change the range of movement at a specific joint by adjusting the machine's settings.

- **Free weights**, such as barbells or dumb-bells, allow an individual to have a constant resistance during a dynamic action. Free weights increase strength in the short term, increase range of movement, specialise in certain movements or muscle groups and some movements aid the training of balance and coordination. Fixed resistance machines and free weights are used to improve muscular strength. Both produce positive results. However, there is a greater chance of injury while using free weights. For safety reasons when using larger weights, helpers (or 'spotters') are required to oversee (or 'spot') for an individual.

- **Medicine balls** – volleyball players throw and catch medicine balls (heavy balls weighing from 1 to 7 kg) to upgrade their spiking ability; basketball players use the balls to improve their passing and rebounding capacities; baseball players toss medicine balls to improve their throwing speed; and all-round athletes cavort with the balls in the hope of enhancing their 'core strength' (muscle strength in the hips, abdomen and back).

- **Circuit training** – in a circuit training session, a number of different exercises (or stations) are organised in rotations. Individuals are set a time period to perform these exercises, such as one minute per station. Between the stations there should be a rest period dependent on the individual or groups completing the circuit.

  A circuit can be designed to improve aerobic endurance, muscular endurance or strength, or a combination of all three. To avoid fatigue, the stations should be structured in a way that consecutive exercises use different muscle groups, for example, repeated sprints (legs) may be followed by press-ups (upper body). To increase progression and overload, the individual may wish to:

  o decrease the rest period

  o increase the number of stations

  o increase the number of circuits

  o increase the time spent at each station

  o increase the number of circuit sessions per week.

- **Core stability training** exercises the deep muscles of the torso all at the same time. It is vital to most sports because the core muscles stabilise the spine and provide a solid foundation for movement in the arms and legs. The core is the centre point for all sporting actions – it reduces postural imbalance and plays an important role in injury prevention.

Benefits of strength training

If you think about how a person's appearance changes after they have been using the gym a lot, you will be able to identify some changes that are a result of strength training and may say that somebody looks 'built' or 'pumped'. These changes in appearance are known as increased muscle tone and muscle hypertrophy. Muscle tone is where muscles have a more defined appearance; whereas muscle hypertrophy is the growth of the muscle and happens when the **muscle fibres** and **myofibrils** increase in size.

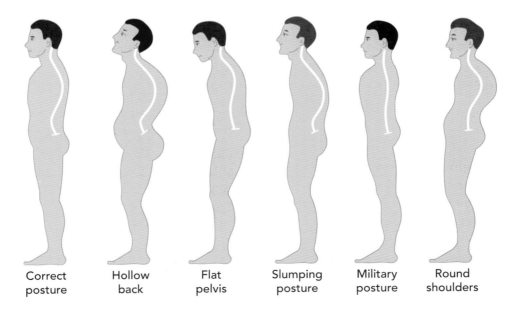

| Correct posture | Hollow back | Flat pelvis | Slumping posture | Military posture | Round shoulders |

Figure 9.2: How do you think core stability training could help these postural deviations?

Benefits of muscular endurance training

Muscular endurance training has similar benefits to muscular strength training in that muscle tone can increase and muscles will experience hypertrophy (although to a lesser extent). The benefits of muscular endurance training are ones that you can't see as they happen within the muscle cell.

The first benefit is that muscular endurance training places stress on the slow twitch muscle fibres and as a result they can increase in size. This means that there is more space for mitochondrial activity. The increase in size and number of the **mitochondria** is important because they are the part of the muscle that produces aerobic energy. By increasing the size and number of mitochondria, you can increase aerobic performance. Another important change within the muscle is that there is a large increase in **myoglobin** content. This is important for aerobic performance as the myoglobin carries oxygen to the mitochondria. If you have more myoglobin you can produce more aerobic energy in the mitochondria. These changes within the muscle can increase VO_2 max by up to 20 per cent which is important in a number of sports.

Key terms

Muscle fibres – the contractile element of a muscle.

Myofibril – the contractile element of a muscle fibre.

Mitochondria – organelles containing enzymes responsible for energy production. Mitochondria are therefore the part of a muscle responsible for aerobic energy production.

Myoglobin – the form of haemoglobin found in muscles that binds and stores oxygen. Myoglobin is responsible for delivering oxygen to the mitochondria.

Flexibility training

Both static and dynamic flexibility can be developed using a range of training methods. The main methods of flexibility training are:

- static stretching
- dynamic stretching
- ballistic stretching
- proprioceptive neuromuscular facilitation (PNF) stretching.

The general principle of flexibility training is to overload the specific muscle group by stretching the muscles beyond what they are used to. The aim is to increase the range of movement, and work must be targeted towards the joints and muscle groups requiring improvement. The movement should not exceed the tolerance level of the tissue. For improvements in flexibility, an individual should increase the time (duration) of stretching and the number of repetitions to allow overload to take place. As flexibility is significantly affected by the temperature of muscles and connective tissues, flexibility training is best completed at the end of a training session or after some form of aerobic training. If using stretching activities as part of a warm-up, you should make sure that the stretching is low intensity and doesn't stretch the muscle or joint too far, too soon.

- **Static stretching** – if you want to improve your flexibility, you could use static stretching. Static stretches are controlled and slow. There are two types: passive and active. Passive stretching is also known as assisted stretching as it requires the help of another person or an object such as a wall. The other person would apply an external force (push or pull) to force the muscle to stretch. Unlike passive stretching, active stretching can be achieved by an individual. It involves voluntary contraction of specific muscles.

- **Dynamic stretching** – think about when you have watched football players, rugby players or basketball players going through their warm-up. You will see them performing a range of movements that are like the sports movements they need during the game. These are dynamic flexibility exercises. Dynamic flexibility is important for sports that have high speed movements and movements that take a muscle or joint past its normal range of static flexibility.

- **Ballistic stretching** improves an individual's flexibility. The individual has to make fast, jerky movements, usually taking the form of bouncing and bobbing through the full range of motion. Ballistic stretching should be specific to the movement pattern experienced in the relevant sporting activity. These stretches can lead to soreness or may cause injury such as strains, so must be undertaken carefully and with the correct technique.

- **Proprioceptive neuromuscular facilitation (PNF) stretching** is an advanced form of passive stretching and is one of the most effective forms of increasing flexibility. The types of movement vary between muscles and muscle groups, but the processes are generally the same:

  o stretch the target muscle group to the upper limit of its range of movement

  o isometrically contract the muscle or muscle group against a partner for 6–10 seconds

  o relax the muscle or muscle group as your partner stretches it to a new upper limit of range of movement (you should be able to stretch it further this time).

  When using this type of stretching remember that pain is the body's signal that you are working it too hard in some way, so when this activity hurts too much you have taken it too far.

Responses to stretching

The improvements that occur because of flexibility training occur because when you stretch a muscle, you stretch the muscle spindle. When you stretch the muscle spindle, a series of signals are sent to your spinal cord. Signals are then sent back, telling the muscle to resist the stretch. After this, your Golgi tendon organ is activated which makes your muscle relax, which allows the muscle to be stretched further the next time. To get this series of reactions, the stretch needs to be held for at least 7 seconds.

Power

There are two common methods of power training:

- plyometrics
- hill sprints.

- **Plyometrics** is designed to improve explosive leg power and is regularly used to increase power in sports. Plyometrics is a useful training method because it engages and stretches the target muscle or muscle groups at the same time. If you stretch a contracted muscle it becomes stronger. Like most elastic tissues, muscles produce more force if they have been previously stretched. Think of your muscle as an elastic band – the elastic band will fire further if you stretch it further back before letting it go. Plyometric activities facilitate this process of force production by taking the muscle through an **eccentric muscle action** before a powerful **concentric muscle action**. This process causes the muscle spindles to cause a **stretch reflex**, preventing any muscle damage and producing maximum force at a rapid rate. Plyometric training is ideal for sports and activities that involve explosive actions, such as a slam dunk in basketball or a sprint start for the 100 metres.

  Different activities are used in plyometric training sessions. Lower body activities include hurdle jumps, single leg bounds, alternate leg bounds, box drills and depth jumps. Upper body activities include plyometric press-ups and medicine ball throws.

- **Hill sprints** – athletes use hill sprints to increase speed, coordination and acceleration. These sprints can be up or down a hill, depending on the content and aims of the session. Hill sprints help to develop

Key terms

Eccentric muscle action – the muscle increases in length while still producing tension.

Concentric muscle action – the muscle gets shorter and the two ends of the muscle move closer together.

Stretch reflex – the body's automatic response to something that stretches the muscle.

Standing calf stretch

Pectoralis stretch

Quadriceps stretch

Standing hamstring stretch

Hip flexor stretch

Double knee to chest

Hip adductor stretch

Piriformis stretch

Trunk rotation

Upper trapezius stretch

Wrist stretch

Figure 9.3: Which athletes would benefit from these types of stretches?

Activity: Plyometrics

Imagine you are working as an assistant to the strength and conditioning coach of your local athletics club. The coach has asked you to produce an information booklet that shows and explains different plyometric exercises that can be used by a range of track and field athletes including jump, sprint and throwing athletes. The coach has asked you to provide:

- a range of both upper and lower body activities
- an image (or series of images) of the different activities
- a step-by-step instruction list for each activity.

power for different reasons. Hill sprints involve a shorter stride length and a longer contact time with the ground than flat sprints; the knee, hip and ankle joints are more flexed during hill sprints and there is greater muscle activity in the gastrocnemius, quadriceps muscle group and gluteus maximus muscle. All of these play a key role in sporting activities that involve sprinting and jumping.

Speed training

Speed is an essential component of fitness in most sports, and good acceleration is vital. Acceleration from a standing position is critical for success in sports such as sprinting and in team-based sports such as rugby league, where a player has to accelerate with the ball past opponents, changing pace rapidly. Interval training and sport-specific speed training benefit speed and acceleration.

- **Interval training** can improve anaerobic endurance. The work intervals for aerobic endurance training tend to be long in duration and low in intensity in order to train the aerobic system. By contrast, for anaerobic endurance, the work intervals will be shorter but more intense (near to maximum). Interval training can help an athlete improve speed and anaerobic endurance (speed endurance). An athlete should work at a high intensity. The principles of overload and progression can be brought into the programme by making changes such as decreasing the rest period (see Table 9.1 on page 242).

- **Sport-specific speed training** – some sports require specific types of speed training to improve performance. For team-based sports you need to concentrate on different distances as players sprint over varying distances and movement patterns by sprinting in different directions to aid agility.

Take it further

Speed training techniques

Using books and the Internet, research the following speed training techniques:

- interval training
- sport-specific speed training
- parachute runs
- hill sprints
- ladders and hurdles

For each one, provide a description of the training method, an example of a training session using that method and a summary of the benefits and limitations of each method.

Assessment activity 9.1

You are working as a fitness trainer for a youth sports team. Your club is launching a new website and would like you to produce some information for the new website that can be accessed by players and coaches of the sports club.

The information for the website needs to include:

1. a description of one method of fitness training for six different components of physical fitness (so six training methods in total). **P1**

2. an explanation of one method of fitness training for six different components of physical fitness (again, six training methods in total). **M1**

Grading tips

P1 To attain P1 provide a general description of each of the different training methods.

M1 To attain M1 give a detailed explanation of each of the training methods that provides examples of exercises that can be used in the different training methods and highlights the benefits of the training methods for the athlete.

2. Be able to plan a fitness training session

📱 2.1 Plan

When planning sessions, you should consider a number of different factors. One of the most important principles when planning individual sessions and full training programmes is the FITT principle.

Frequency, intensity, time and type (FITT principle)

FITT stands for:

Frequency – the number of session(s)

Intensity – how hard the session(s) are

Time – how long the session(s) last for

Type – the activities that you will include in your session(s).

- **Frequency** of a training session or programme refers to the number of training sessions per week. While the frequency of sessions is important, intensity and duration of training are more important. Novice trainers should not train more than three times per week until their levels of fitness can cope with the increased training load. Once your levels of fitness have increased, you could progress to five times per week.

- **Intensity** of a programme is closely linked with the training principle of overload – it is how hard you are working during your training. Intensity is one of the most important factors when designing a training programme and relates to factors such as weight, distance, heart rate percentages and speed.

- **Time** relates to the length of your training session.

- **Type** of exercise you complete will be related to your individual needs. It is the mode of training you will complete, for example free weight training.

2.2 Individuals

When planning your sessions, you need to take into account the type of individual that you are working with. It is not uncommon for personal trainers to work with a combination of elite athletes, trained individuals, untrained individuals or even teams. You need knowledge of each of their circumstances to plan the right type of session for each client.

2.3 Cardiovascular training

Exercise intensities

See Table 9.1 for some general guidelines for cardiovascular exercise intensities.

Guidelines for aerobic training			
Level	Percentage of age predicted maximum heart rate	Duration (per session)	Frequency
Beginner	60	20 minutes	3
Advanced	90	20–50 minutes	5

Table 9.1: Guidelines for aerobic training

Another way of looking at cardiovascular exercise intensities is to see them as zones of training.

- **Warm-up or cool down zone** – the first cardiovascular training intensity is often known as the warm-up/cool down zone. This zone is at around 50 per cent of your maximum heart rate and is mainly for the sedentary or unfit person that wants to start training.

- **Active recovery zone** – this zone is approximately 60 per cent of your maximum heart rate. It is useful for aiding recovery, removing waste products and provides a good next step for those new to cardiovascular training.

- **Fat burning zone** – the fat burning (or weight management) zone is at 60–70 per cent of your maximum heart rate. It is a progression for people from the moderate aerobic zone once they have increased their fitness levels, but is also used by athletes training for long distance events such as a marathon. You may use continuous training when training in this zone.

- **Aerobic fitness zone** – this zone is at 70–80 per cent of your maximum heart rate and is the zone where you develop your aerobic endurance. This zone is suitable for more active or trained individuals.

- **'Target heart rate' zone** – this zone occurs at approximately 60–75 per cent of your maximum heart rate (but has sometimes been known to go as high as 85 per cent). This is the zone that has the greatest benefits for cardiovascular health and for improving the body's ability to use fat as an energy source.

- **Peak performance zone** – this zone occurs at 80–90 per cent of your maximum heart rate and is your highest zone of cardiovascular training. This training zone is geared towards competitive sport and will help you develop speed. It is at this training zone that you will alter your anaerobic threshold. You will often use up-tempo methods such as fartlek and interval training when training through the aerobic fitness and peak performance zones.

- **Anaerobic threshold** – have you ever run for a while and your legs have started to get hot, tight and achy? These are signs that you are close to your anaerobic threshold. Your anaerobic threshold is the point where you can no longer meet your energy requirements of exercise using your aerobic energy

system, so your body produces energy using your anaerobic systems. This is the point that your blood lactate levels increase significantly. Training at high percentages of your maximum heart rate helps to increase this threshold, allowing you to train at higher intensities and longer durations while still using your aerobic energy system. Training close to your **anaerobic threshold** significantly stresses your cardiovascular system so is not suitable for inexperienced trainers.

Key term

Anaerobic threshold – the point at which aerobic energy sources can no longer meet the demand of the activity being undertaken, so there is an increase in anaerobic energy production. This shift is also reflected by an increase in blood lactate production.

Monitoring intensity

When training yourself or working with a client, you must monitor the intensity of the session to ensure that it is as effective as possible and so that your client is not at any risk. Common methods of monitoring intensity include:

- observing your client
- the talk test
- the rating of perceived exertion (RPE)
- age predicted maximum heart rate
- the Karvonen (or heart rate reserve) formula.

- **Observation** – how many times have you been training and ended up tired and red-faced? This is just one of the things that you can look for when observing people while training. Observing people is a subjective way of monitoring progress, but can be very useful. When observing people, look for changes in exercise technique, skin colour, changes in breathing patterns and excessive sweat levels.

- **Talk test** – think about when you're exercising and how much harder it becomes to talk to people as the exercise time continues. The American College of Sports Medicine states that if you are able to hold a conversation at the same time as breathing rhythmically while exercising, you are probably working at an acceptable level for cardiovascular training.

- **Rating of Perceived Exertion (RPE)** is a scale (see Table 9.2) that runs from 6–20 and reflects heart rates that range from 60–200 beats per minute. For example, if you are exercising and you give a rating of 13 (somewhat hard), this gives an equivalent heart rate of 130 beats per minute.

Rate of Perceived Exertion	Intensity	Heart rate equivalent
6		60
7	very, very light	70
8		80
9	very light	90
10		100
11	fairly light	110
12		120
13	somewhat hard	130
14		140
15	hard	150
16		160
17	very hard	170
18		180
19	very, very hard	190
20		200

Table 9.2: Rating of Perceived Exertion (RPE)

It can take some time to learn how to use this rating correctly, so use it with other methods of assessment until you and your client are used to it. One problem with the RPE scale is that it is based on you having a maximum heart rate of 200 beats per minute, which won't always be the case.

- **Maximum heart rate** – monitoring heart rate during cardiovascular training sessions helps you see if you're working hard enough or should work harder. You can use your maximum heart rate and the Karvonen formula to set target training zones and use heart rate monitors to monitor your heart rate and ensure you are within the correct training zone.

You can calculate your maximum heart rate (MHR) by using the simple equation:

maximum heart rate = 220 – age (in years)

This can then be used as part of the Karvonen formula to calculate appropriate training zones (see below).

Activity: Calculating your heart rate zones

For each of the different training zones highlighted above, calculate your training zone based on the percentage of your maximum heart rate.

- **Karvonen formula (heart rate reserve)** was suggested to find target heart rates and training zones for people in cardiovascular training. It uses MHR and resting heart rate (RHR) to calculate your heart rate reserve in the following equation:

heart rate reserve (HRR) = MHR – RHR

Karvonen suggested that a training intensity between 60 and 75 per cent of MHR is suitable for the average athlete. The training heart rate intensity (or zone) is calculated using the equation:

training heart rate % x (HRR) + RHR

This case study below demonstrates how training zone could be used.

Case study: Mike, 20-year-old swimmer

Mike is a 20-year-old swimmer with a RHR of 60 beats per minute. He has been instructed by his coach to train at 60–75 per cent of MHR.

- Training heart rate = 60 per cent
  = 0.60 (HRR) + RHR
  = 0.60 (200 – 60) + 60
  = 84 + 60
  = 144 beats per minute
- Training heart rate = 75 per cent
  = 0.75 (HRR) + RHR
  = 0.75 (200 – 60) + 60
  = 105 + 60
  = 165 beats per minute

From this, you would be able to tell Mike that he needs to be working at an intensity of 144–165 beats per minute and would be able to monitor this intensity using a heart rate monitor.

What are the benefits for Mike of training at this intensity?

If you were in Mike's position and had to train at 60–75 per cent of your MHR, what would your training heart rate be?

Anaerobic threshold

Refer back to page 243 for a description of anaerobic threshold.

Work/rest ratios

You need to get the right work/rest ratio when using training methods such as interval training. Table 9.3 on page 248 demonstrates guidelines for interval training for different type of training sessions.

> ### Remember
>
> You have to work at the correct intensity for the correct period of time to be able to get the correct training effect.

2.4 Resistance training

When designing your resistance training session, find out your primary goal as there are different training sessions for improving strength, power, muscle size or muscle endurance. Try to work on one training outcome per session/programme as this will give you the best results (for example, working on power and muscular endurance produces fewer gains than working on endurance alone).

Choice of exercises

When designing resistance sessions, there are hundreds of exercises to choose from. Make sure that you choose activities that meet the needs of the individual and the sport and keep them as simple as possible. Generally, resistance exercises fall into one of two categories: **core exercises** and **assistance exercises**.

Core exercises:

- focus on large muscle areas such as the chest, back or thigh
- involve two or more joints (called multi-joint activities)
- have more impact on sporting movements.

Assistance exercises:

- focus on smaller muscle areas (such as the upper arm or lower leg)
- involve one joint (single joint exercises)
- have less importance when you are trying to improve sport performance.

> ### Key terms
>
> **Core exercises** – focus on large muscle areas, involve two or more joints and have more direct impact on sport performance.
>
> **Assistance exercises** – focus on smaller muscle areas, only involve one joint and have less importance when trying to improve sport performance.

Number of exercises

The number of exercises you will do during a resistance training session depends on your training goals. Generally you need to ensure that there aren't too many exercises as this could lead to injury. Where you use more than one exercise for an area or muscle group, make sure that you alternate these exercises with other areas or muscles.

Order of exercises

There are different ways to structure your resistance training session but structure exercises so you can create as much force as possible in each exercise, while maintaining correct technique and allowing adequate rest between exercises. Three common techniques used to order exercises are to:

- complete core exercises before assistance exercises
- have exercises that alternate between upper and lower body exercises
- alternate push and pull activities.

Rest between sets

Think about when you have attempted any exercise feeling fine and then when you are tired. You will probably have made more mistakes in technique and performance, had lower effort levels and may have been injured when trying to exercise while fatigued. Allow adequate recovery between sets for performance reasons and health and safety reasons.

Speed of movement

With resistance training, it is not only the repetitions, sets, load and rest that influence the adaptations that the body will experience, the speed of movement is also important. When performing the exercise in a slow and controlled fashion, you will move the joint through the full range of motion and develop the highest force through the full range. This results in the greatest strength gains. Take 4 seconds from the start point of the exercise to the end of the range of motion and 2 seconds to return the resistance to the start point.

Systems of training

There are different systems of training designed to be used by all trainers from novice to experienced. For example, a simple circuit could be used with a novice trainer whereas pyramid training could be used for somebody who wants to increase their power. You should use these systems when planning resistance training sessions for yourself or your clients; and you should use your goals (or the goals of your client) as one of the key factors in your choice of training system. While each of the systems has different benefits and is aimed at people of different levels, one thing that they all share is an aim to help you reach overload which will help you meet your training goals.

- **Simple circuit** – this normally consists of 8–10 exercises, of 15–25 repetitions and with a resistance of 40–60 per cent of your repetition max. It uses a range of multi-joint exercises and works the major muscle groups. This training system is useful for beginners as, through using multi-joint exercises and the major muscles, you will work the smaller muscle groups and develop exercise technique. You can adjust this system of training by altering the number of times the circuit is performed, the number of repetitions, the resistance used and the number of exercises.

- **Pyramids** – pyramid training is a form of multiple set training and develops different components of fitness, depending on whether you use light-to-heavy (ascending pyramid) or heavy-to-light (descending pyramid) methods. Using a descending pyramid is a more advanced training method so is more suited to experienced strength trainers.

- **Super sets** involve performing two or more exercises for the same muscle group in a row or working opposite muscle groups or muscle areas. Performing two or more exercises on the same muscle group (known as compound super sets) increases the stress placed on the working muscle as you can work it from different angles. The benefit of this is that you use more muscle fibres and increase the blood flow to the muscle. Some of the negative elements of this

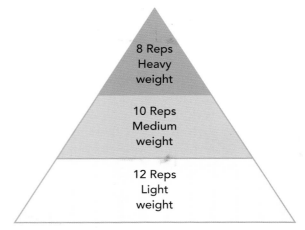

Figure 9.4: Why do you think descending pyramid training is a more advanced method?

training are that it cannot be used in every training session because of the intensity of training and it can carry a high risk of injury and overtraining if you don't know how to do it correctly. Working opposite muscle groups or muscle areas has the advantage that blood is kept in the same area which increases blood flow, carrying more nutrients and oxygen to the working muscle. It is more time-efficient than other training methods as the rest periods are built in to the training (because you are working opposite muscle groups) reducing the overall training time. One key limitation of this training system is that it doesn't increase the overload in the same way as a compound set does, but an advantage is that it increases the demand on the cardiovascular system which helps increase your anaerobic threshold, lactate tolerance and muscular endurance.

Take it further

Research advanced training methods

Using books and the Internet research the following advanced training methods:

- forced rep training
- drop sets
- pre-exhaust
- eccentric training
- split training.

When you are researching, try to find for each method:

1. a description

2. a sample session plan

3. the strengths and limitations.

2.5 Flexibility training

Flexibility training sessions often complement resistance training sessions (and vice versa) because they both improve muscle shape and size. Different factors to consider when designing flexibility training sessions include:

- the choice of exercises
- the number of exercises
- the order of exercises
- the number of repetitions
- the time.

Choice of exercises

When designing flexibility training sessions, relate your choice of exercises to your aims or the aims of your client. Choose from static, dynamic and ballistics flexibility training exercises. A well-designed flexibility session bases the choice of exercises on the results of flexibility tests. If you identify areas of weakness, you will want to focus on these.

Number of exercises

Your flexibility session should include approximately 10–12 exercises.

Order of exercises

Structure your exercises so that your session works different areas of the body to reduce the risk of injury and so that your exercises get progressively harder to help overload the body. For example, dynamic flexibility sessions should start with low speed movements that replicate the sporting actions but don't stretch the muscle or joint to the maximum range of movement. The sessions should then get progressively faster and the range of movement should be pushed further gradually until you reach full speed movement that pushes the limits of flexibility.

Repetitions

If you are a beginner starting a flexibility training programme, start by using three repetitions per exercise. As your flexibility increases, aim to increase this to five repetitions per exercise.

Time

On average, you will spend about 15–30 minutes on a flexibility session depending on the type and number of exercises to be performed. Each stretch should be held for between 6 seconds and 60 seconds, depending on the type of stretch you are doing. For example, static stretching could be held for up to 60 seconds. PNF stretching (see page 97) should have a 6 second contraction followed by 10–30 seconds of assisted stretching.

Activity: Planning flexibility training

Using the guidelines for flexibility training, plan your own flexibility training session. Your session should allow you to improve flexibility in important body parts for your particular sport or activity. When you have done this, ask somebody (for example, a tutor or fitness instructor) to look over your plan to make sure that it is safe and then take part in your session. On completion, write down the good and bad points about your session and try to suggest ways to improve it.

2.6 Speed training

Although there are general guidelines (see Table 9.3 on page 248) for speed-based interval training, the more specific requirements are geared towards the requirements of specific sports and specific positions within those sports. During the training week, speed training should take place after a rest period or low intensity training to reduce the risk of injury or over-training. Within a training session, speed training should take place after the warm-up and any other training within the session should be low intensity.

Time/distance

The time or distance of the sprint is dependent upon your particular sport. In most team sports, acceleration is more important than speed as you don't often hit maximum speed until approximately 50 metres, so most team sports will do speed training over distances of 10–30 metres; whereas an extended sprint athlete, such as an 800-metre runner, may use speed training distances of up to 400 metres at 2–3 seconds faster than their race pace.

Repetitions

As with the time/distance, the number of repetitions is dependent on your sport. Team sports players may use up to 10 repetitions per set but extended sprint athletes, such as 800-metre runners, may only use up to 4 repetitions. A typical speed training session will consist of 5–10 repetitions when aiming to develop maximal speed.

Sets

Depending on the time, distance and repetitions, you will use between 1–5 sets during a speed training session.

Rest between sets

Depending on the intensity, repetitions and sets you are using as part of your training programmes, you may require rest periods of between 1–3 minutes in between sets. These rest periods will be essential for you to replenish energy stores, maintain correct technique and reduce the risk of injury.

Work/rest ratio

A general guideline for maximal speed training is that there should be a work to rest ratio of 1:5, so if you were to have a 10-second maximal sprint, this would be followed by a 50-second rest period. As interval training is used in both running-based cardiovascular training and speed training, you could use the table below to plan training sessions for different energy systems.

Energy system	Time (min:sec)	Sets	Reps per set	Work: relief ratio	Relief interval type
ATP – PC	0:10	5	10	1:3	walking
	0:20	4	10	1:3	
ATP – PC – LA	0:30	5	5	1:3	jogging
	0:40	4	5	1:3	
	0:50	4	5	1:3	
	1:00	3	5	1:3	
	1:10	3	5	1:3	
	1:20	2	5	1:2	
LA – O_2	1:30 – 2:00	2	4	1:2	jogging
	2:00 – 3:00	1	6	1:1	
O_2	3:00 – 4:00	1	4	1:1	walking
	4:00 – 5:00	1	3	1:0.5	

Table 9.3: Guidelines for interval training

PLTS

If you generate ideas and explore different possibilities that could be used in your different sessions (see Assessment activity 9.2 opposite), you could provide evidence of your skills as a **creative thinker**.

Functional skills

If you bring together information regarding different training methods to suit the training programme (see Assessment activity 9.2 opposite), you could provide evidence of your **ICT** skills.

Assessment activity 9.2

You are starting your first day as a personal trainer at your local health club which is used by several types of individuals ranging from elite athletes to individuals on the GP referral scheme.

1. Your manager has asked you to prepare four training session plans, one for each of the following session types:

   • a cardiovascular training session for a trained recreational runner

   • a resistance training session for a boxer

   • a flexibility training session for a youth football player that suffers from tight hamstrings and has been referred to you by the resident sports therapist

   • a speed training session for a 200-metre sprinter. **P2**

2. To meet the merit grade, you must ensure that each of your training session plans is detailed. **M2**

3. Finally, you must justify each of your training session plans. **D1**

Grading tips

P2 To attain P2 produce a session plan for each type of session that says who the session is aimed at, the FITT of activities and shows how you could develop the required components of fitness.

M2 To attain M2 produce detailed session plans plus a range of activities and alternate activities that would benefit each individual.

D1 To attain D1 say why you would use each of the different activities that you have suggested on your session plan. This could be achieved by using physiological and performance related benefits of the different activities.

Use websites such as www.sport-fitness-advisor.com and www.pponline.co.uk to help you with this activity.

3. Be able to plan a fitness training programme

3.1 Collect information

One of the biggest problems for anybody trying to improve their fitness is that they often do the wrong type of training or their training programme is not structured properly. This leads to a lack of motivation for the individual as well as few training gains which will make the training programme useless. Collecting appropriate information about your client, such as goals, lifestyle information, medical history and physical activity history, means you will produce a more effective programme for your client.

Remember

Collecting information about your client is important, not only for the effectiveness of your programme, but also for health and safety reasons and (if you are working as a self-employed personal trainer or fitness instructor) your own insurance purposes.

Short-, medium- and long-term goals

An important part of designing training programmes is the individual's goals – without knowing these, you will not know what to direct your training towards. The programme must be flexible but capable of meeting these goals and personal needs. Each individual has different ambitions and aspirations, and your programme should reflect these. The athlete's goals should be broken up into short-term (up to one month) medium-term (one to three months) and long-term goals (three months to one year).

SMART targets

When designing the training programme, set goals that are based on SMART targets:

Specific – they say exactly what you mean (for example, to improve flexibility in the hamstring muscle group)

Measurable – you can prove that you have reached them (for example, increase flexibility by 5 cm using the sit and reach test)

Achievable – they are actions you can in fact achieve (for example, you can practise and improve flexibility through training)

Realistic – you will be able to achieve them but they will still challenge you (for example, the increase in flexibility must be manageable – a 20 cm increase in two weeks is not achievable)

Time-bound – they have deadlines (for example, to reach the target within six weeks).

Lifestyle

When designing a training programme, you need to know about different lifestyle factors such as alcohol intake, diet, time availability, occupation, family and financial situation; all of these will influence how you design a training programme for clients. The training programme should be built into a routine rather than becoming an extra stress as this will help adherence to the programme and will produce the best results.

Take it further

Why do you think that it is important for the fitness instructor or personal trainer to know about all of the different lifestyle factors?

Medical history

Before you design the programme, find out about the athlete's medical history. Ask them to complete a pre-exercise health questionnaire like the one shown in Figure 9.5 on page 251.

Physical activity history

When designing a training programme, the fitness trainer must gain a picture of the athlete's history, including any health-related issues, asthma or recent illnesses. Previous activity levels are part of this picture. If the athlete has been involved in a structured programme and has a good level of fitness, assessed through fitness tests, then the programme should reflect this. The exercises prescribed should be at a moderate to high intensity. Another athlete may not

have exercised for a long time (one month or more) for reasons such as injury, illness or loss of motivation. In this case, the programme should initially be set at a lower level, in terms of number of sessions per week, duration and intensity.

3.2 Principles of training

Any fitness programme is based on the principles of training. Following these principles results in the greatest gains through your training. The principles of training can be remembered using the acronym SPORTI, which stands for:

Specificity

Progression

Overload

Reversibility/recovery

Tedium

Individual differences.

Specificity

The principle of specificity means that you should plan your training programme around the needs of the sport or activity (such as specific muscle groups, components of fitness or sporting actions) and your individual needs (such as targets that are specific to you rather than just general targets).

Progression

Have you ever heard the phrase 'if you always do what you've always done, you'll always get what you've always got'? This is where progression is important because the only way your body adapts to training is if you keep making training progressively harder (increasing the levels of overload). Without correct levels of overload and progression, your training gains would start to level off (plateau). Be careful when planning progression because poor performances may result from too little progression or a training programme that overloads the system. As well as poor performance, excessive overloading may lead to injury or illness through over-training.

Overload

Overload is stretching the body systems beyond their normal functional level and is an essential aspect of gaining training effects. The following areas can be adapted (increased or decreased) to control the level of overload:

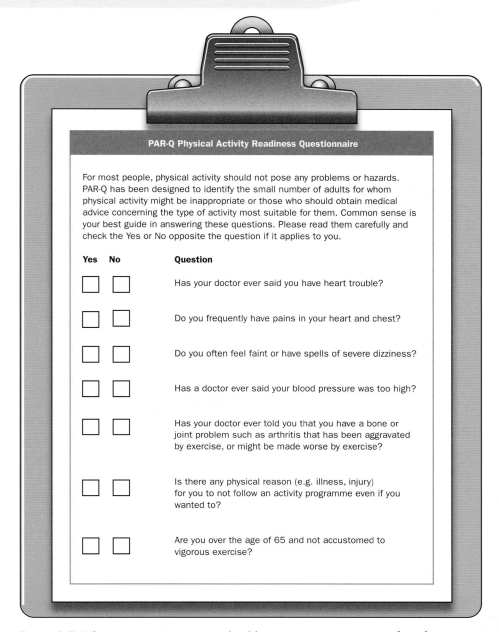

PAR-Q Physical Activity Readiness Questionnaire

For most people, physical activity should not pose any problems or hazards. PAR-Q has been designed to identify the small number of adults for whom physical activity might be inappropriate or those who should obtain medical advice concerning the type of activity most suitable for them. Common sense is your best guide in answering these questions. Please read them carefully and check the Yes or No opposite the question if it applies to you.

Yes	No	Question
☐	☐	Has your doctor ever said you have heart trouble?
☐	☐	Do you frequently have pains in your heart and chest?
☐	☐	Do you often feel faint or have spells of severe dizziness?
☐	☐	Has a doctor ever said your blood pressure was too high?
☐	☐	Has your doctor ever told you that you have a bone or joint problem such as arthritis that has been aggravated by exercise, or might be made worse by exercise?
☐	☐	Is there any physical reason (e.g. illness, injury) for you to not follow an activity programme even if you wanted to?
☐	☐	Are you over the age of 65 and not accustomed to vigorous exercise?

Figure 9.5: Why is using a pre-exercise health questionnaire important for a fitness instructor or personal trainer?

- frequency: the number of sessions a week, for example, increasing from two to four
- intensity: the amount of energy needed to perform a particular exercise or activity
- duration: the total time an exercise session or activity takes, for example, a 20-minute session could be increased to a 30-minute session.

During your training, you will normally be trying to progress the overload to make sure that you keep seeing training effects, but there are times when you would want or need to reduce the overload.

These include:

- signs of over-training or burnout, such as injury, illness or severe decrease in motivation
- different times of the season (for example, off season or close to a major competition).

Recovery and reversibility

Recovery time is essential within any athlete's training programme to allow for repair and renewal of the body's tissues. If you don't give the physiological system that you have been training the time that it needs to recover, you reduce your progression rate. However, a marked decrease in training or complete inactivity (for example during an illness, the off season or a long-term injury) leads to a decrease in functional capacity which is detrimental to performance. This decrease in performance is due to the principle of training called reversibility, which is sometimes known as detraining.

Remember

Reversibility leads to a dramatic and rapid reduction in fitness levels – faster than the improvements gained through overloading over a period of time.

Tedium/variation

One of the biggest reasons for stopping a training programme is if it becomes tedious (boring). This is often caused by following the same style of training on a regular basis. This principle is also known as the principle of variation because, to avoid tedium, you need to vary the training methods used in the programme.

Individual differences

All individuals have different needs, abilities, goals, skills, physical attributes, lifestyles, medical history and exercise preferences. Therefore a training programme should be tailor-made for each individual. Your expectations should be specific to different individuals. Athletes with low levels of fitness will show greater improvement than elite athletes because they have scope for larger amounts of improvement. However, even though elite athletes will show a minimal improvement, it could prove significant. For example, if you have never trained before, you could improve your 1 repetition max by 60 kg after a long period of resistance training. An Olympic weightlifter, however, might increase their personal best by only 1 kg during the same time frame, but this could mean breaking the world record.

FITT

In addition to the SPORTI principles, you also need to consider the FITT (frequency, intensity, time and type) principles (refer back to page 242).

3.3 Periodisation

Most people in sport use a training programme based on a structured cycle. This is known as periodisation. The training cycle is split into:

- **macrocycles** – 1-year to 4-year training cycles
- **mesocycles** – monthly training cycles
- **microcycles** – weekly or individually planned training sessions.

Periodisation can benefit you because it ensures continued physiological and psychological changes, it prevents over-training injuries and boredom and helps to achieve peak performance for key events.

Macrocycle

The first layer of a training programme may be based on a 1-year to 4-year cycle, which is known as a macrocycle. For example, a football player will train based on a 1-year cycle, from June to May, aiming to peak for a weekly or bi-weekly match, whereas an Olympic athlete will have a 4-year macrocycle, aiming for peak performance to coincide with the Olympic games.

Mesocycle

The macrocycle is divided into a number of mesocycles. These normally consist of a medium-term process of 4–24 weeks. The mesocycle is the main method of controlling the work to rest ratios; for example if you had a work to rest ratio of 3:1, this means you would have three working weeks followed by one active rest week. If you are an inexperienced trainer, you would have a ratio of 2:1 but if you are an advanced trainer, you could have a ratio of up to 6:1. Mesocycles can be step loaded. This technique uses a repetitive work to rest ratio; for example, with a 4-week mesocycle, you could have a ratio of 3:1 and repeat this cycle three times but increasing the intensity of the work weeks at the start of each cycle.

Microcycle

Each mesocycle is divided into a number of microcycles. The microcycle is planned with a specific adaptation in mind and should show the details of FITT training. Microcycles typically last for one week, but can range from 5–10 days.

A typical periodised training programme would look like the one in Table 9.4 (opposite).

Individual training sessions

Each microcycle consists of a number of individual training sessions. A training session should include three basic components: the warm-up, the main workout and the cool down.

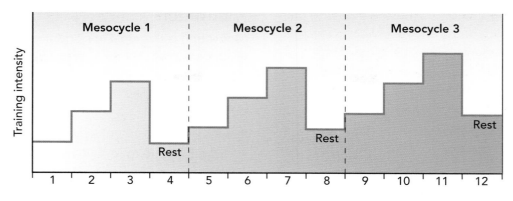

Figure 9.6: Why do you think that step loading mesocycles can improve fitness?

Macrocycle											
Mesocycle 1				Mesocycle 2				Mesocycle 3			
Microcycle 1	Microcycle 2	Microcycle 3	Microcycle 4	Microcycle 1	Microcycle 2	Microcycle 3	Microcycle 4	Microcycle 1	Microcycle 2	Microcycle 3	Microcycle 4
work	work	work	rest	work	work	work	rest	work	work	work	rest

Table 9.4: A typical periodised training programme. What level of athlete do you think that this structure of programme would be suitable for and why?

The warm-up is performed before the main exercise period to prepare you for the main session and to ensure your health and safety. A warm-up is required to:

- lubricate the joints with synovial fluid
- increase the temperature of the body generally, but specifically muscles and connective tissues
- increase blood flow
- take muscles and connective tissues through the full range of movement
- prepare you psychologically for the activity, focusing attention and increasing arousal.

A warm-up consists of: mobility exercises for joints; aerobic activity to increase body temperature and raise the pulse; preparatory stretches for the muscles and groups used in the main session; specific rehearsal activities that mimic the main session content.

The main session – the content of the main session is dependent on the session aims. However, make sure that your session is designed to meet your individual needs and ensure health, safety and welfare.

The cool down is shorter than the warm-up and is based on low-intensity exercises. The main aim of the cool down is to return the body to its resting state, and the main focus is on the aerobic component. Reasons why the athlete should perform a cool down include:

- to remove waste products from the working muscles, which are still receiving the oxygenated blood
- to stretch in order to decrease the chance of muscle stiffness
- to reduce the chances of fainting after an intense session.

3.4 Training diary

When working with athletes, maintain a training diary on a regular basis. The need to keep records of the training programme is often overlooked in the fitness industry, possibly because it is time-consuming. However, it is important for:

- **health and safety** – records can increase a trainer's awareness of previous injuries or illnesses
- **progression** – records allow the fitness trainer to see whether there is progression in the programme

- **communication** – records allow the trainer to gain an understanding of the athlete's history, which should aid communication
- **evaluation** – the information stored can be used as a part of the evaluation process
- **professionalism** – keeping records shows the fitness trainer has a level of competence and is following good practice
- reviewing your training programme.

Date and details of the session

Keeping the dates and details of the different training sessions helps you organise your time and monitor your progression more effectively, and allows you to alter future plans when necessary.

Progression

Progress should be logged so that you can monitor the programme regularly. You may make comments on the following:

- How did you find the intensity?
- Could you have performed more repetitions or sets?
- What were your thoughts on the types of exercises you were performing?
- Do you feel you have progressed from the previous session?
- Any other relevant thoughts.

Attitude

A major part of a training session is based on your attitude or approach to training. You should use the diary to make comments on your attitude so that you can explain the reason for good or poor sessions. To gain a wider picture, the fitness trainer should make comments on the attitude shown.

Why do you think having the correct attitude is important for training benefits?

Motivation

Motivation is the most important ingredient for success when carrying out a training programme. An athlete needs to be motivated in the sessions to maximise training effects. The motivation of an athlete may decrease due to:

- lack of improvement in fitness
- boredom due to repetitive exercise
- poor sporting performances
- external pressures, for example, college work.

Links to goals

Within the diary try to comment on your goal, which you identified at the start of the programme. Consider the following questions:

- How close are you to your goals?
- Are the goals still SMART targets?
- Do the goals need to be revised?
- Is the training too focused on one particular goal?

Competition results

For athletes at all levels, keeping competition results as part of the training diary is an important part of monitoring progress. It has a number of benefits:

- **Motivation:** if you can see improvements then you are more likely to want to experience more success. Alternatively, if you aren't seeing improvements it is more likely to motivate you to review your training to see if it is as effective as it could be.
- **Progression:** if you are seeing an improvement in performance results, this can act as a catalyst for progression in your training programme as the only way to keep improvements going is to keep progressing your training in the correct way.

PLTS

If you generate ideas and explore possibilities for your training programme, you could provide evidence of your **creative thinker** skills (see Assessment activity 9.3 on page 255).

Functional skills

If you present your information in an appropriate manner, you could provide evidence of your **ICT** skills (see Assessment activity 9.3 on page 255).

Assessment activity 9.3

Plan a 6-week training programme for an individual of your choice, such as a friend or family member, that will help them to improve important components of fitness for their activity. Make sure that you incorporate the principles of training and use the periodisation model to structure your programme. **P3**

Grading tips

P3 To attain P3 make sure that your training programme is geared towards individual needs and the fitness requirements of their specific activity. Use each of the principles of training and periodisation to structure the training.

4. Be able to review a fitness training programme

To find out the effectiveness of a training programme, monitor and review your progress throughout it. There are different techniques that you can use.

4.1 Monitor

A training programme is useless unless you know if (and how) it is working. Ways of monitoring your training programmes include the use of training diaries and fitness tests and gaining feedback from your coach or fitness instructor.

Training diaries

Training diaries should be as detailed as possible when used for monitoring. You may want to include some of the details discussed earlier. If you are the fitness instructor or personal trainer, include some of the following in your diary for your client:

- personal contact details in case of emergency – stored confidentially in accordance with the Data Protection Act
- health questionnaires
- accident, injury or illness forms
- copies of any quality check questionnaires given to the athlete to assess the quality of service.

Fitness test results

The only way of monitoring physiological changes is to conduct repeated fitness tests. Record the following details in your training diary to monitor your progression:

- the name of the test
- the component of fitness
- the result

- units of measurement, for example, metres or kilograms
- the comparison of results to normative data rating, for example, very good.

To effectively monitor and evaluate a training programme, fitness testing should take place at the start, during and at the end of the training programme (see Unit 8 Fitness testing for sport and exercise, on page 197).

Coach/instructor feedback

A coach or fitness instructor must record, monitor and review an individual's progress on a regular basis so that they can interpret the effectiveness of the training programme. It is commonplace for fitness trainers to record training details using ICT such as databases, spreadsheets, tables and online journals. Feedback and reviews should take place regularly so that any issues with the training programme can be identified and rectified quickly.

4.2 Review

An individual's training programme should be reviewed regularly to gauge its effectiveness. Through the appropriate fitness tests, the programme should be evaluated to assess whether personal goals and objectives have been met. The review process should involve both the coach/fitness instructor and the athlete. When reviewing training programmes consider:

- the overall suitability of the programme in terms of structure, goals, time and equipment
- achievements – physical, psychological, social and health-related

- negative aspects – issues such as boredom and lack of motivation
- future needs – new or modified goals
- whether the individual has received value for money.

Extent to which programme is achieving set goals

To discover how the training programme is working, fitness test the individual halfway through the programme. To read more about the fitness tests you could use with the individual, see Unit 8 Fitness testing for sport and exercise. If things are going well, maintain the programme or even increase the intensity/frequency of exercise. However, if the individual is unlikely to achieve the goals set, adapt the training programme and/or goals.

Remember

A review halfway through a programme can help to pinpoint any problems and indicate where valuable changes could be made.

Modification of programme to achieve planned goals

The main function of reviewing the training programme is to monitor its effectiveness against achievement of the planned goals. To make the training programme more effective you may need to modify it. This could be for a variety of reasons including:

- injury to the individual
- change in facilities or equipment
- change in motivation level
- lack of progress
- boredom
- achieving goals too quickly.

In these cases, it is important that you consider changing the:

- frequency of sessions or exercises
- intensity of exercises
- type of exercises being performed
- location of training
- overload and progression within the programme.

Assessment activity 9.4

 BTEC

Ask your client to complete the 6-week training programme that you designed as part of Assessment activity 9.3.

1. In order to make sure that your training programme is effective, monitor performance against goals during the six weeks. **P4**

2. At the end of the training programme, write a letter of feedback to your client that describes their strengths and areas for improvement. **P5**

3. In your feedback, make sure that you explain their strengths and areas for improvement. **M3**

4. Finally, evaluate your client's progress and provide them with recommendations for future activities. **D2**

Grading tips

P4 To attain P4 use a range of techniques to monitor progress against the goals of the training programme.

P5 To attain P5 include the client's key strengths and areas for improvement in order of priority.

M3 To attain M3 give specific details of strengths and areas for improvement of your client that are related to specific training goals and norm data for fitness tests.

D2 To attain D2 inform your client how the future recommendations will benefit them. You could suggest how the future recommendations will improve components of fitness further and look at any general sport or health-related benefits that will result from this.

PLTS

If you support your conclusions relating to the success of the training programme using reasoned arguments and supporting evidence, you could provide evidence of your skills as an **independent enquirer**.

Functional skills

If you provide feedback to your client in the correct manner, you could provide evidence of your **English** skills.

Amy Done
Fitness instructor

Amy is 19 and works as a fitness instructor at a local health club. She is responsible for a range of duties including: inducting people into the health club, conducting health screening with new members, setting training programmes for new members, reviewing current training programmes for existing members and providing general training advice for club members.

'Training is really important for both health and sport performance, so I need to make sure the advice that I give is up to date and correct so my clients get the best out of their sessions with me. I get to work with lots of different people as part of my job role which I find really interesting and challenging. On any day, it's quite common for me to be working with clients that range from obese people that need guidance on starting their exercise programmes so that they can lose weight and reduce their risk of associated conditions and diseases, all the way up to experienced weight trainers that just want somebody there to spot them or watch their technique for them. Quite often I'll get to see people develop their training habits over a long period of time and it's good to see that I've helped people to progress.

One of the biggest problems that I face is that, regardless of their level, one aspect of training that people always neglect is their flexibility training. No matter how much I try to encourage them to do it, most people don't bother with it because it doesn't involve lifting weights, running on the treadmill or swimming in the pool, so they don't see it as an actual method of training.'

Think about it!

- If you were in Amy's position how would you try to get people to increase their levels of flexibility training?
- Why do you think it is important for all gym users to understand flexibility training?
- If you could give people one piece of advice regarding their flexibility training, what would it be?
- Is fitness instructing a career you would be interested in and why?

Just checking

1. What are the health-related components of fitness?
2. What are the skill-related components of fitness?
3. Name one training method that can be used to increase each of the components of fitness
4. What does FITT stand for?
5. What does SPORTI stand for?
6. What types of information should you collect from a client before designing a training programme for them?
7. What is periodisation?
8. What are the different cycles within a periodised training programme?
9. Why should you use a training diary?
10. What are the different ways that you can monitor and review a training programme?

edexcel

Assignment tips

- Visit www.pponline.co.uk and www.sport-fitness-advisor.com. You can also use e-journals such as the American College of Sports Medicine Fit Society Newsletter which can be found at www.acsm.org.

- Use a range of specific textbooks for support when you are completing this unit. You may be really interested in a specific aspect of training and would like to read about it in more depth.

- If you know any fitness instructors, personal trainers or strength and conditioning coaches, talk to them about the content of this unit and how it fits in an applied setting.

- When you are completing assessments, provide as many appropriate examples, recommendations and justifications as you can on top of the more general information – this will help you to work at a higher level.

- Check your work with your tutor. They will be able to tell you how close you are to achieving the high grades and offer advice on how to improve your work.

- When you are learning about the different training methods, take part practically in the classes and even outside class. If you are experiencing the different training methods, you will get an understanding of their benefits.

- There are several professional bodies that are associated with fitness training and programming, including the British Association of Sport and Exercise Sciences (BASES), Register of Exercise Professionals (REPS), UK Strength and Conditioning Association (UKSCA) and British Weightlifting Association (BWLA). Visit their websites to investigate careers within fitness training and programming.

10 Sport and exercise massage

Think about when you have started an event and your legs have felt tired and heavy, or when you have finished a race and your legs felt sore shortly after. How many times have you immediately rubbed your legs to make them feel better? What you have started to do is some very basic massage.

Due to the increasingly competitive nature of sport, athletes are exploring every avenue to give themselves the best chance of success. In order to be successful, athletes need to use as many ways as possible to prepare for their competition and to recover from competitive schedules. As a result of this, sport and exercise massage has become more prominent and popular within the sporting world in recent years.

Throughout this unit, you will learn about the effects and benefits of sport and exercise massage before looking at the roles of sport and exercise massage professionals. You will then learn about the different practices involved with sport massage ranging from how to identify the massage requirements of different athletes all of the way through to being able to perform different massage techniques.

Learning outcomes

After completing this unit you should:

1. know the effects and benefits of sport and exercise massage
2. know the roles of sport and exercise massage professionals
3. be able to identify the sport and exercise requirements of athletes
4. be able to perform and review sport and exercise massage techniques.

Assessment and grading criteria

This table shows you what you must do in order to achieve a pass, merit or distinction grade, and where you can find activities in this book to help you.

To achieve a **pass** grade the evidence must show that you are able to:	To achieve a **merit** grade the evidence must show that, in addition to the pass criteria, you are able to:	To achieve a **distinction** grade the evidence must show that, in addition to the pass and merit criteria, you are able to:
P1 describe the effects and benefits of sport and exercise massage **See Assessment activity 10.1, page 265**	**M1** explain the beneficial effects of sport and exercise massage **See Assessment activity 10.1, page 265**	
P2 describe the roles of sport and exercise massage professionals **See Assessment activity 10.2, page 267**		
P3 carry out pre-treatment consultations on two different athletes **See Assessment activity 10.3, page 283**	**M2** explain the sport and exercise massage requirements of two different athletes **See Assessment activity 10.3, page 283**	**D1** compare and contrast the sport and exercise massage requirements of two athletes **See Assessment activity 10.3, page 283**
P4 describe six contraindications to massage treatment **See Assessment activity 10.3, page 283**		
P5 produce a treatment plan for two athletes **See Assessment activity 10.3, page 283**		
P6 demonstrate appropriate sport and exercise massage techniques on two athletes **See Assessment activity 10.4, page 286**		
P7 review the treatment plan for two athletes, describing future treatment opportunities **See Assessment activity 10.4, page 286**	**M3** explain the appropriate sport and exercise massage treatment for two athletes **See Assessment activity 10.4, page 286**	**D2** evaluate the appropriate sport and exercise massage treatment for two athletes **See Assessment activity 10.4, page 286**

How you will be assessed

This unit will be assessed by internal assignments that will be designed and marked by the tutors at your centre. Your assessments could be in the form of:

- written reports
- posters
- leaflets
- presentations
- practical sports and exercise massage routines.

Sophie, 19-year-old sport massage therapist

This unit was really useful for me as I always wanted to be a sport massage therapist. Until I started this unit, I thought a sport massage therapist was somebody who just knew how to give a massage treatment to people, but it is so much more than that! It was really good to get an understanding of the benefits of sport and exercise massage as well as learning about all of the different roles of a sport and exercise massage professional.

This unit also got me thinking about all of the different directions that I could take my work in, how it could link in with sports injuries and how important sport and exercise massage is within sporting environments.

The part of this unit that I enjoyed the most was learning the massage techniques. It was really hands on, practical work which suits how I learn and it helped me to develop the different massage techniques that I use every day with my clients.

Over to you!

1. Which parts of the unit do you think you will find interesting?
2. Which other units do you think would help you throughout this unit?
3. How are you going to prepare yourself for this unit?

1. Know the effects and benefits of sport and exercise massage

Warm-up

What are the benefits of sport and exercise massage?

The basic aim of sport and exercise massage is to maintain or restore normal functioning. The sport and exercise massage professional uses massage to help assist performance and reduce the risk of injury. Why do you think athletes are so keen to use sport and exercise massage professionals in sport?

Due to the effects and benefits of sport and exercise massage, it has become an integral part of the training programmes of many athletes and regular exercisers.

1.1 Effects

Physical and mechanical effects

There are a number of physical and mechanical effects of sport and exercise massage that can be seen in Figure 10.1 below. These include blood and lymphatic circulation, tissue permeability, stretching, reducing and remodelling scar tissue and opening micro-circulation.

- **Blood and lymphatic circulation** – localised blood circulation can be improved as a result of sport and exercise massage. Circulation can be stimulated because the pressure exerted by the massage technique compresses and releases blood vessels which supplements their normal pumping action. When you massage a limb, it stimulates blood flow to that limb and stimulates blood flow to the other limb which makes massage particularly useful for people that have had limb injuries that has left one limb immobilised (for example, a broken leg). Increased circulation as a result of massage has the benefit of increasing the supply of oxygen and nutrients to the area and aids **lymphatic drainage**.

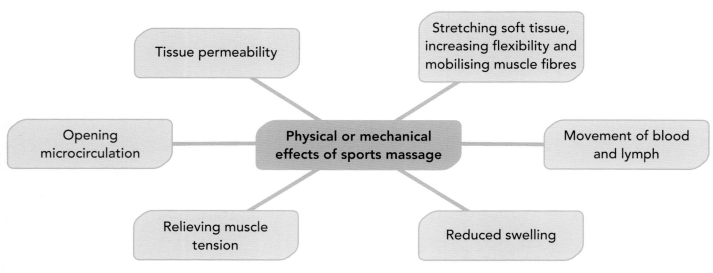

Figure 10.1: How will these effects help you to be a better athlete?

Lymphatic drainage is important because it helps to remove waste products and reduce swelling.

- **Tissue permeability** – massage improves the absorption of substances within the body tissues. It also affects **cell permeability**, which allows nutrients and other substances to enter the cell more readily and allows the removal of waste products from the cell.

- **Stretching** – most of the flexibility within a muscle comes from the surrounding connective tissues and the muscle fibres. With the forces that are applied through massage, muscle fibres can be separated, the connective tissues that surround the fibres can be stretched and the fibres can be stretched longitudinally. These three things, combined with the increased muscle temperature and circulation, make the tissue more pliable and reduces **adhesions**.

- **Reducing and remodelling scar tissue** – as muscle fibres start to heal after being damaged, they start to lose their elasticity and can become rigid – this causes scar tissue. If this is left untreated, it will cause permanent weakness and decreased flexibility in that area. Massage can help this as applying massage techniques across the direction of the muscle fibre can separate fibres that have adhered together and can break down scar tissue.

- **Opening micro-circulation** – massage opens the blood vessels by stretching them, enabling nutrients to pass through more easily.

Key terms

Lymphatic drainage – a massage treatment that uses light pressure and long, rhythmic strokes to increase lymphatic flow. Lymph, a fluid that contains white cells, is drained from tissue spaces by the vessels of the lymphatic system. It can transport bacteria, viruses and cancer cells. The lymphatic system is associated with the removal of excess fluid from the body. It is made up of lymphatic capillaries, lymphatic vessels, lymph nodes and lymph ducts.

Cell permeability – allowing or activating the passage of a substance through cells or from one cell to another.

Adhesions – pieces of scar tissue that attach to structures within the body, limiting movement and sometimes causing pain.

Physiological effects

There are a number of physiological effects of sport massage (see Figure 10.2 below). These will be due in some part to the effects of the massage technique on the autonomic nervous system, which is made up of the sympathetic and parasympathetic nervous systems.

The autonomic nerves are responsible for controlling the functioning of the vital organs in the body. Within this, the sympathetic nervous system stimulates activity within physiological systems, whereas the parasympathetic nervous system inhibits activity. Sport massage therapists use different massage techniques to stimulate the client's sense of touch, and by stimulating this sense of touch you can enhance the effects and benefits of sport massage.

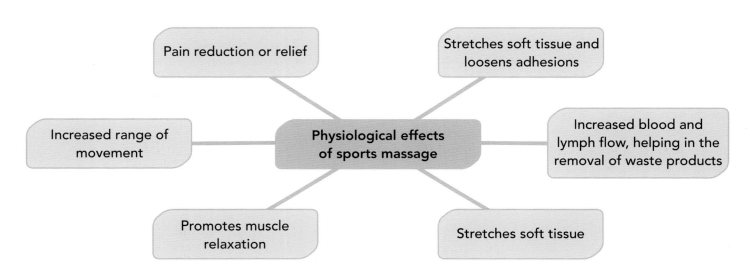

Figure 10.2: What physiological effects does sport massage have on sport and exercise performance?

Massage techniques that are deeper or more vigorous can stimulate the nervous system. Placing a small amount of pressure on the nervous system can also relieve pain by blocking nerve impulses, thus resulting in a numbing sensation in the area. Alternatively, slow, smooth massage techniques can produce a relaxing effect on the nerves. These effects are commonly accepted as the effects of massage on the nervous system, but some research has not found any sympathetic or parasympathetic responses to different massage techniques.

1.2 Benefits of sport and exercise massage

There are a number of physiological and psychological benefits of sport and exercise massage including stress reduction, enhanced wellbeing, improved body awareness, pain reduction and relaxation.

Stress reduction and enhanced wellbeing

Sport and exercise massage techniques can enhance a sense of wellbeing by stimulating the release of **endorphins** and by reducing levels of stress hormones such as **cortisol**.

Improved body awareness

Physiologically, massage can increase body awareness by enhancing nervous system function and giving you a greater awareness of your body. Psychologically, massage gives you an increased awareness of how your body actually looks, rather than how you think it looks, which can lead to a more positive body image.

Pain reduction

When pain occurs in an area, messages are sent to your brain via **afferent nerves**. By massaging the painful area, you stimulate **cutaneous mechanoreceptors** that block the signals before they reach your spinal cord. As your brain never receives the pain signals from the affected area, your perception of the pain is reduced.

Relaxation

Certain massage techniques can have relaxing effects on your nervous system and can release muscle tension, as well as stimulating the release of endorphins which can enhance your mood. This combination leads to a generally pleasant, relaxed feeling.

Key terms

Endorphins – morphine-like chemicals that can reduce pain and improve mood.

Cortisol – a hormone that is associated with stress, anxiety and depression.

Afferent nerves – sensory nerves that usually have receptors at the skin and joints.

Cutaneous mechanoreceptors – sensory nerve endings in the skin.

Remember

To understand the benefits of sport and exercise massage, you need to know how different body systems influence each other. For example, a sprinter may be worried about their performance because they cannot run as fast as normal and are starting to feel more stressed about their performance levels. They have very tight quadriceps and hamstrings which could be compressing the nerves passing through the muscles. When the nerve is compressed, the nerve impulse that travels down the nerve is slowed which will then slow down the overall muscle contraction. Using different massage techniques, the muscle tension is released, which increases the rate of the nerve impulse and the speed of contraction. Ultimately, this increases performance and reduces performance related stress.

Assessment activity 10.1

You have started your own business as a self-employed sport massage therapist and you need to market the benefits of your product to a range of clients. In order to do this, you have decided to design a website that is split into different sections, one of which describes and explains the benefits of sport and exercise massage.

1. Describe each of the different effects and benefits of sport massage. **P1**

2. Explain the beneficial effects of sport and exercise massage. **M1**

Grading tips

- To attain **P1** look at what each of the physiological, physical, mechanical and psychological beneficial effects are.

- To attain **M1** look at how the physiological, physical, mechanical and psychological beneficial effects are interlinked.

PLTS

If you can support the statements you make regarding the effects and benefits of sport and exercise massage, you could provide evidence towards your skill as an **independent enquirer**.

Functional skills

If your work is fit for purpose and communicates your information, ideas and opinions persuasively, you could provide evidence of your **English** skills.

2.   Know the roles of sport and exercise massage professionals

Sport and exercise massage professionals work in a variety of settings including private practice, health and fitness clubs, spas and alongside other professionals such as physiotherapists. When working as a sport and exercise massage professional, you must have a detailed knowledge of the types of work you may do, the different treatments that you can apply and knowledge of your profession.

and you will generally find yourself working with sport or exercise related athletes (although anybody can benefit from sport and exercise massage techniques). Therefore, you must understand the effects of massage on sport or exercise related performance. You are not trained to diagnose medical conditions, so you must always have a referral network of other professionals that you can work with and to whom you can send your clients if necessary.

2.1 Roles

Types of work

When working as a sport and exercise massage professional, you must be confident in your ability to work with clients and be aware of your limitations of practice. Your limitations of practice are the things that you can and cannot do as a sport and exercise massage professional. As a sport and exercise massage professional, you are able to administer sport and exercise massage therapy for its intended purpose

Take it further

Sport Massage Association Code of Conduct

Using the Sport Massage Association Code of Conduct, find out more about the roles of a sport and exercise massage professional and their limitations of practice. Visit the association website (www.sportsmassageassociation.org).

Types of activities

There are a range of activities that you need to do to be an effective professional. Your activities will range from administrative tasks (such as checking and replying to emails, website maintenance, completing stock checks of materials and ordering stationery) to client assessments (such as biomechanical assessments) and treating clients.

Treatments applied

As a sport and exercise massage professional, you can apply several types of treatment dependent upon your experience and training. The main treatments that you could apply are massage, relaxation, strapping and taping, manipulation and electrotherapy treatments.

- **Massage** – the different massage techniques that you could use include effleurage, petrissage, frictions, tapotement and vibrations. These massage techniques involve the manipulation of soft tissue to assist in correcting problems and imbalances that can be caused by sport and exercise to help improve performance, prevent injury and enhance recovery.

- **Relaxation** – sport and exercise massage professionals are trained in different activities to aid relaxation, including massage techniques, stretching techniques and breathing techniques. One such advanced massage technique that combines the use of different strengthening, stretching, massage and breathing activities to elicit relaxation is known as Muscle Energy Technique (MET).

- **Strapping and taping** techniques are used by sport and exercise massage professionals to prevent injury and recurrence while returning to sport. The tape limits the movement in an injured area (such as a joint) to prevent excess or abnormal movement. Tape can also be used to protect unstable joints where repeated or severe ligament damage has resulted in stretching of the ligaments and joint instability. For example, if a taped ankle starts to over-invert (commonly known as 'going over on your ankle') after landing from a basketball jump shot, the tape will restrict excessive movement and inform the body that it needs to contract muscles to prevent too much movement at the ankle. Without this feedback the athlete may be unaware the ankle has started to invert and land on it thus

injuring it again. Tape should support the muscles surrounding the joint that may be under additional strain due to connective tissue injury.

- **Manipulation** – soft tissue manipulation is the stretching or lifting of tissues without lubrication; or the physical manipulation of joints to assist movement. This technique is used to help with the realignment of tissues and/or joint surfaces that have been misaligned as a result of injury. Manipulation should only be used by sport and exercise massage professionals after appropriate training.

- **Electrotherapy modalities** – electrotherapy is a technique that uses electrical currents at different frequencies to aid recovery from injury. Some common modalities of electrotherapy include ultrasound, Transcutaneous Electrical Nerve Stimulation (TENS) and interferential therapy. The use of these techniques requires specialist training.

Take it further

Muscle Energy Technique (MET)

Using books and the Internet, research MET.
1. **How can this technique benefit your massage clients?**
2. **What are some of the dangers of using MET?**

Knowledge

To maintain your reputation and work in the best interests of your client, you must make sure that your knowledge is up to date. You must have specific knowledge of your training requirements, career opportunities and the application of your treatments to sport and exercise.

- **Training** – sport and exercise massage is currently not regulated by law within the UK, but sport and exercise massage professionals do have professional bodies with which they associate themselves. These include the Sport Massage Association (www.sportsmassageassociation.org) and the Society of Sports Therapists (www.society-of-sports-therapists.org). Both of these professional bodies provide lists of accredited training courses on their websites and provide details of the training and experiential requirements to be accredited or be a member of the professional body. Once you are qualified as a sport and exercise massage professional, you need to make sure that you follow a programme of continued professional development (CPD) so that the professional body know that you are improving your knowledge and skills base.

- **Career opportunities** – there are a number of career opportunities for sport and exercise massage professionals which include working:
  - as a self-employed practitioner
  - in health and leisure clubs
  - for sports clubs
  - within the health services.

  Each will have their own training requirements and experience requirements, so it is a good idea to spend time researching what you will need to do to be able to progress into that career.
- **Application to sport** – when you work within sport and exercise massage, you will work mainly (although not exclusively) with athletes actively involved in sport or exercise. Massage can be an integral part of preparation for, and recovery from,

sport or exercise and can be used to increase training benefits, reduce or rehabilitate sports injuries and increase sport performance. You must understand how the different treatments can be applied specifically to sport and exercise.

Activity: Careers in sport and exercise massage

Imagine you want a career in sport and exercise massage but you don't really know how to get there. Spend time researching the different career opportunities so that you have a good idea of the requirements of the different careers. Using the Internet and books, research the different careers that are available in sport and exercise massage and find one that you are interested in. When you have done this, find out what qualifications and experience you will need to be able to progress into that career. Use the Sport Massage Association and the Society of Sports Therapists websites to help you.

Assessment activity 10.2

You have applied for a job working as a sport and exercise massage professional at a major health and fitness chain. As part of your application process, you must demonstrate that you fully understand the job.

Produce a presentation that describes the roles of sport and exercise massage professionals. **P2**

Grading tip

- To attain **P2** describe the types of work and activities undertaken by sport and exercise massage professionals, the treatments they apply and the knowledge they must have.

PLTS

If you communicate your information regarding the roles of sport and exercise massage professionals effectively, you could provide evidence of your skills as a **reflective learner**.

Functional skills

If your presentation is fit for purpose, you will provide evidence of your **English** skills.

3. Be able to identify the sport and exercise massage requirements of athletes

When you start to work with clients you must make sure that your massage is well planned and that you know why you are doing it. To do this, you need to conduct client assessments, keep appropriate documentation and be aware of the different contraindications to massage; and then use all of this information to propose an appropriate treatment plan.

3.1 Assessment

Your client assessment involves using initial consultations, making referrals to practitioners (if required), identifying the treatment area and having a knowledge of different simple injuries.

Initial consultation

During your initial consultation you should complete a client consultation form using questions and answers (a verbal assessment), an assessment of posture (a visual assessment) and an assessment of tension and movement (a physical assessment). Your questionnaire should include:

- key personal details of the client
- medical history history
- any current problems
- lifestyle details
- a diagram to identify areas and level of pain
- a section for therapist's comments
- a consent section where the patient and the therapist sign to show that the information is correct and that consent has been given by the client for treatment.

An example of a consultation form can be seen in Figure 10.4.

During the consultation you must visually assess a client's posture to see if there are any postural problems that could be a factor in injury. Figure 10.3 shows examples of good and bad posture; and the different warning signs to look for.

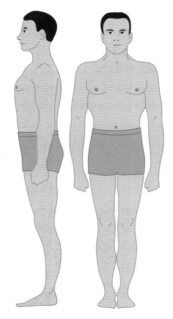

Good posture

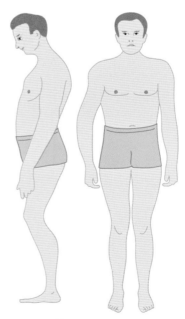

Poor posture

Figure 10.3: How does your posture compare to the images?

Client consultation form

Client name ....
Date of birth ....

Address ....
Occupation ....

....
Marital status ....

....
G.P. name ....

Home telephone ....
G.P. surgery address ....

Mobile telephone ....
....

Email ....

Medical history

Current general health status. (Circle as appropriate.)

Excellent   *Good*   *Average*   *Poor*   *Very Poor*

Any current or recent injuries? Yes / No (if yes, please specify)

....

Do you currently experience any problems with the following areas? (Circle as appropriate.)

Muscular   *Skeletal*   *Circulatory*   *Respiratory*

Are you currently undergoing any medical treatments? Yes / No (If yes, please specify.)

....

Are you currently taking any medication? Yes / No (If yes, please specify name and dosage.)

....

Do you have a family history of any medical conditions? Yes / No? (If yes, please specify.)

....

Lifestyle information

How would you describe your current diet? (please circle)

Excellent   *Good*   *Average*   *Poor*   *Very Poor*

Do you currently smoke? Yes / No (If yes, please specify) ☐ Cigarettes per day

Do you drink alcohol? Yes / No (If yes, please specify) ☐ Units per week

Do you currently use any other form of recreational drug? Yes / No (If yes, please specify.)

Do you currently take part in sport / exercise / physical activity? Yes / No (If yes, please specify.)

....
....

Other information

On the diagram, please indicate the site of pain and give it a level from 1–10.
(1 = not painful at all, 10 = extremely painful)

Is there anything that you can do that makes the pain ease?

....
....
....
....
....

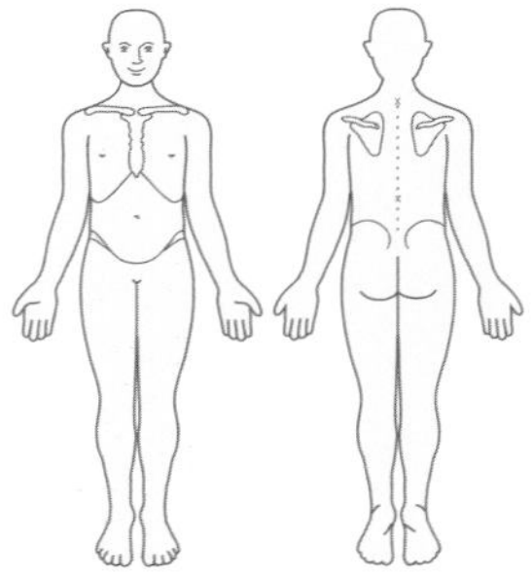

Therapist notes (to include techniques to be used and justification of techniques)

Client signature .... Date ....

Therapist signature .... Date ....

Figure 10.4: Why is it important to have a detailed consultation form?

As well as a general assessment of posture, there are specific areas to look at while observing your client from behind. When you are assessing posture from behind, you should stand approximately 1 metre away (standing closer will prevent you from effectively comparing the left and right halves of the body).

Activity: Postural observation

Observe a friend from behind. Can you see any of the specific postural issues listed below?

- Are the ears level? If not, there could be spinal misalignment.

- Are the shoulders level at the acromio-clavicular joints and is the muscle bulk the same on both sides?

- Are the scapulae (shoulder blades) level? (See Figure 10.5.)

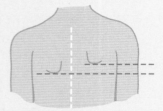

Figure 10.5: Uneven scapulae.

- How does the overall spine alignment look? Is there a straight or curved line between the neck and pelvis?

- Is the 'keyhole' (the gap between the arms and the body) even on both sides? If not, there could be spinal or shoulder misalignment (see Figure 10.6).

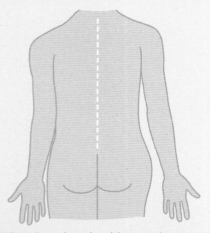

Figure 10.6: Spinal or shoulder misalignment.

- Are there any skin creases at the waist level? Are there more on one side than the other? This could indicate the person has a tendency to lean to one side.

- Is the pelvis level at both sides?

- Are the creases between the buttocks and the top of the hamstrings level? If not, there could be some pelvic misalignment (see Figure 10.7).

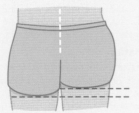

Figure 10.7: Pelvic misalignment.

- Check the number and angles of knee creases and check overall muscle bulk to assess any imbalances in the legs.

- Is the Achilles tendon vertically aligned or is it twisted? Is there any thickening of the tendon? Is the muscle bulk the same at the midline of the calf? These could indicate postural issues in the legs and feet.

- Are the feet pointing forwards when standing relaxed and barefoot? Are there any signs of hard skin? Does the client naturally invert or evert their feet when relaxed or walking?

Take it further

Researching postural terms

When you are conducting your postural assessments, it is good to have as much information as you can. Using books and the Internet, research the following terms and produce a description of each term with diagrams to accompany your description:

- plumb line
- head thrust
- flat back
- kyphosis (type 1)
- kyphosis (type 2)
- lordosis
- scoliosis
- bow legs
- knock knees
- back knees
- flat feet

The final part of your initial consultation is the physical consultation which involves the sport and exercise massage professional palpating (touching) the area to detect any tension in the area; and the client performing different movements so that the therapist can assess the range of movement at different joints and find out if there is any pain or discomfort when performing different activities. When you are assessing pain that is experienced through either palpation or movement, you should ask the client to rate the pain on a scale

from 1 (minimal pain) to 10 (unbearable pain). Palpation is a key part of the initial physical consultation. When you examine your client using palpation, they could be standing, sitting or lying (prone and supine). This part of the consultation has two parts: a general assessment of the tissues within the area and precise palpation to try to find areas of tension, sensitivity or any trigger points. Some different activities that you could use to assess range of movement include:

- Forward bending from the waist with the legs straight. (How easy was it for the client? Are the vertebrae stiff or mobile? Are the hamstrings tight?)
- Side bending from the waist. (How easy was this? Was there any difference between sides?)
- Backward bending from the waist. (How easy was this for the client?)
- Turning head left and right. (Is the chin in line with the shoulders? Is there a difference between left and right?)
- Tilting head forwards and backwards. (Can the chin touch the chest? Can the back of the head touch the cervical/thoracic junction of the spine?)
- Gait analysis. (How does the client walk? Any limping/favouring? Any excessive inversion/eversion?)

Activity: Conducting initial consultations

The initial consultation is an important process as it will give you the information you need to be able to decide on your client's massage requirements. Working with a friend, complete an initial consultation that you could use to draw up a massage treatment plan. As part of your consultation, you need to:

- design and use your own client consultation form (you could use the one in Figure 10.4 as a guide)
- complete a visual assessment of your client, looking at their posture and noting down any areas of concern
- complete a physical assessment of your client including both palpation and range of movement. When you are palpating your client remember these points:
  - Look at the colour of the area that you are palpating and compare it with other parts of the body. Do you notice any differences in colour or any noticeable swelling?
  - Start by touching your client gently. Lay your hand on the area you are palpating and feel

for the temperature (is it too hot/cold?) and moisture of the area (is it damp or dry?).
  - Progress by pressing a little deeper and move the skin over the underlying layers. Do the underlying layers feel connected or loose? Are they pliable? Are there any differences in temperature and moisture?
  - Palpate different areas of the muscle. Do they feel tense or can you feel any knots? Ask your client to let you know about any areas that feel different to normal, for example, ticklish or tender.
  - Pay attention to any non-verbal cues that your client may give you as you palpate including wincing, holding their breath, wriggling or spasms.
  - Palpate for any trigger points but make sure that you don't press too firmly as this could hurt too much.
- record all of the information that you have gained through your initial consultation and store it in a safe place.

Referral to practitioners

By working within the limitations of your practice, you need to know when, and to whom, you could refer your clients if the problem is something that you are not qualified or experienced enough to deal with. Other professionals to whom you could refer clients include GPs, physiotherapists, podiatrists, chiropractors, sports therapists or surgeons. To refer your clients, you may need to write a referral letter to the appropriate professional. An example is shown in Figure 10.8.

When making the decision to refer your client, consider the following points:

- Is the pain sudden and inexplicable (is there no traumatic or overuse cause)?
- Is the injury not responding to treatment?
- Is the injury severely swollen?

Merton College Sports Academy
Sports Injury Clinic
Merton College
Hurst St, Merton, MT3 1JF
Telephone 01897 336 6888

Mr T. Shap
Townhouse Chiropodist and Podiatrist
Argyll St
Merton

Dear Mr Shap,

Re: Jason Burns, Maple Way, Merton

Jason is a competitive footballer suffering from a recurring painful Achilles tendonitis. During recent consultation we discussed his history of stiffness and soreness in the area of the gastrocnemius. Following a biomedical assessment I was aware that he appeared to have a significant genu-varus of his knees that may be causing over-pronation.

In discussion with Jason we agreed that it would be advisable to make this referral for podiatrist assessment.

Yours sincerely

Andre Lee
Sport massage therapist

Figure 10.8: Why is it important to refer to other practitioners?

- In the case of a head injury, does the client have a headache or feel sick?
- Does the injury continue to hurt despite rest?
- Are there continual throbbing and shooting pains, numbness or tingling sensations?
- Is there anything that you do not recognise?

Treatment area

As a sport and exercise massage professional you should be able to identify the correct treatment area using appropriate anatomical terminology. The different anatomical reference terms can be seen in Table 10.1 and are illustrated in Figure 10.9.

Simple injuries

As a sport and exercise massage professional you need an understanding of some simple injuries including the different types of haematoma, muscle tears, tendon injuries, inflammation and ligament injuries. You also need an understanding of how massage can benefit them.

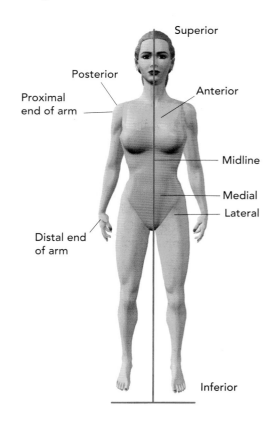

Figure 10.9: Why is it important for therapists to use correct anatomical terminology?

Table 10.1: Anatomical references.

Anatomical reference	Definition
Anterior	The front view of the client
Posterior	The rear view of the client
Midline	An imaginary vertical line that divides the body into symmetrical left and right halves
Superior	A body part that is higher in location
Inferior	A body part that is lower in location
Lateral	The part of the limb or body that is furthest from the midline
Medial	The part of the limb or body that is closest to the midline
Proximal	A body part nearer to the point of reference or to the centre of the body than something else is. For example, the elbow is proximal to the hand.
Distal	A body part further from the point of reference or to the centre of the body than something else is. For example, the elbow is distal to the shoulder.

- **Haematoma** – this is a mass of blood in the tissue caused by an injury when the muscle is squashed between the object of impact and the bone underlying the muscle. There are two types of haematoma:
  - **Inter-muscular haematomas** happen when the sheath surrounding the muscle fibre is ruptured and the blood is able to move into the surrounding tissue, causing bruising, swelling, a loss of power and a loss of range of movement.
  - **Intra-muscular haematomas** happen when the sheath surrounding the muscle fibres stays intact, causing bleeding within the muscle which results in a blood clot within the muscle. Intra-muscular haematomas result in inflammation and a great reduction in range of movement, usually because of the build-up of pressure within the muscle and the associated pain. Bruising is not always evident as the blood is contained within the muscle sheath. This type of haematoma takes much longer to recover. Remember that you should not massage an intra-muscular haematoma as this can worsen it and also worsen a condition called myositis ossificans, where bone cells grow within the haematoma and cause a severe loss of movement. If you suspect myositis ossificans is present, you must refer your client to their GP who will then refer them to a specialist.

- **Muscle tears or strains** – when a muscle is torn (strained), a number of the muscle fibres and their associated capillaries are torn. There are three different degrees of muscle tear, shown in Table 10.2.

Key terms

Inter-muscular haematoma – a haematoma that escapes the muscle sheath through a tear or rupture.

Intra-muscular haematoma – a haematoma that remains trapped inside the muscle sheath.

Table 10.2: Muscle tear classification.

Classification of tear	Fibres torn	Symptoms
Grade 1	Mild tear A few fibres torn	Minor inflammation Minimal pain
Grade 2	Moderate tear Up to 50% of fibres torn	Noticeable inflammation Noticeable pain
Grade 3	Severe tear Up to 100% of fibres torn	Major inflammation Severe pain

- **Tendon injuries** – tendons can become injured either by overuse or by trauma, such as being kicked. Overuse injuries of the tendon (or the paratendon) lead to pain, swelling and loss of mobility (commonly known as **tendonitis** or **paratendonitis**) or the deterioration of the tendon itself (known as **tendonosis**), whereas trauma related injuries can lead to partial or complete tears of the tendon.

- **Inflammation** is the body's response to an injury. The signs of inflammation are heat, redness, swelling, pain and loss of function. There are three different types of inflammation; **haemarthrosis**, **oedema** and **synovial effusion**.

- **Ligament injuries** – the most common injury that sport and exercise massage professionals assist in is the rehabilitation of a sprain. There are different degrees of sprain, shown in Table 10.3.

Key terms

Tendonitis – inflammation of the tendon.

Paratendonitis – inflammation of the paratendon (the tissue surrounding the tendon).

Tendonosis – deterioration of the tendon.

Haemarthrosis – a build-up of blood in the joint.

Oedema – a build-up of blood and tissue fluid within the tissue.

Synovial effusion – a build-up of synovial fluid within the joint.

3.2 Documentation

You must maintain the correct documentation when working with clients to monitor their progress across the treatment. This documentation should be kept in a safe place (such as a locked filing cabinet, or a password protected computer and within an encrypted file). The main documentation you will keep will be your record cards.

Record cards

Your record cards will include a range of information, including:

- the date of treatment
- the treatments proposed/completed (including the type, duration, responses to and effectiveness of treatment) and relevant health and safety information (including the medium used for treatment, such as oil, talc or cream)
- homecare and aftercare advice given to clients
- notes regarding future treatments
- dates of future appointments.

Treatments

Your record card should show details of the treatments that you plan to use with your client (or the treatments that you have used), the details about the treatments (highlighted above) and your justification for using those treatments (see pages 276–278 for details of the different massage techniques and when to use them).

Table 10.3: Classifying sprains.

Classification of sprain	Effects	Symptoms
Grade 1	Minor sprain with only a few fibres torn No joint instability	Minor inflammation Minimal pain
Grade 2	Moderate sprain 50% of fibres torn Minor joint instability	Noticeable inflammation Noticeable pain
Grade 3	Severe sprain Up to 100% of fibres torn Severe joint instability	Major inflammation Severe pain

Relevant health and safety information

Your record card should show details of the medium used for the massage and show that you have checked for any allergies that could prevent the use of a certain medium (for example, some oils are nut based so cannot be used with people with nut allergies). Other health and safety information that could be included on the record card could be a confirmation that you have given the client a basic fire safety induction on their first visit.

Aftercare advice

Your aftercare advice should be included in your treatment plan. The general aftercare advice that you give your client should be to drink plenty of fluids to rehydrate the body as massage can have a dehydrating effect as well as increasing circulation, so water will be needed to aid both of these. You may also need to advise your client to rest after the massage (where appropriate).

Homecare advice

As with aftercare advice, you should provide homecare advice for your client as they will have to manage the injury in between treatments. The homecare that you will provide will be dependent upon the individual, their treatments and their injury. However, some general advice that can be given to most clients is to try to eliminate the cause of the problem (for example, adjust your working position if the problem is lower back pain), attempt to reduce inflammation (for example, give advice regarding the use of ice) and provide home-based exercise (for example, stretching exercises to increase flexibility of muscles and connective tissues to prevent recurrence of the injury).

3.3 Contraindications to massage

A contraindication is a reason to avoid massage treatment. There are a number of contraindications to massage including the client history, the type of injury, the location of the injury, different skin conditions, circulatory conditions and other medical conditions.

Client history

There may be elements of the client's history that mean they should not receive certain massage treatments, for example, a negative reaction to a previous massage

treatment. These contraindications could be local contraindications (a particular body part cannot receive massage treatment) or general contraindications (the client shouldn't receive massage treatment at all). Other factors that would contraindicate the client from massage would be feeling unwell or pregnancy.

Type of injury

There are numerous types of injuries that should not be massaged including:

- acute trauma injuries (24–72 hours post trauma)
- dislocations
- fractures
- swollen, hot, bruised or painful areas
- intra-muscular haematoma.

Location of injury

Massage can be applied to most areas of the body (other than directly to the eyes and genitalia) but you need to take care when massaging the injury site itself.

Skin conditions

Certain skin conditions mean that massage is contraindicated as it could worsen the condition and/or the condition could spread to the therapist. These conditions include:

- acne
- cuts and abrasions
- new scar tissue
- sunburn or windburn
- blisters
- warts
- moles
- infectious skin diseases, such as impetigo.

Circulatory conditions

There are some circulatory conditions that are contraindications to sport and exercise massage as they could increase the chance of blood clots travelling around the body. These include:

- varicose veins
- phlebitis (inflammation of the walls of the veins)
- high or low blood pressure
- thrombosis (blood clots) or deep vein thrombosis.

Table 10.4: Contraindications.

Contraindication	Reason
Multiple sclerosis	Although massage can be beneficial, it can also increase muscle spasm and cause more pain.
Cancer	Although more recent research demonstrates some contrasting viewpoints, it is widely believed that massage can cause the tumour to disintegrate and can influence circulation, causing the cancer to spread more quickly.
Uncontrolled epilepsy (epilepsy not controlled by medication)	Over-stimulation or deep relaxation may result in convulsions. Some types of epilepsy can be triggered by different smells so could react to your massage medium.
Diabetes	Blood sugars tend to drop during and after massage so the client and therapist need to be aware of this and make sure that they are appropriately prepared. Some diabetes patients also suffer from sensory impairment, so they will not be able to give you accurate feedback on the pressure.
Osteoporosis	Brittle bones could be further damaged by deep massage techniques.

Other medical conditions

Other medical conditions that can contraindicate sport and exercise massage can be seen in Table 10.4. If a client with any of these conditions approaches you for massage, you should always seek advice from their GP before starting treatments.

Remember

If you are in doubt about any contraindications, do not massage. Refer your client to the appropriate professional and wait for that professional's permission to commence any treatments.

Activity: Contraindications to sport massage

You are working as a sport and exercise massage professional and have just started marketing your services. You want to include some information on your website for potential clients so that they understand some of the different contraindications and can gain appropriate clearance from their GP before visiting you if necessary. You need to prepare the following information for your website:

- descriptions of the different contraindications
- reasons why they contraindicate massage.

3.4 Proposed treatment plan

Your proposed treatment plan should be based on all of the information that you will have gained through your verbal, visual and physical consultations, and your knowledge of any contraindications, and should be recorded on appropriate documentation. Throughout your treatments, you will use a range of techniques including effleurage, petrissage, frictions, tapotement and vibrations. These techniques will be used as part of overall massage treatments. Massage treatments will generally fall into the following categories:

- pre-event
- inter-event
- post-event.

Massage techniques and procedures

The different massage techniques, their aims and associated techniques are summarised in Table 10.5.

Take it further

Researching massage techniques

Using books and the Internet, find a detailed description and images or videos of each of the different techniques (and their associated techniques) highlighted in Table 10.5. Use the information to produce a booklet or electronic file of the different massage techniques.

Table 10.5: Massage techniques, aims and associated techniques.

Technique	Aims	Associated techniques
Effleurage	Introduces touch to the client Stimulates nerve endings Relaxes the muscles Increases circulation Stretches tissues	Stroking using palm of the hand, pads of the fingers and thumb, heel of the hand, forearm, elbow, ulna border, or clenched fist
Petrissage	Increases mobility Stretches muscle fibres Increases circulation (increases venous and lymphatic return)	Kneading Wringing Skin rolling Thumb sliding Knuckling Heel squeezing
Frictions	Separates adhesions Breaks down scar tissue Realigns scar tissue Stimulates blood flow Relieves pain	Circular frictions Transverse frictions
Tapotement	Warms muscle tissue Increases circulation Improves muscle tone Stimulates nerve endings	Cupping Hacking Slapping Pounding Beating
Vibrations	Relieves tension Provides relaxation Stimulates nerve endings Relieves pain Loosens connective tissue	Static vibrations Running vibrations

- **Effleurage** is usually the first technique used in a massage and is used in pre-event, inter-event and post-event massage. It can be either superficial (light stroking) or deep (pressured stroking). The speed and pressure of stroking can be altered, depending on whether you are performing pre-, inter-, or post-event massage. When you start effleurage, you should work with a light touch in a rhythmical and relaxed manner and progress through to a deeper pressure with slower movements that can help to increase circulation and stretch tissues.

  The direction of the stroke is always in the direction of the heart to encourage venous return and lymphatic fluid drainage. When you use strokes which pass over bony prominences, you must ease the pressure but maintain contact. Effleurage movements can be performed using both hands simultaneously or by using alternate hands. On the return stroke, the hands should maintain light contact but avoid the path taken on the initial stroke.

- **Petrissage** is used to have a deeper effect on soft tissues than effleurage by compressing and releasing the tissue, either by picking up and squeezing the skin and muscle or by applying direct pressure. This technique can be used in pre-, inter- and post-event massage.

  When using petrissage, the pressure is applied in the direction of the heart to encourage venous return, but the overall direction is from proximal to distal. This is achieved by you applying shorter strokes in the direction of the heart to push the blood out of the area followed by deliberately sliding the hands distally to push fresh blood back

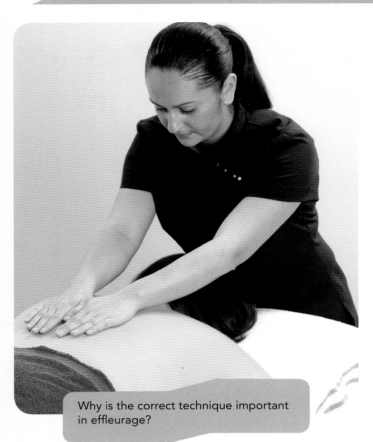

Why is the correct technique important in effleurage?

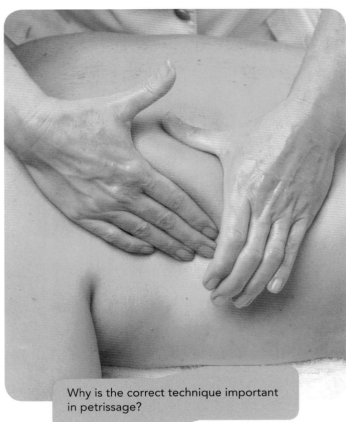

Why is the correct technique important in petrissage?

into the area before starting the technique again. During petrissage, your hands stay in constant contact with the client's skin while moving it over the underlying muscle.

- **Frictions** are techniques that use significantly more pressure than the two previous techniques, and the pressure is more localised to specific areas using the pads of the fingers or thumbs (or the elbow in some cases). Before you use frictions with the client, you must reassuringly warn them that the technique can be painful due to its aims and you may need to help them relax by taking them through some deep breathing activities prior to and during the treatment.

When you perform frictions, your thumb or finger pads must remain in constant contact with your client's skin while you move their subcutaneous tissue over deeper tissue. The thumb or finger pads move in either circular or transverse directions, depending on the technique you are applying and very firm pressure will need to be applied when you are trying to break down scar tissue or separating muscle fibres.

As frictions are classed as advanced massage techniques and can cause pain to your client, you must be sure of three things before you attempt to use them: that you can accurately locate the problem, that you can place the affected area in full stretch by using your knowledge of origins and insertions and that you are confident there will be an overall benefit. Your clients must also be aware that frictions may need to be used two to three times per week and may have to be applied for a period of minutes during the massage session to be effective.

- **Tapotement** techniques use rhythmic movements of the hands to stimulate muscle tissue and nerve endings. The tissue is struck with both hands alternately, but the tapotement technique that you will use will determine which part of the hand is used and the type of contact made. Tapotement techniques are often used in pre- and inter-event massage.

- **Vibrations** are performed using one or both hands and any number of fingers. The technique uses a moderate degree of pressure and involves the fingers being shaken in a fast action so that the vibrations pass through the body part.

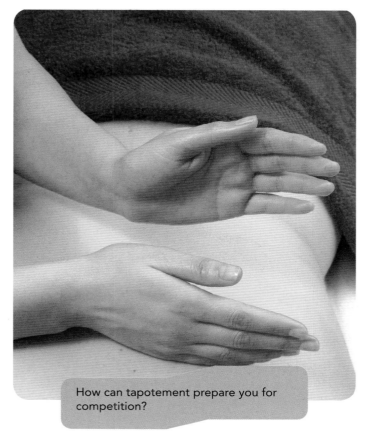

How can tapotement prepare you for competition?

Table 10.6: Massage routines.

Sample positions and sequences of body sections for planning treatments	
Position	**Sequencing of body sections**
Prone	Legs, back, neck, shoulder, lumbar
Supine	Legs, arms, front torso, neck, head
Side – lying	Legs, arms, back, obliques
Sitting	Back, arms, neck, head
Standing	Arms, shoulders, back, legs
Sample sequences for body sections for planning treatments	
Section	**Sequencing of sub-sections**
Arms	Shoulder, upper arm, forearm, hand
Legs	Hip, thigh, knee, lower leg, foot
Back	Sacroiliac joint, lumbar region, thoracic region, shoulder girdle, neck
Progressions in the quality of movements in massage	
Quality of movement	**Progression**
Pressure	Light to heavy
Rhythm	Even to uneven
Pace	Slow to fast
Continuity	Smooth to vigorous transitions
Specificity	General to specific

Massage routines

While the individual massage requirements of different people will vary, there are routines that can be used as a guide when providing massage treatments. The sequencing of routines relates to the sequencing of positions, the sequencing of sections and sub-sections for each position and the sequencing of steps within each section. These can be seen in Table 10.6.

Pre-event massage

Think back to when you have been getting ready to play your sport. You will have rubbed and shaken your legs to try to warm them a little more. If this has been of benefit, imagine how a massage before your event could have helped. A pre-event massage helps to prepare you physically and psychologically, and can be performed anywhere between a few minutes before the event to a few days before the event. Remember that pre-event massage should not take the place of a full warm-up.

Remember

Pre-event massage techniques are often used less deeply and more vigorously, and for a shorter period of time, so that you can be prepared for the demands of your sport quite quickly.

- **Aims** – while the aims of the pre-event massage and the techniques used will vary depending upon when you are performing the massage, pre-event massage has the following general aims of:
  o warming the muscles
  o stretching
  o increasing the range of movement, mobility and circulation
  o psychological preparation.
- **Massage procedures** – effleurage, petrissage and tapotement are the main techniques that you will use in pre-event massage.
- **Massage duration** – pre-event massages normally last for about 10–15 minutes.

Case study: 15-minute pre-event massage

The pre-event massage routine below can be used for a centre–midfielder in football.

Massage the front of the legs with the client lying supine:

- Effleurage with long strokes of the whole leg
- Effleurage on the thigh – fast, short, vigorous movements
- Palmar kneading on the thigh, checking depth and pressure to ensure no bruising occurs
- Wringing of the quadriceps
- Wringing of the adductors
- Palmar kneading of the iliotibial band, checking depth and pressure to ensure no bruising occurs
- Hacking, cupping or shaking of the thigh
- Thumb kneading around the knee joint
- Thumb kneading of the tibialis anterior
- Effleurage lower leg
- Thumb knead ankle around lateral and medial maleolus
- Effleurage the whole leg, finish with shaking

Massage the back of the legs with the client lying prone:

- Effleurage the whole leg
- Short, vigorous effleurage to the hamstrings
- Palmar kneading of the hamstrings
- Wringing of the hamstrings
- Hacking or cupping of the hamstrings
- Effleurage of the hamstrings
- Muscle rolling of the hamstrings
- Effleurage of the calf
- Wringing of the calf
- Hacking/cupping of the calf
- Thumb kneading of achilles tendon
- Effleurage to whole leg, finishing with shaking

1. **Do you think that this routine would be suitable for all sports?**
2. **How could you alter this treatment to meet the needs of different clients such as those with less or greater muscle bulk, younger athletes or older athletes?**

Inter-event massage

Think of a football game that has gone into extra time and penalties, and before the players go back out, somebody massages and shakes their legs – this is inter-event massage. Inter-event massage takes place during intervals in competition, for example at half time in football. You use this type of massage to keep your client physically and psychologically prepared for their sport.

Remember

Inter-event massage should work on the muscles that are going to be used as well as the muscles that have just been used, and may require both stimulating and relaxing massage techniques.

- **Aims** – the main aims of inter-event massage are to:
  - relieve muscle tension
  - maintain body temperature
  - remove waste products.
- **Massage procedures** – effleurage, petrissage and tapotement are the main techniques that you will use in inter-event massage.
- **Massage duration** – inter-event massage can last up to 25 minutes.

Post-event massage

Post-event massage helps the body recover from the stress of the activity and relaxes the client. This type of massage tends to be deeper and can be used to identify any issues that may have arisen during the game (for example, injuries, knots or tension). The massage should be performed at a depth that does not worsen any conditions that happen as a result of the activity (such as delayed onset of muscle soreness (DOMS)), and the depth of techniques should be increased as the muscles loosen and relax. There is some debate about whether a post-event massage can take the place of a cool down, so it is always best to complete a cool down after activity even if you will be having a post-event massage.

- **Aims** – the main aims of post-event massage are to:
  - accelerate the recovery process
  - reduce DOMS

  - remove waste products
  - stretch the muscle tissue.
- **Massage procedures** – effleurage, petrissage, vibrations and stretching activities are the common techniques used within post-event massage.
- **Massage duration** – post-event massage can take up to 60 minutes.

Case study: 5-minute inter-event massage

The inter-event massage routine below can be used for a point-guard in basketball.

Front of the legs:
- Effleurage of the whole leg
- Effleurage of the quadriceps
- Wringing of the quadriceps
- Hacking/cupping of quadriceps
- Effleurage of the whole leg
- Stretching

Back of the legs:
- Effleurage of the whole leg
- Effleurage of the hamstrings

- Wringing of the hamstrings
- Hacking/cupping of the hamstrings
- Effleurage of the whole leg
- Stretching

1. **Do you think that this routine would be suitable for all sports?**
2. **How could you alter this treatment to meet the needs of different clients such as those with less or greater muscle bulk, younger athletes or older athletes?**

Case study: 60-minute post-event massage

The post-event massage routine below can be used for the back, legs and arms of a rugby player.

Back
- Effleurage of the back
- Effleurage of the neck
- Thumb and finger kneading of the upper trapezius and cervical region of the neck
- Knead shoulder area towards axillary lymph node
- Circular frictions of the scapular region to release knots, adhesions or tightness
- Effleurage of the rhomboid region
- Effleurage of the trapezius and both shoulders
- Deep stroking of lateral regions of the back, using the ulna border if necessary
- Knead lateral regions of the back from waist to shoulder

- Transverse and circular frictions of the erector spinae (light pressure)
- Circular frictions of the lumbar region (around L5 and sacrum and into gluteus medius if necessary)
- Effleurage of the whole back, finish with shaking and stretching

Front of the upper legs (with client in supine position)
- Slow effleurage of the thigh (proximal to distal)
- Strong linear stroking of the thigh
- Kneading/ringing of the thigh
- Linear stroking of the tensor fascia latae
- Palmar linear stroking of the iliotibial band
- Effleurage to the adductors with the therapist supporting the knee
- Wringing of the adductors

- Gentle thumb stroking around the knee joint line
- Effleurage to the whole of the thigh, finish with shaking and stretching

Front of the lower legs (with the client in supine position)

- Effleurage to whole of lower leg
- Linear stroking of the tibialis anterior
- Linear stroking of the peroneus longus and peroneus brevis
- Stroking of the medial and lateral borders of the tibia
- Finger kneading of the medial and lateral malleolus and the ankle joint line
- Effleurage to the foot
- Kneading of the arch of the foot
- Effleurage to the whole of the front of the lower leg, finish with shaking and stretching

Back of the upper legs (with the client in a prone position)

- Effleurage to the hamstrings (proximal to distal)
- Linear stroking of the hamstrings
- Circular frictions to the origin of the hamstrings
- Kneading of the hamstrings
- Wringing of the origin and insertion of the hamstrings
- Effleurage to the whole of the hamstrings, finish with shaking and stretching

Back of the lower legs (with the client in a prone position)

- Effleurage to the whole of the back of the lower leg
- Deep linear stroking of the calf region
- Kneading of the calf region
- Wringing of the calf region
- Effleurage to calf region
- Effleurage to the Achilles tendon
- Finger kneading of the Achilles tendon
- Effleurage to the whole of the lower leg, finish with shaking and stretching

Arm

- Effleurage to the whole of the arm (distal to proximal)
- Petrissage to the upper arm, from the elbow to deltoid (including biceps and triceps)
- Shaking of the upper arm
- Effleurage to the lower arm
- Frictions to the tendon insertion at the elbow joint
- Effleurage to the whole of the arm, finish with shaking and stretching

1. **Do you think that this routine would be suitable for all sports?**
2. **How could you alter this treatment to meet the needs of different clients such as those with less or greater muscle bulk, younger athletes or older athletes?**

Assessment activity 10.3

You are the sports therapist for a sports team that has male and female players. You are getting ready to massage one of the clients from a male squad and one of the players from a female squad and need to produce a treatment plan for these two different athletes.

1. Using a male and a female friend as your clients, produce a treatment plan for each of them that is based on pre-treatment consultations. **P3**

2. Explain the sport and exercise massage requirements of each client. **M2**

3. Compare and contrast the treatment requirements of the two clients. **D1**

4. Choose six contraindications to massage that are relevant to your clients and describe them. **P4**

5. Produce a treatment plan for each client based on the information that you have gathered through the consultation. **P5**

Grading tips

- To attain **P3** complete verbal, visual and physical aspects of the initial consultation with your two clients and record your findings on appropriate documentation.

- To attain **M2** include the area to be treated, the simple injuries that you have looked for and any referrals to practitioners that you may have to make.

- To attain **D1** justify why you have chosen the massage treatments for each client.

- To attain **P4** say why they contraindicate massage treatment.

- To attain **P5** say whether you need to use pre-, inter- or post-event massage and plan a massage treatment that includes the duration of the treatment and a description of the massage procedure (the routines and techniques) that you will use.

PLTS

When producing your client consultation form, identifying questions to ask and problems that need to be resolved will provide evidence of your skills as an **independent enquirer**.

Functional skills

If you make effective contributions to the discussion with your client during the verbal element of your initial consultations, you could provide evidence of your **English** skills.

4. Be able to perform and review sport and exercise massage techniques

Your major function as a sport and exercise massage professional is to provide massage treatments for different clients. In order to do this, you need to make sure that the environment in which you work, your client preparation and the different techniques that you use are all up to standard. As a professional, ensure that you review your work so that you can aim for the highest quality of service for your clients.

4.1 Client preparation

After the initial consultation, your client will need to undress and lie on the massage couch. You should

leave the area before they undress and provide them with a towel so that when they lie on the couch, they can cover themselves before you return. You should place additional towels in appropriate places to further protect their modesty, for example when lying prone in place for a back massage, a female client may need additional rolled towels placing along the side of the torso so that her breasts are not exposed.

Health and safety

You need to consider health and safety and hygiene as part of your client preparation. Make sure they know where to find the fire exit and the toilet; provide them with water if they require it and make sure that they are positioned on the couch in a manner that will prevent them from falling.

Sport and exercise massage professionals must also be aware of appropriate health and safety legislation including the Health and Safety at Work Act, COSHH (Control of Substances Hazardous to Health) and PPE (Personal and Protective Equipment).

Hygiene

You must wash your hands before massaging your client. You may also need to clean parts of their body before you massage, for example their feet. This can be done with antibacterial wipes.

4.2 Demonstrate

Safe and effective massage

The massage treatment you use with your client needs to be safe and effective for both you and your client. To achieve this maintain the correct posture when massaging, position your client so that they won't fall off the couch, ensure that the correct technique is used and monitor your client throughout by checking levels of pain and pressure.

Different techniques

Earlier, when looking at your proposed treatment plan, you examined the different techniques that you can use when providing massage treatments, including effleurage, petrissage, frictions, tapotement and vibrations. You should refer back to these (see pages 276–278), the example routines and the work you did for the 'Take it further' activities when you are preparing to deliver your sport massage treatment. You need to ensure correct application of these techniques when you deliver your massage treatment.

Application of techniques

When you are delivering your sport massage treatments maintain the correct technique. Part of this is ensuring you have the correct posture. When delivering massage, you should stand with your feet comfortably apart to maintain good balance, have your back straight and stand close enough to the couch to deliver the massage. If you maintain the correct

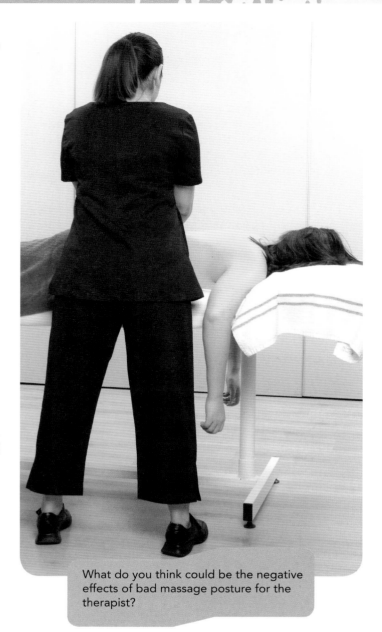

What do you think could be the negative effects of bad massage posture for the therapist?

posture, you will reduce the amount of effort that you need to put into your massage with the result that you will not be as tired and achy at the end of it. In addition to this, you must refer to pages 276–282 for details of the techniques, routines and durations of massage.

Try to develop a rapport with your client. He or she could be quite nervous when having a sport and exercise massage, especially if it is their first time. You need to make sure that you put your client at ease during the treatment by checking the pressure and pain levels resulting from the different techniques as well as chatting to the client about things like hobbies.

4.3 Mediums

The three mediums used during massage are oil, talc and creams.

Activity: Conducting sport and exercise massage

Under the supervision of your tutor, complete the different massage treatments with a partner on their legs, arms and back. Ask your tutor and your client to give you feedback about the quality of your massage.

4.4 Documentation

When you have finished your treatment with your client, complete a record card that shows:

- the date of the treatment
- the type of treatment
- the duration of the treatment
- the response of the client to the treatment
- the dates of any future appointments.

4.5 Review

After your massage treatment, review it against different criteria including speed, depth, rate of sport massage, effectiveness of treatment, liaison with the athlete, timing, adaptation of treatment and recommendations for future treatments.

Speed, depth and rate of massage

During your treatment, you will need to liaise with your client. Ask your client to rate the speed, depth and rate of treatment by asking questions such as 'How is the pressure for you?'. The responses you get will determine whether or not you need to alter your massage treatment for your client. You can use this feedback from your client to review your massage after the treatment has finished.

Effectiveness of treatment

The effectiveness of your treatment can be assessed by asking your client questions during the treatment and getting their feedback and by using the same visual and physical tests that you completed as part of your initial consultation. If there is more mobility in the area, or less tension, or less pain, you could say that your massage technique has been effective. When reviewing the effectiveness of your treatment, it is a good idea to ask your client to fill out a short questionnaire after their treatment so that they can give you some feedback regarding the treatment.

Timing

Different massage treatments have timings that you should try to adhere to. When assessing your massage, you should make a comment about whether you managed to stay on time.

Adaptation of treatment

During your session you may need to adapt your treatment to meet the needs of your client (for example, changing the speed, rate or depth of massage). If you have to do this, make a comment in your evaluation about the changes that you made, why you made them and how they benefited your client.

Table 10.7: Advantages and disadvantages of massage mediums.

Medium	Advantages	Disadvantages
Oil	Longer lasting Additives can be relaxing or stimulating	Quite expensive Can contain nut derivatives Not practical for people with a lot of body hair
Talc	Produces frictions	Can be quite messy Can only be used pre-event
Cream	Generally cheaper than oils Better for people with more body hair Tend to be hypo-allergenic	Can be absorbed quite quickly

Future treatment

After your massage, reflect on any adaptations to the treatment that you needed to make during the session. Think about any changes that you should make for future treatments, including any adaptations of the current treatments and additions to the treatments. Give your client a return date for their next appointment and subsequent appointments (if applicable). The final part of your future treatment section should include some aftercare and homecare advice for your client as they will need to manage the injury or the problem during their treatments (see page 275).

Assessment activity 10.4

1. Using the treatment plan that you produced for Assessment activity 10.3, provide a sport and exercise massage treatment for your two clients. You should complete this treatment under the supervision of your tutor. **P6**

2. Explain the appropriate sport and exercise massage treatments for your two clients. **M3**

3. Evaluate the treatments. **D2**

4. Review the treatment plan for your two athletes and describe future treatment requirements. **P7**

Grading tips

- To attain **P6** prior to the massage, follow appropriate client preparation techniques. Make sure that you are using the correct technique as you go through your treatment, paying attention to the technique that you are using, the application of the technique, following a set routine, using an appropriate medium for your client, adhering to your time limit and talking to your client to make sure that they are OK.

- To attain **M3** explain to your tutor the techniques that you are using for each of your athletes as you are conducting the massage.

- To attain **D2** tell your tutor why you are using different massage techniques with each client.

- To attain **P7** comment on the effectiveness of the treatments you have provided.

PLTS

When reviewing your treatment and deciding on future treatment requirements, you could provide evidence of your skills as a **creative thinker**.

Functional skills

If you are able to make effective contributions to discussions with your tutor and clients regarding the treatment and the effectiveness of the treatment, you could provide evidence of your **English** skills.

Lucy Durell
Sport massage therapist

Lucy is a self-employed sport massage therapist working for a number of sports teams. She is also employed at major sports events including football and rugby matches as well as massaging at the London Marathon and Great North Run every year.

She is responsible for planning and conducting sport massage treatments with a range of clients.

'Sport massage is a great job. I get to work with lots of different people who want to get the best out of their training and competition which is really fulfilling. The skills the course has given me help me to work with my clients as I have a greater understanding of the different massage techniques that can be used with clients, when to use them and what the benefits are. The course has also helped me to recognise the different contraindications to massage. Both of these aspects have helped me to give a higher quality of service to my clients, allowing them to recover from injuries and return to training at an appropriate rate.

Helping people to recover from injuries and get back to training gives me a great sense of satisfaction. It isn't all easy though and there are some difficult parts of the job. One of the biggest problems that I face is recognising and dealing with all of the different contraindications to massage when working within the field. I currently work in a variety of settings with a wide range of clients, so there are a number of different things that I need to take into account when I am planning and conducting massage sessions. One of the issues that I do face regularly at the different charity events is people who have different contraindications but who would still like to receive a sport massage.'

Think about it!

- If you were Lucy, what different contraindications to massage would you need to be aware of?
- How could you deal with these different contraindications?
- What advice would you give to clients who had different contraindications to sport massage?

Just checking

1. What are the physical and mechanical effects of massage?
2. What are the physiological effects of massage?
3. What are the benefits of massage?
4. What are the different treatments that can be applied by sport and exercise massage professionals?
5. What are the main elements of an initial consultation?
6. What information needs to be included on a record card?
7. Name five contraindications to sport and exercise massage and explain why massage is contraindicated.
8. Describe three massage techniques, including their aims and associated techniques.
9. What is meant by the terms pre-event massage, inter-event massage and post-event massage?
10. What are the different criteria that you can use to review your sport and exercise massage routine?

edexcel :::

Assignment tips

- Sport and exercise massage is very 'hands on', so it is always good to practise your techniques under the supervision of your tutor whenever possible so that you can learn the correct technique.

- To help extend your learning you may want to use some specific sport massage textbooks that give a detailed overview of all massage techniques.

- There are some good websites that you can use to help with this unit including physioroom.com (www.physioroom.com), sports injury clinic (www.sportsinjuryclinic.net) and the Sport Massage Association website (www.sportsmassageassociation.org).

- If you know any sports therapists, it could be good to discuss this unit with them. They can talk to you about the different roles that they fulfil and the different clients that they work with.

- If you are interested in sport and exercise massage therapy as a career, you may want to ask your college's work placement office to help you find work placements as this will help you to gain a greater understanding of the world of work in this area.

- Always check your work over with your tutor. Sometimes you may need to clarify the requirements of the higher level grading criteria to make sure that you are doing the right things and your tutor will be able to advise you on this.

12 Sports nutrition

Whether you are an elite athlete preparing for an Olympic event, a semi-professional aiming to continue performing or an amateur participant who wants to improve your performance; a healthy balanced diet and its links to good health and improved sports performance is key to the athlete's lifestyle.

In this unit you will explore the links between nutrition, health and performance in sport and exercise. You will learn about the fundamentals of a healthy diet and develop an understanding of the influence of nutrition on exercise and performance, along with a solid foundation of knowledge on which to develop good eating practices. You will consider factors that affect food intake and choice, and methods of collecting and analysing dietary information to assess nutritional needs. By the end of this unit you should be able to demonstrate the application of nutrition strategies in a variety of contexts through examination of the diets of a range of sports from the amateur athlete to the elite performer.

You will not develop the breadth of knowledge and skills of a sports dietitian or nutritionist upon completion of this unit, but you will gain an appreciation of how diet affects sporting performance before, during and after training and competition.

Learning outcomes

After completing this unit you should:

1. know the concepts of nutrition and digestion
2. know energy intake and energy expenditure in sports performance
3. know the relationship between hydration and sports performance
4. be able to plan a diet appropriate for a selected sports activity.

Assessment and grading criteria

This table shows you what you must do in order to achieve a pass, merit or distinction grade, and where you can find activities in this book to help you.

To achieve a **pass** grade the evidence must show that the learner is able to:	To achieve a **merit** grade the evidence must show that, in addition to the pass criteria, the learner is able to:	To achieve a **distinction** grade the evidence must show that, in addition to the pass and merit criteria, the learner is able to:
P1 describe nutrition, including nutritional requirements using common terminology associated with nutrition **Assessment activity 12.1, page 301**		
P2 describe the structure and function of the digestive system **Assessment activity 12.1, page 301**		
P3 describe energy intake and expenditure in sports performance **Assessment activity 12.2, page 307**	**M1** explain energy intake and expenditure in sports performance **Assessment activity 12.2, page 307**	
P4 describe energy balance and its importance in relation to sports performance **Assessment activity 12.2, page 307**	**M2** explain the importance of energy balance in relation to sports performance **Assessment activity 12.2, page 307**	**D1** analyse the effects of energy balance on sports performance **Assessment activity 12.2, page 307**
P5 describe hydration and its effects on sports performance **Assessment activity 12.3, page 310**		
P6 describe the components of a balanced diet **Assessment activity 12.4, page 320**	**M3** explain the components of a balanced diet **Assessment activity 12.4, page 320**	
P7 plan an appropriate two-week diet plan for a selected sports performer for a selected sports activity **Assessment activity 12.4, page 320**	**M4** explain the two-week diet plan for a selected sports performer for a selected sports activity **Assessment activity 12.4, page 320**	**D2** justify the two-week diet plan for a selected sports performer for a selected sports activity **Assessment activity 12.4, page 320**

How you will be assessed

This unit will be internally assessed by a range of assignments that will be designed and graded by your tutor. Your assignment tasks will be designed to allow you to demonstrate your understanding of the unit learning outcomes and relate to what you should be able to do after completing this unit. Your assignments could be in the form of:

- presentations
- practical tasks
- written assignments and case studies
- a logbook or portfolio of evidence.

Sample assessment activities are included throughout this unit as an example of how you might achieve these learning outcomes.

Harry Archer, an academy rugby player

In this unit I learned how to predict my nutritional requirements and analyse my intake. I worked with my peers to research different diets for different sports and devise nutritional strategies to be implemented before, during and after exercise to optimise performance. I particularly enjoyed evaluating my eating and exercise patterns and planning to improve my nutritional intake. As a rugby player I am concerned about my body mass and size. I now understand the concept of energy balance and its implications on my desire to gain weight, and how I can achieve this through sensible dietary manipulation. I now enjoy a healthier diet and have more energy for my training programme.

Over to you

- **What areas of this unit are you most looking forward to?**
- **How might you apply some of the learning you acquire in this unit to impact on your health, performance or both?**

1. Know the concepts of nutrition and digestion

Warm-up

Factors that affect food intake and choice

Take a few minutes to think about the factors that might influence your food intake and choice. If you can think of 10, this is good going, and 20 or more is excellent. Awareness of these factors will assist you in formulating realistic and achievable dietary goals and plans when meeting some of the assessment requirements of this unit.

All activity stimulates your body's need for fuel and fluid. Knowledge of the nutrients your body requires, along with their different functions, provides the basis for the science of **nutrition**.

Remember

There should be no conflict between eating for health and eating for performance.

1.1 Nutrition

Foods contain varying amounts of the nutrients carbohydrate, protein, fat, vitamins, minerals, fibre and water.

Macronutrients

Nutrients in food are categorised according to the relative amounts required by your body. Carbohydrate, protein and fat are termed **macronutrients**, as they are required in relatively large amounts on a daily basis. These nutrients are also the energy-providing nutrients of your **diet**.

Carbohydrates

Carbohydrates form your body's most readily available source of energy and can be accessed rapidly. One gram of carbohydrate provides approximately 4 kcal of energy. Carbohydrate foods are divided into two basic types and are generally known as either simple or complex.

Simple carbohydrates are essentially sugars. They are formed from single and double sugar units and

Why is it important to have a balanced diet in order to stay healthy?
Discuss your ideas with your peers and tutor.

Key terms

Nutrition – the means by which your body takes in energy and nutrients in food to sustain growth and development, and to keep us alive and healthy.

Food – any substance derived from plants or animals containing a combination of carbohydrates, fats, proteins, vitamins, minerals, fibre, water and alcohol.

Macronutrient – nutrient required by your body in daily amounts greater than a few grams, e.g. carbohydrate, fat and protein.

Diet – a person's usual eating habits and food consumption.

are easily digested and absorbed to provide a quick energy source. The simplest carbohydrate unit is the monosaccharide, the most common of which is glucose. *Saccharide* means sugar, *mono* means one, therefore a monosaccharide is a single sugar unit. Glucose is used to produce adenosine triphosphate (ATP), the compound required for muscle contraction.

Other monosaccharides include fructose, also called fruit sugar as it is found in fruits and vegetables, and galactose, found in milk. Monosaccharides mostly occur combined in carbohydrates. Two monosaccharides together form a disaccharide or double sugar. The most common disaccharide is sucrose or table sugar. Others include lactose (found in milk) and maltose (found in cereals).

Longer chains of simple sugar units are called polysaccharides or complex carbohydrates. These allow large quantities of glucose to be stored as starch in the cells of plants or as glycogen in the muscles and liver of animals. All carbohydrate consumed ends up as glucose to provide energy.

Complex carbohydrates are an important source of energy since they are broken down slowly in your body to release energy over longer periods. They should form the largest percentage of your total carbohydrate intake. Unrefined sources such as wholemeal bread, wholegrain rice and pasta are preferable as they also contain a higher nutritional value by way of micronutrients and fibre.

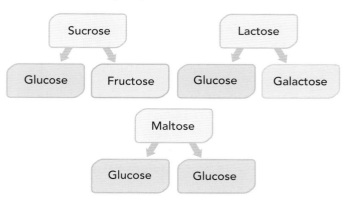

Figure 12.1: Double sugars or disaccharides and their monosaccharides

What sources of carbohydrate do you regularly consume in your diet?

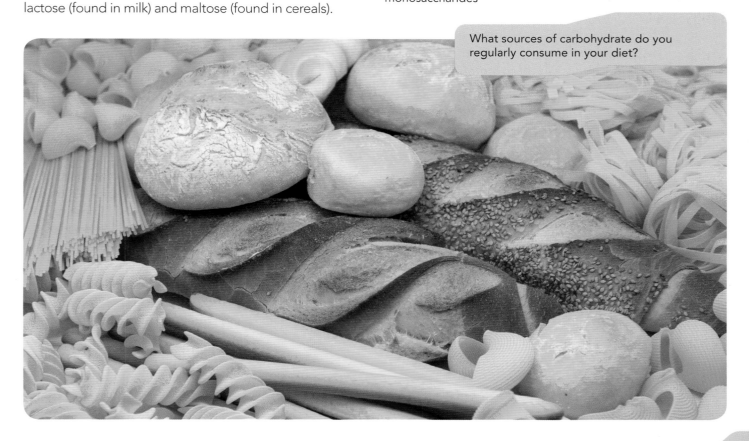

After you eat foods containing carbohydrate your blood sugar level rises, stimulating the pancreas to secrete the hormone insulin. The role of insulin is to normalise blood sugar levels and aid the transport of glucose from the blood to the cells. Glucose is then used directly by the cells for energy or stored as glycogen in your liver and muscles. Glycogen is a crucial source of glucose for fuelling activity.

Simple	Complex
Sugar, syrup, jam, honey, marmalade, sugary fizzy drinks, boiled sweets, fudge, fruit juice, sports drinks, energy gels	Bread, bagels, crispbread, crackers, rice, pasta, noodles, couscous, potatoes, breakfast cereals, pulses, root vegetables

Table 12.1: Simple and complex carbohydrates

Around 80 per cent is stored in your muscles while the rest is stored in your liver, with a small amount of circulating blood glucose. Excess carbohydrate not required to replenish glycogen stores is converted to fat and stored in your body's **adipose tissue**.

Carbohydrate can only be stored as glycogen in limited amounts – approximately 375–475 grams in the average adult, equivalent to approximately 1,500–2,000 kcal. Day-to-day stores of glycogen are influenced by dietary carbohydrate intake and levels of physical activity or training. Regular exercise can encourage your muscles to adapt to store more glycogen. This is an important training adaptation for elite athletes, particularly in endurance-type sports.

Remember

The intensity and duration of exercise influence the rate and amount of glycogen usage. The harder the exercise and the longer its duration, the greater the depletion of glycogen.

Proteins

Proteins are essential to maintaining optimal health and physical performance. The smallest units of proteins are amino acids. It is not necessary for you to be familiar with the names and functions of the individual **amino acids**. The body needs all 20 amino acids to be present simultaneously for protein synthesis to occur, to sustain optimal growth and functioning. Different proteins contain different numbers and combinations of amino acids. The eight that your body is unable to make are called essential amino acids (EAAs) – they are a necessary part of your diet. The remaining amino acids are called non-essential – your body is able to synthesise these if all the essential ones are present.

Key terms

Adipose tissue – commonly referred to as fat tissue, is a type of connective tissue that serves as the body's most abundant energy reserve.

Amino acids – the building blocks of proteins.

The chief role of protein in your body is to build and repair tissue. Proteins may also be used as a secondary source of energy when carbohydrate and fat are limited, such as towards the end of prolonged endurance events or during severe energy restriction that may accompany dieting.

Proteins, like carbohydrates, have an energy value of approximately 4 calories per gram. Unlike carbohydrate and fat, excess protein cannot be stored in your body. All proteins carry out functional roles, so daily protein ingestion is required. If your protein intake exceeds requirements to support growth and repair, excess is used to provide energy immediately or converted to fat or carbohydrate and stored.

Protein foods are classified into two groups (see Table 12.2). The value of foods for meeting your body's protein needs is determined by their composition of amino acids. Foods that contain all of the EAAs are known as first-class or complete proteins. These are mainly of animal origin like eggs, meat, fish, milk and other dairy products, and soya. Foods that are lacking in one or more of the EAAs are called second-class or incomplete proteins. These come from plant sources such as cereals, bread, rice, pasta, pulses, nuts and seeds. Vegetarians and vegans must ensure that they eat a variety of these in careful combinations to ensure adequate intake of all EAAs; for example, beans and wheat complement each other well.

In the context of sports performance does the typical UK diet contain adequate amounts of protein?

Complete	Incomplete
Meat, poultry, offal, fish, eggs, milk, cheese, yoghurt, soya	Cereals, bread, rice, pasta, noodles, pulses, peas, beans, lentils, nuts, seeds

Table 12.2: Protein foods

Fats

Fat is an essential nutrient. Triglycerides form the basic component of fats. Each triglyceride consists of a glycerol molecule with three fatty acids attached. When triglycerides are digested and absorbed by your body they break down into these two substances. Fats are obtained from animal and vegetable sources and are of two main types: saturated and unsaturated.

Fatty acids contain chains of carbon atoms to which hydrogen atoms attach. The number of hydrogen atoms relative to the number of carbon atoms determines whether a fatty acid is classified as saturated or unsaturated. If all the carbons are associated with two hydrogens, the fat is saturated, but if one or more of the carbons is without hydrogen then the fat is unsaturated. Unsaturated fatty acids can be of two kinds: monounsaturated and polyunsaturated.

All fats in your diet are a mixture of these three fatty acid types (see Table 12.3 on page 296). Fats that contain mostly saturated fatty acids are generally solid at room temperature, like butter and ordinary margarine, and are usually found in meat, eggs and dairy foods. The two exceptions are palm and coconut oil, which are plant sources. Fats composed mainly of unsaturated fatty acids are usually liquid at room temperature, like olive or sunflower oils.

Most dietary experts recommend cutting back on fat intake. This is sound advice for athletes as it allows them to consume a greater proportion of energy intake from carbohydrates to maintain glycogen stores, to support training and competition.

The primary function of fats is to provide a concentrated source of energy, forming your body's largest potential energy store. Even the leanest of individuals will have large amounts of energy stored as fat. Fat is more than twice as energy-dense as other macronutrients, yielding 9 calories per gram.

Fats protect and cushion your vital organs, provide structural material for cells and act as an insulator. Animal fats are a source of the fat-soluble vitamins A, D, E and K. Fats add flavour and texture to foods, which can be the reason for over-consumption.

Saturated	Monounsaturated	Polyunsaturated
Full-fat dairy products, butter, hard margarine, lard, dripping, suet, fatty meat, meat pies, pâté, cream, cakes, biscuits, chocolate, coconut, coconut oil	Olive oil, olive oil spreads, rapeseed oil, corn oil, peanuts, peanut butter, peanut oil	Soft margarine, low-fat spreads labelled high in polyunsaturated fats, sunflower oil, safflower oil, soya oil, oily fish, nuts

Table 12.3: Sources and types of fat in the diet

Micronutrients

Vitamins and minerals are referred to as micronutrients as they are required in much smaller amounts – some in minute quantities. Despite your relatively small requirements for these nutrients, many play a critical role in regulating chemical reactions in your body.

Vitamins

Vitamins are vital, non-caloric nutrients required in very small amounts. They perform specific metabolic functions and prevent particular deficiency diseases.

Most vitamins required to maintain health cannot be produced by your body and must be supplied by your diet. The exceptions are vitamin D, which your body is able to synthesise by the action of sunlight on the skin, and vitamin K, which can be produced by the bacteria of the large intestine. Vitamins play essential roles in regulating many metabolic processes in your body, particularly those that release energy. They also support growth and the immune and nervous system functions, and some are involved in producing hormones.

Vitamins are obtained from a variety of plant and animal sources and are broadly grouped depending on whether they are fat- or water-soluble. Vitamins A, D, E and K form the fat-soluble group, with the B vitamins and vitamin C making up the water-soluble group.

Specific vitamins have specific functions and are required in differing amounts. Individual requirements are determined by age, sex, state of health and levels of physical activity. The UK Department of Health has set **Dietary Reference Values (DRVs)** for all nutrients for different groups of healthy people. The Reference Nutrient Intake (RNI) value should meet the needs of 97 per cent of the population. A balanced and varied diet with an adequate energy content should supply sufficient intake of all vitamins.

It is important to note that large amounts of some vitamins can be harmful to health. This is particularly true for the fat-soluble vitamins, as they can be stored in your body. The only situation in which large doses of any vitamin may be beneficial is when the body has a severe deficiency of a particular vitamin or is unable to absorb or metabolise vitamins efficiently.

> **Remember**
>
> Individual vitamin requirements vary and are determined by age, sex, state of health and physical activity level.
>
> Supplementation with high doses of any vitamin should always be medically supervised and not self-prescribed.

- All fat-soluble vitamins have a number of common features. As the term suggests, they are found in the fatty or oily parts of foods. Once digested they are absorbed and transported in the lymph and ultimately reach the blood. As a result of their insolubility in water, they are not excreted in the urine and can accumulate in the liver and adipose tissue.
- Water-soluble vitamins consist of the B vitamins and vitamin C. Many of the B vitamins serve similar functions, facilitating the use of energy within your body. Excesses are excreted via the urine, so your body has only limited stores, necessitating regular intakes. It should be noted that many of these vitamins are destroyed by food processing and preparation.

Minerals

Minerals are non-caloric nutrients that are essential to life, and like vitamins they are required in small or trace amounts. Minerals are classified in terms of the relative amounts required by your body and can be placed broadly into two categories.

- Macrominerals such as calcium are required in relatively large amounts, sometimes as much as several hundred milligrams per day.

- Trace elements such as copper and selenium are required in much smaller quantities (micrograms per day).

All minerals are essential to health and form important components of your body such as bone, connective tissue, enzymes and hormones. Some play essential roles in nerve function and muscle contraction; others regulate fluid balance in your body. Levels of minerals are closely controlled by absorption and excretion to prevent excessive build-up. Some minerals compete with each other for absorption, especially iron, zinc and copper.

Fibre

Fibre is a complex carbohydrate. Non-starch polysaccharide (NSP) is the new scientific term for dietary fibre. NSP forms the main component of plant cell walls, which are the principal component of dietary fibre. They resist digestion by the stomach and small intestine and provide bulk which aids the transit of food through your digestive system.

Fibre is obtained from wholegrain cereals, nuts, pulses, fruits and vegetables. It is thought to help in both preventing and treating certain diseases including cancer of the colon, diabetes, heart disease and irritable bowel syndrome. A high-fibre intake plus a high-fluid intake also helps to keep your bowel functioning efficiently. Adequate amounts may also play a role in weight control by helping to achieve the feeling of fullness.

There are two types of fibre: soluble and insoluble. Soluble fibre can be found in oats, rye, barley, peas, beans, lentils, fruits and vegetables. This is important in the control of blood glucose and cholesterol. Insoluble fibre is found in wholewheat bread, rice and pasta, wholegrain breakfast cereals, fruits and vegetables; it is thought to be important in the prevention of bowel disorders. A healthy diet requires both types of fibre, with adults requiring around 18 grams in total per day.

Remember

Non-starch polysaccharide is the new scientific term for dietary fibre.

Nutritional requirements

The amount of each nutrient you need is referred to as the nutritional requirement. These differ depending on age, sex, levels of activity and state of health. Some nutrients are more essential during different stages of life, such as calcium in childhood and iron during pregnancy.

Essential and non-essential carbohydrates

To support health and performance, it is recommended that around 50–60 per cent of your total daily calorie intake is derived from carbohydrates. Greater intakes may be required by athletes in regular intense training. For example, a marathon runner or a triathlete may need to get 65–70 per cent of their total energy from carbohydrates.

However, the average sedentary individual will require around 50 per cent of total daily calorie intake to be supplied by carbohydrates, of which the majority should be from starchy sources. This would equate to around 250 grams per day for females and 300 grams per day for males. Table 12.4 estimates the carbohydrate requirements that can be prescribed based on activity levels.

Level of daily activity	Carbohydrate per kilogram of body weight (g)
Less than 1 hour	4–5
1 hour	5–6
1–2 hours	6–7
2–3 hours	7–8
More than 3 hours	8–10

Table 12.4: Carbohydrate requirements based on daily activity levels

Whether eating for health or performance, the best approach to achieving an adequate carbohydrate intake is to eat at regular intervals and ensure that all meals and snacks are centred around starchy carbohydrate foods. People with high carbohydrate requirements may need to eat more frequent meals and snacks or consume more simple carbohydrates to achieve their requirements.

Activity: Your intake

Based on your current body weight and level of physical activity, estimate your carbohydrate requirements in grams per day. Do you think your requirements are constant, or do they vary from day to day? What practical strategies could you implement to ensure you achieve your carbohydrate requirements?

Essential and non-essential protein

Active individuals have higher protein requirements in order to promote tissue growth and repair following training and competition. Overall, protein intake should represent between 12 and 15 per cent of your total daily energy intake. The misguided belief that additional protein will automatically help to build muscle has been perpetuated since the times of the ancient Greeks. Regular exercise does increase protein needs, but most people already eat enough protein. Athletes are likely to be eating more to meet increased calorie requirements, and therefore should already be eating enough to meet any theoretical increase in requirements.

Type of activity	Protein per kilogram of body weight (g)
Mainly sedentary	0.75–1.0
Mainly endurance	1.2–1.4
Mainly strength	1.2–1.7

Table 12.5: Daily protein requirements based on type of activity

Essential and non-essential fat

Surveys in the UK have shown that the average diet contains around 40 per cent of calories from fat, a level deemed by experts to be too high. It is recommended that fat intakes are reduced to 30–35 per cent of total calorie intake: around 70 grams per day for females and 90 grams per day for males. Of this, only 6–10 per cent should be from saturated fats. Athletes involved in regular intense activity may need to further reduce their overall fat intake to around 25–30 per cent of total energy consumed to achieve adequate carbohydrate intakes, but in absolute terms this may equate to the same quantity of intake as that of the sedentary individual, as athletes will be eating more calories to meet their increased energy requirements.

Remember

Government guidelines recommend 70 grams of fat per day for the average female and 90 grams per day for the average male.

Common terminology

Recommended Daily Allowance (RDA)

Dietary standards have been used in the UK since World War II. The first set of standards focused on Recommended Daily Allowance (RDA), which aimed to prevent nutritional deficiency by recommending one intake target per nutrient. In the late 1980s, the government set up a panel of experts to review the RDAs of nutrients, and new Dietary Reference Values (DRVs) were established. The phrase 'dietary reference value' is an umbrella term that can be applied to any of the following measures of nutrient intake values:

- Reference Nutrient Intake (RNI)
- Estimated Average Requirements (EAR)
- Lower Reference Nutrient Intake (LRNI)
- Safe Intake (SI).

Remember

DRVs provide a yardstick against which the nutritional adequacy of your diet can be assessed.

Optimal Level

It is thought that some recommended nutrient intakes may be too high or too low. The theory of optimal levels of nutrient intake is grounded in nutritional therapy and attempts to take more account of individual requirements, lifestyle and circumstances such as smoking and stress. Defining optimal nutrient intakes has presented nutrition scientists with considerable challenges. To determine an individual's optimum nutrient intake level requires biochemical screening through the analysis of blood or urine, which is not routine practice.

Safe Intake (SI)

Safe Intake (SI) is a term used to indicate the intake of a nutrient where there is insufficient scientific information to estimate the distribution of requirements within a population. It represents an intake that is thought to be adequate for most people's needs but not so high as to cause undesirable effects on health.

Estimated Average Requirements (EAR)

Estimated Average Requirements (EAR) are the most widely used value in assessing energy requirement. Many individuals require more than the EAR and many require less.

> ## Take it further
>
> To find out more about Dietary Reference Values, look at the Department of Health's *Report on Health and Social Subjects 41: Dietary Reference Values for Food Energy and Nutrients for the United Kingdom*, HMSO, 1991.

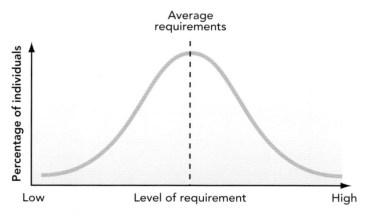

Figure 12.2: The normal distribution curve of nutrient requirements in a population. Where might athletes fit within this?

1.2 Digestion

You have already seen that food provides the energy and nutrients you need to stay alive and in good health. Before your body can make use of this energy and nutrients, the food has to be broken down to release them through the process of digestion.

Structure of the digestive system

Digestion starts in the mouth (**buccal cavity**). Your teeth and jaws crush and grind food to mix it with saliva, which contains the enzyme amylase that begins the breakdown of starch. You then swallow the food, which enters the **oesophagus**, the tube that connects your mouth to your **stomach**. The food bolus is squeezed along the oesophagus by the process of peristalsis. It takes around 3–6 seconds for food to travel from your mouth to your stomach. Your stomach acts as a large mixing bowl, churning the food into a liquid called chyme. Lining your stomach are cells that produce and release gastric juices containing enzymes and hydrochloric acid, which assist in the breakdown of the food and kill any bacteria present in it. Food normally remains in your stomach for 1–4 hours, but fluid may pass through much more rapidly.

From your stomach the chyme passes to your **duodenum** and then to your **small intestine**, a tube about 6 metres long. As the chyme enters your small intestine, it is mixed with more **digestive juices**, this time from the **pancreas**. Pancreatic juice contains bile made by the **liver** as well as **enzymes** to further assist the breakdown of carbohydrate, protein and fat. It is also alkaline to neutralise the acid from the stomach. Your **gall bladder**, a pear-shaped organ, stores and concentrates bile until it is required for digestion. Then it is released into your digestive tract to emulsify fats and neutralise the acids in partly digested food. Peristalsis continues to move the chyme through your digestive system to your **large intestine** (another long tube) and eventually the **rectum** and **anal canal**.

> ## Key term
>
> **Enzymes** – proteins that start or accelerate the digestive process.

As the chyme moves through your small intestine, vitamins, minerals, amino acids, fatty acids and sugars are absorbed by your intestinal wall. Lining the wall of your small intestine are finger-like projections known as villi, which increase the surface area available for absorption and speed up the process.

By the time the chyme reaches your large intestine, it is less fluid and has been reduced to mainly indigestible matter. Your large intestine does not produce any digestive enzymes but continues to absorb water. Bacteria in your large intestine produce vitamin K. The residue (faeces) left behind is eliminated (excreted) from your body through your anus. See page 300 for a diagram of the digestive system.

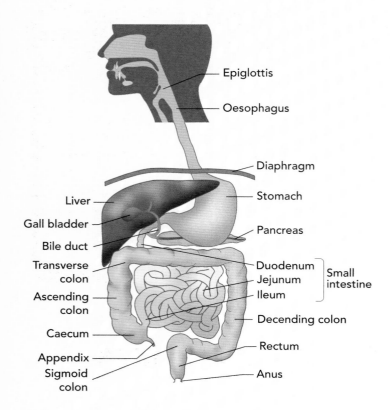

Figure 12.3: The digestive system

Function of the digestive system

Digestion

Digestion can be considered a multi-stage process following the ingestion of raw materials (the food you eat). It involves mechanical and chemical elements in the process that ultimately leads to enzymes in the gut breaking down the larger chemical compounds in your food into smaller compounds that can be absorbed by your body.

Absorption

This is the movement of digested food from your stomach and small intestine into your body tissues and blood. The process of absorption happens in the villi that line your small intestine. These finger-like projections provide a large surface area for absorption

to take place. Each villus has a network of capillaries to quickly absorb nutrients. Amino acids (from the breakdown of proteins) and glucose (from the breakdown of carbohydrates) enter your bloodstream directly. Fatty acids and glycerol (from the breakdown of fats) are taken up by your lymphatic system.

Excretion

Excretion is the removal of potentially poisonous end-products from metabolism, normally in your urine and faeces. In humans the main organs of excretion are the kidneys, through which urine is eliminated, and the large intestine, through which solid or semi-solid waste is expelled.

The kidneys

Your kidneys play a key role in keeping the composition of your blood constant by filtering it to remove excess water and waste products which are then secreted as urine. Every 24 hours your kidneys filter in the region of 150 litres of blood and produce around 1.5 litres of urine.

PLTS

Using a variety of sources to research the processes of digestion, absorption and excretion for Assessment activity 12.1 page 301 will demonstrate your skills as an **independent enquirer**. Evidencing the links between these processes will demonstrate your ability to think critically.

Functional skills

Using information communication technology (**ICT**) to produce your leaflet for Assessment activity 12.1 page 301 will develop your ability to access, search for and select ICT-based information and evaluate its fitness for purpose, and evidence your ability to present information in ways that are fit for the intended audience.

Assessment activity 12.1

1. Produce a leaflet for athletes, describing the importance of good nutrition to health and performance and introducing them to nutritional requirements and common terminology associated with nutrition. **P1**

2. Create a short PowerPoint presentation describing the structure and function of the digestive system. **P2**

Grading tips

P1 You must be able to describe nutrition and nutritional requirements using frequently used terminology. You should be familiar with guidelines recommended by public health sources.

P2 You need to describe the digestive system and be familiar with the enzymes that break down specific food sources, and you should evidence the links between digestion, absorption and excretion.

2.   Know energy intake and energy expenditure in sports performance

2.1 Energy

Energy is obtained from the foods you eat and used to support your basal metabolic rate (the minimum amount of energy required to sustain your body's vital functions in a waking state), and all activity carried out at work and leisure.

Measures

Energy is measured in **calories** or **joules**. As both these units are very small they are multiplied by 1,000 and referred to as **kilocalories** (the UK system) or **kilojoules** (the metric or international system).

Key terms

Calorie – the energy required to raise 1 gram of water by 1 °C.

Joule – 1 joule of energy moves a mass of 1 gram at a velocity of 1 metre per second. Approximately 4.2 joules = 1 calorie.

Kilocalorie – the energy required to raise the temperature of 1 kg of water by 1 °C. Equal to 1,000 calories and used to convey the energy value of food. Kilocalories are often simply referred to as calories.

Kilojoule – a unit of measurement for energy, but like the calorie the joule is not a large unit of energy; therefore kilojoules are more often used.

Remember

- 1 calorie (cal) = 4.2 joules (J)
- 1 kilocalorie (kcal) = 4.2 kilojoules (kJ)
- 1 kilocalorie (kcal) = 1,000 calories (cal)
- 1 kilojoule (kJ) = 1,000 joules (J)

Sources

The potential fuel sources available to exercising muscles are listed below. Their relative value as fuels for activity differs. Protein may be used during prolonged periods of exercise and towards the latter stages of endurance events like the marathon, particularly if fat and carbohydrate as sources of fuel within the working muscles have become limited.

Fats

1 gram fat = 9.0 kcal = 38 kJ

Carbohydrates

1 gram carbohydrate = 4.0 kcal = 17 kJ

Proteins

1 gram protein = 4.0 kcal = 17 kJ

Fat and carbohydrate are the main energy fuels for your exercising muscles. Exercising muscles prefer glucose as a fuel, particularly as the intensity of the activity being undertaken increases. When you exercise, your muscles use energy at a rate that is directly proportional to the intensity of your activity. If this energy is not replaced as it is used up, your muscles will be unable to maintain their rate of work and the intensity of the activity will need to be reduced or stopped.

Measuring requirements

Body composition

The most commonly used method of classification of body type is known as somatotyping, which recognises three basic body types:

- ectomorph – a slim build, long limbs, delicate bone structure, a low body fat and muscle content, and usually finds weight gain difficult
- endomorph – a heavy build, rounded shape, a tendency to gain weight, and generally finds weight loss difficult
- mesomorph – a muscular build and large bone structure.

Most of us have characteristics of each type to a varying degree, and although many women in particular want to be slim and ectomorph-like, it is important to note that it is impossible to alter your basic body type.

Lean body mass

Body composition refers to the lean body mass and body fat that make up total body weight. Lean body mass includes bone, muscle, water, connective and organ tissues. Body fat includes both essential and non-essential fat stores.

Percentage of body fat

People actively engaged in fitness regimes are often concerned about their weight, whether for performance or health reasons. Unlike basic body type, it is possible to alter body composition, with exercise generally having the effect of increasing lean body mass and decreasing body fat.

Methods of assessing percentage of body fat include:

- skinfold analysis
- bioelectrical impedance analysis
- hydrodensitometry (underwater weighing).

All these methods have most merit in measuring changes in body composition over time rather than absolute values. In order to minimise potential errors in measuring changes in body composition over time:

- always use the same method
- ensure the subject is assessed by the same person
- take repeat measurements at the same time of day.

Skinfold analysis

This technique uses callipers to measure the thickness of skinfolds at various anatomical sites, usually the biceps, triceps, subscapula and suprailiac crest. The sum of these measurements is used to calculate percentage of body fat, using equations or tables that take into account the subject's age and gender.

This is a relatively cheap and convenient method but it requires a high degree of skill. It is thought to be generally reliable if performed correctly.

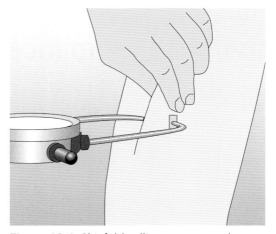

Figure 12.4: Skinfold callipers measure the amount of subcutaneous fat (fat immediately below the skin) in millimetres

Bioelectrical impedance analysis

Bioelectrical impedance analysis (BIA) is fast becoming a standard technique for assessment of body composition, particularly in the health and fitness sector. BIA machines provide a quick, easy and non-invasive method of estimating percentage body fat. Some equipment requires the attachment of electrodes to the hands and feet (Bodystat), others require the subject to stand on specially designed scales (Tanita) or to grip handles (Omron).

BIA measures resistance to the flow of an electrical current through the body, using the fact that different body tissues display different impedance to the flow of the current. Tissues that contain a large amount of water, such as lean tissue, provide a lower impedance than tissues such as bone and fat.

When using BIA techniques a number of assumptions have to be made, and equations applied, to obtain a body fat percentage figure. One potential drawback is that impedance measurements are related to the water content of tissues, so for accurate results subjects must be fully hydrated, and must abstain from exercise and substances which exert a diuretic effect – such as alcohol or caffeine – for at least 24 hours before the test. Invalid results may also be obtained for women immediately before or during menstruation, when the body's water content may be higher than normal.

Hydrodensitometry

This is considered to be one of the most accurate methods of assessing body composition. However, it is expensive and time-consuming and can be stressful as it requires the subject to be submerged in water. The technique measures body density that can be translated mathematically into percentage of body fat. It relies on Archimedes' principle of water displacement to estimate body density.

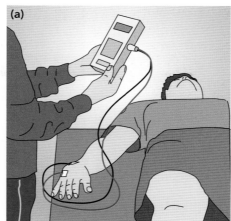
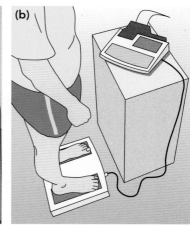
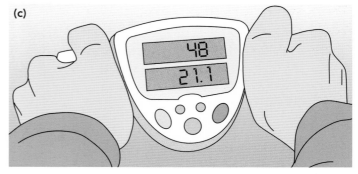

Figure 12.5: Bioelectrical impedance machines: (a) using electrodes, (b) foot-to-foot and (c) hand-to-hand

Take it further

Undertake an Internet search using the term 'body composition assessment'. Evaluate the range of body composition assessment products available in terms of affordability, ease of application and suitability for use with athletes. Be sure to investigate the methods of air displacement plethysmography and dual-energy x-ray absorptiometry.

Body weight

Body weight, more precisely referred to as body mass, is usually measured in kilograms. Some individuals have problems controlling their body weight, often resulting in obesity. Some sports are categorised based on body weight. Energy and nutrient requirements may also be expressed relative to body mass.

Direct and indirect calorimetry

Energy expenditure can be assessed by direct or indirect calorimetry, essentially through the measurement of heat production.

Direct calorimetry (DC) measures the actual amount of heat produced by the body. It uses an airtight chamber where heat produced by the subject warms water surrounding it.

Indirect calorimetry (IC) estimates heat production by measuring respiratory gases. The most common technique is via mouthpiece and Douglas bag collection or mouthpiece and gas analysis system, with energy consumption calculated from the amount of oxygen consumed. The consumption of 1 litre of oxygen equates to approximately 4.8 kcal of energy expended, assuming a mixture of fats and carbohydrates are oxidised.

Take it further

Using the Internet, investigate other measures of energy expenditure including doubly labelled water and motion analysers.

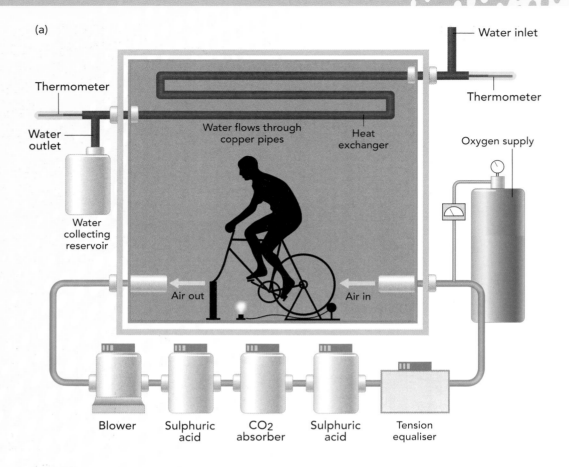

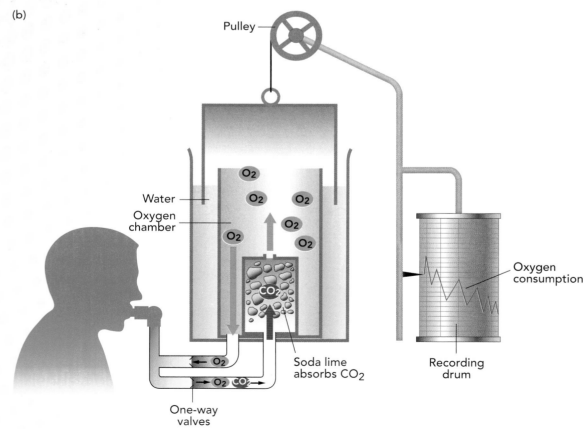

Figure 12.6: (a) Direct calorimetry and (b) indirect calorimetry

2.2 Energy balance

You are in energy balance when the amount of energy you take in as food and drink (energy input) equals the amount of energy you expend (energy output). You will neither be losing nor gaining weight. There are four major components to energy output: resting metabolic rate (RMR), dietary thermogenesis (DT), physical activity (PA) and adaptive thermogenesis (AT).

- Resting metabolic rate can account for 60–75 per cent of total energy output and represents the largest component of total daily energy expenditure. RMR is closely related to lean body mass and so is influenced by body composition. Muscle tissue is much more metabolically active than fat tissue. Gains in muscle mass will result in increases in RMR. RMR is also influenced by your age, sex and genetic background.

- Dietary thermogenesis refers to the energy expended above that of RMR for the processes of digestion, absorption, transport and storage of food. It is influenced by the calorie content and composition of your diet along with your individual nutritional status. High energy intakes and a regular eating pattern are thought to help maintain higher rates of dietary thermogenesis, while skipping meals and restrictive dietary practices lead to a reduction in this component of total energy expenditure.

- Physical activity represents the most variable component of your total energy expenditure. This is the additional energy expended above RMR and DT, and will contribute more to total daily energy expenditure in active individuals. Exactly how much it varies depends on how active your general lifestyle is, how often, how energetically, and for how long you participate in sport and exercise, and what type of activity it is.

- Adaptive thermogenesis is energy expenditure that occurs as a result of environmental or physiological stresses placed on your body, such as a change in temperature that may require you to respond by shivering or stress that causes anxiety or fidgeting.

Nutritional supplements are sometimes used to achieve and maintain energy balance. Investigate a range of supplements that make these claims.

When energy intake exceeds expenditure, this is referred to as **positive energy balance** and weight is gained. If intake is less than requirements, the additional energy required will be drawn from your body's fat reserves and weight will be lost. This is referred to as **negative energy balance**.

Remember

Energy balance is achieved when energy input equals energy output.

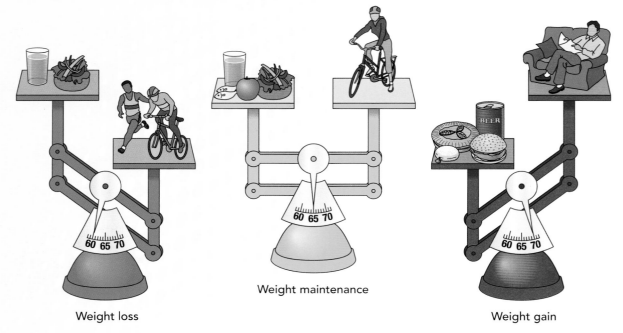

Figure 12.7: Energy balance

(Scales labelled from left to right:) Weight loss · Weight maintenance · Weight gain

Basal metabolism

To estimate energy requirements, you first need to calculate basal metabolic requirements (BMR) in kilocalories per day using the data in Table 12.6.

	Age (years)	Basal metabolic requirements in kilocalories per day (W = weight in kilograms)
Males	10–17	BMR = 17.7W + 657
	18–29	BMR = 15.1W + 692
	30–59	BMR = 11.5W + 873
	60–74	BMR = 11.9W + 700
Females	10–17	BMR = 13.4W + 692
	18–29	BMR = 14.8W + 487
	30–59	BMR = 8.3W + 846
	60–74	BMR = 9.2W + 687

Table 12.6: Calculating basal metabolic requirements (Schofield et al., 1985)

Age

Your basal metabolism reduces with increasing age. After the age of 30, it falls by around 2 per cent per decade.

Gender

Males generally have greater muscle mass than females, so generally have a higher basal metabolic rate.

Climate

Exposure to hot or cold climates causes an increase in basal metabolism to maintain the body's internal temperature.

Physical activity

To estimate your total energy requirements you also need to consider your level of physical activity and training. The simplest method of estimating your total energy requirement is by multiplying your BMR by your **physical activity level (PAL)**. Calculating PALs requires you to make an assumption about the energy demands of both your occupational and non-occupational activity levels (see Table 12.7).

Activity: Skills

Using Tables 12.6 and 12.7, calculate your BMR and total daily energy requirements and record your answers in kilocalories per day.

Once you have calculated an estimate for your total energy requirement, you can predict your carbohydrate, protein and fat requirements. Remember that in general athletes will require an energy distribution of 50–60 per cent of calories from carbohydrate, 12–15 per cent from protein and 25–30 per cent from fat.

Non-occupational activity	Occupational activity					
	Light		Moderate		Heavy	
	Male	Female	Male	Female	Male	Female
Non-active	1.4	1.4	1.6	1.5	1.7	1.5
Moderately active	1.5	1.5	1.7	1.6	1.8	1.6
Very active	1.6	1.6	1.8	1.7	1.9	1.7

Table 12.7: Physical activity levels for three levels (adapted from Committee on Medical Aspects of Food and Nutrition Policy (COMA) 1991)

Assessment activity 12.2

BTEC

1. Hold a group discussion to identify the range of sports participation in your class. In small groups, investigate the energy demands of some or all of these sports and prepare a short PowerPoint presentation to describe energy intake and energy expenditure in sports performance. **P3**

2. Produce a fact sheet for a specific sport to explain energy intake and energy expenditure in sports performance. **M1**

3. Consider the importance of energy balance in sport. Prepare a short PowerPoint presentation to support your views. **P4**

4. Explain the role of body composition assessment in the achievement and maintenance of energy balance in the athlete. **M2**

5. Analyse the effects of energy balance on sports performance. You could use some of the information you have collected in the Take it further activities in this section. **D1**

Grading tips

P3 You need to consider the importance of energy balance in sports performance.

M1 Consider the role of sports drinks, and energy gels and bars on achieving and maintaining energy balance.

P4 Describe energy balance and its importance to sports performance.

M2 Explain the importance of these measures in achieving and maintaining energy balance in the athlete.

D1 Consider examples from different sports and categories of athlete.

PLTS

Researching and analysing the importance of energy balance in a range of sports will develop you as an **independent enquirer** and **reflective learner**.

Functional skills

Discussing energy demands and interpreting energy balance and its importance in sports performance will develop your **English** skills in contributing to discussion, gathering arguments and opinions and making effective presentations.

3. Know the relationship between hydration and sports performance

During exercise, fluid requirements increase according to the type, duration and intensity of the exercise and the environmental conditions under which it is taking place. Understanding the relationship between hydration and sports performance is vital for achieving optimal performance in training and competition.

3.1 Hydration

Water is the main transport mechanism in your body, carrying nutrients, waste products and internal secretions. It also plays a vital role in temperature regulation, particularly during exercise, and aids the passage of food through your digestive system.

Water makes up around 50–60 per cent of your total body weight. Actual amounts vary depending on age, sex and body composition. Muscle has a higher water content than fat tissue, so leaner individuals have a higher water content than fatter individuals of the same body mass.

Water is lost from your body through a number of routes including urine, faeces, evaporation from the skin and expired breath. If water loss is high, your body becomes dehydrated. Under normal circumstances your body maintains a balance between fluid input and output. Table 12.8 illustrates the balance between water intake and water loss.

Signs and symptoms

Water is one of the most important nutrients. You cannot survive more than a few days without it. Losses may be as high as a litre per hour during endurance-type exercise, even higher in hot or humid conditions.

Fluid losses incurred by athletes during training and competition are linked to the body's need to maintain temperature within very narrow limits. During exercise, your body temperature rises and the extra heat is lost through sweating – evaporation of water from your skin's surface. If fluid lost through sweating is not replaced, there is a risk of dehydration and performance may suffer.

Dehydration

Dehydration can reduce strength, power and aerobic capacity. Severe dehydration can cause heatstroke and may be fatal. A loss as small as 2 per cent of body mass can be enough to begin to affect your ability to perform muscular work. For a 75 kg male this would be equivalent to a fluid loss of only 1.5 litres from the body. It is therefore important to minimise the risks of dehydration, and to note that thirst is a poor indicator of your body's hydration status. The warning signs for dehydration include:

- lack of energy and early fatigue during exercise
- feeling hot
- clammy or flushed skin
- not needing to go to the toilet
- nausea
- headache*
- disorientation*
- shortness of breath.*

* These are signs of advanced dehydration.

Daily water input		Daily water output	
Source	Millilitres	Source	Millilitres
Fluids	1,200	Urine	1,250
Food	1,000	Skin	850
Metabolism	350	Lungs	350
		Faeces	100
Total	2,550	Total	2,550

Table 12.8: Daily water balance for a sedentary 70 kg adult male

Hyperhydration

Hyperhydration is a state of increased hydration, producing a greater than normal body water content. Starting exercise in a hyperhydrated state can improve **thermoregulation**, improving heat dissipation and exercise performance. However, this area of sports science research needs to be further investigated.

Hypohydration

Hypohydration is a state of decreased hydration, producing a less-than-normal body water content. Hypohydration increases core body temperature, impairs the sweating response and causes skeletal muscle fatigue.

Superhydration

Superhydration is a state of hydration achieved by manipulation of the ergogenic aid glycerol. When ingested with large volumes of water (1–2 litres), glycerol has been shown to increase water retention in the body. This reduces overall heat stress during exercise in hot conditions, lowering heart rate and body temperature. However, not all glycerol studies have shown improvements in hydration or endurance performance and side effects may include headaches, dizziness, gastrointestinal upsets and bloating.

Fluid intake

To maintain water balance, a sedentary individual requires 2–2.5 litres of fluid per day, the equivalent of 6–8 cups. Around 10 per cent of your daily fluid requirements come from the metabolic processes that release water within your body. The other 90 per cent is derived from your diet. Approximately 60 per cent of this comes directly from fluids and the rest comes from food, particularly that with a high water content.

Pre-event

Athletes should be encouraged to begin fully hydrated and to drink plenty of water both during and after activity. Training should be used as the opportunity to practise fluid-replacement strategies that run smoothly in competitive situations. Drinking 300–500 ml of fluid 10–15 minutes before exercise is recommended.

Inter-event

Many factors can influence the effectiveness of fluid-replacement strategies during exercise. Fluid replacement can be accelerated by drinking still, cool drinks of a reasonable volume. They should not be too concentrated, and they must be palatable to drink. The more intense the activity, the more the absorption of fluid is slowed. Unpleasant symptoms experienced when drinking during exercise usually mean you started drinking too late and your body is already dehydrated. Drinking 150–200 ml every 15–20 minutes during exercise is recommended, especially if the exercise lasts longer than an hour.

Post-event

Weight and urine-colour checks are a useful and simple way of monitoring fluid status during and after training and competition. A weight reduction of 1 kg is equivalent to 1 litre of fluid loss. Frequent trips to the toilet to pass plentiful quantities of pale-coloured urine are an indicator of good hydration, whereas scant quantities of dark-coloured urine indicate poor hydration. These simple checks before and after exercise can be useful in determining fluid requirements post-training or during competition. As a guide, after exercise fluid losses should be replaced 1.5 times within the first 2 hours of recovery.

Sources
Water

Water is considered to be an adequate fluid suitable for most exercise, but some sports drinks may be useful if exercising at higher intensities for longer durations.

Sports drinks

Most sports drinks aim to provide three nutrients: carbohydrates to replace energy, water to replace fluid and **electrolytes** to replace minerals lost in sweat. The carbohydrate is usually glucose, fructose, sucrose or maltodextrins, which are all saccharides that are quickly absorbed. Sports drinks often contain a range of minerals and vitamins, but most often include the electrolytes sodium and potassium; both these macrominerals are lost in sweat. Sodium promotes the absorption of glucose and water. Magnesium is another mineral lost in sweat, and is present in water and most sports drinks.

Key terms

Thermoregulation – the ability to keep the body's temperature constant, even if the surrounding temperature is different.

Electrolytes – salts in the blood, for example, calcium, potassium and sodium.

Hypertonic

Hypertonic drinks contain over 8 per cent of carbohydrate and are absorbed more slowly. Although they provide a source of carbohydrate replenishment, they are not ideal for optimal rehydration and may need to be consumed with other fluids. These are best used in the recovery stage after exercise.

Isotonic

Isotonic drinks contain the same concentration of glucose to water as the blood: 4–8 per cent or up to 8 grams per 100 ml of water. They usually contain sodium, which makes them more quickly absorbed into the bloodstream. They are useful when exercise has been prolonged or during warmer weather. They can also be used before exercise.

Why is it important to minimise dehydration in sports performance?

Hypotonic

Hypotonic drinks have a lower concentration of carbohydrates and are more diluted than isotonic or hypertonic drinks. They contain less than 4 per cent

carbohydrate (4 grams per 100 ml of water) and are generally easily absorbed and well tolerated. Although water is adequate for non-endurance training or when sweat losses are small, these drinks may encourage fluid replacement through enhanced taste.

Before	During	After
300–500 ml 10–15 minutes before activity	150–200 ml every 15–20 minutes	Based on body mass lost; replace losses 150%

Table 12.9: Fluid replacement strategies for exercise

3.2 Effects on sports performance

The greater the **frequency**, **intensity** and **duration** of exercise, the more important fluid replacement strategies become and the more likely that sports drinks will have a useful contribution to make in terms of effects on performance and **recovery**, by providing not only fluid but also energy. Sound nutritional strategies, including those relating to fluid replacement, may have their biggest contribution to make in allowing athletes to train consistently to meet the desired adaptations to training in terms of **specificity** and **progression**.

4.   Be able to plan a diet appropriate for a selected sports activity

4.1 Diet

To be able to plan a diet for a selected sports activity, you need to consider the physiological demands of the activity, the phase of training and the individual's needs. These will help you to plan a **balanced diet** across the food groups. This is also known as **sports nutrition**.

Balanced diet

Foods are popularly classed as good or bad, healthy or unhealthy, with **healthy eating** often viewed as a hardship or a chore. However, it is better to look at the overall balance of foods eaten as either healthy or unhealthy.

> ### Key terms
>
> **Balanced diet** – a diet that provides the correct amounts of nutrients without excess or deficiency.
>
> **Sports nutrition** – the influence of nutritional strategies on sports performance during preparation for, participation in and recovery from training and competition.
>
> **Healthy eating** – the pursuit of a balanced diet to support health and reduce the risks of chronic disease. Healthy eating principles should form the solid foundations on which athletes can build more specific nutritional strategies to support training and competition.

Figure 12.8 A healthy plate – based on the Eatwell Plate

A simple guide to healthy eating:

- eat the correct amount to maintain a healthy body weight
- cut back on your fat intake, particularly fat from saturated sources
- eat plenty of foods with a high starch and fibre content
- don't eat sugary foods too often
- use salt sparingly and reduce your reliance on convenience foods
- ensure adequate intakes of vitamins and minerals by eating a wide variety of foods
- if you drink alcohol, keep within sensible limits
- enjoy your food and do not become obsessed with your diet or dieting.

Carbohydrates

To achieve optimal carbohydrate stores, athletes may need to top up with sugary sources that are more rapidly absorbed like sweets, dried fruit, fruit juice, and sugary or sports drinks.

As a guide, 4–5 grams of carbohydrate per kilogram of body weight should be sufficient if you do less than an hour's exercise each day, 5–6 grams per kilogram of body weight if you exercise for an hour a day, 6–7 grams for 1–2 hours per day and 8–10 grams per kilogram of body weight for heavy training exceeding 3 hours per day.

The best approach is to base all meals and snacks around starchy carbohydrate foods and eat at regular intervals. Glycogen – your body's store of carbohydrate – is replenished most efficiently within the first half-hour to 2 hours after exercise.

Fats

Fat provides a concentrated source of energy and is the predominant fuel for low-intensity activity. In the average UK diet, fat accounts for 40 per cent of total calorie intake. To promote good health it is recommended that intake is between 30 and 35 per cent. Those engaging in regular intense activity need to reduce this further to achieve recommended carbohydrate intakes.

Proteins

Many athletes believe they need to eat large amounts of meat, fish, eggs, pulses and dairy products to build muscle and increase strength, but in most cases this is not necessary. That can only be achieved by the appropriate training. Some of these foods are also high in animal fats, which should be reduced for long-term health. They may also leave no appetite for carbohydrate foods to provide sufficient energy stores to support training. Eating a normal varied diet and meeting energy (calorie) requirements should provide enough protein.

Active individuals require more protein per kilogram of body weight in order to promote tissue growth and repair. The International Olympic Committee's second Consensus Conference on Nutrition for Sport in 2003 recommended an intake of 1.2–1.7 grams per kilogram of body weight per day. The lower end of this range should cover the requirements of most endurance athletes, with the upper end meeting the needs of those engaging in more strength and power activities.

Water

Normal fluid requirements are in the region of 30–35 ml per kilogram of body weight per day, or 1 ml per calorie of energy requirement. Thirst is a poor indicator of dehydration, so drinking before the sensation of thirst is recommended to ensure adequate fluid status.

Fibre

Your daily requirement is 18 grams per day. Athletes with high carbohydrate requirements will need to manage fibre intake because consuming large quantities of fibre-rich carbohydrate food can make the diet bulky and filling, with the potential to limit overall food and energy intake.

Vitamins and minerals

Athletes often believe they need more vitamins and minerals than the average person. There is no doubt that an adequate supply is necessary for health, but whether regular exercise increases requirements is a different matter. The scientific consensus is that exercise does not particularly increase the need for micronutrients, although there may be a case for increased requirements of nutrients involved in energy metabolism. Generally, athletes will be eating greater quantities of food to meet increased energy requirements, and as a result will be automatically increasing vitamin and mineral intakes – as long as nutrient-rich foods are chosen.

4.2 Activities

Different activities require different dietary plans or strategies to optimise performance.

Aerobic

Aerobic or endurance activities will significantly challenge the athlete's energy and fluid stores. The longer and more intense the aerobic training or competition, the more depleted these stores are likely to become. A key goal for aerobic activities should be to maximise glycogen stores. Increasing carbohydrate intake during the 2 or 3 days before competition is a useful strategy. Carbohydrate supplements in the form of energy drinks, bars or gels may be a useful addition to the diet.

Endurance athletes should start exercise fully hydrated. The longer the duration of the activity, the more important it is to consume fluids during it. Sports drinks may be useful as they provide carbohydrate as well as replacing fluids.

Some aerobic activities may benefit from carbohydrate loading. The amount of glycogen available for storage in the muscles is related to the amount of carbohydrate consumed and the level and intensity of activity undertaken. For most sports, a diet consisting of 5–10 grams of carbohydrate per kilogram of body weight will maintain liver and muscle glycogen stores. However, the aim of carbohydrate loading is to increase the muscles' capacity to store glycogen above their normal level. This may be useful to athletes competing in endurance events that last longer than 90 minutes, such as marathon running, triathlons and endurance swimming. Although carbohydrate loading does not benefit all athletes, everyone regularly training and competing in sports should consume a high carbohydrate diet at all times and will benefit from a carbohydrate-rich meal or snack before training or competition.

Remember

The goal of carbohydrate loading is to increase the muscles' capacity to store glycogen above their normal level, usually in preparation for an endurance event.

Anaerobic

In anaerobic activities such as strength, power and sprint sports, the key role of nutritional strategies is to support the development of lean body mass (muscle) as well as to meet energy demands. Although carbohydrate requirements are not as great as for aerobic activities, they are still important. Combining carbohydrate with protein post-exercise promotes an **anabolic** environment and increases protein synthesis that helps to promote muscle development; however, excessive protein intake should be avoided. Some team sports may fall into this category.

Key term

Anabolism – the constructive metabolism of the body – the building of tissue.

Muscular strength and endurance

Many sports can fall into this category depending on the particular physiological demands of the sport. For example, high levels of muscular strength and endurance are required for team sports such as rugby as well as weight category sports such as judo. Nutritional demands will be dictated by the nature of the individual sport and participant requirements, but key nutrients in all cases are carbohydrate and fluid.

Flexibility

For sports that require a good deal of flexibility such as gymnastics, diving and figure skating, weight control is a serious issue. Evidence suggests participants in these aesthetic or appearance-orientated sports, where performance is subjectively evaluated by judges, may be more prone to eating-disorders. Leanness or a specific weight may be considered important for optimal performance, placing greater emphasis on what the athlete eats and how they look. However, it is important to remember that the fewer calories consumed, the fewer nutrients consumed. Calcium and iron intakes are reported to be particularly low in studies investigating the diet of female participants in these sports.

Healthy eating and Eatwell Plate principles apply to the planning of dietary intakes for these sports, but greater emphasis may be placed on a low-fat diet. However, this should not be at the expense of essential nutrients such as carbohydrate, protein, vitamins and minerals. Adequate fluid intake and hydration are also essential to maintain concentration for the technical demands of these sports.

Timing

Many athletes undertake a periodised programme of training. Periodisation represents the organised division of the training year and aims to prepare athletes for:

- achievement of an optimum improvement in performance
- a definite peak in the competition season
- main competitions within that peak.

Training undertaken within the programme is a form of stress to the body. If it is undertaken properly, the athlete adapts to that stress. Good nutritional practices are important in allowing the body to adapt and to deliver performance improvements.

Pre-season

For most sports, pre-season nutritional requirements need to take account of the frequency, intensity, duration and specificity of training. As training progresses in frequency, intensity and duration, it can be expected that the athlete's energy, carbohydrate and fluid requirements will increase. If energy and nutrient demands are not met, the athlete will increase their risk of injury and illness. In addition, reducing post-season weight gain is often a target of pre-season nutritional strategies.

Mid-season

Nutritional demands of the mid-season phase are focused on maintaining energy and fluid requirements as the competition schedule gets underway. During this time, less overall nutrition may be required but more attention may need to be placed on pre-event preparation and post-event recovery strategies to remain free from injury and illness.

Post-season

Post-season presents a window of opportunity where the athlete can relax dietary intake a little but unnecessary weight gain should be monitored. Energy and fluid requirements are likely to be at their lowest during this period.

Pre-event

Many of the principles of preparing for a competition mirror those of the training diet. A pre-competition

Choose a team sport and consider how the changing phases of the training and competition cycle impact on nutritional demands.

meal should aim to top up muscle and liver glycogen stores. Therefore, it should be rich in carbohydrate but low in fat and fibre and should contain a moderate amount of protein. It should be remembered that larger meals take longer to digest and that nervousness can result in delayed digestion.

Competition is not a time to experiment with new foods. The pre-event meal should be made of familiar foods and provide adequate fluids. Solid foods can usually be consumed with comfort up to 2 hours before an event, but liquid meals or carbohydrate drinks can be consumed up to 30–60 minutes before.

Athletes in events lasting longer than 90 minutes should be advised, where possible, to taper training in the week leading up to the event, include a rest day, and consume more carbohydrate and fluid than normal.

Inter-event

During training and competition, fluid loss is a major consideration. During intense training or competition isotonic sports drinks may be consumed. This may be beneficial especially if training or competition lasts longer than 60 minutes. During endurance or ultra-endurance events lasting longer than 4 hours, solid foods may be required. In these instances, energy bars or gels might be useful as a more concentrated source of carbohydrate.

> ### Remember
>
> Regular sports performers should be encouraged to practise their fluid and fuelling regimes in training to ensure that they do not run into any unexpected problems during competition.

Post-event

Good nutrition can make its greatest contribution in aiding recovery between training sessions. For the regular sports performer, performance improvements are the product of the body's adaptation to the demands of training. Sound nutrition has its biggest impact in supporting athletes in training consistently and effectively to achieve the desired adaptations.

What is consumed, how much and how soon after an intense workout or competition can all influence the recovery process. Sensible choices in terms of food and fluids will allow faster recovery for the next training session. It is important to refuel as soon as possible after each workout or competition. The longer refuelling is delayed, the longer it will take to fully refuel. Athletes may find it easier to have small, frequent meals and snacks at regular intervals to help to maximise glycogen synthesis.

To refuel efficiently, a high carbohydrate diet is required. Post-exercise carbohydrates that are easy to eat and digest are preferred. Athletes are advised to consume a high-carbohydrate (at least 50 grams) low-fat snack as soon as possible after training or competition, preferably within the first half-hour – when the muscles' capacity to refuel is greatest. They should eat their next meal, which should be rich in carbohydrate, within 2 hours.

After exercise, rehydration should start immediately. Drinks containing carbohydrates will also assist with energy and glycogen replacement. These may be particularly useful if the activity has been intense and resulted in a suppression of appetite and a reluctance to eat solid foods.

> ### Case study: Meal plan
>
> Jon is 16 years old and is competing in a national badminton tournament tomorrow. Considering Jon's overall nutritional requirements and the demands of his sport, suggest a suitable pre-competition meal plan and give some advice on how he might ensure that he keeps fuelled and hydrated during the tournament.
>
> Suggest ways in which you might monitor or evaluate Jon's nutritional preparation for the competition and the impact of your advice on his performance.

4.3 Planning diets

Before you can safely and effectively plan and implement balanced eating programmes and nutritional strategies to support training and competition for others, you need to be able to critically evaluate your own eating habits and activity patterns and consider the relationship between them.

Appropriate for selected activity

Athletes should pay careful attention to foods that can enhance, not hinder, their preparation for participation in and recovery from training and competition. Most athletes will obtain all the energy and nutrients they need by eating when they are hungry and choosing a balanced and varied diet.

Sports can be categorised into the following groups:

- multi-sprint or team sports, e.g. soccer
- strength sports, e.g. sprinting
- endurance and ultra-endurance sports, e.g. marathon running and triathlon
- weight category sports, e.g. boxing
- aesthetic sports, e.g. diving.

Each category requires sound nutritional strategies to support successful performance. Winning, avoiding injury and illness, and improving fitness are what matter to most competitive sportspeople. With the

intermittent nature of team sports, the intensity at which they are performed can alter at any time. These changes are irregular and can be random, and may draw significantly on the body's glycogen stores. Performance may be impaired towards the end of a match if glycogen stores are running low. Weight-loss methods and restrictive dietary practices are often used by athletes in weight category and aesthetic sports, with potential dangers to both health and performance.

Appropriate for selected sports performer

There are a number of methods for collecting information on what people eat and drink. These include the 24-hour diet recall, the diet history or interview technique, daily food records or diaries, weighed food intake records and food frequency questionnaires.

Remember

Any detailed or complex dietary analysis incorporating major changes, particularly those relating to medical conditions, should always be referred to a qualified state registered dietitian, or an accredited sports dietitian if it concerns an athlete. The usual means of referral to a state registered dietitian are through a general practitioner, consultant or dentist.

- The 24-hour diet recall is quick and easy, but relies heavily on memory. The interviewer questions the subject about what he or she usually eats and drinks. It is useful in assessing the quality of food intake and may reveal imbalances such as a potentially high fat intake. However, it is rarely adequate to provide a quantitative estimate of nutrient intakes to allow for comparison with Dietary Reference Values.

- The diet history or interview is quick and easy to use, but again relies heavily on memory. The interviewer questions the subject about what he or she usually eats and drinks, but over a longer time period. Recollections usually underestimate intake and there is the danger of fabrication to impress the interviewer. The method is, however, useful in assessing the quality of dietary intake and may be able to reveal dietary imbalances in the same way as the 24-hour recall.

- Daily food record or diet diary: this can give a good overall guide to the types and quantities of food and drink consumed. At least 3 days should be recorded, including one weekend day to account for any different food patterns. For a more detailed picture, a 7-day record is recommended. With athletes, the record should include rest and competition days as well as training days.

- Weighed food intake: individual foods are weighed before consumption. This method is time-consuming and intrusive, and could lead to distortion of the overall pattern of foods consumed in order to make weighing and recording easier.

Assessment of needs

When developing sound eating habits and nutritional strategies to support training and competition, the following issues are important:

- the types of food eaten to support training and competition

- the timing of meals and snacks around training and competition

- ensuring a balanced diet is achieved in respect of all nutrients

- maintaining a sufficient fluid intake

- encouraging an adequate calcium and iron intake, particularly for females

- promoting long-term health and reducing the risk of chronic disease

- the problems of travelling to training and competition venues

- minimising the risk of injury and illness.

The nutritional requirements for different sports and individuals will vary according to:

- the type of sport and training methods undertaken

- the intensity of training or competition

- the duration of training or competition

- the frequency of training or competition

- the training status and fitness level of the individual.

The Eatwell Plate principles should be used to plan meals. These principles should form the foundations on which to develop more specific sports nutrition strategies. Athletes should eat sufficient carbohydrate and start refuelling as soon as possible after training, when muscle capacity to refuel is at its greatest. This may not coincide with traditional meal times. Eating may need to be fitted in around the training process, with smaller, more frequent meals and snacks being necessary. Snacks and fluids should be carried in the kit bag at all times.

Rest days are important, and should be used to recover from the stresses of training and competition. A high fluid intake should be encouraged. In many sports, post-match alcohol consumption is traditional, but it is important to rehydrate with other fluids before drinking alcohol. Where an injury has been sustained, alcohol consumption may delay recovery and should be avoided for at least 48 hours.

Weight gain

Weight can be gained by increasing the amount of fat or the amount of lean body mass. Both will register as increases in weight on the scales, but the results will be very different in terms of body composition. Gains in fat weight are relatively easy to achieve – as most people wishing to lose weight would testify – but gains in lean body mass can only be achieved as a result of adaptations to a progressive strength training programme, supported by an adequate diet.

Weight loss

Most athletes are concerned about either attaining or maintaining an optimal body weight. Weight-category sports include body-building, boxing, horse racing, martial arts and rowing. Participants in these sports must compete within a given weight range.

For some sports a low body weight may be crucial, which for some may be below their natural weight. These might be considered as weight-controlled sports, and include distance running, gymnastics, figure skating and diving. These sports may present challenges in maintaining a nutritionally adequate diet while reducing or maintaining weight. Inappropriate weight-loss practices include fasting or skipping meals, laxative abuse, bingeing and purging, and intentional dehydration by the use of sweatsuits or saunas. When most athletes talk about achieving weight loss, they usually mean fat loss, as losses in muscle mass may result in unfavourable changes in their power-to-weight ratio.

Muscle gain

When athletes talk about weight gain, they usually mean muscle gain. In this case strength training provides the stimulus for muscles to grow, while adequate nutrition provides the opportunity for them to grow at an optimal rate.

Rates of weight/muscle gain are dependent on genetics and body type. To gain strength and size, it is necessary to achieve a slightly positive energy balance – somewhere in the region of an extra 500 calories per day – and a protein intake of about 1.4–1.7 grams per kilogram of body mass. A high-protein diet, or supplementing with amino acids (common practice for many athletes wishing to gain muscle bulk and size) will not automatically lead to great increases in muscle size or strength. Achieving an adequate energy intake is more important.

Fat gain

In very few instances the athlete may wish to gain fat weight, such as in contact sports where additional body fat may provide extra protection.

Fat loss

When your diet provides more calories than your body needs for general maintenance and its current level of

physical activity, the excess energy is stored in the form of body fat. The removal of excess fat is by a reversal of the processes that have stored this excess energy. If you burn more energy than you are consuming, the energy stored as fat will be broken down to provide energy.

Nutrition

Macronutrients

Performance in and recovery from exercise are enhanced by optimal nutrition. For most sports, carbohydrate requirements are likely to contribute 55–65 per cent of total energy intake, protein 12–15 per cent and the remainder coming from fat.

Micronutrients

Vitamin and mineral supplementation will not improve the performance of athletes whose diet is already adequate and varied. Those at risk of micronutrient deficiency are people who restrict energy intake, use severe weight-loss strategies or follow a high carbohydrate diet with low micronutrient density. Athletes should aim to consume diets that meet RNI values for micronutrient intakes.

Fibre

Athletes should aim to achieve fibre intakes in line with the sedentary population intake target of 18 grams per day.

Food groups

The Eatwell Plate is the UK's National Food Guide. Originally devised by the Health Education Authority as the Balance of Good Health, a simplified means of helping people understand healthy eating, it has been adopted by the Food Standards Agency. The model attempts to make following a balanced diet easier by identifying the types and proportions of foods required to achieve a healthy, balanced and varied diet, based around the five main food groups.

The model depicts a plate with divisions of varying sizes representing each of these five groups. Foods represented by larger divisions should feature in larger proportions in your diet, while those with the smaller shares should be consumed in smaller quantities or only occasionally (see Figure 12.8 on page 311).

This guide to healthy eating applies to most people in the UK, including those who engage in regular exercise and sport. It does not, however, apply to children under the age of five.

The key messages of the model are that you should aim to:

- base all your meals around starchy foods
- eat at least five servings of fruit and/or vegetables each day
- include milk and dairy foods, if possible three servings per day
- eat smaller portions of meat or fish, and try alternatives such as pulses
- limit your intake of foods with a high fat or sugar content.

Table 12.10 shows the recommended daily amounts and nutrients supplied by each of the main food groups.

Activity: Triathlon

Sayeed has recently taken up the triathlon. His usual diet consists of a macronutrient energy distribution of 40 per cent carbohydrate, 40 per cent fat and 20 per cent protein. He is about to enter his first major competition.

1. What effect could this macronutrient distribution have on his performance?
2. What practical advice could you offer to improve his diet?
3. What could Sayeed do in his preparation for the competition to help to delay fatigue?

Food	What is a serving?	Recommended amount per day	Main nutrients supplied
Grains and potatoes			
Bread, rolls, muffins, bagels, crumpets, chapattis, naan bread, pitta bread, tortillas, scones, pikelets, potato cakes, breakfast cereals, rice, pasta, noodles, couscous and potatoes	3 tbsp breakfast cereal, 1 Weetabix or Shredded Wheat, 1 slice of bread, ½ a pitta, 1 heaped tbsp boiled potato, pasta, rice or couscous	These should form the main part of all meals and snacks About a third of the total volume of food consumed each day	Carbohydrate, NSP (mainly insoluble), calcium, iron and B vitamins
Vegetables and fruits			
All types of fresh, frozen, canned and dried fruits and vegetables (except potatoes) and fruit and vegetable juices	1 apple, orange, pear, banana, 1 small glass of fruit juice, 1 small salad, 2 tbsp vegetables, 2 tbsp stewed or tinned fruit in juice	At least five portions per day About a third of the total volume of food consumed each day	NSP (especially soluble), vitamin C, folate and potassium
Oils			
Butter, margarine, cooking oils, mayonnaise, salad dressing, cream, pastries, crisps, biscuits and cakes	1 tsp butter or margarine, 1 tsp vegetable or olive oil, 1 tsp mayonnaise	These should be eaten sparingly and lower-fat options selected	Fat, essential fatty acids and some vitamins
Dairy			
Milk, yoghurt, cheese, fromage frais	1/3 pint milk, 1¼ oz cheese, 1 small carton yoghurt or cottage cheese	Two or three servings per day About a sixth of the total volume of food consumed each day	Protein, calcium, vitamins A and D
Meat, fish and alternative proteins			
Meat, poultry, fish, eggs, pulses, nuts, meat and fish products (e.g. sausages, beefburgers, fish cakes, fish fingers)	2–3 oz lean meat, chicken or oily fish, 4–5 oz white fish, 2 eggs, 1 small tin baked beans, 2 tbsp nuts, 4 oz Quorn or soya product	Two servings per day About a sixth of the total volume of food consumed each day	Protein, iron, zinc, magnesium and B vitamins Pulses provide a good source of NSP

Table 12.10: Food groups. How might the messages of the Eatwell Plate need to be adapted to meet the needs of a sports performer?

Sources

The sources of each food group are identified in Table 12.10, together with the main nutrients supplied by each food group.

Availability

Several factors influence food availability. These may include physical or environmental factors such as perishability and economic factors such as cost and budgeting priorities. Cooking skills and facilities, and nutritional knowledge, are also crucial factors in the provision and availability of food.

Assessment activity 12.4

1. Create a leaflet targeted at a specific sport to describe the components of a balanced diet to support performance. **P6**

2. Produce a short PowerPoint presentation targeted at a different sport to explain the components of a balanced diet to support performance. **M3**

3. Identify an athlete on whom you can undertake a dietary assessment (you may wish to consider your own diet if you are actively engaged in sport at a competitive level). Use the information you have gathered through the practical activities in this unit. Decide on an appropriate method for collecting information from your subject. **P7**

4. Analyse the information you have obtained and write a report which suggests, where necessary, appropriate modifications or improvements to support health and performance. Use a combination of manual and computer-based methods of processing and analysing nutrient intake information. **P7 M4 D2**

5. Plan a 2-week diet for your subject. Include advice on nutritional strategies to support preparation for, participation in and recovery from training and competition. **P7**

6. Explain the 2-week diet plan in terms of your selection of food and nutritional strategies. **M4**

7. Justify your food selection and nutritional strategies. Find ways of supporting your proposals by referring to relevant published material. **D2**

Grading tips

P6 You should consider the importance of carbohydrate, fat, protein, water, fibre, vitamins and minerals.

M3 You should explain the significance of the various nutrients in a balanced diet.

P7 You need to produce an appropriate 2-week diet plan for a named athlete. This should focus on aspects of achieving adequate fuelling and hydration.

M4 Explain your choice of food selection, fuelling and hydration strategies and their likely impact on training and competition performance. You should carefully consider the status of your athlete (amateur, semi-professional, elite) in explaining your 2-week plan.

D2 You need to justify your selection by being critical and looking for means to support your views. Do this with reference to relevant published material such as the ACSM (American College of Sports Medicine), Position Stand on Nutrition for Athletic Performance or the International Olympic Committee's Consensus on Nutrition for Athletes.

PLTS

Planning an appropriate diet for a selected athlete for a selected activity will develop you as a **self-manager**; interviewing your athlete, determining the physiological demands of their activity and evaluating their nutritional needs and intake will develop your skills as a **critical thinker** and **reflective learner**.

Functional skills

Calculating energy and nutrient requirements, interpreting food logs, devising menus and measuring body composition will require you to select and use a range of **Mathematics** skills to find solutions and advise on appropriate strategies to support training and competition.

Debbie Smith
Sports Nutritionist

I work as a freelance sports nutritionist. On a day-to-day basis I work with a range of athletes, from recreational to elite, to plan and advise on appropriate diets for their sport. I usually undertake a needs analysis interview with clients to ascertain relevant background information, particularly relating to factors that may affect their food intake and choice, and identify their nutritional and performance goals.

Another key element of my work is the assessment of adequacy of nutrient intake. For this athletes keep detailed diet and activity records that I analyse using nutritional analysis software. I then produce reports on their intake and feed this back to the athlete in a one-to-one consultation.

Most athletes, whatever their sport, will usually have weight-management goals, be it to lose, gain or maintain their current weight. It is recommended that if athletes have significant weight management concerns that they refer this to the sports nutritionist rather than trying to self-manage because without careful planning to the adjustments in intake that might be required nutritional inadequacies or imbalances might occur. Another key part of my work is the delivery of group education workshops, and I have from time to time undertaken supermarket visits and cooking sessions with clients.

The best thing about my job is educating clients to work out for themselves how to meet their dietary needs by increasing their knowledge of general nutrition and sport-specific nutritional strategies to aid performance.

Think about it!

If you are thinking about becoming a sports nutritionist:

- What knowledge and skills have you gained in this unit that provide you with an insight into the work of a sports nutritionist?
- What further knowledge and skills might you need to develop in order to pursue this career option?
- Try to spend a day shadowing a sports nutritionist at work, to see how they apply the theory you have learned in this unit.
- Ask a sports nutritionist about any professional training and accreditation that are necessary for the job.

Just checking

1. Define the term 'diet'.

2. Define the term Reference Nutrient Intake (RNI). What is the significance of this dietary reference value?

3. Draw and label a simple diagram of the digestive system.

4. Explain the term 'energy balance'.

5. Explain the components and the relative contributions of total energy expenditure.

6. Describe one method for estimating energy requirements.

7. List four routes of water loss from the body.

8. Because water losses are greater during exercise, athletes need to employ sound strategies for fluid replacement. What might be the signs and symptoms of dehydration and how might they be avoided?

9. What are the advantages and disadvantages of a high carbohydrate content in a sports drink?

10. Describe the skinfold analysis method of measuring body composition. Why is this one of the most widely used field techniques for assessing body composition in athletes?

11. List two micronutrients for special attention in the diet of athletes. Why might these be of particular concern in the diets of female athletes?

12. How soon do you need to eat after a hard training session and why is it so important to eat afterwards?

13. Describe the components of a balanced diet.

14. Describe how you might undertake an assessment of an athlete's nutritional needs.

15. What factors need to be taken into consideration when planning a diet for a selected sports activity?

edexcel

Assignment tips

- An awareness of the factors that affect food intake and choice, along with an understanding of the athlete's lifestyle and nutritional dilemmas they may face, will facilitate your ability to suggest realistic dietary plans to support sports performance.

- Being able to evaluate your own dietary practices and understand the links between your own diet, exercise and performance will help you meet the learning outcomes for this unit.

13 Current issues in sport

Sport contributes to society in many ways; it provides jobs, entertainment, opportunities for endeavour, and improves our health, fitness and well-being. Sport does not exist in a vacuum. It impacts on society and is itself influenced by society; for example, sport is affected by sport in schools, racism, sexism, corruption, drugs, inequality and commercialism. Sport is often used to try and solve social problems, for instance helping deprived children improve their health, and to improve social inclusion.

The media influence on modern-day sport is covered in this unit along with commercialisation and the use of technology.

This unit explores the development of sport from the pre-industrial era to the present day. The UK sports industry is examined in detail and it is related to broader international influences. Sports participation is explored, along with barriers to participation and cultural factors that affect participation.

Learning outcomes

After completing this unit you should:

1. know how sport has developed in the UK

2. know how media and technology influence modern sport

3. know how contemporary issues affect sport

4. understand the cultural influences and barriers that affect participation in sports activities.

Assessment and grading criteria

This table shows you what you must do in order to achieve a pass, merit or distinction grade, and where you can find activities in this book to help you.

To achieve a **pass** grade the evidence must show that you are able to:	To achieve a **merit** grade the evidence must show that, in addition to the pass criteria, you are able to:	To achieve a **distinction** grade the evidence must show that, in addition to the pass and merit criteria, you are able to:
P1 describe the development and organisation of a selected sport in the UK **See Assessment activity 13.1, page 333**	**M1** explain the development and organisation of a selected sport in the UK **See Assessment activity 13.1, page 333**	
P2 describe the influence of the media on a selected sport in the UK **See Assessment activity 13.2, page 337**	**M2** explain the influence of the media on a selected sport in the UK **See Assessment activity 13.2, page 337**	
P3 describe the effect that technology has on a selected sport **See Assessment activity 13.3, page 339**	**M3** explain the effect that technology has on a selected sport **See Assessment activity 13.3, page 339**	
P4 describe the effects of four contemporary issues on a selected sport **See Assessment activity 13.4, page 343**	**M4** explain the effects of four contemporary issues on a selected sport **See Assessment activity 13.4, page 343**	**D1** evaluate the effects of four contemporary issues on a selected sport **See Assessment activity 13.4, page 343**
P5 explain the barriers to sports participation **See Assessment activity 13.5, page 348**		
P6 explain three cultural influences on sports participation **See Assessment activity 13.5, page 348**		
P7 describe three strategies or initiatives which relate to sports participation **See Assessment activity 13.5, page 348**	**M5** explain three strategies or initiatives which relate to sports participation **See Assessment activity 13.5, page 348**	**D2** evaluate three strategies or initiatives which relate to sports participation **See Assessment activity 13.5, page 348**

How you will be assessed

Assessment of this unit can take a varied approach to allow customisation and reflect the nature of current thinking in sport, particularly when applied to the areas of media and technology. Assessments could be in the form of:

- a written report
- a series of leaflets or presentations
- a multimedia presentation
- a web-based article
- witness statements and observation records might also apply.

James McCartney, 16-year-old footballer

When I started this unit and saw how diverse the assessments were I thought this would be a challenge. However, after talking with my tutor it was clear I would have to be careful to select a sport which would cover all the issues asked for in the assessments and there had to be lots of information available about that sport. Being a keen football player I chose the FA.

I chose a sports governing body with a good website and made sure that it was a sport often covered in the media, that technology had changed it and several issues surrounded it. I used our school library to research books on barriers to participation and cultural influences. I also arranged a meeting with a sports development officer from our local leisure department to find out about strategies and initiatives running to help participation locally.

I enjoyed talking with the sports development officer as I might do that for a career. The FA website had plenty of detail for me to study. I learned that there is so much more to providing sporting opportunities than I had thought before.

Over to you!

- As you have to carry out a similar assessment task to James, what can you learn from his method of approaching this task?
- Which parts of this unit do you think you will find especially challenging?
- How might you prepare for tackling this unit?

1. Know how sport has developed in the UK

Inactive people

In 2005 the 'Active People' participation survey from Sport England showed the general levels of participation in sport around the UK were 18–23 per cent. Not a very high percentage compared to Scandinavian countries. Why do you think this is so? Check the 2009 results to see if we have improved since then.

1.1 Development

Early British sport

Early British sport rose out of activities born in countryside leisure, education and military activities. In this section you will investigate different historical periods and social developments that played a role in forming sport in our society today. (See Figure 13.1)

Agricultural society

In the agricultural society of medieval and early modern Britain and Ireland, existence was mainly subsistence – living off the land to survive. There would not be time to take part in leisure activities on a day to day basis. Hard physical work was the norm for many, including children. On market days, or at fairs, there would be an opportunity to pursue leisure activities like drinking, dancing, cock-fighting, bear-baiting, dog-fighting, gambling and bare-fist fighting. The local hostelry would be the focus for village life, and often the place where people might take part in more gentle pursuits such as billiards, bowls and skittles.

The rich were able to travel and hunted on neighbouring estates or went to the coast to sail. They also played real tennis. Ordinary people were prevented from hunting by game laws which made poaching a crime. For the poorer peasants there were sports like mob football and demonstrations of skill in pursuits such as archery.

Much physical activity had traditionally been for military purposes – getting fit to fight, and building strength to wield swords, pikes and axes. Sport was represented by fencing, archery and sparring.

How does this equipment differ from the modern Olympians' archery?

During the Puritan period of Cromwell's protectorate, there was pressure on any kind of sport as the authorities and church preferred people to worship rather than play.

After the restoration of the monarchy in 1660, King Charles II resurrected sports, and tennis, yachting and hunting grew in popularity. Other sports, such as early forms of cricket, skating and fishing, were followed by the rich. Some traditional events that took place are still represented today by surviving country shows and county fairs like the Great Yorkshire show.

Cricket was born around the early 1700s and by the mid century county matches were not uncommon.

Activity: Through the centuries

Identify and discuss other agricultural or animal-based sports and military activities that have carried on through the centuries.

Case study:
The Great Yorkshire Show

One example of these traditions is the Great Yorkshire Show, held in Harrogate every July at the agricultural showground. In 2011 the 153rd show will take place, demonstrating how popular this type of show still is. You can still see some traditional sports and pastimes in the country pursuits and forestry events arenas, such as pole-climbing, show jumping, scurry racing, dog handling and falconry.

1. **Visit the website at www.greatyorkshireshow.com.**
2. **Why do you think there are still some enduring country sports?**

Effects of the Industrial Revolution

In the 19th century cities grew, but life was hard – conditions were often cramped and unsanitary. Work was physically demanding (mining, weaving and other factory work or labouring on building sites) and there was little time off, and no additional earnings available for sport and leisure activities. Despite mechanisation, children were still being put to work to increase family income. Not until the Education Act of 1870 was it compulsory for them to go to school instead.

In cities, sport and leisure opportunities were fewer, and different from country sports, with activities for the working classes being spectator sports such as boxing, wrestling and rowing. Many activities had a gambling dimension and were blood sports brought in from historical country pursuits, such as dog-fighting.

Aristocratic sports flourished among the richer classes, who were benefitting from trade and land ownership. They had leisure time and were able to follow interests such as dancing and stage plays, and to continue their country pursuits such as hunting, riding and shooting.

Britain's trading empire had grown around the world; this meant that many British sports were exported with traders and colonists. For example, the origins of cricket in places like the Caribbean, India and Australia can be traced back to its roots in the days of Britain's imperial rule.

Influence of public schools

'Public' schools were so called because they were originally founded to provide an education outside the houses of the rich. However, the schools and their endowments increasingly became used by the nobility turning the public school system into the one we know today (i.e. independent fee paying schools). This system grew in the early nineteenth century and sports flourished within the walls of the public schools, especially rugby, cricket, tennis and soccer, for the schools were wealthy and had extensive playing fields. Rules were made to help structure sports, and these form the basis of rules and regulations today. Public schools made a great contribution to sport with old boys carrying British sporting traditions and values around the globe.

In the poorer Victorian slums, factory workers and their children had little leisure to speak of other than street and pub games. Their working week would be close to 70 hours. However, there were many more public holidays than now. Bills went through Parliament in the late 1800s which gave us the bank holidays we have today. The Victorians were also very generous, creating parks and gardens in many cities along with libraries, theatres and playing fields and of course Victorian baths.

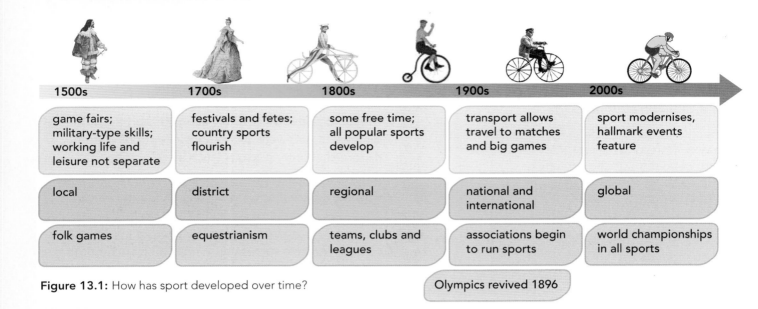

1500s	1700s	1800s	1900s	2000s
game fairs; military-type skills; working life and leisure not separate	festivals and fetes; country sports flourish	some free time; all popular sports develop	transport allows travel to matches and big games	sport modernises, hallmark events feature
local	district	regional	national and international	global
folk games	equestrianism	teams, clubs and leagues	associations begin to run sports	world championships in all sports

Figure 13.1: How has sport developed over time?

Olympics revived 1896

Rationalisation

More general affluence spread and the middle class emerged. They wanted to adopt sports previously only in the realm of the rich. They promoted **rationalisation** of sport and leisure to encourage more organised, structured and 'wholesome' recreation – sports and games with a healthy purpose (like swimming, athletics, lawn tennis and cycling). This was in sharp opposition to the drinking, gambling and blood sports, such as bare-knuckle fights, of the working classes. There are several motives for the 'rational recreation' philosophy:

- Making people healthier – both physically and spiritually.
- Giving them sport and leisure activities to help them forget the drudgery of work.
- Compensating them for hard physical labour.
- Helping them to get fresh air and escape poor working conditions.

Regulation

At this time, the influence of the public schools created a general trend towards the **regulation** of how sports were played – this was called codification. For example, boxing adopted the Queensberry rules in 1867. Sports associations, leagues and clubs began to form too, many being 'works teams' such as Arsenal, the football team formed in 1886 by workers at the Woolwich Arsenal Armaments Factory.

Development in this period gave much more structure and fabric to sport, laying down the modern foundations. City councils also played an active role in providing sports venues for their communities. The beginnings of professionalism were laid down too. The Olympic Games were reintroduced by Baron de Coubertin in 1896.

Key terms

Rationalisation – more organised and structured sport.
Regulation – following rules.

20th century

The start of the last century saw a period of great flux in Britain, with the First World War, then the depression, followed by the Second World War. Between the wars, people were determined to enjoy themselves. There were big sporting events such as the FA Cup Finals, the Oxford and Cambridge Boat Race, the Derbies and Wimbledon, which gave sport and leisure a chance to flourish.

Better working conditions

After the Second World War, the hours of work shortened, giving more leisure time, and wages increased, giving some disposable income. The new-found leisure time of the working classes was

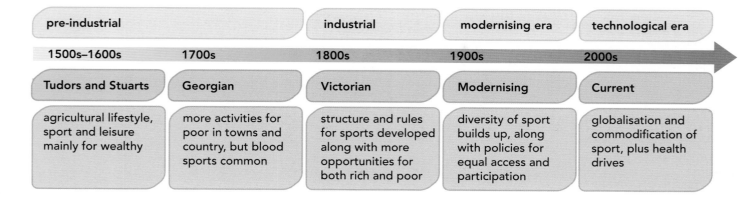

pre-industrial		industrial	modernising era	technological era
1500s–1600s	1700s	1800s	1900s	2000s
Tudors and Stuarts	Georgian	Victorian	Modernising	Current
agricultural lifestyle, sport and leisure mainly for wealthy	more activities for poor in towns and country, but blood sports common	structure and rules for sports developed along with more opportunities for both rich and poor	diversity of sport builds up, along with policies for equal access and participation	globalisation and commodification of sport, plus health drives

Figure 13.2: Can you describe the growth of sports and leisure?

quickly filled with amusements and entertainment, but also with some sports matches taking on the more commercial approach that we see today. Opportunities to play and watch football, cricket and golf grew as stadiums and grounds were built.

Activity: Origins

Investigate your favourite football team – when was it formed and what were its origins?

Influence of war

War has a profound effect on society and this was true for Britain after a series of wars. However, war did bring some benefits for sport and leisure:

- New technology was created.
- People were motivated to compensate themselves after the austerity of war and enjoy and value their leisure time more.
- Sport provided a form of safe, shared competition.
- It provided a bridge to rebuild relationships.
- Sport could carry great national pride, just as armies did.

Women had proved themselves in the war effort, in both world wars, so opportunities began to open up for their participation in sport (although equality was some way off, with most sports being male-dominated).

Outdoor activities

In contrast to urban sport and leisure, interest grew in the outdoors; as transport improved people could get to the coast or into the hills. Some richer people made the 'grand tour' of spas and resorts in Europe, spreading sports and health interests such as skiing, climbing and simply 'taking the waters'. There was sufficient interest in winter sports activities for the Winter Olympics to be created in 1924.

1.2 Key national organisations

In the late 1890s sports governing bodies were set up to organise, control and develop individual sports – including the Rugby Football Union (RFU), the Football Association (FA) and the Lawn Tennis Association (LTA). In the 1990s some new bodies were set up to control and develop sport in a more strategic way (including the English Institute for Sport, UK Sport and Sports Coach UK). This move was designed to help sports governing bodies who had tended to do their own thing and lacked a joined-up strategy. After some poor Olympic performances, the government was keen to change this. Some key organisations and their websites are shown in Table 13.1.

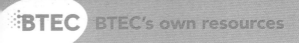
Table 13.1: Key organisations. Add their year of origin to complete your time frame of sports organisation developments.

Sports governing bodies	
Rugby Football Union	www.rfu.com
Football Association	www.thefa.com
Lawn Tennis Association	www.lta.org.uk
Irish Football Association	www.irishfa.com
Welsh Bowling Association	www.welshbowlingassociation.co.uk
British Canoe Union	www.bcu.org.uk
Scottish Hockey Union	www.scottish-hockey.org.uk
England Basketball	www.englandbasketball.co.uk
Strategic organisations	
Department for Culture, Media and Sport	www.culture.gov.uk
Central Council of Physical Recreation	www.ccpr.org.uk
UK Sport	www.uksport.gov.uk
Sport England	www.sportengland.org
Sport Scotland	www.sportscotland.org.uk
Sports Council Wales	www.sports-council-wales.org.uk
Sport Northern Ireland	www.sportni.net
English Institute for Sport	www.eis2win.co.uk
Sports Coach UK	www.sportscoachuk.org
English Federation of Disability Sport	ww.efds.net
Women's Sports Foundation	www.womenssportsfoundation.org

Department for Culture, Media and Sport (DCMS)

The DCMS covers a broad range of sectors under its wing, including the arts, the National Lottery, tourism, libraries, museums and galleries, as well as sport. It has a specific Sport and Recreation division with a Director who briefs the Minister for Sport. The DCMS funds Sport England and supports UK Sport, along with the National Lottery. For example, in 2009 the DCMS committed over £36 million to a scheme called Sports Unlimited, an innovative scheme to try and attract 900,000 youngsters to taster sessions in sport before 2011. In addition, it has supported the new Wembley Stadium project, and the Olympic builds. In June 2008 the DCMS published 'Playing to win – a new era for sport' which sets out the Government's ambition to become a truly world leading sporting nation.

Central Council of Physical Recreation (CCPR)

The CCPR is the oldest sporting body (other than governing bodies). It was formed in 1935 in response to a concern that PE was a low priority and children were not healthy enough. At that time, few young people stayed on at school after 14.

Take it further

Inspect the CCPR

Visit the website of CCPR at www.ccpr.org.uk. How is it structured? Identify its divisions and assess what role they play in delivering sport in this country.

UK Sport

This is one of the UK's newest sports organisations, formed in 1997. UK Sport aims to work in partnership with the home-country sports councils (Scotland, England, Wales and Northern Ireland) and with other agencies to try and attain world-class success. It is responsible for managing and distributing public investment, and is a distributor of funds raised by the National Lottery through the DCMS.

UK Sport's mission is: 'to work in partnership to lead sport in the UK to world-class success'. Its goals can be summed up as to:

- encourage world class performance and to develop home-grown expertise to support our athletes for the London Olympiad
- have an international programme that has a worldwide impact to bring best practice in other sporting nations to the UK
- promote world class standards of sporting conduct and give a strategic lead
- lead a world-class anti-doping programme for the UK and improve the education and promotion of ethically fair and drug-free sport.

UK Sport guides the overall strategy for the whole of the UK. Each country has a sports organisation (previously called a sports council) that is responsible for implementing plans, funding development and supporting all kinds of sports initiatives.

Sport England

Sport England's focus is hinged around three outcomes:

1. Growing the numbers of people taking part in sport.
2. Sustaining these numbers.
3. Improving talent development to help more people excel.

To achieve its aims Sport England has set the following the targets:

- One million people taking part in more sport.
- More children and young people taking part in five hours of PE and sport a week.
- More people satisfied with their sporting experience.
- 25 per cent fewer 16–18 year olds dropping out of at least five sports.
- Improved talent development in at least 25 sports.

Sport Scotland

Sport Scotland's mission is 'to encourage everyone in Scotland to discover and develop their own sporting experience, helping to increase participation (60 per cent by 2020) and improve performances in Scottish sport'. As well as running the Scottish Institute of Sport (www.sisport.com) to support the development of high-performance sport in Scotland, Sport Scotland runs three national centres: Inverclyde (sport), Cumbrae (watersports) and Glenmore Lodge (Europe's leading outdoor centre). It also distributes National Lottery and government money for sports development, makes awards to create links between schools and communities, and supports areas and groups deprived of sporting opportunities.

Sports Council Wales

Sports Council Wales is the national organisation responsible for developing and promoting sport and recreation. It was set up in 1972, and is the main advisor to the Welsh Assembly Government on all sporting matters. It is also responsible for distributing lottery funds to sport in Wales. Its main focus is to increase the frequency of participation by persuading those who are currently sedentary to become more active and to encourage people, young and old, to develop a range of activities through which to achieve healthy levels of activity.

Take it further

Sports Council Wales

Evaluate Sports Council Wales' strategic plan 'Climbing Higher' and its shift in plans for children, women and girls, by visiting its website at www.sports-council-wales.co.uk.

Sport Northern Ireland

Sport Northern Ireland describes itself as the lead facilitator for sport in Northern Ireland. It aims to increase and sustain its commitment to participation in the province, and to:

- raise the standards of sporting excellence
- promote the good reputation and efficient administration of sport
- increase and sustain committed participation, especially among young people

It has a strong drive to improve leadership skills among coaches and helpers so that they can work more effectively in the community. Performance-level athletes are given a range of support and advice.

Activity: Sports councils' goals

Using material from the text and your own research, identify and describe the main similarities and differences of the strategies and goals of the four sports councils.

1.3 National governing bodies

These organisations aim to promote and develop a particular sport. Almost all types of sport have a national governing body. A few examples include:

Basketball

Each country in the UK has its own basketball association. Collectively, they make up the British Basketball Federation (www.british-basketball.co.uk), and from this the Great Britain team is chosen.

Hockey

The Irish Hockey Association (www.hockey.ie) was formed in 2000, as a result of the merger of the two pre-existing unions which governed men's and women's hockey separately. The origins of both the pre-existing unions date back to the late 19th century, when they were formed. Typical work for this association includes their hockey camps.

Canoeing

The British Canoe Union (www.bcu.org.uk) is the governing body of paddlesport and was set up in 1936 to send a team to the Berlin Olympics. It is the lead body for canoeing and kayaking in the UK. It has divisions in all four countries of the UK. An estimated 2 million people take to the water in a canoe or kayak each year.

Cricket

The England & Wales Cricket Board (ECB) state its development aims as increasing:

- participation
- club membership and affiliations
- coaching and volunteering roles
- funding
- equity
- relationships with all counties.

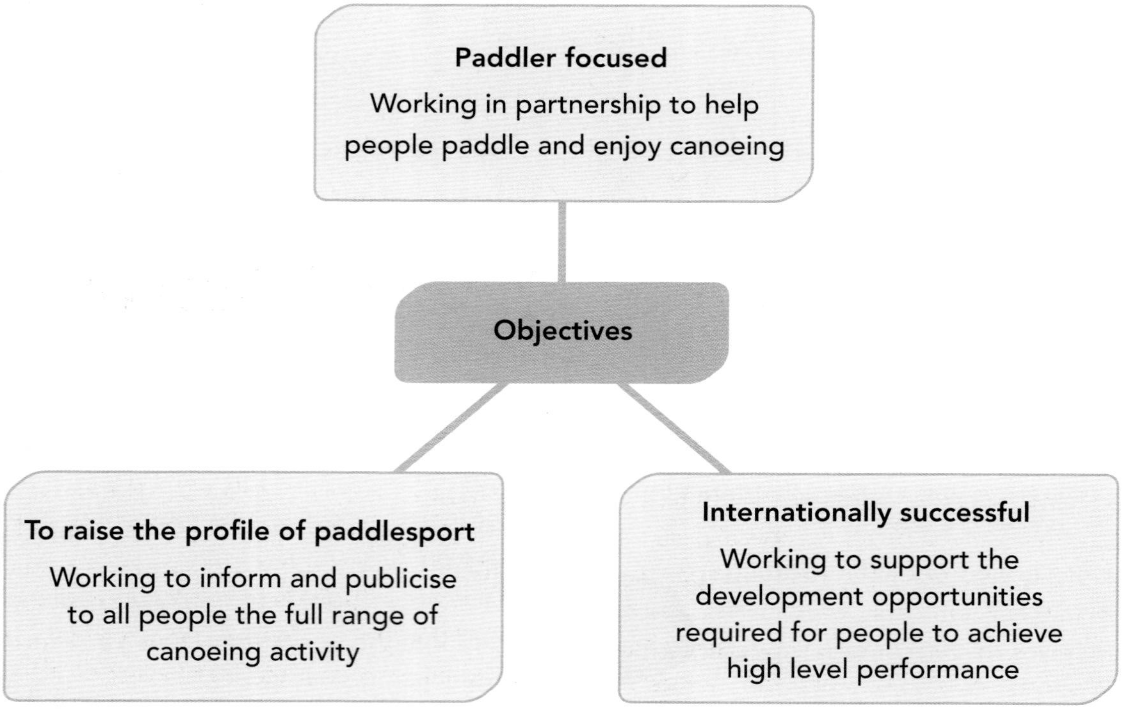

Paddler focused
Working in partnership to help people paddle and enjoy canoeing

Objectives

To raise the profile of paddlesport
Working to inform and publicise to all people the full range of canoeing activity

Internationally successful
Working to support the development opportunities required for people to achieve high level performance

Figure 13.3: Objectives of the British Canoe Union. What issues could prevent the British Canoe Union from achieving its objectives?

Take it further

ECB funding

In 2008, ECB announced a £30 million investment in facilities and in club cricket, the most significant injection of funding ever in cricket in England and Wales. Visit their website at www.ecb.co.uk to learn more or choose them as one of your case studies.

Assessment activity 13.1

Using material from the text and your own research, prepare a presentation using a program such as PowerPoint® to describe or explain the development and organisation of a selected sport in the UK. **P1** **M1**

Grading tips

- To attain **P1** link your description to some of the national bodies and show how it works with others and what issues it might be currently tackling. You might cover scale, structure and provision.

- To attain **M1** clearly explain how the sport you have selected has been developed and is now organised. You might make some historical notes and show links to other agencies.

PLTS

When describing or explaining the development of a selected sport you will be using your skills as an **independent enquirer**. This will also be the case when you describe or explain its organisation.

Functional skills

By researching online and creating this presentation you are providing evidence towards skills in **ICT**. Evidence for **English** could be generated through discussion on what to include.

2. Know how media and technology influence modern sport

2.1 Media

There are several different forms of media and each raises issues for sport, some positive and others negative. The ability of people and organisations to communicate received a massive boost in the late 20th and early 21st centuries, with mobile phones, iPods, satellite television, Xbox Live, Wiis and the Internet. This new technology has brought with it issues for sport as it draws young people away from physical activity.

Television

This has had a huge impact and brings with it considerations of commercialisation, good and bad presentation, reporting and journalism. Satellite television can beam in sport 24 hours a day from all around the globe. The running of many sports events has been geared up to suit television audiences.

Participation might be increased as a result of young people watching a great performance on television and being inspired to take up a sport. This happened with cycling after the Beijing Olympics. Or you might watch a charity run and decide to have a go to raise money for a good cause. On the downside, the increase in childhood obesity through lack of activity might well be linked to computer games and television viewing. People watch television for an average of just over 26 hours per week. Other figures show that commercial television accounts for 64 per cent of total broadcast viewing, with the BBC taking the remaining share. Sports events are an important portion of this.

Sponsorship

Sponsorship is said to have a symbiotic relationship with sport – one can't live without the other. Sponsorship does bring in much-needed cash to a club. However, in football, for example, there never seems to be enough sponsorship money filtering down to lower league sides to help them survive or develop new talent.

Businesses are keen to be sponsors as they will gain media exposure if their event or team is reported. However teams have to be winners to retain their sponsorship and in the credit crunch of 2009 many sponsors withdrew to save on costs.

Advertising

Advertising is a necessity for many professional sports – without it they would not exist. It brings in cash to pay players and to run clubs and stadiums. Television cameras pick up and highlight sponsors' logos. Some of these logos appear in 3D on the pitch.

Spectatorism

The increased coverage of sport means that fewer people will be playing. They might be considered consumers rather than supporters. Many big match crowds are dominated by corporate spectators looking

Activity: Broadcasting rights for national events

Consider these news stories:

- Sky Sports won the exclusive UK rights to screen the Ryder Cup in 2010 and 2012 and extended its coverage of the PGA European Tour for a further four years as the battle for the subscription fees of the UK's golf fans takes another turn.
- Setanta Sports acquired the UK television rights for the Indian Premier League's (IPL) Twenty20 cricket competition in a five year deal with the IPL.
- The International Olympic Committee and the European Broadcasting Union announced that the BBC won the UK television, radio and online rights to cover the 2010 Winter Olympics from Vancouver and 2012 Games.

What issues can you see coming out of these reports under the following headings: access, costs, control, market share/profits, impact on the sport?

for entertainment, leading to fewer true fans in the crowd. Football hooliganism still surfaces to spoil some matches. Test match crowds really do differ from those at football matches. Why do you think this is?

Television offers ways of watching events that would be impossible to attend otherwise, and reaches a far larger audience than could ever fit into a stadium.

Because of the entry fees paid by spectators, plus sponsorship and **broadcasting rights**, players can now be paid more, facilitating the growth of the professional player in sports other than football.

Punditry

Television uses sports **pundits** (an Indian word for an expert) – former players or athletes who give their analysis and opinions on matches. Notable ones might be Alan Hanson or John McEnroe. It is possible that you might have a favourite pundit or commentator.

Narrative technique

Narrative technique is how a commentator describes a sequence of events or paints the picture of the sporting scene on television or radio. This can influence our opinion of an incident. It helps us to imagine how an athlete might be thinking or feeling, capturing the moment, the drama, in words.

> ### Remember
> Narrative technique can bias your interpretation of events.

Key terms

Broadcasting rights – having the contract to televise an event.

Spectatorism – watching sport.

Punditry – so-called expert opinion.

Narrative technique – the style of making a commentary.

Rule changes

Media demands have had an impact on the rules of some sports, for example, the third umpire in cricket or the video referee in rugby whose decision can overturn that of the match official. Hawkeye (invented by Dr Paul Hawkins) has been developed by Roke systems for sports applications. It is used in tennis for decisions on serving and challenges.

In the US, American football and basketball are so reliant on television coverage for their funding that they have adapted and changed their rules and competitions in order to suit television scheduling. In both sports, time-outs and official game stoppages have been built in to allow the television companies to show advertisements.

> ### Take it further
> **Video replay debate**
> Debate in groups whether video replays should be used in football to decide penalties, offsides, handball and bookable offences.

Local and national press

Local newspapers are very good at reporting the progress of local teams. Read any local or regional newspaper and you will find reports and scores for everything that happens locally, from under-11s football and cricket, to the achievements of individuals in cross-country or swimming. These stories and photos are essential to sell local newspapers.

The national press has a strong influence, including the power to damage individuals' careers when journalists comment on performances which are circulated to millions of people. Examples include the departure of the England Rugby Union coach Andy Robinson, or the negative press received by England's cricketers in Australia while trying to defend the Ashes (Figure 13.4).

Magazines

Sport-related magazines cover health, fitness, exercise, diet and the body (see Figure 13.5). They can have a positive influence, with good guidance and interesting articles or programmes to follow. However, many images of slim, fit people puts pressure on others to attain an ideal and this can cause dietary and emotional problems.

Abject England rolls over
FRIDAY JANUARY 5, 2007

The inevitable happened 12 minutes before lunch this morning when Matthew Hayden hit the run that gave Australia victory by 10 wickets in the final test and the 5-0 whitewash they have craved for the last 16 months. Set to score 46, Justin Langer and Hayden took just one ball shy of 11 overs to complete England's biggest humiliation in 86 years....

Figure 13.4: How can the press influence how we think about sport?

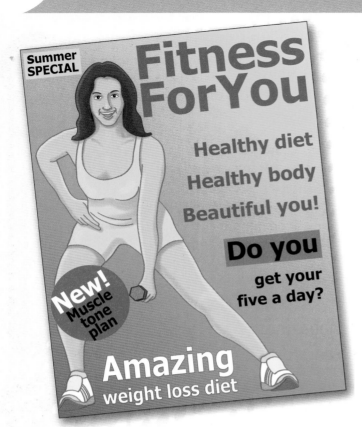

Figure 13.5: How might people feel pressured by the images in magazines?

Sensationalism

Many journalists who work for the tabloid press have been accused of sensationalising the news that they report. That is, blowing it up out of proportion or even, in some cases, making it up. This obviously helps them sell more newspapers, but the downside is that athletes and players can receive 'negative' press, which may affect them personally or may deter a sponsor. Many famous sports stars are pursued by the paparazzi so that they can be caught on camera unexpectedly.

Gender imbalance

The media has a habit of giving male sports much more attention than female sports. This creates a gender imbalance with female sports losing out, not just on publicity, but also on sponsorship as they cannot command the same space in newspapers and on television. When women's sports are reported they will have fewer column inches or maybe just a glamorous photo. In 2009 England's women's teams won the cricket world cup and got through to the final of the European football cup – little was seen in the press but there was some television coverage. Think about why this might be the case.

Jingoism

This term means extreme chauvinism or nationalism. We can identify examples of this in the media when sports programmes focus exclusively on male athletes or on only one country's athletes.

The Internet

The Internet has a huge influence, attracting young people away from active sports to sedentary solo activities. This may be why we have such low levels of participation in sports in the UK. However, it does offer real-time viewing of sport and global coverage, making events more accessible to more people. Plus, the arrival of broadband means that people have faster access to more information than ever before, and are able to catch up with TV programmes they've missed.

Chat rooms give people the chance to communicate over great distances with lots of people. This can spread information and gossip about sports stars. However, despite the opportunity to interact with many people remotely, chat rooms can encourage a sedentary and lonely lifestyle.

On fan sites, people who are keen to follow a sport or club can sign up and receive news of their favourite team or player. A fan site means teams and individuals can have a global presence, for example, the Spurs Singapore fan site. The sites carry advertisements which provide revenue. The typical contents of a fan site include:

- a forum to discuss the team
- blogs from players or fans
- surveys and match analysis
- deals on supporters' kit
- travel and accommodation for away matches
- competitions
- downloadable clips of action
- player profiles.

Merchandising

An important function of the Internet is merchandising. This has boomed in recent years. Almost every kind of sports goods is for sale online, from team kit to specialist footwear or equipment. This has led to the demise of some high street chains and smaller sports shops. All large club stadiums have merchandising shops and these are mirrored with online sales.

Assessment activity 13.2

Using material from the text and your own research, prepare a report which describes and explains:

- the positive influence that the media has had on a selected sport in the UK
- some negative impacts of the media.

Grading tips

- To attain **P2** link your description to real examples you have researched and found. Create a logical set of headings for your report. Make sure you choose an appropriate sport that has plenty of examples.

- To attain **M2** you must clearly explain both the positive and negatives influences, using clear subheadings and real examples. Make sure you choose an appropriate sport that has plenty of examples.

PLTS

When describing or explaining the influences of the media you will be using your **independent enquirer** skills. If you work in a group you can develop your **effective participator** skills.

Functional skills

By word processing your report you are providing evidence towards skills in **English**. If you use the Internet for research, you are using your **ICT** skills and may also do so if your report includes graphics or multimedia content.

2.2 Technology

We live in a technological age – the era of gadgets and instant communication. Many of the devices invented have been sport specific or adapted to be sports' aids.

Clothing

A range of thermally efficient and breathable types of material have been developed for outdoor activities. Other examples are spin-offs from space technology such as waterproof Teflon-coated jackets. Gloves with a 'thinsulate' layer to help insulation from the cold are also available.

Fluorescent garments are often worn by sportsmen and women to improve visibility and safety. Some rugby players use special gloves with a 'grippy' surface to increase their catching ability; climbers wear sticky boots to aid their friction footholds.

Some controversy has also arisen over the buoyancy and slipperiness of some swimsuits, with a call to ban them and revert all records to 2007 levels before they were approved.

Personal equipment

Outdoor sports participants can use a range of devices including hand-held satellite navigation aids and pedometers. Pagers and mobile phones might come into this category as well as personal organisers and notepads. Ski poles have been adapted for older walkers and reaction sunglasses help provide increased protection from the sun. Home-based exercise has improved with the production of modern gym equipment. You can also consider the level of technology that goes into our sports shoes. Lightweight personal protection for high impact sports has been created, including body armour for American football players, padding for cricketers and protection for hockey goalkeepers, and helmets for all.

How do you feel about clothing technology that improves performance?

Cameras

Digitisation has allowed camera technology to move forward massively. The benefits to sport are very obvious, from movement analysis to image creation and the capturing of sporting moments by nano-photography which freezes the action in great detail.

By using camera replay systems, critical incidents can be analysed to give the 'correct' decision or help the referee or umpire to make their decision, for example, rugby tries, cricket shots and run outs. The third eye principle can capture and retain the moment which the human eye and brain cannot achieve in quite the same way. In the 2010 Winter Olympics the use of 'super slo-motion camera work' allowed us to watch the 'aerials' in fine detail so that we could better appreciate their technique and complexity.

Analysis

Analysis in sport has benefited from new technology. Drug testing capabilities have been enhanced in the race to analyse and identify the drug-takers in sport. The world anti-doping agency has benefited as 80 per cent of tests are random and can now be done outside the laboratory. Lord Coe commented that an Olympics in London without drug cheats looks impossible, but added: 'We are winning the battle, the technology is much better, and we will present the best possible environment for a drug-free Games in London.'

Computer and video analysis means that athletes' techniques can be studied carefully, while biomechanics are much more easily understood for those studying in this area. One such system is Dartfish.

You are probably most familiar with Computer Games Applications of new technology. Many are sports-based and interactive giving everyone, even the couch-bound, the chance to take some exercise. Examples include Wii Fit and Wii Sports.

Lactate threshold measurement is another technological advance which helps with training. A small hand-held kit is now available to help measure the maximal lactate steady state (MLSS) that an athlete can continue at for an extended period of time without slowing. Lactate threshold is the best known indicator of endurance performance.

Hyperbaric chambers are available in portable form so that users can breathe higher levels of oxygen. Hyperbaric Oxygen Therapy (HBOT) is a painless procedure in which a person is exposed to increased pressure, thus allowing greater absorption of oxygen throughout the body tissues. This increased pressure allows more oxygen to reach the cells within the body leading to many healing and therapeutic benefits.

Computer software programmes now allow us to transfer data to and from our personal devices or the Internet. This has many applications for sports management such as equipment and facility management, maintenance scheduling and diagnostic tests. There are also secure line options and encryption services to ensure safety and privacy of data.

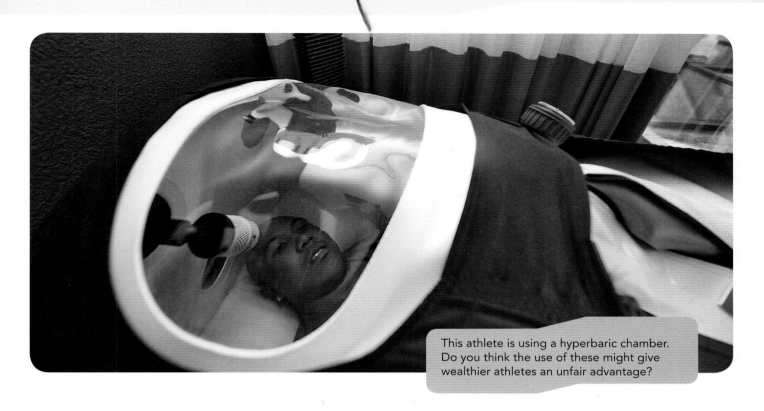

This athlete is using a hyperbaric chamber. Do you think the use of these might give wealthier athletes an unfair advantage?

Assessment activity 13.3   BTEC

Using material from the text and your own research, prepare a magazine article which describes or explains the effects of technology on a selected sport in the UK. **P3** **M3**

Grading tips

- To attain **P3** you might use some pictures, i.e. photos of technology being used by an athlete to help them analyse or improve their performance. Choose an appropriate sport that has plenty of examples.

- To attain **M3** make clear explanations in your article (look at some real ones for guidance). Try to use several technological dimensions.

PLTS

When describing and explaining you will be using your **independent enquirer** skills. If you discuss effects with others, you can develop your **effective participator** skills.

Functional skills

By carrying out research and writing your magazine article you are providing evidence towards skills in **English**. If you use the Internet for research and photographs to illustrate it you are showing evidence of your **ICT** skills. You may also do this by using an electronic medium to support your presentation.

3. Know how contemporary issues affect sport

Sport in society has transformed since the 18th century. But it still carries issues and some are as old as sport itself (racism and sexism to name two); others reflect our technological age (for example, the media and globalisation) and materialism.

3.1 What are contemporary issues?

Contemporary means 'current' and an issue can be described as 'a topic of discussion about which people have different views'. Some of the issues affecting sport our explored below.

Deviance

Deviant behaviour is a recognised violation of social norms – such as hooliganism, violence or verbal abuse. For some people, sport can provide a potential solution, or at least a pathway, to conformity and good citizenship. Many sport development schemes have been used to try and help change negative behaviour. **Deviance** can also be demonstrated in the desire to win or succeed at all costs – some athletes will cheat or use drugs to enhance their performance.

Playing sport is a good way to help with anti-crime initiatives. Sport can help people understand discipline and rules, and may help to build confidence and other social skills. Sports development schemes often adopt an anti-crime agenda – crime rates drop when more constructive sports are available, especially in deprived areas of major cities. Voluntary organisations and police forces have been using this tool for inclusion for many years.

Sport can help tackle **social exclusion**. It has been used successfully to draw people back into normal, healthy habits and give them opportunities to improve their lives.

Remember

The social and economic cost of crime to the nation is enormous – over a quarter of the working age population has a previous conviction, and the annual cost of crime is over £50 billion.

Gamesmanship is the cynical side of sport. With the pressure to win in many sports, gamesmanship has become all too frequent. Can you think of an example?

Case study: Crime reduction through sport

One specific project typifies many others – a partnership scheme between Nacro, the national crime reduction charity, Chelmsford Borough Council, Chelmsford College and other community-based organisations. An extract in 2009 shows some of its aims which again typify many others:

- To provide holiday sports courses for young people during the Easter holiday period.

- To provide sporting activities for young people during the summer holiday period in conjunction with our partners.

- Deliver one-off events throughout the year including an Extreme Sports Day at Essex University and an Anti-Racism Event as part of the FA's initiative to 'Kick racism out of football'.

Source: www.chelmsford.gov.uk

1. **What do you think are the main reasons for young people turning to crime and vandalism in the first place, and why do you think sport is seen as such a good solution?**

2. **What other benefits to society will there be if more people are involved, and have better access, to sport?**

Key terms

Deviance – cheating or bad behaviour.

Social exclusion – feeling as though you are outside normal society.

Gamesmanship – when dubious tactics are employed in a sport to gain an advantage over the opposition, e.g. intimidation (this can be psychological and/or physical) or an attempt to disrupt concentration.

When it comes to taking drugs to enhance sporting performance, we tend to think of the high-level athletes who have been caught, but there are many other players who just want to build strength or body mass. There are many issues here:

- It is unethical to enhance performance using drugs.
- It breaks rules and codes of conduct.
- There could be long-term effects on health.
- The costs of policing it.

Can you think of other doping issues? The list of banned drug classes is shown in Table 13.2.

Some supplements and medicines contain banned substances and this has caught out athletes who have tested positive after taking medication, for example, the Olympic skier Alain Baxter who claimed that a tiny trace of methamphetamine had originated from a Vicks inhaler. Further information can be obtained from the World Anti-Doping Agency (WADA).

Education and sport in schools

Physical education (PE) and sport in schools has become a key issue for everyone involved in education. Targets have been set for schools to create more time for PE (75–90 minutes per week in primary schools). For secondary schools, the amount of time and range of activities are more flexible but most aim for a minimum of two hours of PE per week. The standard types of PE and sport on offer are:

- gymnastics
- invasion games
- swimming
- outdoor activities
- net and wall games
- striking and fielding games.

Table 13.2: Consider the underlying risks for drug takers shown by the side effects.

Drugs/banned substance	Taken to:	Side effects
Stimulants	- increase alertness - improve concentration - increase aggressiveness - decrease fatigue - shorten reaction time	- Increased cholesterol level - Increased risk of heart attack, hypertension, stroke, liver and kidney damage, jaundice, depression, aggression, mood swings, acne and skin disease
Peptide hormones and growth factors	- stimulate growth and cell reproduction and regeneration - increase muscle mass - increase energy levels	- Increased risk of diabetes - Joint swelling - Joint pain - Carpal tunnel syndrome
Anabolic agents	- create lean body mass	- Nausea and dizziness - Headaches - Muscle cramps - Heart flutters
Diuretics	- reduce weight - draw off water to mask other drugs in the body	- Dehydration and cramps - Dizziness - Heart damage - Kidney failure

These activities aim to:

- give pupils skills and confidence
- create a lifelong learning attitude/interest in sport
- give regular activity and exercise sessions
- help pupils to work in a team
- help pupils to learn to follow rules and play fair
- give pupils a chance to take part in activities away from home and outdoors.

Child protection

The safety and security of children has become a major issue for our society. Legislation under the Child Protection Act of 1999 was brought in to give guidance on this. Sports governing bodies and clubs are among the most proactive in terms of child protection. Most clubs must now have a child protection policy in place before they can become affiliated.

Sport England and the National Society for the Prevention of Cruelty to Children (NSPCC) have guidelines for clubs to follow. Every person working with children in a sports context must undergo a Criminal Records Bureau check to determine whether they have a criminal past or record that would make them unsuitable to work with children. Each school or club needs to have a procedure to follow if anything suspicious happens.

Health initiatives

Recently, much attention has been paid to the health risks associated with obesity in young people. Television programmes such as Jamie's School Dinners have highlighted bad eating habits and a lack of exercise as the main causes of obesity. As a result, there have been campaigns to try and encourage young people to eat healthier school meals and take more exercise. Change4Life is one example.

Racism

According to the Commission for Racial Equality, **racism** means 'holding biased or unfair views about other nationalities or ethnically different people, and treating them as inferior'. Unfortunately, incidents of racism in sport and our modern multicultural society are still common – for example, racist comments at football matches directed at non-white or non-UK players. The Football Association has been running a strong campaign for several years called 'Let's Kick

Racism Out of Football' (www.kickitout.org) and in 2000 a Racial Equality Charter for Sport was launched (www.sportingequals.com).

Commercialisation

Commercialisation means making sports into a more marketable 'commodity' that can be sold to audiences, spectators or participants, usually for a profit. Examples include:

- selling the television rights to a big match, e.g. the UEFA Champions League
- selling official team strips and other merchandising
- package deals to travel to a big event, e.g. the Winter Olympics
- the chance to gamble, e.g. online betting.

Sport as a global spectacle

Globalisation is a result of a number of factors – commercialisation, global communications, travel and also professionalism, which allows players to compete around the world in their sport or to play for teams in any country. The sports landscape, takes in the whole globe, and we are now able to watch sport 24/7 from around the world – its big business.

Take it further

Global sport – who wins?

Discuss with a partner, then in a group of three or four, and then as a class:

- Who receives the profits from global sports events? Does globalisation mean that we need huge international federations to run our sports?
- Do the television channels show us everything we want to see – or just what they want us to see?
- Are sport's interests really at the heart of it all?

Politics

In the present sports climate, politics is having an impact in several ways. In a positive way, the support of the UK government has helped to win the bid for the London Olympics. This support continues with funding. In a negative way, governments and human rights campaigners have not always been in favour of athletes competing against other countries which have a poor human rights or safety record, for example, South Africa, China, Uganda and North Korea. You will probably recall the protest about China's human rights record when the Olympic flag was carried through London in 2008. Consider also the withdrawal of the Tongan Football team by their President after the shooting at the African Cup of Nations in Angola in January 2010.

At regional and local levels the evidence of 'political positivism' can be seen by the funding for regeneration schemes that are driven by sport aims, for example, Leigh sports village. However, was this a vote catcher?

Religion and culture

The UK is a multicultural society. Religious and other cultural issues present challenges for sport.

- Muslim women have to wear full body coverage to play and compete and no bodily contact is allowed.
- Other religions may not wish followers to play during specific fasting or prayer periods.
- Many sports facilities now provide prayer rooms.
- Other cultural barriers might be language, lack of education and little or no knowledge of British sports.

Some specific associations have been set up to try and overcome cultural barriers such as the British Asian Rugby Association (BARA) and The Women's Sport and Fitness Foundation (WSFA).

Gender issues

Gender differences in sport have a long history – sport was a male-dominated sector (and some would argue it still is). Women have had to fight to compete in many sports. Men held the opinion that women were too weak or frail to compete in men's sports – or should be looking after the home and children. The Victorians saw women as objects of beauty that should not expose flesh, perspire or be exposed to contact sports.

Participation rates in sport among women and girls are much lower than for men. Reasons for this gender gap can be grouped as practical, personal and social and cultural.

Minorities can face high levels of stigma from their own communities, as well as the wider population. This is particularly so for the lesbian, gay, bisexual and transgender (LGBT) community.

Assessment activity 13.4

Imagine you are a trainee sports reporter for a local newspaper, eager to make a splash with a series of articles over the next few weeks. You have chosen four main areas you will write about to investigate and expose underlying issues.

1. Select from the topic headings in this outcome (see pages 340–343). You should also select one sport to focus on.

2. Prepare four articles for your paper, including the main issues, research undertaken and giving your views on what should be done.

Grading tips

- To attain **P4** you could use previous newspaper articles to help you. But ensure you show the effects and don't just describe the source. Focus on impacts.

- To attain **M4** give good detail and show your understanding of the issues on your selected sport and its effects.

- To attain **D1** evaluate the issues with examples and go on to show the effects clearly and in depth.

PLTS

When you analyse what issues you will focus on you are likely to produce evidence of your **independent enquirer** skills. You will be using your **creative thinker** skills when you review contemporary issues. If you work in a group you can develop your **effective participator** and **team worker** skills. Working independently will produce evidence that you are a **self-manager**.

Functional skills

By describing explaining or evaluating these selected issues and writing these articles you are providing evidence towards skills in **English**. If you use a computer or software to produce your articles and to help you research, you will improve your **ICT** skills.

4. Understand the cultural influences and barriers that affect participation in sports activities

Over the centuries, differences in culture have influenced what, how and why sport is played. There are many barriers which prevent people from playing, some personal, some material, and some cultural. Many agencies have derived strategies and initiatives to help encourage and give access to sporting opportunities in our society.

4.1 Barriers to participation

Time

Lack of time is the most frequently cited reason for not participating or taking exercise. To take part in sport, people may have to juggle priorities such as work, parenting and domestic duties. This creates a spectrum with dedicated people at one end and non-participants at the other – all may wish to participate but some have no free time.

Resources

Resources fall into three main groups: financial, physical and people. The two ends of the resource spectrum show the divide that has always existed in sport and leisure participation (Figure 13.6).

Fitness

Lack of fitness is often the excuse given by people who say they cannot take part in sport. They probably need to build up their fitness to help them participate. Initially, the problem is finding the motivation to do so. This needs to be tackled with a positive mindset and a gradual approach.

Ability

Lack of ability can prevent someone from taking part at a higher level, but it should not prevent them from finding a sport that they can enjoy. Getting some coaching to improve ability, or joining a class with a friend, is a good strategy.

Lifestyle

A busy lifestyle is often a reason for not participating in exercise or sport. We have a culture of long work hours in the UK, where people who are eager to impress colleagues, or get promoted, stay late at work. This eats into their leisure time. Prioritising areas other than work might help them to achieve a better work–life balance. On the other side of the argument, some people will choose certain sports because of their status, for example, golf or sailing. Conversely, this might put others off joining.

Medical conditions

People with genuine medical conditions need to take exercise under supervision or guidance. Many do so under GP referral schemes, where a trained instructor looks after their needs, perhaps at a local gym, after being referred by their doctor. For those recovering from an operation, exercise can be of help, for example, the Walk to Health campaign.

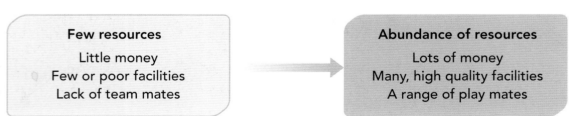

Few resources
Little money
Few or poor facilities
Lack of team mates

Abundance of resources
Lots of money
Many, high quality facilities
A range of play mates

Figure 13.6: How is a lack of resources a barrier to participation in sport?

Walking is Britain's most popular physical activity – which do you think is the next most popular?

4.2 Cultural influences

The influences and differences in our society relating to sports participation stem from four main areas.

Gender difference

This has produced inequality in terms of access to and participation in sport. In the past, and still to an extent today, many women have been stereotyped into domestic roles, leaving fewer opportunities or activities suitable for them to participate in. During the 1980s a more enlightened and equal approach began to emerge, allowing women's participation in sports to blossom in the UK. This may have been spurred on by the equal pay act, feminist activists and the formation of women's only sports federations.

Ethnicity

Ethnicity refers to a population whose members identify with each other, usually on the basis of a common genealogy or ancestry, and who are united by common cultural, linguistic or religious traits. It can influence what or whether we play or succeed in sport, other people's attitudes and progress.

Age

In 2006 new legislation was passed making it illegal to discriminate against anyone on the basis of age. For older people in the sports industry, this means they should be able to continue working for longer if they wish, be just as eligible for promotion as a younger candidate, and have the same terms and conditions of contract.

In terms of participation, as people age they take less exercise so greater encouragement is needed here.

Socio-economic groups

Socio-economic groups are a concept created in the 20th century to help classify society into different types. This is basically a crude measure, based on income and job type, which produces the categories in Table 13.3. These groups can be useful in considering participation rates and reasons for non-participation.

Key terms

Ethnicity – belonging to a group of people who identify themselves as from one nationality or culture.

Socio-economic groups – ways of grouping people according to income and job.

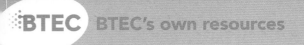

Table 13.3: Socio-economic groups. Discuss which categories are most likely to participate in sport and why.

Classification	Type of job
1.1	Employers in industry, commerce, etc. (large establishments)
1.2	Managers in local and central government, industry, commerce, etc. (large establishments)
2.1	Employers in industry, commerce, etc. (small establishments)
2.2	Managers in industry, commerce, etc. (small establishments)
3	Professional workers – self-employed
4	Professional workers – employees
5.1	Intermediate non-manual workers – ancillary workers and artists
5.2	Intermediate non-manual workers – foremen and supervisors non-manual
6	Junior non-manual workers
7	Personal service workers
8	Foremen and supervisors – manual
9	Skilled manual workers
10	Semi-skilled manual workers
11	Unskilled manual workers
12	Own account workers (other than professional)
13	Farmers – employers and managers
14	Farmers – own account
15	Agricultural workers
16	Members of armed forces
(17)	Inadequately described and not stated occupations

Source:www.gov.statistics.uk

4.3 Strategies and initiatives

A number of sports-related agencies have designed a range of strategies (plans) and initiatives to help people participate.

National

Game Plan was a national government plan for sport, created in 2002. It detailed the government's vision and strategy for sport from a mass participation and a performance perspective up until 2020 (note that it was published before the awarding of the 2012 Olympic Games to London). To research Game Plan, see www.culture.gov.uk. Try to identify whether a new strategy has been put in place after the 2010 election.

Every Child Matters is a government strategy which proposes a range of measures to reform and improve children's care nationally. The aim is to protect children and to maximise opportunities open to young people to improve their life chances and fulfil their potential, particularly through sport and out-of-school activities.

Sporting Equals is a national initiative which is working towards creating a society where:

* people from ethnic minorities can influence and participate equally in sport
* understanding of racial equality issues that impact on sport is high
* providers of sport work towards a fully integrated and inclusive society
* cultural diversity is recognised and celebrated.

The Talented Athlete Scholarship Scheme (TASS) is a national DCMS (government)-funded programme that is a partnership between sport and higher and further education. The programme distributes awards to talented athletes who are committed to combining sport and education.

Plan for Sport 2001 was the 2001 action plan based on the document *A Sporting Future For All*, published by the government in 2000. It was followed by Game Plan and Playing to Win in 2008. These action plans deal with initiatives to develop sport in education, community and the modernisation of organisations involved in sport. This is an ongoing strategy, and the DCMS website gives regular updates on its progress and the Olympics.

Coaching Task Force 2002 was set up by the DCMS to look at ways of improving coaching. It published a report in July 2002, with the following targets:

- to implement a UK Coaching Certificate by January 2007
- to have 45 Coach Development Officers in post by April 2005
- to get 3000 Community Sports Coaches in post by the end of 2006
- research to be produced on 'Sports Coaching in the UK'.

Check their website (www.sportscoachuk.org) to see what was achieved.

Local

Girls First was a scheme run locally in secondary schools in Wales, giving £1000 to each qualifying school to provide after-school activities, specifically targeting girls' participation. It was hoped that by providing enjoyable activities on a regular basis, more girls would be encouraged to form positive habits about exercising and keeping healthy.

TOP Programmes was probably the best known scheme to help develop sport across England. The initiative, led by the Youth Sports Trust, aimed to supply schools with a sports bag and trained leaders, giving them ready access to resources for sport.

Active Sports is an ongoing national development programme, supported by Sport England, that aims to help young people get more from their participation in sport – from grassroots to high-level young performers. The programme is based around targeted sports,

Kiran Matharu is not just unusual for a golfer; she is the first female British Asian sports champion. Which other top sports people come from an Asian background?

including basketball, cricket, girls' football, hockey, netball and rugby union. Each local area is encouraged to devise its own content to suit local needs and facilities. This programme is now coming to an end and being replaced by funding for Whole Sports Plans involving schools and clubs.

Sportsmark is an award made to outstanding schools for sports provision. Derived from the success of Sportsmark, there are several others in operation now too: Activemark for primary schools, Sportsmark for secondary schools and Sports Partnership Mark for independent schools. Schools will receive the award if at least 90 per cent of pupils across the school are doing at least two hours of sport.

Assessment activity 13.5

Imagine you have recently been employed as a sports development officer for a local authority. You have been asked to put together a plan for the multicultural borough that you look after. Carry out the following tasks:

1. Explain the full range of barriers to participation in sports that people of all abilities, age groups, income groups, genders and ethnic types experience. **P5**

2. Explain three cultural influences that have an impact on sports participation. **P6**

3. Describe, explain and evaluate three strategies or initiatives which relate to sports participation. **P7** **M5** **D2**

Grading tips

- To attain **P5** you need to cover a good range of examples in your description, perhaps using case studies to illustrate or support your point.

- To attain **P6** your descriptions of three cultural influences can be drawn from a range. Make sure you are thorough and clear when you present your evidence.

- To attain **P7** there are many strategies and initiatives currently available for you to use. Perhaps try some contrasting ones. Keep your description clear.

- To attain **M5** good explanations will be needed and clear links to participation established.

- To attain **D2** an in-depth analysis will be important. Evaluation means you need to do some analysis and get your facts right.

PLTS

Working independently will produce evidence of your **self-manager** skills. Evidence of your **independent enquirer** skills will come through as you prepare your material explaining the influences and barriers. **Creative thinker** evidence could be found as you explain influences and barriers clearly, maybe making contrasts. If group work is involved that should produce evidence of your **effective participator** skills and some **team worker** evidence too.

Functional skills

By presenting or writing and discussing your plan, you are providing evidence towards skills in **English**. If you use a computer to produce your plan and to help you research, e.g. to produce tables or images, you will provide evidence of **ICT** skills.

Matt Ison
Sports development officer

Matt Ison works for a northern council's sport development department. The district he is responsible for has some rundown estates, but there are a few success stories about professional athletes from his patch who have done well. With the increase in immigration to the area, he has been faced with some new challenges in the last year.

To do his job effectively Matt needs a range of knowledge at his fingertips and lots of contacts.

Matt is regularly in touch with Sport England and local schools' sports partnerships to see where funding might be found or what their development plans are. He also uses the media to help him publicise programmes and events in the borough. He is regularly on the radio on Fridays and often appears in the Saturday sport pages attending these events.

He has had two big challenges recently:

- First of all, he has had to find ways to help new immigrants integrate with local communities. Some football games have helped with this which Matt managed to get sponsored by a local firm.

- The second challenge sees him trying get more kids into clubs to keep them active, but as many of them come from poorer families this has not been easy. He has been able to test their fitness levels before and after playing using some new gadgets – this has helped to keep them interested.

Local politicians have supported Matt in these initiatives and one or two former local players have come back to visit and to help with publicity.

Think about it!

- What other programmes do you think Matt could try for his area?
- Which governing bodies might help him?
- What sort of training do you think Matt went through to get where he is today?

Just checking

1. What was sport in pre-industrial society generally like?
2. How important were the public schools in helping to develop sport for society?
3. Can you explain 'rationalisation' and 'regulation' developments in sport?
4. Give names in full for the following – DCMS, CCPR and NGB.
5. Give reasons why sport is often called 'big business' these days.
6. Name the three main sectors in the sports industry.
7. Give two examples of new technology helping sport to develop
8. Give four ways in which the media can affect sports.
9. Explain how 'racism' and 'sexism' can affect participation in sports, giving examples of each.
10. List five barriers to participation in sports.

edexcel ⣿

Assignment tips

- Some of the issues that affect sport come from society, for example, participation (an example would be that of more children playing on computers and playing less sport).

- Some issues in society are fostered by sport, for example, gambling. Be clear which is which.

- Whichever direction or source the issue comes from there might be positive and negative outcomes – explore both in your work, for example, when considering issues connected to the media.

- There is a government drive to improve social issues through sport. These issues are often deeply embedded – try to uncover them.

- The sporting framework of the UK has grown up in a piecemeal way over centuries so we are left with a fragmented patchwork of provision – that should come across in your work.

- Our multicultural society presents new challenges, especially in city areas. Try to identify and assess these to add value to your work.

- Overall your work will be improved if you: ask questions of your tutor; discuss ideas with others before you begin; read the briefs carefully; carry out thorough research. The information is out there so find it!

Credit value: 10

15 Sports injuries

Sports injuries can be a major cause of physical pain, frustration, heartache and financial loss for players of all sporting disciplines and at a variety of performance levels. However, technological advances in the diagnosis and treatment of injuries are being developed all the time. This is due partly to a dramatic increase in the number of individuals studying a wide variety of sport and exercise disciplines as an academic subject. The huge amount of money involved in sport at the highest level has also contributed to major developments in the sports sciences on a worldwide scale.

In this unit you will investigate the identification of risks and the prevention of injuries. You will also examine the types, causes and symptoms of a range of injuries and the treatments available, identifying which methods are applicable. Putting into practice the knowledge that you will develop, you will produce an initial treatment plan, along with a long-term rehabilitation programme, for two commonly occurring sports injuries.

Learning outcomes

After completing this unit you should:

1. know how common sports injuries can be prevented by the correct identification of risk factors
2. know about a range of sports injuries and their symptoms
3. know how to apply methods of treating sports injuries
4. be able to plan and construct treatment and rehabilitation programmes for two common sports injuries.

Assessment and grading criteria

This table shows you what you must do in order to achieve a pass, merit or distinction grade, and where you can find activities in this book to help you.

To achieve a **pass** grade the evidence must show that you are able to:	To achieve a **merit** grade the evidence must show that, in addition to the pass criteria, you are able to:	To achieve a **distinction** grade the evidence must show that, in addition to the pass and merit criteria, you are able to:
P1 describe extrinsic and intrinsic risk factors in relation to sports injuries **See Assessment activity 15.1, page 358**	**M1** explain how risk factors can be minimised by utilisation of preventative measures **See Assessment activity 15.1, page 358**	
P2 describe preventative measures that can be taken in order to prevent sports injuries occurring **See Assessment activity 15.1, page 358**		
P3 describe the physiological responses common to most sports injuries **See Assessment activity 15.2, page 361**	**M2** explain the physiological and psychological responses common to most sports injuries **See Assessment activity 15.2, page 361**	**D1** analyse the physiological and psychological responses common to most sports injuries **See Assessment activity 15.2, page 361**
P4 describe the psychological responses common to sports injuries **See Assessment activity 15.2, page 361**		
P5 describe first-aid and common treatments used for four different types of sports injury **See Assessment activity 15.3, page 370**		
P6 design a safe and appropriate treatment and rehabilitation programme for two common sports injuries, with tutor support **See Assessment activity 15.4, page 374**	**M3** independently design a safe and appropriate treatment and rehabilitation programme for two common sports injuries **See Assessment activity 15.4, page 374**	**D2** evaluate the treatment and rehabilitation programme designed, justifying the choices and suggesting alternatives where appropriate **See Assessment activity 15.4, page 374**

How you will be assessed

Your assessment could be in the form of:

- presentations
- case studies
- practical tasks
- written assignments.

Don, 18-year-old rugby player

While competing in the national trials I suffered from a sprained shoulder joint. This left me very disappointed as I did not fulfil my full potential and make the squad, and I could not train or compete for a while. Rehabilitation from my injury seemed to be taking a long time and I started to feel frustrated and disillusioned with my physical progress.

Through this unit I have developed a great deal of insight into the different stages of the rehabilitation process. This knowledge has made me realise the need for specific goals during rehabilitation and that my injury had, in reality, improved tremendously. My experiences throughout the unit also developed my appreciation that sports injuries produce both psychological and physical impacts on athletes.

Over to you!

1. Have you ever suffered from an injury and wondered what physiological responses were taking place within your body?

2. After suffering an injury have you ever considered the various treatment and rehabilitation methods available?

3. What aspect of this unit are you particularly interested in?

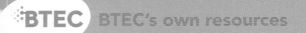

1. Know how common sports injuries can be prevented by the correct identification of risk factors

Warm-up

How can injuries be prevented or minimised?

The type and severity of injuries vary greatly between different sports, with contact sports often having higher rates of traumatic injury. Various individuals, as well as athletes, can help to reduce the likelihood of accidents. The most important issue surrounding sports injuries is how to prevent them, or minimise the severity if they occur. Can you think of ways in which to achieve this?

Sports injuries can be caused by a variety of different factors which fall into two categories – **extrinsic** and **intrinsic**. Identifying the risk factors can dramatically reduce the chances of someone developing the different types of injury.

Key terms

Extrinsic – a risk or force from outside the body. These are external forces, such as from objects or other individuals making contact with someone

Intrinsic – a risk or force from within the body. These are internal forces, which are stresses from within the body.

📱 1.1 Extrinsic risk factors

Coaching

If a coach demonstrates poor communication and leadership methods and suggests incorrect techniques and exercise, this can pose risks for sports players. The rules of sports are designed by the governing bodies, in part, to protect the players. Non-adherence to these will involve risks for both the player breaking the rules and other players participating.

Incorrect technique

Using inappropriate or incorrect techniques is an injury risk. As well as poor sports techniques, incorrect methods of setting up and lifting and handling equipment will cause risks to those involved.

Environmental factors

Weather can have a huge impact on playing conditions in sport. Poor playing conditions potentially increase the risk of injury. For example:

- slips and falls from slippery surfaces
- falling on uneven ground
- cold conditions which make playing surfaces harder and potentially dangerous
- poor conditions may mean the style of play may change, and create further risks to players via the movements that they carry out.

Clothing and footwear

Not wearing the correct equipment for your sport will create major extrinsic risk factors. Examples of incorrect equipment include wearing:

- the wrong footwear for the activity or playing surface
- damaged, or too much or too little, protective equipment
- the wrong protective equipment for the sport.

Safety hazards

It is important for coaches, support staff and players to be aware of hazards and risks associated with the activities being undertaken. Various health and safety considerations must be applied to all activities both before and during participation.

- **Environment** – a safety check of the sporting environment should be carried out before a game or training. It is vital to remove any dangerous objects, or any slippery or uneven areas of a playing surface, along with a general consideration of potential risks.

- **Sports equipment** – the equipment we use as training aids, for protection, and to enhance performance can also act as a potential extrinsic risk factor, and it is essential that equipment is checked by players and coaches before use. A referee should also check equipment before the players enter the playing area (for example, checking studs before a rugby or football match).

- **Misuse of equipment** – the misuse and abuse of equipment will cause risks to sports players – equipment is specifically designed to do a particular job. Tampering with or modifying equipment will make it less useful and often dangerous.

- **First-aid provision** – a lack of preparation for any potential accidents on the sports field may cause undue risks to sports players. Experienced first-aiders and/or medical professionals and, crucially, a fully equipped first-aid kit should be available at all sports sessions.

- **Safety checklist** – this is a useful tool to make sure all activities and equipment are safe.

1.2 Intrinsic risk factors

Training effects

Due to anatomical differences and abnormalities (such as muscle imbalance), undue stresses can be placed on different parts of the body, potentially causing injuries.

Inadequate or poor preparation for sports training and competition places risks on athletes. It is essential to prepare for sport both mentally and physically before participating. The warm-up is an essential aspect of preparation for sport (Unit 14 Instructing physical activity and exercise, on the CD-ROM, pages 10–11). Appropriate flexibility is an important component of fitness, and a lack of flexibility will place physical stress and risk on an athlete. Inappropriate general fitness levels will also yield intrinsic risks. Particularly when combined with other intrinsic risks, overuse injuries are also potential risk factors athletes must be aware of.

Individual variables

Having the correct fitness levels to play your chosen sport minimises the risks of injury. Playing at an appropriate level is also critical, as playing sport with individuals of either superior or inferior fitness levels and/or age and physical development will involve risk to yourself and others.

Your anatomy can predispose you to certain injuries and a history of certain injuries can make you more susceptible to anatomical abnormalities. A history of injury increases the intrinsic risk of that injury recurring during future sports participation. Differences or problems associated with your anatomy are classed as an intrinsic risk factor.

Insufficient sleep before training and competition is another risk. Being alert and refreshed for sport is a key ingredient for focus and success in training and competition. A crucial method of preparing for physical activity is sufficient nutrition (including hydration). Not eating or drinking enough before an activity will cause serious risks to the body (see Unit 12 Sports nutrition).

Postural defects

Abnormal curvature of the spine is a potential risk that can become degenerative and inhibit sporting potential. Examples of such malalignment of the vertebrae include:

scoliosis – a lateral imbalance or sideways bending of the spine

kyphosis – an excessive arching of the upper part of the spine

lordosis – an excessive inward curve at the lower part of the spine.

These problems can occur independently or sometimes together to a certain degree.

Overuse and insufficient recovery following exercise and excessive strain on a body part can also exacerbate injuries and worsen existing postural defects.

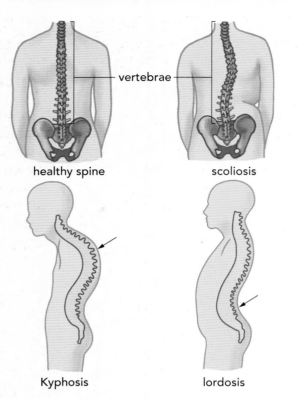

healthy spine

scoliosis

Kyphosis

lordosis

Figure 15.1: What measures can be used to minimise the risks and severity of vertebral malalignment?

1.3 Preventative measures

The role of the coach

The coach will play a major role, particularly for younger athletes, in preventing mishaps on the playing field. As a physical trainer, sports leader or sports coach, you must:

- have up to date knowledge of all your players' abilities, including strengths and weaknesses in their physicality and skills

- have up to date and relevant knowledge and qualifications in the sport that you are coaching

- be able to adapt your coaching style based on ability, age, fitness, gender and motivation of the athletes being coached

- stress the importance of health and safety in well planned training sessions and match situations – communication skills are vital for all coaches

- check that all equipment is safe to use, that it is being used correctly, and that the environment is safe for the activity being undertaken

Activity: Intrinsic or extrinsic?

Complete the table below to check your understanding of the categorisation of risk factors.

Table 15.1: Categorisation of risk factors.

Risk factor	Intrinsic (I) or extrinsic (E)?
Lack of organisation for an event	
Inadequate preparation for a game	
Muscular imbalance	
Postural defects	
Poor technique	
Poor coaching and/or leadership	
Playing surfaces	
Age	
Inadequate fitness levels	
Overuse	
Growth and development	
Environment (weather)	
Insufficient flexibility	
A history of previous injury	
Nutrition	
Sleep disturbances	

- ensure that players are aware of all governing body guidelines and adhere to the rules and regulations that have been set out
- ensure sufficient first-aid provision is available for all training and competition scenarios – this is critically important
- make a detailed assessment of the risks of all activities.

Activity: Risk fact sheet

In small groups, produce a fact sheet explaining the different types of risks associated with sporting activity. Include a section indicating the roles of different individuals in minimising extrinsic and intrinsic risk factors.

Equipment and environment

As previously highlighted, a thorough risk assessment of the training and competition environment must be carried out. It is also important to go through this procedure for the equipment that is used (for example, protective equipment). In many sports, the protective equipment available has changed dramatically over the years. Technological advances in the materials available and biomechanical analysis techniques (research and analysis of movement) have allowed dramatic improvements in the quality of protective equipment available. Advances have been in both specific protection of body parts, and limiting the negative impact of the protection on playing performance (such as excess weight and decreased range of movement).

Sports players need to ensure that specialist protective equipment is used correctly. If it is used incorrectly, this can be a hazard, putting yourself and other players at risk. When using different types of protective equipment, you should:

- ensure that the equipment is thoroughly checked prior to use
- use the equipment only for the sport for which it is designed
- use only the correct size
- not share your personal equipment (for example, boots, pads, etc.) with other people
- not use damaged equipment
- not make modifications to equipment

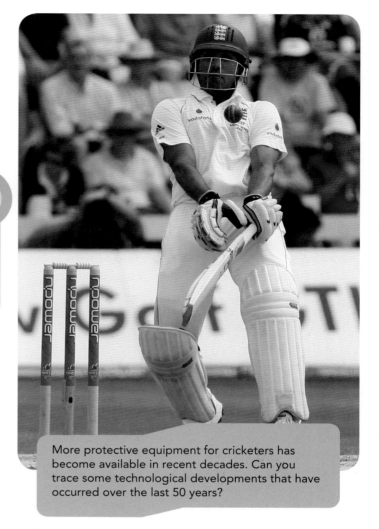

More protective equipment for cricketers has become available in recent decades. Can you trace some technological developments that have occurred over the last 50 years?

- be aware that protective equipment does not make you invincible
- use the equipment for both practice and competition
- be aware that some equipment can protect both you and other players.

Take it further

Research protective equipment

The protective equipment for many sports has changed dramatically over the years. Choose three sports and highlight the developments in equipment.

Remember

Many individuals can play a role in preventing injuries – including players, coaches, support staff and parents, among others.

Assessment activity 15.1

You are a trainee working with the coach of a local youth sports team (choose a sport that is relevant to your background). Considering all the various risk factors associated with sports injuries, you are going to describe the range of measures you could put in place to prevent injuries to players in your team.

1. Describe extrinsic and intrinsic risk factors in relation to sports injuries. **P1**

2. Write a detailed explanation of how risk factors can be minimised with the use of preventative measures. **M1**

3. Describe preventative measures that can be taken in order to prevent sports injuries occurring. **P2**

Grading tips

- To attain **P1** break down your answers into a table of extrinsic and intrinsic risk factors and how they can lead to sports injuries.

- To attain **M1** write a detailed explanation of the relationship between specific preventative measures and the risk factors they relate to.

- To attain **P2** highlight the different individuals involved, and explain their role in injury prevention. Explain the different tasks that should be done before a sporting activity (for example, equipment and playing area checks).

PLTS

If you describe sports injury risk factors and preventative methods you can develop your skills as an **independent enquirer**, **creative thinker** and **self-manager**.

Functional skills

If you describe the range of measures you could put in place to prevent injuries to players in your team you could provide evidence of your **ICT** and **English** skills.

2. Know about a range of sports injuries and their symptoms

Knowledge of the signs and symptoms of different sports injuries is vital to ensure the correct treatment is applied from the onset of the problem. You should try and gain as much knowledge as possible about the injury, as early as possible, so the best care can be implemented at each stage of treatment.

2.1 Physiological responses

Key term

Physiological response – the body's physical mechanisms that respond when an injury takes place. These are initiated to repair and protect the damaged tissue.

Damaged tissue

As soon as an injury takes place, the body responds in a number of ways. Damage to body tissue initiates the primary damage response mechanism. The two main signs and symptoms are pain and inflammation. Causes such as external trauma, overload (this is excessive use of one or more of the FITT principles, see page 242), repeated load, pressure and friction can cause inflammation, which is associated with the majority of sports injuries. Inflammation is caused by a number of factors, which trigger other signs and symptoms:

- accumulation of fluid surrounding the injury

- redness due to an increase in blood flow

- tender to the touch
- impaired functioning and range of motion (ROM).

When you bleed because of an injury, the blood clots to initiate the healing process. Platelets, which are cells within the blood, are activated by chemical reactions when trauma causes blood loss. These platelets make the blood sticky, and quickly cause a clot as they stick to the surface of the blood vessels. The clotting mechanism is important as this process acts as a preliminary phase of the healing process.

Bleeding is a major physiological response to all injuries. When an acute injury occurs to the body, the damaged tissue will bleed into the surrounding tissues. The amount of bleeding that takes place will be specific to the type and severity of injury. There are two types of haematoma:

- intermuscular haematoma – bleeding occurs within the compartment of the muscle, but does not seep into the surrounding tissue
- intramuscular haematoma – blood escapes into the surrounding tissue (for example, different muscle compartments).

Scanning electron micrograph of an activated blood platelet among red blood cells (unactivated platelets are smooth and oval-shaped) – platelets clump together to prevent bleeding and assist in clot formation (magnification: × 10,2000). What other substances are present in blood and what are their roles?

The different types of haematoma are described in more detail on page 363.

Importance of scar tissue in the remodelling process

The remodelling process (the development of scar tissue) restores the tissue at the site of an injury as close as possible to its original state. From the time when an injury takes place, scar tissue starts to form. It is crucial that the correct treatments are applied to regain the original functioning of the body part. The more severe an injury, the more difficult it will be to restore damaged tissue to its original state.

A more detailed explanation of the remodelling process is given on page 371.

Specific to injury

The signs and symptoms of various injuries may differ and this must be considered during initial diagnosis. For example, first, second and third degree sprains and strains will be different, and the physiological responses will be more pronounced.

2.2 Psychological responses

Response to injury

As well as the physiological responses of the body to injury, **psychological responses** can cause stress to an athlete. The way a person deals with an injury varies between individuals and some potential negative psychological responses are listed below.

> **Key term**
>
> **Psychological response** – the mental aspect of how an athlete copes and comes to terms with their injury and treatment.

- Fear – this can take many forms, including the fear of recurrence of an injury, and fear of not returning to full fitness.
- Stress and anxiety – this can be felt by an athlete during competition. If the athlete then suffers an injury, these feelings will be increased. As an injury progresses, concerns regarding the athlete's long- and short-term sporting prospects can become a psychological issue.

- Motivational issues – some injuries can take a long time to heal. As the duration of an injury increases, an athlete's motivation towards their sport may decrease.

- Depression – some athletes may demonstrate symptoms of clinical depression, such as decreased energy levels, constant sadness, withdrawal from social contact, etc.

- Anger – this can be towards oneself, the injury, and also other people (particularly if the injury is the fault of someone else).

- Decreased confidence – this is very common for athletes who are returning to training and competition. An athlete may suffer from a lack of confidence in their own skill levels, and decreased confidence in their fitness and ability to push their body physically.

- Denial – sometimes an athlete may try to deny the severity of an injury, and try to return to their sport too quickly. It is important that those supporting sports players (for example, coaches and family) are aware of the nature of the injury and take guidance from medical professionals.

- Frustration – this is a common issue for many athletes, particularly for long-term injury. The majority of sports players will crave to return to competition, and become frustrated by a lack of physical exercise and/or their specialist sport.

- Isolation from team mates – many team sports players' frustration can be exacerbated by the fact that they will not be involved in competition and training. This can lead to players becoming mentally withdrawn from their team.

Response to treatment and rehabilitation

As well as the athlete's physiological response to the injury, psychological responses also take place during rehabilitation and these can either hinder or assist the healing and rehabilitation processes. They include:

- anxiety – this can occur during many phases of an injury often due to uncertainty regarding the treatment and rehabilitation methods used

- frustration – when an athlete cannot see immediate improvements, or if there is a plateau in progress, frustration will often set in

- need for motivation – athletes will need to remain motivated during the often long road to recovery from injury. Those involved in rehabilitation can often support with such motivational issues

- use of goal setting – to ensure that athletes stay motivated, goal setting strategies are useful to keep track of progress and to see the improvements that have been made.

The psychological responses to a sports injury vary dramatically between individuals. Some may suffer no or few negative responses, whereas others may experience a number of psychological issues.

Remember

Often, when we consider sports injuries, we think of the traumatic injuries that occur due to a mishap on a specific occasion, in a game or in training. But many injuries are caused by an accumulation of stress over a period of time, or to overuse of a body part.

Chronic injuries are long-term injuries that have developed slowly.

Acute or traumatic injuries occur suddenly through instant trauma to the individual.

Examples could be:

- chronic – a runner develops a stress fracture due to repetitive overloading

- acute – an individual suffers a sprained ankle when cockling over while playing badminton.

Note: the severity of the injury is not determined by any of these categorisations.

Assessment activity 15.2

You are a first-aider working for a large local voluntary sports club. Produce a poster to raise awareness of how the body responds to a sports injury. Specifically you must cover the following:

1. Describe the physiological responses common to most sports injuries. **P3**

2. Describe the psychological responses common to sports injuries. **P4**

3. Explain the physiological and psychological effects common to most sports injuries. **M2**

4. Analyse the physiological and psychological responses common to most sports injuries. **D1**

Grading tips

- To attain **P3** you could include some specific examples of sports injuries you are familiar with.

- To attain **P4** think about the types of feeling that you may experience at the time of an injury taking

place and also as time progresses when you cannot train or compete. Brainstorm some ideas and provide a description of how some psychological reactions might affect a sportsperson.

- To attain **M2** you should explain *why* the physiological responses are taking place and their role in the healing process following an injury. You should also explain why any psychological issues occur, and the short- and long-term effects they may have on the athlete.

- To attain **D1** think about how the psychological and physiological factors interact when a sports player suffers an injury. Which individual characteristics may contribute to psychological effects of sports injuries in the long- and short-term? How can the body's physiological and psychological responses change during the different stages of the healing process?

PLTS

By producing a poster raising awareness of the physiological and psychological responses to sports injuries, you can develop your skills as an **independent enquirer**, **creative thinker** and **self-manager**.

Functional skills

By producing your poster you could provide evidence of your skills in **ICT** and **English**.

3. Know how to apply methods of treating sports injuries

Some common trends have emerged regarding the types of sporting injury. Collisions with other performers or objects, and twists or turns beyond the body's capabilities, are common causes of acute injury. Continued excessive force on a specific body part (for example, the knee) is associated with chronic injuries. This section details the anatomy and physiology of some common sports injuries. It is important that you are aware of the types of sport that may cause the different injuries outlined, and the specific preventative measures that can be taken.

Hard tissue injuries are to bones, joints and cartilage, whereas **soft tissue injuries** are to muscles, tendons, ligaments, internal organs and the skin. A combination of both hard and soft tissue injuries can occur, and this must be taken into consideration during the treatment and rehabilitation processes.

Key terms

Hard tissue injury – injury to bones, joints and cartilage.

Soft tissue injury – injury to muscles, tendons, ligaments, internal organs and skin.

3.1 Types of sports injury: hard tissue damage

Hard tissue injuries are particularly prevalent in contact sports such as football, and in individual sports such as skiing, gymnastics and riding. Hard tissue injuries include fractures, dislocations and cartilage injuries. Although sport can cause skeletal injuries, as with other parts of the anatomy, exercise can result in strengthening and thickening of bone, making injury less likely.

Fractures

A **fracture** is a partial or complete break in a bone – a common form of hard tissue injury. The way an injury takes place causes bones to break differently. Most are due to direct impact, but the site of the injury and how it occurs will result in different types of fracture. The treatments for different fractures are slightly different and so the correct category of injury has to be diagnosed. Fractures can be categorised into many different types.

- **Open and closed fractures** – a closed fracture is one where relatively little displacement of bone has occurred, which therefore does not cause much damage to the soft tissue surrounding the injury. An open fracture is one in which the fractured ends of the bone/s break through the skin. Open fractures have a high risk of infection, so it is vital that they are dealt with immediately after injury occurs. All fractures are relatively serious injuries, and specialist professional attention should be sought in all cases.
- **Complete and incomplete fractures** – some fractures do not crack the full length of the bone. This is an incomplete fracture. Fractures where a complete break in the bone occurs (when more than one fragment exists) are called complete fractures.

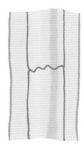

Figure 15.2: An open fracture (left) and a closed fracture (right). How will the treatment differ for each category?

- **Greenstick fracture** – the bone bends and splits without causing a full break in the bone (resembling a bending tree twig). This type of fracture is common among children, because children's bones are not fully developed and not as hard as fully matured bone.
- **Transverse fracture** – a crack that is perpendicular (at right angles) to the length of the bone.
- **Oblique fracture** – similar to a transverse fracture, but the break occurs diagonally across the bone, resulting in sharp ends where the break occurred.
- **Spiral fracture** – very similar to an oblique fracture, but the break is in a spiralling motion along the bone. This often occurs due to a twisting motion accompanied by a high amount of stress to the bone.
- **Comminuted fracture** – produces multiple fragments of bone. With these types of injury, it is often necessary to use screws and wires to assist with healing of the bone, and long rehabilitation is often required.
- **Impacted fracture** – both ends of the bone are forced together in a compression motion. Again, this type of fracture can be complicated, and rehabilitation is needed to restore normal functioning.
- **Avulsion fracture** – a fragment of bone becomes detached at the attachment point (either ligament, tendon or muscle).

Dislocation

A **dislocation** occurs when the correct alignment of bones becomes disrupted, moving them out of their normal position. Such injuries are often caused by impact with another player or object, or by a fall. Typical sites of dislocation due to sports are shoulders, hips, knees, ankles, elbows, fingers and toes. If you suspect that a dislocation has occurred, it is important to seek medical attention to ensure the bones are replaced in correct alignment without damaging the joint. Very often, a dislocated joint will result in ligament damage. The joints in the body are held together by ligaments – when a dislocation occurs they can become stretched, sometimes permanently. If this happens, you become more susceptible to a recurrence of the same injury, particularly in joints such as the shoulder or kneecap.

A subluxation is an incomplete or partial dislocation.

Key terms

Fracture – a partial or complete break in a bone.

Dislocation – a displacement of the position of bones, often caused by a sudden impact.

Stress fracture

This is different from the other forms of **fracture** as it is not caused by a traumatic injury, but develops due to overuse or fatigue. A stress fracture can also be called a fatigue or insufficiency fracture, and generally occurs in weight-bearing bones.

Stress fractures can be particularly difficult to spot using traditional X-ray equipment, particularly at the early stages of development.

Take it further

Types of fracture

Of the different types of fracture, which are more likely to produce an open fracture, and why?

Shin splints

These are another hard tissue injury to the front of the tibia (shin bone). This is often caused by inflammation to the periosteum (sheath around the bone's surface) and is common in runners.

3.2 Types of sports injury: soft tissue damage

Haematoma

A **haematoma** is a pocket of congealed blood caused by bleeding to a specific area of the body. Haematomas may be small bruises, or can be more serious when they occur to different organs (such as the brain), or cause large amounts of blood flow disruption. The majority of haematomas caused by sports injuries occur to the muscles, and are caused by impact or rupture. Muscular haematomas fall into two main types: intermuscular and intramuscular. The size and shape of skeletal muscles vary dramatically, but the general structure remains similar. Muscle fibres

(cells) are bundled together in groups and surrounded by a membrane. These are grouped in further bundles, again surrounded by a membrane. These groups of muscle fibres mean that the structure of a muscle is broken down into a number of compartments. For a more detailed overview of the muscular system, see Unit 1 Anatomy for sport and exercise. Whether a muscular haematoma is inter- or intramuscular depends on where the bleeding takes place.

An intermuscular haematoma is when damage to the muscle causes blood flow within the muscle belly. In this case, the bleeding does not seep into the surrounding tissues, but is restricted to specific compartments within the muscle. An intramuscular haematoma, in contrast, results in blood escaping to the surrounding tissue. With these types of injury, the resultant bruise can spread to areas where the injuries did not occur. Both intra- and intermuscular haematomas can be either superficial or deep (superficial being towards the surface and deep being further inside the muscle).

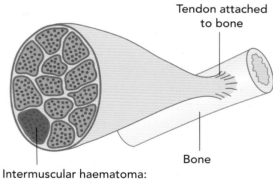

Intermuscular haematoma: bleeding is confined to one bundle of muscle fibres

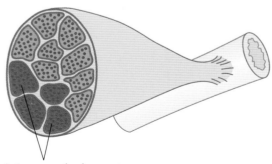

Intramuscular haematoma: bleeding has spread to several bundles of muscle fibres

Figure 15 .3: Intermuscular (left) and intramuscular (right) haematomas. How does the recovery differ for the different types of haematoma?

Abrasion

An abrasion is superficial damage to the skin. In the majority of cases, abrasions (often friction burns) are relatively minor and cover a small area of skin. Many abrasions are caused by contact with a playing surface (for example, falling and slipping), or clothing rubbing on the body.

Sprains and strains

Many people find it difficult to differentiate between a sprain and a strain. It is quite simple, as long as you have a reasonable understanding of basic anatomy:

- a **sprain** is damage to ligaments (stretch or tear)
- a **strain** is damage to muscle or tendon.

Sprain – the causes of a sprain are generally a sudden twist, impact or fall that makes the joint move outside its normal range of movement. Sprains commonly occur to the ankle, wrist, thumb or knee, generally the parts of the body that are at risk when involved in specific sporting activities. The severity of sprains depends on different factors. More than one ligament can be damaged at the same time, and the more ligaments affected, the more severe the injury. Also, whether the ligament is stretched or torn (either partially or fully) determines how severe the injury is. Sprains can be categorised as either first-, second- or third degree, depending on severity:

- first-degree sprain – stretching of ligament (no tear)
- second-degree sprain – partial tear of ligament
- third-degree sprain – complete tear of ligament, or detachment of ligament from the bone.

Strain – a strain is damage to a muscle or tendon caused by overstretching that particular area. Similar to a sprain, a strain can result in a simple overstretching of the muscle or, in more serious examples, partial or even complete rupture. Strains can be common in sports involving dynamic lunging, particularly when combined with sprinting activities, and in contact sports (for example, tackling in football). The severity of a strain is determined by a three-grade categorisation system:

- Grade 1 – relatively minor damage to the muscle fibres (cells) – less than 5 per cent.
- Grade 2 – the muscle is not completely ruptured, but more extensive damage to the fibres has occurred.
- Grade 3 – a complete rupture of the muscle has occurred – in most cases this will require surgery and rehabilitation.

Concussion

Concussion is caused by the brain shaking inside the skull. This causes a temporary loss of consciousness or functioning. Other signs and symptoms include:

- partial or complete loss of consciousness, usually of short duration
- shallow breathing
- nausea and vomiting can occur when the person starts to regain consciousness
- the injured person will often describe 'seeing stars'
- loss of memory of what has happened just before and immediately after the incident
- headache may occur.

Tendonitis

The repetitive and high-impact nature of sporting activity involves continued muscle actions, pulling on tendons, resulting in movement of the skeleton. Tendons will normally glide smoothly with the contraction of the muscles, allowing efficient movements. The varied and dynamic movements involved in sports can, from time to time, place friction on the tendons causing irritation and inflammation.

This inflammation is called tendonitis, and is generally caused by overuse, particularly with increased or different training demands. The symptoms normally subside within a few days, but without care the problem can last weeks or even months. Typical locations of tendonitis could be the achilles tendon and within the complex structures of the shoulder joint.

Tendon rupture

A tendon attaches muscle to bone. A tendon rupture (tear) can be particularly serious depending on the location of the injury and may need surgery.

Blister

Blisters are caused as a defence mechanism to help repair damage to the skin. They are a response to a burn or friction, and are fluid that develops under the upper layers of the skin. Avoid popping a blister, as this will make it more susceptible to infection.

Cramp

Cramp is an involuntary contraction of muscles. Muscles that are particularly susceptible are the gastrocnemius (calf), the quadriceps (thigh), the hamstrings, the abdomen and the feet and hands, depending on the type of activity. Cramp is caused by a lack of oxygen to the muscles, or a lack of water or salt. Deep breathing can alleviate cramp if poor oxygen supply is the cause. In the case of a lack of water and salt, stretching, taking on more fluids and gentle massage can reduce the problem.

Tennis elbow

Symptoms of tennis elbow include pain and tenderness on the outside of your elbow and this may spread to the forearm. Inflammation or a tear to the tendon that joins the forearm muscles to the humerus bone is the cause of tennis elbow.

Back pain

Back pain is a common problem for many people – not just sports players. The back is central to the posture and movements in the majority of sports skills, so pain can cause major disruptions to performance. Four out of five adults have at least one bout of back pain sometime during their lives. In fact, back pain is one of the most common reasons for health care visits and missed work.

Activity: Sports and their injuries

Working in groups, discuss the nature of the following sporting activities and suggest (with appropriate reasons) the types of injury that might be prevalent:

- field hockey
- football
- boxing
- netball
- cricket
- equestrianism.

Based on the injuries you have highlighted, suggest strategies to decrease the risk/likelihood of such injuries taking place. Consider the following:

- protective equipment
- specific rules and regulations
- possible future schemes that could be implemented.

Make a table of your suggestions like the one below.

Table 15.2: Strategies to reduce the risk of sports injuries.

Sport	Common injuries	Protective equipment	Governing body guidelines	Future schemes
Field hockey				
Football				
Boxing				
Netball				
Cricket				
Equestrianism				

Treatment may involve anti-inflammatory drugs, physiotherapy, massage and many other approaches, depending on the specific cause of the pain. Sometimes the actual cause of pain can be very difficult to pinpoint, increasing the difficulty of treatment.

Cartilage injuries

Cartilage comes in different forms, serving various purposes in the body. Cartilage acts as ossification (bone growth) sites, acts as the skeleton for a foetus, keeps tubes of the body open (such as the epiglottis), supports areas of the body requiring tensile strength (such as between the ribs), and lines adjoining bones. Cartilage minimises the impact of internal skeletal forces during sports and general activities. During intense exercise such as running, the forces on the knee, for example, can be huge. Cartilage absorbs the impact of bones while reducing the friction. Damage to cartilage is often due to wear and tear from long-term overuse. Alternatively degenerative conditions (such as osteoarthritis) would also result in chronic cartilage problems. Acute trauma can also cause damage to cartilage, which can occur alongside other injuries (such as a dislocation).

Friction burns

Friction burns are a form of abrasion. In sport these are often caused by falling on playing surfaces or skin rubbing on kit.

3.3 First-aid

First-aid is the immediate treatment given to an injured person. The severity of sporting injuries can vary, from minor cuts and bruises to life-threatening problems. Some knowledge of first-aid can potentially save a person's life, and can also help with minor problems to speed the recovery process and limit potential complications.

Completion of this unit does not qualify you as a first-aider. If you do witness a serious accident, the most qualified and experienced individual should be the one who carries out the first-aid procedures. Do not crowd the injured person, and assist in any way that the first-aider asks.

Remember

Completion of first-aid qualifications can be a great benefit to your sports team. Also, formal first-aid qualifications improve your general employment potential through an enhanced CV.

Emergency/immediate treatment

The priority of first-aid is to preserve life and reduce the risk of further complications from an injury. With potentially serious accidents, a specific primary survey should be carried out.

Primary survey

This is to ensure that a patient is breathing, so it is of paramount importance that it is carried out first.

- **Danger** – check the area for potential danger to yourself. Another casualty will worsen the problem. Also remove any potentially hazardous objects from around the casualty.
- **Response** – check if there is any response from the injured person. If not, call for help immediately. Do not leave the injured person.
- **Airway** – be aware of potential neck injuries. Gently tip the head backwards and check if there are any foreign objects in the person's mouth, blocking the airway.
- **Breathing** – check to see if the person is breathing (up to 10 seconds). If not, send someone for an ambulance (dial 999).
- **Circulation** – check for signs of circulation. If not, cardiopulmonary resuscitation (CPR, see below) should commence.

Secondary survey

A secondary survey should be carried out if an unconscious person is breathing. This is done to check all areas of the body for damage. The process should be carried out quickly and in a systematic way.

- **Bleeding** – check the area, and check the patient head-to-toe for blood.
- **Head and neck** – check for bruising and/or deformity. Gently feel the back of the neck for damage.
- **Shoulders and chest** – compare the shoulders; feel for fractures in the collarbones and ribs.

- **Abdomen and pelvis** – feel around the abdomen for abnormalities and to see if the person feels any pain.
- **Legs and arms** – check legs, then arms, for fracture and any other clues.
- **Pockets** – check the pockets of the person to make sure that when you roll them into the recovery position, items do not injure them. Be very cautious of sharp objects (for example, needles). If possible, have a witness if you remove anything from their pockets.
- **Recovery** – making sure that you don't cause further damage to the person, place them in the recovery position (see below). If a neck injury is suspected, this should be done with the assistance of other people supporting the casualty's whole body.

Be aware of jewellery to make sure it is not worsening the problem – remove it in such cases. Also look for medic alerts (such as diabetes bracelets/necklaces).

Make a mental and/or written note of anything you have observed during the primary and secondary surveys. This information should be passed on to the emergency services to help with treating the patient.

The recovery position is a way of positioning an unconscious casualty, minimising the risk of their airway becoming compromised. Two potential dangers that are avoided are:

- the tongue relaxing and blocking the airway
- the patient vomiting and the vomit blocking the airway.

Figure 15.4: The recovery position – turn the casualty onto their side; lift their chin forward in the open airway position and adjust their hand under their cheek as necessary; check the casualty cannot roll forwards or backwards.

Cardiopulmonary resuscitation (CPR)

CPR is performed when a person is not breathing and does not show any signs of circulation. This process is carried out to keep the vital organs alive until help

arrives. An oxygen supply to the brain is needed to sustain life, and this is done via inhaled air and the movement of blood in the body. If a person is not breathing and their heart is not beating, this will need to be done for them. CPR involves breathing for the casualty and performing chest compressions. This is represented in Figure 15.5.

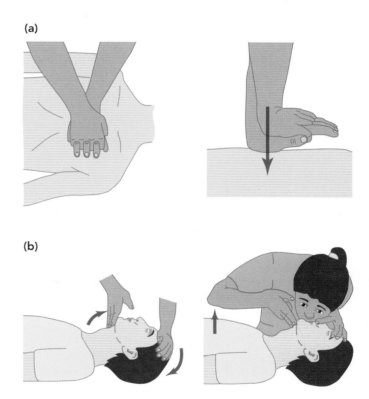

Figure 15.5: The CPR process: (a) chest compressions, (b) rescue breaths. What is the ratio of chest compressions to rescue breaths?

Shock

Shock is caused by a drop in blood pressure or blood volume. Shock can be a secondary reaction to many serious injuries (for example, with major blood loss). There are three classifications:

- cardiogenic shock – the most common type, caused by the heart not pumping effectively
- hypovolaemic shock – caused by a loss in bodily fluids resulting in low blood volume (can be common for traumatic injuries such as major sports injuries)
- anaphylactic shock – caused by a severe allergic reaction.

The signs and symptoms of shock include:

- increased pulse rate (can become weaker as the condition worsens)
- pale and clammy skin, sweating as shock worsens (lips can become blue)
- fast, shallow breathing
- nausea or vomiting
- dizziness
- feelings of weakness
- with severe shock, deep breathing can develop, with confusion, anxiety and possibly aggression
- casualties can become unconscious.

To treat shock:

- the cause of shock must be addressed (for example, a fracture must be immobilised)
- lay the person down and, if possible, raise the legs (keeping the flow of blood to the vital organs)
- keep the person warm
- loosen any tight clothing.

With all cases of shock, the emergency services should be contacted immediately. The casualty should be monitored continuously (breathing, pulse and response).

Bleeding

Loss of blood is common in many sports. Causes of blood loss can vary from minor scratches to serious lacerations and puncture wounds. With all cases of blood loss you should prevent infection in both the casualty and the person treating the wound. Disposable gloves should be worn when dealing with blood. The main priorities of blood-loss treatment are to stop the bleeding, prevent the person from going into shock, and reduce the risk of infection to a wound.

To treat bleeding, direct pressure should be applied to the site of bleeding using an appropriate bandage or gauze. Do not remove any large, impaled objects from a person. If an object is imbedded in a person, pressure can be applied at either side of the object. An absorbent, sterile dressing large enough to cover the wound completely should be applied firmly without restricting blood flow to the rest of the body. Fortunately, the majority of sports injuries are not serious enough to require CPR or treatment for shock. However, appropriate treatment is required for all injuries – if in any doubt, a professional opinion is

required. The correct treatment of injuries is critical to ensure that the healing process can occur without complications.

Further considerations

Special attention needs to be paid in certain situations following an injury.

- For an unconscious casualty you must be aware of the potential of both head injuries and the chance of concealed injuries. These can be identified through the primary and secondary surveys already discussed.
- If fractures are a possibility it is essential to minimise the movement of the injury.
- Where the risk of infection is high it is important to minimise this risk, often through appropriate covering of the injury.
- With any of these injuries, it is important to summon qualified assistance and the emergency services.
- Whether an accident takes place in the workplace or during sporting competition, it is essential to complete an accident report form if treatment of injury is required. This process is a legal requirement for insurance purposes.

3.4 Common treatments

SALTAPS

In assessing sporting injuries, you are likely to have seen the accident take place, and you will already have a reasonable understanding of the specific body part that may be damaged. In this context, some aspects of the primary and secondary survey can become obsolete, and a more specific sports-related assessment is more relevant. One such technique is performed by using the acronym **SALTAPS**.

To ensure the best efforts are made to carry out an accurate assessment of the signs and symptoms, and hopefully diagnose the injury itself, the following specific guidelines are used to assess injured people at the point of occurrence.

Stop – observe the injury.

Ask – ask questions about the injury, where it hurts, type of pain, etc.

Look – for specific signs, for example, redness, swelling, foreign objects.

Touch – palpate the injured part to identify painful areas and swelling.

Active movement – ask the injured person if they can move the injured part of the body without help.

Passive movement – if the person can move the injured part, gently move it through a full range of movement (ROM).

Strength testing – can the player stand or put pressure on the injury? Can they resume playing? If so, make sure you continue to observe them.

Note: with increasingly serious injuries, it is important to stop the SALTAPS process at an appropriate stage.

In the treatment of all sports-related injuries, the most appropriate individuals to give treatment are the most experienced. The aim of the SALTAPS process is to make an accurate assessment of the type, severity and location of an injury. This can be difficult for some sports injuries – even the most experienced practitioners can find an initial on-site diagnosis difficult.

Activity: SALTAPS

You are a first-aider on work experience alongside the sports therapist for a youth football team. During a match, two players collide in a tackle. After the incident, one of the players clutches their leg and is clearly in substantial pain. Following the SALTAPS procedure, highlight some typical responses that you may encounter, and the possible injuries. For the injuries you identify (for example, strains, sprains, fractures, bruises), highlight the point at which you should stop the SALTAPS procedure.

PRICED

For acute but less severe traumatic injuries, the initial treatment should involve the **PRICED** procedure. When soft tissues are injured they become inflamed, and the purpose of treatment is to reduce swelling, prevent further damage and ease pain.

Protect – the person and injured part of the body to minimise the risk of further injury.

Rest – allows healing and prevent any further damage.

Ice – stops the injured area from swelling.

Compression – acts as support and also prevents swelling.

Elevation – reduces blood flow to the area, reducing swelling with the aid of gravity.

Diagnosis – needs to be done by a professional.

Key terms

SALTAPS – procedure for the assessment of an injured person – stop, ask, look, touch, active movement, passive movement, strength testing.

PRICED – procedure for the treatment of acute injuries – protect, rest, ice, compression, elevation, diagnosis.

More common treatments

Common treatments that can be used when dealing with an injury are often used to minimise movement of the injured area and therefore limit further damage. Such methods could include:

- taping
- bandaging
- tubigrips
- splints
- limb supports.

Other common treatments that can be used could include:

- cryotherapy – this is the local or general use of **low** temperature that reduces swelling, prevents bleeding and provides pain relief
- thermotherapy – this is the use of **heat** treatment used to assist the healing process
- anaesthetic spray
- electrotherapy.

Medical referrals for specialist help as appropriate

Depending on the nature of the injury it may be necessary to refer an individual to a specialist. Such individuals could include:

- GP
- physiotherapist
- specialist consultant
- surgeon
- strength and conditioning coach
- nutritionist.

Assessment activity 15.3

 P5 **BTEC**

Working in a coaching, teaching or performance environment will expose you, or other participants, to sports injuries from time to time. In your role as first-aider on work experience alongside a sports therapist, describe the steps you would take when you witness the following injuries taking place:

- a suspected fractured femur
- a head injury resulting in an unconscious casualty
- a potential hamstring tear
- a suspected anterior cruciate ligament tear. **P5**

Grading tips

To attain **P5** choose four contrasting types of sports injury to demonstrate your knowledge of a range of treatment methods. Try to include injuries at different severity levels to show your understanding of a range of treatment methods. Describe how you would approach the injury, and what you would expect to see using the SALTAPS procedure. Indicate at what point you would stop the SALTAPS procedure. Consider the first-aid methods that are most appropriate for each specific injury.

4. Be able to plan and construct treatment and rehabilitation programmes for two common sports injuries

4.1 Treatment

Based on accurate diagnosis

Rehabilitation is concerned with restoring a sportsperson's functionality to a normal state, or as near as physically possible. Progress during rehabilitation is dependent upon accurate diagnosis to enable effective healing processes of damaged tissue. The immediate first-aid and initial diagnosis and treatment of the injury can be critical to the long-term healing of the injury. If rehabilitation is not done effectively, and/or the person returns to activity too quickly, the injured body part is far more susceptible to a recurrence of the injury.

As previously highlighted, GPs, physiotherapists, medical specialists, consultant surgeons, strength and conditioning coaches and nutritionists provide specialist help and advice and this advice can be for the long-term success of a rehabilitation programme. This is particularly important for serious injuries where rehabilitation can be a long, time-consuming, and often painful and frustrating process.

Key term

Rehabilitation – the process of restoring a person's physical functionality to a normal state, or as near as physically possible.

4.2 Rehabilitation

Identification of the stages of rehabilitation

There are five stages of rehabilitation:

1 acute stage
2 re-establishing functional activity
3 strengthening exercises
4 ongoing treatments
5 gradual increase in activity.

These five stages are designed to ensure the functions of rehabilitation are systematically undertaken to ensure the athlete has the best potential to return to normal functional activity. A combination of strengthening exercises, ongoing medical treatments and gradual increases in activity are central components of a programme design. Some important functions of a programme are to:

- ensure correct immediate first-aid is provided
- reduce pain and swelling
- minimise pain in subsequent hours, days and weeks
- re-establish neuromuscular control of the injured area of the body
- restore ROM of the affected joints
- restore lost muscular strength, power and endurance
- develop core stability, posture and balance
- maintain cardiovascular fitness to an attainable level.

The healing process

Many of the physiological responses to injury follow a clear sequence and timescale. The signs and symptoms of an injury can be a clear indicator of the progression of the healing process.

- Inflammatory response phase (see page 358) occurs as soon as an injury takes place, and is the start of the healing process. Inflammation ensures that healing properties in the blood can access the injured part of the body while simultaneously disposing of injury by-products.
- Repair phase – occurs after a few hours of injury, and can last as long as six weeks. Some of the signs and symptoms are similar to the inflammatory response phase. Involves rebuilding the damaged structure and healing the damaged areas. Scar tissue will develop during this phase.
- Remodelling phase – scar tissue development will imitate the original structures prior to the injury. If appropriate care is given to the injury, long-term scarring will decrease, and strength and ROM will improve at the site of the injury.

Remember

Each phase of the healing process can be prolonged by inappropriate management techniques. It is important to encourage movement exercises, as developing scar tissue can shrink over time and can limit ROM.

4.3 Programme

Methods to improve lost range of motion

Restoring flexibility is vital to limit the chances of an injury recurring. With the majority of injuries, inflammation and general damage will have dramatically reduced the movement possible at the joints near or at the site of injury. Potentially, ROM at other joints of the body will also have decreased, because exercise levels will have dropped. Stretching of muscles is an important ingredient of any warm-up and cool down and will minimise the risk of injury (see Unit 14, Instructing physical activity and exercise, pages 10–11). Stretching should be incorporated into a rehabilitation programme to regain ROM.

Advice on the best stretching methods has changed over the years, with some methods being replaced (some can cause damage to different parts of the body, for example, bouncing while touching your toes puts stress on your lower back). Distinctly different methods of stretching are used in ROM exercises:

- dynamic stretching – controlled movements towards the limits of ROM (for example, swinging arms and legs)
- static stretching – holding a stretch at the furthest ROM
- passive stretching – similar to static stretching, but involves stretching using either a piece of apparatus or another person
- active stretching – similar to static stretching, but involves holding a position with only the assistance of the surrounding muscle groups
- proprioceptive neuromuscular facilitation (PNF) stretching – combines stretching with muscular contraction.

PNF is fast-developing and is used in a number of sports (for example, gymnastics and dance) as well as for rehabilitation. A stretch is performed by moving the limb or joint toward the limits of ROM, then force is applied by the person stretching against a resistance (either a partner or apparatus) (see Unit 14 Instructing physical activity and exercise, page 12).

Strengthening and coordination exercises

Strengthening exercises are important throughout rehabilitation, as this aspect of fitness will have deteriorated as a result of an injury. Developing muscular strength, endurance and power is an essential element of rehabilitation. Muscle atrophy is a decrease in muscle size that will take place due to injury and reduced physical training. Static and dynamic strength training methods can be used to address the problem, with increased resistance and impact later in a programme. Resistance machines, free weights and some endurance machines (for example, an exercise bike) can be used for this aspect of rehabilitation. Exercises should be specific to the injured area, but the whole body should be considered to prevent muscular imbalances. Coordination losses will often occur following an injury. A range of coordination training exercises, specific to the injured area of the body, should be incorporated into a rehabilitation programme to complement other treatment procedures. An example is wobble board exercises.

Remember

A rehabilitation programme must be designed specifically to take into account an individual's abilities and characteristics. Depending on the speed of recovery, and any problems that arise, modifications may be needed on a regular basis.

Psychological considerations during rehabilitation

The psychological aspect of how well an athlete deals with rehabilitation and the often slow return to competition is often neglected. Athletes, and any individual who suffers an injury, can experience a very wide range of emotions. Individual differences dictate that athletes will vary dramatically both in the physical aspects of the programme (including pain threshold and speed of recovery) and also in how well they deal with the mental aspects of an injury. Motivation and anxiety are common issues that must be considered during each phase of rehabilitation.

Activity: Treatment techniques

Research the following treatment techniques and identify the stage of the healing and rehabilitation process at which it would be best to use the different methods for different injuries. Working in groups, make a table like the one below.

Table 15.3: At which stage should each method be used?

Method	Inflammatory response	Repair	Remodelling phase
Flexibility stretching			
Taping			
Cryotherapy			
Strengthening exercises			
Coordination exercises			
Electrotherapy			
Massage			
Thermotherapy			
Acupuncture			

Many of the psychological techniques used to enhance performance and other coping strategies can be useful in dealing with the problems associated with sporting injuries. These techniques are covered in Unit 3 Sport and exercise psychology. Such psychological intervention techniques can be implemented alongside a rehabilitation programme to complement the processes.

> ### Remember
> Psychological issues can also influence physical recovery following an injury.

One of the most important aspects of a rehabilitation programme for an athlete is that they can see improvements in the injury and that they are progressing towards competition fitness. It important to set appropriate goals for the athlete to strive towards during rehabilitation. Goal-setting can incorporate both long- and short-term goals. These should be designed in a progressive manner – a number of very specific short-term goals (week by week) are assembled to construct a more generalised set of long-term goals. Goal-setting can be a vital tool enabling a progressive rehabilitation programme, and well planned goals can act as a powerful psychological tool, helping the athlete to see significant progression and to remain focused on returning to fitness.

The need for a careful, structured approach to rehabilitation

The physical and mental strain that can be placed on an athlete during their rehabilitation from injury can elicit motivational issues and also anxiety. Such factors must be acknowledged when designing and modifying programmes to suit individual needs.

Recording documentation and tracking of treatment

When developing a rehabilitation programme you should be proficient in both the practical aspects and the accurate recording of the entire process. The records kept should detail accurately all the factors of the rehabilitation, from the initial injury evaluation to the end of the programme. Things to consider when documenting a rehabilitation programme include:

- background information about the client (for example, medical issues, injury history, specific requirements of rehabilitation)
- the activities undertaken
- the levels and development of the client
- problems or issues arising from the session
- complications (for example, allergies or illness) that affect the quality of the client's progress during the session
- important legal documents and forms such as parental consent for younger sports players
- dates for review/functional testing (aims, objectives, etc.)
- accurate and up to date information that may change during the duration of the treatment
- specific objectives including appropriate and measurable timescales and review dates.

> ### Take it further
>
> **Potential complications**
>
> Research into the potential complications that could arise during the rehabilitation of injury for the following scenarios:
>
> - a 9-year-old football player experiencing a hairline fracture to the fibula and an ankle sprain
> - a 55-year-old, physically healthy man who has developed knee cartilage problems
> - a 17-year-old student representative hockey player who has developed lower back muscular spasms
> - a formerly inactive 32-year-old individual who has developed Achilles tendonitis two weeks after starting at a gym with the intention of losing weight.

Assessment activity 15.4

1. In your role as a first-aider on work experience alongside the sports therapist, design a rehabilitation programme for two selected athletes who have suffered different, common sports injuries. You can do this with support from your tutor. **P6**

2. Alternatively, you can perform this task without tutor support. **M3**

3. Finally, you should evaluate your rehabilitation programme and justify your choice of methods and, where appropriate, suggest alternative methods. **D2**

Grading tips

- To attain **P6** you must demonstrate your research skills and knowledge of a range of rehabilitation protocols. Ensure you provide appropriate timescales for a rehabilitation programme for the two different injuries.

- To attain **M3** you must ensure you do all of the above but independently.

- To attain **D2** explain how unforeseen circumstances may require changes and modifications to a rehabilitation programme. Consideration is needed of how the rehabilitation process will change in response to each specific phase of the healing process. Link the type of activity to the injury and the duration/phase of healing process.

PLTS

By designing your rehabilitation programme, you can develop your skills as an **independent enquirer**, **creative thinker** and **self-manager**.

Functional skills

By producing your rehabilitation programme you could provide evidence of your skills in **English**.

Ian Harris

Physiotherapist

Ian is a registered physiotherapist and leads a small team in a sports injuries clinic. He is responsible for the evaluation and rehabilitation of clients who have suffered a wide variety of sports injuries. The roles and responsibilities that Ian fulfils are very diverse including:

- dealing with professional athletes who have suffered injuries of various severities
- supporting elderly people with a variety of health-related problems and injuries
- treating and rehabilitating young people who have been injured while participating in youth sport
- rehabilitating individuals with long-term chronic injuries requiring technical modifications to their physical movements.

'A common scenario that I sometimes encounter involves elite athletes feeling concerned that they will not be able to compete at the level they did previously and that their injury might be career threatening. In a situation like this I often prioritise both the physiological and psychological demands on the athletes. Furthermore, in cases like this, a team of individuals may be used to support the athlete including me (the physiotherapist), a sport psychologist, coaches, family and team mates.

Based on the physical and mental demands on an athlete it is essential to provide realistic but challenging goals that they can work towards. When an athlete becomes disillusioned with their progress I often find it particularly useful to sit down with them and explain how far they have developed since the injury by reviewing their previous short-term goals.'

A physiotherapist is continually dealing with people and Ian has not only the scientific know-how and academic qualifications but also the interpersonal and counselling skills that are often demanded in his job.

Think about it!

- What steps would you take when dealing with an athlete who has become frustrated with their rehabilitation progress and is considering retiring from their sport?
- What are the skills most often applied by professional physiotherapists? Write a list of the main personal attributes needed to become a physiotherapist and discuss these with your peers.
- Research the qualifications required to become a physiotherapist.

Just checking

1. What is the difference between intrinsic and extrinsic injury risk factors?
2. What steps can you take to reduce your risk of injury before training or competition?
3. What can coaches do to protect their team from injury risk?
4. Provide three examples of the primary damage responses that are likely to occur as a result of a sports injury.
5. Define the following:
   lordosis
   kyphosis
   scoliosis
6. What are the different categorisations of fractures?
7. What is the difference between hard and soft tissue damage?
8. What do the following acronyms stand for?
   PRICED
   SALTAPS
9. Which psychological problems may occur as a result of suffering from a sports injury?
10. Provide three examples of typical procedures that are common during injury rehabilitation.

edexcel

Assignment tips

- Choose to investigate injuries from that are common within sports that you have an interest in.
- Remember that extrinsic and intrinsic sports injury risk can be minimised using a variety of control measures.
- Ensure that you match the appropriate preventative measures to the specific sport.
- Utilise a range of sources of information to help write your treatment programme.
- Keep a record of the different injury classification methods.
- Remember that sport injuries manifest both psychological and physiological responses.

16 Sports coaching

There is more to being a good coach than producing good athletes or excellent teams. The best coaches are those who give athletes a positive experience and motivate them to continue. The role of a sports coach can go beyond that of a skilled and knowledgeable coach who is dedicated to developing athletes. A coach might be called on to act as a fitness trainer, social worker, motivator, disciplinarian, friend, mentor, manager or secretary, as well as many other roles.

The prospect of hosting the Olympic and Paralympic Games in 2012 has boosted sport and coaching in the UK. In 2006 Sport Coach UK in conjunction with Sport England set an agenda to enable all athletes to be coached and educated in sport by a qualified sports coach. This action plan requires thousands of coaches to be trained and educated in a number of different sports. The government has backed this programme and provided funding for coaches in specific sports to obtain qualifications to support this goal. The overall aim of the plan is to increase the number of qualified coaches to develop the provision of sport for all by 2016, building on the London 2012 legacy.

In this unit you will investigate the work of successful coaches, examine the roles, responsibilities and skills and techniques and knowledge base required to develop sports performance. You will plan and deliver a coaching session and after its completion, you will assess your performance and produce a development plan which should support the improvement of your planning and delivery skills.

Learning outcomes

After completing this unit you should:

1. know the roles, responsibilities and skills of sports coaches
2. know the techniques used by coaches to improve the performance of athletes
3. be able to plan a sports coaching session
4. be able to deliver and review a sports coaching session.

Assessment and grading criteria

This table shows you what you must do in order to achieve a pass, merit or distinction grade, and where you can find activities in this book to help you.

To achieve a pass grade the evidence must show that the learner is able to:	To achieve a merit grade the evidence must show that, in addition to the pass criteria, the learner is able to:	To achieve a distinction grade the evidence must show that, in addition to the pass and merit criteria, the learner is able to:
P1 describe four roles and four responsibilities of sports coaches, using examples of coaches from different sports **Assessment activity 16.1, page 390**	**M1** explain four roles and four responsibilities of sports coaches, using examples of coaches from different sports **Assessment activity 16.1, page 390**	**D1** compare and contrast the roles, responsibilities and skills of successful coaches from different sports **Assessment activity 16.1, page 390**
P2 describe three skills common to successful sports coaches, using examples of coaches from different sports **Assessment activity 16.1, page 390**	**M2** explain three skills common to successful sports coaches, using examples of coaches from different sports **Assessment activity 16.1, page 390**	
P3 describe three different techniques that are used by coaches, to improve the performance of athletes **Assessment activity 16.2, page 395**	**M3** explain three different techniques that are used by coaches to improve the performance of athletes **Assessment activity 16.2, page 395**	**D2** evaluate three different techniques that are used by coaches, to improve the performance of athletes **Assessment activity 16.2, page 395**
P4 plan a sports coaching session **Assessment activity 16.3, page 406**		
P5 deliver a sports coaching session, with tutor support **Assessment activity 16.3, page 406**	**M4** independently deliver a sports coaching session **Assessment activity 16.3, page 406**	
P6 carry out a review of the planning and delivery of a sports coaching session, identifying strengths and areas for improvement **Assessment activity 16.3, page 406**	**M5** evaluate the planning and delivery of a sports coaching session, suggesting how improvements could be reached in the identified areas **Assessment activity 16.3, page 406**	**D3** justify suggestions made in relation to the development plan **Assessment activity 16.3, page 406**

How you will be assessed

Your assessment could be in the form of:

- video recordings
- session plans completed for a sports activity session
- observation records of your performance while leading a sports coaching session
- assessment of your own performance while coaching a session
- a development plan which identifies and describes methods for improving performance.

Wayne Pybus, 22-year-old football coach

I have always wanted to pursue a career in sport. When I was younger I thought I would be a professional footballer, but realised when I was released from a football club that professional sport was not for me. After this, I enrolled on a BTEC National Diploma course at my local college. I really enjoyed the course, especially the sports coaching unit.

Through completing this unit I developed a greater understanding of the roles, responsibilities, skills and techniques required to be a successful coach. This was very useful when I went on to complete coaching qualifications in a variety of sports.

The coaching unit was practical and very hands on and enabled me to plan and lead coaching sessions to a variety of groups of athletes. I really enjoyed this part of the unit, especially when we went into a local school and I led a football session and improved the performance of every participant.

Over to you

- **What are your reasons for wanting to play sport?**
- **What could a sports coach do to ensure that all your needs are met in a coaching session?**

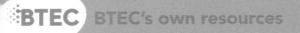
1. Know the roles, responsibilities and skills of sports coaches

In this unit you will examine the roles, responsibilities and skills of a sports coach. You will reflect on how coaches should and do meet the requirements of each of these roles, responsibilities and skills. Remember that in order to be an excellent coach you don't have to fulfil every role, responsibility and skill covered in this unit. Even the greatest coaches may not demonstrate excellence in all the areas covered. As a sports coach you can always improve and should always seek to develop in order to support the athletes you work with.

1.1 Roles

In sports coaching, the desired roles should support the development of athletes at a variety of levels.

Innovator

The term innovation means a new or original way of doing something. As a sports coach you need to search for new techniques to enhance performance or to generate greater enjoyment in a session.

During his management of Bolton Wanderers FC (1999–2007), Sam Allardyce examined methods of measuring and improving players' performance. He introduced the use of Prozone technology to assess players' effectiveness and based training programmes on the results. Allardyce also added nutritionists, sports psychologists, fitness coaches, defensive coaches and attacking coaches to his coaching squad. He turned Bolton Wanderers from a Premier League yo-yo club to an established top ten Premier League team.

Another innovator is Shane Sutton, a coach with the British cycling team in Beijing 2008. Sutton combined scientific, data-based technology with specific training methods, developing a team mentality in a predominantly individual sport that led the British cycling team to enormous success.

Friend

An athlete and coach may spend considerable amounts of time together. Friendships develop, athlete and coach may share positive and negative experiences and because of these common experiences a bond evolves.

When developing a relationship with anyone you learn more about their personality and a sports coach can use this knowledge to help them. Increased understanding of an athlete's personality will support the coach in developing an effective training plan.

When developing friendships with athletes it is important that the coach is aware of their role and clearly states the boundaries of the relationship at the start of the friendship. The athlete's development must be the priority. At times a coach may have to criticise an athlete's performance; as a friend, this information may be easily shared, although athletes may react negatively to criticism.

Manager

You may think of managing a team when you consider sports coaching. It is often the manager's responsibility to coach the team and individual players as well as to manage the fixtures, prepare the equipment and organise transport to the competition or training venues. The principle role of a manager is to lead. Their leadership style will depend on the athletes they are managing.

Coaching style	Characteristics	Advantages	Disadvantages
Command style	Coach makes all the decisions Leader tells the athletes what to do and how to do it	Good for beginners when explaining basic skills and techniques Good method of controlling a group and keeping large groups safe	Only works on single skills in isolation Difficult to examine athletes' prior knowledge and understanding, as session controlled solely by coach
Reciprocal style	Coach decides what is to be delivered in the session, but involves athletes in decision-making process	Good for developed athletes Develops close relationships with athletes Develops communication and athletes' confidence	Time-consuming Problems may occur in large teams when everyone has different opinions and ideas
The guided discovery style	Athletes are in control of the session and make the decisions Coach is a mentor for the athletes when appropriate	Often used with experts or professional athletes Helps develop self-confidence Can increase understanding and develop athletes' decision-making skills Can increase athletes' motivation	Lack of structure to the session Can develop bad techniques without coach's intervention Can take time to meet a desired goal or target

Table 16.1: Different coaching styles and which athletes they are best suited to

Take it further

Think of the different coaches you have worked with as an athlete. Can you identify a coach who used any of the leadership styles described in Table 16.1? Can you evaluate the effectiveness of their coaching for you as an athlete?

A good manager should motivate their team, learn from mistakes, and gain respect from the athletes who play for them. The managers who attain excellence are those whose players want to play for them. Managers generate this desire through a mixture of motivation and respect, which could stem from coaching sessions, team talks, previous successes and their reputation. For an individual sport the manager's role is to monitor the individual's development and do everything possible to obtain their optimum performance. In team sports the manager's role involves team selection and could include choosing the best team from a squad of players, or the best combination of players to beat the opponents. When working with teams the manager has to oversee the relationship between players. Good managers create team cohesion to help players perform to the best of their ability.

In some sports and at the highest levels, a variety of coaches may be employed to develop skills, fitness and tactical awareness, while the **manager's** role is to organise and coordinate training programmes.

The photo shows England team manager Fabio Capello giving instructions to David Beckham during an international football match.

1. List the other roles and responsibilities Capello will have to meet in his role as England football manager.
2. Identify your own sports manager or another team manager from your school or college. List the roles and responsibilities they will have to meet.

Trainer

When a coach takes up a role as trainer they need to be aware of the physical, technical and tactical demands of the specific sport. They should have a bank of activities that can be drawn on to develop the athlete's ability to perform to their optimum. The most common trainer is probably a fitness trainer.

Coaches need to have a good knowledge of health and fitness and training principles (see Unit 9 Fitness training and programming, page 229). As a trainer, a coach should be able to design and implement programmes that are appropriate for the athletes and reflect the sports they compete in. When planning fitness development sessions, coaches should consider the athletes':

* age
* ability
* interests
* experience.

Role model

When leading a sport or physical activity session, a coach is representing that particular sport or activity, and should set an example to the participants. A good coach will demonstrate appropriate behaviour and use appropriate language with athletes at all times. Coaches should accept responsibility for the conduct of the athletes they coach and encourage positive and non-discriminatory behaviour.

To be an effective role model, a coach must set an example with the clothes they wear when coaching. A coach should have sports clothing and footwear and the appropriate equipment to coach the session.

A coach will sell the sport or physical activity session to the athletes, and the more enthusiastic the coach is, the more enthusiastic the athletes are likely to become.

Educator

A coach will educate athletes so that they can develop as performers. When coaching young children and beginners, a coach will start by educating them about the basic skills of the game. As a performer develops in the basic skills, the coach will provide support and develop their skills to enhance their efficiency and effectiveness. A coach needs to understand how people learn. Athletes learn best when:

* they are actively involved, rather than listening and watching the coach playing

* they recognise how, when and where new techniques, skills or tactics can be used
* they are encouraged to build on experiences and skills learned in previous sessions or other sports (for example, catching in cricket could be transferred to basketball, netball or rugby)
* they are interested, enjoying themselves and motivated
* they can see or feel improvements in their performance.

A coach will be aware that athletes develop differently and require a mixture of coaching styles. An effective coach develops a range of styles to deal with a variety of learners.

1.2 Responsibilities

A coach has responsibilities to the participants in their coaching session and also to:

* the participants' parents or guardians
* the club or school that the coach is representing
* other coaches who may be involved in the delivery of the session
* the sport that the coach is representing, for example in a football session a coach will be representing the Football Association and the sport of football.

Legal obligations

Child protection

Children are introduced to sport at very early ages, and coaches must be aware of child-protection procedures.

Prior to working with children in any capacity a coach must be the subject of a Criminal Records Bureau (CRB) check to check the criminal records of a potential employee. Any previous convictions will be listed and a decision will be made by the organisation after they have viewed the CRB's feedback. This will determine whether or not the candidate is appropriate for the work. In some instances those with criminal records will not be able to work with children (this includes people on the sex offenders' registers and those with violent criminal records).

The Children Act (2004)

A coach must be aware of the Children Act (2004) and of the signs and symptoms of child abuse. This act provides a legislative framework for services working with children and young people to improve their health, development and well-being.

The Children Act makes it a responsibility of all agencies working with children and young people to work together and adopt a multi-agency approach when offering services. The act enforces specific duties which must be carried out by the service providers. These include:

- providing care, planned and supervised activities for all children at all times
- publishing adequate information about the services
- reviewing and monitoring the services on offer and consulting with the appropriate bodies, for example professionals who deal with the protection of children
- ensuring that registration is completed for all organisations which supervise activities for children under the age of 18 years.

Before a service can be registered, the suitability of the organisation, all its employees and its premises need to be assessed.

Coaches must be able to recognise the main forms of child abuse, which include:

Physical abuse – physical hurt or injury caused by an adult to a child (could be displayed when a child displays unexplained bruising, cuts or burns)

Sexual abuse – adults, both male and female, using children to meet their own sexual needs (could be displayed when a child demonstrates over-sexualised behaviour)

Emotional abuse – could be a persistent lack of love and affection (this could be displayed when a child becomes reserved and withdrawn from social contact with others)

Neglect – failure to meet the child's basic needs like food and warm clothing (this could be evident from a child's appearance and clothing).

If a child says or indicates that he or she is being abused, or information is obtained which raises concerns that a child is being abused, the coach or anyone receiving the information should:

- react calmly so as not to frighten the child
- tell the child they are not to blame and they are right to tell
- take what the child says seriously
- keep questions to an absolute minimum
- reassure the child
- make a full record of what the child has said
- not promise the child that no one else will be informed
- as soon as the conversation has ended, the person receiving the information should report the findings

to a designated child-protection officer at the school or sports centre, or report the information directly to the police.

As a sports coach you should be aware that coaches have caused harm to children through over-training, bullying and other forms of mistreatment, and that it is vital that a coach always treats children fairly and with respect.

Insurance

Sports coaches are required to have appropriate insurance cover to participate in physical activity as well as to lead a sport or physical activity session. A coach is responsible for the safety of the athletes while they are under his or her supervision. If an athlete is injured during a coaching session, the coach is considered liable and could be deemed negligent.

Professional conduct

A coach should always behave appropriately. As a coach your conduct and behaviour will determine the experience and future behaviour of the athletes you coach. A good coach will:

- demonstrate clear knowledge and experience of the sport
- have appropriate coaching qualifications and relevant experience
- dress appropriately for the coaching session
- speak clearly, using appropriate language at all times
- respect all athletes of all abilities and treat them all equally
- respect and support all officials and their decisions
- promote **fair play**
- promote honesty
- reward effort.

Key term

Fair play – playing as competitively as possible, but always within the rules of the sport as determined by the national governing body.

Many national governing bodies (NGBs) have set specific codes of conduct to promote appropriate behaviour for coaches who are qualified under their coach-education schemes. These codes of conduct determine whether or not a coach is acting professionally.

Take it further

Below is an example of a code of conduct provided by the Football Association for all football coaches, team managers and club officials. For more information about codes of conduct see www.TheFA.com/Respect.

Code of conduct: Coaches, team managers and club officials

We all have a responsibility to promote high standards of behaviour in the game.

In the Football Association's survey of over 37,000 grassroots participants, behaviour was the biggest concern in the game. This included the abuse of match officials and the unacceptable behaviour by over competitive parents, spectators and coaches on the sideline.

Play your part and observe the FA's Respect Code of Conduct in everything you do.

On and off the field, I will:

- Show respect to others involved in the game including match officials, opposition players, coaches, managers, officials and spectators
- Adhere to the laws and spirit of the game
- Promote Fair Play and high standards of behaviour
- Always respect the match officials' decision
- Never enter the field of play without the referee's permission
- Never engage in public criticism of the match officials
- Never engage in, or tolerate, offensive, insulting or abusive language or behaviour

When working with players, I will:

- Place the well-being, safety and enjoyment of each player above everything, including winning
- Explain exactly what I expect of players and what they can expect from me
- Ensure all parents/carers of all players under the age of 18 understand these expectations
- Never engage in or tolerate any form of bullying
- Develop mutual trust and respect with every player to build their self-esteem
- Encourage each player to accept responsibility for their own behaviour and performance
- Ensure all activities I organise are appropriate for the players' ability level, age and maturity
- Co-operate fully with others in football (e.g. officials, doctors, physiotherapists, welfare officers) for each player's best interests

I understand that if I do not follow the Code, any/all of the following actions may be taken by my club, County FA or The FA.

I may be:

- Required to meet with the club, league or County Welfare Officer
- Required to meet with the club committee
- Monitored by another club coach
- Required to attend a FA education course
- Suspended by the club from attending matches
- Suspended or fined by the County FA
- Required to leave or be sacked by the club

In addition:

- My FACA (FA Coaches Association) membership may be withdrawn

Activity: Code of conduct

Produce a code of conduct with your peers for when you are coaching – as a class, make it clear what expectations you have of everyone who coaches at your school/college/sports club.

To support the completion of your code of conduct, each group member should identify what makes a good coach and what makes a bad coach – share and discuss your findings.

Activity: Intrinsic or extrinsic injuries?

Classify each of the following causes of injury as intrinsic or extrinsic.

- overuse
- age
- inappropriate coaching
- environmental conditions, e.g. rain, snow, ice
- poor preparation
- poor technique
- clashes with opponents
- clashes with teammates
- postural defects
- muscle imbalance
- equipment failure
- loose clothing
- inappropriate clothing.

Health and safety

A key responsibility of a sports coach is managing the safety of everyone involved in a coaching session. When working anyone under the age of 18 this responsibility becomes a legal obligation of a **duty of care**. A coach should consider the health and safety of the participants before, during and after the session as a priority. It is often the head coach's responsibility to lead on health and safety, although assistant coaches must also maintain a safe coaching environment at all times.

All sports carry an element of risk of injury; it is the role of the sports coach to:

- assess risk
- protect athletes from injury and reduce the likelihood of risk
- deal with injuries and accidents when they occur.

Although a coach may assess every risk and hazard and implement methods of reducing injury and keeping harm to a minimum, injuries can and will occur during sport and physical activity sessions. There are two major causes of injuries – **extrinsic risks** and **intrinsic risks**.

Key terms

Duty of care – a legal obligation imposed on an individual, requiring that they adhere to a standard of reasonable care while performing any acts that could possibly harm others.

Extrinsic risk – something outside the body that may cause an injury.

Intrinsic risk – a physical aspect of the body that may cause an injury.

Sports coaches may benefit from obtaining a first-aid qualification to ensure they know what action to take if an athlete is injured. If you are not a qualified first-aider, you should make provision for first-aid during coaching sessions, for example by ensuring that a qualified first-aider is present. A coach should ensure that athletes seek professional advice as soon as possible if:

- a major injury is sustained during a session – fracture, severe bleeding, head injury, severe swelling or bruising with pain
- a minor injury is sustained during a session – muscle strain, muscle contusion (bruising), minor cuts or bleeding
- they become ill – vomiting, headache, sore throat, dizziness.

It is vital to ensure that the coaching and playing environment is safe and to know what to do in the event of a serious accident. If you are not sure about anything regarding the health and safety of the participants of your session, you should seek advice from a senior coach or a senior member of staff prior to starting your session.

The photo shows an athlete receiving first-aid. Often the coach is first on the scene of an injury, therefore they must have knowledge of first-aid.
- Identify an appropriate first-aid course that would be suitable for you to complete as a coach.
- Identify the location of the next available first-aid course and the cost of the qualification.

Activity: Dealing with accidents and illnesses

During a coaching session, you may be presented with any of the following:

- a player suffers a minor injury, e.g. cut/bruise/strain
- a player suffers a major injury, e.g. broken bone/concussion/severe bleed
- a player becomes ill, e.g. vomiting/headache.

1. For each scenario, explain what action(s) you would take to deal with the problem.

2. Imagine each scenario occurring in your sports hall – identify the qualified contact at the school/college and explain how they would be contacted and what procedure would need to be followed.

3. Find the nearest first-aid bag at your sports hall – assess the effectiveness of its contents and discuss with your group how they could be improved.

Equal opportunities

A competent coach will ensure that equal opportunities are given to all athletes, spectators, parents and match officials. Ensuring equal opportunities is about recognising inequalities and addressing and solving the issues that surround each one. To achieve equality, coaches should make sure that coaching sessions are accessible to all, without prejudice to age, gender, race, ethnicity, religion, sexuality, socio-economic status or ability.

When planning coaching sessions you as a coach will need to cater for participants with different motives, needs and goals. In order for all groups to achieve what they want, you must be willing and able to adapt the session.

Knowledge of the coaching environment

Sports coaches familiarise themselves with the environment in which they deliver their sessions. This can take many forms, including:

- outdoor pitches
- indoor pitches
- sports halls
- indoor courts
- outdoor courts
- multi-use game areas
- astroturf pitches
- third-generation grass pitches
- gymnasiums
- school halls.

A coach will be aware of the size of the environment and how it can be best used. For example, if a coach is delivering a basketball session in a sports hall and the basketball nets are folded away, the coach will need to know how to unfold them or where to find a member of staff who can help.

The coach should also be aware of the location of changing rooms, toilets, showers, first-aid box or designated first-aid room and member of staff if appropriate. This knowledge will demonstrate to the participating athletes that their coach is well prepared.

The more a coach knows about the coaching environment, the more organisation and professionalism they can demonstrate when running a session. This in turn will increase the athletes' confidence in their coach.

1.3 Skills

Communication

Communication is possibly the most important skill required to coach athletes effectively. Coaches have to exchange information not only with athletes, but also with parents, other coaches, officials, other staff at a sports club, teachers, spectators and many other people. The three main forms of communication used by sports coaches are verbal communication, non-verbal communication, and listening skills.

In **verbal communication** it is important to keep language simple and free from technical and complex jargon. A coach should ensure that what they are to say is correct and appropriate, and that they have the attention of the person/people they are speaking to. After providing the information, they should check for understanding by questioning the audience or observing the performance of the athlete.

Non-verbal communication can take many forms, for example body language. Most body language is unconscious (done without thinking). An athlete will be able to read positive and negative body language and this information will indicate the coach's mood.

Other forms of non-verbal communication used by coaches are hand signals and demonstrations. Hand signals can direct athletes or provide instructions during training and competitions. Demonstrations are used to show the correct technique and model each component of a skill, technique or tactic.

As well as sending out communication, it is important that a coach can receive information. In order to improve their listening skills a coach should:

- concentrate when someone is talking to them
- make eye contact with the speaker
- avoid interrupting the speaker
- ask questions or summarise what has been said to confirm understanding.

Organisation

When planning training programmes and sessions, a coach needs to demonstrate high levels of organisation. An organised session will motivate athletes and maintain interest. In order to be fully prepared and organised for a session a coach should:

- ensure they know how many participants are taking part
- ensure that the activities are appropriate for all the participants (to do this the coach will need to know the ability levels of each participant)
- decide what equipment they will need prior to the event and ensure that it is available and ready for use on the day of the session
- ensure that the facility where the session is taking place is booked well in advance and that they are aware of its safety procedures
- ensure at the end of the session that the facility and equipment are left as they were when the session started
- ensure that they have clear methods of stopping and starting the session. This could be discussed with participants at the start of the session, for example, when the coach blows the whistle, all participants must stop.

When they first start coaching, many sports coaches record each session they deliver and collate their records to make a logbook to which they can refer when planning future sessions. Although these session plans and logbooks are important to demonstrate organisation for the planning and delivery of coaching sessions, coaches need to know how to adapt sessions if activities are not working. It is in these situations that a coach's knowledge, experience and organisational skills will be pushed to the limit.

Analysing

Spectators watching sports live or on television make judgements on what they see. Everyone has their own ideas, which sometimes go against those of the coach of the team they are observing. A coach makes similar judgements, but they are often based on more objective data.

A coach must demonstrate effective analysis skills. Analysis of sports performance is the ability to observe and make appropriate judgements about performers' technical and tactical ability. A coach should assess individual players and/or teams in action and should identify and prioritise performance targets for them.

In order to complete an effective analysis of a player's and/or team's performance, a coach needs to have a clear expectation of the performers at their stage of development. The ability to analyse requires a coach to observe and assess any faults in what they see. This skill takes time and experience to develop. Even the greatest athletes have weaknesses and sometimes these are not spotted by every coach. That is why elite athletes change coaches or seek support from others, or build a team of coaches to work on specific parts of their overall performance.

As well as analysing ability, a coach must be able to analyse the personality and motivation of the athletes they will be coaching. A coach will do the majority of their analysis by watching athletes' performance, behaviour and actions to learn about their personality and motivation, and should be able to read their mood through their body language and gestures while training or competing.

Problem-solving

The coaching environment can be very inconsistent: problems may arise suddenly which will require the coach's attention. Problems can take many forms including:

- participants
- equipment
- facility
- opponents
- transport.

Athletes expecting to participate in a coaching session will often expect any problems to be solved in advance so that the session can proceed according to plan. It is a coach's job to spot when things are going wrong, determine the nature of the problem and find a solution. Often they will have to find a solution on the spot, to allow things to continue as normal.

Activity: Problem-solving

Imagine you are a sports coach and explain what actions you would take to resolve the following problems:

* You have planned a football coaching session with the aim of improving dribbling. The majority of the activities you have planned require each player to dribble with a ball – you have 12 balls but 18 players – what should you do?

* You are coaching a tennis session. You arrive at the local tennis centre and all the tennis courts are booked, but the receptionist tells you that there are two squash courts free – what should you do?

* You are coaching a basketball session; on arrival at the sports hall you find the storage room is locked and no key is available. There are 14 players waiting to participate – what should you do?

Evaluating

Evaluation is observing yourself or someone else and assessing the effectiveness of your, or their, performance. To do this, you need to compare the performance with an exemplar performance at an equivalent level or with equivalent experience and qualifications.

The skills of evaluation should be used by a coach in two different ways. First, they should evaluate their own performance to form the basis of future coaching session plans. An evaluation of every session should enable them to assess what went well and could be used again and what was less successful. The way a coach deals with identified areas of weakness depends on how they develop as a coach. A good coach should be able to reflect on any areas of weakness and plan short-, medium- and long-term targets for their development.

Second, a coach should evaluate the performance of an athlete or a team, and produce a training programme based around their evaluation.

Time-management

The tasks a coach has to carry out prior to delivering a coaching session can demand a lot of time and effort. Many coaches are not professional, so may be juggling the demands of planning and delivering a coaching session around full- or part-time employment. Due to the demands that can be placed on a coach, it is important that they manage their time effectively.

Prior to a coaching session a coach will need to ensure that:

* all athletes attending the session are aware of the location and timing of the session
* the facility is booked
* the equipment required is prepared and ready for use
* the session is planned and all appropriate arrangements are made.

During the session the coach must also ensure that:

* an appropriate amount of time is dedicated to each component of the session
* weaknesses previously observed are worked on
* all athletes will develop technically and tactically (depending on the aims of the session)
* the session is fun and enjoyable
* time is allocated for athletes in a competitive situation to apply the skills covered in the session
* feedback is completed for players and parents or spectators as appropriate
* athletes are aware of future competitions or training.

Assessment activity 16.1 (P1) (P2) (M1) (M2) (D1) BTEC

1. You have been asked to produce a leaflet for prospective volunteer coaches at a local sports club. Your leaflet must describe four roles and four responsibilities of sports coaches, using examples from different sports. **(P1)**

2. In order to meet the requirement for M1 in your leaflet, in addition to the requirements for P1, you must explain four roles and four responsibilities of sports coaches, using examples from different sports. **(M1)**

3. In your leaflet you must also describe three skills common to successful sports coaches, using examples from different sports. **(P2)**

4. In order to meet the requirements of M2, in addition to the requirements for P2, you must explain three skills common to successful sports coaches, using examples from different sports. **(M2)**

5. If you would like to achieve D1 in this activity, in addition to the requirements for P1, P2, M1 and M2, you must compare and contrast the roles, responsibilities and skills of successful coaches from different sports. **(D1)**

Grading tips

(P1) Select four roles and four responsibilities and define each one, stating how sports coaches use each role and responsibility effectively.

(P2) Select three skills.

(M1), (M2) Use examples of at least three coaches from different sports to discuss the effective application of each role, responsibility and skill.

(M1) Explain how each coach selected meets the requirement of each role, responsibility and skill successfully.

(D1) Compare the roles, responsibilities and skills of the selected sports coaches. Say which roles, responsibilities and skills they all use (similarities) and which roles, responsibilities and skills some, but not all, of the coaches use (differences).

PLTS

Researching sports coaches who have fulfilled each role, responsibility and skill selected will help you to develop your skills as an **independent enquirer**.

Functional skills

Describing the roles, responsibilities and skills of sports coaches will help you develop your **English** writing skills.

2. Know the techniques used by coaches to improve the performance of athletes

2.1 Techniques

Observation analysis

A popular technique used by coaches to assess the performance and effective application of the skills, techniques and tactics required in a specific sport is observation analysis. Coaches need to be effective observers to enable them to identify strengths and weaknesses during performance.

Observation analysis is a crucial part of the coach's role, since coaching plans should be informed by analysis. Observation analysis should be used to identify an athlete's needs, with the coach completing a full analysis of their overall performance and then developing a training programme around it, aiming to improve the most significant weaknesses observed.

There are two basic ways of formulating judgements through observation analysis: subjective and objective analysis. Subjective analysis is based on observational judgements, personal interpretations and opinions. Objective analysis involves the measurement and comparison of performance data, for example the ability to perform a basketball free throw could be assessed objectively by counting how many free throws a player scores out of ten. The same assessment could be carried out objectively if a coach compares the player's technique and skill against a mental image of an ideal technique.

The most commonly used method of observation analysis is notational analysis. This requires the coach to record the number of skills completed effectively in a competitive situation. On completion of an objective analysis the coach is able to make subjective observations on the outcome of the athlete's overall performance.

When carrying out observation analysis, a coach must be careful not to be biased. They will have built up a relationship with the athlete they work with, but must view their performance in as unbiased a light as possible.

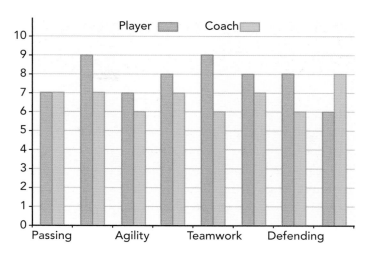

Figure 16.1: A performance profile completed by a coach and an athlete

Performance profiling

In order to complete a full assessment of an athlete's overall performance, a coach needs to carry out a full assessment of the technical, tactical, physical and psychological requirements of the sport. This is called a performance profile.

A performance profile is used by a coach to assess the technical and tactical ability of an athlete. It is

a subjective assessment which is completed using a variety of methods including notational analysis and performance observation. After such an assessment the coach will award the athletes or themselves a grade or mark which should be set against a specific target or goal with regard to development.

For example, a golfer who has a handicap of 16 may compare their performance against a golfer who has an 8 handicap, so on a scale of 1 to 10, 1 may be the attribute of a 16 handicap while 10 may be compared to the skills and attributes of a 4 handicap golfer. It would not be realistic to compare their performance to Tiger Woods because of the difference in ability and skill levels. It is therefore important for a coach to have realistic expectations regarding the developmental goals of athletes.

When coaching a beginner, a coach will complete a performance profile to determine which elements of the performance require development. At this stage of the athlete's career there will be little conversation between the athlete and the coach, as only the coach has the knowledge and experience required to develop performance.

As an athlete develops, the performance profiling should be completed by both the coach and the performer. After the completion of the performance profile, they should discuss the findings and agree a development plan that aims to address any technical, tactical, psychological or physical weaknesses in their performance.

Fitness assessment

Unit 8: Fitness testing for sport and exercise (page 200) introduces a variety of methods of assessing the physical and skill-related fitness components. A coach will use these to assess an athlete's fitness.

After the completion of such tests, the coach will be able to plan a training programme to work on any identified areas for improvement.

Following the training programme, the coach can also use fitness tests to reassess the athlete's fitness and compare the results to see whether improvements have been made.

Goal-setting

Goal-setting should be used by coaches to increase athletes' motivation and confidence. It should be the first stage of the planning process for any coach, as goals should provide both direction and motivation for athletes. Goals may be **short-term**, **medium-term**, or **long-term**.

Short-term goals could extend from one day to one month, for example a target that an athlete wishes to achieve after the next training session, or a specific technique they would like to develop by the end of the next month.

Medium-term goals should progressively support the progress of the athlete and their coach towards achieving the long-term goals. These goals can be measured at specific points in an athlete's season.

Long-term goals are set for and with athletes to help determine what their aims are and the best way of achieving them. A coach should use these to shape their coaching schedule for a season or longer if appropriate. The goals are often set for a season, for example a team may aim to finish the season in the top two positions in the league and achieve promotion. Long-term goals can also run over a number of years, as with an elite athlete who sets themselves a target of competing in the next Olympic Games, which may not take place for the next three years.

Simulation

When athletes have mastered the technical components in coaching sessions, the coach may use simulated practices as a means of advancing the skills developed in the session or previous sessions. Such practices may simulate a competitive environment, for example a simulated practice in a team game would be a conditioned game that would replicate some elements of the game, but where the coach would adapt the rules, number of players, or size of the pitch to try to support the development of specific skills.

Conditioned games will enable athletes to develop more of an understanding of the skills they are working on. If a coach limits the number of defenders when working on an attacking skill, the attackers are more likely to succeed, which will support their motivation. The coach can increase the number of defenders when they feel the performers are ready to be tested, and this will show how the performers cope in a realistic situation.

Simulation can also be used to support athletes to prepare for a specific event. For example, an athlete who is going to compete at a certain time of day at a certain altitude could simulate the environment by training at the same time of day and at the same altitude as the location of the competition.

Modelling

When introducing new skills to athletes, coaches often use modelling to demonstrate exactly what they expect the athletes to achieve. Modelling can be delivered in two forms:

- coach or performer demonstration
- video demonstration.

The model is an example of the skill, technique or activity which the coach would like the athletes to master. For example, when delivering a session with the aim of improving a player's ability to correctly and safely administer a rugby tackle, a coach may use a model of the action to show learners what is expected of them.

Modelling skills should be used to paint a picture in the minds of athletes, and to point out key technical instructions for the skill or activity the coach would like them to achieve.

Dartfish technology provides an opportunity to slow down movements and freeze actions, allowing coaches to demonstrate complex skills. It can also show two performances simultaneously to compare techniques.

Take it further

Dartfish is a video analysis program that can slow down and freeze-frame sporting actions. It is used to analyse sport skills and techniques in action.

This image demonstrates how Dartfish is used to analyse performance and the application of skills.

> Can you think of other sports where this technology could be used to develop performance?

Effective demonstration

Demonstrations are an important tool which should be used by coaches to support and develop athletes of all abilities. One of the first considerations a coach will have to make is whether to use video or still images to support the athlete's development.

For example, when working with a group of children or beginners, the coach should demonstrate the skill they would like the group to achieve during the session. At this stage the group's knowledge of the skill is limited and therefore if the coach has any bad habits these could be amended at a later stage in their development. On the other hand, when coaching elite athletes a coach may choose to use still images or video demonstrations because their own demonstrations at this level may display an inaccurate model. A video can be slowed down and replayed, with the coach highlighting the key factors for the athlete to address in their own application of the skill.

When demonstrating a skill to athletes a coach should:

- determine the purpose and type of demonstration to be used
- ensure that the image the demonstration paints in the athletes' minds is correct and appropriate
- ensure all athletes can see the demonstration
- only demonstrate one or two coaching points at a time
- repeat the demonstration more than once
- invite questions from the athletes at the end of the demonstration

The photo shows an international coach describing and demonstrating a skill to an England cricketer. Why is it important for the coach to demonstrate a skill or technique? Do you think it is ever inappropriate for a coach to demonstrate a skill? If so, when?

- let the athletes practise the skill
- observe the application of the skill and work individually with athletes if possible.

> **Remember**
>
> Demonstration: 'A picture paints a thousand words.'

Technical instruction

As mentioned earlier in this unit (page 387), verbal communication in coaching sessions should be clear and concise. A coach will often convey technical instructions to athletes using both verbal and non-verbal means. Non-verbal communication usually consists of some form of demonstration, while verbal communication involves providing instructions and guidance during and after demonstrations.

An effective coach should have a good knowledge of the technical requirements of the sport they are coaching. They should know how to break down the components of each skill or technique in order to share it with the participants in the session. When instructing athletes it is important to explain the significance and relevance of the instruction in relation to their overall development.

When providing technical instructions a coach should:

- plan what they are going to say and how they are going to deliver the information (this may depend on the audience)
- gain the attention of all the athletes prior to speaking
- keep the instructions simple but ensure the information is accurate
- when possible, use demonstrations/visual examples to reinforce the instructions
- check at the end of the instructions that all members of the group have understood.

As with any learning process, an athlete's ability to take in information will depend on what stage of learning they are at. For each stage, a coach should provide different levels of instructions and support (see Table 16.2).

> **Remember**
>
> When giving instructions, KISS – Keep It Simple.

The stages of learning		
Cognitive	**Associative**	**Autonomous**
Athletes are trying to grasp the basics of the skills/tasks set; they often have few experiences to relate to in the sport being coached. They will demonstrate a lot of errors and technical inefficiencies.	Athletes try to develop skills and techniques. They do this through practice. As they develop, they make fewer errors, although there will still be errors in the application of skills.	Athletes can produce skills with little effort almost 100% accuracy and success. At this stage they should be able to apply skills successfully in competitive situations.
Coach should: • use simple technical explanations and demonstrations • use simple basic drills and practices to develop skills • create fun and enjoyable sessions • encourage performers to practise unopposed • use lots of positive feedback.	Coach should: • use instructions and demonstrations to give athletes more information on the correct application of the skills • simulate training sessions and activities to develop specific skills • provide constructive feedback and promote peer- and self-analysis to assess performance.	Coach should: • use video demonstrations to demonstrate perfect application of skills • use complex technical instructions to fine-tune skills • discuss tactical application of the skills mastered.

Table 16.2: Matching instructions to the appropriate stage of learning

Developing performer coaching diaries

At the start of their career, sports coaches are always encouraged to keep a log of every session they complete and to collate all their session plans. At the end of each session they should reflect on what they and the participants have achieved. This process should continue as a coach develops.

A coach who records the development of each participant in each session will have a record of progress over a season. This can be useful when an athlete and coach reflect on the last season or look ahead and start to plan short-, medium- and long-term goals.

Adapting practices to meet individual needs

A coach must be able to support the varying needs and aspirations of all athletes who attend their sessions, all of whom have different methods of learning. This does not mean producing different session plans for each athlete, but it does mean that a coach should know their athletes, how they learn and which components of their game need support. A coach should be tactful, so that no one feels embarrassed or uncomfortable.

Designing effective practice sessions

A coach should aim to maintain athletes' interest, enjoyment and motivation. To achieve this aim, sessions should balance technical development, simulated practices and competitive situations. Although athletes should enjoy the sessions, it is also vital that the coach develops the application of skills, techniques and tactics in every session that they plan and deliver. Coaching sessions should differ for athletes of different ages or ability levels. However, a coach should also consider individual needs, as mentioned above.

Assessment activity 16.2

1. You have been asked to produce a presentation for all the volunteer coaches who have responded to an advertisement placed by your local sports club. Your presentation must describe three different techniques used by coaches to improve athletes' performance. **P3**

2. In order to meet the requirements of M3 in your presentation you must, in addition to the requirements for P3, explain three different techniques that are used by coaches to improve athletes' performance. **M3**

3. Finally, to meet the requirements of D2 in addition to the requirements of P3 and M3, your presentation must evaluate three different techniques that are used by coaches to improve athletes' performance. **D2**

Grading tips

P3 Select the three techniques you know most about. Describe what each one is and how it is used by coaches to improve performance.

M3 Give examples of coaches who use this technique successfully to develop athletes.

Give examples of coaches who have used these techniques and failed to develop athletes' performance.

D2 Assess the strengths and weaknesses of each technique, commenting on the reliability, subjectivity and validity of each one, as appropriate.

PLTS

Describing techniques used by coaches to improve athletes' performance will develop your skills as a **creative thinker**.

Functional skills

Describing techniques used by coaches to improve athletes' performance will develop your **English** writing skills.

3. Be able to plan a sports coaching session

3.1 Plan

Aims and objectives

All coaching sessions should have a clear **aim**. This should be clearly stated on the coach's session plan and agreed before the start of the session, for example for everyone to be able to execute a chest pass in netball by the end of the session.

In order to achieve your aims, you will need to have **objectives** (one per aim). These should be clearly written on your session plan and should express how you will meet each of them, for example 'In order for everyone in the group to execute a chest pass effectively I must introduce, demonstrate and develop the required technique for the chest pass.'

> ### Key terms
>
> **Aim** – something you want to achieve – a goal.
>
> **Objective** – how you are going to achieve your aim.

SMART (specific, measurable, achievable, realistic, time-bound) targets

A coach uses targets to develop athletes. They should be set around each individual's strengths and areas for improvement. The coach's session plan should focus on particular performers and set realistic targets. Coaches could use the SMART model for setting targets for participants in their session:

Specific – make the target as precise and detailed as possible.

Measurable – define a method of measuring the success of the athlete – set achievement targets – what by when?

Achievable – goal should be able to be attained within a set period of time and should be relevant for the athlete.

Realistic – appropriate for the athlete.

Time-bound – ensure you agree a timescale, even if it includes mini-targets for athlete development.

Roles and responsibilities

When planning a session with more than one coach, it is important to share roles and responsibilities equally. The plan should be recorded and the coaches should meet regularly to discuss the planning and preparation for the session/event and ensure that each coach is fulfilling their designated role and responsibility.

When planning a coaching session on your own, you should consider how you will meet each of your roles and responsibilities; you will be able to prepare for some of these beforehand, others you will have to apply during the delivery of your session.

3.2 Participants

When planning coaching sessions, the coach must consider the participants. They may determine the types of activities and the method of delivery and instruction (as discussed earlier in this unit). All information regarding the participants should be highlighted on the session plan (see Figure 16.3 pages 398–99).

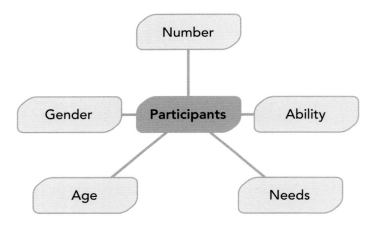

Figure 16.2: Participants

> ### Take it further
>
> Plan a coaching session for a group who are at the associative stage of learning. One has a physical disability and is in a wheelchair.
>
> Set clear aims and objectives for the session and set targets for the disabled participant using the SMART model.

Activity: Sports participants

Observe three different sessions (for the same sport) for boys aged 5–10, girls aged 12–16, and adults (over 18).

For each session, write a report identifying and describing: the coaching style, the types of activities, the levels of technical instruction used by the coach, the motivation of the performers' strengths of the session, areas of the session which could be improved and how.

3.3 Resources

Highlight on a session plan the resources required in each component of the session and how they will be used. There are three different types of resources in coaching sessions: **human, physical** and **fiscal**.

Key terms

Human resources – people involved in the delivery of a coaching session, e.g. coaches, assistant coaches, parents, spectators.

Physical resources – the facility and equipment required to deliver the session.

Fiscal resources – the financial costs of running coaching sessions, this may include facility and or equipment hire and could include depreciation costs or loss or damage costs to the equipment or facility.

3.4 Health and safety

Risk assessment

Sports coaches must exercise their duty of care at all times to provide a safe environment for the athletes who participate in their sessions, in order to comply with all relevant health and safety legislation, e.g. the Health and Safety at Work Act (1974). Assessing risk is not new: every time you cross the road you assess the risks. Risk assessment is an examination of everything that could cause harm and what can be done to reduce the risk of harm or injury to players, spectators and coaches.

Risk assessment requires the coach to examine all equipment and the facility/playing surface where the activity is taking place. Once a hazard has been identified, the coach must eliminate the hazard and/or risk. If the hazard can be eliminated then the session can proceed; if not, the coach must classify the degree of risk. Risks are usually classified as:

- low – no or minimal risk of injury
- medium – some risk of injury
- high – high risk of injury.

If the risk is anything higher than low, the coach must take action to eliminate the hazard, where possible, or reduce it to an acceptable level by reviewing and adding precautions. If a coach encounters such hazards, they must consult a more senior coach or member of staff and discuss whether the session should proceed.

Emergency procedures

When coaching a sports session, a coach needs to be aware of all the emergency procedures for the facility. They should follow these procedures and should also share their knowledge of them with athletes at the start of every session. A coach will therefore need to familiarise themselves with:

- the fire drill at a facility/organisation
- the evacuation procedures at a facility/organisation
- the first-aid procedure at a facility/organisation
- the location of qualified first-aid staff at a facility/organisation
- the location of telephones at a facility/organisation in the event of the emergency services being needed
- the risk-assessment procedure at a facility/organisation.

Prior to a coaching session a coach should carry out last-minute health and safety checks to ensure the facility is prepared and safe for physical activity to commence.

Contingencies

A good coach should be prepared for every eventuality, this is known as contingency planning. When undertaking a contingency plan it is important to:

- consider everything that could possibly go wrong
- do everything you can to ensure that none of these things does happen, so check all equipment, the availability of the facility, the number of participants and specific needs of participants at least the night before the event
- have an alternative plan and be prepared in case something does go wrong.

Figure 16.3 shows a session plan.

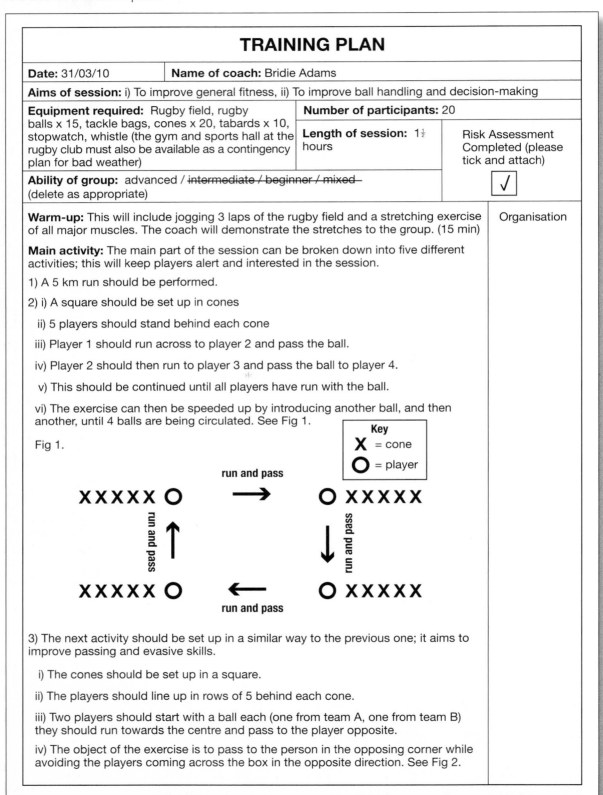

TRAINING PLAN

Date: 31/03/10	**Name of coach:** Bridie Adams	
Aims of session: i) To improve general fitness, ii) To improve ball handling and decision-making		
Equipment required: Rugby field, rugby balls x 15, tackle bags, cones x 20, tabards x 10, stopwatch, whistle (the gym and sports hall at the rugby club must also be available as a contingency plan for bad weather)	**Number of participants:** 20	
	Length of session: 1½ hours	Risk Assessment Completed (please tick and attach)
Ability of group: advanced / ~~intermediate / beginner / mixed~~ (delete as appropriate)		✓

	Organisation

Warm-up: This will include jogging 3 laps of the rugby field and a stretching exercise of all major muscles. The coach will demonstrate the stretches to the group. (15 min)
 	
Main activity: The main part of the session can be broken down into five different activities; this will keep players alert and interested in the session.
 	
1) A 5 km run should be performed.
 	
2) i) A square should be set up in cones
 	
  ii) 5 players should stand behind each cone
 	
  iii) Player 1 should run across to player 2 and pass the ball.
 	
  iv) Player 2 should then run to player 3 and pass the ball to player 4.
 	
  v) This should be continued until all players have run with the ball.
 	
  vi) The exercise can then be speeded up by introducing another ball, and then another, until 4 balls are being circulated. See Fig 1.
 	
Fig 1.
 	
Key
X = cone
O = player
 	
3) The next activity should be set up in a similar way to the previous one; it aims to improve passing and evasive skills.
 	
  i) The cones should be set up in a square.
 	
  ii) The players should line up in rows of 5 behind each cone.
 	
  iii) Two players should start with a ball each (one from team A, one from team B) they should run towards the centre and pass to the player opposite.
 	
  iv) The object of the exercise is to pass to the person in the opposing corner while avoiding the players coming across the box in the opposite direction. See Fig 2.	

Figure 16.3: A plan for a rugby training session

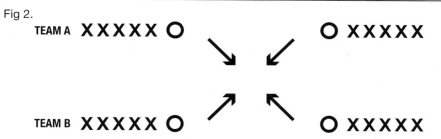

Fig 2.

4) This exercise aims to improve defending and decision-making skills.

i) During this exercise two players must attempt to score a try at the other side of a marked-out box. The defender who is positioned in the box will attempt to stop the try being scored. The two ball carriers are not permitted to stray outside the box.

ii) When the two players enter the marked-out defender s box, they must pass to each other.

iii) The aim of the exercise is for the ball carrier to draw the defender in and either pass/dummy and score a try at the other side of the box without the defender intercepting the pass or tackling the ball carrier.

iv) Two sets of boxes can be set up in different parts of the field, allowing two exercises to be carried out in sequence. When everyone has had a turn, the exercise can be adapted and two defenders can be stationed in the box, then three, etc.

v) Tackle bags can then be introduced for the defenders to hold, this will encourage more physical contact.

(a player defending his/her area)

5) The next exercise uses the whole pitch. The players must be split into two teams; they can then practise match plays and moves on their own with no opposition. Coaches must observe the players and give feedback and advice on their performance.

6) Finally, a friendly game of tag rugby can be played. This should help strengthen team spirit, help the players to interact well together and should also be relaxed and fun.

Cool down: The cool down will include a further 2 laps of the field and stretching out of all muscles and joints. (10 min)

Contingencies

This coaching plan can take place in most weather conditions. If it is raining, slippery or too cold to catch and throw properly, the plan can be adjusted. If necessary, more emphasis can be placed on the physical fitness aim of the session, a longer run could be incorporated which will improve fitness and warm the players up, the gym at the club can also be used. In order to practise ball skills and decision-making, the hall at the club is available and scaled exercises in smaller groups can be performed safely within this space. The exercises that involve physical contact should be eliminated, as these could be dangerous; also as the floor will be a harder surface, any tackling should be avoided.

Figure 16.3: A plan for a rugby training session (continued)

3.5 Components of a session

Having set clear aims and objectives for your coaching session, you can begin to devise the activities that will make up the session itself. Any session you devise will follow a structure broadly similar to the one below.

Warm-up – every coaching session should start with a warm-up to prepare the athletes both physically and mentally. This should last for at least 10 minutes. It should take a methodological approach which:

- initially increases body heat and respiratory and metabolic rates
- stretches the muscles and mobilises the joints that will be used in the session
- includes rehearsal and practice of some of the activities that are required in the sport.

Main body – this could include a variety of activities, depending on the aims and objectives of the session. If the aims and objectives are to develop a technical component of a sport, then the coach will need to include technical drills and skill practices. If the aims and objectives are to develop a specific aspect of fitness, then the session will have to include appropriate fitness activities. The main body of the session often includes a competitive element, which some coaches use to develop the skill or component of fitness covered earlier in the session. To do this a coach may choose to condition the game. For example, if the aim of the session is to develop short passing in football, the coach may choose to condition a competitive game at the end where a team score a goal for completing ten or more consecutive passes.

Cool down – at the end of the session a coach should ensure that all participants spend an appropriate amount of time cooling down. The aim of this is to bring the body gradually back to the pre-exercise condition. It should prevent muscle stiffness, injury and improve flexibility, provided stretches are performed correctly and controlled effectively by the coach.

Sequencing

When teaching a new skill or technique, the coach should consider how the delivery of the skill or technique will be best understood and learned by each athlete. To ensure that participants achieve optimum results in a session, the coach should consider:

- when to introduce skills and techniques
- whether to deliver a skill or technique as a whole practice or by breaking it down into parts
- the method of competition in which performers will be required to apply the skill or technique covered in the session.

Coaching skills and techniques

As mentioned earlier in this unit, a coach can use a number of skills and techniques to develop athletes' performance and ability. When planning coaching sessions a coach should consider the appropriate techniques and skills to use and when to use them.

Feedback

At the end of each activity and throughout a session, time should be allocated for the coach and athletes to feed back regarding the performance of each skill or technique covered.

Coaches are always providing feedback to athletes. This is usually given verbally, although with the development of technology and sports-analysis software, more coaches are using video and objective data.

It is essential for a coach to discuss with the athletes how well they have done in a session and what areas they can develop in future sessions. Inexperienced performers and children are less able to make sense of what happened during the session, so have a greater need for feedback. As athletes gain experience, they are more able to compare their own experiences and actions with previous attempts and thus more able to contribute to a coach-led discussion.

Assessment activity 16.3

The assessment activity for this section of Unit 16 is on page 406.

4. Be able to deliver and review a sports coaching session

When delivering coaching sessions the sports coach has to demonstrate appropriate roles, responsibilities, skills and techniques to support the development of the participants. The coach should ensure that they deliver the session they planned, only making changes when these are demanded by external factors.

The final part of this unit will require you as the coach to be assessed; the delivery of your session will be assessed against the criteria shown in Figure 16.4.

Methods of assessment will vary, but for an exemplar assessment observation sheet used by an assessor, look at Figure 16.7 on page 404. When being assessed it is important that learners fulfil the requirement of each role, responsibility, skill and technique as appropriate.

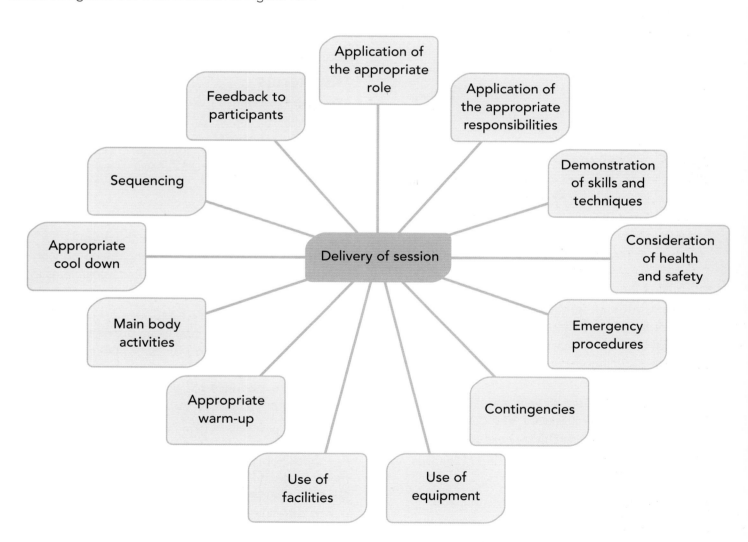

Figure 16.4: Vital factors in planning and delivering a coaching session

4.1 Review

Figure 16.5 shows the process every coach should follow to support their development and future sessions that they deliver. Even top coaches like Arsene Wenger constantly evaluate their own performance while delivering coaching sessions and look for other ways to develop the players they coach and their own practices as a coach. This is part of Wenger's coaching philosophy and one of the reasons why Arsenal have been so successful in spite of having limited resources in comparison to other Premier League teams.

The coaching process

Figure 16.5: The coaching process

The evaluation stage of the coaching process is an important stage where the coach should assess the effectiveness of each session. It should influence the planning of future sessions. The cycle should continue, each time benefiting from the experience of the previous stage.

Following each session, a coach should find time to evaluate how the session went. The questions below should help in assessing the success of a session.

1. Did the session meet the aims and objectives set at the start?
2. Did you meet the SMART targets that you set the athletes?
3. What went well in the session and why?
4. What did not go well in the session and why?
5. What lessons have you learnt as a coach and why?
6. What would you do to improve the session if you had to deliver it again?

Formative and summative assessment

A coach should review their performance at different stages in their development. In a **formative assessment** they will assess their coaching bit by bit and use feedback from learners and observers to assess their effectiveness. This will help a developing coach to plan short- and medium-term goals. **Summative assessment** could come from an external coach or assessor to award a coaching qualification or as a judgement about a coach's overall performance. When any form of assessment takes place the coach should use the feedback to support their development. Even negative feedback is useful: the best coaches are those who respond and come back improved after listening to the advice.

Key terms

Formative assessment – takes place informally and should support the development of a coach.

Summative assessment – takes place formally to assess the performance of a coach. It is often used to assess ability – for example, when trying to attain a coaching qualification.

Feedback

A developing coach should use feedback from participants and spectators regarding the delivery of their coaching sessions. A coach could ask athletes to complete a brief questionnaire like the one in Figure 16.6 on page 403.

Feedback from another coach can provide greater objectivity. See Figure 16.7 on page 404 for an example of an observation checklist that could be used by an experienced coach to assess another's performance.

Strengths

Feedback from participants and observers should enable the coach to identify the strengths of a session. The feedback should consist of summative feedback, plus the athletes' session body language and responses.

Areas for improvement

A coach should be able to ascertain which elements of their performance require improvement. This is the basis on which they should build their efforts to improve their performance. Every coach should seek to improve at every stage of their career.

Even Glenn Mills, the coach of the greatest sprinter of all time, will sometimes reflect on his own development as a coach and set targets for improvement.

- What areas do you think your own sports coach could improve on?
- What advice would you give your coach to develop these identified areas of weakness?

Performer Feedback Sheet

Please circle your answers.

Did you enjoy the session?

Did you enjoy the warm-up?

Did you enjoy the drills in the session e.g. the dribbling between the cones, the shooting into the hockey net?

Did the sports leader communicate clearly?

Did the sports leader demonstrate clearly what you had to do in the session?

Did you feel that your performance improved in the session?

What extra activities would you like to have done in the session?

....

Figure 16.6: An example of a questionnaire on a coach's performance

Assessment of:

Session Plan

Did the learner produce a lesson plan (prior to the start of the session/event?)	YES/NO
Was the session planned appropriately for the needs of the participants?	YES/NO
Will the session/event meet the aims and objectives of the session?	YES/NO

Targets

Did the learner set targets for participants?	YES/NO
Were these targets met during the session/event?	YES/NO
Before the session:	
Did the learner carry out a safety check of the participants and of the venue and equipment prior to the session/event?	YES/NO
Did the learner produce a risk assessment for the event/session?	YES/NO

Delivery

Did the learner communicate effectively throughout the session/event?	YES/NO
Did the learner use the facility and equipment effectively throughout the session?	YES/NO
Did the learner organise the session effectively?	YES/NO
Did the learner demonstrate effective application of the roles and responsibilities of a sports coach?	YES/NO
Did the learner demonstrate appropriate knowledge and language of the sport and the techniques and skills covered in the session?	YES/NO
Which techniques did the learner use to develop the performers within the session?	
Did the learner wear appropriate clothing for the session?	YES/NO
Did the learner motivate the performers throughout the session?	YES/NO
Were the components of the session delivered effectively and appropriately?	YES/NO
Did the learner demonstrate effective sequencing within the session?	YES/NO
Did the learner provide feedback throughout the session?	YES/NO
Did the learner conclude the session with a summary and provide opportunities for feedback to all performers?	YES/NO

Which areas could be improved?

Signed _____ (assessor) Date _____

Figure 16.7: An example of the observation record that the assessor may use when assessing your delivery skills of the coaching session for this unit

4.2 Development plan

After completing the coaching process (see Figure 16.5) a coach should reflect on their performance and consider how to address the feedback obtained. Their conclusions should form the basis of a development plan, consisting of targets they have set themselves.

Opportunities

In their development plan the coach should identify specific goals, for example:

- completing specific coaching qualifications
- working with specific sports coaches
- observing sports coaches working with specific groups.

The plan should clearly identify the methods the coach wishes to use to improve their performance, with a justification of how and why.

Further qualifications

National governing bodies (NGBs) of sport have developed coaching and leadership awards to support developing coaches. Almost all NGBs now have a coach-education structure which produces qualifications from assistant coach level (level 1) up to elite coach level (levels 4 and 5).

A coach should aim to gain the qualifications required to coach and lead the athletes they work with, to ensure that they receive the support and experience recommended by the NGB.

Potential barriers

When producing a development plan a coach must be aware of the barriers that could prevent some of their targets being met. A coach, unlike an athlete, will be left to their own devices to overcome potential barriers and therefore must be aware of what may stand in their way, for example:

- geographical location
- cost
- time
- gender
- ethnic minority.

Activity: Further qualifications

As part of your development as a coach, you should be aware of the location of the NGB for your chosen sport.

1. Research the address and contact details (phone number, email address and website) of the national headquarters of the NGB for your chosen sport.

2. Find out if there are regional offices for the NGB for your chosen sport, make a note of the contact details if appropriate (telephone number, email address and website).

3. Now you have the contact details, research the coach-education structure for your chosen sport:
   - make a note of the title of each qualification
   - make a note of the level of each qualification
   - make a note of the learning hours required to complete each qualification
   - make a note of the location of the next available appropriate course for a delegate with similar experience to you
   - make a note of the cost of the course.

Despite such barriers, Sport England and NGBs are working with community groups to increase the number of coaches. Initiatives such as the McDonalds Coaching Scheme run in conjunction with the Football Association to increase the number of qualified coaches. The scheme offers football coaches an opportunity to gain a coaching qualification for free and is run through the regional FAs to support coaches who may have not been able to access such qualifications in the past.

Assessment activity 16.3

P4 P5 P6 M4 M5 D3

BTEC

You have been asked to demonstrate to volunteers how to plan and deliver a sports coaching session.

1. You should provide the volunteers with a session plan for a specific sports coaching session. **P4**

2. You will then deliver the coaching session with support. **P5**

3. In addition to the requirement of P5, if you complete it independently you will attain M4 criteria. **M4**

4. After you have completed the session you must demonstrate to the volunteers how to review the planning and delivery of a sports coaching session, identifying strengths and areas for improvement. You will do this in the form of a written report which will be sent to each volunteer after the event. **P6**

5. In order to meet the requirements for M5, in addition to the requirements for P6, in your feedback to the volunteers you should also evaluate the planning and delivery of a sports coaching session, suggesting how improvements could be made in the areas identified for improvement. **M5**

6. To meet the requirements of D3, in addition to the requirements of P6 and M5, you must justify suggestions made in relation to the development plan. **D3**

Grading tips

P4 Complete your session plan in a clear format, ensuring that it includes the aims and objectives of the session, coaching pointers and methods of managing health and safety.

Prior to the session, ensure you have arranged questionnaires for the athletes and observers to complete regarding the delivery of the session.

P5 Ensure that your assessor observes your performance and completes an observation record.

M4 Lead your session independently.

P6 Ensure that someone records your coaching session so you can look back on it to develop a self-assessment of your performance.

Observe your coaching session and list your strengths and areas for improvement.

Look through the feedback obtained from the participants and performers and list the strengths and areas for improvement.

M5 Summarise the planning and delivery of the session, what you did well, what you did less well and what you would do if you had the opportunity to deliver the session again.

Produce a development plan, stating how you plan to develop as a coach.

D3 Identify specific coaching qualifications which you could complete to support your development, describing what components of your performance as a coach these will develop.

For each selected coaching course and planned development opportunity, identify how this will support your development as a coach.

PLTS

Reviewing your performance after the coaching session will improve your skills as a **reflective learner**.

Functional skills

Planning a sports coaching session using a computer will develop your **ICT** skills.

Teresa Dodd
Head Netball Coach, Wilberforce Academy

Teresa's team have been consistently high achievers for 5 years, winning the league twice and the cup competition once. This year their form has dipped significantly and they are currently bottom of the Hull and East Riding District League. This is mainly because the team lost a number of players at the end of the last season to another team in the Northern League. These have been replaced with young players with limited competitive experience at this level but exceptional technical skills.

During the last competitive match Teresa carried out an observational analysis of the team's performance. She concluded that a number of players lacked the required aerobic endurance to complete the game. She also noticed that technically all the members of the team matched their opponents. However, their application of the required tactical components was weak, especially when attacking with the ball.

In the past Teresa has allowed the club captain to take the training sessions, as she is an experienced player. However, she noticed that the last training session consisted of a competitive match between the old team members and the players who have recently joined the club. Many players have spoken with Teresa, expressing their lack of motivation to train.

Teresa has decided to take over the training sessions to try to improve the team's performance. Teresa has not coached a session for a long time and is seeking advice on how to support the team and tackle some of the areas for improvement.

Think about it!

- Give Teresa some advice regarding the types of activities she could use to develop team cohesion.
- Advise her on the types of activities she could use to develop the weak areas she noticed in the team's fitness.
- Guide Teresa on types of activities used to support the development of tactical knowledge and its application in competitive situations.
- Produce a session plan for Teresa's first training session that identifies different types of activities and coaching tips she could use.

Just checking

1. List five successful sports coaches and describe why each one has been successful.
2. List six roles a sports coach must try to fulfil.
3. List six responsibilities a sports coach should try to fulfil.
4. What common skills are required by a coach to support athletes' development?
5. What are objective and subjective analysis?
6. What is observational analysis and how is it used by coaches to support performance development?
7. Why would technical instruction support performance development and what knowledge would a coach require to provide effective technical instruction?
8. Provide a definition for each of the following:
   • human resources   • physical resources   • fiscal resources.
9. What is a risk and what is a hazard?
10. What action can a coach take to reduce the risks and hazards in a coaching session?
11. What methods can a coach use to ensure they obtain appropriate feedback from observers and participants?
12. List the courses that could support the development of a coach in your own sport.
13. What other opportunities could a coach undertake to support their development?

edexcel

Assignment tips

- Observe a number of sessions run by local coaches and consider the planning and experience required to become an effective coach.
- When planning coaching sessions you will need to have a good understanding of the sport involved. Choose a sport you are confident to coach and have appropriate knowledge about.
- Make the most of opportunities to plan and lead coaching sessions. Enjoy developing new skills.
- Don't be afraid to tell athletes what you think: remember, your job is to improve their performance, not just to observe them making mistakes.
- Remember to consider the methods of feedback you will use to assess the effectiveness of your session; you should get feedback from performers, peers and your assessor.
- Research the coaching courses available in your selected sport, and examine other methods that could be used to develop your skills as a coach.
- Complete a level 1 coaching award to support your development of the required skills and techniques required to coach in your selected sport.
- Ensure that you read the assignment briefs properly. Take your time and ensure you are happy with the task set. If not, ask your tutor for assistance.
- Attempt all parts of the assignments. If you only attempt the pass criteria, this is all you will achieve. Think big and try it all.

17 & 18

Practical individual sports & practical team sports

The desire to participate in sports continues to grow. People are becoming more aware of the lifelong benefits of a healthy lifestyle, and the legacy of the UK's successful Olympic bid will provide more opportunities for those wanting to take part in sport.

Sport gives individuals an opportunity to push themselves to the limits. This is what motivates them to aim for the perfect performance and achieve the highest accolades. Units 17 and 18 introduce the skills, techniques and tactics required in selected sports. You will have to demonstrate application of these in each of your selected sports. You will also examine the application of the rules of team and individual sports, the methods used to assess sports performance and how to use performance assessments to further develop team or individual performance.

Learning outcomes

After completing this unit you should:

1. know the skills, techniques and tactics required in selected team/individual sports
2. know the rules and regulations of selected team/individual sports
3. be able to assess your own performance in selected team/individual sports
4. be able to assess the performance of others in selected team/individual sports.

Unit 17 and Unit 18 Assessment and grading criteria

This table shows you what you must do in order to achieve a pass, merit or distinction grade, and where you can find activities in this book to help you.

To achieve a **pass** grade the evidence must show that the learner is able to:	To achieve a **merit** grade the evidence must show that, in addition to the pass criteria, the learner is able to:	To achieve a **distinction** grade the evidence must show that, in addition to the pass and merit criteria, the learner is able to:
P1 describe skills, techniques and tactics required in two different team/individual sports **Assessment activity 17.1 page 418** **Assessment activity 18.1, page 419**	**M1** explain skills, techniques and tactics required in two different team/individual sports **Assessment activity 17.1, page 418** **Assessment activity 18.1, page 419**	
P2 describe the rules and regulations of two different team/individual sports, and apply them to three different situations for each sport **Assessment activity 17.2, page 428** **Assessment activity 18.2, page 428**	**M2** explain the application of the rules and regulations of two different team/individual sports, in three different situations for each sport **Assessment activity 17.2, page 428** **Assessment activity 18.2, page 428**	
P3 demonstrate appropriate skills, techniques and tactics in two different team/individual sports **Assessment activity 17.1, page 418** **Assessment activity 18.1, page 419**		
P4 carry out a self-analysis using two different methods of assessment identifying strengths and areas for improvement in two different team/individual sports **Assessment activity 17.3, page 437** **Assessment activity 18.3, page 439**	**M3** explain identified strengths and areas for improvement in two different team/individual sports, and make suggestions relating to personal development **Assessment activity 17.3, page 437** **Assessment activity 18.3, page 439**	**D1** analyse identified strengths and areas for improvement in two different team/individual sports, and justify suggestions made **Assessment activity 17.3, page 437** **Assessment activity 18.3, page 439**
P5 carry out a performance analysis using two different methods of assessment, identifying strengths and areas for improvement in the development of a team/an individual in a team/an individual sport **Assessment activity 17.4, page 438** **Assessment activity 18.4, page 440**	**M4** explain identified strengths and areas for improvement in the development of a team/an individual in a team/an individual sport, and make suggestions relating to development of a team/an individual **Assessment activity 17.4, page 438** **Assessment activity 18.4, page 440**	**D2** analyse identified strengths and areas for improvement in the development of a team/an individual in a team/an individual sport, and justify suggestions made **Assessment activity 17.4, page 438** **Assessment activity 18.4, page 440**

How you will be assessed

Your assessment for each of these two units can be in the form of:

- video showing you applying the appropriate rules, skills, techniques and tactics for selected team or individual sports
- logbooks with records of your achievements and development in each practical team or individual session
- observation records of your performance as a player in selected team or individual sports
- written summaries of the rules, regulations and scoring systems for selected team or individual sports
- written peer- and self-analysis and assessments of your performance in selected team or individual sports
- video showing analysis and assessments.

Team sports: Tom Dawson, 22-year-old schoolteacher

I completed a BTEC National Diploma before gaining a degree in Sports Coaching at university. At school I loved playing sport, and through completing this unit I learned more about the application of the rules and the techniques required to play a sport. This unit gave me a greater appreciation of development, and the things I learned have been really useful now that I am trying to develop young children every day as a teacher.

Part of my development plan was to obtain as many sports coaching awards and certificates as possible, and I started doing this as soon as the college offered us the opportunity to complete the Football Association Level 1 coaching award. After that I got the bug and now have a whole host of coaching awards, which has really helped with teaching.

I am now teaching this unit to my students and trying to communicate the importance of gaining knowledge of all sports, not just one!

Over to you

- **What team sports did you play at school?**
- **For each one, describe the scoring system and major rules.**

Individual sports: Lisa Stockdale, 18-year-old degree student

I have always wanted to be a sports therapist and I believe that this is because of the enthusiasm passed on to me from my PE teacher at school. I enjoyed the practical part of PE lessons, but used to worry that I would play less after I left school because of the lack of organised sport available.

When I discovered that the BTEC National Diploma in Sport at my local college included practical sports as well as the theoretical units, I was keen to complete this course.

At school, I was never as good at sports as some of the other students, but this course has allowed me to continue to play and to learn more about the skills, techniques and tactics of different individual sports and achieve the highest grade possible, without having to be a fantastic performer.

I play badminton at university and I feel the knowledge that I have gained from the course has given me the confidence to play with high-level performers. I hope to continue playing throughout university and beyond.

Over to you

- Examine the provision for playing individual sports in your locality.
- What clubs are there and who do they provide activities for (e.g. beginners, intermediate, advanced)?
- Discuss why sports participation levels drop when children leave school.

1. Know the skills, techniques and tactics required in selected team/individual sports

The earliest evidence of sport includes *tsu chu*, a form of football played in China over 3,000 years ago, and the Ancient Greek Olympics. The Olympics were revived in 1896, and are now enjoyed by participants and spectators from all over the world.

Sport could be defined as 'an organised competitive physical activity, governed by set rules and regulations'. This definition clearly includes sports such as tennis, badminton, athletics and gymnastics, but leaves others such as snooker, pool and darts open to debate.

The debate will continue to grow as the popularity of these sports increases. Often as a sport grows, an international governing body is established to govern its rules, and this is often a determining factor in its classification.

Key term

Sport – the *Oxford Concise Dictionary* defines sport as 'An activity involving physical exertion and skill in which an individual or team competes against another or others for entertainment.'

Sports can be classified as athletic, gymnastic, and games, and as team and individual sports. They can then be divided further, for example within the 'games' category there are net and wall games, invasion games, striking and fielding games, combat games, target games, track athletics and field athletics.

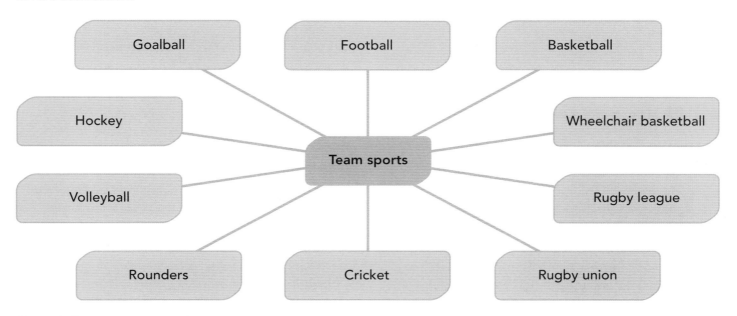

Goalball · Football · Basketball · Hockey · Wheelchair basketball · **Team sports** · Volleyball · Rugby league · Rounders · Cricket · Rugby union

Figure 1: Team sports

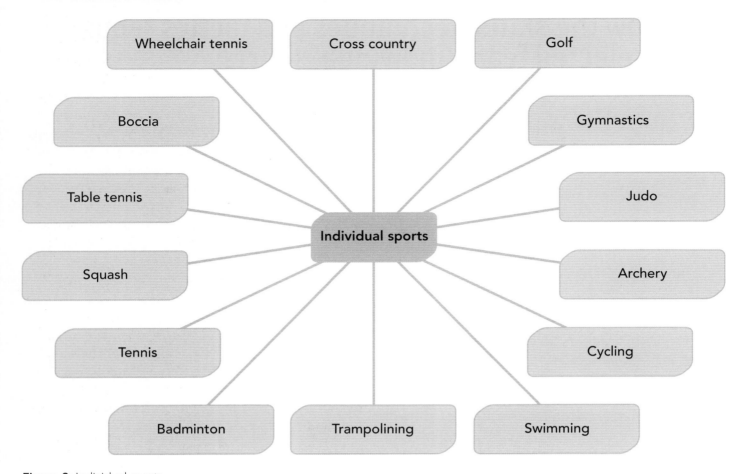

Figure 2: Individual sports

In this unit you will examine both team and individual sports. A team sport involves competition between teams of players with a shared goal of winning. Team sports require athletes to work together to obtain this goal. They are complex, with highly structured rules. An individual sport involves a single athlete competing against other athletes or another single performer. In most individual sports there can only be one winner.

1.1 Skills and techniques

Skills

Skill is defined by Knapp as 'The learned ability to bring about predetermined results with maximum certainty, often with the minimum outlay of time or energy or both.'

A skill in sport is the ability to produce a combination of movements using a variety of muscles and joints to produce a coordinated action. Skills are acquired through learning, and mastered through practice and observation. Athletes develop skills through support and feedback from experienced and knowledgeable coaches and/or athletes. Mastering a skill means being able to continually produce it successfully with little effort.

Skills vary, however some can be transferred from sport to sport. For example, an athlete who masters the skill of catching when receiving a pass in rugby can transfer this skill to other sports that involve catching, such as basketball, cricket or netball.

Activity: Skills transfer

Think of some other sports where skills can be transferred to enhance an athlete's performance.

Skills have been classified into different groups using continuums with opposites at either end and gradually changing characteristics between them.

Open and closed skills

Skills can be classified according to the environment in which they are performed. They may be open or closed.

Open skills are those which the athlete is constantly adapting, according to what is happening around them.

An example of an open skill in a team sport could be when a footballer is dribbling a ball, unaware of the location of all the members of the opposing team. Defenders will challenge the player to try to get possession of the ball. The decisions that the player dribbling the ball will make will depend on the actions of the opponents.

An example of an open skill in an individual sport could be a return in badminton: the receiver is unaware where the shuttlecock will be played by the returnee, so will have to react to their opponent's moves in order to select an appropriate return. The choice of the return shot will also be affected by the position of the opponent on the court.

Closed skills are pre-learned patterns of movements which the athlete can follow with very little reference to the surrounding environment.

An example of a closed skill in a team sport is a rugby player taking a conversion during a match. The movement pattern remains the same every time the player performs the skill.

An example of a closed skill in an individual sport is when an archer takes aim, pulls back the bowstring and releases the arrow towards the target.

We also classify skills by the pace with which the athlete controls the timing of an action. Skills are said to be self-paced, externally paced, or somewhere between the two.

Self-paced skills are those where an athlete controls the timing of the execution of the skill. An example of a self-paced skill in a team sport might be a serve in volleyball: the server decides when to start the action; the timing may depend on the location of the opponents and the readiness of the server.

An example of a self-paced skill in an individual sport might be a golf shot: the golfer determines when to start the swing, and may choose to wait until a gust of wind has dropped prior to taking the shot.

Externally-paced skills are those in which the timing of the skill is determined by what is happening elsewhere. For example, when applying a pass in

hockey, the skill is determined by the location of players on the same team and the opposing team. Likewise, a windsurfer will have to alter the angle of his/her sail, depending on the direction of the wind.

For some skills the athlete can control the start of the action, but thereafter the movement takes place at an externally set pace. An example from a team sport would be a goalkeeper making a save during a football game: the goalkeeper will decide when to dive towards the ball, but once the decision is made, the goalkeeper no longer has any control over the speed at which she/he travels towards the ball. An example from an individual sport might be a 10-metre board diver who decides when to start the dive, but having left the board is unable to control the rate at which she/he heads towards the water.

To achieve success in sport, an athlete has to successfully master a range of skills. For example, a basketball player will have to perform the following skills successfully: dribbling, passing, free throws, jump shots, lay-ups, rebounds, blocking, stealing. A tennis player must successfully perform serves, volleys, forehands, backhands, slices and top spins.

Modern technological advances have affected sport just as much as other aspects of our lives.

Fine and gross body involvement

Skills can also be classified by the muscles involved. On this continuum, skills are defined as fine and gross.

Fine skills involve small movements of specific parts of the body. For example, taking a close-range shot at goal in netball will only require the goal shooter and goal attack to move their fingers and wrist to produce the required skill. An individual shooting a rifle on a shooting range will only have to move their trigger finger.

Gross skills involve large muscle groups and movement from the whole body. An example of this form of skill in a team sport is the bowling action in cricket, while an individual example is the javelin throw.

Continuous, discrete or serial skills

Continuous skills are those which have no obvious beginning or end; they can be continued for as long as the performer wishes, with the end of the skill becoming the beginning of the next, for example, running.

A **discrete skill** has a clear beginning and end. The skill can be repeated, but the athlete will start the full action again in a controlled and timely manner. An example of a discrete skill in a team sport is a rugby conversion, while an individual example is a golf putt.

A **serial skill** is a series of discrete skills put together to produce an organised movement. The order of the movement is often important, but the requirements of each part of the skill will require specific development. An example from a team sport is when a footballer dribbles with the ball, steps over it to beat a defender and then shoots at goal at the end of the movement. An example from an individual sport is a gymnastic tumble.

In groups, identify whether a golf shot is:

- an open or closed skill
- a fine or gross skill
- a self-paced or externally paced skill
- a continuous, discrete or serial skill.

List the skills in your own sport and identify which categories they fall into.

An athlete needs to understand the requirements of the skills in their sport and the correct application of each one, and must remember that coaching and practice are key elements in improving their performance and their ability to perform the necessary skills. Even the greatest athletes continually seek to improve their performance, through attending coaching sessions and listening to the advice of their coach.

Footballer Wayne Rooney taking advice from his manager, Alex Ferguson. Listening to advice is a key process in the development of an athlete.

Golfer Sergio Garcia on the follow-through of an approach shot to the green during a competition.

Techniques

A **technique** is the way an athlete performs a skill. In some sports, players use different techniques to produce the same outcome. For example, David Beckham and Cristiano Ronaldo have different techniques when taking direct free kicks, and Andy Murray and Rodger Federer will have different serving techniques.

The most effective way to consider a technique is to consider how the skill can be broken down. For

Key term

Technique – a way of undertaking a particular skill.

example, a long lofted pass can be broken down into its component actions as follows: run-up (preparation stage), alignment to the ball, feet position, body position, contact with the ball and follow-through. An example from an individual sport might be a tennis serve broken down into its component actions: feet position and movement, body position, action of the racket-holding arm, action of the other arm, ball toss, racket swing and follow-through.

Breaking down skills like this develops athletes' understanding of how to improve their application of each skill. The technical elements for each component will be different for each individual, but the components of the skill will remain the same.

Tactics

Tactics are the skills a player uses in any type of sport to be able to win, for example during a hockey or tennis match, each team or player will apply specific tactics and strategies to try to beat and outwit their opponent(s).

While techniques are the way we apply skills in a selected sport, tactics are how we apply skills successfully in competitive situations. The most skilful and talented performer can lose if they do not apply the skills strategically in specific situations.

Tactics in sport are mostly concerned with attacking and defending. Factors that affect tactics include the opposition, the playing conditions and possibly the timing of the game, match, or tournament in a season. Some tactics are determined before the event starts, these often target a player's or a team's weaknesses. Pre-event tactics can include carrying out research on an opposing player or team.

Tactics are often categorised into attacking strategies, used to attack opponents, and defensive strategies, used to prevent opponents scoring points or gaining ground. Each sport has strategies for attacking and defending, for example in a game of netball, one

team may spot a weakness in one of the opposing players and as a team try to exploit this to gain an advantage. On the other hand, if a netball team is suffering because of a particular player in the opposing team, changes may be made to mark that player very closely. Likewise, in a game of tennis a serve could be seen as an attacking shot, but the application of the skill alone cannot guarantee this. The player performing the serve may adjust their serve to disadvantage their opponent.

It can be difficult to coach athletes in applying tactics in a competitive environment. Such knowledge is developed through experience, although coaches try to develop the knowledge and ability to apply appropriate strategies through simulating specific practices. When athletes have experienced specific scenarios, they will be able to react appropriately.

Key term

Tactics – the skills and strategies a player uses in any type of sport to be able to win, for example during a hockey or tennis match, each team or player will apply specific tactics and strategies to try to beat and outwit their opponent(s).

Remember

The main factors affecting the application of tactics in team and individual sports are:

- attacking and defending
- the situation in the game – are you winning or losing?
- your own/team's strengths – what parts of the race/game are you stronger in and which parts of your game are weaker?
- your opponents' strengths and weaknesses.

Assessment activity 17.1: Skills, techniques and tactics of selected individual sports

You should now complete a number of practical sessions for at least two individual sports. In each session you should be introduced to a skill, technique and tactic for a sport. Your tutor should support you in understanding the correct application of each skill, technique and tactic in each of your selected sports.

1. For each session you participate in, you should complete a practical log or diary in which you describe the skills, techniques and tactics required in two different individual sports. **P1**

2. In order to achieve M1 criteria, in your practical logs you must also explain the skills, techniques and tactics required in two different individual sports. **M1**

3. At the end of each session you should also ensure that you demonstrate the appropriate skills, techniques and tactics in at least two different individual sports. **P3**

Grading tips

P1 After each session, complete your practical log/diary booklet.

Ensure you make notes regarding the correct application of each skill/technique.

Record your performance in each sport when applying specific defending and attacking strategies.

M1 In your diary, explain how the effective use of each skill can develop performance in a competitive situation.

P3 Record your application of each technique/skill.

Describe the different strategies used within each selected individual sport to defend and attack.

Ask your tutor to complete a witness statement that records your achievements.

PLTS

Researching the skills and techniques appropriate to two individual sports will develop your skills as an **independent enquirer**.

Functional skills

When completing a written practical log describing techniques, skills and tactics covered within each practical session for each individual sport, you will develop your **English** writing skills.

Assessment activity 18.1: Skills, techniques and tactics of selected team sports

You should now complete a number of practical sessions for at least two team sports. In each session you should be introduced to a skill, technique and tactic for a sport. Your tutor should support you in understanding the correct application of each skill, technique and tactic in each of your selected sports.

1. For each session you participate in, you should complete a practical log or diary in which you describe the skills, techniques and tactics required in two different team sports. **P1**

2. In order to achieve the M1 criteria, in your practical logs you must also explain the skills, techniques and tactics required in two different team sports. **M1**

3. At the end of each session you should also ensure that you demonstrate the appropriate skills, techniques and tactics in at least two different team sports. **P3**

Grading tips

P1 After each session, complete your practical log/diary booklet.

Ensure you make notes regarding the correct application of each skill/technique.

Record your performance in each sport when applying specific defending and attacking strategies.

M1 In your diary, explain how the effective use of each skill can develop performance in a competitive situation.

P3 Record your application of each technique/skill.

Describe the different strategies used within each selected team sport.

PLTS

Researching the skills and techniques appropriate to two team sports will develop your skills as an **independent enquirer**.

Functional skills

When completing a written practical log describing techniques, skills and tactics covered within each practical session for each team sport, you will develop your **English** writing skills.

2. Know the rules and regulations of selected team/individual sports

2.1 Rules and regulations

As mentioned earlier in the unit, a sport must have governed rules and regulations. These are organised and regularly updated by the appropriate governing bodies at the highest level, and are then enforced by officials who represent the governing bodies, both national and international. An athlete needs to be aware of the rules and regulations of any sport in which they participate.

Researching the rules and regulations of their sport can help to make players more competent and better role models for others. The better an athlete understands the rules and regulations of their sport, the more they will appreciate the work of the officials who implement them.

In team sports, the number of participants per team is restricted and in order for a game to be as equal as possible it is usual for each team to have equal numbers of players. For example, in a game of rugby union, each team is allowed to start with a maximum of 15 players; a side starting with fewer players will be at an obvious disadvantage. Each team has to rely not only on the application of skills from individual players but also on teamwork and the correct tactics. The rules, laws and regulations of a sport are set to provide players with standards to adhere to and ensure that they all play fairly.

Some rules do not differ much from sport to sport, for example in rugby league and rugby union the rules regarding losing control of the ball and knocking the ball forward are similar; likewise in table tennis and tennis the rules regarding the number of times a ball is allowed to bounce are similar. However, most sports' rules differ quite considerably. This section will look at some components of sports which remain constant although varying from sport to sport. This includes the start of a competition, scoring or methods of victory, the competitive environment and time. These are examples of rules which are managed and maintained by national governing bodies (NGBs) and international sports federations (ISFs).

The rules and regulations of sports are normally established and governed by the NGB and when appropriate by ISFs.

Individual sport	National governing body	International sports federation
Boxing	Amateur Boxing Association	International Boxing Association
Badminton	Badminton England	Badminton World Federation
Judo	British Judo Association	International Judo Federation
Gymnastics	British Gymnastics	Fédération Internationale de Gymnastique
Athletics	UK Athletics	International Association of Athletics Federations
Cycling	British Cycling	Union Cycliste Internationale
Rowing	British Rowing (formerly Amateur Rowing Association)	Fédération Internationale des Sociétés d'Aviron
Tennis	Lawn Tennis Association	International Tennis Federation
Sailing	Royal Yachting Association	International Sailing Federation
Table tennis	English Table Tennis Association	International Table Tennis Federation

Table 17.1: The national governing body and international sports federations for ten individual sports

Team sport	National governing body	International sports federation
Football	The Football Association	Fédération Internationale de Football Association (FIFA)
Rugby Union	The Rugby Football Union	International Rugby Board (IRB)
Rugby League	The Rugby Football League	Rugby League International Federation (RLIF)
Volleyball	English Volleyball Association	Fédération Internationale de Volleyball (FIVB)
Basketball	England Basketball	Fédération Internationale de Basketball (FIBA)
Hockey	England Hockey	International Hockey Federation (FIH)
Cricket	England and Wales Cricket Board	International Cricket Council (ICC)
Rounders	Rounders England	National Rounders Association (NRA)
Netball	England Netball Association	International Federation of Netball Associations (IFNA)
Lacrosse	English Lacrosse Association	Federation of International Lacrosse (FIL)

Table 18.1: The national governing body and international sports federations for ten team sports

Take it further

Find and research the website and location of each of the national governing bodies listed in the two tables – if your sport is not listed, research its NGB and ISF.

NGBs work closely with international sports federations to ensure that the rules, structure and development of a sport are managed appropriately.

In the past decade a number of sports have undertaken some changes to the rules and regulations to make them more entertaining for spectators. For example, in 1992 FIFA adapted the laws of football regarding allowing a goalkeeper to pick up a ball that has been passed back to them by a player on the same team, and in 2006 the Badminton World Federation adapted its method of scoring to ensure that for every successful shot a point was awarded to the player(s) who completed it. The process of changing the rules requires a trial period; once the ISF agrees that the rule change was appropriate, the change is sanctioned, the rules and laws of the sport amended and the appropriate information passed to the national governing bodies. This information would be expected to be passed on to officials, clubs, coaches, performers, teachers and spectators, and applied in all future competitions and events.

In most sports, rules and regulations are updated regularly, and it is the responsibility of everyone involved in a sport to have a thorough knowledge of these changes.

The rules and laws decided by national governing bodies and international sports federations determine how a sport can be won or lost. All sports have different rules, regulations and laws, however the goal in all sports is to achieve and win.

The assessment that you will carry out as part of Unit 18 will require you to describe the rules for two selected team sports, and for Unit 17, you will be asked to describe the rules of two individual sports. The text below will introduce you to some categories that the rules of your chosen sports will fall into. However, there will be other rules in the sports you describe, that will be fundamental to how they are played. You must ensure that your descriptions include the core rules and regulations.

2.2 The start of a game/race/competition

Any competition has to have a clear beginning and end. In all sports, the start will be administered by an official who will tell the players when to begin. For example, in a game of basketball a player from each of the two teams will compete to gain possession through participating in a tip-off conducted by the umpire. Before a game of cricket, the umpire must allow the captain from one of the two teams to decide who is going to start the batting or the bowling: this is decided by a toss of a coin. The winner of the toss then decides whether their team will bat or bowl first. In a 100-metre sprint race the start is controlled by the starter: the athletes will go when they hear the gun or starting signal. Before a tennis match, the umpire tosses a coin, and the winner of the toss chooses whether to serve first, and which side of the court to start the game.

2.3 Scoring

In some sports, scores are given for achieving a goal, while in others success is assessed by a time or a distance. The points, games, time, or distance determine who wins and who loses.

A cricket team will win a game if they score more runs than the opposing team. There can be restrictions on the number of overs a team may bowl in order to obtain a set number of runs (limited overs cricket) but some matches (test matches) can have unlimited overs but are restricted to a set number of days. In a sailing regatta, the winner will be the team which completes the race in the fastest time. A 100-metre sprinter will win the race by attaining a faster time than all the other athletes in the race. In tennis, on the other hand, a player has to win a certain number of points to win a game, a certain number of games to win a set and a certain number of sets to win the overall match.

Scoring in a team sport e.g. Cricket

Below is an example of how to score runs in cricket. The rules regarding scoring are set by the International Cricket Council (ICC) and governed in England by representatives (officials) of the England and Wales Cricket Board (ECB).

In cricket, teams score by obtaining units called runs. A run is completed when a batsman hits the ball and then runs to the other end of the cricket pitch, getting past the **crease**.

The non-striking batsman also has to run to the opposite end. The batsmen can run as many times as they like, but they may be out if a fielder hits their **stumps** with the ball before the batsmen reach the crease.

Runs can also be scored in the following ways.

- Boundaries are scored when the ball is hit and touches or goes past the outer edge of the field.

> **Key terms**
>
> **Crease** – in cricket a bowling crease, a popping crease and two return creases are marked in white at each end of the pitch. Bowlers must bowl within these limits and batsmen must remain within the area to ensure they do not get stumped or run out. Within this area the batsman is safe from being run out and stumped.
>
> **Stumps** – three sticks of equal size around 90 cm tall, with 5 cm separating them. Bails (small pieces of wood) are balanced on top of the stumps.

- Four runs are scored when the batsman hits the ball and it hits the ground before reaching the outer edge of the boundary.
- Six runs are scored when the ball is hit and goes over the boundary without touching the ground.
- No-balls, when the bowler oversteps the crease, bowls in a dangerous manner or incorrectly. A no-ball is worth one run (it can be worth more, depending on the competition rules).
- A wide is scored when the ball goes outside the line of the pitch before coming in line with the batsman. This is also worth one run (it can be worth more, depending on the competition rules).
- A leg bye is scored when the ball hits the batsman but doesn't come into contact with his bat and he then proceeds to run.
- A bye is scored when the batsman runs without the ball having come into contact with the batsman or his bat.

Scoring in an individual sport e.g. Tennis

Below is an example of how a tennis match is scored, following the rules set by International Tennis Federation (ITF) and governed in the UK by the Lawn Tennis Association (LTA).

In tennis, points are awarded as follows:

- **Love** is called when a player has **no** points
- **Fifteen** is called when a player has won **one** point in a game
- **Thirty** is called when a player has won **two** points in a game
- **Forty** is called when a player has won **three** points in a game
- **Game** is called when a player has won a **fourth** point or **winning an advantage** from a deuce – see below.

The server's score is always given first. So for example if a server wins the first point of a game, the score will be **fifteen – love**. However, if the server then loses the next two points the score will be **fifteen – thirty**.

Deuce

During a game, if the players score three points each, instead of being forty-all, the score is said to be deuce. The game then continues until one of the players has won the game by two clear points. If the server wins a point at deuce, the score is advantage to the server, who then needs to win another point. If the server fails to win the next point, the score then returns to deuce.

Set

To win a set, a player must win six games. In an 'advantage' set (these are only used in grand-slam events, when a game goes into a final set), if the score reaches five-all, the player must win the set by two games ahead to win (so a game could go on to 9–7 if appropriate, as when Rafael Nadal beat Roger Federer in the 2008 Wimbledon Championship). In a 'tie-break set' if the score reaches six games-all, a tie break is played.

Match

The maximum number of sets in a match is five for men and three for women. Normally both men's and women's tournaments (apart from major tournaments) are played for the best out of three sets. However, tournament organisers decide on the number of sets per match.

Usain Bolt at the end of a race. In the background you can see the time in which he has run the race. An athletes' performance is measured by time. Think of the measures of performance in your own sports and discuss your findings with the rest of the group.

2.4 Boundaries for participation

The area where sport is played may have many names, such as court, pitch, ring, course or track.

In order for a sport to be governed and the rules to be administered by officials, a set boundary is often required. In most sports this will be a closed environment such as a football pitch, basketball court or rugby pitch in team sports, and tennis court, badminton court or boxing ring in individual sports. In some sports the boundaries are more open, although there are still restrictions regarding the route or course an athlete has to take. For example, a sailing race will have limited boundaries and a specific route, but due to the nature of the event the boundaries are flexible.

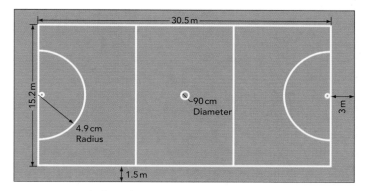

Figure 3: Netball pitch. Example of a competitive environment where athletes are expected to perform within the boundaries as stated by the NGB or ISF

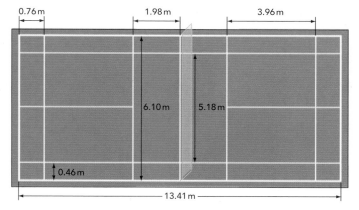

Figure 4: Tennis court. Think of the boundary within which you are confined to participate in your individual sport – draw and label the competitive environment for your sport

2.5 Facilities and equipment

As mentioned earlier in this unit, sports have specific boundaries within which their rules apply. These boundaries remain the same, although some sports can be played both inside and outside them, and the surfaces may differ. For example, association football can be played on either grass or third-generation grass surfaces, and tennis can be played on a variety of surfaces in a variety of facilities (indoor or outdoor). However certain surfaces, such as clay, are generally only suitable for outdoor use, whereas other surfaces are used both indoors and outdoors, e.g. hard court.

Sometimes rules have to be amended to suit the competitive environment, and players and officials must be aware of the rules regarding the use of different facilities. Before a match or event takes place, it is the responsibility of the official in charge to ensure that the facility is suitable. Some sports require a lot of equipment, such as American football, while sports such as volleyball require very little. The equipment must also meet specific rules and regulations.

As technological developments affect sports equipment, governing bodies must approve new products to ensure that they will not give users an unfair advantage. For example, when Adidas introduced its 'Predator' football boots, FIFA initially conducted a number of tests to ensure that they did not give too much of an advantage to any player wearing them. The boots could only be used in competitions after FIFA had approved them. Likewise, when metal woods were first introduced to golf, the Professional Golf Association banned them from all major competitions until testing had been carried out.

2.6 Time

Many team sports limit the length of time a game/match can last. Some include breaks, to give the players a rest and to allow coaches and managers the opportunity to discuss the application of tactics and strategies.

In basketball there are four quarters or two halves; the amount of time per quarter/half depends on the age of the players. If a match ends in a tie, extra time, called 'overtime', is added in order for one of the two teams to win the match.

The rules of some sports demand that there must be a winner at the end of a match, whereas in other sports, such as hockey, if a match ends with an equal score on both sides, a draw will be declared, equal points will be awarded to each team and added to a tally of points. The formulations of these points are governed by the appropriate NGB.

Few individual sports have time constraints, although some combat sports such as boxing and judo do. In boxing, a set number of rounds are agreed (a maximum of twelve is allowed for championship matches, though amateur bouts usually have four). If a bout goes the full number of rounds, the winner will be the boxer who has landed the most punches and obtained the most points (awarded by the officials/adjudicators). Sometimes a winner may be declared before the end of the allocated time; this could be due to a knockout or a stopped fight by the ring or match official.

2.7 Officials

Sports may have referees, umpires, judges, starters or timekeepers, each of whom has clear roles and responsibilities regarding the application of the rules and regulations.

Child protection

At the start of their career, officials will tend to work with younger performers, hence they need to be aware of child protection and the importance of safeguarding children at all times. As well as keeping them free from injury, an official should be aware of the signs and symptoms of child abuse (see Unit 16 Sports coaching page 383) and understand what to do if they notice anything suspicious. Anyone working with children must undergo the appropriate checks, which will be carried out by the organisers of the competition or the league. For more information on child protection in sport, see Unit 16 Sports coaching.

Health and Safety

A key responsibility of an official is managing the safety of everyone involved in a competitive situation. When working with anyone under 18 this responsibility becomes a legal obligation of a duty of care. They should ensure that the playing area meets the required regulations as stated in the sports rule book. Prior to starting a competitive situation, the referee will check the pitch, equipment and players. If they notice any hazards or risks to the participants, they will ensure that appropriate amendments are made. For more information on health and safety in sport, see Unit 16 Sports coaching.

Insurance

Officials are required to have appropriate insurance cover to participate in physical activity as well as to officiate a sport. An official has complete control over a group of athletes when refereeing/umpiring, so is responsible for their safety while they are under his or her supervision. If an athlete is injured during a competition and the official has not applied the laws/rules of the sport, the official could be considered liable for the accident and could be deemed negligent.

Activity: Health and safety

For the sport you play, list the checks that the head official will carry out before the start of a competitive situation and what sanctions or actions they will carry out if they find specific risks or hazards.

Administration

In some sports, the referee/umpire also has to carry out appropriate administration during and on completion of the competitive situation. They may have to keep a scorecard and submit the completed paperwork to the competition organiser or the NGB on completion of the match. The scorecard is so important in some sports that a designated official is appointed to complete it. For example, in cricket the official in control of completing the scorecard is in their own right part of the officiating team. Similarly in basketball, the table officials are responsible for scoring and recording player and team fouls. In other instances the official may be required to submit a match/game report, possibly because specific rules have been broken and sanctions may have been taken against specific performers.

2.8 Unwritten rules and etiquette

Unwritten rules and **etiquette** are the ethics and values which all athletes are expected to follow, both in training and in competitions. The concept of fair play revolves around equality, not just the desire to succeed. The founder of the modern Olympics, Baron de Coubertin, is believed to be one of the earliest exponents of the concept of sportsmanship; his words express the importance of a moral intention in all sports:

> 'The most important thing in the Olympic Games is not to win but to take part, just as the most important thing in life is not the triumph but the struggle.'

Key term

Etiquette – the rules that govern how people behave with others – in sport, etiquette is also known as sportsmanship and fair play.

The rules, regulations and laws of sport are written down and provided for all participants and officials, as well as the spectators. They exist to define what constitutes a victory. There are other rules which are not governed but which all sports performers are nevertheless expected to observe.

Sportsmanship is the belief that all athletes should conform to both the written and unwritten rules of their sport. Fair play means treating an opponent as an equal, and adhering to the rules at the same time as striving to win.

Remember

The concept of fair play includes:

- respect towards other players
- respect towards coaches and spectators
- respect towards officials
- playing within the rules of the sport
- equality for all players.

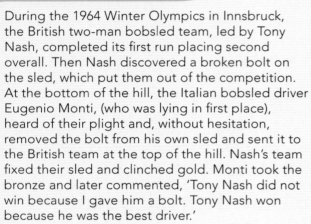

Case study: Unit 17
The unwritten rules in individual sports

During the 1964 Winter Olympics in Innsbruck, the British two-man bobsled team, led by Tony Nash, completed its first run placing second overall. Then Nash discovered a broken bolt on the sled, which put them out of the competition. At the bottom of the hill, the Italian bobsled driver Eugenio Monti, (who was lying in first place), heard of their plight and, without hesitation, removed the bolt from his own sled and sent it to the British team at the top of the hill. Nash's team fixed their sled and clinched gold. Monti took the bronze and later commented, 'Tony Nash did not win because I gave him a bolt. Tony Nash won because he was the best driver.'

1. What unwritten rules do you think have been applied in this scenario?
2. Can you identify any other acts of sportsmanship which have been applied in individual sports recently?
3. Is there a place for sportsmanship and fair play in individual sports today?
4. Discuss the phrase 'nice guys finish last'. Do you agree, if yes, why? If not, why not?
5. Can you identify five ways people can cheat in individual sports?

Case study: Unit 18
The unwritten rules in team sports

Paolo di Canio against Everton

In a Premier League clash in 2000, Paolo di Canio (West Ham United) displayed an unexpected but welcome example of sportsmanship. In injury time, Paul Gerrard, the Everton goalkeeper, went down injured in the penalty area. West Ham continued playing and Trevor Sinclair crossed the ball to di Canio in front of an open goal. Instead of tapping it in to score the winner, di Canio caught the ball and signalled that the writhing Gerrard, who it later turned out had only twisted his knee, needed some urgent attention. This earned him a standing ovation from supporters.

1. What unwritten rules do you think were applied in this situation?
2. Can you identify any other acts of sportsmanship that have been applied in team sports recently?
3. Do you think there is a place for sportsmanship and fair play in team sports today?
4. Discuss the phrase 'Winning isn't everything, it's the only thing.' Do you agree, if yes, why? If not, why not?
5. Can you identify five ways people can cheat in team sports?

2.9 Situations

Every athlete needs to have a good knowledge of how the rules are applied in various situations within their sport. This will give them the necessary understanding of what actions are within the rules and which are illegal. It will also explain any sanctions that may be imposed when they or another player breaks the rules.

A greater understanding of the rules and regulations will increase athletes' appreciation of the officials within the sport and the job they do. All sports demand a high level of respect towards the officials who enforce the rules in competitive situations, and in many sports, any athlete who fails to respect these individuals can expect to have sanctions imposed on them.

Activity: Unit 17 Applying the rules in individual sports

For each of the individual-sport situations described in the table below, say what sanctions and actions an official would impose.

Sport	Situation
Badminton	The shuttlecock lands before the service line when the server is attempting a short serve during a competition.
Athletics	An athlete makes a false start during a 100-metre heat in the Commonwealth Games.
Tennis	One of the players is injured at the change of ends.
Boxing	A boxer hits their opponent below the waistline during an amateur bout.
Swimming	A swimmer makes a false start at the start of a 100-metre butterfly final in the Olympics.

Activity: Unit 18 Applying the rules in team sports

For each of the team-sport situations described in the table below, say what sanctions and actions an official would impose.

Sport	Situation
Football	A defender commits a foul on an attacker in the defender's penalty area and prevents a goal-scoring opportunity.
Rugby Union	The fullback knocks the ball on in the goal area.
Cricket	A fielder catches the ball on the boundary, then steps over the boundary with the ball still in his grasp.
Basketball	The final buzzer goes to signal the end of the match and a shot that was made prior to the buzzer is scored.
Volleyball	A team serves and the referee has noticed that the receiving team has one extra player on their team.

Assessment activity 17.2

Rules and regulations and the correct application of the rules in individual sports

In order to support the development of selected sports, a local high school is trying to increase students' awareness of the rules and regulations of some individual sports.

1. Select two individual sports and describe their rules and regulations in the form of a promotional leaflet.

2. In addition, you should provide an information video which demonstrates how to apply the rules to three different situations in each of your two chosen sports. Ensure that you provide a voiceover describing the correct application of the rules in each situation. **P2**

3. In order to meet the requirements of M2 in your video voiceover, you must explain the application of the rules and regulations of two different individual sports in three different situations. **M2**

Grading tips

P2 Summarise the major rules and regulations of two individual sports.

Select three situations for each individual sport, and describe how the rules are applied in each situation by appropriate officials.

Describe possible sanctions and the specific rules which have been broken.

M2 Explain the actions of each of the officials involved in the decision-making process, including hand signals and methods of communication.

PLTS

Considering how to apply the rules to three different situations for each sport will develop your skills as a **creative thinker**.

Functional skills

When you are searching the Internet for the rules and regulations of selected sports, you will be developing your **ICT** finding and selecting information skills.

Assessment activity 18.2

Rules and regulations and the correct application of the rules in team sports

In order to support the development of selected team sports, the sports-development department at a local authority is trying to increase young adults' awareness of the rules and regulations of these sports.

1. Select two team sports and describe their rules and regulations in the form of a promotional leaflet.

2. In addition, you should provide an information video which demonstrates how to apply the rules of each of your two chosen sports to three different situations. Ensure that you provide a voiceover describing the correct application of the rules in each situation. **P2**

3. In order to meet the requirements of M2 in your video voiceover, you must explain the application of the rules and regulations of two different team sports in three different situations. **M2**

Grading tips

P2 Summarise the major rules and regulations of two team sports.

Select three situations for each team sport, and describe how the rules are applied in each situation by appropriate officials.

Describe possible sanctions and the specific rules which have been broken.

M2 Explain the actions of each of the officials involved in the decision-making process, including hand signals and methods of communication.

3. and 4. Be able to assess your own performance and the performance of others in selected team/individual sports

Athletes are constantly seeking to develop and improve their performance. A pivotal person in this process is the coach. However, as an athlete develops, they should also take responsibility for their own development.

In order to develop, athletes must be made aware of the correct applications of skills and techniques in their sport. They also need to learn the correct use of strategies and tactics in competitive situations. This knowledge may be developed through observing elite performers and also through feedback from their coaches.

As an athlete becomes more reflective about their performance, they should follow the performance cycle shown in Figure 5.

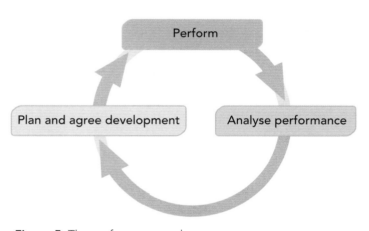

Figure 5: The performance cycle

In this section of the unit, you will examine a variety of methods that you can use to assess the performance of other athletes, but more importantly, you will learn how to assess your own performance and draw conclusions from your findings regarding self-development in individual sports.

3.1 and 4.1 Self-analysis and performer analysis

To support their own development an athlete must demonstrate effective analysis skills. Analysis of performance is the ability to observe and make appropriate judgements, including the technical and tactical elements of a specific performance.

An athlete should be able to identify strengths and prioritise performance targets for their own and other athletes' development.

In order to complete an effective analysis of performance, the observer needs to have a clear understanding of what to expect from an athlete at each stage of their development. Analysis requires the observer to assess any faults from what they see in the whole performance, a skill which takes time and experience to develop.

Take it further

Think about the last time you watched sport on television – did you make a judgement about an athlete's performance? If you made a negative judgement, who or what were you measuring the performance in question against?

Even the greatest athletes have weaknesses which may not be spotted by everyone; even their own coaches may not spot their faults. That is why elite athletes may change coaches or seek support from others, or build a team of coaches to work on specific parts of their performance.

Video analysis is an excellent way to assess performance. A recording is an objective record of what happened during the performance, which can be used as a basis for detailed analysis. The athlete or observer can study their earlier perceptions, thoughts, and decisions about the performance and draw appropriate conclusions regarding strengths and areas for development and improvement.

Specific to sport

When analysing the performance of an individual athlete, the assessor/observer should be aware of the demands of the sport they are assessing. For example, the skills and physical requirements of basketball and football, or of snooker and boxing, are very different and the assessor/observer will have to take this into account in order to make an appropriate judgement on the performance.

Application of skills

When carrying out an assessment the assessor/observer must understand the correct application of each skill ('the perfect model'). Without this understanding, the quality of feedback will be limited. For example, when assessing netball an assessor/observer should be able to compare the application of the players' skills, techniques and tactics to an ideal application of the technique/skill being observed. This comparison against an ideal will enable the assessor/observer to examine the performance for strengths and areas for improvement. If the assessor/observer is unable to spot any weaknesses in the performance, then the athlete should consider consulting a more knowledgeable and experienced coach/assessor/observer.

Techniques analysis and assessment

The skills in many sports are built up of complex contractions and actions, such as the volleyball serve or the tennis serve. To gain a greater understanding of these skills, they are broken down into smaller stages to allow a clear assessment of each stage of the technique.

This method of analysing an athlete's skills may require the assessor/observer to slow the action down (video analysis would be helpful here) and assess each part of the technique. For example, at full speed the service of a volleyball or tennis player may look fine, however slowing it down may show that the ball toss is too far away from the body of the server, which may weaken the player's overall performance.

Technological advances have developed the ability of coaches and analysts to assess performance, see the section on innovation in Unit 16 Sport Coaching (page 380).

Tactical analysis and assessment

It is important when analysing an athlete's performance that the assessor/observer understands the tactics and strategies. They should compare the performance they are watching against an ideal. The athlete must understand what is required and be able to execute the strategy effectively.

Achievements

When analysing the performance of an athlete or a team, it may be useful to look at their previous achievements, which are likely to form an impression prior to the observation. An assessor/observer may find it helpful to look back at recent matches to see if there is a pattern in the wins/losses, and whether this is related to the performers' physical attributes.

Such information may not always be helpful, but it may help to paint a picture prior to any assessment of performance.

> **Remember**
>
> The famous sporting cliché 'You're only as good as your last performance.'

Strengths

The feedback collated during the observational analysis should be drawn from the observer's subjective and objective views. The subjective views are their opinions of the performance and the objective views may come from data compiled during the observation. With this information, the observer should be able to identify the strengths of the performer observed.

Areas for improvement

Like the strengths identified during a performance analysis by an assessor or self-analysis by the athlete, areas for improvement should be identified from the observations made regarding the performance and, if appropriate, the data produced from the observation.

For example, in the 2006/2007 season, Manchester United won the Premier League title. The following season 2007/2008, they retained this title and added the Champions League title to it, proving that even the best teams continually seek to improve.

Likewise, who would have thought that Usain Bolt could have run the 100 metres any faster than he did in the Beijing Olympic final in 2008? However, by developing elements of his performance throughout a season, he managed to beat his own world record in the World Championships in Berlin in 2009.

3.2 and 4.2 Assessment methods

There are four areas of performance to assess: the physical, psychological, technical and tactical demands placed on a performer in a competitive situation. The methods used to assess sports performance are important if weaknesses are to be identified and worked on. To ensure that the best results are obtained from the analysis, the assessor/observer should select the most appropriate assessment method. The method may depend on the sport, the area of performance being analysed, their knowledge of the sport and even of the player(s) they are observing.

Objective performance data

An observer/assessor may choose to assess a team's or individual's performance 'live' at a training session or competition, or on video after the event.

Some observers/assessors like to make assessments by collating statistical data on a performance in a competitive situation. This data can take many different forms, and will allow the performer to make an objective assessment based on the use of numerical data or statistics. For example, if during a football match a team has 15 shots at goal, only three of which are on target, the observer/assessor may conclude that the team need to work on shooting. This data can be collated for teams, but is also used to assess the effectiveness of individual players within a team and athletes in individual sports, for example if a boxer landed 37 left jabs out of 43 attempts and only 23 right jabs out of 53 attempts in a bout, the observer/assessor may conclude that the boxer's strength is their left jab and their weakness is their right.

It is possible to collect objective performance data using notational analysis. This enables an observer/assessor to record data by completing tallies. See Table 17.2, which shows how notational analysis could be used to assess the effectiveness of a tennis player's first and second service during a game.

Number of first serves in	Number of first serves out
HHH HHH HHH HHH II	HHH HHH HHH HHH HHH HHH IIII
Number of second serves in	**Number of double faults**
HHH HHH HHH HHH HHH HHH II	II

Table 17.2: How notational analysis could be used to assess the effectiveness of a tennis player's first and second service during a game

From this data the observer/assessor would conclude that this tennis player needs to develop their first service. However, this information can be used to highlight the issues that may be encountered when using objective performance data: the player may have hit 22 aces from each of the first serves they landed, and therefore the first serve may not be as much of a weakness as the data suggests.

Table 18.2 shows how notational analysis could be used to assess the effectiveness of a footballer's passing ability.

Completed passes in the final third	Failed passes in the final third
HHH HHH HHH HHH II	HHH HHH HHH HHH HHH HHH IIII

Table 18.2: How notational analysis could be used to assess the effectiveness of a footballer's passing ability

From this data the observer/assessor would conclude that this footballer needs to develop their passing in the final third of the pitch in order to improve their own performance and that of the team. Again, this information can be used to highlight the issues that may be encountered with objective performance data: the player may have completed 22 passes and set up three goals from three of the passes they completed. The 34 incomplete passes may have been the result of excessive marking from the opponents after the impact of the earlier passes on the game, so the player's passing ability may not be as much of a weakness as the data suggests.

The collation of data does not always assess technical efficiencies, as it does not include observation.

Activity: Unit 17 Individual sport data analysis

In groups of two or three, watch a game of badminton and record simple information such as:

- successful forehand returns
- successful backhand returns
- number of serves
- number of successful serves
- points won on service
- points won on return of serve.

Analyse the data you have collected. What does it show? Discuss the findings with the rest of your group, then:

1. Discuss what was good about the method of objective data analysis that you used.
2. What problems did you encounter?
3. How could the information you collate in the future be more accurate and effective for the analysis you have to complete?

Activity: Unit 18 Team sport data analysis

In groups of two or three, watch a game of football and record simple information such as:

- successful passes
- shots on target
- shots off target
- number of corners
- successful tackles
- goals scored
- goals conceded.

Analyse the data you have collected. What does it show? Discuss the findings with the rest of your group, then:

1. Discuss what was good about the method of objective data analysis that you used.

2. What problems did you encounter?

3. How could the information you collate in the future be more accurate and effective for the analysis you have to complete?

Many performance observations and assessments combine objective performance data and subjective observations. For example, an observation of a basketball player may include notational analysis of their application of each skill during a match, then the coach may observe their performance and compile feedback based on both these things.

Use of technology

Over the past decade a range of technology has been introduced to support the process of assessment.

Prozone is a computer program that analyses performance and generates data. It can provide post-match performance information for both home and away games, allowing the assessor/observer to analyse every aspect of team and player performance.

Prozone provides post-match analysis that enables coaches to supplement their own subjective observations with objective performance data.

Take it further

For more information regarding Prozone and its use in a variety of sports, visit the Prozone website: www.prozonesports.com.

Subjective observations

Subjective observations and assessments of a team or an individual are based on the observer's/assessor's judgements, interpretations, opinions and comparison against an ideal performance.

Observation analysis is a popular technique for assessing performance and effective application of skills, techniques and tactics. All coaches need to be effective observers, to enable them to identify strengths and weaknesses during performance.

Observation analysis should be used to identify the needs of a team or individual, and should inform a coach's plans to develop performance. An observer's/assessor's full analysis of overall performance should form the basis for a training programme with the aim of addressing the most significant weaknesses.

An example of how Prozone can be used to analyse the performance of a player/team in action.

Discuss how this could be used to develop a player's performance.

Can you think of any other technology that could support the assessment of a player?

An example of how Dartfish can be used to freeze the performance of a player in action.

Discuss how this could be used to develop a player's performance. Can you think of any other technology that could support the assessment of a player?

Another technological advance that can be used to assess the effective application of skills and techniques in sport is Dartfish technology. This program can slow down a movement and freeze-frame each component of a skill to enable an assessor/observer to assess the effective application of a technique at each stage.

Kandle technology is another form of video analysis software which is used to support coaches' observation of performance. The more complex the skill, the greater the requirement for software to enable sports coaches to analyse it in greater detail.

SWOT (strengths, weaknesses, opportunities, threats) analysis

SWOT analysis is used to evaluate the strengths, weaknesses, opportunities and threats involved in the performance of a player or team. The observer should understand the performance demands of the sport they are analysing. Normally, only experienced coaches carry out this process, although as athletes develop it is beneficial for them also to carry out SWOT analyses so that they can compare and contrast their findings with those of their coaches and agree on targets for future performance.

Strengths – the observer/assessor should identify the player's or team's strengths in a SWOT grid like Table 17.3. This information could come from objective data or subjective observations. The coach should compare the

Remember

When assessing the performance demands of a sport, it is important that all four key elements of the performance are assessed: physical, psychological, technical and tactical.

performance against an ideal model for each performance demand. It is important the observer/assessor has clear criteria against which to assess the performer(s) when carrying out the performance and SWOT analysis.

Weaknesses – with the support of the data, the assessor/observer should identify any weaknesses such as technical inefficiencies in the performance of specific skills, or the incorrect application of tactics and strategies in a game or a simulated practice.

Opportunities – the assessor/observer should note any opportunities that the player or team have to develop their performance, such as access to training sessions or specific coaches to support technical development. It may also include information about any opponent(s), such as objective data on previous performances (times, results, etc.) or subjective assessments of their effectiveness, possibly in the form of a scouting report.

Threats – the assessor/observer should identify any short- or long-term threats to the performance of the player or team.

Strengths	Weaknesses
• Good overhead clear • Good agility on the court • Excellent court coverage • High fitness levels	• Inconsistent short and long serve • Poor backhand technique, clear, smash and drop shot • Late to react to opponent's position on the court • Poor shot selection
Opportunities	**Threats**
• Developed short serve through intensive coaching sessions • Opponent also has a poor drop shot • Ability to move around the court gives performer an advantage when returning shots and generating rallies	• Opponent is a better player • Mental strength – easily frustrated after a poor shot • Wrong shot selection in long rallies

Table 17.3: SWOT Analysis of Darren Milner, badminton player

Strengths	Weaknesses
• Good defensive organisation • Excellent centre (country standard) • High fitness levels for all sports performers	• Inconsistent results • Space awareness • Poor shooting
Opportunities	**Threats**
• Developed attacking tactics • Opponents are weak in attack • Recently appointed new head coach (very experienced with lots of ideas)	• Opponents have two county netball players: wing attack and goal attack • Mental strength – easily frustrated after a poor performance • Relegation from the league

Table 18.3: SWOT Analysis of West Side Netball Team

Testing

Tests can give an objective picture of an athlete within a team's current performance levels. For example, psychometric tests may be used to assess an athlete's mental state, and fitness tests may be used to assess the physical and skill components of fitness required.

An example of a psychometric test is the 'profile of mood states' test (POMS). This measures an athlete's mood during training and can indicate whether they are overtraining. It is predominantly used for athletes who are looking jaded in performance or showing a lacklustre attitude when training, and is designed to examine the reasons behind the problems. Unit 8: Fitness testing for sport and exercise (page 200) discusses a variety of tests used to measure athletes' fitness levels.

Interviews

One of the easiest methods of analysing performance is to interview an athlete after a training session or a competition. This gives valuable feedback on how they felt their performance went, and what areas of their performance they feel require further development and improvement. Using the athlete's own views on their personal strengths and areas for improvement will allow them and their coach to develop training strategies to help future performances.

Performance profiling

In order to complete a full assessment of their performance, an athlete may choose to carry out a performance profile: a full assessment of the technical, tactical, physical and psychological requirements of their sport.

A performance profile uses a variety of assessment methods including notational analysis and performance observation. The assessor/observer will award a grade or mark which should be set against an achievable target performance or goal relating to the athlete's development.

It is important for athletes and coaches to have realistic expectations regarding developmental goals. For example, a 10-year-old footballer may compare their performance against that of another player in the same league who is the top goal scorer in the league, so on a scale of 1 to 10, 1 may be a player who has scored no goals in the season, while 10 may be a player who has scored 30 goals. It would not be realistic to compare their performance to that of Wayne Rooney because of the difference in age, ability and skill levels.

Similarly, a golfer who has a handicap of 16 may compare their performance against a golfer who has an 8 handicap, so on a scale of 1 to 10, 1 may be a 16 handicap while a 10 may be compared to a 4-handicap golfer. It would not be realistic to compare their performance to that of Tiger Woods, because of the difference in ability and skill levels.

When coaching beginners, a sports coach will need to complete a performance profile to determine which elements of their performance require development. As an athlete develops in age and ability, the performance profile should be completed by both the coach and the athlete. After the completion of the performance profile, both athlete and coach should discuss the findings and agree a plan that can be followed to develop any technical, tactical, psychological or physical weaknesses in their performance.

3.3 and 4.3 Development plan

Following a performance analysis, the player or team and the observer/assessor should agree a development plan which takes into account the findings from the analysis. This is essential, as without a development plan and agreed goals and targets for future performance, an athlete's or team's performance could plateau.

Aims and objectives

Before formulating a development plan, a team/player and coach should agree clear aims. These should consist of things they would like to achieve, e.g. promotion to the higher league, or improving sprint starts, by the start of next season.

In order to achieve their aims, a team or athlete will also need to have objectives that express how they will meet each of their aims. Each aim will need to have an objective, e.g. 'In order to improve our league position we will have to work on defending', or 'To improve my sprint start I am going to have to work on my reaction time and leg power.'

Goals

After the completion of performance assessments and player or team analysis, the observer and the team should agree specific goals for future development. Goal-setting should be used by individuals and teams to increase their motivation and confidence for future sports events. Goal-setting should be the first stage of the planning process for any team and coach, as through setting goals they can set clear targets for personal development. Goals should provide both direction and motivation. Goals are often set over various periods of time: teams can set short-, medium-, and long-term goals.

Short-term goals are set over a short period, between one day and one month. A short-term goal could be a target that a team or performer wishes to achieve after the next training session, or a specific technique they would like to develop by the end of the next month.

Medium-term goals should progressively support the team or individual achieving the long-term goals. These goals can be measured at specific points within a season.

Long-term goals are set for and with a team or individual to help them determine where they want to go, what they want to achieve and the best way of getting there. A coach should use these goals to shape their coaching schedule for a season or longer if appropriate.

SMART targets

Wherever objectives and goals are set for teams or individuals, they should be SMART:

- **S**pecific – the goals set should be as precise and detailed as possible for the team or individual.
- **M**easurable – the goals set should define a method of measuring the success of the team or individual. They should set achievement targets – what by when?
- **A**chievable – the goals set should be able to be attained within a set period of time and should be relevant for the team or individual.
- **R**ealistic – the goals set should be appropriate for the team or individual.
- **T**ime-bound – ensure you agree a timescale, even if it includes mini-targets for athlete development (short-, medium- and long-term goals).

Opportunities

Formulating a plan for future development may open new doors for teams' and individuals' personal development as well as sporting achievement.

It may be a requirement or an agreed target that an athlete will attend courses and obtain qualifications that involve them learning new skills and techniques, or developing knowledge about a specific area of their sport. They might learn about the treatment and prevention of sports injuries, technical requirements of a sport, sports nutrition or tactical development.

Take it further

In your own sport, find out about appropriate courses and/or qualifications an athlete could take to improve their knowledge about the areas listed below. Give the name of the course, provider, location and cost.

- treatment and prevention of sports injuries
- technical requirements of a sport
- sports nutrition
- tactical development.

For example, if an athlete has suffered a number of injuries, their coach may think it would be beneficial for them to attend a sports injury and rehabilitation course where they will learn about different methods of treating sports injuries, and where they may also learn how to avoid or prevent injuries. By completing these courses an athlete can increase their portfolio of qualifications.

The development plan agreed between the coach and the team may also introduce a team or individual to new methods of training and possibly new coaches. This may freshen up the current methods and develop further motivation. It may also provide an opportunity to develop overall performance.

Possible obstacles

Although the development plan produced for a team or individual may cover every possible eventuality and provide some excellent opportunities, unforeseen circumstances may arise and hinder progress towards attaining the set goals. These could include:

- injury and illness
- bad weather
- lack of funding
- failure to qualify for competitions/events
- family pressure
- peer pressure.

When participating in a training programme, athletes should be given every opportunity to meet their goals and targets. Athletes can seek support from within their club, or from their sport's NGB if appropriate. This support may deflect any obstacles that threatened to prevent them attaining the targets set.

Assessment activity 17.3: Self-analysis in individual sports

In order to support the development of gifted and talented athletes at their school, a local sports college has asked you to demonstrate how performance analysis can be used to develop performance.

1 The college would like you to carry out a self-analysis using two different methods of assessment, identifying strengths and areas for improvement in two different individual sports. **P4**

2. In order to meet the requirements of M3 in this task, in addition to the requirements of P4 in your summary of the assessments, you must explain identified strengths and areas for improvement in two different individual sports, and make suggestions relating to personal development. **M3**

3. Finally, in order to meet the requirements of D1 in this task, in addition to the requirements of P4 and M3, you must analyse identified strengths and areas for improvement in two different individual sports, and justify suggestions made. **D1**

Grading tips

P4 Record your performance in two selected individual sports in competitive situations.

Select two methods of assessment to analyse your performance in two individual sports.

Observe your performance in two individual sports and comment on the strengths and areas for future development.

M3 Summarise your findings in a conclusion, explaining the identified strengths and weaknesses and summarising the methods for addressing the areas of development for two individual sports.

D1 For each individual sport:

- produce a development plan for your own performance
- set aims and objectives for the development plan
- set appropriate long-, medium- and short-term goals
- identify SMART targets for development
- identify opportunities for development
- identify possible obstacles to achieving the goals set.

PLTS

When you are carrying out a self- or peer-analysis using two different methods of assessment, identifying strengths and areas for improvement in two different individual sports, you will develop your skills as a **reflective learner**.

Functional skills

Completing a notational analysis of your own or another individual's practical performance will develop your **Mathematics** skills.

Assessment activity 17.4: Peer-analysis in individual sports

P5 **M4** **D2** **BTEC**

After the completion of your own self-assessments, the sports college would now like you to complete a performance analysis and development plan for one of their gifted and talented sports performers.

1. They would like you to carry out a performance analysis using two different methods of assessment, identifying strengths and areas for improvement in the development of an athlete in an individual sport. **P5**

2. In order to meet the requirements of M4 in this task, in addition to the requirements of P5 in your summary, you must explain identified strengths and areas for improvement in the development of an athlete in an individual sport, and make suggestions relating to the development of an individual. **M4**

3. Finally, in order to meet the requirements of D2 in this task, in addition to the requirements of P5 and M4, you must analyse identified strengths and areas for improvement in the development of an athlete in an individual sport, and justify suggestions made. **D2**

Grading tips

P5 Record the performance of a selected athlete from an individual sport.

Select two methods of assessment to analyse the individual's performance and assess their performance from a recording.

Observe their performance and comment on the strengths and areas for future development after your assessment.

M4 Summarise your findings in a conclusion, explaining the identified strengths and areas for development and suggesting how the athlete could develop in the selected sport.

D2 Produce a development plan to help the athlete improve their skills, techniques and use of tactics in the selected sport.

- Set aims and objectives for their development plan.
- Set appropriate long-, medium- and short-term goals for the athlete.
- Identify SMART targets for the athlete's development.
- Identify opportunities for the athlete's development.
- Identify possible obstacles that may prevent the athlete achieving the goals set.

PLTS

When you are carrying out a self- or peer-analysis using two different methods of assessment, identifying strengths and areas for improvement in two different individual sports, you will develop your skills as a **reflective learner**.

Functional skills

Completing a notational analysis of your own or another individual's practical performance will develop your **Mathematics** skills.

Assessment activity 18.3: Self-analysis in team sport

A local sports team has asked you for support regarding their performance. Their manager would like you to show the players what a performance analysis is, what it entails and how feedback is used to develop performance.

1. The manager would like you to carry out a self-analysis using two different methods of assessment, identifying strengths and areas for improvement in two different team sports. **P4**

2. In order to meet the requirements of M3 in this task, in addition to the requirements of P4, in your summary of the assessments you must explain identified strengths and areas for improvement in two different team sports, and make suggestions relating to personal development. **M3**

3. Finally, in order to meet the requirements of D1 in this task, in addition to the requirements of P4 and M3, you must analyse identified strengths and areas for improvement in two different team sports, and justify suggestions made. **D1**

Grading tips

P4 Record your performance in two selected team sports in competitive situations.

Select two methods of assessment to analyse your performance in two team sports.

Observe your performance in two team sports and comment on the strengths and areas for future development.

M3 Summarise your findings in a conclusion, explaining the identified strengths and weaknesses and summarising the methods for addressing the areas of development for two team sports.

D1 For each team sport:
- produce a development plan for your own performance
- set aims and objectives for the development plan
- set appropriate long-, medium- and short-term goals
- identify SMART targets for development
- identify opportunities for development
- identify possible obstacles to achieving the goals set.

PLTS

When you are carrying out a self- or peer-analysis using two different methods of assessment, identifying strengths and areas for improvement in two different team sports, you will develop your skills as a **reflective learner**.

Functional skills

Completing a notational analysis of your own or another team's practical performance will develop your **Mathematics** skills.

Assessment activity 18.4: Peer-analysis in team sports

After the completion of your own self-assessments, the manager of the local sports team would now like you to complete a performance analysis and development plan for his team.

1. He wants you to carry out a performance analysis using two different methods of assessment, identifying strengths and areas for improvement in the development of a team in a team sport. **P5**

2. In order to meet the requirements of M4 in this task, in addition to the requirements of P5 in your summary, you must explain identified strengths and areas for improvement in the development of a team in a team sport, and make suggestions relating to development of a team. **M4**

3. Finally, in order to meet the requirements of D2 in this task, in addition to the requirements of P5 and M4, you must analyse identified strengths and areas for improvement in the development of a team in a team sport, and justify suggestions made. **D2**

Grading tips

P5 Record the performance of a selected team from a team sport.

Select two methods of assessment to analyse the team's performance and assess their performance from a recording.

Observe the team's performance and comment on the strengths and areas for their future development after your assessment.

M4 Summarise your findings in a conclusion – explaining the identified strengths and areas for development and suggesting how the team could develop.

D2 Produce a development plan to help the team improve their skills, techniques and use of tactics.

- Set aims and objectives for the team.
- Set appropriate long-, medium- and short-term goals for the team.
- Identify SMART targets for the team's development.
- Identify opportunities for the team's development.
- Identify possible obstacles that may prevent the team achieving the goals set.

PLTS

When you are carrying out a self- or peer-analysis using two different methods of assessment, identifying strengths and areas for improvement in two different team sports, you will develop your skills as a **reflective learner**.

Functional skills

Completing a notational analysis of your own or another team's practical performance will develop your **Mathematics** skills.

Darren Singh
Voluntary sports leader

Darren is a voluntary sports coach for a local mixed hockey team. While studying on the BTEC National in Sport at a local college Darren completed both Unit 17 and Unit 18. The practical units developed Darren's appreciation of the skills, techniques and tactics required to play a wide variety of team and individual sports. Before attending college and while at college Darren had always enjoyed playing hockey for a local team but had no intention to run one of the many teams at his club.

Through developing more of an appreciation of the sport while studying at college Darren became more involved at his local club and started to help one of the club coaches out. Initially Darren's role was as an assistant coach but as his confidence grew he became more and more involved. Eventually the head coach at the club asked Darren if he would be interested in completing some coaching courses which Darren accepted.

After completing his Level 1 assistant coaching award Darren started to become more involved in the delivery of training sessions and more recently the head coach has approached Darren again and asked him to be more involved in the analysis of some of the senior players at the club. In order to do this Darren will need to observe the senior team and make subjective judgements on the performances and provide feedback to the head coach on the performance of specific team players.

Think about it!

To support Darren to complete his performance analysis:

- List the core skills and techniques required to play hockey.
- List the tactics which he will need to use when observing the senior team.
- Provide two different methods of assessment that could be used to analyse the performance of these performers at the hockey club.
- Describe the strengths and weaknesses of each method of assessment.

Just checking

1. Define 'sport'.
2. What is a skill?
3. What is an open skill?
4. What is a discrete skill?
5. What is a serial skill?
6. What is a gross skill?
7. What is a technique?
8. What is a tactic?
9. What is an externally paced skill?
10. List five team sports and five individual sports.
11. What are the national governing bodies for each of the sports on your lists?
12. What four factors determine the performance demands of a sport?
13. What does SWOT stand for?
14. What is a subjective assessment?
15. Name two different types of objective data assessments used to analyse sports performance.

Assignment tips

- To complete Unit 17 or 18 successfully you will need to develop your knowledge about individual or team sports. In order to do this you should try to observe a variety of different sports in action. Observe a number of sports and make a list of the skills, techniques and tactics required to perform each sport.
- You are also required to perform in two team or two individual sports to complete either Unit 17 or 18 successfully. Each session that you participate in should cover a skill, technique and tactic required to perform effectively within that sport: you will be required to describe and demonstrate effective application of each of these skills, technique and tactics.
- You should learn the rules and regulations of each sport and develop your ability to apply these rules during competitive situations. You should observe officials from your selected sports in action.
- Ensure you enjoy the opportunities you will be given to participate in practical sessions and to develop skills which you may not have been introduced to before now.
- Develop an understanding of performance analysis through practice and observation. Try to get a model in your mind of an elite sports performer applying each skill, technique and tactic and use this to analyse performance.
- Be confident to observe other sports performers participating in your selected sport and comment on the effective application of each skill, technique and tactic.
- Remember to carefully consider which methods of analysis you will use to assess the effectiveness of yourself and other sports performers.
- When carrying out self-analysis you should first ask someone to visually record your performance in each sport and then watch back the performance comparing yourself to the model performance.
- Research the variety of coaching courses available in your selected sports. Also examine other courses and methods which could be used to develop your skills as a sports performer and develop your knowledge of the sport. You could discuss these with the coaches/tutors who deliver the sessions to you.
- Complete a Level 1 coaching award to support your development of the required skills, techniques and tactics required to perform effectively in your selected sport.
- Ensure that you read the assignment briefs properly. Take your time and ensure you are happy with the task you have been set. If not ask your tutor for additional assistance.
- Make sure you attempt all parts of the assignment briefs. If you only attempt the pass criteria then you can only achieve a pass grade. Think big and try to complete all of the assignment.

21 Applied sport and exercise physiology

Have you ever wondered why footballers do not overheat when running around a pitch for 90 minutes? Why it is that some athletes train at altitude? Do you consider this to be more 'performance-enhancing' than taking anabolic steroids?

This unit investigates these kinds of issues: how temperature, altitude and age affect performance and the implications of race when considering performance. Are girls naturally better gymnasts than boys? Will athletes of West African origin have a natural advantage over athletes of Asian origin when it comes to the 100 metre Olympic final in London in 2012?

Understanding these issues will allow you to answer a number of complex and often controversial questions that the world of professional sport faces today, such as are males better at sport than females and are Africans better runners than Europeans?

Learning outcomes

After completing this unit you should:

1. know how temperature and altitude affect exercise and sports performance
2. know about the physical differences between people of different gender and race and their effect on exercise and sports performance
3. know the impact that the physiological effects of ageing have on exercise and sports performance
4. know the effects and implications of using ergogenic aids for exercise and sports performance.

Assessment and grading criteria

This table shows you what you must do in order to achieve a pass, merit or distinction grade, and where you can find activities in this book to help you.

To achieve a **pass** grade the evidence must show that you are able to:	To achieve a **merit** grade the evidence must show that, in addition to the pass criteria, you are able to:	To achieve a **distinction** grade the evidence must show that, in addition to the pass and merit criteria, you are able to:
P1 Describe the responses of the body to temperature, and their effects on exercise and sports performance **See Assessment activity 21.1, page 452**		
P2 Describe the responses of the body to high altitude, and their effects on exercise and sports performance **See Assessment activity 21.1, page 452**		
P3 Describe the physiological differences between athletes of different gender, and their effects on exercise and sports performance **See Assessment activity 21.2, page 460**	**M1** Explain the effects of the physiological differences between athletes of different gender on exercise and sports performance **See Assessment activity 21.2, page 460**	**D1** Analyse the effects of the physiological differences between athletes of different gender and race on exercise and sports performance **See Assessment activity 21.2, page 460**
P4 Describe the physiological differences between athletes of different races, and their effects on exercise and sports performance **See Assessment activity 21.2, page 460**	**M2** Explain the effects of the physiological differences between athletes of different races on exercise and sports performance **See Assessment activity 21.2, page 460**	
P5 Describe the impact of the physiological effects of ageing on exercise and sports performance **See Assessment activity 21.3, page 463**	**M3** Explain the impact of the physiological effects of ageing on exercise and sports performance **See Assessment activity 21.3, page 463**	**D2** Analyse the impact of the physiological effects of ageing on exercise and sports performance **See Assessment activity 21.3, page 463**
P6 Describe the effects and implications of six different ergogenic aids used for exercise and sports performance **See Assessment activity 21.4, page 468**	**M4** Explain the effects and implications of six different ergogenic aids used for exercise and sports performance **See Assessment activity 21.4, page 468**	**D3** Analyse the effects and implications of six different ergogenic aids used for exercise and sports performance **See Assessment activity 21.4, page 468**

How you will be assessed

This unit will be assessed by an internal assignment that will be designed and marked by the staff at your centre. Your assessment could be in the form of:

- presentations
- case studies
- practical tasks
- written assignments.

Charlotte, 18-year-old mountain climber

This unit taught me about the factors that affect mountain climbing. I never understood why I got out of breath the further up a mountain I climbed, or why my body shivered and my extremities got colder the higher I climbed. But what really interested me were the implications of race and gender.

It wasn't until I went climbing in Kenya that I realised race can have an impact on climbing. A group of climbers walked to the summit of Mount Kilimanjaro. Due to the thin air, I found it hard to breathe, and then I noticed a group of Kenyan climbers who were fine. I thought they were much fitter than me. Only after studying this unit did I realise that, because East Africans live at a higher altitude, they have increased levels of haemoglobin which allows them to assimilate oxygen when the air is much thinner.

I was also interested in the effects of ergogenic aids. I didn't know there were so many substances that can influence sports performance. I'm going to stick to my climbing, eat healthily and get plenty of rest.

Over to you

1. Which section of the unit are you most looking forward to?
2. What preparation can you do in readiness for the unit assessment(s)?
3. Can you think of examples of recent sports news that apply to this unit?

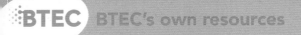

1. Know how temperature and altitude affect exercise and sports performance

How do differences in climate affect sporting performance?

Daily temperature during the Beijing Olympics was estimated at approximately 25°C. However, temperatures often reached over 30°C. The heat was relentless and humidity levels averaged around 75 per cent. Contrast these conditions with those of London, where the daily temperature in August is 22°C – a difference of nearly 10°C. How do you think British athletes coped with Beijing temperatures and humidity and what precautions do you think they took?

An elite athlete expects to compete around the world, from London in the UK to Auckland in New Zealand. This global competition means elite athletes need to cope with numerous diverse conditions. Temperature and altitude can vary depending on where you are. For example, tennis players could be in Dubai playing in 40°C and the following week in Stockholm, where the temperature can be below freezing.

1.1 Temperature

A challenge for any athlete is maintaining a suitable body temperature, so that their body can perform and function effectively while training or competing. Depending on the environment, athletes try to avoid overheating (hyperthermia) or losing body temperature (hypothermia). Table 21.1 indicates an athlete's body temperature (not environmental temperature) and the likely effects on the body.

Responses of body to high temperature

The body's thermoregulatory system enables an athlete to cope with temperature changes. During exercise, the body's metabolic rate can increase twenty fold and this increase in energy consumption raises the body temperature significantly.

- **Sweating** involves the secretion of sweat on to the surface of the skin. It provides an effective cooling process as the sweat on the surface of the skin evaporates.

- **Function of the hypothalamus** – the **hypothalamus** has different roles; its most important is that of the body's thermostat. The hypothalamus contains the central point within the body for temperature regulation. A group of specialised neurons at the base of the brain helps to regulate body temperature within a narrow band around 37°C. The hypothalamus receives a more generous blood supply than any other brain structure. It is mainly through this increased blood supply that it watches over or administers body temperature by initiating responses when that temperature changes. These heat regulation mechanisms are activated in the following ways.

  o Thermal receptors located in the skin provide information to the hypothalamus.

  o Temperature changes in the blood contact the hypothalamus directly, stimulating temperature control.

- **Methods of heat loss** – athletes dissipate heat in different ways including through conduction, evaporation, radiation and respiration. Each has a different level of efficiency depending on characteristics such as age, race, gender and training.

  o **Conduction** involves warming air molecules surrounding the body or warming any cooler surfaces in contact with the skin. Conduction involves the transfer of heat through a liquid, solid or gas by direct contact. The rate of heat loss depends on the temperature difference between

Body temperature (°C)	Effects
26	Death
28	Severe heart rhythm disturbances; breathing may stop
31	Comatose; shallow breathing; serious heart rhythm problems
32	Hallucinations; delirium; progressive comatose; no shivering
33	Confusion; sleepiness; loss of shivering; slow heart beat; shallow breathing
34	Severe shivering; loss of movement in fingers; some behavioural changes
35	Hypothermia; intense shivering; numbness and bluish tint to skin
36	Mild to moderate shivering
37	Normal body temperature
38	Sweating; feeling uncomfortable
39	Severe sweating; flushed and very red; fast heart rate; exhaustion
40	Fainting; dehydration; weakness; vomiting; profuse sweating
41	Fainting; vomiting; severe headache; dizziness; palpitations; breathlessness
42	Convulsions; vomiting; delirium; comatose
43	Brain damage; convulsions; shock; cardiorespiratory collapse
44	Death

Table 21.1: Body temperature and its effects on the body.

the skin and the surroundings. The quicker the air moves around the body, the greater the quantity of heat conducted from the body.

o **Evaporation** is the body's major defence against overheating. Water vaporisation lost via breathing or sweating transfers heat from the body to the environment. In response to overheating, the sweat glands secrete lots of saline solution (NaCl dissolved in water) which forms sweat. The cooling process occurs when sweat reaches the surface of the skin and evaporates. As the air surrounding the body becomes saturated with the evaporated fluid, new air arrives to accept further evaporated sweat. In hot and dry environments, the limiting factor for evaporation as a method of heat loss is the rate of sweat production. Ensuring the athlete is hydrated properly is vital in these conditions. In humid conditions, the capacity of the environment to receive moisture is slight (as the air is already saturated with moisture). Athletes must be careful they do not overheat when exercising or competing in hot and humid conditions.

o **Radiation** is the transfer of heat from one object to another without contact. During radiation heat loss, the athlete radiates heat towards cooler objects. The closer the two temperatures (those of the athlete and the object) the less heat the athlete loses. At rest, radiation is the main method of dissipating body heat. The naked body loses approximately 60 per cent of its heat by radiation. Breathing mechanisms and the expulsion of waste air from the lungs allow for a small amount of heat loss via an athlete's exhaled breath.

o **Respiration** combines the processes of evaporation (moisture in the lungs) and convection (displacement of warm air from the lungs by cold air from the surrounding environment). Moisture is lost when it is exchanged with drier air of the surrounding environment. In addition, a small percentage of body heat is lost when warming the cold air entering your lungs.

Key terms

Hypothalamus – region of the brain responsible for many behavioural patterns, especially those concerned with regulation of the body's internal environment.

Conduction – transfer of heat from one object to another through direct surface contact.

Evaporation – conversion of liquid into vapour (for example, sweat into vapour).

Radiation – emission or transfer of radiant energy as heat waves or particles.

Respiration – emission of waste gases and water vapour via the respiratory system.

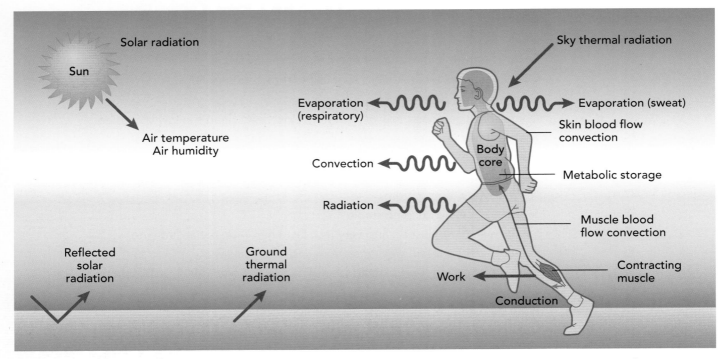

Figure 21.1: For an athlete to perform effectively, excess body heat must be dissipated to the environment to regulate core temperature; this is done by conduction, evaporation, radiation and respiration.

Remember

Once the humidity level passes beyond 70 per cent, the benefits of sweating drop significantly. When you exercise on a humid day you are much more likely to develop heat stroke.

Take it further

Major sources of heat loss

Research what you think are the major sources of heat loss – conduction, evaporation, radiation or respiration – for the following sports. Justify your answers.

- **Swimming 200 metre freestyle**
- **Marathon running in a hot climate**
- **Bodybuilding competition (static pose)**
- **Downhill skiing**

Key terms

Hyperthermia – an unusually high body core temperature greater than 40°C.

Hypothermia – an unusually low body core temperature less than 35°C.

Core temperature – temperature of the inner body, particularly the internal organs.

Dehydration – depletion of fluids that can impede thermoregulation and cause a rise in core body temperature.

Effects of high temperature

Overexposure to hot and humid conditions can result in the normal heat loss processes becoming ineffective. **Hyperthermia** is likely to follow, resulting in the hypothalamus being compromised. A **core**

temperature greater than 40°C increases metabolic rate, which increases heat production. The skin becomes hot and dry as the temperature rises to an extent that organ damage is possible. This condition is called heatstroke and can be fatal if measures are not implemented immediately. These involve cooling the body in water and administering fluids. Heatstroke develops when the body cannot lose excess heat being produced because of the environment and exercise. Early symptoms of heatstroke include excessive sweating, headache, nausea, dizziness and hyperventilation.

Dehydration is a condition of excessive water loss. When water output exceeds intake and the body is negative in its fluid balance, dehydration results. A serious consequence of dehydration is a lowering of blood plasma levels (blood plasma is 90 per cent water), which leads to an inadequate blood volume to maintain normal cardiovascular function. In high temperature environments, approximately 60 per cent of an athlete's cardiac output can pass through the skin for cooling and sweat production. Dehydration is best avoided by drinking plenty of water. Drinking water beyond the body's needs is not a risk as the kidneys remove any excess as urine. However, when a large amount of water is lost through perspiration, maintaining electrolyte balance becomes an issue for the athlete resulting in salt depletion. This can cause further symptoms beyond that of dehydration that include tiredness, irritability, fainting, cramps and an overall loss of performance.

Effects of high temperature on sports performance

Too much body heat generated during exercise reduces performance. As body temperature rises, blood flow to the skin increases, and the body attempts to cool itself by sweating. During intense exercise, the body temperature can rise as high as 39°C and muscle temperature slightly higher. These temperatures make exercise difficult because the body and muscles are competing for blood. As the body temperature rises, oxygen becomes increasingly sought after due to increased circulatory demands. Oxygen is needed for the cooling process, and reduces the amount of oxygen available for vital organs, which can lead to severe health risks as well as a drop in athletic performance.

Responses of body to low temperature

Hypothermia is a condition where low body temperature results from exposure to cold. This causes the body's core temperature to drop. Breathing, blood pressure and heart rate decrease and drowsiness sets in. If uncorrected, hypothermia can be fatal as body temperature approaches 28°C. Hypothermia develops if the rate of heat loss from an athlete's body exceeds the rate at which the body is producing heat. There are three types of hypothermia including:

- immersion: severe cold stress due to the bodily immersion in cold water

- exhaustion: less severe cold stress due to low temperatures involving wet and windy conditions
- urban: cold is relatively mild but prolonged (generally associated with the elderly or infirm but rarely encountered in a sports capacity).

There are three stages of hypothermia, as seen in Table 21.2.

Stage	Body temperature	Effects
1	Drop of 1°C–2°C below normal	Mild to strong shivering occurs; blood vessels in the outer extremities contract, lessening heat to the outside environment; unable to perform complicated tasks with hands
2	Drop of 2°C–4°C below normal	Shivering becomes more violent; poor muscle coordination becomes apparent; movements are slow and mild confusion is shown; extremities become pale
3	Drop of more than 4°C below normal	Shivering stops; cellular metabolic process shuts down and skin becomes blue; major organs fail as pulse and respiration rates decrease; slowly heading towards brain death

Table 21.2: The three stages of hypothermia.

When an athlete is exposed to a cold environment, the hypothalamus reacts and a number of involuntary responses, for example, shivering and vascular adjustments, are triggered to increase core temperature.

- **Shivering** means a series of involuntary muscle contractions that produce heat in response to a cold environment.
- **Vascular adjustments** – blood vessels in the skin constrict, resulting in blood being restricted to the deep body organs and largely bypassing the skin. Because the skin is separated from internal organs by a layer of fatty tissue, heat loss from the core body areas is reduced, and skin temperature drops to that nearer the external environment. Restricting blood flow to the skin is not a problem for short periods. However, if this continues over a

long period of time, skin cells deprived of oxygen and nutrients begin to die, a condition known as frostbite.

In addition, in order to stop their body overcooling, athletes can:

* wear appropriate clothing for the conditions (for example, sweatshirt, hat, gloves)
* drink hot fluids
* increase physical activity to generate heat.

Effects of low temperature

The effects of hypothermia are far reaching: it affects vital functions such as breathing rate, blood pressure and heart rate, while decreasing cellular function. Drowsiness is a common symptom of hypothermia, followed by a feeling of comfort, regardless of how cold the person is. Shivering ceases when the body core temperature drops below approximately 32°C. If uncorrected and the body temperature lowers to around 24°C, death by cardiac arrest is likely.

Effects of low temperature on sports performance

The effects of cold in sport can be more harmful than the effects of extreme heat. One danger is the increased risk of torn muscles or tendons. The greatest risk to sports performance is hypothermia. Exercising in cold weather causes the body to maintain its core temperature by shunting blood away from the body's extremities, minimising heat loss. Moderate hypothermia causes muscular fatigue, poor coordination, numbness and disorientation. Severe hypothermia can result in cardiac arrest.

Activity: Hypothermia and hyperthermia

To help you differentiate between these two important terms, list as many symptoms of both hypothermia and hyperthermia as you can.

Hypothermia	Hyperthermia

1.2 Altitude

Altitude is the measurement of elevation above sea level and has a number of effects on sports performance. However, these effects are rarely encountered by many as most of the world's population live at an altitude close to sea level. Atmospheric pressure decreases as altitude increases. This has implications for athletes because a fall in pressure can lead to a shortage of oxygen (hypoxia). When altitude is encountered by athletes it is usually in competition, as at the 1968 Olympic Games in Mexico City. Athletes experienced (many for the first time) factors such as thinner air (i.e. lower oxygen concentration). The high altitude of Mexico City (2240 metres above sea level) compared with London (sea level) made it especially difficult for endurance athletes to adapt to the low oxygen concentrations.

Responses of body to high altitude

* **Hyperventilation** involves increased ventilation of the lungs caused by impaired gaseous exchange in the lungs. In the UK, the majority of the population live between sea level and 500 metres above sea level. The differences in barometric pressure within this range are not enough to cause problems. When breathing normally, the breaths are varied to maintain normal carbon dioxide levels and supply appropriate levels of oxygen to the body's tissues. This is done automatically by measuring the carbon dioxide level in the blood. At altitude the air is oxygen-deficient, so resulting low carbon dioxide levels cause the brain's blood vessels to contract. This reduces blood flow to the brain accompanied by spells of dizziness or light-headedness. When an athlete leaves sea level and goes to a mountainous region, where air density and pressure are much lower, the body responds in a variety of ways. Headaches, dizziness and nausea due to the respiratory adjustments are common. In time, the athlete will adjust to the new environmental surroundings, a process known as acclimatisation.

* **Tachycardia** is a resting heart rate that is higher than normal (more than 100 beats per minute). Tachycardia can occur as a consequence of low body temperature. There are, however, other causes of tachycardia such as stress, heart disease and drugs.

Effects of high altitude

- **Reduction in partial pressure of oxygen** – decreases in arterial oxygen pressure cause chemoreceptors to become more responsive to an increase in carbon dioxide. This leads to an increase in ventilation as the brain attempts to restore gaseous exchange to a normal level. As less oxygen is available at high altitude, this always results in lower than normal haemoglobin saturation levels in an athlete's blood. At 5000 metres above sea level, for example, the oxygen saturation in blood is approximately 70 per cent (compared to 98 per cent at sea level). If an athlete has not acclimatised to these conditions, the lack of oxygen available from blood may seriously impair physical activity.

- **Reduced maximum oxygen uptake (VO_2 max)** – there is an estimated drop in VO_2 max of 2 per cent for every 300 metres above 1500 metres above sea level. This drop in VO_2 max means an athlete's oxygen uptake decreases, which can (and often will, without acclimatisation) adversely affect athletic performance, particularly during endurance-based events.

Adaptation to altitude

Problems arise when athletes undertake activity and the demands of the cardiovascular and respiratory systems are increased. Unless the athlete has undergone a period of acclimatisation the body's tissues may become **hypoxic**. There are three major changes that occur following acclimatisation:

- Increased haemoglobin concentration: during acclimatisation, there is an increase in red blood cell count and an increase in haemoglobin concentration. The increase in red blood cell count is caused by an increase in the manufacture of red blood cells in the bone marrow as the body's response to the altitude.

- Increased breathing rate: to compensate for the decrease in the partial pressure of oxygen in the lungs, the athlete's breathing rate increases.

- Cellular changes: altitude causes an increase in the myoglobin and mitochondria content within cells.

Key term

Hypoxic – inadequate supply of oxygen to respiratory tissues.

Effects of high altitude on sports performance

At high altitude there is less oxygen which creates a problem for sports performance. Anaerobic events require little adaptation so the focus of sports performance is on endurance training. A number of physiological changes occur when competing or training at high altitude at rest and during exercise, which help offset the lower partial pressure of oxygen.

High altitude training is an effective performance-enhancing tool, as the ability of an athlete to utilise greater amounts of oxygen improves performance. The physiological benefits of high altitude training continue for several weeks after the return of the athlete to sea level training conditions. Following the Mexico City Olympics in 1968 it became apparent that the reduced wind resistance and drag upon the athletes' bodies in the thin air permitted movement with greater efficiency. If an event did not involve specific use of the aerobic energy system (for example, long distance running) an athlete could perform better at high altitude. A moving body encounters reduced air resistance and any object thrown (for example, a javelin) travels further in the thin air.

Remember

VO_2 max is the maximum amount of oxygen an individual can extract from the atmosphere and then transport to use in tissues. It is expressed as the volumes of oxygen (ml) consumed per minute (min) per kilogram of bodyweight (kg). The average VO_2 max for a 20-year-old male is approximately 36–44 millilitres per kilogram per minute, or 36–44 ml/kg/min.

Assessment activity 21.1

P1 P2 BTEC

A semi-professional cricket team is going to Pretoria in South Africa during March. The team coach has asked you to prepare a short presentation on the effects of temperature and altitude to show the players prior to departure.

To emphasise the effects of temperature, your presentation should compare the differences in temperature between Pretoria and the UK.

Your presentation should detail the effects of temperature on the body and the body's responses to altitude. You should cover methods of heat loss, effects of high and low temperature, responses and adaptations to training at altitude and, in particular, the dangers the players may face during exercise. Research the average temperatures in Pretoria (and your home town in the UK) during March and the region's height above sea level to determine the altitude. **P1 P2**

Grading tips

- To attain **P1** indicate why body temperature is such an important factor in human physiology, how sports can in some cases put tremendous stress on body temperature and how the body deals with this. Mention the impact of environmental surroundings too.

- To attain **P2** ensure you explain what happens to the body at high altitude with particular reference to an athlete's breathing and oxygen count.

Functional skills

By developing a presentation on the effects of altitude and temperature on sports performance you could provide evidence of your **ICT** skills.

2. Know about the physical differences between people of different gender and race and their effect on exercise and sports performance

Gender refers to attributes that are categorised as male and female. Race, on the other hand, refers to a group of people who share common ancestry. To understand the physical differences between gender and race requires an examination of the anatomical and scientific evidence, as well as the sociological trends of the modern world.

2.1 Gender

Females differ in some ways from males with regard to sports performance and levels of physical ability. However, sociological thinking tends towards increasing equality, with females taking on more traditional male roles, and the differences between the sexes closing.

Physical differences

Females tend to be about 10 per cent smaller than males in most physical variables such as heart size, blood volume and haemoglobin concentration. Females carry approximately twice the body fat of males. The net result is a total aerobic capacity less than males. However, females are capable of significant improvements in muscle gains when training.

- **Body size** – the female skeleton is smaller and lighter than a male skeleton. Females have shorter appendicular components, which results in a smaller height and weight when compared to males. These skeletal differences have many implications. For example, smaller, lighter and shorter bones are helpful in events such as gymnastics when performances demand balance, flexibility and agility. By contrast, male gymnastics events make primary use of strength and explosive speed (for example, rings and pommel horse).

- **Body composition** – females have a greater percentage of body fat than males, with females averaging 25 per cent and males 12.5 per cent. Although this is an advantage in sports events such as long distance swimming (increased buoyancy and heat insulation) increased body fat is a distinct disadvantage in weight-bearing endurance events on land (for example, marathon running). Increased body fat raises the amount of work necessary to support and propel the body efficiently. It decreases VO_2 max when it is measured per kilogram of body mass and decreases the efficiency of heat loss over the skin by conduction, convention and radiation. However, trained females can be exceptionally lean and their body fat percentage can be below that of untrained males. Females can reduce their body fat content well below what is considered normal for their gender.

- **Muscle mass** – skeletal muscle has the same components and muscles respond and perform in the same way. The major reason females do not develop skeletal muscles of a similar size to males is because of higher **oestrogen** levels in most females. Oestrogen deters skeletal muscle from becoming large and bulky. Males have high levels of **testosterone**, which allows them to build skeletal muscle mass more easily and in greater quantities. Muscle mass is closely related to muscular strength and muscle mass for females is approximately 20 per cent less than for males. When comparing the muscular strength of males and females, males are naturally stronger than females in all muscle groups. Given the smaller muscle mass of females, there is less **phosphagen** available for maximal muscle contractions. Therefore, the peak power on average is approximately 20 per cent less for females.

Take it further

Male versus female

Serena Williams has won over 30 women's tennis titles during her career. Do you think she could adequately compete against male professional tennis players?

- **Testosterone levels** – testosterone is a hormone that occurs naturally in both males and females. In males testosterone is the main sex hormone that is secreted from the testes and controls muscle size, increases red blood cell count, decreases body fat and promotes male sex characteristics. In females, testosterone is secreted in small amounts from the ovaries, but its effects are outweighed by oestrogen, the main female sex hormone also secreted by the ovaries which controls the menstrual cycle, increases fat deposition and promotes female sex characteristics.

- **Haemoglobin levels** – males have slightly higher concentrations of haemoglobin in their blood than females. In theory males have an increased capacity for oxygen delivery to the working muscles.

Key terms

Oestrogen – the female sex hormone.

Testosterone – the male sex hormone.

Phosphagen – a member of a group of energy-rich phosphate compounds such as phosphocreatine.

Take it further

Advantage male?

Given that extended periods of exercise are supplied largely by the aerobic energy system, do males have a physiological advantage over females in aerobic events? Might this explain why the men's world record for the marathon is quicker, or is it more to do with males having larger skeletal muscles?

- **VO_2 max** – untrained females have lower VO_2 max values (generally between 20 per cent and 30 per cent lower) than untrained males. Endurance-trained females have VO_2 max values closer to those of endurance-trained males. Females are proven to excel in endurance events and currently hold many world records in long distance swimming.

Part of this success may be because of additional buoyancy afforded by the additional body fat found in females. However, at present, the physiology of this performance is not yet fully understood – it may be linked to improved fat metabolism and a greater tolerance of temperature variations.

- **Thermoregulation** – females generally sweat less than males because they start to sweat at higher skin and core temperatures. Despite a lower sweat output, females show heat tolerance similar to that of men and this is largely due to fact that females rely more on circulatory mechanisms for heat dissipation, whereas males make greater use of convection and evaporation. This allows females greater protection from dehydration during exercise at higher temperatures. Females tend to cool quicker than males through their smaller body mass across a relatively large surface area. Males have a smaller surface area to mass ratio given their greater concentration of skeletal muscle tissue.

- **Heart size** – females have smaller hearts than males because their body tends to be smaller. Genetics dictate that heart size is often relative to body size. Because men have larger muscle mass and larger internal organs (such as liver and lungs), their hearts require a larger stroke volume to accommodate the various functions.

- **Flexibility** – flexibility is an important component of fitness that has many contributory factors. It is affected by the composition of a given joint, the length and position of tendons and ligaments, and the elasticity of both the muscle tissue and the skin. Females tend to be more flexible than males.

- **Training differences** – there are few differences between the training responses of males and females undertaking similar activities. However, given the physiological differences between males and females, there are other factors which may influence training that merit further discussion. Men risk greater trauma in sporting contests in their genitalia, and the reproductive physiology of female athletes can be susceptible to the stress of competition and training. Exercise can affect menstruation, particularly among females involved in high-intensity training and competition sports.

Female athletes can develop **amenorrhea** (an abnormal cessation of menstruation) during training and competition. Excessive weight loss through a reduction in body fat is believed to be a cause of amenorrhea among female athletes. Menstruation can lead to iron deficiency in certain cases. Under these conditions, there may not be the full oxygen-binding capacity within the haemoglobin levels in a given volume of blood. This may have a detrimental effect on aerobic performance, so training adaptations or iron supplementation may be required.

Key term

Amenorrhea – absence of blood flow during the menstrual cycle.

Effects

- **Recovery periods** are dependent on an individual's level of fitness, regardless of gender. However, females have a tendency to have a slightly lower haemoglobin count than males, which may lessen female recovery rates.

- **Anaerobic capacity** – short-term high intensity exercises that involve anaerobic power often show a significant difference between the capabilities of both male and female athletes. Male athletes have a greater capacity for anaerobic power due to muscular strength and other neuromuscular factors. All these are fed by a ready supply of ATP.

- **Aerobic capacity** – females have lower natural haemoglobin counts, which means the oxygen-carrying capabilities of their blood are less than those of males. However, trained females are successful in certain endurance-based events. The fact that females carry more fat tissue than males means, for trained athletes, that there is an additional fuel supply on hand in greater quantities than in males. This ultimately is of benefit in endurance-based events.

2.2 Race

Athletes come from different racial types based on convention with relation to ethnicity, geography, skin colour and body form. Examples are West African, East African, Caucasian and Asian. Why not look at blood groups, muscle fibre types or other genetic traits? The reason you don't is largely sociological. The distribution of one physical or genetic characteristic is not necessarily the same as that of another, such as blood group or muscle fibre type. Some racial types are known to perform extremely well in certain sports. So you need to consider just how accurate or how closely aligned these social conventions and genetics actually are, and their impact on applied sport and exercise physiology.

West African origin

West Africa comprises the western-most region of Africa, occupying approximately one-fifth of the continent and composed of states including Nigeria, Gambia, Ghana, Senegal and Côte d'Ivoire. West Africa has a complex history. An important aspect of that history (in the context of future sport) was the colonial period during the eighteenth and nineteenth centuries in which France and Britain controlled nearly the entire region. During the slave trade many indigenous West Africans were transported to the Caribbean and North American continent to work on agricultural plantations. African-Americans are descendants of these people. The Chelsea striker Didier Drogba is of West African origin. He was born in Abidjan in Côte d'Ivoire, but moved to France with his family at the age of five.

East African origin

East Africa comprises the eastern-most region of Africa and includes nations such as Kenya, Tanzania, Uganda and Ethiopia. The unique geography and suitability for farming made East Africa an appealing target for European colonisation in the nineteenth century. Former world 800 metre champion Wilson Kipketer is of East African origin. He was born in Kenya in 1972, but later applied for Danish nationality after studying there for many years.

Figure 21.2: West Africa encompasses a huge area on the Atlantic coast of the African continent.

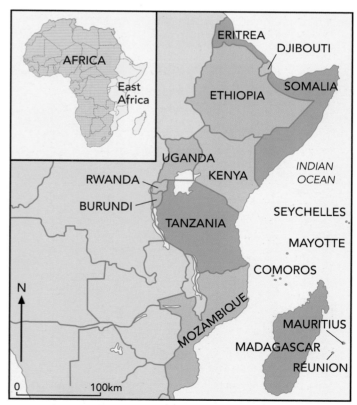

Figure 21.3: East Africa countries have large areas of high altitude where many of the world's top endurance athletes originate.

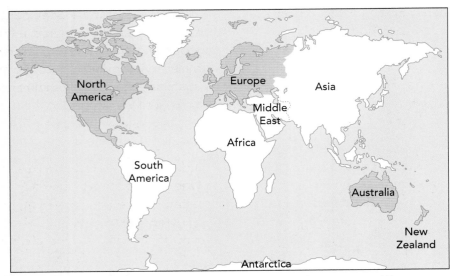

Figure 21.4: The Caucasian race is the majority in North America and Europe, Australia and New Zealand.

Caucasian

The term 'Caucasian' refers to people whose ancestry can be traced back to Europe, the Middle East and some regions of Asia. The physical characteristics of Caucasian athletes tend to be light to brown skin pigmentations and a variety of physical forms. Former seven-time Formula 1 world champion Michael

Schumacher is of Caucasian origin. He was born in Germany in 1969 and went on to become the most successful Formula 1 driver to date.

Asian

The term 'Asian' refers to people from Asia. The meaning varies by country and person, much like the term Caucasian. In the US, for example, Asian refers

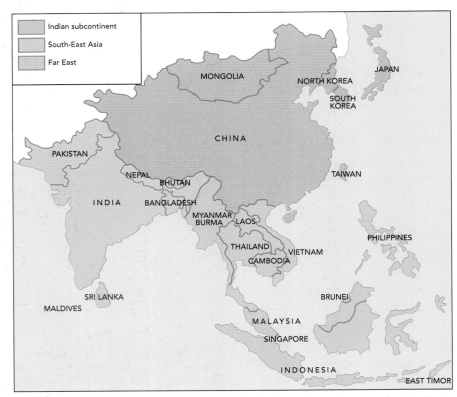

Figure 21.5: Asia covers a vast area from the Indian subcontinent to the Far East and South-East Asia. Asians remain the majority race in these areas.

to people of predominantly East Asian (for example, China and Japan) or South-East Asian origin (for example, Thailand and Vietnam). On the other hand, in the UK Asian generally refers to South Asia (for example, India and Pakistan). Former women's Olympic 100 metre breaststroke gold medallist Luo Xuejuan was born in China in 1984, and set a new Olympic record during her 2004 Olympic triumph. She has retired from competition following heart surgery.

Physical differences

The human race evolved in Africa and spread over the continents. Over time, populations became geographically separated as the human race spread across the world. These populations gradually evolved different physical characteristics to accommodate new surroundings. West African, East African, Caucasian and Asian races all display physical differences as a consequence of adapting to their environment. As a general rule, West African athletes tend to be black skinned and well-muscled, whereas East African athletes have a narrower skeletal frame and a leaner muscle structure. Caucasian athletes have a light skin colour, a lighter hair colour and a fairly muscular frame. Asian athletes tend to have black hair, darker skin and a smaller physical frame than Caucasians. These racial differences occur as a consequence of the processes of mutation, natural selection and genetic drift, and geographical separation.

- **Muscle fibre types** – East African athletes win approximately 50 per cent of endurance races in elite athletics. East Africans living at altitude are born with a high number of slow twitch muscle fibres. Seventy to 75 per cent of their muscle fibres are slow twitch. The interesting point from a physiological viewpoint is that many of these athletes trace their ancestry to the 2000–3000 metre altitude highlands of the East African Great Rift Valley. Evolution has granted East African athletes a distinct physiological advantage when it comes to competing in endurance events as their cardiovascular systems are able to function efficiently using air that has a lower oxygen pressure, ensuring a significant aerobic advantage. Many West Africans or African-Americans trace their ancestry to low-lying areas towards the Atlantic coastal regions. Consequently, they have far fewer slow twitch muscle fibres but a higher concentration of fast twitch muscle fibres, which are ideal for explosive events such as sprinting.

- **Body composition** is often discussed in terms of somatotypes. These describe the characteristic shape and physical appearance of an individual athlete, disregarding size. The most common form of somatotyping involves three types:
  o endomorph
  o mesomorph
  o ectomorph.

Individuals are rated on a scale of 1 to 7 for each type: 1 is a minimal rating and 7 is a maximal rating. The sequence of numbers this gives refers to components in the following order: endomorph, mesomorph and ectomorph. For example, looking at the photo of Haile Gebrselassie, his somatotype rating would be approximately 1–3–6.

Given his East African ancestry, Haile Gebrselassie's body composition is largely ectomorphic. How does this give him a physiological advantage when it comes to endurance events?

East African athletes tend to be ectomorphs, short in stature with long slender limbs. This makes them perfect for endurance events such as distance running. West Africans, on the other hand, tend to be mesomorphs, reasonably tall in stature with well-muscled limbs and torso, making them perfect for explosive events such as sprinting. Caucasians tend to fall in between ectomorph and mesomorph. They have upper body strength, making them suitable for events such as weightlifting and field events. Asians tend to be similar to Caucasians in terms of body composition, only smaller. Their more ectomorphic build allows them to excel in events where flexibility is key, such as springboard diving and gymnastics.

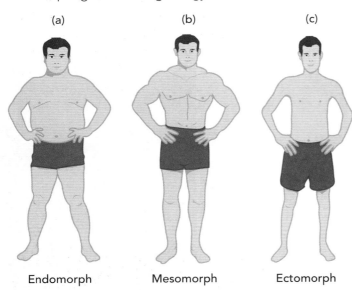

(a)　　　　　(b)　　　　　(c)

Endomorph　　　Mesomorph　　　Ectomorph

Figure 21.6: The three somatotypes:
a) endomorph, b) mesomorph and c) ectomorph.

- **Lung capacity and haemoglobin levels** – Kenyan success in endurance running is partly due to the fact that many Kenyan runners come from a high altitude region. Kenyans from low altitudes tend not to do well in the classic long distance events, so it is not necessarily about being Kenyan

or originating from East Africa that contributes to success in endurance events. It is more about living or having genetic ancestry in high altitude areas. South Korea is increasingly becoming a force in endurance running. Athletes of Asian origin were not considered a threat to the East African dominance. However, much of South Korea is mountainous terrain at high altitude, so this is no longer the case. Further proof of this is the emergence of Ecuadorian athletes as an endurance-running force. Ecuador is a high altitude country in South America. Given the propensity of athletes from altitude to assimilate oxygen in regions of low oxygen pressure, these athletes tend to have increased levels of haemoglobin. This is not the case for West African athletes and most Caucasian athletes, although Asian athletes from mountainous regions of China, Japan and Korea do.

- **Body types** (somatotypes) generalise that West Africans tend to be squat and muscular (i.e. the classic mesomorph) whereas East Africans tend to be tall and slender (i.e. the classic ectomorph). Caucasians, on the other hand, tend to be a mixture (depending on where each Caucasian is descended from).

Remember

Caucasian is a general racial description whereas West African and East African are geographical indicators. Asians tend to be smaller than Caucasians.

Effects

- **Heat tolerance and cold tolerance** – heat retention is facilitated by having a short and muscular frame. This is the case in many northern European and north Asian regions, where the climate is

Activity: Somatotyping

In groups, identify the somatotype rating for at least three different athletes from three different sports using a copy of the table below. Remember that 1 is a minimal rating while 7 is a maximal rating.

Name	Endomorph rating (1–7)	Mesomorph rating (1–7)	Ectomorph rating (1–7)	Sport

predominantly cool. If you evolved in East Africa, where the environment is hot, then heat loss is facilitated by being long and lean or ectomorphic.

- **Sprinting ability** – all the sprinters who featured in the 100 metre final at the Beijing Olympics in 2008 can trace their ancestry to West Africa. Yet despite their wealth of distance runners, the current Kenyan 100 metre record stands at 10.28 seconds, which ranks virtually nowhere. Most of the world record holders in the 100 metre event are of West African origin. Interestingly they also tend to be West African-Americans whose race has been mixed over the generations. Therefore, it is not easy to categorically say whether being of West African descent is a factor in being able to sprint, or whether it is the mixed race of West African with other races that has helped them become so fast. Where is the evidence for this? If you examine successful sprinters they all trained in the US, Canada, the UK or the Caribbean. However, if you examine West African countries where these successful sprinters' ancestors hail from, none of these countries (Nigeria, Côte d'Ivoire, Ghana, etc.) have ever produced world records or Olympic titles. Explanations such as wealth and resources cannot be used as a reason for lack of success, particularly as less wealthy countries such as Kenya and Ethiopia regularly produce world records and Olympic titles at distance events. Asian countries such as China and Japan also produce talented sprinters, so the fact that most of the world record holders in the 100 metre event are of West African origin may not be the case in future. Are our scientific assumptions based on race false? Only time will tell, but it will take an exceptional athlete to beat Usain Bolt's record of 9.58 seconds.

- **High altitude tolerance** – people who are indigenous to areas of high altitude, such as East Africa or countries like Bolivia, possess greater concentrations of haemoglobin in their blood. This allows them to deliver a larger amount of oxygen to tissue under low oxygen pressure (at altitude). Consequently, it is believed that these athletes have a greater aerobic capacity and, therefore, excel at endurance events.

Remember

The top ten fastest male 100 metre sprinters of all time have been athletes of West African origin. Of the ten fastest female sprinters, eight have been of West African origin and two have been Caucasian.

How much of Usain Bolt's sprinting success is down to his ancestry?

Assessment activity 21.2

Following a successful pre-season tour to South Africa, the cricket team has made excellent community links with local cricket clubs in Pretoria and Johannesburg. These clubs have asked if some of their players might travel to the UK to train and play here. The UK cricket coach has agreed and a group of under-18 local players (male and female), mostly from the surrounding township areas, are flying back to the UK under an exchange programme.

The coach has asked you to prepare a poster that helps to explain the physiological differences between male and female, and Caucasian and South or East African cricketers, and the effects these differences may have on performance.

1. Your poster should make reference to the following and how they might affect batting, bowling and overall performance on the cricket field:

   a physiological differences and effects on performance of gender **P3**

   b physiological differences and effects on performance of race. **P4**

2. Further explain on your poster the effects of the physiological differences between male and female on performance. **M1**

3. Further explain on your poster the effects of the physiological differences between different races on performance. **M2**

4. As an addition to the poster, produce a leaflet which coaches can take away that analyses the effects of the physiological differences between gender and races on sports performance. **D1**

Grading tips

- To attain **P3** you must be able to describe the physiological differences between male and female athletes that involve factors such as body size and composition, muscle mass, hormone levels, haemoglobin levels, VO_2 max, thermoregulation, heart size, flexibility and training differences. Then go on to describe how these differences might impact on sports performance, specifically training, recovery periods, and aerobic and anaerobic capacities.

- To attain **P4** you must be able to describe the physiological differences between races such as different muscle fibre types, body composition, lung capacity, haemoglobin levels and body type. Then go on to describe how these differences impact on sports performance, specifically heat tolerance, cold tolerance, sprinting ability, and high-altitude tolerance.

- To attain **M1** keep your explanations in the context of the effects of the gender on sports performance covered in **P3**, especially in a cricket context.

- To attain **M2** keep your explanations in the context of the effects of the race on sports performance covered in **P4**, especially in a cricket context.

- To attain **D1** the distinction level means you must analyse or break up the components of the assignment covered in **P3** and **P4**, addressing both the key differences and similarities between gender and race, and their impact on exercise and sports performance.

PLTS

Describing the physiological differences between athletes of different gender, and their effects on exercise and sports performance, can develop your skills as a **creative thinker** and as an **independent enquirer**.

Functional skills

Developing a presentation researching physiological differences of athletes could help develop your **ICT** skills.

3. Know the impact that the physiological effects of ageing have on exercise and sports performance

Ageing is associated with a degenerative process that includes a reduction in muscular strength, weakening of the skeletal structure and longer reaction times. This process has an effect on exercise and physical performance at some stage, although when this process begins and how rapidly it takes hold depends on the fitness levels of the individual.

3.1 Physiological effects of ageing

The physiology and performance abilities of older people are different from younger athletes. Are these differences due to natural biological processes, sociological constraints (such as diet) or the opportunity to exercise regularly? During childhood, girls and boys follow similar growth patterns, resulting in similar amounts of muscle tissue, bone mass and body composition. From about 7–9 years of age, balance, coordination and agility begin to improve as the child's central nervous system develops. Once adolescents reach maturity, ageing affects individuals through changes in cell structure and organ function. From a physical peak at about 25, there is a progressive deterioration in physical capabilities. This is due to a decrease in the efficiency of the body's major systems and how it adapts to exercise. The ageing process includes restricted joint flexibility, increases in body fat, muscle **atrophy** and osteoporosis. Probably the most influential factor of ageing on the body is the formation of additional **collagen fibres** throughout major organs and skeletal muscles.

Key terms

Atrophy – loss of mass or wasting away.

Collagen fibres – most abundant of fibres found in connective tissue.

Sarcopenia – loss of muscle mass.

Maximum heart rate

Maximum heart rate decreases at an average rate of 1 or 2 beats per year. Extra collagen fibres form between the heart's muscles fibres, reducing the heart's elasticity and stroke volume. A rough approximation of the change in maximal heart rate with age is expressed by the following formula:

maximum heart rate = 220 – age (in years)

The older someone gets, the lower their maximum heart rate will be. This lower heart rate means maximum cardiac output is reduced. Contributing to this reduced blood flow is the reduction in the heart's stroke rate. Whether or not these changes are as a result of the ageing process or as a consequence of modern living and sedentary lifestyles is a topic of debate. Age affects an athlete's blood pressure. A normal blood pressure reading for a healthy adult is 120/80 mm Hg. However, arterioles lose their elasticity with age and this raises peripheral resistance. Therefore, the pressure generated by cardiac output remains high. This can lead to high systolic levels of blood pressure as the heart has to apply extra force to propel the blood around stiffened arterioles. Age-related stiffening of the arterioles can lead to a condition known as arteriosclerosis, which reduces the blood supply to vital organs and reduces an individual's exercise capabilities.

Lung volumes

Extra collagen fibres formed in the lungs decrease elasticity, which reduces lung volumes, affecting the respiratory system's ability to carry out gaseous exchange, especially under heavy exercise workloads.

Flexibility

As an athlete ages, the cross-linkages between the collagen fibres increase. This results in stiffening throughout the body's skeletal muscles and tendons. This stiffening is as a result of the muscle sheaths becoming thicker and stiffer. By the time you reach 30, a loss of muscle mass known as **sarcopenia** occurs, as muscle proteins start to degrade more rapidly than they can be replaced.

Thermoregulation

The ability to cope with moderate temperature change does not deteriorate with age. Some research has indicated that the onset of age sometimes assists with acclimatisation involving heat toleration. However, age is a limiting factor during vigorous exercise in heat due to an apparent delay in sweating.

3.2 Impact

Training

Regular exercise helps reverse sarcopenia. Those who did not exercise when younger often witness an increase in muscle mass and muscular strength when they train during middle age.

> ### Remember
>
> Exercise is a potent stimulator of bone deposition, which increases both bone mass and density. This delays the onset of diseases such as osteoarthritis and osteoporosis.

Recovery periods

The impact of ageing on recovery periods is determined by the physical condition of the athlete. The ageing process affects a number of key physiological processes.

- A reduction in the ability to synthesise protein results in a loss of lean muscle mass. This loss reduces the **basal metabolic rate** (BMR). Therefore, although there is no increase in food intake, body fat levels may rise. When combined, both these factors mean that smaller muscles have less capacity to store glycogen and will have to work with more intensity to exercise a body containing increased fat levels. The results of this are that glycogen levels may be depleted more readily so the recovery process, as the muscles refuel, is likely to take longer.

- A loss of nerve cells in the brain affects all aspects of body movement, so the ageing process can result in a decrease in the control of complex motor units. This, in turn, places more burden on the reduced skeletal muscle mass and further depletes their energy sources due to their increased inefficiency. Glycogen levels may be depleted more readily so the recovery process, as the muscle refuels, takes longer.

> ## Key term
>
> **Basal metabolic rate (BMR)** – energy demand of the body at rest.

Aerobic and anaerobic capacity

Ageing has an impact on an athlete's aerobic capacity. As you get older, your maximum heart rate decreases. As the stroke volume lessens, an increase in resting heart rate is necessary to satisfy the needs of the cardiovascular system. This is further hampered by hardening of the arteries, which increases the resting systolic blood pressure. When taking these factors into account, recovery after exercise takes longer. The onset of age impairs the ability of the body to utilise oxygen. VO_2 max reaches its peak for an athlete between the ages of 18 and 25 years. After age 25, the VO_2 max declines steadily so that by the age of 55, an individual's VO_2 max will have declined by approximately 25 per cent. However, as research into this area progresses, it is apparent that those undertaking physical activity – whether recreationally or at an elite level – are more likely to maintain a healthy VO_2 max than those who do not. Anaerobic capacity does not escape the ageing process. The decline in anaerobic abilities includes muscle and strength atrophy and a shift towards a greater concentration of slow twitch fibres. A thinning of the myelinated sheaths around muscle tissue lengthens reaction times.

Overheating

There is no definitive link between age and an increased risk of dehydration leading to hyperthermia (overheating), so the likelihood of an older athlete overheating before a younger athlete, whatever the circumstances, is minimal. Overheating is an advanced stage of heatstroke or sunstroke during which the body absorbs more heat than it can dissipate. It usually occurs as a result of overexposure to excessive heat, especially in competition. The heat controlling mechanisms of the body eventually become overwhelmed and unable to deal with the heat appropriately. As a consequence, the body temperature rises to a dangerous level.

Activity: Age and training

Imagine you are a fitness instructor who has been given the task of writing a training programme for a 60-year-old female who wishes to run a marathon for the first time. Using a table like the one below, list the likely effects age will have on your client's physical abilities in the left column, and the potential benefits from training in the right column. Compare your results with your classmates for discussion.

60-year-old female

Effects of age on physical capabilities	Likely benefits of training

Assessment activity 21.3

The pre-season tour and exchange programme proved a success for the cricket club. Its profile has risen and now has enough interest to field a veteran team of players, aged over 40, to play in a regional league.

1. The coach has asked you to compile a short guide that describes the physiological effects of ageing on exercise sports performance. The guide is to be handed out to players, so he's asked for something easy to understand. He suggests a double-sided piece of A4, which can then be laminated for safekeeping. **P5**

2. Make sure that your guide also explains the impact of the physiological effects of ageing in exercise and sports performance. **M3**

3. Further analyse the physiological effects of ageing on performance in your guide. **D2**

Grading tips

- To attain **P5** your guide must describe the impact of the physiological effects of ageing on exercise such as maximum heart rate, lung volumes, flexibility and thermoregulation. Then go on to describe how these impact sports performance in terms of training, recovery periods, aerobic and anaerobic capacity, and overheating.

- To attain **M3** explain the impact of the physiological effects of ageing on performance, but bear in mind tact may be required, given those reading your work may be affected.

- To attain **D2** you must analyse the important points concerned with ageing that others might overlook, as well as identifying faults and making realistic suggestions as to how to accommodate the effects of ageing.

PLTS

Describing the impact of the physiological effects of ageing on exercise and sports performance can develop your skills as an **independent enquirer**.

Functional skills

The production and presentation of your guide could give you a chance to display your **ICT** skills.

4. Know the effects and implications of using ergogenic aids for exercise and sports performance

Ergogenic aids are any method or factor which enhances exercise and sports performance. They are often thought of as performance-enhancing drugs, but include everyday items such as vitamins and minerals, and psychological techniques such as mental rehearsal or playing music.

Key terms

Ergogenic – a factor that enhances physical performance.

Anabolic – changes include the growth and development of body tissues, most notably muscle.

4.1 Ergogenic aids

Athletes and coaches are continually searching for ways to gain a competitive advantage to improve athletic performance. It is therefore unsurprising that ergogenic aids are marketed and sold to athletes at all levels. There is a vast range of ergogenic aids on the market. Some are commercially available and legal, others are available on prescription only while others are illegal and their use and possession will result in criminal investigation. In response to the legal issue and moral arguments surrounding cheating or doping, the International Olympic Committee (IOC) has formulated the list in Table 21.3 which divides banned or illegal drugs into categories.

Drug type	Examples
Anabolic agents	Anabolic steroids
Peptide hormones	Human growth hormone, EPO and insulin
Diuretics	Caffeine and slimming agents
Masking agents	Blood doping
Drugs subject to restriction	Beta blockers
Stimulants	Amphetamines
Narcotics	Codeine and morphine
Anti-oestrogen agents	Tamoxifen

Table 21.3: International Olympic Committee banned or illegal drug categories.

Anabolic steroids

Society loves a winner and the rewards are huge, both socially and financially. It is perhaps unsurprising that many athletes resort to performance-enhancing products if it means a chance of success, regardless of whether or not they are legal. Anabolic steroids are designed to mimic the effects of testosterone (the male sex hormone). Testosterone is produced in both the male testes and the female ovaries, although it is present in much higher concentrations in males than females. The anabolic properties of steroids include the growth and development of many body tissues, especially muscle tissue. Use of anabolic steroids may lead to temporary infertility in males, the suppression of sex hormones and an impairment of sperm production.

During the 1988 Olympics in Seoul, Ben Johnson was crowned 100 metre champion, smashing the existing world record as he powered to victory in a time of 9.79 seconds. Shortly afterwards he gave a urine sample that proved positive for stanozolol, an anabolic steroid. He was later stripped of his medal and the title and his time was erased from the record books.

Severe penalties are imposed by the IOC and other sports bodies if anabolic steroids are detected. The penalties of a positive drugs test may have serious

How many other top class athletes and sports people have tested positive after drugs tests?

repercussions for both the athlete and the public image of the sport. Anabolic steroids have been associated with strength-related sports such as weightlifting. However, the current extent of anabolic steroid use extends to sports such as swimming, cycling and sprinting.

Growth hormone

Human growth hormone, also known as somatropin, is secreted by the pituitary gland. Growth hormone affects the growth of every organ and every type of tissue found in the human body. It increases protein synthesis, producing an anabolic effect. Growth hormone also stimulates the synthesis of fat as a source of energy, thus sparing muscle glycogen. Athletes using growth hormone as a performance-enhancing drug do so to increase their size and strength. However, side effects have included skeletal changes, enlargement of internal organs, the development of diabetes and a thickening and coarsening of the skin. Human growth hormone is often taken by athletes also using anabolic steroids and is banned by the IOC.

Creatine

In sports such as sprinting, the rate of ATP resynthesis is more important than the capacity for energy production. The rapid resynthesis of ATP occurs as a result of the degradation of **creatine phosphate**. Creatine supplementation is perfectly legal and is believed to increase the resynthesis of creatine phosphate, resulting in an increased capacity to perform explosive or strength-related exercises. The source of most natural creatine is from foods such as meat and fish. However, creatine monohydrate is the supplement used and 1 gram is the equivalent to the creatine content in 1 kg of fresh meat.

Key term

Creatine phosphate – an energy-rich compound used in the production of ATP from ADP in muscle cells.

Insulin

Insulin is a hormone that stimulates the liver, muscles and fat cells to remove glucose from the blood for use or storage. Insulin production falls during strenuous exercise. However, in trained athletes, it does not fall as much during exercise as in untrained athletes. This allows more energy to be derived from free fatty acids. Consequently, injecting insulin prior to exercise can enhance endurance-based competition and is banned by the IOC.

Caffeine

Caffeine is one of the most common and frequently used stimulants available. It is found at various levels of potency in tea, coffee and many soft drinks. Caffeine is a common addition to cold and flu remedies. Despite being freely available and not illegal, caffeine is a potent and potentially addictive drug and is banned in large quantities by the IOC. Its use has been linked to a number of adverse effects including tremors, anxiety headaches and cramps. The performance-enhancing effects include an increase in heart rate, stroke volume, cardiac output and blood pressure, an increase in alertness and a decrease in the perception of fatigue. Caffeine is proven to increase the contractile nature of skeletal muscle and metabolic rate. Other research has suggested that caffeine may enhance the utilisation of fats, thus sparing glycogen stores.

Blood doping

An increasingly popular form of ergogenic aid is blood doping. This involves injecting red blood cells to enhance the blood's aerobic system. The method involves the athlete donating blood (1 to 2 litres depending on body size) prior to training or competition. This blood is frozen and kept in storage. In response to this loss of blood, the body replaces the red blood cells by way of natural reaction. Prior to training or competition the athlete receives the stored blood by venous injection, thus raising the total red blood cell count in his or her body. The disadvantages of blood doping are extensive. As well as the possible risk of infection, blood clotting is a heightened risk, especially if the athlete becomes dehydrated during the event. This injection (or doping) raises the red blood cell count well above normal and temporarily increases the oxygen-carrying capacity of the blood. This is highly advantageous for endurance-based events. Blood doping is a process that is banned by the IOC, although artificial blood boosting is difficult to detect.

Erythropoietin (EPO)

Erythropoietin (EPO) is the hormone responsible for red blood cell production and is produced in the kidneys. Although EPO has benefitted many anaemia sufferers, it has also been used as a blood doping agent to give healthy athletes a competitive advantage. EPO works by increasing the oxygen-carrying capacities of blood, which improves the aerobic respiratory capacity of skeletal muscles. EPO has been popular with professional cyclists and long distance runners, but its use is banned by the IOC. EPO is dangerous as it increases the viscosity of the blood and blood pressure. Both these symptoms can lead to heart failure or stroke.

Altitude training

Altitude training is used by athletes to gain a future competitive edge. The body adapts to the lack of oxygen available at over 2000 metres by increasing the concentration of red blood cells and haemoglobin levels in the blood. When athletes return to sea level to compete, they maintain the higher concentration of red blood cells for several weeks. This concentration of red blood cells allows more oxygen to be supplied to the muscles, improving performance.

Glycogen loading

Glycogen loading (also known as carbohydrate loading) is used by athletes to maximise the storage of glycogen in skeletal muscles. Glycogen loading involves increased carbohydrate intake (in the form of pasta, rice and cereals) and decreased training for approximately three days prior to competition. Glycogen loading is based on a regular, controlled diet and is legal.

Beta blockers

Beta blockers are used to treat a wide range of medical conditions such as **hypertension**, **cardiac arrhythmias** and migraines. Beta blockers prevent adrenaline and noradrenaline from exerting their effects on the body. This has the effect of reducing anxiety and muscle tremors. Beta blockers can enhance performance in certain sports such as archery, shooting and diving, so they are on the IOC's list of banned substances. Beta blockers are unlikely to enhance endurance events, which require prolonged periods of high cardiac output.

Key terms

Hypertension – high blood pressure, when systolic blood pressure is above 140 mm Hg and diastolic pressure is above 90 mm Hg.

Cardiac arrhythmia – an irregular heart beat.

Marijuana

The effects of marijuana include decreased motivation for physical activity, decreased motor coordination and changes in perception. Persistent use of marijuana is incompatible with serious sport participation because it tends to demotivate athletes, taking away their will to win. Marijuana is listed on the IOC's banned list and is illegal in the UK.

Amphetamines

Amphetamines are a class of synthetic stimulant drugs invented to suppress appetite. Amphetamines are powerful stimulants of the central nervous system, producing feelings of euphoria, alertness, mental clarity and increased energy. The implications for most sports are obvious, and the effects on an athlete would prove far reaching for events ranging from football to track and field. The disadvantages of amphetamines are an increased heart rate and blood pressure, and nausea and fatigue once the effects have worn off. Amphetamines are on the IOC's banned list and their possession is illegal in the UK.

Cocaine

Cocaine has significant effects on mood. These affect levels of friendliness, arousal, elation and positive mood states. Cocaine also has a significant effect on the brain, which includes increased activity at the neural synapses. Consequently, if cocaine is used repeatedly, the effects on behaviour can become exaggerated. Cocaine is a Class A drug in the UK, so possession is illegal. In addition, it is classed as a stimulant and is therefore on the IOC's banned list.

Remember

The International Olympic Committee (IOC) compiles and updates the list of banned substances with the World Anti-Doping Agency (WADA), an affiliate organisation of the IOC. The complete and current list of WADA banned substances can be found at www.wada-ama.org.

4.2 Effects of ergogenic aids

Positive effects

- **Decreased heart rate** – this is likely to be beneficial to sports requiring fine motor skills and prolonged levels of concentration. Beta blockers work by preventing adrenaline and noradrenaline from exerting their effects on the body and the heart in particular. However, events requiring prolonged periods of cardiac output may be severely hindered by taking beta blockers.

- **Decreased recovery time** – this is beneficial to any athlete as it means they can compete or train much sooner than predicted. Glycogen loading will replace that used during training, but whether or not this can significantly decrease recovery time is debatable. Certain anabolic steroids (such as nandrolone decanoate) are known to invigorate exercised muscle so that they feel less sore or fatigued after exercise. Other ergogenic aids such as EPO have the ability to increase an athlete's blood cell count. This means oxygen and nutrients are able to reach the fatigued muscles and cells far quicker post-exercise.

- **Increased mobilisation of fatty acids** – substances such as caffeine, insulin and human growth hormone are believed to increase the mobilisation of fatty acids. This allows for a more plentiful supply of energy from the fatty acids, placing less dependence on glycogen, both of which can enhance endurance-based activities.

Negative effects

- **Heart palpitations** – substances such as amphetamines and cocaine can induce heart palpitations – a rapid series of heartbeats (tachycardia) often accompanied by symptoms including sweating, faintness, dizziness or even chest pains. Palpitations are likely to be detrimental to any form of exercise and the likely benefits of taking ergogenic aids such as caffeine or cocaine (not least because the latter is illegal) are likely to be outweighed by the symptoms of heart palpitations.

- **Reduced fertility** – anabolic steroids in most forms are proven to reduce fertility in certain circumstances. The use of anabolic steroids may lead to temporary infertility in males, the suppression of sex hormones and an impairment of sperm production.

- **Cancer** – anabolic steroids are known to increase the risk of liver cancer.

- **Skin disorders** – anabolic steroids are known to increase acne and male pattern baldness.

- **Increased blood pressure** – both EPO and anabolic steroids are known to increase systolic blood pressure.

- **Breathing difficulties** – beta blockers are known to cause breathing difficulties, especially in individuals with asthma.

- **Muscle cramps** – creatine has caused muscle cramps with some users, though controlled studies have yet to document any significant side effects.

- **Kidney failure** – anabolic steroids are known to increase the risk of kidney failure.

Take it further

Banned substances

Research a recent case in which a high-profile athlete has failed a drugs test and subsequently been banned from competition. Examine their reasons or motivations for taking banned substances and whether or not they were aware of the potential dangers to their health.

Assessment activity 21.4

The cricket coach is concerned about recent press reports of professional cricketers testing positive for banned performance-enhancing substances. He has asked you to prepare a poster for display in the pavilion that educates the players on the variety of ergogenic aids available.

Your poster should explain which aids the cricketers should never consider taking and which may prove beneficial.

1. Your poster should describe the effects and implications of six ergogenic aids. **P6**

2. Explain the effects and implications of your chosen ergogenic aids. **M4**

3. Further analyse the effects and implications of your chosen ergogenic aids. **D3**

Grading tips

- To attain **P6**, as a guide, you might look at the following:

    o banned ergogenic aids including anabolic steroids, EPO and amphetamines

    o approved ergogenic aids including creatine, altitude training and glycogen loading.

- To attain **M4** explain the effects and implications of your chosen six different ergogenic aids used for exercise and sports performance.

- To attain **D3** you need to break up the components of the question and respond to them with critical insight. In other words, spot the important points that others might miss.

PLTS

Describing the effects and implications of six different ergogenic aids used for exercise and sports performance can develop your skills as an **independent enquirer**.

Gemma Knight
Youth worker

Gemma works as a youth worker and is responsible for:

- promoting increased sport participation
- giving talks at schools
- checking emails, verifying information and responding to queries
- working with parents and community groups to win support for important social causes.

'There is no typical day for me, but my day starts when I arrive at the youth centre first thing in the morning. I deal with any outstanding administration or phone calls, then I get out and visit schools and sports clubs – that's the part I enjoy the most. Given my background in sport, my role is concerned with increasing sports participation and educating teenagers on the dangers of drugs and illegal substances. I first became interested in the subject of illegal ergogenic aids as a student. I learned a great deal about the different types of illegal substances (for example, anabolic steroids, marijuana, etc.) and their physiological effects.

'I enjoy meeting and helping young people. Educating young gym users – usually males aged between 16 and 19 – about the dangers of anabolic steroids is a difficult task, but when you are able to explain in detail the potential harm they could do to their bodies, such as an increased chance of developing liver cancer or high blood pressure, they start to take your comments seriously.

'It's a difficult role and, because I'm a female working in the macho world of gym users, it can be a bit frustrating sometimes. However, I've had a couple of success stories – people who were steroid users but understood what damage they were doing to their bodies and stopped. They sometimes accompany me now when I give talks at schools and tell their own stories.'

Think about it!

- What areas have you covered in this unit that provide you with the knowledge and skills used by a youth worker?
- What further skills might you need to develop? Think about how you might discuss harmful performance-enhancing drugs to a group of Year 11 pupils. Discuss your approach in small groups.

Just checking

1. What is normal human body temperature?
2. List the four types of heat loss and briefly describe the key characteristics of each.
3. List three physiological differences between males and females that might affect sports participation.
4. People living at altitude have a higher concentration of what compound in their blood?
5. List the three somatotypes and briefly describe the key characteristics of each.
6. Why do males generally have a larger stroke volume than females?
7. Explain why an increase in collagen fibres due to ageing might affect sports performance.
8. At what points on the temperature scale in degrees Celsius (both hot and cold) would you expect athletes not to be able to perform their sports effectively?
9. List the potential side effects of taking anabolic steroids.
10. List the possible side effects of taking a) amphetamines and b) large amounts of caffeine.

Assignment tips

- Acquire a professional textbook on physiology. It's better to have more than one view or description of the same subject, that way you can 'compare and contrast' and improve the standard of your assessed work.

- Read sports magazines and their websites – Magazines like *Health & Fitness*, *Ultrafit* or *Athletics Weekly* often contain articles relating to gender, race, age, environment and ergogenic aids.

- Speak to physiologists or fitness instructors and ask why they think knowledge of environment, gender, age, race and ergogenic aids is important.

- If you use ergogenic aids such as creatine or glycogen loading, keep a training diary detailing your improvement in running times or lifting strength, and comment why you think these changes have occurred.

- Compile your own portfolio of evidence. There has been considerable research done on the areas covered in this unit; some of that research is quite controversial. The issue of race is particularly topical and there are many arguments going on in the academic world regarding the importance and relevance of race in sport. Find these articles and keep them for debates you might have with your class.

- Keep a physiology portfolio of evidence. You will revisit the concepts in this unit in other units such as Unit 8 Fitness testing for sport and exercise, Unit 9 Fitness training and programming and Unit 10 Sport and exercise massage.

23 Work experience in sport

This is your chance to discover what it is like to work in the sports and leisure industry. The aim of the unit is to provide you with the skills to complete a work experience placement for a minimum of ten days. There are many career opportunities related to sport including management positions, coaching and fitness, sports development, sports science jobs, teaching, sports attendants and lifeguards. Sport and leisure is a growth industry with diverse opportunities. Work experience gives you the chance to progress your career. It looks great on your CV – it is an opportunity for somebody to give you a glowing reference and it will help you make career decisions.

In this unit you will look at different jobs in the industry and reflect on your key aims, objectives and targets for your career and your potential placements. You will look at different ways of applying for a job and interview skills. You will complete your work experience and reflect on your aims, objectives and targets and review them in relation to your career.

Learning outcomes

After completing this unit you should:

1. know about the opportunities for work-based experience in sport
2. be able to prepare for a work-based experience in sport
3. be able to undertake a work-based experience in sport
4. be able to review a work-based experience in sport.

Assessment and grading criteria

This table shows you what you must do in order to achieve a pass, merit or distinction grade, and where you can find activities in this book to help you.

To achieve a pass grade the evidence must show that you are able to:	To achieve a merit grade the evidence must show that, in addition to the pass criteria, you are able to:	To achieve a distinction grade the evidence must show that, in addition to the pass and merit criteria, you are able to:
P1 describe four realistic opportunities for appropriate work-based experience in sport **See Assessment activity 23.1, page 478**	**M1** explain four realistic opportunities for appropriate work-based experience in sport **See Assessment activity 23.1, page 478**	**D1** evaluate the opportunities for appropriate work-based experience in sport **See Assessment activity 23.1, page 478**
P2 select an appropriate work-based experience in sport and complete the application process **See Assessment activity 23.2, page 485**		
P3 demonstrate interview skills as an interviewee **See Assessment activity 23.2, page 485**		
P4 prepare for a work-based experience in sport, identifying targets, aims and objectives **See Assessment activity 23.2, page 485**	**M2** justify identified targets, aims and objectives of work-based experience in sport, suggesting how they can be achieved **See Assessment activity 23.2, page 485**	
P5 undertake a selected appropriate work-based experience in sport **See Assessment activity 23.3, page 488**		
P6 maintain a record of activities and achievements during a work-based experience **See Assessment activity 23.3, page 488**		
P7 present evidence of activities and achievements during work-based experience **See Assessment activity 23.4, page 490**		
P8 review a work-based experience in sport, identifying strengths and areas for improvements **See Assessment activity 23.4, page 490**	**M3** explain identified strengths and areas for improvements and make suggestions relating to own further development **See Assessment activity 23.4, page 490**	**D2** justify identified strengths, areas for improvement and suggestions relating to further development **See Assessment activity 23.4, page 490**

How you will be assessed

You will be assessed through:

- presentations which could be oral, multimedia, ICT- or video-based
- interview demonstration and practice
- a log of your placement which could be a diary, observation record and witness statements
- your application for a job (to include, for example, an application form, covering letter and CV)
- video evidence of your work and written assessments.

Jacob, 16-year-old enthusiastic sport student

I like all sports. I love keeping fit, working out, running, cycling and swimming. I knew I wanted to work in sports so decided to do my work experience in a secondary school and really enjoyed it. I am now working hard to get a good grade so I can go to university to study to become a PE teacher.

During my placement I cleaned out the cupboard, helped with team practices, took warm-ups, ran skills sessions, helped with lessons, compiled my own noticeboard, sorted out the kit and was generally helpful. The hardest thing was finding the placement; I had to find and approach the contact and attend an interview. I kept a record of my placement by making a video diary each day.

My placement made me realise how much work teachers do apart from teaching. They have to do practices, prepping, report writing, marking, planning, organising trips, washing kit and of course making tea! The atmosphere in the PE office was excellent! The best bit was teaching a non-swimmer to swim – it made me feel really good.

Over to you!

1. **What areas of this unit might you find challenging and what are you most looking forward to?**
2. **What preparations can you make in readiness for the unit assessment(s)?**

1. Know about the opportunities for work-based experience in sport

Warm-up

Work placements

Think about work experience from the point of view of the different people involved. How much time will the management at the placement have to invest? What will they worry about? How many work experience students will they have? What will the staff at the placement have to do?

1.1 Opportunities

The sports industry is a growth industry with many exciting opportunities for employment. The BTEC Level 3 National Diploma in Sport is a vocational qualification and so work experience is a vital part of your course.

Sectors

There are many different sectors in the sports industry, most will involve irregular hours. Many people have their leisure time in the evening and at the weekends; therefore these are the times you might be most likely to work.

- **The health and fitness** sector has a holistic approach to the mind and body. Many people go to centres where they can go to the gym, swim, eat a healthy meal, have their hair cut, enjoy a massage, take a class of their choice and read the papers. There are many health and fitness centres varying in size, with a range of jobs available.

- **The sport and recreation** sector includes coaching jobs in a range of specialist sports such as football and ice skating. This sector includes general leisure centre work, physical education teaching and sports development officers. The government have realised that sport and recreation has not been emphasised enough in recent years and now there is more investment in sports opportunities.

- **Outdoor education** is a growth area in the sports industry. There are many centres around the country where you can take part in activities such as sailing, surfing and rock climbing. These centres are run by a team of staff with specialist skills, knowledge

and qualifications in their chosen sports. Many large companies send their staff on training days to develop their teamwork. More people now take exercise classes outside such as British Military Fitness.

- **Sport and exercise science** is a specialist area of sports provision which works on:
  - the psychology of the game
  - analysis of how the body works
  - suggesting and refining small areas of technique to improve performance
  - injuries
  - improving and changing nutritional habits
  - muscle function (tests would be performed by a physiologist).

Remember

If the hours and the idea of shift patterns do not appeal, you must think very carefully about whether or not you are selecting the right industry for your future employment.

Providers

Sport and leisure in the UK is mainly organised into three sectors providing this service. These are the **public**, **private** and **voluntary** sectors. Dual use and partnership centres are also growing sectors of provision.

- **The public sector** is one of the largest providers of sport in this country. The facilities are usually owned by the local council or local authority (your borough). They can be run by organisations that the councils have selected or run by the council. They are open to the public and are not usually membership only – you can usually pay per visit. They will have a policy of making sport accessible to all sections of the community, particularly those who traditionally have not taken part in sport. Providing a service to the local community will be their primary aim.

- **The private sector** has enjoyed the largest growth over the last few years. Private centres are usually for the use of members only. They aim to provide an excellent service to members who may pay an initial joining fee followed by monthly membership fees. Members are normally tied to a minimum one year contract. Sometimes the centres will be specialist, such as a tennis, snooker or squash centre, but in the main they will provide a wider service. They aim to make a profit for the owners and most of the management team will have a performance-related pay agreement. They also reward their investors through dividends. They improve the service for their customers and employees will also enjoy enhanced conditions. Private sector organisations are usually owned either by individuals or shareholders (for example, David Lloyd Leisure Centres and Fitness First). Some centres are owned and run on a franchise basis; this allows for corporate marketing and branding and the benefit of a personal service.

- **The voluntary sector** provides a lot of sport in this country. It is run by volunteers who enjoy sport and want to develop their club or team. Examples include local football teams who play at weekends, swimming clubs, basketball teams, etc. They welcome all ages and usually cover their costs by collecting subscriptions (subs) each week. They do not normally own their facilities but rent them from local councils or local private facilities. The largest voluntary organisations are the scouts and the guides.

- **Partnerships** usually arise when more than one organisation is involved in the funding, operation or use of a facility. This can be beneficial as it might mean that a new facility can be built when there was no opportunity in the past; it can also be fraught with difficulties because more than one organisation (management committee) has a say in how it operates.

Sometimes, when local authorities grant planning permission for a large shopping centre, they do so on the condition that the organisation makes a contribution to a community facility, such as a leisure centre – this is called a 'planning gain'. It can lead to a partnership between the public and private sectors.

- **Dual use centres** are often schools that close their 'educational' service at 6 p.m. and open as a public facility during early mornings, evenings, weekends and holidays. This provides an excellent local service and maximises the investment in the school. It also provides opportunities for community links.

Key terms

Public – owned by the public sector, local councils providing a 'sport for all'.

Private – owned and run for profit (members usually pay on a monthly basis to belong).

Voluntary – run by volunteers for the good of the club.

1.2 Types of occupation

There are many different opportunities for employment in sport. Here are a few ideas for jobs in the different sectors.

Activity: Jobs in sport and leisure

List the careers or jobs you might want to do in the sports industry. Where can you do these locally? Search the Internet or the Yellow Pages and make a list of the name, number, address and contact at each placement you are interested in.

Record six different possibilities.

Health and fitness

Table 23.1: Examples of jobs in the health and fitness sector.

Job	Outline of role
Sports masseur	Gives massages to sports people – pre-performance massage, post-performance massage and injury rehabilitation.
Personal trainer	Normally works one-to-one with a client encouraging and motivating them through their personal workout and exercise plan.
Sports therapist	Works with individuals helping to rehabilitate them from injury.

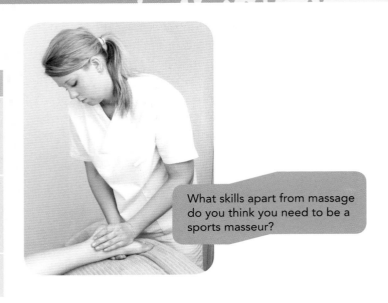

What skills apart from massage do you think you need to be a sports masseur?

Sport and recreation

Table 23.2: Examples of jobs in the sport and recreation sector.

Job	Outline of role
Sports attendant/ recreation assistant	Puts out equipment and tidies it away. They keep the centre clean, deal with customers and have a good awareness of health and safety. They may work on poolside.
Fitness instructor	Most centres have a fitness instructor based at their gym to advise clients about their training programmes and progression.
Sports centre management	Runs the centre on a day to day basis. They will open and close the building, deal with any problems, organise the staffing, be responsible for cashing up and developing the centre.
Sports development officer	Responsible for the development of sport in a local area. They will try and improve sports participation. They may specialise in a particular sport such as netball and provide the opportunities to participate in that sport.
PE teacher	Will have been to university and completed a degree. They will have QTS (Qualified Teacher Status) and may have completed a PGCE (Post Graduate Certificate in Education). They will have a range of knowledge and abilities in a wide variety of sports that they will be expected to teach in a secondary school. There are now PE specialists in some junior schools who are responsible for PE across the whole school.
Sports coach	Usually specialises in one sport such as football or rugby. They will coach it to a range of different age groups and at a range of different levels. Professional football teams will have a coach for their first team and will also have another coach for the reserves, the under 18s, etc.
Coaching and fitness instructor	Works with a team or individual to improve the team's performance with drills and fitness tests specifically designed for that sport.
Professional sports performer	Will have a talent for a particular sport such as cycling and will train, usually full time, in that sport to achieve the highest standard possible. They will set their goal on reaching a particular event, such as the 2012 Olympics.
Sports promoter	Could represent a particular performer or team and arrange the team sponsorship deal. They may represent an event to raise its profile, such as the rugby world cup.

Sport and exercise science

Table 23.3: Examples of jobs in sport and exercise science.

Job	Outline of role
Exercise physiologist	May provide scientific support to sportsmen and women in a club or team setting or might work with cardiac rehabilitation patients and chronic diseases, providing expert advice.
Bio-mechanist	Uses the scientific principles of mechanics to study the effects of forces on sports performance. They will use this information to improve, refine and develop techniques for sports.
Sports psychologist	Helps with the mental/ cognitive components of the performance of sports performers.
Sports dietician	Devises nutritional programmes to help the sports performer to reach their potential by adapting their diet.
Sports scientist	Helps to maximise the performance of an individual, working on small areas of technique or fitness and devising programmes to improve performance.
Sports medicine	A qualified doctor who has decided to specialise in sport. They will diagnose, make recommendations and prescribe and refer.

Outdoor education

Table 23.4: Examples of jobs in the outdoor education centre

Job	Outline of role
Specialist sports instructor	Specialises in a sport such as canoeing. They could teach children, people with disabilities and adults on a range of courses.
Ground facility worker	Has a specialist knowledge of the physics of the ground. All sports grounds need to be maintained.

This person loves their job as a water sports instructor. Do you think you would like to work outside all day?

Considerations

- **Location** – when planning your work-based placement it is advisable that you go there before your first day. Find out where it is and familiarise yourself with the required transport.
- **Travel** – once you have found the venue you will then need to consider how you are going to arrive on time for your first day of the placement (and all subsequent days). You will need to consider the transport options available to you and be aware of how long it will take to get there. If you start work in the morning you may have to consider rush hour traffic. This can add a lot of time to the journey.

Prior to your first day, plan your bus, train, bicycle or car journey. Have a few trial runs to ensure that your journey is achievable in the time you have allocated.

- **Cost** – you will also have to consider the cost of transport to and from the venue for the duration of your placement and other expenses which you may be faced with. For example, equipment and the cost of refreshments.
- **Hours** – you will also have to consider the hours of work (these may be different to your hours at college/school). The hours you work may affect the transport on offer to you and the options you have. Prior to your placement you should agree the hours

which you can work with your placement provider and ensure that you can get to and from the venue of the placement on time and get home safely.

- **Regulations** – you will be subject to the regulations (rules) of the place where you are on work experience. If you have been given a uniform and told to wear it, then you will be obliged to do so. You will be told about various regulations of the placement very early on and you must abide by them.

- **Health and safety** – there are many laws controlling health and safety in the workplace. When you are on work experience you will be subject to them. You will told about some of them on your arrival. When you are on placement you could make a list of all the different laws that are mentioned.

- **Role and responsibilities** – your roles and responsibilities as a student on placement are to do as asked by the management and to be punctual, reliable, trustworthy, willing, helpful, honest and enthusiastic. If you are all these things you will be trusted to take on more roles and responsibilities.

- **Progression** – there are opportunities for progression in the industry. The roles and responsibilities are varied but most work in sport involves working with people so you must be a good communicator. All sections of the industry are subject to statutory regulations and laws. NVQs provide the chance for staff in the industry to upgrade their qualifications while working within the job. Short courses and additional qualifications such as the governing body coaching and officiating awards form part of what is known as Continued Professional Development (CPD). Most organisations ensure that staff have plenty of opportunity for CPD. Staff must be kept up to date with changes in industry practice and in the law.

Take it further

Placements and jobs

Visit www.leisureopportunities.com for ideas about placements.

Research on the Internet about different jobs and the opportunities they offer for CPD.

Assessment activity 23.1

 **BTEC**

Imagine yourself in five years' time in the workplace. What sport-related job are you doing?

1. Make a table and describe four realistic opportunities for appropriate work-based experience where you could get a taste of that job. **P1**

2. Explain these four work placement opportunities. **M1**

3. Evaluate these opportunities. **D1**

Grading tips

- To attain **P1** select four quite different opportunities to evaluate as it is easier if they are very dissimilar.

- To attain **M1** you need to explain each of the four placement opportunities in detail discussing what you think it will offer you.

- To attain **D1** you need to think about what could be good as well as what could be bad about your selected work-based experiences.

PLTS

Describing the four opportunities for placement will help you demonstrate **independent enquirer** and **creative thinker** skills.

Functional skills

Researching the four placements will give you the opportunity to use your **ICT** skills.

2. Be able to prepare for a work-based experience in sport

In this section you will examine different ways of applying for work experience and jobs. To help you do this you will look at the process of applications and study how to reach the interview stage.

2.1 Application process

The application process for jobs in the sport and active leisure industry is much the same as with any job. You will need to make sure that you have carefully researched the jobs you would like to apply for and understand what the job would entail and how you can convince the employer that you are the best person for that role.

Job specifications

A **job specification (or description)** describes the duties and responsibilities of a particular job. You may find a job specification is contained in the advert for the vacancy or it may be sent to you when you apply for a job along with the **person specification** and the application form.

Key terms

Job specification/description – lists the duties of a particular job.

Person specification – based on the job description, it describes the best person for the job.

Freetown FC

Employer	Freetown FC
Job Title	Strength and Conditioning Coach
Sector	Coaching, Training & Medical
Sub-Sectors	Fitness Coach
Salary	£35,000 per annum
Benefits	plus football success-related bonus of up to 50%
Town/City	Freetown
Contract Type	Permanent
Passport/Visa Required	Must be eligible to live and work in the UK

Job Description

JOB TITLE: Strength and Conditioning Coach

REPORTS TO: Club Doctor

JOB FUNCTION:

- To provide fitness conditioning services to the first team squad as required.
- To assist in the preparation of players prior to first team matches as required.
- To take responsibility for the monitoring of the progress of all players' body strength with the use of weights and body weight exercises.
- To assist as required in carrying out fitness testing.
- To explain correct use of gym equipment to players.
- To liaise with and assist in the conditioning of reserve and youth players as required.
- To provide advice and guidance to the Head of Youth and Development Coaches in respect of the conditioning and fitness of under age players involved in the Club's development system.
- Generally to provide such conditioning and fitness services as required by the Doctor, Manager and coaches.
- To liaise with all members of the sports medical and sports science team to assist in the multi-disciplinary approach.

Qualifications required   Must have relevant experience in a professional sporting environment, ideally in football.

Figure 23.1: An example of a job description.

A job description is likely to include:

- the job title
- location
- who you would report to, for example, an assistant manager
- who you would be responsible for
- a brief summary of the job.

A person specification is based on the personal skills, knowledge, qualities, attributes and qualifications needed to do the job described in the job description. Subheadings might include:

- Personal attributes
- Personal qualities
- Vocational qualifications
- Academic qualifications
- Competence and experience
- Duties.

These will be listed as essential or desirable and it will indicate on the person specification whether or not the interviewer is going to find that information from the application form, the interview or the reference. The main reason for using job descriptions and person specifications as part of the recruitment and selection process is to ensure that the interviewer has a clear and objective basis on which to assess each candidate. Personal opinions and preferences are minimised.

Take it further

Job descriptions and specifications

Research the Internet for job descriptions and person specifications. Compare them and see if you match the criteria they are asking for.

Activity: Job descriptions and person specifications

Write a job description and a person specification for a job of your choice. Prepare 12 questions for mock interview practice. Work in groups with three on the interview panel. Plan the introduction and the completion of the interview. Carry out and feed back to each other how well you each did.

Preparing required application documents

There are three main ways to apply for a job or work experience:

1 curriculum vitae (CV)
2 application form
3 letter of application.

- A CV should be typed on a single side of A4, although as you gain more experience this will extend. There are no strict rules about layout but it must be neat, logical and look pleasing and distinctive. It should be easy for the prospective employer to find the information and you should use subheadings in bold. The content of the CV is your decision but as a rule it should contain:
  - name
  - address
  - date of birth
  - phone numbers including mobiles
  - email address
  - personal statement including your skills, qualities and attributes and your ambitions
  - employment record, most recent first with dates and a summary of your duties
  - education to date, most recent first with dates including short courses
  - other achievements, hobbies and interests
  - referees (check with your referees that they will write you a reference before you put their name down).

Adapt your CV to suit the job you are interested in; emphasise the relevant experience and skills that you have for that job. Leave out information that is irrelevant or reflects badly on you. This is your CV and there are no definitive rules about its content as long as what you write is true.

Remember

Your CV is a reflection of you. How it is presented will show your prospective employer many things about you. Make sure the spelling and grammar are accurate, present your work with pride and put the most recent education and employment first.

Your name
Your address
Your telephone number
Your email address
Your date of birth

Personal statement

In a short paragraph descried your best qualities and abilities. Use words such as **reliable**, **enthusiastic** and **responsible** and mention your skills, for instance that you have good communication skills, and work well in a team.

Education

List the most recent first, give the name of the school or college, the dates you were there, the qualifications you took and the grades you got.

School/college	Date	Qualifications
Endsley College of Further Education	2009-2011	BTEC National Diploma Sport Development, Coaching and Fitness
All Saints High School	2002- 2009	GCSEs English C Maths B PE A* Geography C Food tech B

Awards

List the most recent first, where you got them, the qualification and dates.

From	Date	Award
All Saints High School	2009	First-aid at Work
All Saints High School	2008	FA Level 1

Employment

List the most recent first. Include work experience if you have not had a job.

Position	Organisation	Dates	Responsibilities
Football coach	Hampton Soccer School	2008–present	Coach under-11s team Mentor young players
Waiter	Chino's Grill	2007–2009	Taking orders Providing good customer service

Other interests

Include information about yourself. For instance you mention that you play for a team. Highlight achievements like being made captain. Outline an occasion where you have taken responsibility, and include any voluntary work you may do or have done.

Referees

You should give your most recent employer and college tutor. Choose people who will say positive things about you.

Figure 23.2: You can adapt this CV template to suit you. Remember, your CV should take up one side of A4 paper.

- **An application form** is a set form you may be asked to complete for work experience and you must answer all questions fully and accurately. Application forms are the most common way of applying for a job so it is good practice. They are fair because all candidates complete the same form.

When completing an application form:
- write with a black pen
- check to see if they ask for block capitals
- write legibly or type if you have it electronically
- read the question carefully first before answering the question

- have a personal statement prepared (see below) that you can adapt to the job (most jobs will ask for one – you can adapt from your CV
- use the job description or person specification as a guide to what you should include in the statement (if one or both of these have been sent to you)
- sell yourself but do not waffle
- identify key statements from the advertisement, job description or person specification and talk about them on your form (you will be shortlisted based on these)
- if you make a mistake cross it out neatly and carry on
- do not lie – you are signing it as a true and accurate reflection of yourself
- try not to leave it until the last minute
- post in plenty of time or deliver by hand

Your address
Your phone numbers
Your email address

Name of contact
Company name and address

Date

Dear Sir or Madam (or Mr/Ms X)

Subheading in bold to show the position being applied for (e.g. Recreation Assistant, Emily Leisure Centre, Work Experience Placement)

Body of letter...
- Introduce yourself; mention what course you are doing, where you are doing it and why you have to do work experience as part of your course.
- Give reasons why you are interested in the work experience with their company.
- Give details of the skills, qualifications and experience you can offer.
- Please find enclosed my... (CV or application form).
- I look forward to hearing from you.

Yours faithfully (if you started with Dear Sir or Madam)

Yours sincerely (if you started with their name)

Your signature

Your name (typed)

Figure 23.3: What skills and qualifications would you talk about in your covering letter?

- make sure you have the right name on the envelope – this is especially important in a large organisation.

- **A letter of application** sets out all the information found on a CV but in letter style. Some employers ask for this method of application to see if a candidate is committed enough to write a letter. These will normally be completed on computer but some will ask for them to be handwritten. When you send your CV or your application form you need to send a short letter to accompany it (this is sometimes called a covering letter). It is set out in business style (see Figure 23.3 below). The letter needs to be accurate and well presented.
- **Personal statements** – most application forms will give you a full side to complete your personal statement; this will be similar to the information you wrote for your CV or put in your application letter. A personal statement must outline your strengths, skills, attributes, achievements and any other relevant information for that particular job that you have not put on the form for another question. They might want you to handwrite it. Prepare one in advance in rough to minimise the amount of mistakes.
- **Letters of acceptance/decline** – when you have been made a job/work experience offer you may be asked to reply in writing. This letter should be short and well presented thanking them for their offer and accepting or declining the job. It should be set out in business style.

Interviews

An interview will be based on the job description and the person specification. The interview panel will interview you using these two documents and (if appropriate) the answers you gave on your application form.

Prepare well for an interview. Make sure you know your route so that you know where you are going and how long it will take. Arrive early and dress smartly – be outgoing, confident and enthusiastic.

2.2 Interview skills

We can all improve at interviews; the more you practise, the better you will become. Mock interviews are good practice to ensure that you are relaxed and at ease. During mock interviews you can go through the job description and the person specification and try and work out questions that you might be asked based on these documents. When you practise, go through the whole process from beginning to end to become accustomed to the introduction process. Practise 'active listening'; this is when you look at the person talking to you and follow what they are saying while looking interested throughout.

Verbal communication

Your verbal communication skills need to be good in an interview – you need to be clear and you must not use slang or jargon. You need to be confident and use appropriate language for the industry. If you are not sure what the question is you can ask for clarification from the interviewer. Asking questions that are relevant is very important as it shows that you have given thought to what is expected of you. The interview should have a prepared format and will probably be carried out by more than one person. The format and questions should remain similar for all candidates as the panel will compare the answers.

There are a number of different types of questions you can be asked during an interview and some are easier to answer than others. Table 23.5 lists some of the different styles of questions you might be asked.

How do you cope with the pressure of an interview?

Table 23.5: Interview question types.

Question type	Description
Closed	To find out specific information (requires yes/no answers) For example: Have you worked shifts before?
Open	To encourage the interviewee to open up on a topic For example: Why do you carry out fitness tests?
Probing	To find out more on a particular point For example: Could you explain to me why you would use a Eurofit step test?
Clarifying	To check understanding For example: What do you mean by equal opportunities?
Scenario	To test the interviewee's ability to apply their knowledge For example: A child breaks their arm in your session. What do you do?
Rambling	Rambling questions are bad practice but they are often asked! You have to listen carefully to the long question and try to work out what they are asking. For example: When you have been at work, or not at work, what customer service or customer care skills and tips have you developed to help you in and out of work?
Multiple	Asking more than one question in the same question For example: What do you see yourself doing in three years' time – what do you hope to achieve and how are you going to achieve it?

Non-verbal communication

Non-verbal communication is very important. Sit forward and sit up straight – don't cross your arms and make sure you smile. Look as though you are interested. Your body language, facial expressions and posture will indicate your interest to the interviewer. Dress sensibly, smartly and appropriately.

Appropriate presentation

When you are going for an interview you need to dress in a suitable manner – don't wear jeans and opt for smart/casual. For an interview a tracksuit would be inappropriate – avoid large logos and pictures – low cut tops are also inappropriate.

Take it further

Interview questions

Research the type of interviews and questions the staff at your college and at the local leisure centre have been asked. Practise answering them.

Case study: Work experience interview

Siân Griffiths is outgoing and enthusiastic. She went for a work experience interview to work with a personal trainer. It is what she wants to do for a career but she was so nervous in the interview that she answered the questions much too briefly and didn't represent herself well.

1. **What could Siân do to overcome her nerves in interview?**
2. **How can she 'sell' herself more?**

2.3 Prepare

After you have completed your work experience search, telephone, write or email the places you have identified. Be very careful how you speak to staff on the 'phone. Begin the conversation by saying 'good morning/ good afternoon', introduce yourself and ask to speak to the person who deals with work experience. If they are not there, ask what their name is and when it will be convenient to call again. They probably have a lot of enquiries for work experience so remember to 'phone back and if possible leave a message (although do not rely on them returning your call). When you ring again, ask for them by name, make sure you introduce yourself, what course you are doing, where you are doing it, what the work experience requirement is and what the dates are. Have a pen ready to take down any information you may need. Always be polite, enthusiastic and interested in the organisation.

Aims and objectives

Aims are 'large' in size and relate to your career and life aims. They are usually challenging such as 'I want to be a PE teacher and I am going to find a work experience placement in a school to find out what it is like to teach'. Objectives are 'medium' in size and are related to how you will achieve your aims. They are medium-term and achievable, such as 'I am going to contact three schools by the end of the week and send my CV with a covering letter' or 'I want to be able to run a whole session by myself'. You will usually have more objectives than aims.

SMART (specific, measurable, achievable, realistic, timed) targets

Targets are short-term, realistic and achievable; as they relate to your work experience they could be 'I am going to ring and follow up my letter' or 'I am going to ask what I am expected to wear on my placement' or 'I am going to ask to help with extra curricular practices and go to matches'. They will relate to your objectives. Your targets must be set against the SMART principles.

Personal

What personal targets are you setting yourself?

- **Knowledge development** – how do you want to increase and improve your knowledge?
- **Skills development** – what new skills do you want to learn?
- **Personal improvement** – how do you want to improve?

Table 23.6: SMART targets.

S	Specific	Your targets should relate to something you want to achieve.	I want a work experience placement in a leisure centre.
M	Measurable	They should be able to be measured.	I want to find ten contacts for work experience placements.
A	Achievable	They have to be achievable for you to reach.	I am going to set myself a task and a date that are real so that they will be met and not ignored.
R	Realistic	You must set your sights on something you can achieve otherwise you will be put off.	I must be realistic – will I be able to find myself a placement with a PE teacher in a secondary school?
T	Timed	You must set deadlines that can be met.	I want a placement by 3 January.

- **Qualifications** – find out what qualifications the staff at your placement have achieved. Many people move into the industry through a variety of routes. Decide what might help you the most.
- **Organisational** – how can I develop my organisational skills to prepare for work?

- **Relating to qualification/study** – what information can I gather while on work experience that will help me on my course?
- **Supplementary evidence** – what evidence can I gather that will support my work?

Assessment activity 23.2

1. Select an appropriate work experience placement and complete the application process. **P2**
2. Demonstrate your interview skills as an interviewee. **P3**
3. Prepare for a work experience placement, identifying targets, aims and objectives. **P4**
4. Justify your identified targets, aims and objectives suggesting how they can be achieved. **M2**

Grading tips

- To attain **P2** decide on the job you are applying for when you complete your application form, CV and covering letter. This will help you to remain focused on the application.
- To attain **P3** film yourself being interviewed in your groups that you formed for your panel interviews and reflect on your performance.
- To attain **P4** create a table for your aims, objectives and targets of work experience.
- To attain **M2** add a column to your table; justify them and suggest ways in which they can be achieved.

PLTS

Independent enquirers, **reflective learners** and **creative thinkers** will be able to complete the aims, objectives and targets well. Writing CVs, letters and application forms will help you demonstrate **reflective learner** skills.

Functional skills

Letter writing, CV writing and filling in application forms will demonstrate **ICT** and **English** skills.

3. Be able to undertake a work-based experience in sport

This is it – you are now going to start your work experience! This could be a life changing time. Make sure you know how you are going to the placement and how long the journey takes. Be early! Take a diary with you to make notes about what you have done during the day.

3.1 Carry out

Before you start your placement you need to check what time you start, who you report to and what you are expected to wear. It is always better to ask than to arrive in the wrong kit, in the wrong place and at the wrong time!

Planned activities

Ask your placement supervisor what they want you to do. Be enthusiastic, reliable and helpful and use your initiative. If, for example, you are on work experience in a school with a PE teacher, ask if you can take warm-ups. Plan them, show your plans beforehand, discuss them and refine them. Build on this and by the end of your placement you might be allowed to run a whole session.

Case study: Rhianna's work experience

Rhianna Mair managed to find a placement in her local leisure centre. She was given a rota of general duties around the centre. Whenever she was in reception she sat in the receptionist's seat and the receptionist had to ask her to move out of her chair every time. This upset the receptionist and she complained to the manager.

1. **What should Rhianna have done?**
2. **Why should she move out of the chair?**
3. **Rhianna held her FA level 1 Coaching badge and offered to do an after school club at the centre. Who could she approach? What could she do to convince the management team that this was a good idea?**

Considerations

Always remember you are a visitor in the workplace; act in a mature manner as you are now a member of staff. Staff might need privacy to speak to management so

use your initiative and leave the room. Be sensitive to other people's needs and you will fit in well.

- **Codes of practice** – some organisations will require that the staff employed within the organisation adhere to certain behaviours in specific situations. As a temporary employee of the organisation you will also be expected to adhere to such codes. If this is the case, you should request copies of the codes prior to your placement to familiarise yourself with the provider's behaviour expectations.

- **Customer care** – in some instances your placement may involve you working with customers. When this is the case you must make sure you deal with customers appropriately. When dealing with customers you should always:
  - greet the customer politely
  - listen to the customer
  - respond politely
  - deal with a customer's complaint (or find someone who can)
  - be helpful.

- **Health and safety, legislation and regulation** – when you start your placement you will have to undertake a health and safety induction. This induction process will show you the health and safety procedures which are followed within the centre. The staff will show you what to do in the event of a number of incidents, for example, a fire alarm or major or minor injury to an employee or customer, etc. If you are required to set up equipment you should be shown how to do this in a safe and effective manner prior to having to do this independently. If you ever feel at risk of injury, or causing injury, you should must seek support and advice from the staff at the centre.

- **Equal opportunities** – by law all employers should treat their employees equally regardless of gender, race, religion, sexual orientation and ability. If an employer failed to treat all employers equally then they would be subject to criminal proceedings. It is important that, as an employee of an organisation, you also treat everyone within the organisation equally. Failure to comply with this could result in you being asked to leave the placement instantly.

- **Quality assurance** is the process of verifying or determining whether products or services meet or exceed customer expectations. As an employee of a company who carries out quality assurance of the services provided it is important that you follow the required guidelines and procedures effectively. It is possible that the employer will assess your ability to meet their expectations – this is also a measure of assuring quality of the service provided by you.

- **Specific skills** – when working within some organisations it may be a requirement that you possess specific skills, qualifications or experiences. If this is the case, prior to starting the work experience, you will need to ensure that you have obtained the required skills, qualifications or experiences so that you are not out of your depth and can carry out the requirements of the position while you are there. For example, prior to working for a coach in the community, he or she may request that you obtain a Level 1 coaching award in a specific sport to ensure that you are insured to support coaching sessions and that you have the required skills to support the delivery of such sessions. Failure to obtain the qualification could mean that you are not insured to work alongside children and the coach will not be able let you start your placement.

Take it further

Risk assessments

How does the risk assessment at your work experience compare to the risk assessment you use at college or one you have found in your research?

3.2 Record

Diary of daily activities

When on placement, record your experiences in the form of a daily log book. You should record the achievements which you have attained for each day of the placement and the areas which you could improve upon. You should identify in your diary what you have learned and exactly what you did during each day.

Achievement of goals, aims and objectives (personal, organisational, relating to qualification/study)

When you are on work experience, remember to learn as much as you can about as many different aspects of the sports industry as possible. You will be asked to review the aims, objectives and targets you set before you went on your placement. Have you achieved them? Set yourself new ones for your work experience. Relate them to your personal and organisational targets and those relating to your course and other qualifications you may be taking.

Activity: Diary of daily activities

While you are on your work placement, find out some information.

1. What does the organisation do and who are its customers?
2. What is the organisation's customer service policy?
3. Apart from those that you are studying, find out what other qualifications would be useful to the organisation.
4. Give six examples of the organisation's rules and regulations (Code of Practice).
5. What is the organisation's health and safety policy?
6. What is the emergency evacuation procedure? Where are the fire alarms and muster points?
7. Who is the first-aid officer and where is the first-aid kit?
8. What is a risk assessment and why would you carry one out?

Assessment activity 23.3

You are now on work placement – enjoy it and keep a record of everything you have done. Reflect on your performance each day in your diary; this could be kept in a variety of formats including MP3, video diary, by email or in writing.

1. Undertake a selected appropriate work-based experience. **P5**

2. Maintain a record of activities and achievements during your work-based experience. **P6**

Grading tips

- To attain **P5** enjoy your experience and make the most of all the opportunities you are given.

- To attain **P6** report your experiences for the day every day, as you will soon forget the details of each day if you leave it until later.

PLTS

Team workers, **effective participators** and **self-managers** will do well at maintaining a record of their work experience.

Functional skills

Maintaining your record will utilise your **English** and **ICT** skills.

4. Be able to review a work-based experience in sport

This is your time to reflect on your work experience. Be honest with yourself about where you performed well and where there are areas for improvement. Include photographs that you have taken of yourself at work.

4.1 Present

You will need to make a presentation to your group about work experience.

Activities

Introduce the placement by explaining what the organisation does, where it is located and by giving general information. Explain the activities you did and expand on the points individually. You could write each point on a postcard to help you.

Achievements

What did you achieve when you were on work experience? What did you do that you were pleased with? What was a personal achievement for you? It may appear to have been a small achievement such as dealing with a complaint, helping a customer or motivating a reluctant 13-year-old girl to participate in a sports session. Remember you were only there for

a short time so any achievements are good. List your new experiences and at the end of your placement evaluate your performance and analyse what you have learned. The final question you need to ask yourself is 'Do I want to do this as a full-time career?'. If so, what do you need to do to achieve your aim?

Formats

You can deliver a presentation in a variety of formats. An oral presentation is perhaps the most traditional and straightforward format. You could make a written presentation with handouts and you can use your computer skills. The most common and popular method of computerised presentation is PowerPoint®. This consists of a sequence of slides that you can animate. You can include special effects and you can import pictures either taken by you on work experience or imported from the Internet (make sure you cite where you found the photos with the website address in your presentation). During your presentation handouts are very useful. Exhibits, work and leaflets from your placement all add interest. You can also use a whiteboard or flipchart which you can write on as you go along.

4.2 Review

You need to evaluate your performance during work experience. When you are doing this you need to critically analyse what you have done, what you can learn from the situation and how this will be useful in terms of building your skills and knowledge of the industry.

Remember

If you find it difficult to evaluate, imagine you will have to do your work experience placement again. What could you do differently to improve your performance and your opportunity to learn new things?

Activity: Work placement evaluation

1. List ten duties that you carried out.
2. What elements of the work did you enjoy and why? List three.
3. What aspects did you not enjoy and why? List three.
4. What new skills have you learned? List three.
5. Would this type of work interest you as a career? Why?
6. What advice would you give to a student who is about to start their work experience at your placement?
7. Is there anything that could have made the placement more useful than it was?
8. Were you prepared for this placement?
9. Was there anything extra that you needed to know before you started?

Activities

Review the activities that you did on work experience – were they what you expected? Did you do what you hoped to do? Were you given more responsibility than you expected? Did you feel as if you were an unpaid member of staff? Did you feel challenged, but not abandoned?

Achievements

What did you achieve? Were you pleased with what you achieved?

Achievement of goals

Before you went on work experience you listed your goals. Now you should analyse your achievements against your goals. Did you achieve them all? How many did you achieve? Did you achieve them fully or partially?

Aims and objectives

Review the aims and objectives you set for yourself for your work experience – did you achieve them? Has your placement changed your mind about what you want to achieve?

Strengths and areas for improvement

After having completed your work experience, what do you consider to be your strengths and what are your areas for improvement? Here is a list of competencies to help you:

- Communications
- Organisation
- Customer service
- Using initiative
- Dealing with problems
- Teamwork
- Coaching and teaching.

Evidence and techniques

When reviewing your work experience placement, reflect on how you could use evidence to support your work, such as photographs or video footage of you at work.

Interviews and use of witness testimony

Take the opportunity to interview staff about your placement and about your performance. A witness testimony is a statement of what you did, written by your supervisor. This should outline briefly what you did and it should be signed both by the supervising member of staff and by you. Interview the staff – how did they reach that position? What qualifications have they got? What is their biggest achievement to date?

Further development

On completion of the work-based placement you should complete a personal development plan which will reflect upon the attainment of the aims and objectives which you set at the start of the placement. The development plan should support the development of your overall career ambitions as well as those aims and objectives set prior to the work-based placement.

At the end of the placement you should consider what you could do next to support your development and attain your overall goal. To do this you will need to consider what else you could have done to achieve the aims and objectives that you set for yourself prior to the placement. This could include further time at the placement or seeking part-time employment

- **Experiences** – you should consider what other experiences you could pursue in order to fully meet your career ambitions or aims and objectives previously set.

- **Training** – after the work experience you may have been made aware of specific training courses which you could undertake to support your development and achievement of your aims and objectives. These could be included in your personal development plan.

- **Qualifications** – as well as specific training courses there may also be specific qualifications which you have to obtain in order to pursue the job or career of your dreams. In your development plan you should highlight these qualifications and provide yourself with targets of how and when you wish to attain these qualifications and where.

Assessment activity 23.4

1. Having completed your work experience you now have to present the information to your group telling them about your activities and achievements. **P7**

2. Now you need to review your work experience, identifying strengths and areas for improvement. **P8**

3. Explain the strengths and areas for improvement you have identified, making suggestions relating to your further development. **M3**

4. Justify everything you explained for M3. **D2**

Grading tips

- To attain **P7** you must present evidence, such as photographs, of the placement.

- To attain **P8** go back to the aims, objectives and targets you set in the first assignment and review them.

- To attain **M3** make suggestions relating to your own further development, such as attending a level 2 FA coaching course (aim) as you want to develop your coaching skills (objective) and you are going to contact someone to organise your course by May (target).

- To attain **D2** remember to reflect on your achievements and areas for improvement and justify them in detail. What did you learn from your work experience? Relate it to what you want to go on to do now.

PLTS

Reflecting on and presenting your work experience will show evidence of your skills as an **independent enquirer**, a **reflective learner**, an **effective participator** and a **self-manager**.

Functional skills

When you make your presentation and reflect on your placement, you will demonstrate your skills in **English**.

Jordan Evans
Leisure centre duty manager

Jordan completed ten days' work experience at his local leisure centre. He had just passed his NPLQ at college and was offered a job as a lifeguard and sports attendant. He finished his National Diploma and now works full-time as duty manager.

Jordan has worked hard and taken every opportunity that was presented to him. He arrives at the centre at 6 a.m. to open up at 6.30 and closes it late at night – the centre shuts at 11 p.m. and he aims to leave at 11.30 p.m. depending on his shift. He cashes up and has very good customer service skills. He has completed his Pool Plant course, a management development course and managed to complete four governing body awards. He is 19 and wants to apply for the job as manager. The shifts he does are either an early or a late and he has one weekend in three off (but he does have time off during the week to make up for it). The skills he uses most are customer service skills, organisation and management techniques.

'I love being in contact with the public and being responsible for the smooth running of the centre. I particularly enjoy it when we have events like wedding receptions.

I really enjoy managing and organising the staff – it's like a complex game of chess! And it's great when it all comes together – I thrive on the challenge of working to a deadline and getting the set-up perfect. I have some training but now I want to learn about how to manage.'

Think about it!

- What does Jordan need to do to prove he is suitable for the manager position?
- What will he need to prepare for the interview?
- How can he make himself stand out from the other candidates?
- How can he persuade the interview panel that, at 19, he is ready for the manager's position?

Just checking

1. Who are the customers in public sector facilities? Who funds them?
2. Who are the customers in private sector facilities? Who funds them?
3. Who are the customers in voluntary sector facilities? Who funds them?
4. What is a dual use centre and what is a partnership centre?
5. What is the difference between a job description and a person specification?
6. What is a covering letter used for?
7. What is a letter of application?
8. What is the difference between aims, objectives and targets?
9. Have you reviewed your work experience?
10. What do you understand by evaluation?

edexcel

Assignment tips

- Set your aims, objectives and targets clearly — this will help in Assessment activity 23.4 when you have to review them after your work experience.
- Remember that work experience is meant to be fun. Enjoy the experience and be open to trying new things and working hard.
- Record what you do every day as you will soon forget. It also reminds the people you are now working with that you are there for a college course and you have to do work. It also gives you something to do when you have a few minutes to yourself.
- Be helpful and take some initiative on your placement. This will help you to enjoy it more and, if you enjoy it, you are more likely to perform better.
- Learn from the staff at the placement. Watch them carefully. They will all be experienced and have plenty to teach you. Talk to them and gather information from them to assist with your assignments.
- Ensure that you properly read the assignment briefs. Take your time and ensure you are happy with the task set for you. If not ask your tutor for additional assistance.

Glossary

Absolute VO$_2$ max – maximum oxygen consumption expressed in litres per minute (l/min).

Accuracy – how close a measurement is to the true value.

Acromion – roughened triangular projection atop of the scapula.

Adhesions – pieces of scar tissue that attach to structures within the body, limiting movement and sometimes causing pain.

Adipose tissue – commonly referred to as fat tissue, is a type of connective tissue that serves as the body's most abundant energy reserve.

Aerobic – requires oxygen.

Aerobic endurance – the ability of the cardiovascular and respiratory systems to supply the exercising muscles with oxygen to maintain the aerobic exercise for a long period of time, for example over two hours during a marathon.

Afferent nerves – sensory nerves that usually have receptors at the skin and joints.

Aim – something you want to achieve – a goal.

Amenorrhea – absence of blood flow during the menstrual cycle.

Amino acids – the building blocks of proteins.

Anabolic – changes include the growth and development of body tissues, most notably muscle.

Anabolism – the constructive metabolism of the body – the building of tissue.

Anaerobic – does not require oxygen.

Anaerobic threshold – the point at which aerobic energy sources can no longer meet the demand of the activity being undertaken, so there is an increase in anaerobic energy production. This shift is also reflected by an increase in blood lactate production.

Anthropometric – the science of measuring height, weight, size of component parts, including skinfold thickness, of the human body to study and compare the relative proportions under normal and abnormal conditions. Also called anthropometric measurement.

Anthropometry – the scientific study of physical dimensions, proportions and composition of the human body, as well as the related variables that affect them.

Articular (or hyaline) cartilage – smooth, slippery covering over bones that reduces friction.

Articulating surface – acts as a cushion between joints.

Assistance exercises – focus on smaller muscle areas, only involve one joint and have less importance when trying to improve sport performance.

Atrophy – loss of mass or wasting away.

Attribution – the reason you give to explain the outcome of an event.

Auditory – you concentrate on the different sounds that you associate with a sporting movement (for example, hitting the sweet spot on a cricket bat).

Balanced diet – a diet that provides the correct amounts of nutrients without excess or deficiency.

Basal metabolic rate (BMR) – energy demand of the body at rest.

Blood pH – measure of acidity or alkalinity of a solution.

Blood pressure – can be measured using a digital blood pressure monitor, which provides a reading of blood pressure in mmHg (millimetres of mercury).

Bone marrow – fat or blood-forming tissue found within bone.

Broadcasting rights – having the contract to televise an event.

Calorie – the energy required to raise 1 gram of water by 1 °C.

Cancellous bone – lightweight, honeycomb bone with a spongy appearance found at the ends of long bones and also in the centre of other bones.

Capillary bed – an interwoven network of capillaries.

Capillary exchange – where oxygen, carbon dioxide, nutrients and metabolic waste pass between blood and interstitial fluid by diffusion.

Cardiac arrhythmia – an irregular heart beat.

Cardiac muscle – specialised muscle of the heart.

Cardiac output – volume of blood pumped out of left ventricle in one minute: cardiac output = stroke volume × beats per minute.

Catharsis – the release of aggression through socially acceptable means, such as sport.

Cell permeability – allowing or activating the passage of a substance through cells or from one cell to another.

Cellular adaptations – changes within the cell structure (for example, an increase in mitochondrial size).

Cognitive anxiety – the thought component of anxiety that most people refer to as 'worrying about something'.

Collagen fibres – most abundant of fibres found in connective tissue.

Compact bone – forms the dense outer shell of bones. It has a smooth appearance.

Concentric muscle action – the muscle gets shorter and the two ends of the muscle move closer together.

Conduction – transfer of heat from one object to another through direct surface contact.

Connective tissue – (tendon) is used to attach muscles to bones, and is used for structure and support of the skeleton.

Contraindication – a physical or mental condition or factor that increases the risk involved when engaging in a particular activity. Contra means 'against'.

Coordination faults/losses – these occur when players do not connect with their play, the team interacts poorly or ineffective strategies are used. Generally, sports that require more interaction or cooperation between players are more susceptible to coordination faults or losses.

Core temperature – temperature of the inner body, particularly the internal organs.

Core exercises – focus on large muscle areas, involve two or more joints and have more direct impact on sport performance.

Coronary heart disease (CHD) – also known as coronary artery disease (CAD), is caused by fatty deposits lining the walls of arteries, causing them to thicken and harden (atherosclerosis). This results in less oxygenated blood reaching the heart, leading to chest pain (angina), or if the artery becomes totally blocked, a heart attack (myocardial infarction).

Cortisol – a hormone that is associated with stress, anxiety and depression.

Crease – in cricket a bowling crease, a popping crease and two return creases are marked in white at each end of the pitch. Bowlers must bowl within these limits and batsmen must remain within the area to ensure they do not get stumped or run out. Within this area the batsman is safe from being run out and stumped.

Creatine phosphate – energy-rich compound used in the production of ATP from ADP in muscle cells.

Curvilinear motion – movement in a curved line (for example, 200 metre sprint race in athletics).

Cutaneous mechanoreceptors – sensory nerve endings in the skin.

Degree of freedom – used as a correction factor for bias and to limit the effects of outliers, and based on the number of participants you have.

Dehydration – depletion of fluids that can impede thermoregulation and cause a rise in core body temperature.

Delayed-onset muscle soreness (DOMS) – the pain or discomfort often felt 24–72 hours after exercising. It subsides generally within 2–3 days.

Descriptive – saying what you see in the sport performance.

Deviance – cheating or bad behaviour.

Diabetes mellitus – a metabolic disorder resulting in high levels of sugar in the blood. Diabetes results from a lack of insulin produced by the pancreas, so sugar is not broken down to release energy. If untreated it can result in diabetic coma and death. Treatment is by dietary control and doses of insulin. Long-term effects include thickening of the arteries.

Diastole – cardiac-cycle period when either the ventricles or the atria are relaxing.

Diastolic blood pressure – the lowest pressure in the bloodstream, which occurs between beats when the heart is in diastole (relaxing, filling with blood).

Diet – a person's usual eating habits and food consumption.

Diffusion – a substance moves by diffusion from a region of higher concentration to a region of lower concentration until equilibrium is reached.

Dislocation – a displacement of the position of bones, often caused by a sudden impact.

Distress – extreme anxiety related to performance.

Duty of care – a legal obligation imposed on an individual, requiring that they adhere to a standard of reasonable care while performing any acts that could possibly harm others.

Dynamic flexibility – the range of movement that a muscle or joint can achieve when in motion.

Eccentric muscle action – the muscle increases in length while still producing tension.

Ectomorphy – the 'leanness component', characterised by small bones and poor muscular development, the shoulders may droop. Abdomen and lumbar curve are flat, shoulders are narrow and there is a lack of muscle bulk.

Electrolytes – a substance (usually salts) dissolved in water. Also salts in the blood, for example, calcium, potassium and sodium.

Endomorphy – the 'fatness' component. Characteristics include a predominance of the abdomen over the thorax, high square shoulders and a short neck.

Endorphins – morphine-like chemicals that can reduce pain and improve mood.

Enzymes – proteins that start or accelerate the digestive process.

Epinephrine – a chemical in the body used for communication between cells in the nervous system and other cells in the body.

It works with norepinephrine to prepare the body for the 'fight or flight response'.

Ergogenic – a factor that enhances physical performance.

Ethnicity – belonging to a group of people who identify themselves as from one nationality or culture.

Etiquette – the rules that govern how people behave with others – in sport, etiquette is also known as sportsmanship and fair play.

Eustress – 'beneficial' stress that helps an athlete to perform.

Evaporation – conversion of liquid into vapour (for example, sweat into vapour).

External imagery – imagining yourself doing something as though you are watching it on a film so that you can develop an awareness of how the activity looks.

Extrinsic – an external factor, for example a risk or a force from outside the body or a reward. These are external forces, such as from objects or other individuals making contact with someone.

Fair play – playing as competitively as possible, but always within the rules of the sport as determined by the national governing body.

Fibroblast – connective tissue cell that makes and secretes collagen proteins.

Fibrocartilage – tough cartilage capable of absorbing heavy loads.

Field of view – the area you are recording that contains the sporting action.

Fiscal resources – the financial costs of running coaching sessions, this may include facility and or equipment hire and could include depreciation costs or loss or damage costs to the equipment or facility.

FITT – frequency (how often), intensity (how hard), time (how long) and type (how appropriate).

Flexibility – the ability of a specific joint, for example the knee, to move through a full range of movement. As with muscular endurance, an athlete can have different flexibility levels in different joints.

Focus group – a group-based interview where the group interaction is an essential aspect of data collection. This tends to be a semi-structured interview.

Food – any substance derived from plants or animals containing a combination of carbohydrates, fats, proteins, vitamins, minerals, fibre, water and alcohol.

Formative assessment – takes place informally and should support the development of a coach.

Fracture – a partial or complete break in a bone.

Free fatty acids – the parts of fat that are used by the body for metabolism.

Gamesmanship – when dubious tactics are employed in a sport to gain an advantage over the opposition, e.g. intimidation (this can be psychological and/or physical) or an attempt to disrupt concentration.

Golgi tendon – a proprioceptor located within the muscle tendon.

Haemarthrosis – a build-up of blood in the joint.

Haematoma – a collection of clotted blood due to bleeding in a specific area of the body.

Haemoglobin – oxygen transporting component of red blood cells.

Hard tissue injury – injury to bones, joints and cartilage.

Health – as defined by the World Health Organization, is a state of complete physical, mental and social wellbeing and not merely the absence of disease and infirmity.

Healthy eating – the pursuit of a balanced diet to support health and reduce the risks of chronic disease. Healthy eating principles should form the solid foundations on which athletes can build more specific nutritional strategies to support training and competition.

Horizontal scaling – providing a scale of measurement that will allow you to convert on screen measurements to real-life measurements.

Human resources – people involved in the delivery of a coaching session, e.g. coaches, assistant coaches, parents, spectators.

Hypertension – high blood pressure, which is when systolic blood pressure is above 140mm Hg and diastolic blood pressure is above 90mm Hg.

Hyperthermia – an unusually high core body temperature greater than 40°C.

Hypothalamus – region of the brain responsible for many behavioural patterns, especially those concerned with regulation of the body's internal environment.

Hypothermia – an unusually low body core temperature less than 35°C.

Hypoxic – inadequate supply of oxygen to respiratory tissues.

Informed consent – the knowing permission or agreement of your participants (or legal representative in the case of a child) to take part in the research as you have described it to them. The participant must be willing and should not be unfairly persuaded into taking part.

Insertion – a muscle's insertion is attached to the moveable bone.

Inter-muscular haematoma – a haematoma that escapes the muscle sheath through a tear or rupture.

Internal imagery – imagining yourself doing something and concentrating on how the activity feels.

Intra-muscular haematoma – a haematoma that remains trapped inside the muscle sheath.

Intrinsic – internal factors, for example a risk or force from within the body or enjoyment felt from taking part in a sport. These are internal forces, which are stresses or emotions from within the body.

Job specification/description – lists the duties of a particular job.

Joule – 1 joule of energy moves a mass of 1 gram at a velocity of 1 metre per second. Approximately 4.2 joules = 1 calorie.

Kilocalorie – the energy required to raise the temperature of 1 kg of water by 1 °C. Equal to 1,000 calories and used to convey the energy value of food. Kilocalories are often simply referred to as calories.

Kilojoule – a unit of measurement for energy, but like the calorie the joule is not a large unit of energy; therefore kilojoules are more often used.

Kinaesthetic – you concentrate on the feel of the movement.

Kinanthropometry – the scientific study of the relationship between the structure of the human body, specifically when applied to human movement.

Krebs cycle – a series of chemical reactions occurring in mitochondria in which carbon dioxide is produced and carbon dioxide atoms are oxidised.

Lactate – product of lactic acid which occurs in blood.

Lymphatic drainage – a massage treatment that uses light pressure and long, rhythmic strokes to increase lymphatic flow. Lymph, a fluid that contains white cells, is drained from tissue spaces by the vessels of the lymphatic system. It can transport bacteria, viruses and cancer cells. The lymphatic system is associated with the removal of excess fluid from the body. It is made up of lymphatic capillaries, lymphatic vessels, lymph nodes and lymph ducts.

Macronutrient – nutrient required by your body in daily amounts greater than a few grams, e.g. carbohydrate, fat and protein.

Maximal exercise – level of training intensity when an athlete approaches their maximal heart rate and performs exercise to an increasingly anaerobic level.

Mean – the measure of central tendency that is calculated by adding up all of the values and dividing the answer by the number of values. You may also know this term as the 'average'.

Median – the middle value in a series of numbers.

Member checking – allowing the participants of the study to check your interpretations and conclusions for validity purposes.

Mesomorphy – characterised by a body that is heavily muscled. The thorax is large, the waist is relatively slender and shoulders are broad. Abdominal muscles are well toned.

Minute ventilation – tidal volume × frequency of breaths per minute.

Mode – the value that occurs most frequently.

Motivation – the direction and the intensity of your effort; it is critical to sporting success.

Motivational faults/losses – these occur when some members of the team do not give 100 per cent effort.

Muscular endurance – the ability of a specific muscle or muscle group to sustain repeated contractions over an extended period of time.

Mitochondria – organelles containing enzymes responsible for energy production. Mitochondria are therefore the part of a muscle responsible for aerobic energy production.

Muscle fibres – the contractile element of a muscle.

Myofibril – the contractile element of a muscle fibre.

Myoglobin – the form of haemoglobin found in muscles that binds and stores oxygen. Myoglobin is responsible for delivering oxygen to the mitochondria.

Narrative technique – the style of making a commentary.

Neurotransmitters – chemicals used to carry signals or information between neurons and cells.

Non-parametric tests – statistical tests that use ordinal or nominal data.

Norepinephrine – a chemical in the body used for communication between cells in the nervous system and other cells in the body. It works with epinephrine to prepare the body for the 'fight or flight response'.

Notational analysis – analyses of sport performance involving counting different observations of performance, for example, how many shots were successful versus unsuccessful.

Numerical model – a model of sport performance based on numerical factors.

Nutrition – the means by which your body takes in energy and nutrients in food to sustain growth and development, and to keep us alive and healthy.

Objective – how you are going to achieve your aim.

Oedema – a build-up of blood and tissue fluid within the tissue.

Oestrogen – female sex hormone.

Olecranon process – forms part of the elbow; located at the end of the ulna.

Olfactory – you concentrate on the different smells that you associate with a sporting action (for example, the smell of freshly cut grass on the first game of the season for your football team).

One-tailed test – a test that assumes one group will be better than the other, or at least no worse than the other. For example, girls will be better than boys.

Origin – a muscle's origin is attached to the immobile (or less moveable) bone.

Oxygen dissociation – graph illustrating the relationship between oxygen saturation in blood and partial pressure of oxygen.

Oxygen saturation of blood – measure of oxygen dissolved or carried in blood.

Parametric tests – statistical tests that use interval or ratio data. They assume that the data is drawn from a normal distribution and has the same variance.

Parasympathetic nerve – slows heart rate through the release of acetylcholine.

Parasympathetic nervous system – part of the system that helps you to relax.

Paratendonitis – inflammation of the paratendon (the tissue surrounding the tendon).

Partial pressure – pressure exerted by a single gas in a mixture of gases (for example, the pressure of oxygen is different from the pressure of air).

Pedometer – a portable electronic device usually worn all day on the belt which counts each step taken.

Performance analysis – the provision of objective feedback to performers trying to achieve a positive change in performance.

Performance criteria – aspects of sport performance which, if performed well, should lead to successful sport performance.

Performance profiling – a process of identifying important psychological skills training objectives that can help to increase the motivation of athletes due to their involvement in the process.

Person specification – based on the job description, it describes the best person for the job.

Personality – the sum of the characteristics that make a person unique.

Perspective error – an error where objects seem to get bigger or smaller as they move towards and away from the camera and you can't effectively judge their position.

Phosphagen – member of group of energy rich phosphate compounds such as phosphocreatine.

Physical resources – the facility and equipment required to deliver the session.

Physiological response – the body's physical mechanisms that respond when an injury takes place. These are initiated to repair and protect the damaged tissue.

Pilot study – a smaller scale version of your study used to check the data collection and analysis procedures.

Polysensorial – involving as many of your senses in the imagery process as possible.

Power – the ability to generate and use muscular strength quickly over a short period of time.

Precision – how fine or small a difference a measurement can detect.

Prehypertension – means you don't have high blood pressure now but you are likely to develop it in future.

PRICED – procedure for the treatment of acute injuries – protect, rest, ice, compression, elevation, diagnosis.

Private – owned and run for profit (members usually pay on a monthly basis to belong).

Psychological response – the mental aspect of how an athlete copes and comes to terms with their injury and treatment.

Pubic crest – portion of the pelvis next to the pubic arc.

Public – owned by the public sector, local councils providing a 'sport for all'.

Punditry – so-called expert opinion.

Qualitative analysis – uses descriptions and words to describe sporting performance.

Qualitative model – a model that uses words, rather than numbers, to examine performance.

Qualitative research – a more subjective form of research that tries to explain differences, relationships or causality using non-numerical data such as words.

Quantitative analysis – uses numerical data or statistics to describe sporting performance.

Quantitative research – a formal, objective and systematic process in which numerical data is used to obtain information.

Radiation – emission or transfer of radiant energy as heat waves or particles.

Rationale – the reason for completing the research project.

Rationalisation – more organised and structured sport.

Rectilinear motion – movement in a straight line (for example, 100 metre sprint race in athletics).

Regulation – following rules.

Rehabilitation – the process of restoring a person's physical functionality to a normal state, or as near as physically possible.

Relative VO$_2$ max – maximum oxygen consumption expressed relative to the individual's body weight in kg. The units of relative VO$_2$ max are ml of oxygen per kilogram of body weight per minute (ml/kg/min).

Reliability – the consistency and repeatability of the results obtained. That is, the ability to carry out the same test method and expect the same results.

Repeated measures – using more than one data collection session to assess the reliability of your research.

Respiration – emission of waste gases and water vapour via the respiratory system.

SALTAPS – procedure for the assessment of an injured person – stop, ask, look, touch, active movement, passive movement, strength testing.

Sample – the participants in your study.

Sarcopenia – loss of muscle mass.

Scalar quantities – a quantity that only has a magnitude (for example, speed).

Scope – who and where your research is applicable to.

Semi-structured interview – an interview that follows the guide but allows scope for probing further with your questions if a topic of interest is brought up. This is a good technique as it allows you to get deeper information from your participant through additional questioning as well as giving the participant the opportunity to discuss things further.

Skeletal muscle – voluntary muscle with obvious striations that attaches to the body's skeleton.

Smooth muscle – muscle with no visible striations found mainly on the walls of hollow organs, veins and arteries.

Social exclusion – feeling as though you are outside normal society.

Social learning theory – states that individuals learn in sporting situations through two processes: modelling and reinforcement.

Socio-economic groups – ways of grouping people according to income and job.

Soft tissue injury – injury to muscles, tendons, ligaments, internal organs and skin.

Spectatorism – watching sport.

Speed – the ability to move a distance in the shortest time.

Sport – an activity involving physical exertion and skill in which an individual or team competes against another or others for entertainment.

Sports nutrition – the influence of nutritional strategies on sports performance during preparation for, participation in and recovery from training and competition.

Sprain – a stretch or tear of ligaments.

State anxiety – a temporary, ever-changing mood state that is an emotional response to any situation considered to be threatening.

Static flexibility – the range of movement that a muscle or joint can achieve.

Strain – an injury to muscle or tendon.

Strength – the ability of a specific muscle or muscle group to exert a force in a single maximal contraction to overcome some form of resistance.

Stretch reflex – the body's automatic response to something that stretches the muscle.

Stroke volume – the amount of blood pushed out of the heart in one contraction. It is volume of blood pumped out of left ventricle per beat.

Structured interview – a set interview guide that you adhere to without change in light of participant responses.

Stumps – three sticks of equal size around 90 cm tall, with 5 cm separating them. Bails (small pieces of wood) are balanced on top of the stumps.

Subjective – a performance analysis based on your own opinion.

Summative assessment – takes place formally to assess the performance of a coach. It is often used to assess ability – for example, when trying to attain a coaching qualification.

Sympathetic nerve – speeds up heart rate through the release of noradrenalin.

Sympathetic nervous system – part of the system responsible for the 'fight or flight' response.

Synovial effusion – a build-up of synovial fluid within the joint.

Synovial joints – freely movable joints that allow movement. A synovial capsule between the bones prevents bones rubbing together and lubricates the joint cavity.

Systole – cardiac-cycle period when either the ventricles or atria are contracting.

Systolic blood pressure – the highest pressure within the bloodstream, which occurs during each beat when the heart is in systole (contracting).

Tactics – the skills and strategies a player uses in any type of sport to be able to win, for example during a hockey or tennis match, each team or player will apply specific tactics and strategies to try to beat and outwit their opponent(s).

Tactile – you concentrate on your sense of touch throughout the movement.

Technique – a way of undertaking a particular skill.

Tendonitis – inflammation of the tendon.

Tendonosis – deterioration of the tendon.

Testosterone – male sex hormone.

Test variable – this is any factor which could affect the validity and/or reliability of fitness test results.

Thermoregulation – the ability to keep the body's temperature constant, even if the surrounding temperature is different.

Trait – a stable and enduring characteristic that is part of your personality.

Trait anxiety – a behavioural tendency to feel threatened even in situations that are not really threatening, and then to respond to this with high levels of state anxiety.

Triangulation – using more than one data analysis method to ensure the validity of results.

Triglycerides – the most concentrated energy source in the body. Most fats are stored as these.

Two-tailed test – a test that assumes there will be a difference between both groups, but doesn't say which will be better. For example, there will be a difference between girls and boys.

Type A personality – typified by a strong competitive urge and a lack of patience. These people rush to finish activities, multi-task successfully under time constraints, lack tolerance towards others and experience higher anxiety levels.

Type B personality – people with this personality type are relaxed and reflective. They have higher levels of imagination and creativity and experience lower anxiety levels.

Unstructured interview – this type of interview has a start question and then the conversation goes from there. You must be skilled at focusing your conversation to get a lot out of this type of interview.

Validity – the accuracy of the results. This means whether the results obtained are a true reflection of what you are actually trying to measure.

Validity – whether you are measuring what you are supposed to be measuring.

Vector quantities – a quantity that has a magnitude and a direction (for example, velocity).

Vertical reference – as for horizontal scaling, but on a vertical plane.

Visual – you concentrate on the different things that you can see during the movement.

VO_2 max – the maximum amount of oxygen that can be taken in by, transported in, and utilised by the body during incremental exercise. Also, a measure of the endurance capacity of the cardiovascular and respiratory systems and exercising skeletal muscles.

Voluntary – run by volunteers for the good of the club.

Wellness – can be viewed as our approach to personal health that emphasises individual responsibility for wellbeing through the practice of health promoting lifestyle behaviours.

Xiphoid process – forms the end of the sternum.

Index